T0270910

JAPAN'S ECONOMIC PLANNING AND MOBILIZATION IN WARTIME, 1930s–1940s

Most economists, political scientists, and historians believe that the Japanese government's economic conduct of war from the 1930s in China through the end of World War II was largely efficient, if not ultimately effective. Yoshiro Miwa has long argued that this perspective is mistaken. Following Nobel Laureate George Stigler's distinction between state competence and its aims, Miwa contends that the Japanese government did not have the competence and institutional means to direct resources to the extent that many analysts claim. His painstaking research in historical materials, which include government archives, allows him to document the gaps between military objectives and those of economic planning, structure, and mobilization as the Japanese government prepared itself for the conflict. He finds that the government – despite its reputation for industrial planning – was ill prepared and draws from this study sophisticated lessons about the ability of governments to plan their economies.

Yoshiro Miwa is Professor of Economics at Osaka Gakuin University and Professor Emeritus at the University of Tokyo, where he obtained his BA, MA, and PhD. He writes on a wide variety of subjects, but much of his work has been in industrial organization. His current research concerns the effect of government involvement on economic activity in the 1930s and 1940s. Professor Miwa's publications include *Firms and Industrial Organization in Japan* (1996); *State Competence and Economic Growth in Japan* (2004); and *The Fable of the Keiretsu* (2006), coauthored with J. Mark Ramseyser.

Japan's Economic Planning and Mobilization in Wartime, 1930s–1940s

The Competence of the State

YOSHIRO MIWA

Osaka Gakuin University and the University of Tokyo

CAMBRIDGE
UNIVERSITY PRESS

CAMBRIDGE
UNIVERSITY PRESS

32 Avenue of the Americas, New York, NY 10013-2473, USA

Cambridge University Press is part of the University of Cambridge.

It furthers the University's mission by disseminating knowledge in the pursuit of
education, learning, and research at the highest international levels of excellence.

www.cambridge.org
Information on this title: www.cambridge.org/9781107026506

First published 2015

A catalog record for this publication is available from the British Library.

Library of Congress Cataloging in Publication data
Miwa, Yoshiro, 1948–
Japan's economic planning and mobilization in wartime, 1930s–1940s : the
competence of the state / Yoshiro Miwa.
pages   cm
Includes bibliographical references and index.
ISBN 978-1-107-02650-6 (hardback)
1. World War, 1939–1945 – Economic aspects – Japan.   2. Sino-Japanese War, 1937–
1945 – Economic aspects – Japan.   3. Industrial mobilization – Japan – History – 20th
century.   4. Japan – Armed Forces – Mobilization – History – 20th century.   5. Japan –
Economic policy – 1918–1945.   6. Japan – Military policy.   7. Military planning – Japan –
History – 20th century.   8. Japan. Navy. Air Force – History – 20th century.   I. Title.
HC462.8.M474   2014
940.53′1–dc23   2014020400

ISBN 978-1-107-02650-6 Hardback

Contents

Preface

I. The Competence of the State

Several years ago, I published a study of state competence based on data from late-twentieth-century Japan (*State Competence and Economic Growth in Japan*, Routledge Curzon, 2004). In it, I explored how well the Japanese government had planned and implemented growth-promoting policies – and found the government to have been largely ineffective. In work with J. Mark Ramseyer (*The Fable of the Keiretsu*, University of Chicago Press, 2006), I next asked whether the government would even have had the power to enforce such policies – and found it did not. In this book, I extend these studies to the 1930s and early 1940s. More specifically, I ask how competently the Japanese government planned and executed its wars against China and the United States.

In examining state competence, I draw on a literature begun by George Stigler in the 1960s. Adam Smith had expressed an abiding mistrust of government two centuries earlier, of course (Smith, 1776, p. 437). But as Stigler noted, Smith did not mistrust the government's ability (Stigler, 1965). Instead, he mistrusted its goals. Smith brought to his mistrust, explained Stigler, an undocumented and fundamentally unwarranted confidence in the competence of the state. Smith assumed that governments could implement their policies efficiently and effectively, however inappropriate they might generally be. And in making that assumption, Stigler concluded, Smith made his most fundamental mistake.

For all their vastly increased technical sophistication, Smith's followers, who include most professional economists today, retain his fundamental faith in state competence. Crucially, however, they adduce no evidence that governments can effectively plan or control economic activity. Sharing little skepticism about governmental ability, they continue to expect the best of governmental intervention.

Granted, economists expect less of government today than they did a half-century ago. The collapse of the Soviet empire caused nothing if not an increase in academic skepticism toward government control. Economists pushed, successfully, the deregulation that one sees today in the advanced market economies. Expect too much of government, most economists now realize, and people can suffer. Even this, however, is not a uniformly held consensus. Some scholars still attribute the Soviet collapse to specific government missteps. The Soviet empire did not fail because of any inherent government inability to plan and direct economic ability, they suggest. It collapsed because the Soviet state made a series of specific policy errors.

I do not advocate a libertarian agenda, and I do not write this book as a partisan polemic. The smooth operation of the modern economy entails government intervention at a wide variety of levels. To choose the appropriate foci for government policy, however, one needs to understand accurately what governments can and cannot do. That understanding requires an empirical basis. And those empirics demand the careful study of when, how, and to what effect governments have intervened in the past. As one step in that broader empirical project, this book supplies a case study that contributes to a fuller understanding of government competence.

For Japan, World War II began with the invasion of North China in the 1930s and continued into the next decade with the war against the United States. That war offers an intriguing "laboratory" to study Japanese governmental competence. After all, governments direct wars. They decide whether to prepare for them, when to initiate them, how to execute them, and the terms on which to end them. Toward that end, the public sometimes grants them as much power as it can feasibly grant. And in Japan during World War II, the public did grant the state that maximum power.

What is more, many scholars assume that the Japanese government brought to the war an extraordinary ability to plan the economy. The economy had grown rapidly in the decades leading up to the war, and historians routinely attribute that growth to planning. Bureaucrats pursued the vision captured by the contemporaneous motto, "rich nation, strong army," historians argue, and the national growth reflected the success with which they did so.

The Japanese economy also grew rapidly in the 1960s, of course, and social scientists attribute that growth to government plans as well. Just as bureaucrats grew the prewar economy to realize a rich nation and a strong army, they grew the postwar economy through all-encompassing "industrial policy." If this is true, then the government that entered the War with China and exited the war with the United States was a government with extraordinarily solid competence.

Although the past literature on other countries has sometimes mirrored this story, modern scholars have begun to question it. More specifically, they have begun to reevaluate the role that the 1930s governments played in Germany, the USSR, the UK, and the United States. Through this book, I extend this inquiry into Japan. Just as scholars of prewar governments in the West have begun to challenge assumptions of state competence, I do the same for the East.

Scholars of the wartime Japanese government conventionally begin with accounts of its strength. At least initially, according to this account, the government enjoyed widespread popular support. To execute the war, it arrogated to itself extraordinary powers. With that support and power, it planned for the war. Once the war began, it executed it according to its plans. It supplied its military machine by intervening in the economy and mobilizing its resources. And throughout the war it maintained close control over both the economy and the hostilities themselves.

Other than the government's own self-serving accounts, however, these scholars advance virtually no evidence for these claims. Nor, I find, could they have done so. The bureaucrats may have planned, but they did not implement most of the plans they made. When they did implement a plan, it seldom worked as anticipated. What the conventional account misses is the way wars rarely develop as governments anticipate. Once the fighting begins, events proceed in a fashion so unanticipated that the surprises swamp the preparations. The country that wins a war is rarely the one that plans most elaborately. It is usually the one that responds to the vicissitudes most sensibly and expeditiously.

In this book, I show that the Japanese government did not plan. It did not plan seriously for war with China. It had not bothered to collect the information it needed to mobilize the country. Once the war began, it did not exploit the resources it had. It had no real hope that the war would end, and if it did end it had no real idea how to structure events thereafter. It could see no credible reason for the war. It could identify no effective way to wage the war. Any plans it had made in advance it did not implement. In truth, it made its choices on an ad hoc basis, and the war itself quickly became a dead-end, a drifting war of attrition.

If the government did not plan for the War with China, neither did it plan for the war with the United States. Not having planned for the war, it mobilized its resources no more effectively than it had against the Chinese.

It had opened a second front that no one in the leadership thought it could win. With little information and no plans, it could not raise the supplies it needed. And with no plans, it faced unbalanced supplies, bottlenecks, and shortages.

The Japanese government did no better in Manchuria. From time to time, scholars have argued that its puppet regime in Manchukuo successfully implemented a planned economy. They argue that it built a massive manufacturing base for the Japanese military. In fact, once again the government implemented no substantial plans. The few supplies it produced in Manchukuo had little effect on the war it waged.

Indeed, government leaders could not even induce their Army and Navy to cooperate. The two military branches had long competed for control. Once the wars began, the chronic competition became an open dispute.

This leadership vacuum appears in the turnover within the government. Consider the period from July 1937 (when the War with China began) to December 1941 (Pearl Harbor). By the end of this period, the Army Central Command was on its sixth Strategy Section Chief, fifth Strategy Division Chief, and sixth Deputy Central Command. The Army was on its fourth Minister, its fifth Deputy Minister, seventh Military Bureau Chief, third Military (*gunji*) Section Chief, and fifth Military (*gunmu*) Section Chief. Indeed, the country itself was on its seventh Prime Minister (though Fumimaro Konoe held the post on three of those occasions).

Aircraft and strategic bombing played a crucial role in this war, and here too the Japanese government played an ineffective role. To build that air power, the Navy needed to develop and produce a wide variety of aircraft and equipment. It needed new technology. It needed raw materials. It fell to the government to foster that development and production. Yet this was a role in which the government failed.

That the government planned for the war incompetently casts doubt on the accounts of the decades before and after the war as well. Historians may claim that it structured the prewar growth to promote a policy of "rich nation, strong army." Social scientists may claim it structured postwar growth through industrial policy. But if – with vastly more authority and power than at any time before or since – it could not coherently prepare for war, then perhaps it did not plan much for peace either.

II. Myth of the Competent Japanese State

The preceding pages may surprise some readers, particularly if they are familiar with the dominant view about Japan during World War II, its wartime economy, or its postwar recovery and high growth, which was established immediately after the war, under the Allied (or U.S.) occupation. This view remains the conventional wisdom even today, after more than half a century. It is symbolized in the enthusiasm and excitement both in Japan and abroad over John W. Dower's *Embracing Defeat: Japan in the Wake of World War II* (1999).[1]

The War with China began in July 1937. Despite the forecast of most Japanese leaders, it escalated rapidly to a full-scale, protracted war. With most soldiers on the Chinese front, the Army was trapped in a situation that seriously jeopardized the defense of the national border with the USSR. Even when Japan reached the limit of its war mobilization capacity in the autumn of 1938, the end of the war was nowhere in sight. Japan found itself in a long, drawn-out war of attrition from which it could not extricate itself and which rapidly drained its resources. Within a few years, Japan, by now economically exhausted, began the Pacific War against the United States and the UK.

Because of success stories about "democratization" under the Allied occupation after World War II, readers may be surprised to learn that Japan had become a democracy before the war. The conventional wisdom is that the Japanese government was competent enough to plan and enforce effective policies for postwar recovery and high growth. Yet that same bureaucracy – indeed, almost all the same bureaucrats – implemented the "war mobilization" with "wartime control" efforts.

This book is not a study of Japanese military history. It is a study of state competence. I am interested in the history of the war only to the extent that it enables us to understand what a government can and cannot do. Neither do I study the Japanese government of the time as a unique historical phenomenon: I study it to inform the debate on the competence and role of the state. As always, in order to be useful in informing policy, a study needs to have internal validity as well as external validity.

Many believe that the government, or the state, led not only the recovery and subsequent high growth in postwar Japan but also the remarkable economic development of prewar Japan. Implicitly, they believe that the Japanese government was competent enough to accomplish this. Although this apparently competent government led the country into a war of aggression that ended in a crushing defeat and chaos, the conventional wisdom asserts that it then led the country back to immediate recovery and high

---

[1] On this point, see Miwa and Ramseyer (2009a, pp. 364–6). For more details, see Miwa and Ramseyer (2005a, 2009a, 2009b).

growth. This is part of the package that development economists have urged the governments of developing countries to adopt. At the same time, however, seeing the ongoing stagnation in the Japanese economy, some economists now protest confusion over where the competent government has gone.

The more strongly readers believe stories of Japan's economic success, the harder they may find it to read this book to the end. Perhaps they are interested in Japan's success because it occurred outside of the West, outside of the formerly European colonies, outside of the Christian zone, and in a place quite remote from Western Europe. Perhaps they are interested in it because it was not accomplished by white Europeans. I wrote in the first of my books to be published in English (Miwa, 1996, p. 29): "Since the thirteenth century, when the description of Cipango or Zipangu in Marco Polo's book *Il Millione* set a definite goal for Columbus in his journey, Japan has been a rich source of imagination and myth, particularly for Westerners. Even today Japan still remains full of misunderstanding and mythification. I hope that this volume will push us in the direction of a fuller, more proper understanding of the Japanese economy."

III. Source Materials

This is a long book, and it is written to be read from beginning to end. For various reasons, however, many readers may find it hard to proceed smoothly through Part II on the government's plans and policies and then read the study of the Navy Air Force in Part III. The Introduction and Part I are written for them.

I based this book both on a monograph I published in Japanese (Miwa, 2008) and a companion paper (Miwa, 2007). The English-language audience obviously brings a different set of interests and approaches the topic from a different intellectual environment. Accordingly, neither this book nor its title is a straight translation of those earlier publications. Instead, I draw on discussions in the Japanese monograph that will most strongly interest the audience in the West.

Some readers may wonder why the book includes so much detail. I take this approach primarily because this book investigates state competence (rather than motives), for which it is necessary and appropriate to conduct detailed empirical studies. Three other factors argue for this level of detail: first, most issues under study are based on materials that were confidential during wartime and are unknown even today, primarily because of the predominance of the conventional wisdom; second, the conventional wisdom about Japanese wartime control, assuming an outstandingly competent state, was established and widely accepted when state planning and control were believed to be effective and efficient; and third, this conventional wisdom about Japanese wartime control and postwar economic growth has been very persistent. Many readers will recognize that most literature advocating the conventional wisdom, such as Ando (1972), Nakamura (1989), Calder (1993), and Oishi (1994), rarely refers to detailed factual evidence. Instead, the authors rely heavily on a few principal stories.

Most source materials I use in this book are written in Japanese and have rarely been referred to in the past literature, particularly the English-language literature. Since the war, a large amount of source material has been translated into English. Obviously, however, it is only a selected part of that material. More importantly, the material translated reflects a bias consistent with the conventional wisdom that became established immediately after the war. Unfortunately, even many Japanese historians and political scientists have never referred to those materials.

In wartime Japan, most key information was kept confidential behind the wall of military secrecy. When the war was over, the (military) government ordered all military documents to be burned before the Allied occupation began. The Allied Powers, including the United States, the UK, and the USSR, eagerly amassed scattered materials and information and translated them into English. Obviously only a selected portion of that material has been published; more importantly, what has been translated and published reflects a bias consistent with the conventional wisdom that became established immediately after the war. One reason why I include many references and quotations is to provide basic materials in English, otherwise not a few would be frustrated with scarce materials available in English to think over the issues by themselves.

Readers may become skeptical to find so many references provided by former military personnel. This book is neither a war history nor a history of operations. Instead, focusing on systematic war preparations, war mobilization, and economic control, it pays major attention to central policies and decision making. As a result, most materials referred to here, such as Boeicho, *senshi-sosho* (Library of War History), and NAFHistory (*The History of the Japanese Navy Air Force*), are drawn from information and memoirs of key individuals, from those published for private circulation during the occupation period to those published in the 1990s. All have been subjected to careful cross-checking to establish their consistency and reliability.

Japan recovered independence in 1952, after which the Japanese government amassed the scattered war-related materials and information, notably establishing Senshi-shitsu (the War History Chamber) in Boei kenshujo (the National Institute for Defense Studies) of Boeicho (the Japanese Defense Agency). In the 1960s and 1970s, it published "*senshi-sosho* (Library of War History)" in 102 volumes, each averaging 600 pages, a collection of materials on a variety of topics related to the War with China and the Pacific War. *Senshi-sosho* is not an official war history; it devotes more space to the Army than to the Navy, and only a little space to the Navy Air Force. For this reason, particularly in Part III on the Navy Air Force, I rely heavily on *The History of the Japanese Navy Air Force* (1969), published in 4 volumes, each averaging 1,000 pages, written by a group of former Naval Air Force personnel.

IV. Acknowledgments

Some readers may think it strange that an empirical (micro-)economist, specializing in the fields of industrial organization, regulation, and law and economics, should have written this book. Those who know the other books and research papers I have written, mostly in collaboration with Professor J. Mark Ramseyer, on prewar Japan and postwar government policies, will realize that I am finally tackling the one big issue I have left untouched. I may be an economist, but "if economists told stories about the economy they would be historians" (McCloskey, 1990, p. 40) – so I am a historian.[2]

I already had an interest in the function and role of the government and its policies in the mid-1960s, when I was a first-year undergraduate at the University of Tokyo. Professor Takafusa Nakamura showed specific evidence that was sharply critical of the dominant view about the Japanese economy from the second half of the 1920s to the 1930s. For me, this was the beginning of recognizing both the danger of easy acceptance of dominant views and the importance of evidence-based verification. It was also the beginning of my interest in the Japanese economy of the 1930s.

In Professor Ryutaro Komiya's class in the Economics Department, I learned that the effectiveness of a government's actions, especially its economic policies, should be confirmed by careful investigation: this set and defined the direction, content, and style of my academic life since my graduate student days. Because of this foundation, Stigler's (1965) basic message that it is more important to focus on "the competence of the state" than its "motives" resonated strongly with me.

---

[2] For more details, see subsection 1–2–1 of Miwa (2008). Also, for my commentary and evaluation of existing literature on relevant issues by "historians" and "economic historians," see subsection 2–5–2.

In 1998, after a long period of communication and cooperation, I began a ten-year joint research project with Professor J. Mark Ramseyer of Harvard Law School. This was a very fertile experience producing more than thirty articles and five books in English and Japanese. This book started as part of the joint work, but by mutual consent, after a certain point, I continued to develop it on my own. I obviously owe much to Professor Ramseyer's inspiration, from problem setting to development and conclusion. As an English editor, he made a tremendous contribution to the substance, style, and readability of this book.

Professor Leslie Hannah, now at the London School of Economics and Political Science, was a colleague in the Department of Economics at the University of Tokyo for three years until the spring of 2007. From him I learned a great deal, particularly about the conditions in Europe during the first half of the twentieth century. In various chapters of this book, readers will find evidence of a close encounter with his logical and transparent problem setting, breadth of vision, and wide knowledge.

A long time has elapsed since the original idea for this book began to grow. Over that period, many friends in many institutions have shared their ideas with me, both in conversation and through their comments on my drafts. Those who were particularly generous with their time and thoughts include Fumio Akiyoshi, Yoshitaka Fukui, Arnold D. Harvey, Shigeo Hirano, Hideki Kanda, Yoshitsugu Kanemoto, Motonari Kurasawa, Katsuji Nakagane, Hiroshi Ohashi, and Kazuo Wada. Above all, Professor Daniel F. Spulber of Northwestern University encouraged and supported me to write this book in English, and from him I received many helpful substantive and stylistic comments.

I gratefully acknowledge the permission of Yuhikaku and *Keizaigaku ronshu* to revise and include my earlier works in this English version. I received financial support from the Research Fund Grant of the Economics Department of the University of Tokyo and from the Academic Research Support Fund of the Japanese Bankers Association (also for the publication of Miwa [2008]).

Only half jokingly, I am often asked, "How do you ever begin to think of those problems, and develop and finalize all your papers and books?" I can only respond by referring to the dedication to my father in Miwa and Ramseyer (2006): "*To the memory of Shizuo Miwa – someone who behaves as I do never could have been raised without a dad like him.*"

Last, but by no means least, I thank my wife, Kazuko, for her understanding and forgiveness through the many evenings and weekends lost while writing this book. It is to her that I affectionately dedicate this book.

Abbreviations

AAF	Army Air Force
ACCom	Army Central Command
ACCommander	Army Central Commander
ACE	administrative-command economy
AM	Army Ministry
BNDP	Basic National Defense Policy
Boeicho	The Japanese Defense Agency
BOO	Basic Outline of Operations
CAC	Combined Air Corps
FY	fiscal year
FYOP	fiscal year operation plan
GM	general mobilization
GOCO	government-owned, company-operated
IH	Imperial Headquarters
IH-AD	Imperial Headquarters–Army Division
IH-ND	Imperial Headquarters–Navy Division
JSW	Japan Steel Works
KIAss Order	Imperial Order for Key Industry Associations
KICAct	Key Industries Control Act or the Act for the Control of Key Industries
MAP	Ministry of Aircraft Production
MCE	manufacturing capacity expansion
METI	Ministry of Economy, Trade, and Industry
MHI	The Manchurian Heavy Industries
MIM	Munitions Industry Mobilization
MIMAct	Munitions Industry Mobilization Act
MITI	Ministry of International Trade and Industry
MMPlan(s)	Materials Mobilization Plan(s)

NAF	Navy Air Force
NAFHistory	*The History of the Japanese Navy Air Force*
NCCom	Navy Central Command
NCCommander	Navy Central Commander
NGMAct	National General Mobilization Act
NM	Navy Ministry
NSC	National Strength Council (*kokusei-in*)
OR	Office of Resources
PCE	production capacity expansion
PCECmt	Production Capacity Expansion Committee
PCEPlan(s)	Production Capacity Expansion Plan(s)
PCEPolicies	Production Capacity Expansion Policies
PPS	Priority Production Scheme
SMR	South Manchurian Railways Company
"Special Aid" Act	Act on special aid for the weapons manufacturing business
TFCAct	Temporary Funds Coordination Act
TIEGAct	Temporary Import-Export Grading Act
TOMC	Temporary Office for Materials Coordination
WM	War Mobilization

Introduction

I

The Administrative-Command Economy Under Stalin's Dictatorship

The Soviet administrative-command economy was the most important social and economic experiment of the twentieth century. Its failure continues to reverberate throughout those countries in Europe, Asia, and Latin America that adopted it, either forcibly or voluntarily.... The former administrative-command economies have had to confront their pasts as they make their transition to market economies. Empirical studies show that the heavier the imprint of the administrative-command system, the more difficult has been the transition. (Gregory, 2004, p. 1)

The confusion-to-collapse process of the administrative-command economies of the countries that were once part of the former Soviet Republic paralleled the development of deregulation in the majority of developed market economies, led by the United States and the United Kingdom.

What we witnessed in the former Soviet republics around 1990 demonstrated that an administrative-command economy will end in failure in the long run. "The opening of the formerly secret Soviet state and party archives in the early 1990s was an event of profound significance" (Gregory, 2001, p. vii). It enabled rapid progress in clarifying and understanding the reality of the mechanism of the Soviet economic regime during the period from the 1930s to the beginning of the 1950s, often referred to as Stalin's command economy. Berliner (2001) concludes: "[T]he archives have confirmed that the sources available to foreign scholars in the past, though not abundant and heavily censored, enabled them to draw a fairly accurate picture of the USSR in Stalin's time.... [O]ur understanding is now, because of the archives, much more complete, detailed, and nuanced."[1]

The picture of the USSR in Stalin's time confirmed by the archival evidence had not been widely accepted before the archives were opened. Unfortunately, this remains much the case, despite the newly revealed evidence.

The reality of administrative-command economy differs substantially from the one assumed in the economic regime controversy that had flourished since the 1930s. Its operation was by far more difficult than had been supposed. Facing tough realities of operating the economy, the government (or the state) as the planner from the start virtually adopted a decentralized system. A multilayered complex administration hierarchy was formed inside the government, through which its authorities were delegated to lower subplanners. High-layered planners' control over lower-layered subplanners was neither easy nor necessarily strict. Economic agents such as producers, targets of planners' commands, were left great room for flexibility.[2] Direct transaction between "producers" did not disappear. Administrative commands with detailed specifics of the central government did not cover the whole economy, with which the content of its "plans" was strictly limited. Function and role of "plans" were limited as well.[3]

---

[1] Gregory and Harrison (2005, p. 724) write: "In terms of the real character of high-level decision making in the Stalinist state, archival documentation has given us completely new knowledge. This regime was indifferent to calculation, preoccupied by the need to punish and deter its enemies, and bent on implementing its decisions through a complex administrative hierarchy of agents motivated by threats and promises."

[2] Spulber (2003, p. xxi) writes, for instance: "After the collapse of Tsarism, the Bolsheviks nationalized all the means of production – creating in fact a *sui generis* state capitalism – instituting a centrally controlled system of employment on the basis of centrally fixed wages.... The Bolsheviks, rebaptized as Communists, assumed the whole power, but willy-nilly had to create a vast strata of managers and administrators – the *nomenklatura*. Notwithstanding its theoretical complete dependence on the Communist Party's commands and directives, the *nomenklatura* felt increasingly capable of cheating the system, falsifying the results of its assignments, and finally asserting extensive controls over the activities of their enterprises particularly in the 1980s."

[3] Gregory and Harrison (2005, p. 724) write: "Research in the archives has shown how decision-makers at every level actually allocated resources. They made it up as they went along, using intuition, historical precedent, and common sense. As befits a bureaucracy, there were plenty of formal rules, but the rules were constantly revised or overridden. Those at higher levels made formal rules, only to break them. Those at lower levels, unable to live without rules, relied on customary norms or rules of thumb. The flaws in this planned economy became apparent to its leaders almost immediately. Before the archives, we believed that official proposals for decentralizing economic reform began to circulate after Stalin's death: the first serious reform experiment actually dates back to 1932 and bears a strong resemblance to reform proposals after Stalin's death. But, like all those that followed, it was quickly frustrated."

From approximately 1932 until his death in March 1953, Stalin was a true dictator: he had his way on every matter and was not afraid to abuse and humiliate those on whom he depended most closely (Gregory and Harrison, 2005, p. 724). Coupled with the memory of the "purges" in which he eliminated rivals, challengers, and opponents,[4] until recently the conventional wisdom about the Soviet economy had been widely accepted: First, it was an administrative-command economy under Stalin's dictatorship; second, it operated efficiently as a "planned economy." "The prevailing view of Gosplan[5] before the archives exaggerated its role, at least for the Stalin period, Gosplan was not an all-powerful director of resources; the power belonged to the dictator" (Gregory and Harrison, 2005, p. 728).

Germany and the United States

During Stalin's dictatorship, and in particular in the first half, public confidence in the function and role of the market was undermined all over the world. Simultaneously, government intervention was strongly demanded and enforced. The conventional wisdom that the government played an active and important role in the market in Germany and the United States as well prevailed for many years in the postwar period. In either country, however, has this view been critically reviewed.

The conventional wisdom about the Germany of this time was that when Hitler came to power in January 1933, during a severe recession, full-scale rearmament began.[6] Its critical review, however, began to appear very early

---

[4] "The Soviet regime's brutal treatment of its own personnel, party, state, and military officials during the Great Purges of 1936–9 had no parallel in the history of the Nazi regime" (Rees, 2001, p. 59). It is often called the "Great Terror" (Rees, 2001, p. 57). The "attempts to reform the system were brought to a halt by the purges of 1936–1938. In every government department a large number of senior officials were dismissed, arrested, and often executed. In the State Bank, Mar'yasin was arrested in July 1936 and subsequently executed. The purges affected its whole staff" (Davies, 2001, p. 75). "1936 saw the beginning of great purges in Russia: practically every old Bolshevik leader was executed or imprisoned, thousands – perhaps millions – of lesser Russians sent off to Siberia. In the following year the purge extended to the armed forces: Tukhachevsky the chief of staff, three out of five marshals, 13 out of 15 army commanders, and many others were shot after a secret trial or none at all" (Taylor, 1964, p. 112). The results of Stalin's purge of the military that began in May 1937 "were catastrophic. The Soviet Union's secret police devastated the air force's officer corps and caused a paralysis that delayed the transition to a new generation of aircraft until 1941" (Murray, 1999, p. 115).

[5] Gosplan was the committee responsible for economic planning in the Soviet Union.

[6] "The Nazi government, it was commonly believed, had for six years concentrated the country's resources on preparations for war. This was a tacit assumption of the diplomacy of the period, and a point of major emphasis in the voluminous writing on Germany" (Klein, 1959, p. 3).

after the war. In fact, Germany actually began full-scale rearmament after its economic recovery, around 1936.[7]

Overy (1994, pp. 16–17) writes: "This process should not be seen in isolation. State intervention and 'planism' was on the increase in all European economies. Arguments over the nationalization of industry emerged in Italy, France, and Britain in the 1930s.... Nor should this development be seen as a crude 'dualism', state on one side, and industry on the other." He concludes, "The Nazi regime after 1936 was determined to transform the economy in ways which would serve the drive for empire and conquest."

The same applies to the United States.[8] The major turning point in the growth of the federal government was the New Deal. "There was an ideological shift – from widespread skepticism about the ability of the central government to improve the functioning of the economy to widespread faith in the competence of the government" (Rockoff, 1998, p. 125). To shed light on the ideological preconditions for the New Deal, Rockoff explores the attitude of economists toward government intervention in the decade preceding the depression, and concludes: "Virtually all of the reforms adopted in the 1930s – minimum wages, social security, unemployment compensation, the Civilian Conservation Corps, and so on – had been championed by economists. When the depression came, moreover, economists played a major role in bringing their reforms into being by writing the legislation, testifying in support of it before Congress, and implementing the new programs....There is no justification at all for viewing the economists in the 1920s as doctrinaire defenders of laissez-faire" (Rockoff, 1998, pp. 125–6, 133).

---

[7] Taylor (1964) represents the beginning of the critical review of the conventional wisdom about the origin of World War II, including German rearmament in 1936–9 (the first edition was published in 1961). On this point, see Watt (1965). Klein (1959), which became widely known particularly through Taylor (1964), declared: "[e]ven a cursory examination of the official German data recently made available shows that the validity of these propositions is questionable." This declaration follows the statement (p. 1): "Nearly all the economic and political studies of prewar Germany agreed on three major propositions: (1) that in the period before 1939 Germany had succeeded in building up a military machine whose comparative strength was enormous; (2) that a substantial part of the increase in production from the low level of the depression was channeled into the construction of huge war potential; (3) that all economic considerations were subordinated to the central task of preparing for war." The study on which Klein (1959) was based was completed during 1946–8, and published as Klein (1948). On his work, see also Overy (1994, p. 18).

[8] The same also applies to the UK. Conventional wisdom about the UK has been critically reviewed and under reconstruction, concerning not only the one for interwar and war period with "disarming," "appeasement," and "liberal internationalism," but also the one for its whole history of the twentieth century with "welfare state," "declinist," and "two cultures." See the introduction in Edgerton (2006), p. 5~ in particular. One historian observes there is a sort of history of the UK that "explains an outcome which never happened ... by a cause that is equally imagined" (Hannah, 1995, p. 248).

Upon a careful review, Rockoff (1998, pp. 146–7) concludes:

[O]n the eve of the depression the economics profession (or at least an important segment of it) was ready with an arsenal of reform plans, ranging from minimum wage laws to industrial reserve armies, for the New Deal to use in its war against the depression. The general assumption that lay behind these plans was that markets frequently fail to produce socially desirable results, and that the central government was normally competent to diagnose and correct the problems created by unfettered markets. This assumption, massively reinforced by the depression itself, inevitably structured the debate over subsequent reforms, and constituted one of the most enduring legacies of the depression.

"In the postwar era", he continues (p. 147): "the evolution of opinion (both professional and public) about the appropriate economic role of the federal government followed the inverse of the path described in the preceding sections. In particular, just as the depression of the 1930s encouraged the public to adopt the enthusiasm for government intervention already prevalent among leading economists, the stagflation of 1970s encouraged the adoption of a new skepticism about government already evident among economists at an earlier date."

Conventional Wisdom About Japan

A similar conventional wisdom became dominant in Japan. Here, however, there is very little sign of critical review or reconstruction, even in the twenty-first century.

The conventional view is that from September–October 1937, after the beginning of the War with China in July 1937, Japan's economic system rapidly came under direct state control. "Plan" and "planning" are the key words that characterize this era. This remains the dominant view today, both in Japan and abroad. The eight volumes of *The Japanese Economic History*, by leading Japanese economic historians, were published in 1989, as the former USSR collapsed. Takafusa Nakamura, the editor of the seventh volume, entitled *"Planning" and "Democratization,"* which covered the period 1937 to 1954, explained the historical background that prompted the government to put controls into action. Nakamura (1989, p. 9) argued that "because ordinary policy measures were recognized to be ineffective there was no other choice than to adopt direct control." What is more, he added, "wide support for criticism of the capitalist system and pervasive negativity toward a laissez-faire economy" played a critical role.[9]

---

[9] Nakamura (1989, p. 9). For more details, see section 3–2.

Immediately after the end of the Pacific War, under the U.S. occupation, this became the dominant view: the coalition government, led by the Socialist Party, implemented effective plans and planning, and interventionist policies such as *keisha seisan seido* (the Priority Production Scheme, PPS) were highly successful. Under the U.S. occupation, the experience (and success) of New Deal policies in the United States was accepted with enthusiastic support in Japan.[10]

What is peculiar to Japan is the persistence and influence of the conventional wisdom, and the strong support the idea of a socialist planned economy receives ("the praise of socialist planned economy"). While there was some weakening of support in the 1960s at the latest, this belief still remains strong in the twenty-first century. Little has been said in Japan about the reality of the Soviet economy under Stalin's dictatorship; likewise, critical reevaluation over several decades of the economic policy and rearmament in the Nazi Germany, the U.S. New Deal policies, and the whole history of twentieth-century UK is little known in Japan. The substantial wall of conventional wisdom has effectively impeded the flow of information and the acceptance of alternative views.

The direct focus of this book is on Japan's economic policies from the second half of the 1930s to the first half of the 1940s, its so-called systematic war preparations, war mobilization, and economic control. I also examine the competence of the state that conditioned them. The dominant view of the effective economic policies of this era characterized by such key words as "plan" and "planning" enforced by the competent Japanese government has indeed faced few serious questions leading to a critical review and reevaluation. As the dominant view, even today it receives wide public support, and its position as the dominant view remains solid.

The conventional wisdom about the effectiveness of plans and planning and the economic policies of wartime Japan are two sides of the same coin, mutually reinforcing each other.

II

Three Lessons from the Soviet-Type Administrative-Command Economy

Considerable time has now passed since the collapse of the Soviet Union forced the formerly socialist countries to make the transition from an

---

[10] See Miwa and Ramseyer (2009a, b), and for details, see Miwa and Ramseyer (2004a, 2005a).

administrative-command economy (ACE) to a market economy. Until the 1960s, many people in Japan – particularly young people – regularly debated such topics as "When would the political balance between conservative and progressive forces be reversed?" "Capitalism or socialism?" "When would the capitalist system collapse?" "What are the ways and measures for promoting smooth transition to socialism?" For this reason, many Japanese who were young at the time may have a strong resistance to this observation and its long-lasting political influence as a bitter reminder.[11]

This book, which reviews the state's actions and economic policies in wartime Japan, and its overall competence, will prompt a similar reaction. The war is for many readers "the past they hate to remember." However, this period of our history and these phenomena have been shelved for a long time. This book will newly investigate the reality and performance of these policies and undertakes a fundamental review of that era and phenomena.

Three lessons can be drawn from the failure of the former Soviet-type ACE and applied to economic policies in prewar and wartime Japan.

Lesson 1: An Infeasible Request Beyond the Competence of the State

Reviewing the ACE under Stalin's dictatorship amounts to more than detailing how it ended in failure. The ACE was an economic regime adopted by many countries for a significant period of time. People all over the world became firmly convinced, in the 1930s at least, that the USSR's adoption of the ACE had been a huge success, and that it operated efficiently and effectively (the praise of the socialist planned economy). Many countries, fully or partially, followed suit. In other countries that did not adopt the policy, including Japan, many argued that it should be adopted – indeed, some still do so today.

What was the cause of the failure? Could the collapse have been circumvented by improving the operating mechanism? If the collapse was avoidable, then the failure was specific to the Soviet Union and the result of mismanagement.

---

[11] This book discusses neither socialist economy and the theory of socialist economic systems nor the "praise of socialist planned economy." On these issues, readers who read Japanese should see Nakagane (2007, 2010). The former discusses the Chinese economic system, which closes (pp. 76–7) as follows: "If Churchill had lived twelve years longer, he would have said before his death, 'the greatest misery of the Chinese people was that Mao Tse-tung was born in their country … and the next one was that he had lived too long.'"

The first lesson to be drawn from the experience of the ACE under Stalin's dictatorship is that it applies to ACE-type economic systems in general. The cause of the failure of the former Soviet ACE was not any defect or failure in management. Enforcing an efficient and effective socialist planned economy is an infeasible request beyond the competence of the state.

Lesson 2: A Clear View of the Details

The failure of the ACE system was brought to light in the 1990s, after the opening of the formerly secret Soviet state and party archives. From the time of its adoption, the ACE system had consistently failed, even during Stalin's dictatorship. Even before its full adoption, the people concerned should have predicted the difficulties they would face with the system. However, the problems did not become evident immediately. The process from the detection of the problems to the adoption of countermeasures must have been long and complicated.

So what policy measures were adopted before the failure became evident to everyone? What was the consequence of individual policy measures that were adopted? What lessons did people draw from them?

From the initial stage of its adoption, a significant number of people clearly understood that it would be impossible to operate a full-scale ACE system effectively and efficiently. For this reason, from the start the ACE system actually adopted differed from the idealized ACE that most presume, in which an organization or institution such as Gosplan formulates the central plan that covers the whole economy, on the basis of which the government controls and operates the whole economy. Moreover, the system initially adopted had been continuously revised as needed.

Lesson 2 is twofold. First, the ACE system actually adopted had been from the start substantially different from the widely accepted idealized one. It had been continuously revised in response to difficulties and troubles. Second, to understand adequately the working mechanism and performance, it is of critical importance to look straight at the specific details of ACE system in action, including plans and planning.

The disregard and neglect of this lesson mean that the public has paid a high cost by leaving huge wastage unchecked for a long time. The conventional wisdom had support from a wide spectrum of public opinion, perpetuating a myth that substantially deviates from the reality of the Soviet-type ACE under Stalin's dictatorship. Under the Soviet system, from the beginning, the function and role of plans was limited, and features of a decentralized system were adopted.

Lesson 3: Misunderstandings Are Frequently Adopted as Conventional Wisdom

In the first half of the 1930s, the declaration that the USSR's first Five-Year Plan had achieved a remarkable success was widely accepted throughout the world. In many countries, it had an enormous influence both at the time of and even after the war.

In Japan, its influence became stronger after the end of the Pacific War. In the second half of the 1940s, the praise of socialist planned economy, together with success stories about plans and planning, became widely accepted and is still maintained today. If we call a view that deviates substantially from reality a bubble, both the conventional wisdom that the ACE system operated effectively and efficiently and belief in the effectiveness of a socialist planned economy are bubbles on a magnificent scale.[12]

Why did this misunderstanding about the alleged success of the ACE – which was not actually adopted – gain currency and wide acceptance? Why did it have such wide support for so long? It should make us wonder how many similar cases might have existed around us.[13]

III

The Competence of the State

The (ultimate) focus of my investigation is "the competence of the state" (Stigler, 1965). In some ways, this book is an extension of my *State Competence and Economic Growth in Japan* (Miwa, 2004). As George Stigler pointed out in his 1964 presidential address to the American Economic Association (Stigler, 1965, p. 4), Adam Smith distrusted not the competence of the state but its motives: The legislature is directed less often by an extended view of the common good than by "the clamorous importunity of partial interests" (1776, p. 437). What Stigler (1965, p. 4) considers "to be a

---

[12] Miwa and Ramseyer (2001, p. 431) wrote: "with its long lifetime, strength and depth of support, and vital force expected to continue for some time in the future, the 'keiretsu' bubble is the very foundation of a group of the conventional wisdom about Japan. Comparing with this, 'mainbank' bubble is at most a mini-bubble, 'a baby tortoise on the back of her mother.'" See also Miwa and Ramseyer (2002c, e, and 2006).

[13] As Stigler (1988, pp. 111–12) wrote, once widely accepted and established, the dominant view "is guaranteed a measure of immortality. Its decline in popularity is more often due to changing interests than to contrary evidence, no matter how powerful that evidence may be." The fourth question (for the reader) may be, "How large is the cost to have supported the conventional wisdom which is a misunderstanding, and to continue to support it further?"

more important weakness in Smith's position. however – his undocumented assumption that the state was efficient in achieving mistaken ends – was not only accepted, but emphatically reaffirmed by his followers."

Smith's intellectual heirs did little to advance this state other than to repeat his claims endlessly. It was Stigler who noted that we lacked a usable theory of social and political control of economic activity. Both by exhortation and example, he urged us to study state intervention in economic activity empirically. To do all this when so many scholars and voters seem to support "big government" took extraordinary intellectual courage, but this was courage typical of Stigler.[14]

The Competence of the Japanese State: War Preparations and Mobilization

Like my previous work, Miwa (2004), which placed the ultimate focus on the competence of the state, this book focuses directly on the behavior and function of the state related to its competence.

In Part I of Miwa (2004), I investigated the reality of the state's function and role in promoting the machine tool industry that formed the basis of the wartime economy, and evaluated its performance. This new book investigates the reality of the state's function and role – that is, policies as a whole, called "plans," "preparations," "mobilization," and "control," in relation to wars (and national defense) during this era, often expressed as systematic war preparation, war mobilization, and economic control – and evaluates its performance. Unfortunately, because of Japan's defeat in war, and in particular the "postwar processing," including the dismantling of the military, it became extremely difficult to conduct this kind of ex-post investigation and evaluation.

Concerning the selection of examination objects, I wrote in Miwa (2004, p. xix):

If ever there were circumstances that would have given regulators the resources they needed to implement national policy, they were there in the early years of the

---

[14] Unfortunately, the state lacks many of the incentives to avoid inefficient (or simply infeasible) projects that individuals and firms face. Myriad empirical questions follow. When can the state competently fill a public order? How does a given agency behave when it receives an order that it cannot competently fill? Will it refuse to supply it or try to dissuade legislators from making demands? When might an agency pretend to fill an order that it understands to be impossible but later report as a success on the basis that most people have long forgotten the order? Will the public in fact have forgotten? When will it remember? More broadly, when and how will voters monitor the state? For more detail on this issue, see Miwa (2004, pp. xvi–xviii).

war. Under the exigency of military need, regulators in those early years enjoyed massive public support, largely compliant legislators, and enormous government resources.

It is that military exigency that makes the early wartime years the ideal laboratory of state competence. To measure the force of gravity, we need to observe falling objects in a vacuum, where air resistance will not slow the acceleration toward the Earth. To measure the theoretical competence of the state, we need to observe its behavior under favorable government control, where neither public resistance, inadequate funding, nor inappropriate statutes will dampen its effectiveness.

Because this book questions the status of conventional wisdom about Japan's war preparations and policies, its results and conclusions may surprise many readers.

The conventional wisdom about war mobilization at this period is consistent with the conventional wisdom that the state had made a significant contribution to Japan's spectacular economic development since the Meiji Restoration in 1868 through the policies of *fukoku-kyohei saku* (rich nation, strong army policy) and *shokusan-kogyo seisaku* (encouraging new industry policies). It is consistent also with the conventional wisdom that the state's market intervention or policies such as the PPS and the industrial policy made a great contribution to high postwar growth.

The conclusion of this book, therefore, will lead readers not only to redefine the conventional wisdom characterized by key terms such as "systematic war preparation," "war mobilization," and "economic control," but also to make it easy to understand and accept a series of arguments by Miwa and Ramseyer (for instance, see Miwa and Ramseyer, 2002a, 2006), which raise fundamental questions about the conventional wisdom that Japan's economic development since the Meiji Restoration had been state-led).

IV

Misunderstandings About Plans and Planning

Even in the twenty-first century, plans and planning are the key words that characterize the view of Japan during the period from the 1930s to the first half of the 1940s.

I begin the discussion with a critical review of the conventional wisdom that Japan began and developed the war on the basis of systematic war preparation and smoothly and effectively enforced war mobilization and economic control. At the beginning of my investigation of the reality and performance of war-related policies, I faced the seemingly invulnerable barrier of conventional wisdom that has for a long time made it extremely hard even to raise appropriate and matter-of-course questions about the dominant view.

As a result, the substance of the perception of systematic war preparations, as well as its validity and persuasiveness, has been neither thoroughly examined nor confirmed. The same holds for the reality and the actual function and role of plans and planning, and the behavior and competence of the government. All these dominant views assume a highly competent state. For this reason, the evaluation of the real function and role of policies in this era is useful for evaluating the competence of the state in Japan.

"Wars, when they come, are always different from the war that is expected" (Taylor, 1964, p. 116). Even for the state or government that began a war on the basis of carefully planned preparations, it is indispensable to have the capacity to make an appropriate and swift response to unexpected situations. In waging a war, the state is expected to have a different capacity from the one needed for operating a socialist planned economy. The Japanese government of the time had not systematically prepared for war. It did not manifest either the competence to operate a (socialist-like) planned economy or the ability to respond swiftly and appropriately to unexpected situations.

Some Essential – and Obvious – Questions

Thus we must endeavor to answer the following basic questions:

1. What was the war that the conventional wisdom argues that Japan began and developed upon carefully planned systematic preparations? Does it include all the events from the Manchurian Incident to the end of the Pacific War, for instance?

2. Did plans and planning, and the mobilization and control based on them, anticipate accurately the process after initiating the war? Did they prepare a precise menu with itemized quantities of weapons and war-related materials necessary for achieving the goal of the war (presumably victory)? Did they demonstrate that goal's feasibility and prepare specific means to achieve it? From that viewpoint, were prepared plans useful in achieving the goal? Were they well enough specified to work effectively? Suppose they were somewhat less than perfect, either in the accuracy of anticipation or in the degree of feasibility and specificity of means to achieve the goal. Where and how were they imperfect? How did those imperfections affect the usefulness and effectiveness of plans, mobilization, and control?

3. Did the government always make appropriate and swift responses to unexpected situations? Was there a framework that would enable it to

do so? From this viewpoint, did the state plan and prepare carefully and well?

4. Were plans, mobilization, and control enforceable, as the planners and people in charge expected? Was a careful enforcement framework planned and prepared? Was the framework prepared before the war flexible and competent enough to respond swiftly to unexpected situations that appeared in the lead-up to the war and during it? Did the relevant economic agents, including munitions companies, respond as expected? Did the government prepare means, such as providing incentives, to obtain their cooperation?

5. Did the individual government organizations that made up the enforcement framework work as the planners and people in charge of enforcement expected? Did the means to obtain the cooperation of relevant parties work as expected?

6. Did plans, mobilization, and control actually make a substantial contribution to the achievement of the goal of the war, which the state began and developed on the basis of systematic preparations, as the conventional wisdom argues? Where, how, and to what degree did they make contributions?

Let's work on the general assumption that "the war" covers the whole stream of events from the Manchurian Incident in 1931 to the Pacific War that ended in 1945. It then follows that Japan, on the basis of carefully planned systematic preparations, began and developed a war that would end in total defeat. It's inconceivable that Japan planned a war that would end in that way. Many readers must be frustrated with the conventional wisdom, without reference to unexpected situations aroused after formulating plans (or beginning the war). Such a basic consideration should be enough for readers to think it necessary to investigate in detail the validity and persuasiveness of the conventional wisdom.

The Need for Reassessment

As I will show, the answers to these questions indicate that the conventional wisdom is full of nonsensical phrases and extremely ambiguous substance. There is very little logical foundation or empirical evidence to support the conventional wisdom. I have been unable to find either logical foundation or empirical evidence to support the basic assumption that Japan began the war on the basis of carefully planned systematic preparations and exerted war mobilization and economic control smoothly and effectively.

It is important to critically review and eliminate the basics of this conventional wisdom. But this is not in itself the ultimate goal. For the (ultimate) focus of this book, its importance and usefulness to the evaluation of the competence of the state are also limited. Even when not based on plans formulated before the war, war mobilization and economic control enforced along different plans may have made a significant contribution to waging war. To investigate this point, we have to go into specific details of war mobilization and economic control. For this purpose, I focus on the competence of the state in mobilizing and inducing relevant economic agents such as munitions companies, rather than its competence in exerting policies based on earlier planning.

It seems that the performance of the Japanese government as a planner during this period was no better than that of the governments of any of the major countries that took part in World War II. This book gives a low grade to the Japanese government, both for its performance in establishing systems and organization for the formulation and enforcement of effective plans and for its implementation of effective and efficient mobilization of resources for its policy goal – victory.

The reality of the Soviet ACE under Stalin's dictatorship was substantially different from both the conventional wisdom that pertained until very recently and the basic view on which the economic system controversy concurrently flourished. Facing tough realities in operating the economy, the Soviet government (the planner) adopted factors of a decentralized system virtually from the start. During the period when Japan's economic system shifted rapidly to one under state control, the conventional wisdom argues, public confidence in the function and role of the market was undermined all over the world and government intervention, including planning, was strongly demanded and enforced.

As I show later, the conventional wisdom about Japan's systematic war preparations, carefully exerted under government direct control, is a misunderstanding that deviates substantially from reality. The robustness of this conventional wisdom is based on the same factor as the content of the conventional wisdom and the robustness of its status about the reality of planned economy under Stalin's dictatorship.

V

War Mobilization and Economic Control, 1931–1945

World War II began on 1 September 1939 with the German invasion of Poland and escalated to involve most of the major countries of the world.

The war had been foreseen by many, and most major countries maintained huge armed forces and armaments at the beginning of the 1930s, although these were far below the peak figures of World War I. During that decade, those countries systematically prepared for war. In that sense, systematic war preparation was common to all countries, and Germany and Japan were no exception.[15]

The overriding aim of a war policy is victory. If war preparations were planned and enforced systematically, their performance should be evaluated by their contribution to the victory in any war that the government began and developed.

Cairncross (1991, p. 3) summarized Ely Devons' thesis about the role of the government in war. (Devons was his boss in the Planning Department in the Ministry of Aircraft Production): "War … is a great centraliser. It is the government that conducts the war, decides what strategy to follow, and determines how the country's resources can best be used if the war is to be won. For this purpose it assumes in total war all necessary powers, taking control over the entire economy and acting as 'the sole consumer of the products of the economic system', even to deciding what should be left for civilian consumption. Civilians are regarded as instruments for carrying on the war rather than as 'individual persons with separate and different objectives of their own'." My evaluation of the reality and performance of government functions and roles is consistent with this understanding.

I assume that there is a central organization that designs the system for policy enforcement, is responsible for the reconciliation of interest among relevant economic agents, and integrates the whole system for policy implementation. I call this the government. Therefore, unless otherwise stated, the Prime Minister, the Cabinet, the Diet, the Army, the Army Ministry (AM), the Army Central Command (ACCom), the Navy, the Navy Ministry (NM), and the Navy Central Command (NCCom) are all part of the government.

The capacity of the government to respond to policy concerns decisively depends on the reality of power, implying the degree of concentration of power, and its stability.[16] Obviously, the mere existence of a strong (or prominent) leader, or dictator, is not enough.[17]

During this period in Japan, the degree of concentration of power and its stability were so very low that they rarely appeared as topics of discussion

---

[15] In this context, see the view of Taylor (1964, p. XVI), to which I will refer in note 1 of Chapter 2.

[16] See "The Five Issues of Governance" in Gregory (2004, pp. 52–3).

[17] See Chapter 4 of *The Nazi Dictatorship* (Kershaw, 2000), entitled "Hitler: 'Master in the Third Reich' or 'Weak Dictator'?"

even after the war. It makes no sense to think that the Japanese government could have had a high capability of responding to the policy objective of achieving victory in the coming war.

Government Performance in Wartime Japan and the UK

In its state of preparedness for a major war, the swiftness and appropriateness of its response to situations after the outbreak of war, and its development of a relevant wartime framework, the UK government showed the better performance. Neither a Soviet-type ACE nor admiration for a socialist planned economy has ever won overwhelming support in the UK.[18]

The UK government distinguished itself in the development, production, and deployment of wartime aircraft (particularly the application of large-scale bombers to strategic bombing), which played a decisive role in World War II. When Winston Churchill became the Prime Minister in May 1940, he established the Ministry of Aircraft Production (MAP) on the basis of long-standing preparations. "[Churchill] had been Minister of Munitions in the First World War, was firm believer in taking away from Service departments responsibility for production of the weapons they used and took steps to put an end to the exercise of this responsibility by the Air Ministry" (Cairncross, 1991, p. 7).[19]

Cairncross notes that a "more elaborate system of planning" became necessary because "by 1941 MAP was working on a scale far beyond that of prewar years" and because it needed to change priorities as the war changed

[18] Toye (2003) begins the "Conclusion" of *The Labour Party and the Planned Economy* (p. 66):
"When the Labour Party left office in 1951, it was still committed to economic planning, and indeed claimed to have undertaken such planning when in government. Nevertheless, the party's thought about the nature and scope of the planned economy was radically different from the planning policies and programmes which had been consequent upon its far heavier defeat twenty years earlier.... There had been a clear departure from the grand aspiration of the past. Labour's commitment to the planned economy had reached a crescendo in the aftermath of 1931. This died away to diminuendo in the Cripps and Gaitskell eras. And however noisy the drums surrounding later developments, like the Wilson government's national plan of 1965, the main theme of the thirties – comprehensive planning based on wholesale nationalisation and extensive physical controls – would in future be reduced to the merest echo."

[19] Edgerton (2006, p. 74) writes, however: "This picture of energetic civilian ousting the complacent air marshals and putting production to the fore has long been doubted by historians. Rightly so, ... there were also important continuities in personnel. Indeed it is important to note that these new ministries grew out of the service ministries.... However, the retrospective case for separate ministries seemed compelling in the light of the standard picture of utterly inadequate interwar armament production and rearmament."

course in 1940. MAP "invited John Jewkes, then head of the Economic Section of the War Cabinet Office, to prepare a report on [the idea of planning department] in May 1941 and Jewkes in turn asked Norman Chester and me [Cairncross], as colleagues of his in the Economic Section on the War Cabinet Offices, to lend a hand" (Cairncross, 1991, p. 8). By December 1941, he succeeded in building up a new department of programs and statistics with a small professional staff of about a dozen, all of them with degrees in economics.[20] "Nowadays we associate production programmes with long production runs of standardized goods, often consumer durables, with extensive tooling, line production, and careful design of the product, backed by research and development" (Cairncross, 1991, pp. 13–14, 8).

In Japan, as we have seen, the degree of concentration of power was low. In addition, at every stage until the end of the war, systematic use of economic resources for centralized planning operated poorly in almost every aspect of the development, production, and deployment of weapons, munitions, aircraft, and basic materials. This was also the case for establishing the framework, institutions, and organizations needed to realize systematic use.

At any stage of the war Japan took part in over a long time, I can find no indication that Japan began the war on the basis of carefully planned systematic preparations. The Japanese government did not realize an effective use of economic resources by swiftly and appropriately responding to unexpected situations that occurred in succession. Any plan prepared before the war was not based on accurate predictions of what might happen after the war began. Clearly, whatever plans there were, Japan did not prepare the specific means to respond appropriately to the situations and events that actually occurred.

Focusing on the war mobilization and economic control enforced after the outbreak of war, both in the speed and scale of mobilization and in the degree of effective and efficient use of materials I find no reason to think that the Japanese government achieved an excellent performance. Focusing on the framework for implementing systematic war preparations, war mobilization, economic control, and the war leadership's capacity to respond, I

---

[20] "Jewkes was no great admirer, then or afterwards, of central planning in principle and none of us had a very clear idea what planning aircraft production would involve in practice" (Cairncross, 1991, p. 8). "Most professional economists were hostile to planning, especially perhaps those who were directly involved in industrial planning and programming. . . . Thus Lionel Robbins was the head of the economic section of the Cabinet Office, a notable anti-planner. The successive directors general of planning in the MAP were Manchester liberals – John Jewkes and Ely Devons" (Edgerton, 2006, p. 72).

find no reason to think that the performance of the Japanese government was better than the government of any other major country involved in the war.

War Mobilization, Economic Control, and Administrative-Command Economy

The principal decision maker concerning war-related issues must be the government. Plans developed by another agent would have been ineffective, unless adopted by the government, and would have no connection with systematic war preparations.

Even today, plans and planning are the key words that characterize Japan from the 1930s to the first half of the 1940s. At the time, in many quarters, but particularly inside and around the government, long-term plans were developed, some of which attracted tremendous interest (and still gather attention today). Documents entitled plans demonstrate an endless variety of concreteness, enforceability, effectiveness, accuracy, and reliability, but many of them had very little substance.

In Japan in the mid-1930s, it was generally understood that the first Soviet Five-Year Plan was a huge success and that the second plan would work equally well. It was widely believed that Hitler's long-term plan for Germany would also be extremely successful. In the context of this prevailing conviction, many Five-Year Plans were developed in Japan, primarily by the Army.[21]

In the period immediately after the war, the view gained support that those long-term plans had been effectively enforced and had resulted in success. Manchukuo was smoothly and successfully constructed, and on the basis of that successful experience, long-tern plans were developed and implemented in Japan (and China). This view is encapsulated in phrases such as "systematic war preparations" and "total war regime," and represented symbolically by the Production Capacity Expansion Plans. The view that Japan began and developed the war on the basis of systematic

---

[21] Horiba (1962) represents the atmosphere in the Army of the time. Colonel Horiba was a chief of staff of war leadership in the ACCom when the War with China began. After graduation from Army War College, at the time of Manchurian Incident, he joined the ACCom. Then, as a resident officer, he stayed in the USSR and Poland for three years and carefully studied the USSR under Stalin, particularly its Five-Year Plan, which attracted world's attention (p. 3). Returning from the USSR in February 1937, he obtained a position at the War Leadership Section in the ACCom. Strategy Section Chief Ishiwara asked him to develop a five-year industrial development plan in Japan and Manchuria and national defense policies in particular. For more details on this point, see section 4–1 of this book.

preparations, and that carefully prepared war mobilization and economic control were enforced effectively and efficiently, became the dominant view, which is widely accepted even today.[22]

VI

Challenges for the Administrative-Command Economy

Only bureaucrats can think that planning work ends with the creation of the plan. *The creation of the plan is only the beginning.* The real direction of the plan develops only after the putting together of the plan. (Stalin, 1937)[23]

The difficulties that the (socialist) planned economy faced were far more serious and tough than the conventional wisdom has assumed, and in response the government adopted a system substantially different from the one widely accepted as a (socialist) planned economy for avoiding (or postponing) a collapse.

---

[22] As a historical background to the appearance and acceptance of the dominant view, the rise of both socialist political forces and Marxist political thought was of critical importance. More generally, together with the chaos and adversity of postwar Japan and strong reaction to wartime experiences, worldwide support for socialism, planning, plans, and the planned economy was also important. The content of Schumpeter (1947) and its acceptance in Japan symbolizes the atmosphere of the time. The final chapter of its first edition, published in 1942, ends (p. 375): "[I]t is only socialism ... that is so predictable. Nothing else is. In particular there is little reason to believe that this socialism will mean the advent of the civilization of which orthodox socialists dream. It is much more likely to present fascist features. That would be a strange answer to Marx's prayer. But history sometimes indulges in jokes of questionable taste." "A little more can now (July, 1946) be added to what was said in the last section about the effects of the war on the social structure of our epoch and on the position and prospects of orthodox (i.e. non-Communist) socialist groups," with which Schumpeter begins newly added Chapter 28, "The Consequences of the Second World War" (p. 376): "It was obvious in July, 1942, that, whatever the fate of particular socialist *groups*, there would be another great stride toward the socialist *order*, and that this time the stride would be taken also in the United States." Part II, "Can Capitalism Survive?" and Chapter XII, "Crumbling Walls," in particular, is the basis for the preceding view. In many countries, including Japan, this book attracted huge number of readers for several decades. It was in 1951 when Japan was under the U.S. occupation that the third edition of this book by the Harvard professor of economics was translated into Japanese by two well-known Japanese economists, Ichiro Nakayama and Seiichi Tohata, who wrote (p. 32 of the Japanese translation): "This book concludes that it is a worldwide basic trend to head along the gradual path to socialism, studying the character of managed capitalism, capitalism that would be coordinated and controlled by the society – the means toward democratic socialization, and that the U.S. is no exception". The translation was revised in 1962, and the one I now have was printed in 1968, the sixteenth printing. Recall here Stigler's (1988, pp. 111–12) comment, to which I refer in note 13.

[23] This is from Gregory and Harrison (2005, p. 730; italics in the original text).

To see what these difficulties were, let's begin with a review of influential criticism of the time. "Mises and Hayek's critique of a 'pure' planned economy are undoubtedly valid: The center cannot plan and price millions of goods and services; the coordination and incentive problems of such a complex organization would have been overwhelming; extracting reliable information from reluctant subordinates must have been a nightmare. Yet this system survived for more than sixty years!" (Gregory, 2004, p. 5). An overwhelming majority of supporters of the planned economy rarely understood it.

Gregory's next point is important:

Early writers on the administrative-command economy, ranging from Hayek and Mises to contemporary writers such as Mancur Olson..., paid little attention to the manner in which the dictatorship would organize its bureaucratic staff to manage producers. Mises and Hayek spoke vaguely of a central planning board that would deal directly with enterprises. Students of dictatorship also simplified it by assuming "costless coercion"; namely, that the dictator could costlessly persuade subordinates to do his bidding.... The dictator must oppose horizontal relations among industrial ministries, or among factories, because they weaken control, particularly when they form into organized interest groups. (Gregory, 2004, p. 133)[24]

Any government that adopted planning policies must have faced serious difficulties of this kind. The same applies to systematic war preparations, war mobilization, and economic control, which most major countries had exerted since the mid-1930s. However, I find very little discussion

---

[24] "Neither Stalin nor Hayek and Mises anticipated that the dictatorial interlocking directorate itself would inevitably be split into "them" (those representing narrow interests) and "us" (the relatively few representing "encompassing" interests). The number of top party officials who could occupy encompassing positions, independent of branch or regional interests, was limited" (Gregory, 2004, p. 135).

Hayek wrote in 1945 (Hayek, 1945, pp. 524–5): "If we can agree that the economic problem of society is mainly one of rapid adaptation to changes in the particular circumstances of time and place, it would seem to follow that the ultimate decisions must be left to the people who are familiar with these circumstances, who know directly of the relevant changes and of the resources immediately available to meet them.... We must solve it by some form of decentralization. But this answers only part of our problem. We need decentralization because only thus can we ensure that the knowledge of the particular circumstances of time and place will be promptly used. But 'man on the spot' cannot decide solely on the basis of his limited but intimate knowledge of the facts of his immediate surroundings. There will remain the problem of communicating to him such further information as he needs to fit his decisions into the whole pattern of changes of the economic system." For the details of its implications for war mobilization, see section 2–4–3, "The Meaning of the Scenario that the Military Led War Mobilization," in Miwa (2008, pp. 112–19). Also, for its application to supplier-assembler relationships in the motor industry, see Miwa (1996, ch. 4).

and information about such serious difficulties, and in particular their implementation, in Japan's economic history. As a result, these difficulties and the means for overcoming them never became a significant policy concern in Japan either during wartime or in the postwar period.[25]

Overvaluation of the Competence of the State

Socialist planned economies, which were "the most important social and economic experiment of the twentieth century" (Gregory, 2004, p. 1), do not work. Nevertheless, in many countries, including Japan, the concept was given strong if not overwhelming support over several decades, and in some countries this still continues.

Support for a socialist planned economy assumes both an undervaluation of the difficulties posed by its policies and an overvaluation of the competence of the state when it comes to their implementation. Yet that support has acquired an extraordinary vital force, despite the collapse of ACE in full view of everyone. It seems that very few people are prepared to confirm the collapse of a house of cards built on false assumptions and insist on a reevaluation of its foundations. Instead, they continue to repeat success stories (or myths) about the planned economy.

The Perpetuation of Myths About the Planned Economy

In Japan, a classic, idealized picture of a socialist planned economy, one that deviates substantially from reality, still garners overwhelmingly strong

[25] The Japanese government of the time must have faced with the same troubles as the Soviet government, as introduced in Gregory and Harrison (2005, pp. 729–30). What "the most important industrial leader of the 1930s expressed" as his frustration is symbolic: "They give us every day decree upon decree, each one is stronger and without foundation." They continue: "Ministries and enterprises insured themselves against interventions by holding back obligatory information and submitting their own plan proposals at the last minute to avoid duplicating this work later; ministries often proposed relatively modest targets to Gosplan while quietly imposing tougher assignments on their own enterprises.... Ministries fought for generalized plans and tried to avoid divulging enterprise plans to Gosplan; in April 1933, for example, Gosplan complained that ministry plans 'suffered from such incompleteness that it is impossible to use them.' ... The ministries withheld information from Gosplan and financial authorities on ground of national security.... For producers, the best plan was either no plan at all or a plan so general that it left all the real decisions to them. Gosplan even uncovered cases of 'nonplanning': 'Enterprises [large enterprises located near Moscow] declared to our representatives that they had not seen annual plans for a period of years.'" In Part II of this book, readers will find similar observations regarding Japan.

support.[26] *The Japanese Economic History*, mentioned earlier, sold well in the 1990s. Even now, most books on the Japanese economy or its economic history written in English are fiercely loyal to the conventional wisdom, which is still dominant among non-Japanese (readers).[27]

In Japan in the mid-1930s, a phenomenon emerged known as the planning boom, which was expanded and reinforced in postwar Japan. Under environmental conditions such as the war defeat, occupation, and political and economic chaos, the planning boom thrived for a considerable period of time.

The essence of the postwar planning boom is revealed in the way "plans" and "planning" have become the key words that characterize the Japanese economy from the mid-1930s to the second half of the 1940s. During the planning boom, the argument that plans and planning achieved great results in Japan during the period from the 1930s to the first half of the 1940s became widely accepted.

VII

Part I. The Reality of Systematic War Preparations, War Mobilization, and Economic Control

The subject of this book is the war-related policies established during the period from the 1930s to the first half of the 1940s. The book is based on Miwa (2008) and a companion paper, Miwa (2007). The majority of readers in the West are unfamiliar with the historic background to the conventional wisdom about Japan's preparedness for war.[28]

Part I sets the scene for Parts II and III and provides an approach to the research on long-neglected issues hidden behind the barrier of the conventional wisdom. Part II, "Materials Mobilization and Production Capacity Expansion Plans," investigates the details of representative plans and policies for war mobilization and economic control in wartime Japan. Because

---

[26] Japan seems not to be an exception. Gregory (2004, p. 3) writes: "The worldwide appeal of Marxism, communism, or the Radical Left was remarkably unaffected by the collapse of communism." See also note 6 on the same page.

[27] For example, Reischauer (1977), Johnson (1982), Calder (1993), Okazaki and Okuno-Fujiwara, eds. (1999), and Hoshi and Kashyap (2001) are widely accepted as standard reading today, and representative of the situation.

[28] Readers who are interested in further details of the conventional wisdom, its foundation and historical background, and the measures I took to liberate Japanese readers from its spell should see Part I of Miwa (2008). Unfortunately, this book is available only in Japanese.

those particular policies were primarily for basic materials, Part II places more emphasis on governmental rather than military competence. Part III is a study of the Navy Air Force, in which I investigate plans and policies for development, production, and the use of aircraft. Because aircraft were one of the weapons that played a key role in the war, Part III focuses on the military rather than the government.

For those investigations, we need at least a minimal understanding of the contemporary and historical environment and background to the issues I address in this book, including international relations, the reality of wars and battles, and the state of technology and function of aircraft and the roles they performed. For instance, many readers will be surprised to know that Japan had been at war with China for four and half years and was almost collapsing before the Pearl Harbor in December 1941.

As I declare at the beginning of Chapter 1, it is reckless, dangerous, and futile to accept straightforwardly the conventional wisdom that Japan began and executed "the war" upon systematically "planned preparations."

Chapter 1, "War Planning and Mobilization During the First Half of the War with China," discusses the reality of war mobilization that the Japanese government began in earnest with the outbreak of the War with China, the development of the laws and institutions concerned, and the performance of the war mobilization effort. The focus of discussion is the period of a little over a year from the outbreak of the war in July 1937. This chapter identifies and evaluates the reality of war preparation, in terms of the function, role, and performance of the individual organizations that were assigned roles in war planning and mobilization.

It concludes: "Over two decades before the outbreak of the war a diversity of phenomena associated with 'systematic war preparations' were continuously observed. However, most of them, lacking substance and specifics, did not function when needed as preparations. The war neither began upon careful 'preparation' nor developed along the 'plans' deliberately prepared. No 'preparations' were 'planned' and put into action before the war. Any 'preparations' completed before the war did not contribute to the implementation of 'war mobilization.'"

Chapter 2, "Operation Plan, War Plan, and Basic National Defense Policy," discusses the details of the decision-making process in Japan. It is widely accepted that a handful of military (Army) personnel controlled the decision making on critical issues during the 1930s and early 1940s. This chapter leads readers to reexamine the conventional wisdom about Japan's history, politics, economy, society, and life during this period. Once this is shown to be groundless, a wide variety of issues will emerge for reexamination.

The focus is on the details of the decision-making process on critical issues connected with war. It is not on whether plans were formulated but on the substance and effectiveness of government decision making. This chapter deals with two cases of decision making connected with the revision of the basic policies of national defense and policies on the War with China. I discuss decision-making issues connected with war mobilization and economic control in Part II. The existence of "plans" and "visions" and their effectiveness in performing important roles are completely different things. A key question is not whether "plans" existed, but their effectiveness and the roles they performed.

VIII

Part II. Materials Mobilization Plans, Production Capacity Expansion Plans, and Economic Control

Four chapters in Part II investigate the details of representative plans and policies for war mobilization and economic control in wartime Japan. In these chapters, I investigate the reality of the government's planning, control, and mobilization for basic materials and in key industries. I do so to evaluate the competence of the state under conditions as close as realistically possible to those of an experimental laboratory (on this question, see the discussion on planned economy under Stalin's dictatorship in section 3–2).

As I mention in Part I (subsection 2–4–2), with the lessons of the World War I and considerable development of aircraft capability and military usage, the total war theory or the national-defense-first theory became dominant. Recognizing the situation, "the Army commenced studies toward a full-fledged rearmament plan in 1934. From FY1937 it launched its 'first armament plan' and began building 41 divisions and 142 squadrons" (Boeicho, 1975c, p. 117). However, this was just before the beginning of the War with China. At first, the government (including the Army leadership) announced a nonexpansionist policy. Even after the escalation of the War with China, the government's basic policy was to resolve it promptly. In December 1941, more than four years after the war began, however, Japan began a war with the United States.

The Strategy Division Chief of the NCCom at the beginning of the Pacific War later recalled: "Modern warfare is a total war, and war potential is equivalent to national capacity. Everybody should have understood that a country with little national capacity could not challenge a country with a lot" (Fukudome, 1951, pp. 182–3). Modern warfare, as in the War with China and the Pacific War, is an all-out and long, drawn-out war of attrition. The competence required of a state undertaking this kind of war is twofold: to prepare for the war before its beginning, and to be prepared for unforeseen events and to respond swiftly and adequately to them.

Four chapters in Part II apply the discussion in Part I to specific plans, policies, and economic control. Those chapters provide readers with the information needed to address the question of how a socialist planned economy under Stalin's dictatorship might have worked had there been no Stalin.

Chapter 3 first discusses the historical background and general situation in the 1930s, including the wide support for planning and a planned economy, and then "control" as an expression and its substance, control laws and systems. Chapter 4 investigates in detail the reality and effectiveness of the Materials Mobilization Plans (MMPlans), while Chapter 5 investigates the details of the Production Capacity Expansion Plans (PCEPlans) and policies. Although conventional wisdom identifies the PCEPlans as the backbone of systematic war preparations, the cabinet approved only the "Outline" of PCEPlans in January 1939, eighteen months after the beginning of the War with China. Chapter 5 focuses also on Japanese production capacity expansion policies outside the PCEPlans. Chapter 6 studies PCEPolicies in Manchukuo (Manchuria).

The competence of the state in Japan in a situation where its realization and manifestation were crucial does not deserve a high score. The performance of this allegedly competent state – even when performance mattered most – was desultory at best.

IX

Part III. The Navy Air Force: A Study of a Central Japanese Player

Part III is a study of the Navy Air Force, in which I apply the analytic framework and discussion from Parts I and II to a specific aspect of the war and confirm their validity. In contrast to Part II, Part III focuses on military rather than government policies, looking at the air forces (and weaponry), including carrier-based fighters and land-based attack aircraft (or bombers) that were developed, produced, and used primarily by the Japanese Navy. During the period 1937 to 1945, the Navy (not the Army) Air Force dominated Japanese air warfare. Part III examines and evaluates the competence of the state in a situation where its realization and manifestation were most crucial.

The battle of attrition over Guadalcanal Island in 1942–3 is discussed in detail in Chapter 9, and is used as a case study of the competence of the state in responding to unforeseen events.

The study of the Navy Air Force in Part III confirms that the conventional wisdom about Japanese preparedness for war is a myth that deviates fatally from reality. It confirms that such conventional wisdom is dangerous and harmful in impeding empirical historical inquiry, and that the competence of the state of Japan at this time fell a long way short of the level that conventional wisdom has long taken for granted.

PART I

THE REALITY OF SYSTEMATIC WAR PREPARATIONS, WAR MOBILIZATION, AND ECONOMIC CONTROL

Part I sets the scene for Parts II and III, and provides an approach to the research on long-neglected issues hidden behind the barrier of the conventional wisdom.

1

War Planning and Mobilization during the First Half of the War with China

1-1. Overview

Section 1-2 offers three opening remarks on the conventional wisdom that Japan began and executed the war following systematically planned preparations. Those remarks on Japan's war production, the reality of systematic, long-term war preparations, and "inconvenient timing" raise serious questions about the grounds of the conventional wisdom.

Section 1-3 reviews the rapid development of institutions and systems relevant to war mobilization during the year following the outbreak of the War with China. In this section, I examine Japan's additional war needs and the areas in which the military found serious shortages. I focus on preparations for the military control of munitions factories, which were to serve as a foundation for war mobilization.

Section 1-4 investigates the war preparations that are supposed to have been systematically conducted before the outbreak of the War with China. This is a critical investigation into the substance of the historical observations that inform the dominant view of Japan's preparedness for war. First, I review the reality of the various plans related to war mobilization and the vicissitudes of the organizations that took charge of the planning tasks, together with their functions and roles. I divide the period into two parts, before and after 1927, the year the Office of Resources was established and discussion of the general mobilization plan began. Next, I focus on long-term plans, such as the Five-Year Plan for Munitions Manufacturing Industries and the Outline of the Five-Year Plan for Key Industries (Army Plan), which led to subsequent production capacity expansion plans. Last, I examine closely the reality of preparations for the military control of munitions factories. I find no support for the dominant view.

Section 1–5 studies the performance of war mobilization during the year after the outbreak of the War with China. Despite rapid improvements in relevant institutions and systems after the beginning of the war, the extent of war mobilization in this period fell far short of the level demanded and expected. In addition, within a year after the outbreak of the war, Japan had already reached the limits both of its military force and its national capacity for production. These observations imply two things. First, neither prewar planned preparations nor efforts toward war planning after the outbreak of the war – irrespective of whether they were conducted carefully and systematically – achieved satisfactory outcomes. Second, the Japanese government could not appropriately address the circumstances and critical issues it faced after the outbreak of the war. Section 1–6 concludes the chapter.

1–2. Three Opening Remarks on the Conventional Wisdom

1–2–1. Japan's War Production

In the years after 1937, Japan's war production increased rapidly. As Table 1–1 shows, of the total military spending from FY1931 to FY1945, only 4.8 percent is accounted for in the years FY1931–FY1936. Because the War with China that began in July 1937 was fought primarily on the continent, production of Army weapons in particular expanded markedly during the war.[1]

Tables 1–2 and 1–3 show the annual indices and annual weights in Army weapons production in value for the years 1931 to 1944. Figures 1–1 and 1–2 exhibit the annual production of Army's major arms (Figure 1–1) and Navy's major arms and Army-Navy aircraft (Figure 1–2) in volume for the years 1931 to 1945.

1–2–2. Reality of Systematic, Long-Term War Preparations

Focusing on the dominant view that Japan began and executed the war following systematically planned preparations, this book evaluates the function, roles, and performance of war planning, mobilization, and economic control, and ultimately the competence of the state in Japan. Unfortunately,

---

[1] For more details, see Miwa (2008, section 2–5, pp.146–54). In Japan, the fiscal year (FY) begins in April.

Table 1–1. *Army's weapons production (in value) in FY1931~FY1945*

Unit: 1,000Yen

	Before the war with china	During the war with china	During the pacific war	Total	Ratio (%)
	FY1931~FY1936	FY1937~FY1941	FY1942~FY1945		
Firearms	23,410	287,970	570,000	881,380	7.3
Artillery	64,830	255,600	489,000	809,430	6.7
Ammunition and explosive	257,590	2,511,500	1,939,000	4,708,090	39.0
Tank	82,730	501,800	767,000	1,351,530	11.1
Automobile	100,530	685,950	546,000	1,332,480	11.0
Chemical weapon	14,300	52,070	178,500	244,870	2.0
Communication equipment and optical weapon	7,800	23,660	371,000	402,460	3.3
Special-purpose vessels*	–	94,180	431,000	525,180	4.3
Instruments**	5,240	67,380	242,000	314,620	2.6
Air weaponry***	5,120	32,160	466,000	503,280	4.2
Air ammunition****	31,620	262,030	716,000	1,009,650	8.4
Total	593,170	4,774,300	6,715,500	12,082,970	100.0
Ratio in total	4.8	39.5	55.6	100.0	

Notes: * – various ships for landing operation; ** – various instruments including flame gun, hydrophone, searchlight, and transportation vehicles; *** – typically aircraft machine-guns; **** – ammunition and explosives for aircraft.

Source: Toyo keizai shimpo-sha (1950, p. 565).

Table 1–2. *Annual indices in army's weapons production (in value), 1931~1944*

Weapons	Average						Average in 1936–40 = 1.0				
	(1931–6)	1937	1938	1939	1940	(1937–40)	1941	Average 1942	1943	1944	Average (1941–4)
Light arms and machine guns	0.1	0.3	0.8	1.3	1.6	1.0	3.2	5.5	10.9	23.3	10.3
Cannons	0.4	0.6	0.8	1.1	1.5	1.0	1.9	3.3	4.4	5.2	3.4
Ammunition (excluding explosives)	0.1	0.2	1.0	1.3	1.4	1.0	1.6	2.6	4.0	4.2	3.1
Underwater weaponry	0.4	0.7	0.9	1.1	1.2	1.0	2.2	2.6	2.9	6.1	3.4
Specialized military vehicle	0.2	0.4	0.5	1.0	2.1	1.0	3.6	4.5	4.7	3.9	4.2
Military automobile	0.1	0.4	0.5	1.2	1.9	1.0	1.8	1.4	1.6	1.3	1.5
Communication and electric weapons	0.5	1.0	0.9	1.0	1.0	1.0	1.2	4.1	6.6	16.1	7.0
Optical and navigation weapons	0.4	0.7	0.8	1.0	1.5	1.0	3.4	4.3	9.5	14.2	7.9
(Total of the above)	0.2	0.4	0.9	1.2	1.6	1.0	2.0	2.9	4.4	5.9	3.8
Explosives	0.2	0.5	0.8	1.3	1.3	1.0	1.9	2.9	3.4	3.3	2.9

Source: Boeicho (1970, p. 823).

Table 1–3. *Annual Weights in Army's Weapons Production (in Value), 1931~1944*

Unit: %

Weapons	Average					(1937–40)		Average			Average
	(1931–6)	1937	1938	1939	1940	(1937–40)	1941	1942	1943	1944	(1941–4)
Light arms and machine guns	3.7	4.7	6.2	7.5	7.3	6.9	11.1	12.8	17.4	26.3	19.0
Cannons	16.3	12.2	7.3	7.3	8.2	8.1	7.8	9.1	8.4	7.5	8.2
Ammunition (excluding explosives)	29.0	28.2	53.6	46.7	40.9	44.1	35.9	38.9	40.9	33.4	37.0
Underwater weaponry	10.2	8.0	4.7	3.9	3.5	4.3	4.7	3.8	3.0	4.7	4.0
Specialized military vehicle	8.8	9.0	4.8	6.5	11.0	8.1	14.4	12.3	9.0	5.6	9.1
Military automobile	10.7	13.4	8.4	14.1	17.7	14.3	12.9	6.9	5.2	3.2	5.8
Communication and electric weapons	10.0	9.3	3.9	2.9	2.4	3.5	2.0	4.9	5.5	10.2	6.7
Optical and navigation weapons	3.4	2.8	1.4	1.2	1.4	1.5	2.5	2.2	3.3	3.7	3.1
Explosives	7.9	12.4	9.7	9.9	7.6	9.2	8.7	9.1	7.3	5.4	7.1
Total	100.0	100.0	100.0	100.0	100.0	100.0	100.0	100.0	100.0	100.0	100.0

Source: Boeicho (1970, p. 823).

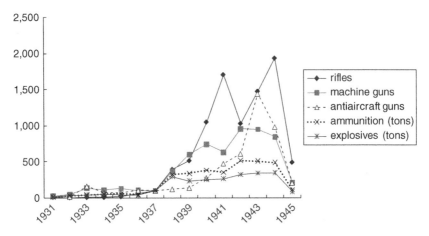

Figure 1-1. Annual Production of Army's Major Arms: in volume (1931–1945). Data from Shoko-gyosei-shi kanko-kai [1955] Table 11.

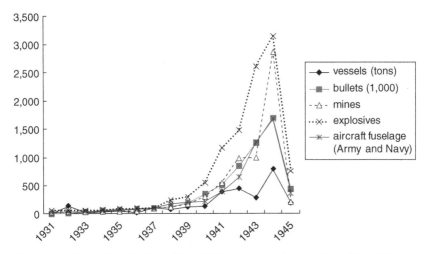

Figure 1-2. Annual Production of Navy's Major Arms and Army-Navy Aircraft: in volume (1931–1945). Data from Shoko-gyosei-shi kanko-kai [1955] Table 11.

the war planning or planned war preparation that has been so forcefully highlighted has no clear definition or substance. There is neither clear argument nor persuasive evidence supporting the view that the military prepared for war in advance. Even the identity of the war that was so systematically prepared for is unclear, and it has not been confirmed that the war that was prepared for was the war that was actually fought.

These considerations alone indicate that it is reckless, dangerous, and futile to accept unquestioningly the conventional wisdom that

Japan began and executed the war following systematically planned preparations. Three further important points should also be taken into consideration.

First, in the mid-1930s, military leaders, particularly those in the Army, urged the government to begin systematic, long-term war preparations. But military leaders assumed that the USSR, rapidly strengthening armament toward the east, would be the enemy. Just as the subsequent military expansion plan was initiated, the War with China began and implementation of the plan was suspended. Army leaders, fearing prolongation of the suspension, strongly opposed the escalation of the War with China – a war for which they had made no plans at all.

Second, both the Army Central Command (hereafter, ACCom) and the Cabinet adopted and maintained a nonescalation policy in the initial stages of the war. At every stage of the ensuing escalation, there were serious clashes of opinion both within the military and between the military and the government. As a result, a war that began without systematic preparation escalated without organization, planning, or coordinated mobilization. After the capture of Hankou in October 1938, a little over a year after the outbreak, the war ran into an impasse. With the so-called Konoe declaration (22 December) of "the creation of new order in East Asia," the Japanese government prepared for a long, drawn-out war. Yet the outbreak and escalation of the War with China retarded the implementation of any long-term war preparation. As the war progressed and Japan was faced with the limits of its military strength and national productive capability, the conflict of opinion inside the Army over the fate of its substantially retarded military plans against the USSR worsened markedly.

Third, from the end of 1938 to December 1941, the clash of opinion over the relative importance of the War with China and the Soviet threat continued, and the military (particularly the Army) and the government found themselves unable to make coherent plans. Long-term plans, such as the Production Capacity Expansion Plans (PCEPlans) that were finally approved in 1939, depended on massive imports of raw materials and production equipment from the United States – not only oil but also high-grade machine tools and steel scrap needed for munitions and aircraft production. This dependency shows that those long-term plans could not have factored in a war with the United States. Many military leaders later recalled that even in mid-1941, they did not anticipate such a war. Even if there were carefully planned systematic war preparations in Japan, the assumed belligerent country was not the United States.

1–2–3. "Inconvenient Timing"

In the conclusion of *Army War Mobilization (2)*, Boeicho (the Japanese Defense Agency) (1970, pp. 828–9) described the reality of prewar planned preparations in a section titled "Inconvenient Timing":

First, no organization of the government had ever attended to this kind of long-term plan. Second, therefore, to realize its "fully fledged armament enhancement plan" the Army itself formulated the Five-Year Plan for Munitions Manufacturing Industries, which it forwarded to the Planning Agency together with the "Outline of Five-Year Plan for Key Industries (Army Plan)." Third, in June 1937 the Army forwarded "the Plan" with "the Outline" to the Agency. When the war began one month later, neither the Plan nor the Outline had been specified in detail or put in action. Fourth, the "wartime mobilization plan" in the Army's "fully fledged armament enhancement plan" that began just before the war included a program to store operational materials for only one battle. Moreover, the plan prioritized the creation of troops, with the procurement of materials to be dealt with in later years. Fifth, with the outbreak and rapid escalation of the War with China that "the Army had never expected," the Army had to procure at one and the same time munitions to replenish supplies consumed in the War and munitions for armament enhancement.

Boeicho's description continued (pp. 829–30):

In preparation for the swift changes in the international situation, in 1940 the Army produced the Revised Armament Enhancement Plan. Just as it decided to start the three-year plan for 1941–43, the international situation changed radically once again. In June 1941 the war between Germany and the USSR began, and in July the Army launched so-called "Kwantung Army Special Exercise, *kan-toku-en*." In late July, the U.S., the U.K., and others froze Japan's foreign currency deposits in their countries, and in early August imposed a complete embargo on Japan. On September 6, in preparation both for war and peace, the Conference in the Presence of the Emperor approved "The Outline of Imperial National Policy Implementation," with which Japan decided to pursue diplomatic negotiation with the U.S. while simultaneously completing its war preparation against that country ... and on December 8 Japan finally began the war against the U.S., the U.K., and the Netherlands. Expansion of munitions manufacturing capacity as part of the Revised Armament Enhancement Plan was still only half complete.

1–3. Outbreak of the War with China and War Mobilization

1–3–1. Overview

At midnight on 7 July 1937, the military forces of Japan and China clashed at Lukouch'iau (Marco Polo Bridge) near Beijing. Expecting no such confrontation, the Japanese occupation forces at that time had only one brigade in China.[2] Army mobilization for war did not begin until 6 October, three months after the incident. The clash was not the result of carefully worked-out preparation, and Japan did not respond immediately with smooth war mobilization.

Concurrently with the incident, the Kwantung Army (the Japanese Army in Manchuria) and the Japanese Army in Korea notified Tokyo that they were preparing to send some of their forces if necessary. This was an emergency step based on official directives from the year's operations plans. Major-General Kanji Ishiwara, the Strategy Division Chief of ACCom, insisted that they should concentrate on the development of Manchukuo and the completion of defensive preparations against the USSR, and should not confuse their priorities by becoming involved in China. The Strategy Division decided on a nonescalation policy. On the evening of 8 July, the Army Central Commander (hereafter ACCommander), Kan'in-no-miya,[3] gave an order to the commander of the occupation forces in China to avoid further use of military force in order to prevent the escalation of the incident. At an extraordinary Cabinet meeting on 9 July, Army Minister Sugiyama said that they were planning to send three divisions from Japan – but the Cabinet deferred its decision. Thus, both the government and the ACCom decided to adopt and maintain a nonescalation policy.[4]

Despite continued efforts to resolve the conflict locally, negotiations between the Chinese and Japanese forces failed to reach agreement, and on 25 July, armed conflict resumed. Rescinding the previous order, the ACCom chief ordered the Army to use military force when necessary. On 27 July, the Army Minister asked the Cabinet to mobilize three divisions from home; the motion was accepted. On the same evening, the Army issued a mobilization order.[5]

The seventy-first special session of the Diet convened on 23 July, and, in addition to approving the budget for the First North China Incident (calculated before the 25 July conflict), agreed to the budget for the Second North China Incident that enabled the Army to mobilize and send military divisions from home. The approximately 400 million yen of the Army Ministry budget for the North China Incident included over 100 million yen for ammunition, but producing such a vast amount of

---

[2] Boeicho (1970, p. 23).
[3] Kan'in-no-miya (Taruhito) was a member of Imperial family, as "miya" suggests.
[4] Boeicho (1970, p. 23).
[5] Boeicho (1970, p. 26).

ammunition in a short time was a big problem. The Army's total budget for armament procurement for the fiscal year 1936 was at most 50–60 million yen.[6]

Immediately after the 7 July incident, the Army Ministry, particularly those sections directly in charge of war mobilization, began to prepare for further escalation of the situation and discussed the need for mobilization and how it would be implemented.[7] The government maintained its policy of conflict limitation, however, and the budget for the Incident remained an emergency step until the Second North China Incident. War mobilization remained haphazard.

The Equipment Bureau of the Army Ministry now had the money to increase ammunition production, but this would have to be done rapidly to avoid a shortfall in supply that would restrict operations planning. Realizing that it would be hard to produce a huge amount of ammunition in a short time, it concluded that war mobilization was the best way to achieve its objective.[8] It also had informal assurance from the ACCom that ten divisions would be available.

The Equipment Bureau (the War Preparation Section in particular) lobbied strenuously for war mobilization, but the Military Bureau stubbornly opposed its proposal, and neither Army Minister Sugiyama nor Deputy-Minister Umezu accepted it. Firmly maintaining the nonescalation policy, they hoped for a prompt resolution of the conflict. They worried about the negative impact of war mobilization on the Japanese economy. Without a clear forecast of the huge long-term budget for war expenditure, they realized they could not make realistic plans.[9]

The war broke out in Shanghai on 9 August, with the Navy becoming involved. The government and the ACCom now abandoned the nonescalation policy. The seventy-second extraordinary session of the Diet convened on 14 August, and the government started the process of giving shape to an emergency budget for war expenditure. With these developments, the Army finally decided mobilize for war.[10]

---

[6] Boeicho (1970, pp. 29–30).

[7] Major Kikusaburo Okada, who was to transfer in the spring to the Military Bureau but for the Ministry's reasons postponed the transition, stayed as the War-Mobilization Subsection Chief of the War Preparation Section in the Equipment Bureau and on 1 August was appointed again to the Equipment Bureau. This was indeed an exceptional event in personnel management (Boeicho, 1970, p. 31).

[8] Boeicho (1970, p. 31).

[9] Ibid.

[10] Ibid.

Army Policies and the Diet

The seventy-second extraordinary session of the Diet (4–8 September) was the defining Diet that transformed Japan from a quasi-wartime to a wartime posture.[11] The Diet created a Special Account for the Emergency Budget, and passed an emergency war budget. It passed legislation for war mobilization, including the act that enabled application of the Munitions Industries Mobilization Act and the Temporary Import-Export Grading Act.

The Planning Council (*kikaku-in*) that took charge of the formulation and implementation of Materials Mobilization Plans (hereafter MMPlans) was established on 25 October, and on 16 January the Cabinet approved the 1938 MMPlan, which focused on the allocation of funds for imports. It was in January 1939, one year later, that the Cabinet approved the Outline of Production Capacity Expansion Plans.

On 18 February 1938, the Cabinet approved the General Mobilization Act, which passed the Diet on 31 March and came into law on 1 April. This original act, however, needed an amending law that took effect in March 1941, three years later, imposing stricter penalties on vicious crimes.

These events occurred after the Incident, as the government, notwithstanding the nonescalation policy it initially adopted, responded hastily to the rapid development of the war. The government was not systematically prepared before the war.

The Army's Decision to Mobilize for War

The War Preparation Section drafted "The Outline for Implementing Army War Mobilization for the North China Incident," which, once agreed upon between relevant sections in the Ministry and the ACCom, obtained the Minister's approval on 21 August. With the budget and war legislation approved by the seventy-second extraordinary session of the Diet, this outline put Japan on a war footing.

As the war developed, the Army decided to act and mobilized about half the forces budgeted for in its fiscal year 1937 Mobilization Plan. It should be noted that the Army drafted the new "Outline," mentioned earlier, instead of applying the established plans for FY1937. In addition to its immediate need for munitions procurement, the Army's major concern was directed to extending the foundations of national power, symbolized by "The Outline of Five-Year Plan for Key Industries (Army Plan)," which the Army proposed to the government in June 1937. Although the war was developing,

---

[11] Boeicho (1967b, p. 620).

the Army still maintained its nonescalation policy. Still fearful of the effects of war on the economy, it limited mobilization to the minimum necessary.

Major Kikusaburo Okada, the War Mobilization Subsection Chief of the War Preparation Section, recalled after the war[12]:

We had FY war mobilization plans, which were exclusively to replenish munitions lost in operations. At that time we were at the stage of procuring munitions for the six-year armament expansion plan we had started that year. We were not allowed simply to follow the FY mobilization plan. The enemy we faced in the Incident was a very different enemy from that which we had anticipated when we made the plans for organization and equipment. In addition, the expansion in the key industries that the Army had proposed had not yet begun. Expecting to bring the situation under control in half a year, we placed paramount importance on not restricting the ACCom's mission during this period. Considering the characteristics of the Incident, however, we prepared new plans for replenishing lost munitions and procuring munitions for armament expansion.

Japan faced an unexpected war against an unexpected enemy. In addition, expecting a prompt resolution, it implemented mobilization plans of an entirely different type from those in the "plan" scheduled to start. This mobilization was not systematically prepared.

1–3–2. Preparations for the Control of Munitions Factories

Invoking war mobilization does not automatically lead to the achievement of the government's objectives. At the very least, the government must prepare carefully for the effective and efficient control of munitions factories.

Preparations for Application of the Munitions Industries Mobilization Act and the Control of Munitions Factories

The Requisition Order, first enacted in 1882 and still effective in 1937,[13] allowed the government to procure "what is currently available." In 1918, the Diet enacted the Munitions Industries Mobilization Act (MIM Act), and, as mentioned previously, the seventy-second extraordinary session of the Diet passed the Act for Applying the MIM Act. The government needed a wide variety of legal conditions in order to invoke the act effectively. The Army quickly prepared the Army Factory Control Order (Imperial Order), the Army Guidance on Munitions Factory Control for the China Incident

---

[12] Boeicho (1970, p. 38).
[13] Boeicho (1967b, p. 1).

(Army Transmittal), the Army Munitions Control Officer Order (Imperial Order), and so on.

The Army Factory Control Order, based on article 2 of the MIM Act, spelled out the basic rules and procedures for the control of munitions factories. The order, enacted on 24 September and signed into law the next day, specified "issues the competent Minister must prospectively consult with the Prime Minister," "items to be listed on the control order document," the "start, alteration, and removal of control," "guidance for controlling and supervising business owners," "guidance for claim handling by factories under control," "issues related to military secrecy," and so on.

Citing the order, the Army and the Navy issued an oral statement in which they said[14]:

> The primary purpose of control for munitions procurement is to improve the efficiency of factory use in order promptly to achieve the maximum production capacity. We will supervise and provide subsidy to factories for improving technology, enhancing the workforce, and procuring materials.... *As before, factory management should be entrusted to the originality and ingenuity of factory owners. That is, control never implies coercive enforcement, but it replaces the order-supervision system of peacetime with production order and process supervision.* We will make every effort not to obstruct business activities, for instance by stopping or canceling important orders from the private sector. (My italics)

The Army and Navy invoked the order to take over some munitions factories on 17 January 1938. With this first-round designation, the Army placed ninety-seven factories under control. Prior to the invocation, on 16 January they declared[15]: "We have decided to control some munitions factories, under the terms of the MIM Act.... The purpose of military control is to realize government–private sector cooperation for adjusting munitions production in accordance with military requirements.... Today, we believe, people no longer worry needlessly about the military control of factories. After all, the Army and the Navy have made careful preparations for such control. Factories under control will be able to devote themselves comfortably to wartime production."

Clearly, the forces were most concerned that the business community should not worry needlessly about military control.[16] War Mobilization Subsection Chief Okada's comment is indicative[17]: "At that time, *there was a strong mood on the private business side not to welcome military control of the*

---

[14] Boeicho (1970, p. 56).
[15] Ibid., p. 108.
[16] Ibid., p. 109.
[17] Ibid.

factories. In addition to distaste for constraints on business freedom under the capitalist economic system, *businessmen worried about the expected loss that would occur with the prompt resolution of the Incident*" (my italics).

Army Guidance on the Control of Munitions Factories for the China Incident

The Army's preparations for munitions factories' control were made step by step, by enacting the Army Factory Control Order, reaching an agreement between the Army and the Navy concerning the control of munitions factories, and establishing the Munitions Control Officer Order.

On 21 October 1937, the Army transmitted the "Army Guidance on the Control of Munitions Factories for the China Incident" to relevant troops. This stipulated the rules and procedures for the Army's control of munitions factories, applying the MIM Act and the Army Factory Control Order. This document defined the framework for the control of munitions factories for the first time; it had not been previously prepared.

The Army Munitions Control Officer Order

The Army decided to appoint a control officer to each munitions factory who would take charge of technology and accounting in relation to munitions order placement. However, the Army had no Imperial Order that approved the position and role of control officers.

When war mobilization began, orders for munitions increased dramatically. The Army had to appoint and dispatch control officers to munitions factories and in order to do so drafted an Army Munitions Control Officer Order. After consulting the Cabinet Legislation Bureau, on 29 September the Army asked the Cabinet to approve the draft order. However, it was not until 14 January 1938 that the Army Munitions Control Officer Order was finally enacted. The delay was due both to the hope that the Incident would be resolved promptly and to concern about the economic consequences of military control of munitions factories.[18]

On 17 January 1938 the Army began to take over munitions factories, invoking the Factory Control Order enacted on 25 September 1937. The Army Munitions Control Officer Order was enacted on 14 January 1938, three days previously. Clearly, the Army could not have trained many competent control officers when control of the factories started.

Control officers were determined to entrust the business management of the factories to the originality and ingenuity of the owners. However, when

[18] Ibid., pp. 64, 107.

necessary, officers could constrain the owners' choices and issue requests and commands. They would compensate losses incurred as a result of their control and could command the factory floor. But officers were not allowed to offer owners incentives to induce their proactive participation and cooperation.

Of course, the "Army Guidance on the Control of Munitions Factories for the China Incident" transmitted to troops on 21 October 1937 offered no assurance that the war mobilization would be effective or efficient. In subsection 1–4–4, I show that none of the information that would be indispensable for the efficient and effective running of those factories was collected or prepared.

1–3–3. Agreement Between the Army and the Navy on Munitions Mobilization

The War Mobilization Conference (Gunju-Doin Kaigi)
On 5 October1937, the Army Minister officially announced war mobilization for the China Incident, and on 17 October called up the commanding officers in charge of war mobilization and convened an extraordinary war mobilization conference.

War Mobilization Subsection Chief Okada drafted the invocation directive, and later recalled[19]:

We had developed a war mobilization plan every year since FY1920, but had never implemented one. Those plans were stored in the vault as paper plans.... We had no opportunity to draw lessons from their actual enforcement, and we seriously worried that we would face a huge variety of problems in implementing them. War mobilization plans are composed of extremely complex factors that are organically integrated.... If one of them were flawed, the plan would not work smoothly....The war mobilization for the China Incident was implemented not with the developed war mobilization plan for FY1937, but with the "Outline for Implementing Army War Mobilization for the North China Incident." Implementing war mobilization for the Incident was a really big undertaking, and the Minister, accepting a proposal from the authorities directly in charge, convened an extraordinary war mobilization conference. (My italics)

Okada continued[20]:

We knew that the Army's military budget for the China Incident, for the time being, supposed "prompt resolution in six months using fifteen divisions." The magnitude

---

[19] Ibid., p. 70.
[20] Ibid., p. 68.

of war mobilization that the main mobilization manager intended was based not only on the expeditionary force to China, but also on the overall mobilization that took the participation of the USSR into consideration. Unlike military mobilization during war, in times of peace we prepare no facilities or workforce for war mobilization. We had to implement overall war mobilization if we intended to replenish and enhance munitions for fifteen divisions and satisfy some of the military requirements against the USSR. We had to make an effort to obtain resources and allocate goods on a massive scale.[21]

Okada also recalled the conflict between the need to prepare for Soviet aggression and the need to pursue the War with China[22]: "With the escalation of the war, we had to worry about the further expansion of expeditionary forces to China. We had to obtain the munitions necessary for operations in China, but we also had to complete the defense buildup plan against the USSR. Therefore, in principle we did not allow the diversion of troops before the mobilization to China. We decided in principle to supply China with newly procured munitions only after mobilization, and continued to prepare for military action against the USSR."

War mobilization began with the invocation of the Army directive on 5 October 1937 of the war mobilization for China Incident. It faced a huge variety of constraints. The content of mobilization depends on the character of the war and the operations and battle conditions. Achieving the objective took a long time. It also necessitated overcoming a large number of impediments, some of which were unexpected. Obviously, preparations were needed before war mobilization could begin. In the statement of reason attached to his approval on 21 August of "The Outline for Implementing Army War Mobilization for the North China Incident," the Army Minister Sugiyama wrote[23]:

We have to prepare both for overall operations in China and for the participation of the USSR. We strive to make the best use of munitions procurement capacity, which takes a long time to realize. Before the start, we should settle various preparatory issues, such as reaching an agreement with the Navy if possible, smoothing the transition from peacetime to wartime, balancing the need of individual munitions depending on urgency, and particularly preparing for material procurement and an explosive increase in labor demand. The time has come for the Army's top leaders

---

[21] He continued further, "Basically the magnitude of the mobilization is determined by the budget. Because the industrial capacity of Japan was so small, for several months following the invocation, it made no difference whether the mobilization was partial or full. We did not declare full mobilization, which would have caused unnecessary friction with the government sections concerned, including the Office of Resources."

[22] Boeicho (1970, pp. 68–9).

[23] Boeicho (1967b, p. 619).

to implement war mobilization. We have to bring the budget into shape effectively and deliberately, and to prepare for its prompt implementation when passed by the Diet.

The Army invoked mobilization six weeks later. The Army Minister convened the War Mobilization Conference on 7 October, and the Army Factory Control Order was first invoked on 17 January 1938.

The Army-Navy Munitions Factory Mobilization Agreement on Aircraft Manufacturing Plants for FY1937

"Viewed from the munitions procurement perspective, the Army and the Navy were independent and stood on an equal footing, which meant it was highly probable that rivalry and confrontation between them would make it hard to implement the plans."[24] Reliable Army-Navy agreement had long been considered indispensable for precise implementation of munitions procurement without encountering unanticipated obstacles. The Army-Navy Munitions Factory Mobilization Agreement on Aircraft Manufacturing Plants for FY1937 reached on 16 June 1937, just before the outbreak of the War with China, was the first accomplishment. However, until the end of the war, Japan suffered seriously from lack of communication and from conflict between the Army and the Navy. The scope, content, and effectiveness of the agreement were woefully insufficient.

For FY1934, the Army War Mobilization Plan was formulated for the first time.[25] For FY1935, the plan was thoroughly revised, and the FY1936 Plan followed it closely. A thoroughly revised FY1937 Plan was transmitted to the sections concerned on 30 November 1936. The direction on transportation for the FY1937 Army War Mobilization Plan was transmitted on 16 January 1937, after which each war mobilization unit formulated its plan and reported it to the Minister.[26]

For the FY1937 War Mobilization Plan, the Army-Navy Munitions Factory Mobilization Agreement on Aircraft Manufacturing Plants for FY1937 was formulated. In order to ensure smooth implementation of munitions factory mobilization, since 1923 the Army and the Navy had continued discussion through the Army-Navy Committee on Munitions Factory Mobilization Agreement. Because of the sensitivity of the agenda, which related to war preparation and operations plans, the discussion

---

[24] Boeicho (1970, p. 17).
[25] On 19 December 1933, the Army Minister transmitted the order to formulate the FY1934 Army War Mobilization Plan to sections concerned, with which from FY1934 the Army War Mobilization Plan was formulated every year (Boeicho, 1970, p. 16).
[26] Boeicho (1967b, pp. 528–9).

always faced such difficulties that the committee failed to achieve concrete results. The scope of agreement was limited to plants for manufacturing or repairing aircraft bodies and engines, leaving out aircraft manufacturing, weapons, and fuel plants.

Major Okada, who was appointed War Mobilization Subsection Chief on 1 August 1936 and who proposed and consolidated the foundation of the agreement, recalled after the war[27]:

At that time, no clear basic policy for national defense was established, and there was no agreement between the Army and the Navy on munitions factory mobilization. The Army kept "Operations to the North" exclusively in mind, and the Navy "Operations to the East." Importantly, neither a unified decision nor an agreement of any kind existed about which set of operations would take priority. Everybody understood that the national productive capacity would not allow them to pursue both operations at once. With immediate problems of direction and content of armaments expansion involved, however, no decision was made to the effect that "we must not execute two operations simultaneously." Neither was any decision made that "in principle, in the Operation to the North the Army would be the primary and the Navy secondary, and in the Operation to the East the Navy the primary and the Army secondary." To put it strongly, the Army and the Navy respectively calculated their military demand taking their own duties into consideration, which the government simply added up to calculate total demand and formulate general mobilization plans (my italics).

The content of the agreement depended on the choice of operation plans, and simultaneously constrained them. On each side, there was overwhelming opposition even to starting negotiations.[28] The agreement itself was epoch-making.

Other Army-Navy Munitions Factory Mobilization Agreements

The Army and the Navy agreed essentially in the fall of 1936 and ultimately in June 1937 on the mobilization of aircraft manufacturing plants for FY1937. Following the initial agreement, the authorities directly in charge made efforts to negotiate the same type of agreement in other areas. They began with the use of a 10,000 ton press machine installed at the Muroran factory of the Japan Steel Works (JSW). Since after the end of World War I, the Navy had the press machine and used it exclusively, while the Army had no such facilities and suffered as a result. Partly because of the delay in reaching the final agreement in June 1937, the

---

[27] Boeicho (1967b, p. 533).
[28] It was the practice at the time that the government did not intervene squarely in command issues, understanding that it had no authority (Boeicho, 1967b, pp. 524–5).

War with China had begun while negotiations between the Army and the Navy were still under way.

Throughout the war, over thirty private firms produced artillery carriages for the Army under the guidance of the Osaka Artillery Arsenal. For availability and technological reasons, the number of firms producing gun barrels was much smaller. Several firms could source their own supply of gun barrel material, but only the Muroran factory could provide the materials for large-caliber guns.

The Army had no facilities for producing large-caliber guns such as anti-aircraft weapons. In wartime, the contract with the company gave the Navy's orders precedence; the company had to obtain the Navy's permission before accepting orders from other government sections or the private sector. In peacetime, any party placing an order had to pay a usage fee to the Navy. Following the initial agreement in 1936, "fortunately the Army could start negotiations with the Navy for the preferential treatment of the Army's orders."[29]

The Army-Navy Munitions Factory Mobilization Agreement on JSW, relating to the use of all JSW, including the Muroran factory, took effect on 12 December 1937, when it was signed by two Ministers.

Before the outbreak of war in 1937, negotiations for Army-Navy munitions factory mobilization agreements made little progress. With the outbreak of war, the success of the agreement on the use of aircraft plants pioneered a series of agreements, including the one on JSW. However, those agreements were not systematically prepared ahead of the war.[30]

1–3–4. Implementation of Munitions Factories' Control

Aircraft Manufacturing Plants
The Army-Navy munitions factory mobilization agreements were critically important as preparation for smooth and effective fully fledged war mobilization implementation, particularly the control of the munitions factories.

The agreement regarding air armament developed as follows. The Army-Navy Agreement on Air Armament for Current Deployment of Troops signed on 25 August 1937 covered only basic principles. Authorities directly in charge on both sides negotiated about individual plants and reached an

[29] Boeicho (1970, pp. 103–4).
[30] Boeicho (1967b, pp. 541–2). For more details, see Chapters 2 and 3 of Boeicho (1970).

agreement on 18 November. In addition to administration partition and peacetime use, the agreement assigned to the Army and the Navy baseline both capacity and its increase in wartime in each plant respectively. For example, Mitsubishi Heavy Industries' Nagoya aircraft manufacturing factory consisted of three plants, of which the Army airframe plant was entirely for the Army, and the Navy airframe plant entirely for the Navy, and the engine plant was shared on a fifty-fifty basis.[31]

The munitions factory control that started in 17 January 1938 expanded the span of control step by step. The sixth order invoked on 16 September 1938 expanded control to aircraft manufacturing factories. Of twenty-one factories newly placed under control, four were exclusively for the Army's use and six for the Navy's, with eleven given joint control.

Because of the agreement of June 1937, and because there was very little private demand, neither the Army nor the Navy had required military control over aircraft manufacturing factories. Military control started at this time for three main reasons[32]: (1) With the need to make arrangements for a long war, long-term increased aircraft production had to be anticipated, and expansion would be ensured under military control. (2) At first, there was strong opposition to military control from private businesses. As time went on, however, the mood changed, as businesses came to recognize that they would make a profit through the preferential treatment they received in areas such as funds, materials, and workforce. (3) Over time, it became more difficult to secure materials and workforce, and military help and control were needed to help production.

This sixth order almost completely followed the Army-Navy agreement reached on 18 November 1937, mentioned previously.[33]

1–4. War Mobilization and Plan: Expression and Substance

1–4–1. Munitions Industries Mobilization Act, Munitions Bureau (*gunju-kyoku*), and Mobilization Plans for Munitions Industries

Before the outbreak of the War with China in July 1937, Japan (its government, Army, and Navy) had apparently developed a wide range of systematic war preparations that symbolically formulated various types of war (or

---

[31] For the details of the agreement, see Boeicho (1970, p. 92 and after).
[32] Ibid., pp. 194–5.
[33] For an illustration of munitions factory control, see Miwa (2008, pp. 306–8), which exemplifies the case of the Japan Steel Works.

general) mobilization plan.[34] In the preceding section, I suggested that the allegedly systematic war preparations that preceded the war did not work well. In this section, I look at those preparations in more detail and confirm that proposition.

Over the two decades that preceded the outbreak of the war, a diversity of phenomena associated with systematic war preparations were continuously observed. However, most of them lacked substance and specifics and did not function when needed. The war neither began on the basis of careful preparation nor developed following deliberately prepared plans. No preparations were planned and put into action before the war. None of the preparations made before the war contributed to the implementation of war mobilization.

The MIM Act of 1918 was a symbolic kickoff. In response to the outbreak of the war two decades later, Japan had quickly to formulate a war mobilization plan. In addition, it had to enact war legislation such as the Act for Applying the MIM Act.

Army War Mobilization Plans

In section 1–3–3, I mentioned that the direction on transportation for FY1937 Army War Mobilization was transmitted on 16 January 1937, after which each war mobilization unit formulated its plan and reported it to the Minister.

This raises two questions.

First, in response to the direction, which war mobilization units reported to the Minister? War mobilization units are intermediaries that supply military goods to satisfy the final user's demand. The units would recruit suppliers as necessary to meet the military demand they received from final users. The system differs in the military goods required, the rate of demand increase, and time pressure. The units should have conducted careful research and collected information about potential suppliers. How much preparation had they done?

Second, the MIM Act was enacted in 1918, at which point collecting information about potential suppliers should have started. What information was actually collected? How specific and precise were the plans formulated based on the information gathered? How was the act affected by government policy, including foreign policy and the budget, and how did it connect with it? The information collected in preparation should

---

[34] Both "plan" and "program" correspond to the Japanese word "keikaku," and in principle in this book I translate Japanese word "keikaku" as "plan."

have corresponded to any likely wars. Naturally, the effectiveness of the preparation critically depended on the validity of the assumptions made about those projected wars. The Army war mobilization plans were prepared systematically and on a continuous basis on the assumption of a war against the USSR. This meant that the Army plans were fundamentally unsuited to meeting the demands of the War with China, which began in July 1937.

The specific content and real meaning of Okada's recollection is critical: "*We had developed a war mobilization plan every year since FY1920, but had never implemented one. Those plans were stored in the vault as paper plans*" (italics in the original text).[35] Also critical is the question of who formulated the plans. "Basically the magnitude of mobilization is determined by the budget,"[36] and the Cabinet's relationship with the Diet (which determined the budget) must also have been important. Between 1920 and 1937, there were not only disarmament treaties such as the Washington Naval Treaty and the London Naval Treaty but also days of administrative restructuring and armament reduction.

Establishment of the Munitions Bureau and Munitions Council

The MIM Act was enacted on 16 April 1918. On 31 May, the government instituted the Munitions Bureau system and Munitions Council system to implement the act.

The Munitions Bureau was placed under the office of the Prime Minister and exercised control over the mobilization of the munitions industries. The Prime Minister served as Bureau President, and the Army Minister and the Navy Minister were the Vice-Presidents. Participants and administrative officers were appointed by the Cabinet from civil servants (or bureaucrats) in the ministries concerned.

To establish the bureau, the Munitions Bureau Clerical Rule was published on 5 June. The bureau had three sections: Clerical, the First Section, and the Second Section. The First Section took charge of research and industries mobilization planning, and the Second Section drew up regulations and determined compensation, profit guarantees, and subsidies.

The Munitions Council also was under the control of the Prime Minister and took charge of affairs relating to calculating compensation, profit guarantees, or subsidies and determining sale prices, following the stipulation of the MIM Act (Article 15–1). In consultation with the Prime Minister,

---

[35] Boeicho (1970, p. 70).
[36] Ibid., p. 68.

it investigated and deliberated issues relating to the implementation of the act.

On the Prime Minister's recommendation, the Chairman and Vice-Chairman were appointed by Imperial Order, and councilors appointed by the Cabinet from among civil servants in the ministries concerned and academic experts.

When the Munitions Bureau was created on 5 June, the Prime Minister showed his enthusiasm for the structure by issuing a Cabinet-level set of instructions. The instructions tracked the general tenor of the act.[37] The bureau was actively to engage in investigating relevant resources at home and abroad, preparing industry mobilization plans, enhancing munitions production capacity (through encouragement and subsidy), and drawing up wartime regulations.

Thus, in 1918 the MIM Act was enacted, and the Munitions Bureau and the Munitions Council began their activities. The MIM Act became the foundation of war mobilization for the 1937 war. Before its use, however, the Diet had to pass the Act for Applying the MIM Act, and the Army had to prepare such orders as the Army Factory Control Order. For twenty years, all these issues had been left unspecified.

Enactment of War-Industry Survey Order (Gunju Chosa-Rei)

With the implementation of the MIM Act, some necessary subsidiary rules were established. Two points are important.

First, the act was also applied to Korea, Taiwan, and Sakhalin. Munitions industry mobilization in Kwantung Leased Territory and the district affiliated with the South Manchurian Railway were also deemed to be covered by this act.

Second, the War-Industry Survey Order was enacted. This Imperial Order faced serious challenges for a number of reasons, and it took some considerable time to produce the final draft. Army munitions industry mobilization plans, or control-operation plans of the nation's full potential, existed to coordinate demand and supply most efficiently, in quality, quantity, and time. So it was critical to collect accurate and recent data about all the relevant resources. Response to the survey conducted for this purpose, therefore, had to be made mandatory, and the procedures and format of the report had to be simple and clear.[38]

---

[37] Boeicho (1970, p. 4).
[38] Ibid.

It was the autumn of 1919 before a formal draft was produced, eighteen months after the establishment of the Munitions Bureau. The order was finally promulgated on 15 December 1919.

It was complicated, with twenty-eight articles and twenty-three charts. The survey covered plant, workplace, vessel, railway, and transport equipment, and collected information about manpower, equipment, machinery and appliances, raw materials, fuel, and engines. In addition, it surveyed business connections in the industry and depositories of munitions-related goods. Respondents were required to complete the survey and send it to the local provincial governor. The situation was reviewed at the end of December each year, and respondents were required to file their reports by 15 February of the following year.

From 1919, this happened systematically.[39]

Response of the Army: Guidance for Munitions Industries
Mobilization Plans and Munitions Industries
Mobilization Fiscal Year Plans
In response to the establishment of the Munitions Bureau, the Army and Navy each created a section that took charge of issues related to munitions industries mobilization: the Procurement Policy Section (*kosei-ka*) of the Armament Bureau (*heiki-kyoku*) in the Army Ministry and the Sixth Section of the Ships Bureau (*kansei-kyoku*) in the Navy Ministry.

The Procurement Policy Section was placed at the top of the Armament Bureau; its lineup was richer than that of other sections, and it was the largest section in the Army Ministry. In addition, a lieutenant-colonel (or major) in the section doubled as a member in the Military (*gunji*) Section of the Military Bureau that administered Army military policy in general. He was charged with coordinating the planning and implementation of war mobilization with organization, equipment, recruitment, and budget.

For the Procurement Policy Section, the critical issues were, first, formulation of Army munitions industries mobilization plans and, second, substantive implementation of the Munitions Bureau's affairs. Section Chief Yoshida and Senior Officer Suzuki doubled as officers in the Munitions Bureau.

Formulating Army munitions industries mobilization plans was seriously challenging. By the autumn of 1919, the final draft of the 1920 Fiscal

---

[39] The War-Industry Survey Order was abrogated on 1 December 1929, with the implementation of the Resource Survey Act and the Resource Survey Order. For example, the Manchurian Incident began on 18 September 1931.

Year Guidance for Munitions Industries Mobilization Plan was produced, and was approved by the Army Minister on 10 January 1920.

The guidance defined the sequence of plan formulation, method, scope of plans, and responsibility for work schedules among the sections in the ministry; spelled out military items; and designated troops that would plan munitions industries mobilization.

The Procurement Policy Section next made an effort to formulate the invocation draft for the 1920 fiscal year guidance for the munitions industries mobilization plan. This invocation draft set specific standards for munitions industries mobilization plans, such as schedules for the types and volumes of military items needed. These schedules would be closely connected with each fiscal year's operations and mobilization plan. Moreover, the Section was to make realistic preparations for supply needs, taking wartime demand and supply capacity into consideration. Thus, the standards were determined for coordinating the supreme command's supply capacity and needs.

On 1 May 1920, the draft was implemented. The 1920 Fiscal Year Guidance was the Army's first mobilization plan. It faced serious challenges in environments that did not allow completion, but was finally established. [40]

For fiscal years 1921 and 1922, the Army munitions industries mobilization plan was formulated following the same guidance and draft. In October 1922, with the benefit of three years' experience, the Army formulated the Army Guidance for Munitions Industries Mobilization Plans, which stipulated general basic items and was of a permanent character. It consisted of sixty-eight articles in ten chapters.

After FY1923, the Army formulated munitions industries mobilization plans repeatedly, with minor or major revisions, based upon this guidance and the invocation draft for fiscal year plans. This guidance formed the backbone of the Army's munitions industries mobilization plans until the Army War Mobilization Plan Order was established in 1933.

Consolidation of the Munitions Bureau into the National Strength Council (NSC, Kokusei-in) and Its Dissolution

The jurisdiction of the Munitions Bureau covered so broad an area and was so complicated that effective implementation was highly problematic. The War Industry Survey Order was finalized in October 1919, but the bureau had to continue its efforts to investigate war mobilization planning and policy measures, such as subsidies for promoting armaments industries.

---

[40] Boeicho (1970, pp. 5–6).

On 15 May 1920, the government expanded and strengthened the Munitions Bureau by consolidating it with the Cabinet Statistics Bureau to form the National Strength Council (NSC). The Munitions Bureau became Part Two of the NSC, with four separate sections on institutions, plants, military items, and industries.

The NSC's life was short, however. It was dissolved and Part Two abolished at the end of October 1922. The major achievements of the NSC were strengthening the authority of the Prime Minister on the implementation of the MIM Act and obtaining agreement among ministries concerned on the implementation of the MIM Act.

The former, an exception to the Cabinet system of the time, authorized the leadership of the Prime Minister and gave him the authority to issue orders to ministries concerning the implementation of the MIM Act.

The Munitions Bureau started the process for the latter in January 1920. The agreement was not only related to a broad range of issues but also affected the responsibilities of the ministries concerned, particularly the strategy and mobilization plans of the Army and the Navy. After deliberation over a period of twenty-two months and more than two hundred revisions, agreement was reached in November 1921. The long, drawn-out process symbolizes the substance and difficulties involved in munitions industries mobilization.[41]

The agreement was established, but the NSC was dissolved before it could formulate munitions industries mobilization plans. The League of Nations was created in 1919, and the Naval Arms Control Pact (Washington Naval Treaty) was concluded in 1922. In Japan, mired in a postwar depression, the government ardently pursued administrative readjustment and arms control.[42]

When the NSC was dissolved and Part Two abolished at the end of October 1922, both the Munitions Council Order and the authority of the Prime Minister on the implementation of MIM Act were annulled.[43] No munitions industries mobilization plans had been formulated.

After FY1920, the Army formulated an Army munitions industries mobilization plan every fiscal year. In response to the abolition of the Part Two

---

[41] Ibid., p. 7.
[42] After the Army Ministers of the time, arms controls of the Army were called Yamanashi arms control (1922) and Ugaki arms control (1925).
[43] The abolition of these two Imperial Orders would cause trouble with the MIM Act. New orders were issued later, for the latter in November 1937 and for the former in September 1939. This observation implies that, before the outbreak of the War with China, there was no need to resurrect them, that is, no need to use the act.

of NSC, the Army also decided to formulate an Army Munitions Industries Mobilization Central Plan after FY1924. This central plan included countermeasures to fill the gap created by with the abolition of Part Two. The central plan was established as an agreement between the Army Ministry and the ACCom. It was regarded as being of prime importance, but was confidential outside the Army.[44]

1–4–2. Establishment of the Office of Resources and the General Mobilization Plan

In 1927, the Office of Resources (OR) and the Resources Council were established as general mobilization organizations. The activities later called general mobilization plans began here. The operations envisioned, however, were broad and complicated. From the start, these weak organizations confronted the hard task of coordinating the conflicting interests of the bodies concerned. As I show in section 1–4–3, when the Army presented the Outline of the Five-Year Plan for Key Industries (Army Plan) to the government, it also presented the general framework it drafted as a guide for its implementation, assuming that the government had insufficient capacity to execute the proposal.

Establishment of the OR and Creation of the Procurement
Bureau (seibi-kyoku) in the Army Ministry
Both houses of the Diet recommended that the government create organizations for general mobilization. Facing serious difficulty in reaching an agreement among the ministries concerned on the implementation of the MIM Act in 1922, the Cabinet approved on 22 April 1926 the preparatory committee to establish an organization for general mobilization. The committee carefully investigated the form and task of organization and measures of enforcement and coordination with the bodies concerned. The government then included budget expenses for the creation of the new organization in the FY1927.

New orders were issued on 26 May 1927 for the OR and on 18 July for the Resource Council. With this, the central organizations for general mobilization were revived.

Yet these were not simple revivals of the Munitions Bureau and Munitions Council. The Munitions Bureau (and the NSC) had seen general mobilization as fulfilling military demand. The main task of the OR was to complete

---

[44] Ibid., p. 8.

the control and use of national resources and meet military and private demand. It viewed general mobilization as its primary task, and military demand fulfillment as a subsidiary. Indeed, general mobilization was the basic goal of both these organizations.[45]

They were, however, based on the MIM Act of 1918. The General Mobilization Act was established in 1938. The OR was consolidated into the Planning Council (*kikaku-in*) in October 1937.

On 30 September 1926, alongside the government's effort to create new organizations, the Army Ministry also engaged in restructuring the Army Ministry in response to general mobilization and munitions procurement, concentrating on the reorganization of the Military Bureau and the creation of the Procurement Bureau (*seibi-kyoku*).

The Procurement Bureau, into which the Procurement Policy Section of the Armament Bureau was dissolved, also absorbed part of the Military Bureau's task. The lineup of the bureau was almost the same as the Armament Bureau without the Procurement Policy Section, and was located between the Military Bureau and the Armament Bureau. The Procurement Bureau consisted of two sections, the Mobilization Section (*doin-ka*) and the Control Section (*tosei-ka*).[46]

Enacting Regulations for the Resources Survey

From the start, the OR actively addressed issues such as developing a resource survey system, formulating a framework for control and use of plans for resources (general mobilization), and investigating wartime regulations. With the transition of focus from the fulfillment of military demand to general mobilization, the task of the OR expanded tremendously and

---

[45] Ibid., p. 10.

[46] Takeo Iwaguro served several years after 1928 in the Control Section of the Procurement Bureau and was recalled after the war (Iwaguro, 1977, pp. 23–9). In 1921, a meeting on materials for operations was established in the Army Ministry, where related parties from the Army Ministry and the ACCom checked on materials for operations, such as weapons, clothes, and food. As a result, Ugaki arms control was realized by reducing the number of divisions but increasing the equipment expenses. Then the permanent Procurement Bureau was created. "At that time the number of material items needed for operations was over 50,000 (now, in the 1970s, 1 million), for each of which we determined the allocation volume, the unit price, and the necessary budget. During wartime, in addition to peacetime needs, assuming procurement was increased on a temporary basis and newly manufactured if unavailable, we formulated both production and requisition plans for wartime and procurement plans for peacetime. At the beginning 100 people worked for five years. When I was serving, the task was enormously simplified. More than 20 people worked in the Control Section and divided the work over 50,000 items every day."

became complex. That complexity, in turn, made the achievement of these goals more difficult.

Resources for direct military use were surveyed under the War-Industry Survey Order of 1919. The OR, which was to complete the control and use of national resources and fulfill military and private demand, had to survey a much broader range of resources. Following the report of the Resource Council on 12 August 1927, the Cabinet approved the general line of resource survey for control-and-use plans of national resources. The OR now started drafting the resource survey bill and the resource survey order. Following Cabinet approval on 5 February 1929, the bill was submitted to the Diet and approved. The Resource Survey Act, with seven articles, took effect on 11 April 1929.

Drafting the resource survey order – which would specify in detail the entity of the resource survey act and prepare the implementation structure, together with related cabinet orders, ministry ordinances, and announcements – was also very difficult. The resource survey order took effect on 1 December 1929. The distinctive character of the order lay in its appendix, which contained a detailed survey sheet for the ministries in charge, occupying fifty-four pages of the statute book.[47]

Establishing the Clerical Outline for Formulating General Mobilization Plans

Also on 5 May 1929, following a report from the Resource Council, the Cabinet approved matters on formulating plans for control-and-use of resources. On 18 June, the Cabinet approved the Clerical Outline for Formulating General Mobilization Plans, and from this moment plans for control-and-use of resources were called general mobilization plans (hereafter, GM plans).

The Clerical Outline planned to formulate both the "basic outline" and "each ministry's plan" for the "basic plan for GM" and the "period plan for GM." The basic plan was ongoing, and the period plan was a plan for each fiscal year.[48]

The Clerical Outline was the outline of clerical works, indicating generally the scope of task of the OR and the division of work between the OR and

---

[47] Ministries included Foreign Affairs, Interior, Finance, Education, Agriculture, Commerce, Communication, and Railways. The Cabinet announcements, ordinances and announcements from the Commerce Ministry, ordinances from the Ministry of Interior, and those from the Ministry of Communication altogether made up 128 pages. Boieicho (1970, pp. 12–13).

[48] For more details, see Boeicho (1970, pp. 13–14). In brief, see Miwa (2008, pp. 318–19).

each ministry. The substance of scope and division would be determined through the process of formulating GM plans. The OR would formulate a "basic plan" and a "basic outline." Each ministry would then formulate its own plan for the "basic goods" and "basic issues" in its charge. The OR was not expected to plan issues in the other ministries' charge.

The OR was put under the control of the Prime Minister, so matters concerned with supreme command were out of its hands. The Army's strong support greatly contributed to the establishment of the OR, which did not change the situation. For GM plans to be realistic and effective, it was essential to specify the environments and constraints that conditioned them. The specific content of the circumstances for mobilization (or war) that GM plans assumed and their counteracting operation, a specific list of weapons to prepare, and the aim and goal of GM plans were at the center of those essential factors. But these were basically under the supreme command. Unless the bodies responsible for the supreme command (the ACCom in the case of the Army) expressly provided the OR with the factors underlying their plans, the work of the OR could be neither specific nor reliable. Each ministry formulated plans about goods and issues in their charge, and it was essential to provide each ministry with those key factors from the supreme command. However, as I will show in the next chapter, the situation inside the Japanese government of the day fell far short of satisfying this condition. The situation did not improve for the whole course of the war.

Formulation of an Interim Period Plan for GM and an Emergency GM Plan

In formulating a GM plan for the first time in Japan, the Clerical Outline stipulated that it be formulated tentatively for FY1930 to FY1932. This three-year plan was named the Interim Period Plan for GM and applied for three years from FY1933.

Though the plan was limited in scope and depth, formulating this first GM plan and mobilizing the full capacity of the OR and other ministries was a big undertaking. For the Interim Period Plan for GM, the GM Planning Conference[49] was held four times, in order to promote communication and integrate ideas. Unexpected circumstances such as the defeat of

---

[49]   The conference was hosted by the President of OR. The first conference on 10 and 11 April 1930 began with the Prime Minister's instructions, where deputy ministers of ministries concerned attended. Twenty members from the Army attended, including the Military Bureau Chief, the Procurement Bureau Chief from the AM, and two representatives from the ACCom.

the related budget for FY1931[50] and the outbreak of the Manchurian war on 18 September 1931 had grave consequences for the process.

The government pressed on with the process, with further simplification and expedient measures. The outline of the interim period plan for Cabinet discussion, with its main body and seventy-seven reports, was tentatively finalized on 30 June 1932. The President of the OR then sent it to the sections concerned, requesting replies by 15 July. This outline was not submitted immediately to the Cabinet. The Army Ministry, which enthusiastically promoted the process, reserved its own reply.

It was at the end of May 1933, almost a year later, that upon making reference to the ACCom the Army Ministry finally drafted its reply. Taking the Army's voice into consideration, the OR submitted the revised version to the Cabinet, which approved it on 21 July 1933.

When it tentatively finalized the outline of the interim period plan, the OR began preparation for the next plans: instruction of details to ministries concerned with the interim period plan for GM, and guidance for formulating emergency GM plans in response to the current situation.

On 1 and 2 July 1932, the OR hosted the fourth GM Planning Conference.[51] This initiated the formulation of emergency GM plans in response to the situation, while individual ministries formulated demand-supply plans for the resources in their charge. The focus of the planning work in the OR was to formulate emergency GM plans for FY1934 and FY1935 with the cooperation of the bodies concerned, on the assumption that they would be applied in those years. In addition to specific resources that were urgently needed, such as technical personnel and workers, the OR's agenda included controlling key industries for war, policies for key industries that would suffer large damages from war, security for GM, preparation of intelligence organization networks, the organization of headquarters for GM and transformation from peacetime organization, and preparations of wartime regulations.[52]

On 30 May 1934, after presenting them to the Prime Minister, the President of the OR submitted Emergency GM Plans (twenty-two volumes) and books for reference (thirty-two volumes) to the Army Ministry, together with a brief overview of the plan formulation process. Some "unprojected items" remained pending for the next interim period plans.[53]

---

[50] The Hamaguchi Cabinet that came into office in July 1929 was eager to pursue arms reduction and fiscal austerity, and its tight budget policy reached a peak at the FY1931 budget. The London Naval Treaty was signed on 22 April 1930.

[51] This conference also began with the Prime Minister's instructions.

[52] Boeicho (1967b, p. 431).

[53] The report on the process suggested that the plans were far from completion (Boeicho, 1967b, pp. 434–). "Unprojected items" included technical personnel, plants, and

What is most remarkable and critical here is that the plans were never completed, and that only those in their last stages were presented to the Prime Minister. No specific policies were decided based on those plans, nor were any of the plans put into action.

Formulation of the Second Period Plan for General Mobilization (GM)
Following the emergency GM plans, the government decided to formulate the Second Period GM plan in FY1934 and FY1935, planning to apply it in FY1936 and FY1937. On 7 June 1934, the OR determined the work plan, which with the Prime Minister's approval was put into action. On 26 June 1936, the OR finalized the draft of the Second Period GM Plan, a gigantic document of 104 volumes including appendices and materials.

In the six and a half years since the formulation of the Interim Period Plan for GM in the spring of 1930, the government finalized the draft of the Second Period GM Plan. The lengthy process indicates how complicated and arduous it was to formulate GM plans.[54]

Three points are important. First, all the plans finalized before the outbreak of the 1937 war included tentative drafts. Second, even though the plans described fully "the physical national power" (Boeicho, 1970, p. 18), they presented neither effective means to achieve the given targets nor specific manner and methods of general mobilization. Third, no plan was put into action – that is, no specific government decision or action, including policy making and implementation, was drawn from those plans.[55]

1–4–3. Long-Term Plans: Five-Year Plan for Munitions Manufacturing Industries and Outline of Five-Year Plan for Key Industries (Army Plan)

The War with China began just as the long-term plans for production capacity expansion and the five-year plan for Manchurian industry development

---

preparation of GM institutions. The OR conducted preparatory studies on technical personnel, but could not even begin planning. For plants, the OR merely prepared a list. The report's authors were not at a stage where they were able to give a presentation on GM institutions. Security for GM was still under investigation, and control of key industries had not yet reached a conclusion.

[54] Boeicho (1970, pp. 18–19).

[55] As a member of the OR, Kikusaburo Okada, the War Mobilization Subsection Chief of the War Preparation Section when the War with China began, took direct charge of food and lumber planning. After the war, he recalled (Boeicho, 1967b, p. 524): "Because of an underlying unreasonable assumption, the Second Period GM Plan lacked feasibility, too. The plan envisaged putting 'the Army's Operation to the North and the Navy's Operation to the East into simultaneous, full-scale action.' Japan's national power allowed a plan to be made for only one of them."

were given shape. The enemy that those plans envisioned was not China, of course, but the USSR. The long-term plans did not cover the contingency of a Sino–Japanese war. Even if they were put into action, they were inadequate preparation for that conflict.

From Army Munitions Industries Mobilization (MIM) Plans to Army War Mobilization (WM) Plans

As I showed in section 1–4–1, after FY1923 the Army basically maintained MIM plans with revisions every year.

In the spring of 1930, the government began the three-year process of formulating the Interim Period Plan for GM. With this plan, it intended to control and allocate all the resources of the nation to meet both military and civilian demands. In response, the Army decided to expand the scope of its plans. It established the order for Army WM plan on 24 May 1933, with which the "guidance for MIM plan" was amended to the "order for Army WM fiscal year plan" (Boeicho, 1967b, pp. 485–6).

The order for FY1934 Army WM plan was promulgated on 12 December 1933. "Each WM unit respectively first formulated 'its order for WM unit plan and WM plans for assigned forces, both basic and for permanent use,' with which for the first time the Army WM plan was formulated." After FY1934, the Army WM plan was formulated every year. For FY1935, the plan was thoroughly revised, and maintained for FY1936 with little modification (Boeicho, 1967b, pp. 485–6).

On 30 November 1936, the FY1937 Army WM plan was thoroughly revised and promulgated. Thus, "for FY1937 this Army WM plan and the Second Period GM Plan assumed to apply for FY1936 and FY1937 were somehow prepared, gathering the collective wisdom of the time" (Boeicho, 1967b, p. 531).

"Those plans had never envisaged the war that actually began" in July 1937. Faced with the need to implement the Army WM as the war developed, the Army newly drew up "the invocation of WM for the China Incident, corresponding to Army WM order," without implementing the Army WM Plan (Boeicho, 1967b, p. 528). As we saw at the beginning of section 1–3–3, Okada recalled after the war that they had developed a WM plan every year since FY1920, but had never implemented one. Those plans were stored in the vault as paper plans (Boeicho, 1970, p. 70).

It was the Army that formulated the FY1937 Army WM plan. It was not a plan that the OR, in cooperation with other ministries, intended to formulate. It seems that the collaborative relationship that must have been established among the relevant ministries was never established among the

Army Ministry and the others. As a consequence, it is unlikely that this Army plan included more concrete programs than the Second Period Plan for GM. It was not a policy adopted by the government. Obviously it had no budgetary support. Nobody evaluated its compatibility with the Navy's plans.

From the Army to the Government: Presentation of Five-Year Plans

The war began just after the start of both the Army's "fully fledged armament enhancement plan" and the Navy's "landmark replenishment plan."[56] In order to prepare for its successful implementation, the Army had formulated independently a Five-Year Plan for Munitions Manufacturing Industries and an Outline of a Five-Year Plan for Key Industries (Army Plan) and presented them to the government a few weeks before the outbreak of the war.

The Army launched the formulation of its armament enhancement plan with the following content, starting in FY1937 (Boeicho, 1967b, pp. 545–6)[57]: "[Force size in wartime] to build by FY1942 approximately 40 divisions and corresponding units, and approximately 140 air squadrons and corresponding units; [Force size in peacetime] to build by FY1942 10 divisions in Manchuria and 17 divisions and corresponding units at home and in Korea, approximately 140 air squadrons and corresponding units, and to enlarge capacity for replenishment, mobilization, education, and health: [Material for operations] to prepare between FY1937 and FY1942 most materials for operations that would be necessary with increase in wartime force size and improvement in organization and equipment."

The Navy also launched its third replenishment plan, with which in five years (four years for air squadrons) from FY1937 it planned to supply an

---

[56] We will see the details and background of those plans in Chapter 2.

[57] The Army's "full-fledged armament enhancement plan" and the Navy's "landmark replenishment plan" were determined as starting in FY1937 at the end of 1936, after negotiation with financial authorities. The budget for those plans was approved by the seventieth session of the Diet (from 26 December 1936 to 31 March 1937; Boeicho, 1967b, pp. 542–7). The ACCom at first planned to complete the armament enhancement by FY1940. This budget, however, enabled them to attain only half of the goals. Moreover, the force size in wartime at the completion was forty-one divisions, fewer than the forty-eight divisions in the initial plan. Taking the size and growing speed of the Soviet Army in the Far East into consideration, within the ACCom there was an outpouring of comments that they could not guarantee national safety. It was argued that enhancement speed was only a quarter of that which was needed. When the War with China began, Kanji Ishiwara, then the Strategy Division Chief of the ACCom, strongly pursued "the nonescalation policy" because preparedness for war against the USSR was in such a miserable state (Boeicho, 1967a, pp. 406–8).

additional sixty-six naval vessels, in total approximately 270,000 tons, and fourteen land-based air squadrons (bringing the total to fifty-three).

The authorities at the Army Ministry recognized that to satisfy the increasing demand for munitions, it was necessary not only to adopt drastic policies for munitions manufacturing industries but also to expand the production capacity of defense industries to provide their ground-level support. On this occasion, the Army decided to expand munitions manufacturing industries dramatically and drafted the Outline of the Five-Year Plan for Munitions Manufacturing Industries.[58]

On 23 June 1937, the authorities printed the final decision plan, which Army Minister Sugiyama approved on June 29. This Five-Year Plan proposed to expand aircraft production capacity to 10,000 per year, increase weapons production capacity fourfold, and extend tank manufacturing capacity to 1,580 per year.[59]

The War with China began before the Army fleshed out the details of the Five-Year Plan, and the plan was never executed.

In May 1937, in order to integrate and coordinate key policies, the government reorganized the Cabinet Council and the Cabinet Research Bureau, both of which had been established in May 1935, into the Planning Agency. (In October 1937, the Planning Agency was consolidated with the OR into the Planning Council, *kikaku-in*.)

The key defense industries were under the control of the Cabinet. Therefore, the Army Ministry drafted independently the Outline of a Five-Year Plan for Key Industries, which it transferred to the Cabinet for prompt realization. After due consultation between the ACCom and the Army Ministry, the Outline (Army Plan) was finalized on 29 May 1937 and approved by the Army Minister on 14 June. On 17 June, Deputy Army Minister Umezu met with the Deputy General-Director of the Planning Agency, to whom on the same day the Army Ministry forwarded "requests regarding the Five-Year Plan for Key Industries."[60]

The Outline (Army Plan) stated, in principle (Boeicho, 1970, p. 21): "We promote the development of key industries for national defense. By around

---

[58] The Army strongly recognized this point even in 1918, when the Munitions Industries Mobilization Act was enacted (Boeicho, 1967a, p. 43).

[59] The focus of the plan was on aircraft; weapons; ammunitions; tanks; and military motor vehicles, primarily aircraft (Boeicho, 1975c, p. 153). Actual aircraft demand both from the Army and the Navy for FY1937 (FY1938) was 1,375 (2,000). See Boeicho (1970, p. 20).

[60] At that time, the Cabinet Research Bureau (the Planning Agency) stood to "investigate and discuss important policies in response to the consultation of the Cabinet," but the bureau, because of both its size and lineup, was not potent enough to play such an important role effectively (ibid., p. 21).

1941 we expect Japan, Manchuria, and North China to supply all the key resources we need. At the same time, we will realize a considerable development of peacetime national power, with which we shall strengthen our ability to lead East Asia."

The Outline set annual production objectives as fifty thousand units of machine tools, 10 million tons of steel, 3.3 million kiloliters of gasoline, 110 million tons of coal, 100,000 tons of aluminum, and an annual production capacity expansion to ten thousand airplanes and one hundred thousand automobiles.

The Planning Agency immediately became involved. But as it started its deliberations, the War with China began. With the expansion of the war, it was in January 1939 that the Outline (Army Plan) was finally approved by the Cabinet as "The Outline of Production Capacity Expansion Plan" (Boeicho, 1970, p. 21).

One focus of this book is the investigation of the substance and effectiveness of "planned" war preparation and its implementation. This Outline (Army Plan) for the Five-Year Plan was practically the first plan or policy for war preparation from a long-term perspective. As I stated previously, the basic framework was approved by the Cabinet in January 1939, and an implementation plan was determined with "Guidance for Formulating FY1939 Implementation Plans" on 17 March. The Cabinet formed the Production Capacity Expansion Committee, where the Planning Council, through subcommittees, was to coordinate the plans formulated by individual government sections in their jurisdiction.[61] Even if these sections performed their jobs and implemented policies concerned properly, the "planned" war preparation actually adopted for the first time was this plan adopted for FY1939, two years after the outbreak of the war.

If our criterion for the effectiveness and existence of "planned" war preparation is whether effective "plans" or "policies" were actually put into action in a long-term perspective, we have to conclude that planned warfare preparation did not exist – because no such plan was implemented. Not only was none implemented before the outbreak of the War with China, but none was implemented for the first half of that conflict. The Production Capacity Expansion Plans and related policies did not work effectively, either, as I will show in the following section.[62]

---

[61] MITI (1964, pp. 213–35).

[62] The Planning Council and the government sections concerned drafted the plan, and the discussion within the committee was kept entirely secret from the outside world. No representative from the business community was allowed to participate in the process. Producers in those key industries were merely required to submit a vast volume of

The Five-Year Industry Development Plan in Manchuria

Subsequently, Boeicho (1970, p. 21) wrote: "Both the Five-Year Plan for Munitions Manufacturing Industries and the Outline of the Five-Year Plan for Key Industries (Army Plan) emphasized expanding the production capacity of the munitions industries or key industries on the continent, particularly in Manchuria. The Army as the intermediary was to guide the Manchukuo, upon 'the Outline of Japan-Manchukuo Economic Controls and Policies' determined in March 1934. It formulated 'The Five-Year Industry Development Plan in Manchuria,' which in January 1937 the Commander of the Kwantung Army (who also held the post of Ambassador to Manchukuo) demanded that Manchukuo government would implement. The Manchukuo government formulated the Five-Year Industry Development Plan to FY1941 and began enforcement in FY1937."

Boeicho concluded, "Thus, just when the Japanese government, and the Army in particular, intended to implement policies to dramatically expand munitions manufacturing capacity and as its foundation to develop and strengthen key industries both in Japan and in Manchuria, the war began.... Without expanding key industries or increasing munitions manufacturing capacity, Japan had to deal with the war, and subsequently plunged into the Greater East Asian War."

Hardly any information exists on the details and effectiveness of the Five-Year Plan that the Manchukuo government began enforcing in FY1937. The statement in Boeicho (1970, p. 21) that "without expanding key industries or increasing munitions manufacturing capacity, Japan had to deal with the war, and subsequently plunged into the Greater East Asian War," suggests that the Five-Year Industry Development Plan in Manchuria had no substance and was ineffective. It is implausible that the Japanese government, busy with a war and postponing its own production capacity expansion plan, could effectively enforce a plan in Manchuria. With poorer preparations than in Japan, enforcement in Manchuria would have faced much greater difficulties.

The Five-Year Industry Development Plan in Manchuria "was incorporated almost entirely into the Outline of the Production Capacity Expansion plan approved by the Cabinet in January 1939" (Boeicho, 1967b, p. 612).

---

planning materials, and later received allocated materials for the production quota for which they were responsible (MITI, 1964, p. 222). It is unimaginable that such a plan could work effectively and ensure the active participation of private companies.

Japan's production capacity expansion plan, however, was "a painted rice-cake" (Nakahara, 1981, p. 140).[63] I will discuss this point and the details of the role of plans in Manchuria in Chapter 6.

1-4-4. Surveys of Munitions Factories for Army Control

As I showed in sections 1-3-3 and 1-3-4, munitions factory control started on 17 January 1938, and the span of control expanded incrementally. In order to designate munitions factories swiftly and control them effectively and efficiently, it was absolutely necessary to conduct *ex ante* surveys and collect multifaceted and detailed information on the actual conditions of factories, including size, organization, business, technology, equipment, and works. Precise information was indispensable for providing appropriate directions based on exact knowledge of technical feasibility and adopting effective policies, such as supplying appropriate incentives, for ensuring cooperation and coordination among the agents (factories and others) concerned. Directions from the government (or the military) would not be enough to achieve these objectives. The assumption of "costless coercion"[64] would not hold here, either.

Furthermore, it would be hard to expect the military to develop an *ex ante* system and conduct surveys to collect relevant information for factory control. However, the Army did conduct surveys as part of its WM plans. I review their objective and substance next.

1-4-5. "Survey of Factories for Army Control"

In section 1-4-1, I described how, after FY1923, the Army basically maintained munitions industries mobilization (MIM) plans with annual revisions.

---

[63] Nakahara, after working at the Osaka Army Arsenal and the Headquarters of Army Arsenals, was assigned in January 1939 to the staff of the Military Bureau in the Army Ministry, where he took charge of the basic plan for preparing and replenishing Army munitions. The title of Chapter 11 of Nakahara (1981) is "Competition Between War Supplies and Manufacturing Capacity Expansion (MCE)." On the second page, he wrote: "There is an old saying: 'If you chase two rabbits, you will lose them both.' It was possible to say that we were able to chase two rabbits, war supplies and MCE, in FY1938 when the General Mobilization Act was enacted and in FY1939. But, after that, with the escalation of the war, we lost both." He continues that the second MCE plan from FY1942 was "a castle in the air": "The primary reason was the shortage of steel, the staple of the industry and the heart of the economy. The supply of steel decreased, but the demand from the Army and the Navy for war supplies increased explosively, with raw material taken for munitions reducing dramatically the raw material available for the industry.... The Army and the Navy took 25% of the total steel supply in FY1938, and in FY1941 they took 50%" (ibid., p. 141).

[64] See Gregory (2004, p. 133), mentioned in section VI of the Introduction.

Following the major revision of the implementation of the FY1931 MIM plan, during 1932 and 1933 the Army surveyed the munitions factories it planned to control and those already under its direct control. This was to prepare for WM plans, and the order for FY1934 Army WM plan was implemented on 12 December 1933.

Army Minister Araki formulated the Guidance for Survey of Factories for Army Control. On this basis, on 15 September 1932 he ordered "a survey of munitions supply capacity and so on, and a report by the end of February 1933." The guidance specified (Boeicho, 1967b, p. 462): "... 2. Each WM unit shall conduct a field survey of factories that it is scheduled to control, and investigate and report the production capacity and the feasibility of plans, primarily on the volume of individual items specified therein; 3. In a field survey, particular attention should be paid to competition with other units using the factory. If there is no competition, the survey should focus on the maximum capacity."

The field survey of factories was to reveal information on "the production capacity and the feasibility of plans." It was confined to the capacity for items specified at that time. It did not assume any coordination with surveys conducted by other units. Each WM unit submitted to the Army Minister its survey reports at one time or successively.[65]

On 3 May 1933, when the survey was close to an end, the Army Ministry directed WM units to survey the production capacity of factories under their direct control. Units included Artillery Arsenal, Clothing Arsenal, Food Arsenal, Air Headquarters, Engineering Headquarters, Science Institute, and Hygiene Products Arsenal.

The survey consisted of three types of questionnaire. The first surveyed the total amount (in value) of materials used, amount (in quantity and value) of specific materials used, fuel and power used, workforce consumption (number of workers per day, average daily work hours, and workdays), and total amount of wages paid. The second surveyed the volume of production and inventory (quantity and value by item). The third surveyed the number of employees by categories of clerical work, engineers, and workers (by sex and age group); the number of persons in the military (in the Army and the Navy, respectively); engines (by type, power, and number in operation, and halt); and operating machines and equipment (by type, numbers in operation, and halt). The Army Ministry organized the reports, which on 25 September it shared with the OR.

---

[65] Boeicho, 1967b, pp. 461–2. The Army Air Headquarters, for instance, surveyed fifty-five factories.

Detailed surveys notwithstanding, it is absolutely impossible that the information collected through these surveys was useful enough for effective control of munitions factories after designation for factory control.

The Army Survey on Munitions Manufacturing Capacity

The 1932–3 Survey of Factories for Army Control was not the first survey of munitions factories. In the spring of 1931, the Army conducted a Survey of Munitions Manufacturing Capacity, which was based on the Resource Survey Act of 1929. Article 1 of the act stipulated that the government could, if necessary, order individuals and corporations to report their human and nonhuman resources. The Survey of Factories for Army Control had no such legal foundation.

In response to the inquiry on the proposal for the act, on 17 January 1929, in response to a query from the President of the OR about the proposal for the Resource Survey Act, the Army Ministry agreed to accept it on condition that the military could issue independently an order based on Article 1, if necessary, to survey specific resources. The Army formulated the Army Military Demand Survey Rule and the Army Ministry Order on Army's Survey of Munitions Manufacturing Capacity. The former was confidential and the latter was made public (Boeicho, 1967b, p. 325).

The rule that stipulated the survey items on which the Army Minister could order a report was issued on 23 March 1930. On 8 October, the Guidance for Planning Resource Survey was issued; by 20 December, each unit had to submit to the Army Minister its resources survey report on relevant issues for acquiring necessary materials, fuel, and major supplies, such as production volume, production districts or factories, producers, and transfer conditions. By mid-December, each unit had reported to the Minister with a document detailing that year's and the next year's plan (Boeicho, 1967b, pp. 326–7).

The order determined the survey guidance concerning "manufacturing and repairing capacity of munitions the Army Minister designated" among the industries on the Commerce Ministry section of the resource survey order list. Specifically, it stipulated that at the end of February every year, each unit would survey a factory's capacity for manufacturing and repairing munitions that the Army Minister designated and submit the report by the end of May.

The survey was conducted annually from 1931 to 1934. It is remarkable that prior to the first survey, a courteous letter from the Deputy Army Minister was sent to factory owners to call for cooperation (Boeicho, 1967b, p. 455).

Unlike the industries upon the Commerce Ministry order to investigate the current state of factories, this survey studied each factory's "manufacturing and repairing capacity of munitions the Army Minister designates." One wonders whether Army Headquarters and the units concerned had enough capacity, competence, and time to conduct effective surveys efficiently.[66] Even after the war began, "there was a strong mood on the private business side not to welcome the military control of factories" (Boeicho, 1970, p. 109). Factory owners had little incentive to provide precise answers, which the Army Ministry recognized.[67]

Even if these surveys were conducted effectively, obviously the information collected was insufficient for the Army to "control" munitions factories effectively and efficiently.[68]

As this illustrates, at the time the state of surveys backed by the commanding Resource Survey Act in Japan was not impressive and performance was poor. Surveys without backup from a commanding authority or surveys in districts such as Manchuria, where security was poor and the status and authority of the government were low, could not be very effective. Thus, in Japan or Manchuria, we find no evidence that planning and policies were well prepared and implemented for war.

1–5. Performance of War Mobilization in the First Year of the War with China

1–5–1. War Mobilization in FY1937

The Situation after the Outbreak of the War
The War with China began when the fully fledged armament enhancement plan was finally ready to start – but it was postponed. The nonescalation

---

[66] The manufacturing capacity of 257 factories was surveyed, of which the Air Headquarters, the Weapons Arsenal, and the Artillery Arsenal surveyed 27, 35, and 32, respectively. Among the remarks from the units concerned, we find a comment from the President of the Artillery Arsenal: "We hope that, before conducting the survey, Headquarters will regulate duplicate use of factories between units" (Boeicho, 1967b, pp. 454–5).

[67] Even this was not the first survey of the current state of war industries. The Munitions Bureau put the war industry survey order into force in December 1919. En route, the Army Ministry, sending to the relevant parties a list of big private factories of interest to the Ministry, requested a survey of equipment and manufacturing capacity (Boeicho, 1967b, p. 75).

[68] Recall the captive view of industry regulation, which suggests that the regulation process is strongly influenced by the regulated industry through maneuvering information that the regulator acquires. In this case, the regulator was the Army Ministry.

policy, initially adopted not only by the government but also by the military, was altered with the development and escalation of the war. The Army, maintaining the nonescalation policy, limited mobilization as much as possible, hoping to keep the negative influence on the economy to a minimum. On 5 October, three months after the outbreak of the war, the Army Minister implemented war mobilization, and on 17 January 1938, more than three months later again, both the Army and the Navy began munitions factory control.

A policy of putting a prompt end to the war was firmly maintained. As the war escalated, the Japanese government repeatedly expressed its plans for a prompt resolution. Eventually, in December 1941, four years and five months after the outbreak of the War with China, the war with the United States began, ending in August 1945 with Japan's defeat.

This section focuses on the performance of Japan's war mobilization at an early stage of the war, FY1937 and FY1938 in particular. With a rapid escalation of the war that few had expected, the demand for munitions soared. However, almost no preparation (or planning) had been implemented, in either the public or the private sector. War mobilization faced serious challenges.

War Mobilization in FY1937
The Japanese Army captured Nanjing on 13 December 1937. A peace overture made by the German ambassador to China, in response to a request from the Japanese government (Foreign Minister Hirota), ended in failure, as Japan's claims escalated in celebration of its victory (I talk about this in more detail in section 2–5–2 in the next chapter). Prime Minister Konoe, overriding the opposition of the ACCom, proclaimed: "From now, we will not deal with the Nationalist Chinese government. We shall cooperate with the emerging Chinese government and revitalize new China" (Boeicho, 1970, pp. 105–6).

Boeicho (1967a, pp. 528–9) explained the situation: "The Konoe Cabinet, ignoring the intention of the ACCom, which was unsure about planning operations, abandoned the prompt resolution of the war.... The ACCom, attaching importance to the political risk of Cabinet collapsing, finally accommodated a policy decision about which they were strategically unconvinced. They thus abandoned the last resort they were allowed under the so-called independence of supreme command." The explanation ends with a recollection of ACCom Strategy Section Chief Kawabe, that "the people were the most aggressive, the government was next, and the ACCom, concerned about the country, was the least [aggressive] and most hesitant." Thus, hopes of prompt resolution were dashed, and Japan proceeded on its way to a long war.

At an early stage, the state-operated Army artillery arsenals responded promptly to the increased demand for munitions. The total number of employees increased steadily, from 3,578 at the end of July, 47,441 at the end of October, to 61,114 by the end of 1937.[69]

"We predicted that war mobilization would face the most serious difficulties during the first six months of implementation. During this period, we had to deal with many demanding tasks for transforming a conventional stance to a war standing. We needed rapidly to enhance production equipment in artillery arsenals, to convert privately owned plants to military production, to recruit and train workers, and to acquire production materials promptly" (Boeicho, 1970, pp. 118–19).

Army Minister Sugiyama's Report to the Emperor

With the Overview of War Mobilization in Munitions Supplies for the China Incident, on 2 June 1938 the Army Minister reported to the Emperor on the actual performance of war mobilization in the first six months of the war.[70] Points 3 through 6, particularly 5 and 6, of the following summary deserve attention; no more detailed or relevant information is available.

1. The initial phase of war mobilization, started in October 1937, was to provide troops centered on fifteen divisions with six-months' worth of extraordinary munitions supplies. With special materials needed for operations and furnishing materials for the newly mobilized troops, this amounted to 1.06 billion yen in total, approximately 1.6 times more than calculated for the war mobilization plan for FY1937.

2. By this stage, the number of workers in state-owned Army factories had increased to 120,000, four times the number under usual conditions. The number of privately owned factories used had also increased to 3,800, 2.5 times the number in peacetime. Of these, the Army selected 150 as particularly essential and placed them under its control.

3. Presenting its needs in advance, the Ministry demanded that the Planning Council secure materials for munitions supply. Spending the budget flexibly, it imported large amounts of crucial material in advance. It also made every effort to purchase machine tools, and to

---

[69] For more details, see Table 5–4 of Miwa (2008, p. 335), adapted from Boeicho (1970, p. 111).

[70] See Boeicho (1970, pp. 119–23; 1967b, pp. 626–8).

recover and reuse materials from the battlefield. With the start of war mobilization, however, materials allocation became erratic, and the Ministry became concerned about the troubles that could lie ahead. In cooperation with other government divisions, it enforced measures such as: (a) imposing agile and appropriate exchange control; (b) strengthening materials allocation control, economizing on consumption, and controlling prices to encourage export; and (c) enhancing the production capacity of materials essential to national defense.

4. The Army Ministry's primary focus was on expanding the capacity of the Army's arsenals. It had already spent 46 million yen on the First War Mobilization, removing bottlenecks in existing facilities and enhancing production capacity for guns and bullets. (It was currently enhancing capacities for the Second War Mobilization, with 120 million yen.) Following mandates, requests, or orders from the Army, privately owned munitions factories had considerably increased their capacity.

5. For various reasons, the actual/planned production ratios in the First War Mobilization were 70 percent in firearms, 60 percent in bullets, 66 percent in airplanes, 27 percent in tanks, 43 percent in lightweight armed vehicles, 12 percent in radios, 100 percent in steel helmets, and the residuals were still work in progress. Highly regrettably, the Ministry had been unable to achieve the desired level of provision of essential munitions such as firearms, bullets, airplanes, and tanks.

6. The causes of this poor performance were as follows. FY1937 was the first year of the plan to improve war preparation, by innovating airplanes, expanding production capacities, and expanding the storage depots network to the continent. That same year, the government also started the so-called Five-Year Industry Development Plan, intending to facilitate a great leap forward in industries essential for national defense. In addition, war mobilization – the size of which had exceeded the fiscal year plan and the content of which was complicated and diversified – faced many serious difficulties. It was Japan's first experience in implementing war mobilization, and, despite every effort, the policies were neither flexible nor consistently enforced. Materials allocation was also erratic.

7. However, since the beginning of the war the Ministry had been able almost fully to meet the demand for supplies to troops in operations against China.

Boeicho (1970, p. 123) commented: "Despite the round-the-clock efforts of each war mobilization unit, we could not reach the planned targets. The magnitude of mobilization, even at this point of time, exceeded the national capacity, particularly for natural resources and industrial potential."

1–5–2. War Mobilization in FY1938

The Japanese government's proclamation of 16 January 1938, "From now, we will not deal with the Nationalist Chinese government...," eradicated any hope of a prompt resolution of the war. The National General Mobilization Act was enacted as a basic law of war mobilization, and the seventy-third ordinary session of the Diet approved the enormous budget of 4.85 billion yen. Under the circumstances, FY1938 war mobilization was planned and implemented. The Army Minister confidentially transmitted to mobilization units on 31 March 1938 "The Direction on the Army Second War Mobilization Implementation for the China Incident" (Boeicho, 1970, p. 169).

The outline was set down in the report to the Emperor mentioned previously (Boeicho, 1970, p. 119): "The second stage of war mobilization was begun at the end of March 1938 and is in place now. It has not only to prepare the munitions necessary for a year's operations for 17 divisions and other troops concerned, but also urgent and indispensable materials for the entire Army and the new divisions that will be founded. The budget is enormous with 2.3 billion yen, and the quantity per month of major munitions items is twice or three times larger than that of the first."

On 17 January 1938, the Army and the Navy began to take control of munitions factories. The expansion of capacity, however, was significantly delayed despite the issue of production and capacity expansion orders to individual factory owners from the Army Minister. "One factory after another failed to complete on time" (Boeicho, 1970, p. 189).

Factory owners pleaded for more time. Boeicho (1970, p. 189) commented on their reasons: "[They] included difficulty in obtaining machines because of delays both in home production and in undelivered imports, and difficulty in recruiting workers. Some noted that they had to pull down private houses on the premises in order to build factories.... For operations involving with a huge variety of components, like factory capacity expansion, we had to prepare well-balanced policies, coordinated with all the relevant parties."

"At that time ... most worried about was the expected loss that could occur through prompt resolution of the incident" (War Mobilization Subsection Chief Okada's postwar recollection, Boeicho, 1970, p. 109). The military wanted capacity expansion, as well as increased production. The "worry about the expected loss" must have been so profound that the flood of requests (or excuses) for delay from the owners was not surprising.

Summary of the Second War Mobilization for the China Incident by the Head of Weapons Arsenals

"Almost no document is available telling the state of war mobilization during this period" (Boeicho, 1970, p. 239). Boeicho includes the Summary of War Mobilization with the Direction on the Army Second War Mobilization Implementation for the China Incident drafted on 30 June 1939 by the Head of Weapons Arsenals. Taking charge of some munitions procurement himself, the Head received, stored, and supplied weapons, ammunition, and equipment that other war mobilization units procured. This is a valuable document giving an overview of the Second War Mobilization, excluding the Air Force.

"The Summary of Procurement Performance, Excluding Ammunition" goes as follows (Boeicho, 1970, p. 243): "In spite of serious difficulties in distributing materials and machine tools to the factories and in recruiting engineers, we could improve the rate of mobilization ... We could fill most of the demands from the military, and adapt ourselves to their operations. The ratio of munitions we received to the munitions ordered for the mobilized troops was, on average, 60%."

Among the arms that they received from artillery arsenals, the summary reports on firearms that "the procurement ratio rarely fell below the 60% level and is gradually improving," but on tanks and armored vehicles that, "though performance is gradually improving, production volume does not keep pace with the rapidly increasing demand." On artilleries, it reports that "on average the procurement ratio stayed at the 60% level, but it does not apply to low-caliber artilleries." On observation equipment, it reports that, "because of production slump in optical weapons, the performance in general was extremely bad."

"Performance in ammunition procurement" reports a more serious situation (Boeicho, 1970, pp. 243–6)[71]: "During the first half of the fiscal year, ammunition supply did not fill the demand. With low inventories the supply primarily depended on production, with which the military operations sometimes were under restraint. In the second half, however, while supply to the front increased after the capture of Wuhan and Guangdong,

---

[71] The performance list is shown in Boeicho (1970, pp. 244–5). At the time of the Battle of Lake Khasan (the *Choko-ho* Incident in Japanese) of July 1938, the volume of ammunition in stock usable in a war against the USSR was not enough in a battle with fifteen divisions (ibid., p. 187).

production increased as did the quantities in stock in the arsenals. Though we suffered from insufficient production capacity and inventory, we have made every effort to promote specific actions, such as removing capacity to the continent and building structures on a temporary basis."

The "Opinions" that follow the preceding "Summary" are particularly informative and interesting (Boeicho, 1970, pp. 246–7)[72]:

(1) Guiding policies on production capacity expansion: Basic conditions for capacity expansion in munitions factories are reliable long-run production plans and a regular supply of materials for equipment enhancement, including machinery, and production. At present, however, factory owners are expressing concern about unpredictability and compensation for future damages. Together with the disruption in materials distribution, this has seriously inhibited the expansion of capacity. Therefore, first, the direction on war mobilization implementation should be firmly based on the allocation of basic materials in the materials-mobilization plans in order to bring performance close to the mandated figures. Second, we should make it clear that the mandated figures must be met, for which we should allow the people in charge the freedom to choose their methods. Last, we should give instructions for munitions supply to the factories for the next three to five years; this guidance will provide the factories with a solid foundation and be persuasive; (2) From the perspective of production-and-use, we must standardize the types and specifications of weapons, and adapt production methods accordingly; (3) We should revise our rule to be able to sell off materials to private factories.

"The General Overview" of the "Conclusion" first summarizes the report as follows. "This Incident began unexpectedly, which strongly conditioned the actual achievement of war mobilization. We could not afford to obtain materials to meet the war demand from the military. Although we are not

---

[72] After a year of war mobilization, each mobilization unit, reviewing the achievement, summarized its opinions for the future and reported to the Head. *Annual Survey of Mobilization: Reference and Opinions for the Future*, drafted by the Technology Headquarters (16 December 1938), lists the following five points in "1. Points to note in guiding private factories in order to make them observe delivery time of '7. Issues concerning procurement': (1) Having no policy or plan, the management of private factories is left to chance. The process management in particular is extremely primitive, and needs improved guidance. (2) Some factories, disregarding their capacity limit, receive excessive orders, most of which are outsourced to subcontracting factories. To prevent excess allocation of orders, we should make direct use of the better-quality subcontracting factories. (3) We should supervise and guide parent factories so that the orders they place with subcontractors match their capacity. (4) Intermediating materials acquisition should be prompt and precise, as this has a great effect on delivery time. (5) Precision machinery and bearings are most difficult to obtain. We have to increase their production, and make even better efforts to supply them directly and intermediate their acquisition" (ibid., p. 232). At the end of 1938, three years before the outbreak of the war with the United States, Japan already faced serious difficulties in obtaining precision machinery, including machine tools and bearings.

yet at the stage where we need to lay the whole national power on the line, we suffer from serious shortages of various materials." And the overview remarks on three specific points (Boeicho, 1970, pp. 250–1):

(1) Because of insufficient human resources for production and difficulty in recruiting engineers and skilled workers, we are not well prepared to meet the explosive demand for munitions production capacity expansion. We have to do our best in training and maintaining skilled workers for the human resource development necessary for future production; (2) [Physical resources] The shortage of raw materials has become serious. Control of their production and distribution, however, has not been strong enough, and everywhere people are either scrambling for materials or withholding them. For smoother munitions production, we should immediately establish a strong central control institution that takes charge of the acquisition and distribution of raw materials. This would enhance manufacturing of major resources of which there is a serious shortage but which are indispensable for munitions production, such as steel, coal, nonferrous metals, and machine tools. It would also encourage and guide private companies to increase production of raw materials for those industries, and when necessary increase their imports; (3) [Guidance of private munitions factories] In times of peace, private factories are managed for profit, and their facilities and equipments conform to this. We cannot expect them to expand production capacity in immediate response to military demand. In the future, therefore, we have to control management, prohibit factory owners acting as free enterprises, and help them prepare for their future production capacity expansion.

Of the "Summary" by the Head of Weapons Arsenals of 30 June 1939, the following three points are particularly important: (1) The War with China "began unexpectedly," and neither the military nor the government of Japan, had made preparations for it; (2) even though "we are not yet at the stage when we need to lay the whole national power on the line, we suffer from serious shortages of various materials," and "could not afford to obtain materials to fulfill the war demand from the military"; and (3) "still we must make further dramatic improvements in human and physical resource management and in 'guiding' private munitions factories."

The Head's three main points covered training and maintaining skilled workers, the need to impose stricter controls on raw materials and increase production of them, and maintaining better guidance of private munitions factories by "control management, [and] prohibit factory owners acting as free enterprises." At the time of reporting, in the early summer of 1939, a series of "preparations" and "policies," independently of their feasibility and effectiveness, had not been implemented. This undermines the dominant view (or conventional wisdom), which argues that the war was begun on the basis of "well-planned preparations," and that those "policies" were implemented at an early stage and strengthened further "by design" as the war escalated.

I therefore conclude the following:

1. Irrespective of whether they were deliberately prepared and implemented, neither prior "systematic war preparations" nor "planned war implementation" efforts after the war outbreak achieved satisfactory outcomes.
2. Irrespective of whether they were "unexpected" events, the Japanese government did not appropriately address the circumstances and challenges it faced after the outbreak of the war.

1–6. Summary of Chapter 1

For at least two decades before the outbreak of the War with China in July 1937, a diversity of phenomena associated with systematic war preparations were continuously observed, kicked off symbolically by the Munitions Industries Mobilization Act of 1918. During this time, such terms as "national defense," "national power," "war mobilization," "general mobilization," "resource mobilization," "production capacity expansion," "plan" or "planning," "control," and "management" were frequently used. New "organizations" were established one after another, including the Munitions Bureau, Munitions Council, Armament Bureau of the Army Ministry and its Procurement Policy Section, National Strength Council (the Part Two), OR, Resource Council, Procurement Bureau of the Army Ministry, General Mobilization Planning Conference, and Planning Agency. Many laws and rules were enacted, such as the Munitions Industries Mobilization Act, War-Industry Survey Order, Resource Survey Order, and Clerical Outline for Formulating General Mobilization Plans. And many "plans" were also formulated – the Army Munitions Industries Mobilization Fiscal Year Plan, Period Plan for General Mobilization, Five-Year Plan for Munitions Manufacturing Industries, Outline of Five-Year Plan for Key Industries (Army Plan), and Five-Year Industry Development Plan in Manchuria.

When the War with China began, however, the systematic war preparations that conventional wisdom claims to have been well designed and implemented did not function. In response to the outbreak of the war, Japan quickly had to make a war mobilization plan. In addition, it had to enact "war legislation" such as the Act for Applying the Munitions Industries Mobilization Act, the Temporary Import-Export Grading Act, and the National General Mobilization Act. The control of munitions factories started in January 1938, six months after the outbreak of the war. However, relevant information on those factories, indispensable for their effective control, had not been collected.

In light both of the actual condition and performance of "war mobilization" and of the reality of developments in institutions and organizational environments and their functions at the initial stage of the war, it is impossible to support the conventional wisdom that Japan began the war on the basis of well-planned preparations. "Wars, when they come, are always different from the war that is expected" (Taylor, 1961, p. 116), and so was the War with China. Faced with a cascade of "unexpected situations" and "unpredictable events," the Japanese government could not respond effectively. It repeatedly declared "a nonescalation policy" and "local resolution of the conflict," yet it rushed to prepare laws and institutions for "war mobilization." "War mobilization" implementation fell into disorder. Plans carefully prepared, as the conventional wisdom claims, lacked specifics and did not play the role of preparations.

The "Summary" of the Head of Weapons Arsenals at the end of June 1939 on the performance of war mobilization in FY1938 stated, "Although we are not yet at the stage where we need to lay the whole national power on the line, we suffer from serious shortages of various materials," and "could not afford to obtain materials to fill the war demand from the military." After the capture of Hankou, the war ran into an impasse, and with the Konoe Proclamation on 22 December of moves "toward the creation of a new order in East Asia," the Japanese government prepared for a "long, drawn-out war."

2

Operation Plan, War Plan, and Basic National Defense Policy

2–1. Overview

A basic premise of "operation plans" was a "war plan" that is closely linked to both political and military strategies. This plan is the metric by which military operations should be prepared. The government and the Imperial Headquarters acted together to formulate a "war plan" by which to carry out "war objectives," "operations," "diplomacy," the "maintenance and cultivation of the national capacity for the conduct of the war," and a "strategy for ending the war." ... In Japan the government and the Imperial Headquarters studied those issues, but as a whole it is hard to say that they formulated "carefully structured war plans."

The Greater East Asian War is said to have been a war without war plans, a war without a precise war vision, a war without a clear vision of operations for the second and later stages in particular.... This is a fact that no future historian can challenge, I believe.... Looking back on the process toward the start of war, I find that, having fallen step by step into an impasse, Japan was forced to choose "peace or war", and had no choice but to start the war. To my regret, I cannot quarrel with the evaluation that the war started "without war plans" and "without clear prospects". If the top leaders of the state (and the highest command of the armed forces) had thoroughly formulated war plans for emergencies and the basic outline of operations, Japan would not have been forced into the war as national policy. Instead, it could have avoided starting the war, which was after all the worst outcome possible (Sejima, 1995, pp. 111, 175).[1]

---

[1] See the following excerpt from Taylor (1964, p. XVI): "Hitler certainly directed his general staffs to prepare for war. But so did the British, and for that matter every other, government. It is the job of general staffs to prepare for war. The directives which they receive from their governments indicate the possible war for which they are to prepare, and are no proof that the government concerned have (*sic*) resolved on it. All the British directives from 1935 onwards were pointed solely against Germany; Hitler's were concerned only with making Germany stronger. If therefore we were (wrongly) to judge political intentions from military plans, the British government would appear set on war with Germany, not the other way round....It is dangerous to deduce political intentions from military plans."

These excerpts are from the memoirs of Ryuzo Sejima (Sejima, 1995), who served in the Strategy Section of the Imperial Headquarters Army Division until the last months of the war from December 1939 to June 1945 (IH-AD, virtually the Army Central Command, ACCom).[2]

Another member of the Strategy Section recalls the situation in the Section before the start of the Pacific War (Imoto, 1978, p. 526)[3]:

> With the imposition of the US economic embargo on Japan, the situation reached a crisis. With 'The Outline of Imperial National Policy Implementation' approved on September 6 at the Conference in the Presence of the Emperor (*Gozen-kaigi*), Japan virtually decided to begin the war against the US and the UK.... The task of the Strategy Section was to mobilize all available resources to complete the operations to the south (against the US, the UK and the Netherlands). Since the previous October I had directed all my attention to China. That was no longer allowed. My primary task was to supervise and summarize the completion of operations to the south and to arrange for cooperation with the Navy. Over a month, from September to October, all the Strategy Section members, staying in the Army-Navy Assembly House at Miyakezaka, devoted all their energies night and day to this task.

I quote these recollections of former Army general staff officers to emphasize two points: (1) the meaning of terms such as "plan," "operation," "forecast," "vision," "measure," or "strategy" varies widely depending on their intended (or unintended) use; and (2) we must be cautious when investigating the association of those expressions with war and their relevance.

Historians note the establishment of the IH, the existence of Strategy Sections in both the ACCom and the Navy Central Command (NCCom), and the drawing up of all kinds of operations, plans, visions, measures, and

---

[2] See also the recollection of Kenryo Sato (Sato, 1976, pp. 286–7), the Military Section (*gunmu*) Chief at the beginning of the Pacific War, alleging that they had no clear prospects or strategy toward ending the war. Or see Miwa (2008, 3–2–4, pp. 169–70).

[3] It was after July 1941, when Japan's overseas assets were frozen by the United States and other countries, that Sejima, who had previously considered war against the United States and the United Kingdom to be unrealistic, began to think it would be unpreventable and decided to do his best in preparing operation plans for such an event. IH-AD Strategy Section members called an initial set of operations (scheduled to end in five months), such as a surprise attack on Hawaii and capturing fortresses in the southern area, "First Stage Operations" (Sejima, 1995, pp. 175, 110~). Imoto recalls (Imoto, 1979, p. 120): "Neither the Army nor the Navy determined operation plans after completing operations to the south. The Army's operation plans in particular did not discuss the issue. The Navy's operation plan stipulated that after securing an occupied area through the First Stage Operations it would establish an invincible self-contained regime; however, there was no specific plan or measure for accomplishing this. They had no consultation with the Army on the issue, either. In short, judging that the war would become a contest of endurance, the Army's and Navy's common policy was to establish an invincible, self-contained regime, upon which they would execute operation plans after the operation plans to the South."

outlines. Yet these observations do not justify the conventional wisdom that Japan began the Pacific War on the basis of a Basic National Defense Policy, a war plan, or an operations plan. The same applies to the War with China.

At the beginning of the Pacific War, there were remarkably few military leaders who thought it would end in victory for Japan. The recollection of the beginning of the war by the Strategy Division Chief of the NCCom captures the situation (Fukudome, 1951, pp. 182–3)[4]:

Without *kamikaze* (divine wind), there was no chance of victory for Japan in this war. Every single factor contributed to our defeat.... With hindsight, I see no reason why Japan should have won. I find many reasons why it had to lose. Modern warfare is total war, and war potential is equivalent to national capacity. Everybody should have understood that no country with little national capacity can challenge a country that has a lot. Japan had worthy government institutions like the Planning Council, and we, the military, did our best to assess the capacity of the various nations.

In Chapter 2, I do not discuss why Japan began the War with China or the Pacific War or whether it could have circumvented them. The focus of the chapter is on the details of the decision-making process on critical issues connected with Basic National Defense Policies, armament enhancement plans, and other issues connected with war.

It is widely accepted that a handful of (Army) military personnel controlled the decision-making on critical issues during the 1930s and early1940s. This discussion leads me to reexamine the conventional wisdom about Japan's history, politics, economy, society, and life during this period. Once this conventional wisdom is shown to be groundless, a wide variety of issues emerge for reexamination.

This chapter deals with two cases of decision making connected with the revision of the Basic National Defense Policies and policies on the War with China. In Part II, I discuss decision-making issues connected with war mobilization and economic control, looking at specific plans and policies such as materials mobilization plans and production capacity expansion plans.

---

[4] For more information, see Miwa (2008, 3-2, pp. 162–70). Nishiura, a high official at the Military (*gunji*) Section in the Army Ministry (AM) who would become the Military Section Chief just after the outbreak of the Pacific War, recalls about the situation in the second half of 1940 (Nishiura, 1968, pp. 301–2): "Focusing on the ocean shipping capacity, we started to study whether it was possible to begin the war against the U.S. Even in the War with China, Japan had to use most of their armed forces. It could not expect a favorable result in the war with the U.S. The Army had outwardly expressed consistently a bullish scenario, but...."

Section 2–2 reviews the basic decision-making system and process. Section 2–3 focuses on the discussion and negotiation process concerning the revision of the Basic National Defense Policy (BNDP) in the mid-1930s. During this period, the Army's fully fledged armament enhancement plan and the Navy's landmark replenishment plan were approved. As shown in section 1–4–3, at around the same time the Army also formulated its Five-Year Plan for the Munitions Manufacturing Industries and its plan for strengthening key industries. As the foundation for the latter, it drafted the Outline of a Five-Year Plan for Key Industries (Army plan) and sent it to the Planning Agency. Discussion and negotiation about the revision of the BNDP were part of the foundation and preparation for those long-term plans. Section 2–4 investigates the details of the process and the substance of important decisions at the initial stage of the War with China. My primary focus is on the peace overture that started in October 1937 and ended in failure after the capture of Nanjing. Section 2–5 concludes that the supreme decision-making body in Japan was a motley collection of representatives from different parties and that it was unclear who occupied the position of ultimate leadership in war. It focuses on the connection between war leadership and planned war preparations.[5] In an appendix to this chapter, I raise several questions: Why didn't Japan stop on the road to war? Could it simply not do so? Suppose it had recovered peace on the way. Could it have been maintained? If so, for how long?

2–2. Decision-Making Systems and Processes in Japan

2–2–1. Overview

Under the Japanese constitution of the time, the supreme decision-making body was a motley collection of representatives from different parties, and it was unclear who occupied the position of ultimate leadership in war (Tanemura, 1979, pp. 21–2).

Tanemura captures the war leadership and decision-making system in Japan from the 1930s to the mid-1940s. As Cairncross (1991, p. 3) says, "War … is a great centraliser. It is the government that conducts the war, decides what strategy to follow, and determines how the country's resources can best be used if the war is to be won." In Japan, "nobody occupied the position of supreme national leader," who, "facing a threat to national security, could

---

[5] I do not review here the dominant view (or the conventional wisdom) that Japan started and developed the war on the basis of planned preparations. For the details of my review and criticism, see Part I of Miwa (2008).

devote his best efforts to determining strategies to follow in politics and war, and could lead the war" (Tanemura, 1979, pp. 21–2). This vacuum in leadership shaped the conduct of the war from the beginning to the end. It was not only victory or defeat that was conditioned, but also the substance and effectiveness of war preparations, war mobilization, and economic control. It was outside the bounds of possibility that Japan could effectively implement systematic war preparations before the war.

Under the Japanese constitution of the time (the Meiji Constitution), as Tanemura points out, decisions were made by "a motley collection of representatives from different parties." This does not imply that individual constituent units or members of each unit could make decisions according to their preferences. Basically, each unit and its members discharged their duty as instructed by rules.[6] I therefore focus this investigation on the process that shaped the behavior of the constituent units and their members. Naturally, the form and substance of the system and the mechanism of communication and coordination between constituent units are matters of considerable concern.

In this book, I discuss war mobilization, economic control, and preparations for it, together with the substance and roles of various plans, the system, its working process, and its decision-making mechanism. To this end, we need information about the ACCom, NCCom, Army Ministry (AM), Navy Ministry (NM), Cabinet, and Diet. We need to understand the organizational structure of each institution, the division of roles among constituent units, and the allocation of roles among these institutions. Because we are interested in the actual implementation of systematic war preparations, war mobilization, and economic control, we focus (for illustrative purposes) on the Strategy Section of the ACCom.

Decision-Making and Consensus-Building Mechanisms

Under the 1889 Meiji Constitution, the Army Central Commander (ACCommander), the Navy Central Commander (NCCommander), the Army Minister, the Navy Minister, the Prime Minister, the Foreign Minister,

---

[6] Actually rules were not often violated. For instance, Army ministers such as Itagaki, Hata, and Tojo, together with Navy Minister Shimada and Finance Minister Kaya, approved expenditures under their jurisdiction in given rules (*Tokyo Tribunal of War Criminals, Shorthand Record*, vol. 96, 23 October 1946). See Miwa (2008, p. 141, note 51). By "violation of rules" I do not mean the behavior of economic agents who failed to follow under instructions from above, as symbolized by the flourishing black market. Obviously, the scarcity of violations does not imply that they circumvent the evils of the "motley collection" of the supreme decision-making body.

and the Kwantung (Manchuria) Army Commander all reported directly to the Emperor. A distinctive feature of Japan's administration of the time was, in today's parlance, an extreme vertically segmented administrative system.

The military leaders who reported to the Emperor needed to communicate, coordinate their views, and establish consensus with each other. With a few exceptions, they failed to do so. The national defense and operations controlled by the ACCom had a close connection with the military administration controlled by the AM. On national defense policies and its operations, the ACCom had to communicate closely with the AM (or with the government through the AM), especially on the budget. The same applies to the relationship between the NCCom and the NM (Sejima, 1995, pp. 70–1).

As we will see in the next section, in the 1930s the ACCom hoped to build an effective defense against the USSR. However, it gained little support toward that end from the divisions concerned, including the NCCom, and it was eventually forced to abandon its plans almost entirely. The Army's fully fledged armament enhancement plan to make up for lost time started with the FY1937 budget, but its magnitude was far below what the ACCom had envisaged.

The ACCom, or its Strategy Section, could not have dominated the decision-making process of the Japanese government. It could not even have led decision making on war-related issues, both because of the basic character of the supreme decision-making body as a motley collection of representatives from different parties and because of the process by which the government made its decisions. With few exceptions, important decision-making issues required a number of parties to coordinate their views and obtain agreement. For this reason, the system and mechanism for coordinating views and consensus building deserve special attention.

Even on important issues concerning war leadership and war mobilization, coordinating views and consensus building among relevant parties rarely progressed smoothly. Exchanging and sharing relevant information was a very slow process. I find no reason to think that the situation was different during the period in which Japan allegedly planned and prepared systematically for the war.

The Supreme National Leader and War Leadership

The first focus of investigation is the role and function of the Emperor, to whom the head of each division reported directly. The standard view is: "The Meiji Constitution stipulates that governance, supreme command,

and decisions about the commencement of war belong to the Emperor. In fact, however, he never exercised this power" (Tanemura, 1979, p. 21). Only rarely did the Emperor express his own view, intervene on specific issues, or coordinate conflicting views.[7]

Tanemura, writing about the ACCom, described the reality of war leadership in Japan (Tanemura, 1979, p. 22):

Before and during the Pacific War period, Japan's war leadership was divided between three people: the Prime Minister, the premier political assistant to the Emperor, and the ACCommander and the NCCommander, premier assistants in the supreme command. The Prime Minister could neither decisively control the Cabinet, nor express his view on matters concerning the supreme command. He presided over the Cabinet, which included the Army and the Navy Ministers, who controlled both forces, and the Foreign Minister. Each Cabinet member reported directly to the Emperor, whose consent the Prime Minister needed before making decisions on issues in his charge and appointments and dismissals. The official rule of the Cabinet stipulated that Cabinet resolutions needed unanimous agreement.[8]

Tanemura (1979, pp. 22–3) concluded that "the independence of the supreme command and the antagonism between the Army and the Navy were the most common causes of difficulty in war leadership," and recounted the following symbolic episode:

When the War with China broke out, Prime Minister Konoe knew almost nothing about the supreme command, including how far the armed forces would advance and what they intended to achieve. He could do nothing but watch what the Army and the Navy did. It was the Army Minister and the Navy Minister who took charge of cooperation between the supreme command and the politicians. Given the independence of the supreme command, the Prime Minister was not allowed to intervene in what it planned.[9]

---

[7] "Under the Meiji Constitution the Emperor governed Japan. But the Emperor was in a position with no responsibility, and governance was conferred upon the government of the day. It was exercised with the support of ministers, who were responsible for the consequences. The same applied to the supreme command. The ACCommander and the NCCommander assisted the Emperor with the supreme command. They were responsible for the consequences" (Hattori, 1965, p. 138).

[8] See Minobe (1927, pp. 270–7), or Miwa (2008, p. 349, note 6).

[9] He continued: "Under such circumstances, even Mr. Konoe could not resolve internal conflicts. When the IH was formed in November 1937, the liaison conference between the IH and the government was formed in order to reach an agreement on important issues. It was a special wartime measure with no grounds in the Constitution. The rule was so restrictive that it allowed a meeting to take place only upon the joint signature that the operation was extremely tight and uncomfortable. With serious inconveniences for close cooperation through the liaison conference, the IH-government Liaison Council was established in December 1940. It held weekly meetings. Communication now became much easier and mutual understanding was much improved, but with the supreme command's continuing independence, there was almost no occasion to discuss issues concerning that command."

The Army and Navy

After the Navy split from the Army following the Russo–Japanese War of 1904–5, the two forces began to form conflicting concepts of national policy. On an equal footing, they competed against each other in armament enhancement and the use of national power. They formed distinct strategies and frequently mistrusted each other. This conflict continued through the War with China into the Pacific War.[10] Together with "the independence of supreme command," "this was the most common cause of difficulty in war leadership" (Tanemura, 1979, p. 22).[11]

As we will see in the next section, ever since the first BNDP was established in 1907, the Army and the Navy had seen different countries as their primary enemy. As a result, they never reached an agreement on Basic National Defense Policies, or even on the relative threats facing the nation. They failed to reach an agreement not only on several revisions of BNDP but also on the mid-1930s debate about revising the BNDP and basic outline of operations. The Army continued to insist that the basic outline of national defense policy placed top priority on armament against the USSR and the Navy on guidance for national defense that aimed at "defense toward the North, aggression toward the South."

Conflict and Coordination within the Organization

There was often a serious conflict of opinions not only between the Army and the Navy but also within the forces themselves. As a result, an enormous amount of time and energy was spent on coordination. Obviously, this was not peculiar to the Army or the Navy at the time.

Like all large enterprises and authorities today, the Army and Navy were huge hierarchical organizations, and decisions were made on the basis of that structure. The Army and Navy allocated authority and responsibility to individual units at lower levels and delegated to them the issues under their jurisdiction.

Nothing changed remarkably with the establishment of the IH in the relation between the ACCom and the NCCom or corresponding sections in each institution. In this respect, its establishment was of no special significance. The IH-AD and the IH-ND, respectively, continued to use the buildings of the ACCom and the NCCom as their offices. See Boeicho (1967a, p. 499).

[10] See Imoto (1978, p. 38).

[11] With the exception of a very few issues that required mutual consultation, each made their own decisions about command and administration, free from restraints from the other side. By keeping these secrets to themselves, neither could understand what the other was thinking and doing (Tanemura, 1979, p. 23). For more details, see Miwa (2008, 3–9, pp. 209–12).

This principle was maintained rigorously until the end of the war. Susumu Nishiura was the Military (*gunji*) Section Chief of the AM Military Bureau from April 1942 to December 1944, following a long career within the section. He explained the authority of the Military Bureau to intervene in military operations (Nishiura, 1980, pp. 192–4)[12]:

After the war, the power and capacity of the AM to control specific operations were discussed at every opportunity. The AM was prohibited from making direct remarks about troops in operation, and it was impossible for it to express and enforce its plans about operations. As a result, it was extremely difficult to transmit the intentions of the military administration to the troops on the ground through the supreme command. Conversely, issuing an order or directive from the IH (AD) required the alignment of the military administration authority. Though aligned, we [the military administration authority] did not always share the same opinion about the entire plan of operations.

He continued:

In general, the military administration authority presented three types of misgiving to the supreme command's schemes: First, given the constraints of budget, materials, or manpower we sometimes considered the feasibility of a scheme very low. Second, we sometimes thought it poorly matched to Cabinet policy. And third, as soldiers, we sometimes thought the planned operations inappropriate. Even in such cases, however, the opinion of the military administration authority was ineffective.

With the first type of misgiving, unless there was an absolute shortage, it was practically impossible to control an operation that the supreme command considered high priority. Even in such exceptional cases as a serious deficiency in ships or railway construction material, the supreme command could insist that the operation was feasible and carry it out. The military administration authority could never succeed with the third type of misgiving. Theoretically, any division could express its opinion about the supreme command's schemes, but only the supreme command could enforce them. This had been true since ancient times, and anything else was prohibited as interference with the supreme command.

Therefore the military administration authority could only ever express an opinion about the second type of problem, which might arise when the supreme command's

---

[12] Nishiura was a secretary to Army Minister Tojo when the Pacific War began. See also Nishiura (1968, p. 319). His recollections as the Military Section Chief reveal a stark contrast with the popular view, represented by Joho (1979, p. 9): "During the period from the beginning of the 1930s to the mid-1940s – throughout the process of war development from the Manchurian Incident to the Shanghai Incident, from the War with China to the Pacific War – it was the Military Bureau as a unit representing the AM that the general public called 'the military' and worshipped. The czar of the power structure, the Military Bureau was the national institution that formed the nucleus of power and decided the conduct of the war."

scheme conflicted with what the Army Minister had decided in the Cabinet, for instance.

He concluded, "There was always discussion about all kinds of operations in the Greater East Asian War at the start, but in the end the military administration authority accepted the original schemes of the supreme command."

Supreme Command and Administration: Cooperation and Confrontation

Not only was cooperation haphazard between the Army and the Navy, but also between the ACCom and the AM (and between the NCCom and the NM). It was not that one party controlled the other. Rather, it was that the mechanisms to coordinate the two did not always work smoothly.

The NM and the NCCom were independent institutions. They did not act together. When necessary, a committee might be organized with staff from the NM and the NCCom to study specific questions. During the period from the mid-1930s to the mid-1940s, two committees deserve attention: the Committee to Study Naval Policies and Institutions, which existed from March to December 1936 (see 2-3-2), and the Naval Committee on National Defense Policy that existed from 12 December 1940 to the end of the war. The Navy organized the former in order to counter the Army's policy of promoting its operations to the North (Boeicho, 1975b, pp. 288–90).

The Kwantung Army

Until just before the beginning of the Pacific War in December 1941, national defense against the USSR was the Army's biggest challenge. The Kwantung Army assumed that the defense of Manchukuo (its client state in Manchuria) would be the first stage of its defense against the USSR. Therefore, the position and roles of the Kwantung Army, particularly the relationships between the Kwantung Army Commander and the AM and between the Armed Forces Chief of the Kwantung Army and the ACCommander, deserve special attention. In neither case did the former act under the orders of the latter.

As a result of the Russo–Japanese War, the Japanese Army began to station troops in South Sakhalin, Kwantung Leased Territory, and Korea. This transformed the national defense of Japan. On 16 September 1905, an agency was established for the defense of Kwantung Leased Territory. Its governor-general would now report directly to the Emperor, control troops, and take charge of the defense of Kwantung Leased Territory (Boeicho, 1967a, p. 129).

With the founding of Manchukuo on 1 March 1932, a mutual-defense treaty was established between Japan and Manchukuo. The assignment of the Kwantung Army Commander, the top commander of the Japanese Army in Manchuria, now changed. He now became the top commander of the Japan–Manchukuo allied forces as well (Boeicho, 1969a, p. 104). An order dated 16 June 1932 defined the Kwantung Army Commander's assignment:

Order: The Kwantung Army Commander takes charge of assignments provided in the Kwantung Army Command Ordinance, and also takes charge of security in key areas in Manchuria and the protection of Japanese people. The details will be specified through the ACCommander.

Direction: The Kwantung Army Commander, when he intends to dispatch troops outside the area of Hunchun, Mudanjiang, Yi-Lan, ... and Dixiing'anling, must report in advance to the ACCommander.

This restriction was eliminated by a further direction on 6 December 1932. When necessary, the Kwantung Army Commander could now dispatch troops outside the designated area and, if necessary, dispatch and station troops anywhere in Manchuria (Boeicho, 1969a, p. 105).

For example, when the Marco Polo Bridge Incident occurred, the Kwantung Army Commander reported to the ACCommander that, in view of the situation in North China, he was preparing to send out immediately the main force of the First and Eleventh mixed brigades and part of the Air Force. The Kwantung Army Command issued the statement at night, indicating its extraordinary preoccupation with the North China Incident.[13]

2–2–2. The Organization of the Strategy Section of the ACCom

ACCom (NCCom) and Supreme Command
Neither the ACCom nor the Strategy Section (nor Kanji Ishiwara, who was the Strategy Section Chief from October 1935 and Strategy Division Chief

---

[13] As the Kwantung Army Commander reported directly to the Emperor, this initiative was not illegal or grotesque, even if highly unusual. The Korean Army Commander and the Armed Forces Chief of the Korean Army behaved similarly. The ACCom, the Strategy Division in particular, considered the enhancement of national defense and power at home to be its absolute priority, in order to improve Japan's national defense on the continent. They did their best to control the influence of the Kwantung Army in North China. On 13 January 1936, they presented the "Outline for Handling the North China Problem" to the North China Occupation Forces Commander. This proposed that the North China occupation forces, rather than the Kwantung Army, would support self-government in this area (Boeicho, 1967a, pp. 432, 372–3).

when the War with China began[14]) led the whole decision-making system. Instead, each component unit acted with considerable independence. "The Army Minister and the ACCommander were both in a position to assist the Emperor. They were independent of the supreme command in the broad sense and on an equal footing with it. In addition, the Army Minister was a member of the Cabinet in charge of general national affairs, and this sometimes placed him in the awkward position of conflicting with the ACCommander and the supreme command" (Boeicho, 1967b, p. 131).

The same applied to the relationship between the Navy Minister and the NCCommander:

The ACCommander and the NCCommander reported directly to the Emperor, and were not routed through either the Cabinet or the Prime Minister. This institution of 'the independence of supreme command' was peculiar to Japan.[15] The ACCommander and the NCCommander, each head of an institution assisting the Emperor, were the highest officers in supreme command. Even chief commanders under the direct control of Emperor had to deliver an opinion through the ACCommander or the NCCommander, and were not allowed to report directly to the Emperor. (Hattori,[16] 1965, p. 138)

Constitutionally, the ACCom was an independent institution that assisted the Emperor in his role as supreme commander. The AM, as part of the Cabinet that supported his control over national affairs, directed Army administration. As mentioned previously, however, national defense and the operations that the ACCom directed had a close connection with the military administration directed by the AM. On national defense policy and army operations, the ACCcom had to work closely with the AM, particularly on budget issues. The same holds for the relationship between the NCCom and the NM (Sejima, 1995, pp. 70–1).

Intermediate issues that fell between military command and military administration were termed "composite issues" or "supreme command issues in the broad sense." In the Army, "depending on the content, the Army Minister, the ACCommander, the Education Commissioner, and on rare occasions the Army Air Commissioner took charge of composite issues. The same held also for the Navy" (Hattori, 1965, p. 138).

[14] He resigned his job on 28 September 1937 – see section 2-4-1.
[15] This view is controversial. Fukudome (1951, pp. 10–11), the Strategy Division Chief of NCCom at the beginning of the Pacific War, argued after the war: "The independence of supreme command was formulated in 1882 by Hirobumi Ito who, having been sent to Europe to study constitutions, considered it right and adopted the German model." For the details of Fukudome's view, see Miwa (2008, p. 354, note 10).
[16] Hattori was the Strategy Section Chief of the IH-AD at the beginning of the Pacific War.

The IH-AD (ACCom)

That was how the ACCom operated in peacetime. The Imperial Headquarters (IH) had been temporarily established for the Sino–Japanese War (1894–5) and the Russo–Japanese War (1904–5) to assist the heads of the supreme command of the Army and the Navy. Once the IH was established, the ACCom (the NCCom) became the IH-AD (IH-ND), and the ACCommander (NCCommander) became the Head of IH-AD (IH-ND). The Army (Navy) Minister who did not join the ACCom (NCCom) in peacetime nevertheless worked with the IH staff in wartime. The IH-AD (IH-ND) used the ACCom's (NCCom's) buildings as its office (Sejima, 1995, p. 71).

The IH was established in November 1937, four months after the beginning of the second Sino–Japanese War. From the end of 1939 to August 1945, Suketaka Tanemura served as a staff officer in Subsection 20 (War Leadership) under the direct command of the Vice-Chief of the IH-AD (vice-ACCom). Tanemura was engaged in communicating administrative issues emerging from conferences among the Emperor, the AM, the NM, and the other ministries. He recalled (Tanemura, 1979, p. 24), "A big sign of the IH-AD (IH-ND) was put up over the door of the ACCom (NCCom) office, which was maintained until the end of the war. The substance stayed about the same, and the establishment of the IH contributed nothing to cooperation either between the Army and the Navy or between national affairs and the supreme command."[17]

The ACCom Strategy Section

The ACCom originated from the General Staff Division (*sanbo-bu*), established in July 1871 within the Military Ministry (*heibu-sho*). After a series of revisions, by 1908 its organizational structure had settled into the shape it maintained until almost the end of the Pacific War.[18]

At the beginning of December 1939, when Captain Sejima arrived at his new post at the Strategy Section of the IH-AD, the ACCom, under the supervision of the ACCommander and the Vice-Chief, was organized into five divisions: the General Affairs Division – general affairs, education (the first section); First Division – strategy, organization and mobilization, and homeland security; Second Division – information; Third Division – traffic

---

[17] For the ACCom's Strategy Division Chief Simomura's similar view, see Boeicho (1967a, pp. 495–6).
[18] For the details, see Takeyama (1971, pp. 420–3).

and communication; and Fourth Division – military history and combat instruction.[19]

The First Division, strategy, consisted of three sections (2–4). Section 2, the Strategy Section, was divided into three subsections – Strategy, Aviation, and Logistics – under the Section Chief, and consisted respectively of seven or eight, three, and eight members (including the Subsection Chief). The Strategy Section had fourteen to fifteen members in total (including the Section Chief). "The Strategy Section was the nerve center of the ACCom or the IH-AD and embraced a small elite policy" (Sejima (1995, p. 73).[20]

To ensure close collaboration between the Army and the Navy, four IH-ND Strategy Section staff officers held the post in the IH-AD Strategy Section and three IH-AD Strategy Section staff officers in the IH-ND Strategy Section. In no other bureau or section was a mutual exchange of this type found (Sejima (1995).[21]

Inside the Strategy Subsection, tasks were assigned flexibly. At the time of Sejima's arrival, it was divided into two groups: "in charge of fronts," such as to the north (operations toward the USSR, Kwantung Army) and to operations in China; and "responsibility for tasks," such as the plan of operations for overall Army and application of armed forces.[22]

Tanemura (1979, p. 40) outlined ACCom's internal decision-making process concerning issues under individual units' jurisdiction:

Quintessentially, determining the outline of national policies starts with detailed plans at the proposing unit. This then proceeds step by step obtaining approval of units at higher levels. An ACCom proposal, the Outline for Coping with the Current Situation (proposed by the IH at the IH-government Liaison Conference on 27 July 1940), was first drafted by the section in charge, discussed at the meeting of Section Chiefs and the meeting of Division Chiefs (usually attended by the ACCommander and Vice-Chief), and eventually became an ACCom proposal.

[19]   See Sejima (1995, p. 72). Sejima and Tanemura, arriving at IH-AD at almost the same time, also left at almost the same time.

[20]   There were fourteen or fifteen commissioned and noncommissioned officers affiliated with the Strategy Section. They were highly capable officers selected from throughout the Army and supported the tasks of section members (Sejima, 1995, p. 73).

[21]   Nishiura (1968, pp. 252–4) says that a similar exchange was found in the Fortress Section and the Vessel Section. In exceptional cases, officers such as Sejima doubled the staff of the Combined Fleets on active service; however, this type of mutual exchange was almost always useless.

[22]   Sejima (1995, p. 101) includes the organization chart of the Strategy Section in July 1941. Takushiro Hattori was the Section Chief, and Sejima was a member of a group in charge of north front affairs (three members) and doubled as the assistant to the Strategy Subsection Chief. Lieutenant-Colonel Imoto (1978, 1979) led south front affairs (five members) and supervised this group.

Then, discussing it with the AM and the Navy, the IH presented it as its own plan to the Liaison Conference for final decision.[23]

Each unit (the Strategy Section, for instance) was assigned tasks and allocated specific duties. Even the most influential and capable Section Chief found it extremely difficult to make a task outside his jurisdiction a recognized part of the ACCom's proposal. There were even more hurdles to clear before it could be made an IH-government Liaison Conference decision.

Tasks Assigned to the Strategy Section

The ACCom (IH-AD) supported the Emperor in his role as supreme commander. Together with the NCCom (IH-ND), it was one of the offices of supreme command, the primary task of which was to formulate the basic outline of operations for national defense. Within the ACCom, the function of the Strategy Section was to formulate basic practices that required collaboration with other units (divisions and sections) inside the ACCom.

The specific affairs allocated to the ACCom in wartime were different from those in peacetime and varied as conditions changed. In 1940, the principal task of the Strategy Section (consistent in both wartime and peacetime) was to formulate fiscal year operation plans based on the BNDP and the basic outline of operations (Sejima, 1995, pp. 80–3). Its second task involved operations in China, and its third related to stationing troops in North French Indochina. Both these latter tasks reflected the exigencies of the time.

Apart from this, the ACCom, as one of the offices of central command (ACCom and NCCom) and alongside the IH and the government, played an important role in formulating national defense. The Strategy Section assisted the ACCommander in this process.

By association, the Strategy Section played a key role in communication and coordination among the units in the nerve centers of the Army, the ACCom, and the AM, and with important forces under the direct control of the Emperor, such as the Kwantung Army and the Expeditionary Force to China. Communication with the Navy, particularly with the NCCom (typically the Strategy Section of the Strategy Division), was also an important task.

Inside the Strategy Section, tasks were divided among units and also among members. On important issues, however, all the members received

---

[23] Basically there is no clear difference between the decision-making process inside the ACCom at that time and the process in today's government ministries in Japan. Readers interested in the latter should see Miwa (2004, pp. 281–9).

proposals and explanations from the member in charge of the issue, deliberated about the question involved, and helped the Section Chief make his final decision (Sejima, 1995, pp. 80–2).

The ACCommander and the ACCom Strategy Section

The ACCommander and the NCCommander assisted the supreme commander – the Emperor – and had no authority to lead military forces directly. Instead, they had the authority to implement Imperial orders, which in the Army were called the Imperial Headquarters (IH) Army Orders and in the Navy the IH Navy Orders. These orders were drafted by IH-AD or IH-ND and approved by the Emperor. The ACCommander or the NCCommander received them and transmitted them to the parties concerned.

The IH Army (Navy) Orders ended with a statement: "The ACCommander (NCCommander) shall issue directions over matters of detail." Reporting to the Emperor was therefore an extremely important task. The backbone of the implementation of the supreme command was national defense, and for that the Strategy Section took primary responsibility. Before the beginning of the Pacific War in December 1941, the ACCommander reported to the Emperor two or three times a week, and after that almost every day (Sejima, 1995, pp. 82–3).

The ACCommander was charged in the ACCom Regulation of March 1889 to head the ACCom and "to take control over the planning of supreme command and national defense operations and the exercising of control over Army staff officers." Moreover, he was to serve "under the direct control of the Emperor and to participate in the supreme command and to supervise the administrative duties of the ACCom." The Strategy Section of ACCom was a part of the administrative duties of ACCom, which was in turn under the supervision of the ACCommander. In this way, the relationship between the ACCommander and the Strategy Section was basically the same as that of the Minister (the Minister of International Trade and Industry, or MITI, for example) and the individual sections (such as the Industrial Structure Section) of the MITI (now the METI) in postwar Japan.

2–2–3. Military Control of Japanese Politics

"Gekokujo" in the 1930s

The Manchurian Incident (1931) marked the rapid rise of the military's vision of an all-out war system.... On the process of fascist restructuring of the system since the

2.26 Incident in 1936 it was accredited by leaders both in politics and business with the formation of "military-business embracing" (Oishi, 1994, p. 14).

As this quotation suggests, the idea that the military (the Army) dominated Japanese politics has been accepted as conventional wisdom, particularly after an attempted coup d'état in 1936 (the 2.26 Incident). At the core of this notion lies the practice of *gekokujo* (lower-level personnel dominate their nominal superiors) within the Army in the 1930s.

Consider a comment from Shidehara (1951), Foreign Minister at the time of the Manchurian Incident, and the recollections of four others, all of whom served within the mainstream of the military during the 1930s and whose perspectives have been almost entirely ignored by scholars since.

Shidehara (1951, pp. 184–5) recalled:

Observers comment that the Manchurian Incident escalated because the leaders of the government and the military were indecisive. If they had enforced orders, however, a revolt by the military would have broken out much earlier in Japan. Others may argue that if the government had refused the spending necessary for the military's reckless campaigns, the military could not have begun the war. Although I see the logic in that, under the conditions at the time it would only have aggravated the discontent within the military. Inside the military *gekokujo* prevailed, and even the Army Minister could not control the junior officers when they acted in concert. This was due to the defect of the Meiji Constitution, under which the top of the military chain of command was the ACCommander or the NCCommander. Even the Prime Minister did not come into the picture. Therefore, ... there was no other way to control the military except for generals like Kanaya to stand together and risk their lives.[24]

Shidehara's recollection has become central to the conventional wisdom. Fukudome was serving as Strategy Section Chief of the NCCom when the War with China began and as Strategy Division Chief at the beginning of the Pacific War. He recalled, however (Fukudome 1951, p. 17): "I was in the NCCom for a long time, and I don't agree unconditionally with these politicians' babbles. We recognize that strategy and operations during the War with China were poorly executed. Even if the Army dominated the decision making involved, however, the main cause of the war was the government's politically motivated actions, which ignored battle plans. On not a few occasions it was the government that was at fault for putting too much emphasis on its politically motivated decision."[25]

---

[24] General Hanzo Kanaya was the ACCommander at the time.

[25] He continues, however: "No one denies that the independence of supreme command caused Japan much greater evil than good and that it facilitated militarism."

Nishiura (1968, pp. 240–3), the Military (*gunji*) Section Chief from April 1942 to December 1944, contrasted "mainstream" with "minor trends." The "mainstream's intention" was reflected in the opinions of "persons in charge," such as "the Minister, Vice-Minister, and Bureau Chiefs, and in the ACCom the Vice-ACCommander, the Strategy Division Chief, and the Strategy Section Chief." Quite often the person in charge relied heavily on his clerical assistants as his executive officers. "This staff system was *gekokujo* – if you can call it *gekokujo* – since the most efficient and active staff were the most influential." Even the most competent Minister could not deal with everything in his charge. But he usually considered his subordinates capable – as "good, efficient, and reliable staff," not "inexcusable fellows doing just what they want."

Inada (1969, p. 265) served as Strategy Section Chief of the ACCom during the War with China, from March 1938 to October 1939. In Japan, he wrote, "the better generals supported their junior officers, saying 'Uh-huh, OK. Do a good job.' As a result, a proponent who originated a plan, typically a lieutenant-colonel or a major, often held a strong position."

Iwaguro (1977, p. 204) was the Military (*gunji*) Section Chief of the AM from February 1939 to February 1941. "What I regret as a main cause of mistakes is that the superior officers were not strong enough to contain their subordinates. Senior officers were eager to gain popularity among juniors, while juniors understood their superiors to be men who acceded to their staff. We misidentified those superiors who, not having their own opinions, accepted subordinates' opinions as those of 'great men.'" He continues that "it was a big mistake to applaud men like Iwao Oyama and Nanshu Saigo as 'great,' when, having no clear opinions, they simply approved anything proposed." [26]

The Military and Japanese Politics: Perceptions and Reality

Table for the moment the question of who traditionally constitutes "the military" and the Army. Here I review the appropriateness of the dominant

---

[26] Concerning this point, see Miwa (2008, p. 95, note 3), which introduces comment from Inada (1969, pp. 190–1), including "inside the Army it was the age of rival warlords." Concerning himself as the Strategy Section Chief of the ACCom, Inada (1969, p. 281) writes: "The Section Chief is a planner. After formulation, to implement my plans I flew to the field, where I explained the details to important people in order to instill the idea firmly." The Section Chief was so busy that on many occasions he needed the help of his own clerical assistants. Concerning the work of the Military (*gunji*) Section Chief, Iwaguro (1977, p. 188) recalls: "I had to meet at least 50 people every day, 100 people when busy. One to three minutes per person. About 85 of 100 people were for his benefits, 10 were enemies, and only five were friends."

view that a small group within the military (in collusion with a small group of bureaucrats, politicians, and businessmen) controlled decision making on political issues, including military affairs, diplomacy, and economic policies.

As I have examined in detail elsewhere,[27] there are almost no clear definitions of key concepts. As a result, many terms remain ambiguous, and the conventional wisdom is almost impossible to evaluate. As no literature argues the appropriateness of the dominant view upon a clear logic and persuasive evidence, it is impossible to evaluate it by standard means.

Here, I simply present several observations that may help readers clarify the substance of the dominant view and question its appropriateness.

Personnel Changes in Top Military Posts

In Japan in this period, no notorious dictators, like Hitler or Stalin, appeared. No strong leaders like Roosevelt, Chiang Kai-shek, or Churchill appeared either. Hideki Tojo's term as the Prime Minister lasted two years and nine months, from October 1941 to July 1944, and his term as Army Minister lasted four years, from September 1940 to July 1944. (Fumimaro Konoe's term as Prime Minister lasted two years and ten months, from June 1937 to January 1939 and from July 1940 to October 1941.)

Consider the period from July 1937 (when the War with China began) to December 1941 (Pearl Harbor). By the end of this period, the ACCom was on its sixth Strategy Section Chief, fifth Strategy Division Chief, and sixth Vice-ACCommander. The Army was on its fourth Minister, its fifth Vice-Minister, seventh Military Bureau Chief, third Military (*gunji*) Section Chief, and fifth Military (*gunmu*) Section Chief.[28] A claim that a Strategy Division Chief or a Strategy Section Chief of the ACCom, for example, consistently led the war or invasion is inconsistent with the observation that the people occupying those positions changed frequently.

As the next two cases suggest, the Strategy Division Chief or Strategy Section Chief could not always realize their claims. They also suggest that strong conflicts of opinion arose between Army leaders.

Kanji Ishiwara is often presented as leading systematic war preparation. Yet, as the next section will show in detail, Ishiwara did not hold an important position in central Army command until August 1935. That month, he

---

[27] See Miwa (2008, section 2–2, pp. 92–100), where I present "eight questions for clarifying the 'conventional wisdom.'" The first question begins by asking, who are the military? Is there common understanding and wide agreement among supporters of the dominant view or the conventional wisdom (p. 94)?

[28] See Nihon kindaishi kenkyu-kai, ed. (1971).

was appointed Strategy Section Chief of the ACCom. Two years later, he opposed the deployment of additional troops to Shanghai and resigned in protest.[29]

On 16 January 1938, Prime Minister Konoe proclaimed: "From now, we will not deal with the Nationalist Chinese government." In the period between the capture of Shanghai and Nanjing (13 December 1937) and this proclamation, there had been a clash of opinion among Army leaders about the basic policy for operations in China. As we will see in section 2–4, the top leaders in the AM and most major staff officers in the ACCom insisted on an aggressive policy. Others believed that a long, drawn-out war in the occupied territory would ensue. The Strategy Section of the ACCom held the latter opinion, supported by the Vice-ACCommander.

The Strategy Division of the ACCom was responsible for leadership in war operations, and the Strategy Section was its nerve center. With its superior understanding of the limits of total army capacity, the Strategy Section could not support an aggressive policy. Section Chief Kawabe strongly advocated a nonescalation policy in China. After the Konoe Proclamation, he proposed a seven-month delay in enforcing more aggressive operations, for which he secured the consent not only of the ACCom and the AM but also of the Navy. The main guidelines for the operations were approved on 16 February at the Conference in the Presence of the Emperor, and Kawabe made a trip to the front to transmit them to commanding officers in the field. What awaited him at ACCom on his return, however, was not an order to implement the guidelines but a letter appointing him to Flight Training School at Hamamatsu. With the dismissal of the Strategy Section Chief, the nonescalation policy collapsed, and the Shandong and Xuzhou campaigns began.[30]

---

[29] His appointment as Strategy Section Chief was strongly supported by Military Bureau Chief Tetsuzan Nagata of the AM; however, Nagata was killed by Lieutenant-Colonel Aizawa in his office the day before Ishiwara's arrival. Nagata was the Military (*gunji*) Section Chief at the time of the Manchurian Incident, in which Ishiwara played a pivotal role as a staff of Kwantung Army. See Joho (1979, pp. 318, 396).

[30] See Imoto (1978, pp. 199–203). "With 'the independence of supreme command' it was the strategy line of the ACCom that took control of pure supreme command (national defense and operations). Once they determined a policy and pushed it through, open opposition to it was no longer permitted, not even by the AM. There was no other way to change the passive policy than to replace personnel in the strategy line" (p. 203). "The Army Ministry had authority over personnel issues in the Army in general. It was under the jurisdiction of the Personnel Bureau of the AM, within which personnel issues of staff officers (central and local) were to be determined by the General Affairs Division Chief of the ACCcom on consultation and liaison with the Personnel Bureau Chief of the AM" (Sejima, 1995, p. 73). Nishiura (1968, p. 150) gives a more detailed explanation. Personnel

In addition, at least twice in the 1930s, just after the attempted coup d'état in February 1936 and after the 1940 invasion of Northern French Indochina, top administrators were replaced simultaneously.[31] In the AM in 1936, the Minister, Vice-Minister, the Military Bureau Chief, and the Military (*gunji*) Section Chief all switched positions, as did the Vice-ACCommander and the Strategy Division Chief in the ACCom.[32] This is inconsistent with the notion that a small group of military leaders controlled important decision making on military affairs, diplomacy, and economic policy.

Army leaders were divided over the invasion of Northern French Indochina in the summer of 1940. The AM and the Second Division (Information) of the ACCom pushed for peace talks, while the First Division (Strategy) of the ACCom insisted on military action. Repeatedly, the expeditionary force on the scene lost touch with IH and failed to negotiate with the local government. The IH policy had been to "make entry consistently in peace, and to resort to military action only when encountering strong resistance." Strategy Division Chief Tominaga was dismissed on 25 September, after an official trip to French Indochina and South China. He was blamed for the failure of the expeditionary force to follow the directions of the ACCommander and the Vice-ACCommander. In addition, Second Division Chief Dobashi, together with Strategy Section Chief Okada and the Strategy Subsection Head Arao and the AM members, were transferred when they tried to keep their more aggressive counterparts in

issues of staffs before the unification adopted after the 2.26 Incident was as follows. The ACCom (General Affairs Section) had authority over staff personnel issues, which were discussed with the ACCom and the AM (Personnel Bureau). Nishiura, a graduate of the Army War College and therefore staff personnel, was on the table of this discussion when he was a lieutenant or a major. The unification was at least partially for form's sake, and not only his immediate superior in the AM but also the ACCom possessed the personal record of Nishiura while he served at the Military Bureau of the AM.

[31] When the Nomonhan Incident (Battle of Khalkhin Gol) in the summer of 1939 had been settled, many top leaders both in Tokyo and the Kwantung Army were also replaced. In the ACCom, the Vice-ACCommander and the Strategy Division Chief went into reserve and the Strategy Section Chief was replaced. In the Kwantung Army Command, the commander and the assistant chief of staff went into reserve, and several strategy staff officers, including the Strategy Section Chief, moved out of staff work (Imoto, 1978, pp. 387–91). The Strategy Section Chief that Inada replaced on this occasion had been appointed to this position after the removal of Torashiro Kawabe in March 1938. For more details, see Nishiura (1968, p. 317) and Inada (1969, pp. 201–3). As we will see later in section 2-3-3, when the ACCom and the AM became entangled in the armament enhancement budget in November 1936, all the people responsible for armament enhancement left the ACCom after cleaning up the mess.

[32] As mentioned in Chapter 1 (note 3), the ACCommander, Kan'in-no-miya (Taruhito), was a member of Imperial family. He was in position from 23 December 1931 to 3 October 1940.

check. In the wake of the personnel changes, the ACCommander and the Vice-ACCommander also resigned (Tanemura, 1979, pp. 41–55).

Frequent Changes in Political Office

Political leaders, especially Cabinet members, changed frequently as well. Consider the period from July 1937 to December 1941. By the end of this period, the Cabinet was on its seventh Prime Minister, twelfth Foreign Minister, ninth Interior Minister, eighth Finance Minister, and ninth Commerce Minister (as well as its fourth Army Minister and fourth Navy Minister).

Let's take a longer period, from the end of 1931 to the end of the war in August 1945. The last Prime Minister, Kantaro Suzuki, was the sixteenth (plus two temporaries by proxy). There were twenty-nine names on the list of Foreign Minister during this period, twenty Interior Ministers, nineteen Finance Ministers, and twenty Commerce Ministers. The average term served by a Prime Minister during this period was less than a year.[33]

Did "the Military," Particularly the Army, Control Politics?

The following observations from Nishiura (1980), are inconsistent with the conventional wisdom that the Army (or a small group of Army officers) controlled politics as they liked.

The first is related to the appointment of General Shunroku Hata as Army Minister of the Abe Cabinet that succeeded the Hiranuma Cabinet in August 1939:

Around that time, the remarks of an Army officer, whether official or private, could carry much weight, and the so-called 'inclination of the military' could strike an unexpectedly deep response. On the morning of a Cabinet meeting, I met Lieutenant Colonel Tomita, a high official in the Military (*gunmu*) Section. He said that, with the recommendation of leaders including ex-Army Minister Itagaki, the Army had sent a telegram to Lieutenant General Hayao Tada, then the Commander of the Third Force in Manchuria. Political observers in the Military Section seemed shocked to receive a nomination list from the Emperor indicating that the incoming Army Minister would be Hata or Umezu. Thus, Army Minister Hata appeared on the scene. Having won a high reputation as Chief Aide-de-Camp, on his appointment as the Army Minister General Hata told the senior officials in the Ministry, "We have to be the Army the Emperor trusts." That statement sums up the atmosphere of the time, I believe. The Emperor did not think favorably of the Army about either the three-party alliance, "the Nomonhan Incident," or the political issues at home. (pp. 133–4)

---

[33] For the list of major Cabinet members during this period, see Table 6–1 of Miwa (2008, p. 365).

The second is related to the Abe Cabinet and the subsequent Yonai Cabinet (p. 137):

Having supported the formation of the Abe Cabinet, the Army quickly turned cool toward it. This shift was partly a consequence of the actions Abe took on his appointment, including the dismissal of the Military (*gunmu*) Section Chief. It was also because of Army Minister Hata's confrontational attitude toward officers inside the Ministry. The Abe Cabinet collapsed before the Diet opened in 1940, and the Yonai Cabinet followed. Incoming Prime Minister Mitsumasa Yonai had been hostile to the Army since the three-party alliance movement and Army Minister Hata remained in his post. Anti-U.S. and UK pressure grew, however, and a group of Army officers who had promoted the three-party alliance now tried to push Yonai to dismiss Hata.

He continued, "The argument for the three-party alliance had waned since the birth of the Abe Cabinet. But with the succession of the Yonai Cabinet, pressure grew within the Army to oust Hata and topple the Yonai administration. This atmosphere naturally provided an opening for political adventurers. Support grew for the so-called Imperial Rule Assistance Association (*taisei yokusan-kai*) with Konoe as its head, and with it the number of visitors to Konoe's villa at Karuizawa increased."

Akira Mutoh was Strategy Section Chief in the early stages of the War with China. Representing the majority view within the Army, he fought Strategy Division Chief Kanji Ishiwara. When the Pacific War began, he was serving as Military Bureau Chief within the AM (30 September 1939–20 April 1942). Consistent with the attitude of the Military Bureau and Bureau Chief, Mutoh argued with "those who make disparaging comments that the Military Bureau Chief intervened too much in politics and business" (Joho, 1979, pp. 460–2)[34] that

[a]s a state minister, the Army Minister was necessarily involved in politics. Politics could not be completed in the Cabinet but had to be implemented through the duties of the office. For this implementation, the Army Ministry had to consult with other ministries and negotiate with the legislature. The Military Bureau was

---

[34] Joho (1979) also offers following commentaries. "Even to a military figure accustomed to politics like Mutoh it seems hard to get involved in them. It symbolically provides evidence of the tremendous difficulty that a serviceman, a graduate of the Imperial Japanese Army Academy and the Army War College, and a complete amateur in politics and business, was faced with when he intended to intervene in politics" (p. 460). Mutoh remarked when he was transferred from the Military Bureau to be commander of the Household (*konoe*) Second Division, "You never know how uncomfortable it is to be the Military Bureau Chief," on which Joho (1979, p. 482) comments: "Military Bureau Chief was such a formidable post that even Mutoh, who saw himself as 'contumelious and hubristic,' could use those words about it."

primarily in charge of this process. At stake was not politics itself, but the duties of the office that implemented the political process. When the Army was small, for example, most equipment could be manufactured in ordnance factories. Food and clothing could be manufactured in its own factories. Because the manufacturing occurred primarily in the private sector, [as the demands of the Army grew,] the Army naturally had to become involved in the economy. Even with these economic policies, however, the Military Bureau intervened only on basic issues like policy and programs, and left specific issues to other bureaux' administration.

Mutoh continued:

It is acceptable to criticize Army officers for intervening in politics. After all, they were prohibited from becoming involved in politics.... But given the political process, someone had to execute the duties of the office that implemented that process.... In my view, it was precisely those military personnel who visited high government officials and lawmakers and loudly criticized "the involvement of Army officers in politics" who were involved in it. They seem to have been strangely unaware of this irony. Furthermore, they held positions that did not allow them to become involved in the duties of political office. Looking back, I unhesitatingly declare that I never took any actions that constituted political involvement, other than the duties of the office that implemented the political process and to which I had been assigned. (Joho, 1979, p. 462)

Tojo: A Dictator?

The figure of Hideki Tojo, Prime Minister and Army Minister at the beginning of the Pacific War and concurrently ACCommander from 21 February 1944, personifies the perception that the Army consistently controlled politics as it liked. The documentary evidence, however, does not support this theory.

Kenryo Sato, who served Army Minister Tojo as Military (*gunmu*) Section Chief and subsequently Military Bureau Chief, made this assessment of Tojo (Sato, 1976, pp. 398–400):

Tojo was nothing like a dictator. He did not have what it takes to be one. He was a man of circumspection, and a self-willed overachiever. He was aggressive and had enough ability to push through his views, and he never listened anyone other than those in charge of each agenda.... On the surface he looked like a dictator. He held great power, so that's how he was perceived by the public. But he had a feeble mind. He had such a strong sense of responsibility that he always appeared to be intimidated by the amount he had to bear.

Tanemura (1979, pp. 226–7) captures this contradiction:

General Tojo, seen by the public as a dictator, in fact lacked one vital element of a dictator's power. He could do nothing at all about the Navy's operations or military administration and always behaved obsequiously toward the Navy. If trouble arose between the Army and the Navy, his subordinates in the AM were extremely hesitant to consult him, because whenever they did, the Army lost out. When the Navy was depressed over the heavy loss of warships in the spring of 1944, the Army transferred 20,000 tons of its steel allocation to the Navy as a token of sympathy. Yet the Navy was very far from being pleased.... Everyone remembers clearly that, at meetings with generals and chiefs of staff, Tojo always declared that crisis in war leadership in Japan arose either when the Army and the Navy were in conflict, or when the USSR entered the war against Japan. General Tojo always kept in mind that the Cabinet faced a crisis when the Army and the Navy fought.... As the ACCommander, he suppressed what the Navy planned to do after the Battle of Saipan.[35] In turn, this increased the pressure on him and led to the collapse of his Cabinet.[36]

Comments from the Strategy Division Chief of the NCCom at the beginning of the Pacific War illustrate Tojo's weakness (Fukudome, 1951, pp. 226–7). Together with the recollection of Imoto (1979, pp. 117–18) of the ACCom's Strategy Section, they suggest that Tojo did not recognize that the war "lacked a precise war vision," as mentioned in the excerpts at the beginning of this chapter, and that he lacked the support of several key staff.

Imoto (1979, pp. 117–18) recalls:

The nerve centers of the Army thought that with the completion of the first-stage operations the primary mission of the Army in this war was tentatively accomplished. Obviously the war would continue, but it would be fought against the U.S. Navy in the Pacific Ocean, which was the exclusive province of the Navy. They thought there would be no room for the Army to play a leading role.... The Army rationalized as follows. Maintaining the occupied areas with operations to the South, and emboldened by the victory in China, they would increase pressure on the enemy as much as possible in order to force them into submission. In Manchuria, strengthening the defenses against the USSR, they would forestall their preparations and conspiracies to Japan. In addition, they would to their best to separate the UK from the U.S., and finally force the UK's submission, by making an impact on India through politics, use of force, and other means toward Burma.... They placed too much expectation on German war development, to which they expected the UK's submission. The nerve center of the Army in earnest thought and expected this.

Fukudome comments:

The occupation of the southern area, the so-called Great East Asia Co-prosperity Sphere, was completed in March 1942. This was the first stage of the IH's plan of

---

[35] From 21 February to July 1944, Tojo combined his role with that of ACCommander. The battle of Saipan ended on 22 July and the Tojo Cabinet resigned as a body on 18 July.

[36] Tanemura continues: "General Tojo was not most inept toward the enemy; he was most inept toward the Navy.... The dictator had a fragile and feeble backbone. It was a tragic fate, and the natural consequence of Japan's national organization. There was nothing Tojo could do to improve it."

operations, scheduled to end in approximately three or four months. Immediately after it was achieved, Tojo emphatically reported to the Diet, that "we have completed the occupation of regions politically and economically necessary to us, and have established a strong defense." He made a public commitment that he would not increase mobilization further, would not lower the draft age, and would not reduce the student-exemption from military service. Moreover, he declared that he would cut the Army mobilized in the south from 350,000 to 200,000 men and bring the other 150,000 home.

Fukudome continued, "From an operational viewpoint, the first stage of the operations had simply captured the places of strategic importance. It was obvious that battles to maintain this vast southern area would continue. And it was obvious that the Army needed urgently to increase substantially, rather than reduce, the size of its forces. The Navy's need for air and marine forces was similarly pressing.... But General Tojo, from his unique perspective, never conceded as much."

At the meeting of 18 July 1944, the Tojo Cabinet resigned en masse, nominally because of its inability to obtain the cooperation of senior statesmen (*jushin*).[37] General Yoshijiro Umezu succeeded Tojo as the ACCommander on the same day. He then rejected a proposal to retain Tojo in the post of the Army Minister, and insisted that he retired from active duty. Marshal Sugiyama, who just the day before had assumed the Office of Education Commissioner, became the new Army Minister.[38]

2-3. National Defense: Policy, Plans, and Controversy in the Mid-1930s

2-3-1. National Defense Policy and National Defense Plan

In June 1937, just before the beginning of the War with China, the Army's fully fledged rearmament plan and the Navy's landmark replenishment plan began to be implemented, as scheduled. Both these plans had been formulated in late 1936 after negotiation with the finance authorities. The

---

[37] For a brief account of the process and background of Cabinet resignation, see Miwa (2007, 7–6). See also Okada (2001, pp. 222–47). For a wider contemporary view and the historical background to this event, see Inomata (1959).

[38] Tanemura (1979, pp. 223–6). See also Sato (1976, pp. 385–98) and Imoto (1979, pp. 554–64). Imoto was secretary to Army Minister Tojo from the fall of 1943 to 18 July 1944. Tojo succeeded Umezu as Army Vice-Minister in May 1938 and was appointed Army Minister in July 1940; Sugiyama was Army Minister from February 1937 to June 1938. Tojo became ACCommander in February 1944, taking over from Sugiyama, who had held the position since October 1940.

requisite funds had been approved in the session of the seventieth regular Diet that ended in March 1937. Intending dramatic expansion of the munitions manufacturing industry, the Army formulated its Five-Year Plan for Munitions Manufacturing Industries. In order to strengthen the key industries at its foundation, Army leaders drafted the Outline of a Five-Year Plan for Key Industries and sent it to the Planning Agency. This plan had not been implemented by the beginning of the war, although it did obtain Cabinet approval in January 1939 in the form of the Outline of Production Capacity Expansion Plan.

In this section, I review the particular system and mechanism of decision making concerning those plans, and the environmental factors (including the historical background) that conditioned them. I will show that the decision making followed predetermined rules. Contrary to what has long been thought, it was not determined by a small group of military leaders who made whatever decisions they wanted or relentlessly pursued preparations for future wars.

Details of the National Defense Policy

The Basic National Defense Policy (BNDP), requisite force size, and the Basic Outline of Operations (BOO) were treated as top-level military secrets.[39] Partly because of this, the position and role of individual plans and their relationship to each other are not always clear. Here I present a bird's-eye view of the plans, following an exposition by a member of the Strategy Section (IH-AD) of the ACCom (Sejima, 1995, pp. 76–7).

Any country that approaches defense policy rationally will have a dominant principle of national defense that integrates politics and strategy on the basis of national credo and policy. The requisite force

---

[39] The BNDP was kept wholly confidential. Four copies were made of it and the accompanying BOO, of which three went to the Imperial Court, the ACCom, and the NCCom, while the fourth was sent to the Prime Minister for preview and kept in the Imperial Court. In the ACCom, the Strategy Section took charge of the documents, which were kept in a vault, supervised by an apprentice staff officer (a staff officer served as an apprentice for a year before becoming a section member). Strategy Section members and apprentices could view them freely, but nobody outside the Section was allowed to access them (Joho, 1979, p. 337). Strategy Section members in ACCom or NCCom had to access them at least once for official reasons, but only tens of people had ever seen them. Nobody recalled clearly the first BNDP, formulated in 1907. All these documents were destroyed by fire at the end of the war, and there is no way to verify exactly what they were. Moreover, no complete original material on the BNDP and BOO revised in 3 June 1936 is available. However, around 1939 a member of the Strategy Section of ACCom copied almost all the original documents in his notebook, which is the source referred to here. See Boeicho (1967a, pp. 158, 394) and Sejima (1995, p. 77).

size is determined upon this principle, taking various constraints into consideration, including national budgets. Together with diplomatic tactics, this defense strategy then forms the foundation of national defense and security.

In Japan, once the BNDP and requisite force size were determined, the BOO for deploying forces during an emergency was decided and used by the Army and Navy to formulate an annual fiscal year operation plan (FYOP) for emergencies. Subsidiary details were also formulated annually.

After discussion and agreement between the government and the supreme command, both BNDP and requisite force size were ratified by the Emperor. The BOO and details of FYOP were formulated, agreed upon between the ACCom and the NCCom, and approved by the Emperor.

The Imperial BNDP, the requisite force size, and the BOO were first formulated in 1907 and revised in 1918, 1923, and 1936. All versions of these documents were classified as military secrets of the highest level and kept in the Strategy Section vault (see note 39).[40]

The Army also prepared an emergency recruitment plan, an armament procurement plan, a war mobilization plan, an education-training plan, and a personnel program based on the BOO and FYOP. It was important to keep the plans consistent with each other. If either went slightly off track, national forces would no longer operate smoothly and effectively in an emergency.[41] Most of the plans described in Chapter 1 were formulated in this way.

---

[40] Among the secret documents were the minutes of Kanji Ishiwara, the Strategy Section Chief at the time the BNDP was revised in June 1936. Sejima recalls that Ishiwara wrote (Sejima, 1995, p. 77): "Japan should devote every effort to the construction of Manchukuo. For this purpose, the Army should augment forces to prepare for a potential threat from the USSR, and the Navy for the threat and interference from the U.S. We must entirely avoid exhausting our national capability on other fronts."

[41] Naturally the same applied to the Navy. The commentary of the Strategy Section Chief of NCCom at the time of the revision is more specific (Fukudome, 1951, p. 107). "The NCCommander, as an assistant to the Emperor in supreme command, took charge of formulating plans for national defense including basic policy and war establishment, and the Navy Minister took charge of formulating an armament plan and war preparations for the implementation of which the government should assist the Emperor.... Requisite force size was a goal of the Navy's armament development, and Naval development plans were formulated for the construction and refitting of vessels.... Armament plans were implementation programs with a restricted implementation term, and so differed from requisite force size, which was a long-term goal. Two or three years were needed to construct a battleship, so naturally every Navy armament plan spanned several years.... But, as implementation was strictly conditioned by the national budget, a five-year, long-term armament plan was not feasible."

Preparing for War Against the USSR

The BNDP was formulated for the first time in 1907,[42] two years after the Russo–Japanese War of 1904–5. The Army, anticipating revenge from Russia, predicted a second war,[43] and assumed that Russia would be its enemy. At the time, however, NCCom did not agree. Instead, the Navy anticipated conflict with the United States. In December 1906, the ACCommander and the NCCommander were ordered to formulate the BNDP, to which end ACCom and NCCom met for counsel and reached an agreement in forty days. They listed Russia, the United States, and France as potential enemies.[44] The Army insisted that the

---

[42] Aritomo Yamagata was the virtual Army leader during this period. Lieutenant Colonel Giichi Tanaka (then senior officer of the ACCom Strategy Section), who was supposed to be Yamagata's successor, participated in the BNDP's drafting. He recognized that, "during the first half of the Russo–Japanese War, Japan consistently suffered from lack of weapons and ammunition, as a result of which we often missed chances. This was because we had depended primarily on the private economy for our armament supply." Tanaka thought they should first define national policy, and then formulate a basic defense policy, for which they should maintain an appropriate force size. Otherwise, they should tone down their policy. He insisted that armament enhancement unrelated to clear basic policies would endanger Japan's national defense (Boeicho, 1967a, pp. 135–6).

[43] In October 1906, Marshal Duke Yamagata appealed to the Emperor, stressing the urgent necessity of formulating a Basic National Defense Policy (Boeicho, 1967a, p. 142): "In formulating war plans, as before, we have to define Russia as the primary enemy. As all informed persons understand, along with its everlasting quest for nonfreezing ports, once it recovers from the after effects of defeat and calm domestic convulsion, Russia will vigorously revive its movement southward. Obviously, it is self-deceiving to say either that Russia has given up its strategies to the east or that it will be unable to undertake a war of vengeance against Japan for at least a decade or more. They neglect entirely the experience of the Russo–Japanese War." Boeicho (1967a, p. 176) also wrote: "Because of domestic affairs and internal discord Russia conceded victory to Japan in the Russo–Japanese War. Nobody knows what would have happened if Russia had staged a counterattack around Halpin, with strong determination to continue. Army leaders at the ACCom understood this well but it was difficult to get others to see it. The Legislature, government, and the Navy all thought that Army leaders were stricken with Russia phobia, or conversely that they were intending to mount an imperialist invasion into Korea and Manchuria. In fact, the Army was fully occupied with making an unbeaten level of military preparations. In succeeding years, too, Russian armament against Japan showed no sign of easing. Defining Japan as an anticipated enemy, Russia (the USSR) steadily strengthened the armament year on year."

[44] Boeicho (1967a, pp. 140–55). Although the Navy assumed the United States as a potential enemy, this policy was not as well established and robust as the Army's policy against Russia. Aware of the speed and size of naval expansion in the United States and Germany, the Japanese Navy was making a frantic effort not to fall behind in armament expansion. Around that time, the United States determined Japan to be its primary expected enemy, and formulated War Plan Orange in 1904 (Boeicho (1967a, pp. 155, 157). It was around this time that Lea (1909), raising an alarm against Japan, created a commotion.

government promise an equivalent military force both to the Army and the Navy.[45]

As a result, for several decades the major targets of Japan's national defense had been Russia (the USSR) and the United States. The Army took the leading part in defense against the USSR (operations on the continent), and the Navy cooperated. The Navy took the lead in defense against the United States (operations in the Pacific), and the Army cooperated.[46] These were tumultuous decades: all this occurred concomitantly with the First World War, the Siberian intervention, the Russian Revolution, the naval arms control pacts, and the rise of the USSR.

By the time of the Manchurian Incident (18 September 1931), the USSR had forcibly conducted its first Five-Year Plan.[47] It deployed only six sniper divisions and two cavalry divisions in the area east of Krasnoyarsk (1,000 kilometers west of Lake Baikal). As the battle lines extended over Manchuria in the spring of 1932, however, the USSR began to enlarge the transportation capacity of Trans-Siberian Railway. It increased its military force in the eastern coastal area (now called Primorsky Krai) with airplanes and tanks. The Japanese ACCom was deeply concerned.[48]

War Plan Orange decided in 1911, was the foundation of the US war plan in the Pacific before the outbreak of the WWII. However, the plan was fatally flawed in the 1930s and 1940s, the age of the air force. It emphasized the role of troops in the Philippines. In case of attack from Japanese troops, they planned to send reinforcements from the West Coast. But crossing the Pacific took several weeks or months. In October 1941 a memorandum from the Armed Force Chief Marshall was sent to General MacArthur, stressing that it was supremely important to deploy a strong air force, including B-17 bombers, in the Philippines by May 1942. US troops in the Philippines encountered an attack before this could be implemented, and in accordance with predetermined plan (Rainbow 5) withdrew to Bataan Peninsula. See Costello (1981, pp. 31–2, 104).

[45] Boeicho (1967a, p. 156). The Army and the Navy had different sense toward the USSR and the United States as expected enemies, and respectively the Army assumed the USSR as an expected enemy and the Navy the United States. Moreover, the Army and the Navy broke apart, conflicted with, clashed with, and obstructed each other (Boeicho, 1967a, p. 156).

[46] Sejima (1995, p. 79).

[47] Winning a domestic power struggle after Lenin's death in 1924, in December 1928 the USSR adopted a Five-Year Plan for industrialization, embodying Stalin's policies for the annihilation of rich farmers, collectivization of agriculture, and rapid industrialization. It was based on the idea that without sufficient industrial foundation for national defense, it was impossible to maintain the independence of the USSR. And without highly developed industrial technology, it was impossible to establish the industrial foundation indispensable for national defense. The implementation of the Five-Year Plan was accelerated, and it was completed by the end of 1932, in four years. The USSR carried out its foreign policy, supported by rapidly enhancing national capacity. See Boeicho (1967a, pp. 292–3). As we will see in Chapter 3, the basic idea of Japan's Production Capacity Expansion Plans (PCEPlans) looks conspicuously like that of the Soviet's Five-Year Plan.

[48] Boeicho (1967a, pp. 338–9).

On 31 May 1933, a cease-fire (the Tanggu Truce) was concluded, and the Kwantung Army was able to concentrate on maintaining order through-out Manchuria.[49] The Soviets further increased their military forces in the Far East, however, until their number in June 1934 stood at 230,000. This was comparable to the total size of Japan's Army around that time. Japan's military forces in either Manchuria or Korea were less than 30 percent of the size of Soviet's forces in the Far East, and "a balance of military forces in the Far East continent between Japan and the USSR was completely dis-rupted, and Japan's national defense fell into a perilous condition." On 21 October 1933, the Japanese government announced officially that it "would strengthen the national defense when our sense of security is threatened and finances allow." However, the Army's demand that the government dra-matically increase military force in Manchuria was not accepted (Boeicho, 1967a, p. 353).

Rivalry Between Japan and the USSR

In the spring of 1933, the USSR began constructing forts along the Manchuria–Soviet border. "The chief motive of the Soviet government is extreme fear of a Japanese invasion, arising out of the expansion of Japan's operations to all parts of Manchuria.... Together with sending military forces to the east and enlarging the transportation capacity, it has decided to reinforce the foundations of its offensive capability. Correspondingly, we strongly feel the necessity to strengthen armament against USSR" (Boeicho, 1967a, p. 342). "Before the establishment of Manchukuo in March 1932, traffic across the border was largely free. To some extent, the USSR was able to collect information on Manchurian domestic affairs. After March, however, the border was closed, and information became hard for the USSR to obtain. As a result, the USSR began actively spying along the border" (Boeicho, 1967a, p. 356).

The memory of the Siberian intervention in the last year of World War I had grave consequences. On 3 March 1918, the USSR negotiated a sepa-rate peace with Germany. Germany-Austria was now able to transfer mili-tary forces to the Western Front in Europe. With the intention of creating a Uralian front to contain the transfer of forces, at the request of the UK, the United States, France, and Italy, Japan dispatched its troops to Siberia. [50]

---

[49] In fact, the Kuwantung Army would not have had enough time to suppress rebellious forces in Manchuria, and could have done almost nothing to prepare for operations against the USSR. Its first priority was to restore civil order, and its second to construct a railway (Boeicho, 1967a, p. 342).

[50] For more details, see Boeicho (1967a, pp. 224–35).

This long-term continuing rivalry decisively conditioned the actions of the countries involved.[51] The Nomonhan Incident (Battle of Khalkhin Gol) of the summer of 1939, for example, followed Soviet strategy and "should be called the Second Russo–Japanese War" (Boeicho, 1967a, p.623). "The USSR concentrated its military forces in the Nomonhan area to deal Japanese troops a crushing blow. By preventing an attack on their Japanese front, they would then be able to commit to their strategy towards Europe" (Boeicho, 1967a, p. 605). Despite pressure from Germany, however, the Soviets' invasion of Poland was significantly delayed by a Japanese counter-offensive in Nomonhan. On the day after the September 15 cease-fire, "the Soviet troops crossed the border into Poland to reap a share of the German invasion.... From Nomonhan, automobiles and tanks were sent west by the Trans-Siberian Railway. The USSR needed far more urgently than Japan to end the Nomonhan conflict" (Boeicho, 1967a, p. 613).

After the beginning of the Russo–German War (the Eastern Front) in 1941, Japan concentrated its military forces and waited for an opportunity (the so-called Kwantung Army Special Exercise, *kan-toku-en*). In response, the USSR did not transfer its troops to the west. These developments gravely influenced the actions of those countries during World War II. "At a late stage of the Greater East Asian War the strength of the Kwantung Army had deteriorated tremendously.... However, its mere existence was able to maintain some peace in the north for an extended period" (Boeicho, 1967a, p. 613).

2–3–2. The National Defense Policy Controversy in the Mid-1930s

The Rise of the Controversy

The mid-1930s saw an increase in debates over national defense policy. Negotiating the revision of the BNDP and BOO (that is, the third revision

---

[51] In November 1936, the Anti-Comintern Pact was concluded between Germany and Japan. This pact was "a ringing declaration of principle which committed neither side to action. Being directed solely against Communism, it was not even an alliance against Russia; and, as things turned out, the two countries were never allies in an anti-Russian war. But the Pact looked as though it were an anti-Russian alliance. The Soviet leaders were made fearful; and, if there be a key to their policy, it is to be found there. They were convinced that they were about to be attacked – perhaps by Germany, perhaps by Japan, perhaps by the two combined. Their greatest, and most immediate, fear was of war in the Far East between themselves and Japan. By a wild irony, such as history often produces, this was the one war, foreseen at the time, which was never fought" (Taylor, 1964, p. 111). See note 86 later in this chapter.

of the Imperial BNDP) in early 1936, the Army's "general outline of national defense policy" placed top priority on armament against the USSR. This ran counter to the Navy's "guidance for national defense" aiming at defense to the North, aggression toward the South. Failing to reach a consensus, the negotiations stalled (Boeicho, 1967a, p. 392).

As Boeicho (1967a, p. 358) described it:

From around 1935 the USSR drastically increased its military forces in the Far East and augmented its railway transportation capacity. As a result, it gained an advantage over Japan, an advantage it would be able to maintain and expand, and to which overwhelmingly dominant air power was crucial. At the end of 1935, Soviet military forces in the Far East reached 240,000, including 14 sniper divisions, 3 cavalry divisions, and about 850 tanks, 950 airplanes, and 20 submarines. In contrast, Japan had only 3 divisions in Manchuria ... Even including its forces in Korea, it had only 80,000. It was far outnumbered by the Soviets.

Introducing the FY1936 operations plan toward the USSR as "similar to the previous fiscal year's plan," Boeicho (1967a, pp. 359–60) commented: "As the gap in peacetime military forces (particularly the Air Force) widened, we formulated a program, with help from naval air forces, to destroy Soviet airplanes and suppress their activities. Setting up airports in North Korea and making them available to Navy Air Force, we arranged with the Navy to share in any attack on Soviet airplanes in Vladivostok. We had no choice but to cooperate with the Navy Air Force if we were to recover from the gap caused by our inferior air power."

Boeicho continued, "Thus, from beginning to end the Soviets had maintained military dominance in the Far East; Japan's traditional advantages were lost. We had to adopt drastic measures to improve the situation, by revolutionarily increasing military force on the continent and establishing self-sufficiency on the continent in human-physical resources."

It was widely known that, with rise of dictatorship in Germany, Italy, and the USSR, and the expiration of Washington Naval Treaty, a global crisis would occur in 1935–6 (Boeicho, 1967a, p. 345). Moreover, "with the lessons of World War I and considerable development of aircraft capability and military usage, the total war theory or the national-defense-first theory became dominant" (Boeicho, 1975c, p. 117).

Recognizing the situation, the Army developed its First Armament Plan (Boeicho, 1975c, pp. 117–18):

In addition to Japan's internationally isolated position after the Manchurian Incident, the Army at the time was most seriously concerned about the rapid enhancement of Soviet military force. In response, the Army began working toward a fully fledged rearmament plan in 1934. In FY1937 it launched its First Armament Plan and began building 41 divisions and 142 squadrons. Meanwhile, the basic concept of use of the Army's Air Force shifted. In the past, the major task of the Air Force had been to coordinate with ground operations. Around 1933, the Army began studying the possibility of destroying the enemy's airplanes from the air at the start of a conflict. With the FY1936 operation plan, this became policy.

Boeicho (1975c, pp. 117–18) continued: "The First Armament Plan was based on the premise of a dramatic development in the aircraft industry. For this reason, in June 1936 the Army formulated its Five-Year Plan for Munitions Manufacturing Industries. In the same month, it urged the government to strengthen key industries that would form the foundation of a munitions manufacturing industry."

The focus of armament plans was on Air Force production capacity, the aircraft industry in particular: we will see more of this in Chapter 4. With the outbreak of the War with China, establishing the details of this project was postponed.

"A balance of military forces between Japan and the USSR in the Far East was completely disrupted, and Japan's national defense fell into a perilous condition" (Boeicho, 1967a, p. 353). In response, the Army commenced studies toward full-fledged rearmament in 1934.[52] It aimed to establish the general outline of national defense policy to address the current situation, replacing the earlier national defense policy by reviewing the BNDP and BOO.

The basic understanding of ACCom was that

The BNDP had been revised several times since its establishment in 1907. However, it still remained a military national defense plan, and lacked a close connection with national policy. In addition, it only listed anticipated enemies, and provided no long-term policy for resolving defense issues involving multiple countries. Given our international isolation and current national capacity, we could not undertake our job of national defense against multiple countries. In short, the national defense policy had become outdated and diminished. It was time to establish a general outline of national defense policy to address the current situation, and to replace the BNDP. (Boeicho, 1967a, p. 392)

---

[52] Before the 1935–6 crisis, at a time when drastic restructuring of military organization was intended, the nerve center of the Army decided to hold a series of leadership conferences within the ACCom and the AM. They would study methods of self-defense, still on the assumption that the USSR was Japan's dangerous enemy. At the first conference in June 1933, nobody objected to this view. However, in September 1933 the Army Minister Araki, preparing the Basic Outline of Imperial National Policy as an agenda for the coming session of the Diet, began discussion in the Five Ministers Conference (Prime Minister, Army, Navy, Foreign Affairs, and Finance Ministers) to obtain approval (Boeicho, 1967a, pp. 345–50).

ACCom's National Defense Policy

Colonel Kanji Ishiwara famously symbolizes the ACCom's perspective on the general outline of national defense policy and the baseline of national policy. In August 1935, he became the Strategy Section Chief of ACCom, succeeding Colonel Suzuki. His appointment came a year after the recognition that "Japan's national defense on the continent had fallen into a perilous condition" (Boeicho, 1967a, p. 353).

In 1933 and 1934, Colonel Suzuki had held tactical exercises in Manchuria designed to give promising young staff officers in ACCom and the Army Ministry a firsthand idea of the need for policies in response to developments in the Manchurian situation and for dramatic rearmament. They had no great effect. Suzuki made a major concession and proposed the refurbishment of only one further cavalry brigade within the current fiscal year. When even this policy was not adopted, despite the government's promise that it "would strengthen national defense when our sense of security is threatened and finances allow" (Boeicho, 1967a, p. 353), he resigned as Strategy Section Chief.

After the Manchurian Incident, a rapid increase in armament toward the USSR was called for, but Japan could not respond. The Kwantung Army, on the front line of defense against the USSR, was in a particularly worrisome situation. The Seventh Comintern Congress, held 25 July–10 August 1935 in Moscow, officially endorsed its antifascist policy, specifying fascism in Germany and Japan, and arguing that communist parties should form a Popular Front with all other antifascist parties. On 1 August 1935, leaders of the Chinese Communist Party, then on the Long March to Yan'an, published their "Message to All Compatriots in the Resistance against Japan and Regarding National Salvation (1 August Declaration)." In it, they proposed that all Chinese, of any class or party, should unite and organize a "national defense government" and an "anti-Japanese allied force for national salvation" (Boeicho, 1967a, pp. 366–7).

Under these circumstances, the ACCom, and Ishiwara in particular, set out to promote the following policies (Boeicho, 1967a, p. 376).[53] "To

---

[53] Army leaders had selected Ishiwara to succeed Suzuki. Obviously, the policy Ishiwara promoted was not different from the basic view of key members of the Strategy Division and the ACCom. Ishiwara didn't go out of control, either. On 20 December 1906, thirty years earlier, the ACCommander and the NCCommander had been ordered to formulate a national defense policy. At the conference held for this purpose, Colonel Yasuharu Matsuishi, the Second Division Chief of the ACCom, submitted "an opinion on a dominant principle of national defense," arguing that, "although we have plans for the southern islands and central-south America in the future, for the next few decades we have to secure national defense to the North, preparing for the possibility of a Russia–Germany

reconstruct the national defense against the USSR and achieve peaceful cooperation with China, we must above all establish a new policy based on a clear recognition of our existing mistakes and defects. We must promote policies consistently and with great determination, on behalf of the entire military. To that end, it is crucial for the government to establish a national defense policy." However, as I will show, after repeated compromises, he was largely unsuccessful (Boeicho, 1967a, p. 393).

Ishiwara was most shocked by the inadequacy of Japan's military forces: "Our Army and Navy have operation plans, but no war plan. As a result, they cannot fulfill our mission of national defense. Today, world powers are approaching war, and condition their diplomacy and rearmament upon their national defense policies....We must formulate a war plan and establish the general outlines of our national defense policy immediately" (Boeicho, 1967a, pp. 370, 377).

The ACCom acknowledged the need to establish a general outline of a national defense policy:

In revising the BNDP and the BOO in 1918 and 1923, we studied whether we should anticipate a short war – like the Sino–Japanese and the Russo–Japanese wars – or a much longer one. All our anticipated enemies, the U.S., USSR, China, and the UK, are strong powers. Against any of these, we have no winning strategy. We must plan for a long, drawn-out struggle. Given our current national capacity, however, it would be difficult to endure a war of attrition. Consequently, we must expand our national defense capacity immediately. Should a war break out tomorrow, we would have no choice but to wage a short war. Keeping the goal of the war to a minimum, we would have to pursue a way to end it, leading to surrender or cease-fire under extremely generous conditions. *The enemy, however, with its superior power, will probably wage a war of attrition. So, we must prepare for a long war. A war of attrition is a war of national power, but this is not within the scope of the BNDP and the BOO. Therefore we must couple a general outline of national defense policy with a national war plan.* (Boeicho, 1967a, pp. 393–4, my italics)

As I will show, developments forced the ACCom to abandon this basic vision, which is often termed the "Ishiwara Vision," after the Strategy Section Chief.[54]

---

alliance" (Boeicho, 1967a, pp. 151–4.) Matsuishi's opinion seems extremely close to the so-called Ishiwara Vision.

[54] See Boeicho (1967a, pp. 376–9) for the details of the Ishiwara Vision. There seems to have been no really serious investigation and discussion about the plausibility and substance of the view that "any war would finally be a war of attrition," a basic tenet of the Ishiwara Vision. Inada (1969, p. 257) commented: "There was no war plan in Japan, just operation plans. The government needed war plans, but it left wars entirely to the military. The root cause of all the errors in those operation plans was that they were not based on a war plan." Budget Subsection Chief Nishiura of the Military (*gunji*) Section at the AM (for

For restructuring the national defense on the continent, Japan had first to grow its national defense capacity, all the while working not to antagonize other countries. However, even inside the Army it was not easy to reach a consensus. After the Manchurian Incident that began in September 1931, Japan externally promoted an aggressive policy. The Strategy Division of the ACCom tried hard to stop the Kwantung Army from intervening aggressively in North China, but the Information Division (Second Division) of the ACCom did not agree. Some officers inside the AM strongly supported the incursions into the North China (Boeicho, 1967a, p. 372).

Army leaders reached a consensus only to the extent of assigning the role of supporting the North Chinese government to the Japanese troops stationed in China, and to withdrawing the Kwantung Army from its central strategic position. On 13 January 1936, the Outline for Handling North China was transmitted to the troop commander there. But the Kwantung Army remained as aggressive as ever, and the instructions from the Army leadership were largely ignored (Boeicho, 1967a, pp. 372-3). Ironically, many leaders, particularly in the Strategy Division of ACCom, were enthusiastic about this policy. In order to inhibit the Kwantung Army from expanding into North China by claiming to support the weak Japanese Army presence, on 18 April 1936 the Army leadership doubled the troops it stationed there.[55] This increase in the Japanese military force in China, however, created the impression that Japan was about to invade North China (Boeicho, 1967a, p. 375).

---

the position and role of this subsection, see Miwa, 2008, p. 93, note 3) commented more acrimoniously (Nishiura, 1968, pp. 190–1): "The Budget Subsection Chief faced a specific question such as, 'What we should do for the next plan?' There was an abstract political debate like 'expansion or nonexpansion.' The Procurement Bureau, for example, eagerly demanded to start war mobilization. But nobody gave us concrete instructions about what to do. Their operational plan for China involved only a few projects in North China, and politically motivated plans to dispatch small numbers of troops to Shandong or Shanghai in an emergency. No one had ever studied seriously an operation that would use 10 divisions in China. Political discussion took the lead excessively, and operation plans followed. For the case to capture Nanjing or Hankou, we did not adopt such careless operations if we had made a carefully investigated, thoughtful total plan, with specific size of necessary forces and its cost. Staff officers with long careers, education, and training in the Strategy Section had had no leading role to play in the War with China since it had begun. So to speak, adopted children used the bequest of the former masters. Those who had been educated in the Strategy Section would not execute such operations."

[55] The standing troops in North China had originally been established as part of the cease-fire treaty in the Boxer Rebellion (the Righteous Harmony Society Movement, or the North Qing Incident, 1899–1901). There was no limit on their number, which was determined in discussion with treaty countries (Boeicho (1967a, p. 375).

Naval Opposition and Abandonment of the Ishiwara Vision

The review of national defense policies before the summer of 1936 and discussion of the current situation continued. In 1907, the BNDP had listed Russia and the United States as its anticipated enemies. After that, the Army assumed that the primary enemy would be Russia, whereas the Navy assumed it would be the United States. When China was added to the list of anticipated enemies in 1918, both the Army and the Navy thought it possible to defend against China with part of their forces. After the Russian Revolution, the threat to Japan from the United States increased. At that point, Japan revised its BNDP and defined the United States as the primary anticipated enemy. With Japan facing the unexpectedly quick rise of the USSR (Russia), however, together with encounters with Soviet forces during the Manchurian Incident, a sense of crisis over defense against the USSR grew. As the Naval Arms Control Pact expired in the end of 1936, Japan faced additional urgency in its rearmament needs.

Recognizing both the inadequacy of its armament against the USSR and the current state of Japan's national defense and capacity, Strategy Section Chief Ishiwara concluded: "It is most pressing at the moment to complete the cultivation and reinforcement of Manchukuo. Meanwhile, we must eliminate the threats from the North by emphasizing our rearmament against the USSR, avoiding catastrophe within China, and maintaining as peaceful a cooperation as possible with the U.S." (Boeicho, 1967a, p. 380).

It became a matter of first priority for the Army to reach a consensus with the Navy on national defense policy. On 17 December 1935, discussion between the Strategy Section Chiefs from the ACCom and the NCCom began. Ishiwara asserted that "over the coming decade we should not try to exert national power beyond Manchukuo." The Navy disagreed, and insisted that Japan maintain its policy of "defense to the north, aggression toward the south" (Boeicho, 1967a, p. 380).

In order to strengthen its forces against the USSR, the Army submitted a budget for national defense to the Cabinet on 25 February 1936, the day before the attempted coup d'état. Once the coup had been suppressed, Ishiwara tried to promote his defense policy. He sought to reach agreement with the Kwantung Army. He negotiated with the Navy – but the Navy refused to compromise, and he was unable to formulate a consensus.[56]

---

[56] See Boeicho (1967a, p. 381), and also for the ACCom's plan. As mentioned previously, after the 2.26 Incident, most leaders of the ACCom and the AM were reshuffled. But Strategy Section Chief Ishiwara remained in his post.

On 9 March, Navy Minister Osami Nagano of the new Hirota Cabinet warned Army Minister Terauchi "not to let the Army in the field pursue the traditional policy toward China." Terauchi agreed. On 19 March 1936, the Navy leadership organized a Committee to Study Naval Policies and Institutions with leaders from both the NM and the NCCom, headed by Navy Vice-Minister Kiyoshi Hasegawa. The committee would address the general outline proposed by the Army and its guidance for national defense and international politics.[57]

Nagano agreed to let the leaders form the new committee. Under the terms of its charter, the committee would study Naval policies on the assumption that the "Army might start a war with the USSR, and we must stop it. We must instead pursue the people's development to the south."[58] The Navy leaders were deeply worried about a war with the USSR, an attitude that the Army understood all too well (Boeicho, 1975d, pp. 291–2, 295).

Recognizing that the discussion with the NCCom about the Basic National Defense Policy "had the opposite effect of heightening the Navy's momentum toward the south and exacerbating the disintegration of a coherent national policy," the ACCom decided to create a new section, the War Leadership Section, which would investigate and establish a Basic National Defense Policy. It also decided to turn to the Emperor when the Navy refused to agree to its plans (Boeicho, 1967a, p. 388).

Following the reorganization of the ACCom in early June 1936, Ishiwara became the chief of the new War Leadership Section, taking charge of "war leadership and assessment of the situation."[59] The ACCom formulated

---

[57] For details of the committee, see Boeicho (1975d, pp. 288–305).

[58] There was widespread agreement among Navy leaders about the committee's charter. See Miwa (2008, p. 380, note 48).

[59] Inada, who was Leadership Subsection Chief, March–August 1937, recalled that despite its name, the Subsection's real task was the promotion of the Five-Year Industry Development Plan (Inada, 1969, p. 132). Nishiura, an officer of the Military (*gunji*) Section of the AM, contrasted the War Leadership Section with the Military Section or Strategy Section of the ACCom, which could supposedly do their job relying on their own authority – the former on its authority to control the budget and the latter on its authority to move soldiers (Nishiura, 1968, pp. 162–3): "The War Leadership Section was a research section, without any authority or money. It bothered nobody seriously even if that Section did not agree. The Section attracted attention and had some power because its Section Chief was Ishiwara, who had bright ideas and foresight. When this genius left, attention from the other parties also depreciated, saying that 'leave alone such a section always speaking something like a dream (or, ignore them, they're living in Cloud Cuckoo Land).' The War Leadership Section had no real power to promote the Five-Year Plan. The Plan moved to the implementation stage in March 1937. In April and May, discrepancy gradually appeared between Ishiwara and Military (*gunji*) Section Chief Shin'ichi Tanaka of the AM and Strategy Section Chief Akira Mutoh of the ACCom."

the general outline of the national defense policy, but when it was once again unable to obtain the agreement of the NCCom, it turned to the ACCommander, Kan'in-no-miya (Boeicho, 1967a, p. 388).[60]

The General Outline of National Policy was finally formulated, based on a compromise between the Army and the Navy, and adopted more of the spirit of the Navy's guidance for national defense (Boeicho, 1975d, p. 298). On 30 June, the General Outline was submitted by the Navy Minister to the Prime Minister and the Army, Foreign, and Finance Ministers. All agreed with its basic thrust. On 7 August, the four Ministers (excluding the Finance Minister) formally confirmed the new Imperial Policy on Diplomacy, and with the agreement of the Finance Minister adopted the General Outline of National Policy (Boeicho, 1967a, pp. 389–90).[61]

The ACCom's Basic Idea Was Not Reflected in the Revised BNDP and BOO

Since February 1936, the Army and Naval officers directly in charge of the supreme command had been studying and formulating a bill of Imperial policy on national defense. The ACCom advocated treating only the USSR as the anticipated enemy, but the NCCom disagreed and also objected to the ACCom's attempt to reorder national threats, on the grounds that it treated the Navy as a subordinate branch. The NCCom and ACCom compromised, and the BNDP and the BOO obtained the approval of the Emperor on 3 June (Boeicho, 1967a, p. 393).[62]

The BNDP was "quickly to achieve the war objective in an emergency. For this purpose, considering the state of affairs, the Empire must maximize the effect of its initial operations. Future wars would be large-scale and long-term, however, so preparations to maximize endurance were essential. The anticipated enemies were primarily the U.S. and the USSR, along with China and the UK." In addition, the BOO stated that "the Imperial Army, following the BNDP, must do its best to resolve disputes promptly through preemptive actions that involved Army-Navy cooperation" (Boeicho, 1967a, p. 39).

---

[60] For the final version (30 June 1936), see Boeicho (1967a, p. 388). For the reasons for the NCCom's disagreement, see Boeicho(1975d, p. 298) or Miwa (2008, p. 381, note 51).

[61] "In the traditional understanding of the Navy, 'national policy' was to be determined by the government, rather than the supreme command" (Boeicho, 1975d, p. 298). See Inada's comment in note 54.

[62] "With a series of concessions, the spirit of the general outline of national defense policy Colonel Ishiwara proposed remained only in name" (Boeicho, 1967a, p. 393).

During the War with China, there were calls to revise the BNDP and BOO. However, Japan proceeded to the Pacific War without ever making those revisions.[63]

Thus, the ACCom's idea did not materialize and neither did the Ishiwara Vision. There are three points to note: (1) The Army's view that Japan should formulate a general outline of a national defense policy was abandoned because of an inability to obtain the Navy's agreement; (2) the Army also failed to define the USSR as the primary anticipated enemy and to place top priority on its preparations against it; and (3) the Army failed to adopt avoidance of war as a basic policy until preparations could be completed. Recognizing that the next war would likely be a war of attrition, it had hoped to place the top priority on cultivating the capacity to endure a sustained conflict.

On 26 November 1936, almost six months after the Emperor approved the BNDP and BOO, the Army leadership unofficially announced its First Armament Plan. Rearmament would take place after FY1937 (Boeicho, 1967a, pp. 393, 403). Both the Army's First Armament Plan and the Navy's landmark replenishment plan took effect just before July 1937, when the War with China began.[64]

2-3-3. The BNDP, Armament Enhancement Plans, and Decision Process

The BNDP

The rearmament plans were formulated only after the BNDP.[65] The force size in the BNDP was a target rather than an action plan, and it was sufficiently large that it could not be realized immediately. It was a target required from the operations viewpoint, for which Japan had neither the budget nor the materials. By mutual agreement, the ACCom and the NCCom took charge of drafting a plan, with the Army and Navy Ministers in an advisory position. The Strategy Section in each organization set pen to paper.

After reaching a consensus between the ACCommander and the NCCommander, the plan was reported to the Emperor. After due formalities, such as consultation in the Marshals Council (*gensui-fu*), the

---

[63] See Boeicho (1967a, p. 397). For more details, see Boeicho (1975d, pp. 328–30).

[64] For the armament development after the beginning of the war, see Miwa (2008, 3-7-2, pp. 196–7).

[65] Section 2-3-3 relies on the testimony of ACCom staffs Kumao Imoto and Yutaka Imaoka, reported in Joho (1979, pp. 336–41).

Emperor approved and ratified the plan. It was accepted practice to allow the Prime Minister, the sole person on the government side, unofficially to view the BNDP. The Prime Minister usually reported to the Emperor that he endorsed it, but it was usual for him to add that he would make an effort to execute it as much as possible, taking the national capacity into consideration.

Armament Enhancement Plans

Drafting a rearmament plan was different from drafting the BNDP. The former process started when momentum toward rearmament built among Army leaders in response to change in circumstances.

Like the Basic 1936 Policy of Rearmament, the process started with the ACCom's presentation (by the Strategy Section, then headed by Kanji Ishiwara) of the requisite force size. Assuming war with the anticipated enemy, the Strategy Section investigated the operation plans and calculated the size of force that would be needed. To prepare the proposal, the Strategy Section consulted with the Organization and Mobilization Section of the ACCom, which always had views about feasibility that to some extent inhibited the Strategy Section's request.

When the two sections reached a consensus, the basic plan was drafted by the Strategy Section and presented to the Military (*gunji*) Section of the AM for its opinion. At this stage, the document was written for administrative negotiation rather than as a draft armament enhancement plan.

The Military Section studied the ACCom's basic plan in light of national budget, conditions of military administration, and materials, and expressed an opinion about its feasibility. This was a binding assessment, and the ACCom and AM took equal roles in the process.

The negotiation was repeated several times. When the two sections approached an agreement, each section reported to its superior and obtained its approval. In addition, it solicited opinions from the sections concerned. At this stage, the AM negotiated with the Ministry of Finance and ensured feasibility in light of the national budget. Therefore, before reaching a consensus between the ACCommander and the Army Minister, it was almost certain that the plan would be approved by the Diet.

When the ACCom and AM reached an agreement, the Organization and Mobilization Section of the ACCom drafted it to the document as a rearmament plan, which the ACCommander and the Army Minister jointly took to the Emperor. With his approval, the plan became final. At this stage, however, it still needed the approval of the Diet for its budget.

The Financial Bureau of the AM took primary charge of drafting the budget plan for the Imperial Diet, although the Military Bureau was also involved.

With the approval of the Diet, the plan was put into action. For each newly created troop, details of organization outline were presented in the form of a military order to the troop commander.

Drafting the military order was divided according to the division between the ACCom and the AM. In the ACCom, the Organization and Mobilization Section drafted the parts concerning the organization and mobilization of troops. In the AM, under the control of the Military Bureau, relevant bureaus were involved in drafting the parts concerning personnel procurement and delivery of weapons, materials, and funds.

Complications over Rearmament

In November 1936, a complication arose between the ACCom and the AM concerning the budget for rearmament. The authorities in both directly in charge of rearmament issues maintained close coordination. However, when the AM found it hard to realize all the ACCom's requests in budget negotiations with the Finance Ministry, Army Vice-Minister Umezu suggested to the Budget Subsection Chief of the Military (*gunji*) Section that the budget should be reduced. The AM reached an agreement with the Finance Ministry, which the AM reported to the ACCom.

General Affairs (*shomu*) Section Chief Kyoji Tominaga of the ACCom, who was in charge of rearmament and budget, was furious. He protested to Umezu, and – together with all the Section members – submitted his resignation to the ACCommander. On 24 November, the ACCommander reached a tentative settlement with the dissatisfied officers.[66] On 1 December, the ACCommander and the Army Minister reported to the Emperor about the rearmament.

In the personnel shuffle of January 1937, the Strategy Division Chief, the General Affairs Section Chief, and two Section members moved out of the ACCom. The Vice-ACCommander also moved out to become the Household (*konoe*) Division Commander. In fact, all the people responsible for rearmament moved out of the ACCom.[67]

---

[66] "It was a norm in the Army that each member was allowed to offer an opinion about his task to his direct superior, but not directly to his higher superiors" (Imoto, 1978, p. 484).

[67] In March, Colonel Ishiwara became Strategy Division Chief, Colonel Torashiro Kawabe the War Leadership Section Chief, and Colonel Akira Mutoh the Strategy Section Chief. They were the leaders of the Strategy Division of the ACCom when the War with China began four months later.

2-4. The War with China

In this section, building on the discussion in section 2-3, I first take a close look at the process by which Japan abandoned its nonescalation policy (section 2-4-1) and the decision-making process concerning the war leadership on the War with China around the capture of Shanghai and Nanjing (section 2-4-2). I then review the reality of the decision-making process of the time (section 2-4-3).

2-4-1. Abandonment of the Nonescalation Policy

The greatest concern of the Japanese government (the military, the Army, and the ACCom in particular) when the War with China began was to enhance armament against the USSR. The War with China began "unexpectedly" in July 1937, when the rearmament program, although inadequate, had just started. With the Five-Year Plan for Key Industries, "Japan had begun a long-term project to build a breakwater against the USSR. But little strokes fell mighty oaks. Before it had grown even an inch, termites had made many holes in it" (Sato, 1976, p. 124).

Contrary to the expectation of most government leaders, including leaders in the ACCom and AM, the unexpected war with China extended throughout China within a year. Suddenly, Japan was faced with the limits of its national capacity.[68] It is not feasible that Japan began the war on the basis of carefully planned, systematic preparation. The outbreak and development of the War with China, contrary to the expectation of most Japanese government leaders, made it almost impossible to execute systematic war preparations and the orderly implementation of war mobilization.

At first, the government (including the Army leadership) announced a nonescalation policy. Even as the War with China increased, the government's basic policy was to resolve it promptly. In December 1941, more than four years after the outbreak of war, however, Japan initiated a war against the United States.

In the mid-1930s, the greatest military concern of the Japanese government was rearmament against the USSR. The War with China started when that rearmament had hardly begun. To the Army leaders at least, the country's fatal lack of preparedness for a full-scale war with China was obvious.

---

[68] See section 1-5-2, in which I quoted the Head of Weapons Arsenals, who said in June 1939, "Though we have not yet reached the stage of war to lay the whole national power on the line, we suffer from serious shortages of various materials."

The ACCom (IH-AD), in the initial stages, was the most critical of the war. "The strategy line of the ACCom took control of pure supreme command (national defense and operations). Once it determined a policy and pushed it through, not even the AM was allowed to oppose it openly" (Imoto, 1978, p. 203). Strategy Division Chief Kanji Ishiwara strongly opposed the escalation of a war that would inhibit the execution of the rearmament against the USSR, the greatest concern of the ACCom. Having lost support step by step, even inside the ACCom, Ishiwara resigned his post in September 1937. As I show in the next section, Strategy Section Chief Kawabe of the ACCom, who advocated a long, drawn-out war as the leading principle for war leadership around the capture of Nanjing, was dismissed.

The Situation After the Lukouch'iau Incident

The Lukouch'iau (Marco Polo Bridge) Incident occurred on 7 July 1937. The military leadership decided upon a basic policy of nonescalation and local resolution. At 6:42 P.M., 8 July, an Imperial Order was transmitted to the Commander of the Stationary Troops in China: "To prevent the spread of the Incident, you must avoid further use of military force." On 9 July, the Vice-ACCommander made enquiries to the chief of staff of the local troops about the policy of negotiation with China. Both the government and the military leadership took action against the expansion of the Incident (Sugita, 1987, p. 74).[69]

The military leadership's basic policy for Incident resolution, which it believed could be achieved "with nonescalation and local resolution" was transmitted as an order from the ACCommander to the local troops in China. They and the representative of the Chinese Twenty-Ninth Army held negotiations to deal with the situation. At 8:00 P.M. on 11 July, a local cease-fire agreement was established. Late that night, having received a report that China accepted all the Japanese demands, an expectation that the conflict would be contained and resolved locally became dominant among Army leaders.

While local negotiations continued on the details of the cease-fire agreement, conflict between the hawks and doves intensified on both sides of the conflict. With a series of small military clashes, Japan increased its armed forces in Beijin-Tianjin area, and the Chinese Central Army moved north. After the Kuanganment Incident of 25 July and the Langfang Incident of 27 July, Japan came to the conclusion that China had no intention of fulfilling

---

[69] For the details of the process toward expansion of the war, see Boeicho (1967a, pp. 425–516) and Imoto (1978, pp. 85–108).

the conditions for resolution. On 27 July, the ACCom decided to use force and dispatched three divisions from Japan to North China. At that time, the assignment of the Commander of the Troops in China was to discipline the Chinese Army in Beijing-Tianjin area and restore tranquility there. The operation was limited to that area (Hara, 1987, pp. 44–5).

Nonexpansionist versus Expansionist

During this period, nonexpansionists and expansionists were at logger-heads. Strategy Division Chief Ishiwara represented the former, and Strategy Section Chief Mutoh the latter.[70] But even an expansionist, as an Army leader, understood that Japan was not prepared for a full-scale war with China.

Ishiwara thought at the time that Japan would never begin a war. In the second half of 1936, he lowered the Army's demand for policies toward China and proposed dropping the policy of separating and governing North China that had been adopted by the Hayashi Cabinet. However, this kind of nonexpansionist (or nonescalation) theory, however, "was viewed by many as contrary to the consensus view of the nation, at least of the Army" (Imoto, 1978, p. 83).[71]

The substance of escalation theory is important. Imoto (1978, pp. 83–4) commented:

It involved the use of force against China. At this point, however, it meant, finishing China at one blow and achieving the Army's established goal toward China, which was mainly to separate and govern the North, and which was thought to be 100% realizable.... They had never dreamed of the situation that they actually faced with full-scale war with China, evolving into a hopeless mess. This theory, together with their conventional wisdom about China, was dominant across the Army, and shared by Ishiwara at the time of the Manchurian Incident in 1931. They firmly believed that China was weak and that the Central Government of Chiang Kai-shek would surrender when threatened. If not, they would certainly do for it with one blow and a small number of Japanese troops.

What Strategy Division Chief Ishiwara had feared most occurred. He was busily engaged in persuading Army leaders in the ACCom and AM to

---

[70] After serving at the Military (*gunji*) Section, for less than a year Mutoh was engaged in intelligence activity in the Kwantung Army. Then, with the recommendation of Strategy Division Chief Ishiwara in March 1937, he became the Strategy Section Chief (Joho, 1979, p. 442).

[71] In the ACCom, the AM, and the field there were supporters of the nonexpansionist theory. In any of them, supporters of expansionist theory were dominant. Strategy Section Chief Mutoh, an immediate subordinate of Ishiwara, the principal nonexpansionist, was impressive and influential, with conflicting views to Ishiwara's (Imoto, 1978, pp. 84–5). See also Inada (1969, pp. 131–41).

maintain the nonescalation policy, arguing that expansion of the conflict would inevitably lead to a long war. He made the same pleas to government leaders. He often came to the Strategy Section office, and argued: "Today's China is not the old China. Already unified, China can exercise a strong power as a national union. War with this China would be long, drawn-out, and lead to chaos. We must circumvent war. Unless we devote all national power to rearmament, following the BDNP, we cannot execute a mission of national defense against either the USSR or China" (Imoto, 1978, p. 88).

Serious clashes of opinion emerged about the consequence of exercising force against China relating to the belief and expectation (the so-called one-blow theory) that China was weak.[72]

On 10 July, ACCom leaders decided to dispatch an additional division to the Stationary Troops in China, a decision with which Ishiwara agreed (Imoto, 1978, pp. 90-1):

(1) Japan adopts a non-escalation policy, but China might challenge us; (2) In this case the small number of Stationary Troops in China might be overwhelmed by the Chinese Army, which would increase the confusion and make it hard to protect Japanese residents. In order to eliminate this concern, it is necessary to dispatch the necessary forces to North China; (3) Also, the anti-Japanese movement is active outside North China. Taking violent changes in the situation into consideration, we must prepare to protect residents; (4) Under the present circumstances there is no possibility of either the European countries, the U.S. or the USSR participating in the war.

The mobilization of inland troops was postponed several times and announced officially on 27 July.[73]

---

[72] The Strategy Division made its own judgments about the situation. The General Affairs Division Chief of the ACCom and the Military (*gummu*) Section Chief of the AM were dispatched to the scene. Both reported a quiet local situation, and expressed the opinion that the situation would calm down without the need to dispatch three additional divisions. On 19 and 27 July, the Information Division of the ACCom concluded that "our daring blow would trigger momentum toward surrender on the Chinese side" (Sugita, 1987, p. 74).

[73] The Strategy Section Chief of the NCCom at the time of Lukouch'iau Incident commented on the decision-making process to dispatch three divisions (Fukudome, 1951, pp. 224–5). In his understanding, it was not an issue with which the supreme command should become involved, and ex ante it did not: "Immediately after the Incident, Army Minister General Hajime Sugiyama asked for Cabinet approval of the mobilization and dispatch of three divisions. After opposition from Navy Minister Yonai, the Cabinet decision was postponed for two days. Following Sugiyama's emphatic statement that with three divisions they would attain their goal easily and quickly, and were confident about limiting operations in North China, the Cabinet approved dispatch, under the condition of the so-called non-escalation policy that restricted operations in North China.

This operation was not based on the necessity of national defense. Instead, it was a political mobilization to assure a political objective, about which the supreme command

Meanwhile, at the Lushan Conference on 19 July, Chiang Kai-shek gave his famous "Final Juncture" speech, declaring that he would hold out to the end against Japan and never surrender.[74] "In sum, together with the Nanjing government's determination at the time and its attitude toward Japan, China had already been unified. In this situation, there was no possibility of reaching an agreement, if Japan, in a small area of North China, negotiated with the East Hobei Autonomous Council (chaired by Song Zheyuan who then led the Chinese Twenty-Ninth Army) and insisted on getting its own way" (Imoto, 1978, p. 100).

North China to Central China

"It was inevitable that the North China situation would spread to Central China" (Hara, 1987, p. 45).[75] The Army Headquarters decided on 15 August to send two divisions to Shanghai. "Under the terms of the cease-fire treaty after the first Japanese–Chinese conflict in Shanghai in 1932, a specific region in the north of Shanghai jointly held concessions became a demilitarized zone. The Chinese Army, approximately 50,000 in size, marched into this region and on 14 August began to attack the Japanese Naval landing force of only 4,000 men. Japanese residents who had recently withdrawn from

did nothing *ex ante*. The decision to dispatch forces was within the government's authority, and the supreme command was not involved beforehand. The government, however, should have taken the supreme command's operations forecast into consideration when making its decision. Instead, the Cabinet directly approved the dispatch of three divisions to North China. When it received the request for operation plans consistent with 'non-escalation' policy, the supreme command was extremely embarrassed.

At the time, there was an almost total consensus across various fields, including the supreme command, that it would be totally impossible to dispatch forces and still restrict the operation area in the North China."

The person in the ACCom with whom Fukudome kept in close communication was Strategy Division Chief Ishiwara.

[74] For the details of this speech, see Boeicho (1967a, pp. 450–2). This Lushan Conference is different from the one held in 1959, which was an informal discussion about the Great Leap Forward.

[75] On 11 July, the decision to dispatch forces to North China was postponed. Judging that "once we use military force in North China it will be highly possible to spread rapidly throughout China"; however, the Navy prepared countermeasures. For details, see Miwa (2008, p. 441, note 26). As the situation in North China became critical, anxiety heightened in areas along the Yangtze River, from which the wives and children of Japanese residents began to withdraw from 20 July. In response to the full operation in North China from 28 July, Navy Headquarters issued an order for the Third Fleet concerning withdrawal from the upper reaches of Hankou and executed it (for example, Japanese residents withdrew from Chongqing on 1 August). On 6 August, residents in downstream reaches of Hankou were given orders for unqualified withdrawal. For details, see Boeicho (1974, pp. 282–304).

the upper reaches of Yantze River, including Hankou, gathered together in Shanghai" (Hara, 1987, p. 45). Hara continued, "The Army headquarters, still maintaining its nonescalation policy, stuck to the line to prevent the spread of the war to the Central China. However, in response to a nonrepudiable request for support from the Navy because of the deterioration of the situation in Shanghai, on 15 August the Army decided to dispatch two divisions of troops, exclusively for 'the security of Imperial residents'."[76]

It was on 31 August in North China and 7 November in Central China that political dispatch was transformed in name and reality into war leadership. On these dates, the North China Army Group and the Central China Army Group, respectively, were given a job description: "Destroy completely the enemies in central Hebei (or Shanghai region), terminate the enemy's fighting spirit and bring the war to a rapid conclusion."[77]

Meanwhile, Strategy Division Chief Ishiwara resigned on 23 September. He disagreed with the vociferous demand to dispatch additional troops to Shanghai, even when a fierce battle opened there, explaining that it would not help much. With the ACCom order of 11 September, however, he had no choice but to send additional troops. When the decision was made to send an additional five divisions, he proffered his resignation and resigned on 23 September. The Military Bureau Chief of the AM also resigned on the same day.[78]

The Imperial Headquarters (IH) was established on 20 November. On 5 October 1937, three months after the outbreak of the war, the Army

---

[76] For more details, see Boeicho (1967a, pp. 464–70). The ACCom tried hard to limit operations in North China, to stop them spreading to Shanghai or Tsingtao. On 9 August, however, Sublieutenant Oyama was shot dead by the Chinese Safety Forces (Boeicho, 1967a, p. 465). Facing with an uneasy atmosphere both in the Shandong Peninsula and the areas along the Yangtze River, on 6 August the NCCom recognized the necessity of preparing to dispatch Army troops and asked the NM to obtain Cabinet approval. The following morning, Navy Minister Yonai put the proposal to Army Minister Sugiyama. Hanging his hopes on the ongoing diplomatic negotiations, Yonai expected desirable results in a few days. Thus, Yonai requested Cabinet approval to prepare for prompt action for an emergency, but wanted to wait for a while rather than dispatching troops immediately. See Boeicho (1974, pp. 313–14).

[77] Hara (1987, pp. 45–6). At the Cabinet meeting of 17 August, however, the Army Minister remarked (Boeicho, 1967a, pp. 471–2): "Even at present it is inappropriate to suggest a change in the nonescalation policy. Officially we must maintain this policy. However, in doing so we may find ourselves one step behind in dealing with the Incident. Militarily we will be passively placed, and the consequence of that would be to prolong and expand the Incident. From now on, we must deal with the Incident independently and voluntarily. When Army troops were sent to Shanghai, the Incident reached a delicate stage. We should recognize it as a process of all-out war."

[78] See Boeicho (1967a, pp. 476–7).

Minister implemented war mobilization, and on 17 January 1938, more than three months later, both the Army and the Navy began munitions factory control.

2-4-2. From Shanghai to Nanjing: The Peace Effort and Its Defeat

Shanghai

The ACCom devoted its utmost efforts to confining operations to North China, preventing their spread to Shanghai or Tsingtao. After 11 August, however, the situation in Shanghai rapidly worsened. Even after Army Minister Sugiyama agreed to send troops to Shanghai, Strategy Division Chief Ishiwara advocated maintaining the nonescalation policy. On 15 August, the Army decided to dispatch two divisions of troops. The Navy began bombing Nanjing and Nanchang. Soon they bombed Hankou, at which point operations in Central China rapidly expanded and turned into all-out war. With the bombing of Nanjing, countries such as the United States took a tougher line toward Japan, criticizing the illegal bombing of a demilitarized city (Boeicho, 1967a, pp. 465–9).

On 24 August, Army Minister Sugiyama held discussions with party leaders. Explaining the general situation, he emphasized the importance of dealing an immediate and decisive blow to end the conflict promptly. Unlike Ishiwara's long, drawn-out war theory, his idea was to attack quickly and end the war. This strategy was supported by most leaders in the AM and some in the ACCom (Boeicho, 1967a, p. 472). The war spread to Shanghai, where the battle intensified. Ishiwara resigned on 23 September.[79]

---

[79] For details, see Imoto (1978, pp. 145–65). This volume is neither a war history nor a history of operations. Instead, focusing on war preparations, war mobilization, and economic control, it pays major attention to the policies and decision making at the center. Most sources referred to here, such as Boeicho, *senshi-sosho* (*Library of War History*) and NAFHistory, *The History of the Japanese Navy Air Force*, are related to the information and memoirs of people who actually took part in those central processes. From the beginning of the War with China to its expansion, we observe impressive ambiguity, zigzags, and conflict of opinions in central policies and decision making. These observations also apply to scenes of battle such as Shanghai and Nanjing, where such ambiguity, zigzags, and conflicts caused confusion and serious lack of preparation. However, these issues are not the major objects of this volume. I refer to them only when they represent a decisive lack of systematic war preparation and consistent war plans. General Iwane Matsui, who from reserve duty was appointed as the Commander of the Expeditionary Force to Shanghai, was surprised to learn that the size of the force sent to Shanghai, besieged by the Chinese Army of two hundred thousand, was only twenty thousand. He was troubled by the substance and ambiguity of decisions at the center. By the same token, examination of policies

On 20 September, the ACCom reported the outline of the armed forces' operation plan to the Emperor. At that time, the ACCom's operation plans in China only went as far as the end of October[80]:

There is little need to worry about the USSR's participation. Unless we quickly settle the Chinese issues, however, the USSR will move in November. By that time we will have aggressively settled the Incident. In case operations in North and Central China do not accomplish our objective and the situation changes, we will cease aggressive land operations against China. Instead, using all other means we will destroy the will of China for a long, drawn-out war. At the same time, we will reduce the forces directly engaged in operations in China, increase our forces in Manchuria, and prepare for operations against the USSR. Concluding aggressive operations against China by the end of October, we would switch to a long, drawn-out war. That is, we think the offensive will be over by the end of October at the latest. (Boeicho, 1967a, p. 478)[81]

From Shanghai to Nanjing

After sending troops to Shanghai, the ACCom expected to destroy the fighting spirit of the Chinese with battles in Hebei. The Chinese Army, however,

---

and decisions of the Chinese Nationalist Party's Army is not an object, either. For example, I do not examine the reasons why they, after retreating from Shanghai, stayed in Nanjing and battled over the castle. For those issues, see, for example, Hayase (2007). Imoto was a staff officer in the expeditionary force to China for a year from September 1939, and Imoto (1978, ch. 4, in particular section 5, on "difficult negotiations between the Expeditionary Force to China and the Center") is based on his experience.

[80] On 20 September, Strategy Section Chief Mutoh of the ACCom visited the NCCom. In addition to the Army's operation plans, he explained that, given the present state of operations against China, the Army would formulate a rainy-day operation plan against the USSR and report it to the Emperor, which the NCCom approved. The plan was as follows (Boeicho, 1975b, pp. 300–4). In China, they had eight divisions in the North, five in Shanghai, and one controlled directly by the center. If they kept three divisions in reserve for China in Japan, there would be a shortfall of ten divisions according to the existing armament plan toward the USSR. This shortage meant that the allocation would be three divisions on the Eastern Front (instead of eight divisions in the existing armament plan), three on the northern front (instead of four), three divisions on the Western Front (instead of three), and four divisions under the direct control of the commander (instead of eight). If war began with the USSR, shifting the operations in China into defensive stance with four divisions in North China and three in Shanghai, the Army would reallocate the seven divisions saved to restore the allocation to the original size on both the eastern and northern fronts, keeping four divisions in reserve in Japan. At that time, the size of the force sent to China was 370,000 in the North and 190,000 in Shanghai.

[81] It continued, "During the offensives, in North China we will destroy the Chinese Army in central Hebei with eight divisions (nine if necessary). In the Shanghai area, we will use five divisions, as before, with which we will destroy the Chinese Army in the outskirts of Shanghai, confining the operations as planned."

adopted an evacuation strategy, and Japan failed to build the momentum to end the war. The main Chinese military force was in Central China, on which Japan concentrated five divisions. The military situation made no progress. On 5 November, the Japanese Tenth Army, with three divisions, landed at Hangzhou Bay to reinforce the Expeditionary Force to Shanghai and improve the military situation (Boeicho, 1967a, pp. 491–2).[82] At that time, there was no plan to capture Nanjing. After Ishiwara's resignation on 23 September, most leaders in the ACCom were aggressive, but Vice-ACCommander Tada "from the standpoint of war leadership inhibited the unconfined progress of pure strategy" (Boeicho, 1967a, p. 482).

On 7 November, the ACCommander issued an open order, in which he commanded the Central China Army Group "to destroy the enemy's fighting spirit and build the momentum to conclude the war, in cooperation with the Navy, and wipe out the enemy in the Shanghai region." It also directed the Group to confine "the operation area of the Central China Army Group to the east of the line connecting Suzhou and Jiaxing." The original assignment of the Expeditionary Force to Shanghai was extremely limited. It was to wipe out enemies in the Shanghai region and occupy important places in Shanghai and adjoining regions to the north, in order to protect the Japanese residents. Now, however, it was thought necessary to crush the enemy's morale and move to a speedy conclusion of the conflict, and for that it was "preferable not only to wipe out the enemy in the Shanghai region but also further afield." Tada, fearing escalation of the war, did not consent to the direction, and argued that it was unnecessary to advance to the line connecting Suzhou and Jiaxing. Strategy Division Chief Shimomura persuaded the group that it was inappropriate to fail to provide guidelines to the armed forces' action, and instructed the order to confine fighting (Boeicho, 1967a, pp. 500–2).[83]

---

[82] When the Japanese military captured Dachans-town (*daijo-chin*), a climax of the battle in Shanghai, on 26 October, the Army's lack of preparedness became apparent. When the Japanese military occupied the Beijing-Tianjin area, Chiang Kai-shek launched a scorched earth strategy. The Chinese abandoned as much space as needed – for which the enemy paid a high price in personnel and material resources – to buy time. With this strategy, the Japanese military was lured deep into inland China. With the escalation of the war, transport routes were extended, making it difficult to ensure security. It is said that Chiang Kai-shek believed the overconfident Japanese military would certainly collapse under this war of attrition. See Boeicho (1967a, p. 493). See also Miwa (2008, 3–6, pp. 185–92).

[83] From December 1931 to October 1940, Imperial Prince Taruhito (Kan'in-no miya) was the ACCommander. Therefore, the Vice-ACCommander was virtually at the top of the administration in the ACCom. When the War with China began, Vice-ACCommander Imai was severely ill. On 10 July, arriving at the entrance by car, he was taken to his office

Three days later on 11 November, the Chinese military began to retreat on all fronts. If the Japanese Army were to remain behind the confinement line as ordered, it could not pursue the Chinese. On 20 November, the Center received a report from the Tenth Army that it had ordered to pursue the enemy toward Nanjing. At that time, the ACCom did not include Nanjing in its operational mission. Instead, it had directed the Tenth Army, together with the Expeditionary Force to Shanghai, to wipe out the enemy in the Shanghai region. In deep astonishment, Tada immediately canceled the order. On 21 November, the following day, the Chief of Staff of the Central China Army Group notified the ACCom that Tada had canceled the order. Finally, on 24 November, the ACCom abolished the "confinement line" (Boeicho, 1967a, p. 503).

On 20 November, the Imperial Headquarters was established, and on 24 November it held the first Conference before the Emperor (*gozen-kaigi*). "At this Conference there was neither any question from the Emperor nor questions and answers. No issue was raised for the Royal Judgment, either. It was held only for reporting to the Emperor the operation plans of the Army and the Navy" (Boeicho, 1967a, pp. 503–5).

The Japanese captured Nanjing on 13 December 1937. Vice-ACCommander Tada had been strongly opposed to the capture of Nanjing, whereas Strategy Division Chief Shimomura had promoted this action aggressively.[84]

Peace Overtures

Since the beginning of the War with China, there had been several peace overtures,[85] none of which succeeded. Instead, the war escalated. On 1 October, Prime Minister Konoe, Foreign Minister Hirota, Army Minister Sugiyama, and Navy Minister Yonai (at the Four Ministers Conference) discussed how they would handle the growing war in China. Simultaneously, they unified the framework of conditions for peace. On 27 October, Hirota arranged meetings with foreign diplomatic representatives in Tokyo, to whom individually he explained the conditions from the Japanese side and

on the second floor on a stretcher and presided over the meeting, reclining on a chair (Imoto, 1978, p. 90).

[84] Many argue that, regardless of its feasibility, at this time Japan should have offered and promoted peace. However, as I show later, operations progressed rapidly, beyond all expectations (Boeicho, 1967a, pp. 506–7). See also the appendix to Chapter 2 (section 2-7).

[85] Examples were plans for Prime Minister Konoe or Foreign Minister Hirota to visit Nanjing suggested by Strategy Division Chief Ishiwara in mid-July, Konoe's plan in late July to send Ryusuke Miyazaki, and a relief program of the Ministry of Foreign Affairs in early August for cease-fire and national-border negotiation (Boeicho, 1967a, pp. 516–17).

asked for fair peace mediation by a third party. He sensed that Germany would mediate.[86]

The German ambassador to Japan, Herbert von Dirksen, received a special request from Foreign Minister Hirota that he lead the negotiations. Recognizing the time was right, on 6 November von Dirksen conveyed the Japanese conditions to Chiang Kai-shek through the German ambassador to China, Oscar P. Trautmann. At the end of November, Chinese leaders discussed the Japanese peace conditions, taking Trautmann's advice. On 2 December, Trautmann discussed peace with Chiang in Nanjing. On 7 December, Dirksen visited Hirota and reported that, subject to maintenance of the territorial integrity, Chiang Kai-shek agreed "to open peace talks on the basis of the Japanese peace conditions," and asked whether those conditions had changed (Boeicho, 1967a, p. 517).[87]

---

[86] In November 1936, Mussolini loudly announced the Rome-Berlin Axis. In the same month, the German–Japanese Agreement and the Anti-Comintern Pact were concluded between Germany and Japan, whom Italy joined in 1937. (The agreement evolved into the Tripartite Pact of 27 September 1940.) "Hitler was following the same policy at this time with Japan. Here also the two Powers did not see eye to eye in practical affairs. Hitler wanted to push Japan forward to Russia and Great Britain, without sacrificing Germany's close connexion with China, whose army was still organized by German generals; Japan would no more tolerate Germany in the Far East than any other European Power. Each intended the other provide the conflict so that it could collect the reward" (Taylor, 1964, p. 111). See also note 51 of this chapter.

A former staff officer of the ACCom's information division recalled that Japan was ignorant (Sugita, 1987, p. 57): "Germany from early on had sent leading military advisors to China, supplied military aid over a long time, and helped China enhance its armament against Japan." At the end of 1927 Chiang Kai-shek invited German military advisors to China for the first time to enhance armaments and provide training for soldiers. Since 1935 in particular, when Lieutenant-General Alexander von Falkenhausen (who had been Chiang's advisor since 1930) became the Chief of Advisors, remarkable progress was made in establishing an air defense system, building coastal artillery, and constructing munitions arsenals, with which trade with Germany expanded. "In a sense, the War with China was a battle between Japan and Germany (or between their soldiers). After the Anti-Comintern Pact of November 1936, German military advisors were to withdraw from China. But, its realization was in February 1937, and even after that some remained in China and helped the Chinese military" (Sugita, 1987, pp. 57–8). Major sites for constructing air defense systems and coastal artilleries were along the Yangtze River, such as Shanghai and Nanjing (often called the Seeckt Line), which saw the fiercest battles of the first half of the war. See also Miwa (2008, 3–10, pp. 213–18).

[87] For the details of the process and consequence of the mediation by Trautmann, see Ishii (1950, pp. 294–301). The author then was the East Asia Bureau Chief of the Foreign Ministry. On the Four Ministers' agreement to accept fair advisory mediation by a third country, on 27 October Hirota explained the conditions for peace to the individual ambassadors from the UK, the United States, France, Germany, and Italy and expressed his hope for peace mediation. From mid-November, the Japanese made remarkable progress in battles in the Shanghai region, and were confidently expected to capture Nanjing. The Nationalist Chinese government declared a resolution for a full-scale war of attrition and

On 13 December, the Japanese captured Nanjing. The resulting sense of euphoria among the Japanese public had a huge effect on the peace conditions, and became "the primary cause of failure in promptly restoring peace between Japan and China" (Boeicho, 1967a, p. 517).

In an article entitled "Journalism, the Public, and the Diet," the East Asia Bureau Chief of the Foreign Ministry recalled after the war (Ishii, 1950, pp. 288–91):

From the outbreak of the War with China, newspapers and magazines took positions that accommodated the military and glorified the aggressive position of the government. We saw almost no article that questioned the need to inflict "punishment" on China, or to take "resolute actions." In personal stories, middle-ranking soldiers were hailed as "bearers of the country's tomorrow," mocking civilians and government clerks.... Belligerent in nature and inspired by newspapers, magazines, and radio, the general public enjoyed the war unreflectingly and with high excitement.... Mass meetings calling for the punishment of domineering China gained popularity.

He continued:

The government proclaimed that "Japan had no territorial ambitions in China," but the public did not take this seriously. They thought it a matter of course that, as punishment, Japan would take rich areas in North and Central China. A representative of the Foreign Ministry on an official trip to a local area was told clearly by the key personalities: "If the government concludes such a peace as to part with territories we have occupied in this holy war, we will barge into the Foreign Ministry in large groups to protest strongly." ...All over Japan, the country was filled with voices demanding punishment for China.

The Capture of Nanjing and the Transformation of the Peace Overture

On 14 December, the day after the capture of Nanjing, the Cabinet and the IH-government Liaison Conference reexamined the conditions for peace, in response to Chiang Kai-shek's query. The process took the following form (Ishii, 1950, pp. 291–301).[88]

The Four Ministers Conference was held immediately after the offer from Dirksen was received, and the participants agreed to accept the offer and move on. Next, a meeting of the three leading Bureau Chiefs, from the

relocation of the capital to Chongqing, for the time being retaining three departments in Hankou – Domestic Affairs, Foreign Affairs, and Finance. Most diplomatic envoys in Nanjing moved to Hankou at the request of the Chinese government. General Chiang remained in Nanjing, declaring his resolution to defend the city at all costs. Trautmann and the Deputy Chief of the Chinese Foreign Affairs Department traveled from Hankou to Nanjing and began mediation for peace talks.

[88] See also Boeicho (1967a, pp. 517–19).

AM, the NM, and the Foreign Ministry, was held. They discussed the peace conditions, in order to be able to notify the ambassador unofficially of their terms. They then put together the final draft of the peace proposal, which was almost the same as the unofficial version. The only difference was the addition of one item about claims for damages. It was considered reasonable to demand compensation for the damages that China had inflicted on Japanese interests in the country, such as the burning of Japanese cotton-spinning factories in Tsingtao. However, on the following day Army Minister Sugiyama visited Hirota and told him that he declined the offer of German mediation, as did the Prime Minister. Hirota agreed, too.[89] But as the result of pleas over the next two days from the NM and the Foreign Ministry, the Army finally agreed to accept the mediation.

The next challenge was to obtain agreement both at the IH-government Liaison Conference and the Cabinet meeting, particularly the former. The Liaison Conference scheduled on 13 December (the day Nanjing was captured) was called off at the request of the Prime Minister. Instead, it was convened on the afternoon of 14 December in the Prime Minister's office, following the Cabinet meeting.

Few at the Cabinet meeting and the Liaison Conference supported the original draft sent to the German ambassador. Home Minister Suetsugu[90] was the most hard-line opponent. Posing the question, "Will the people be satisfied with these conditions?" he implied adverse influences on security issues. Only Navy Minister Yonai and Vice-NCCommander Koga faithfully supported the original draft. Participants such as Vice-ACCommander Tada, Suetsugu, Sugiyama, and Finance Minister Kaya suggested additional conditions. From beginning to end, Prime Minister Konoe kept silent.[91]

---

[89] Ishii (1950, p. 298) commented on the Army Minister: "he was such a slob... [H]e was an Army Minister of swings and roundabouts, as uncontrolled inside the Army went by," and on the two ministers: "embarrassingly unreliable ministers." Tooze (2007, p. 203) writes on the first page of Part II: "the uneasy balance was destabilized on 6 March 1936 by the overthrow of the liberal Japanese Prime Minister Okada Keisuke and his replacement by the pro-war Foreign Minister Hirota Koki." This was just after the 2.26 Incident (the attempted coup d'etat in February of that year).

[90] Relieving the ailing Eiichi Baba, on this same day (14 December) Full Admiral Suetsugu became the Home Minister.

[91] Ishii (1950, p. 299). See Ishii (1950, pp. 300–1) for the details of additional conditions, contrasted with the original. A senior official at the Military (*gunji*) Section (Inada, 1969, pp. 184–9) recalled that they clearly understood that they must follow a nonescalation policy. But they were in ecstasy over the capture of Nanjing. Having no confidence in making up the situation with such conditions, they began an investigation, saying, "Let's look at this closely." Hearing of the process, junior staff in every corner began to send orders about things such as compensation and concessions along the Yangtze River. "The Navy

On 21 December, the Cabinet reached a decision about the reply to be sent to the German ambassador in Tokyo. It was to be the original draft, together with conditions added at the Liaison Conference. The next day, looking over the document, Ambassador Dirksen expressed a sentiment that, because of the substantial differences between the new and the original conditions, he had little hope they would be accepted by the Chinese (Boeicho, 1967a, p. 519).

There were two trends toward peace in the AM and the ACCom, hardline and reconciliatory. The AM, with which the government agreed, represented the former. The War Leadership Section of the ACCom represented the latter, which was finally abandoned.[92]

On 26 December, the conditions were transmitted through Trautmann to the Nationalist Chinese Government.

The Defeat of Peace Overture and Konoe's Proclamation, January 1938

Boeicho (1967a, p. 522) explained the situation after the capture of Nanjing: "On 14 December, the provisional government of Republic of China was established in the North, while in Central China, the movement to establish the revitalized reform government of the Republic of China gained impetus. Because the conclusion of peace between Chiang Kai-shek and Japan would jeopardize these new governments, those who had hopes for them advocated taking a hard line toward Chiang's government. They began to denounce the IH-AD as weakhearted."

The IH-AD intended to fix the peace conditions, which had varied and escalated as the war progressed. In order to stem the growing demand to refuse to negotiate with Chiang Kai-shek's government, it asked for agreement among three ministries (Army, Navy, and Foreign) on the basic principles for dealing with the China Incident. They reached a consensus on this by the end of the year. After approving this "principle" at the IH-government Liaison Conference on 9 January 1938, they decided at the Conference before the Emperor on 11 January to declare it fixed national policy. But, "there appeared to be a difference in true intentions between

---

was the prime example of this opportunism, demanding concessions in South China. The Navy had never given consent to the Incident. They agreed simply because they used the China Incident to solidify the foundation of the Navy in China.... Once related to their interests, the Navy became more hard-line than the Army."

[92] For the details, see Boeicho, 1967a, pp. 516–21. The War Leadership Section members, sharing the role, visited the Vice-ACCommander and the Army Vice-Minister and persuaded them to undo the Cabinet decision on the issue. For the details, see Horiba (1962, pp. 112–21).

the Army, which aimed to realize peace promptly, and the other parties, including the Navy. The difference appeared in the attitude toward Chiang's government" (Boeicho, 1967a, pp. 524–6).

"When the movement to establish a provisional government in North China gained momentum, the demand that Japan refuse to negotiate with the Chiang's government became more pronounced. Anticipating that Chiang's government would accept a peace offer before the capture of Nanjing, they postponed the establishment of that provisional government until the city was captured." The capture of Nanjing on 13 December strengthened the position of those opposing talks with Chaing. Hoping for mediation through Ambassador Trautmann, the government continued to talk with Chiang. Nonetheless, a movement to limit the negotiations to the current year gained momentum. By holding the Conference before the Emperor, and so forth, the government had killed the radicals' time limit proposals of 5 January and 10 January. Nevertheless, they decided to impose a reply deadline of 15 January on the Chinese. Japan did not reply to an inquiry received on 13 January from the Foreign Affairs Department Chief of the Chinese government, requesting that it disclose further details of its peace conditions (Boeicho, 1967a, p. 526).

The IH-government Liaison Conference was held on the morning of 15 January. Vice-ACCommander Tada, representing the ACCom, disagreed with the government. He advocated postponing the decision to shut out Chiang's government and waiting for a reply from the Chinese. He argued that without this, Japan should not move toward a long war, for which the prospects were quite bad.[93] Given the conflict between the government and the IH, and between the AM and the ACCom, the conference failed to reach a conclusion by the end of the day. Finally, the Military Bureau Chief

---

[93] Because both the ACCommander and the NCCommander were members of the Imperial family, at the government's request the Vice-ACCommander and the Vice-NCCommander attended the conference from the supreme command (Boeicho, 1967a, p. 526).

When a Strategy Section Chief was asked, during the War with China, "What was the influence of Kan'in-no-miya as the ACCommander?" (Inada, 1969, pp. 240–1), he replied, "None at all." His answer to "What happened if not an Imperial family was the ACCommander?" was, "it would be cumbersome." To, "Was there no voice demanding resignation of such a person as member of Imperial family?", he commented: "It must be so…, however, there was no such a voice." And he continued: "Nobody was reliable. Hajime Sugiyama was no exception. Nobody was reliable during the War with China." He also commented: "Kan'in-no-miya never attended a conference as the ACCommander." Nishiura (1968, p. 96) commented on Kan'in-no-miya's arrival in December 1931 as the ACCommander (until October 1940): "At the beginning we simply thought it great. After a while, especially once the War with China began, a voice requesting his prompt resignation became dominant in the Army."

of the AM put full responsibility on the Vice-ACCommander, declaring that "unless the Vice-ACCommander accepts the plan, the Cabinet will resign."[94] After careful discussion with Division Chiefs of the ACCom in the evening, Tada conceded: "The IH-AD cannot agree with the proposal. Recognizing the negative effects of a Cabinet collapse, however, we do not dare offer a dissenting opinion" (Boeicho (1967a, pp. 526–7).[95]

The next day, 16 January, the government issued a formal statement (the so-called Konoe Proclamation) that included, "From now on, we will not deal with the National Chinese government."[96] On 18 January, it issued a supplementary statement (Boeicho (1967a, pp. 527–8): "From now on, we will not deal with the National Chinese government is a stronger expression than that we refuse to recognize the government. Basically, from the viewpoint of international law, it is enough for the denial of the National Chinese government to approve the new government. The provisional government

---

[94] At that time, the Army overvalued the Konoe Cabinet. They thought it indispensable for war leadership, and the ACCom made concessions (Nishiura, 1968, p. 211). See also Inada (1969, pp. 186–8). Many Army leaders placed hopes on the second Konoe Cabinet formed in July 1940, but he was "not such a reliable person" (Iwaguro, 1977, p. 179). For the Tripartite Pact signed immediately after the institution of the second Konoe Cabinet, see Taylor (1964, p. 18) or Miwa (2008, p. 169, note 13).For the Chief Cabinet Secretary Akira Kazami of the second Konoe Cabinet, see Miwa [2008, p. 95, note 3]. He was famous for criticizing 'the Umuzu-Tojo line' for stubbornly objecting to the appointment of Itagaki to the Army Minister. Inada [1969, pp. 190–1] commented on Kazami: "This Chief Cabinet Secretary was a dominant cause of the wishy-washiness of the Konoe Cabinets. He knew nothing about military, serious military in particular, and he suspected men without reason. What people said about the 'xx-line' or 'xx-*batsu* (clique)' was mostly false. I don't say there were no such things. But it is a bad habit of newspaper reporters to tell this kind of story and then use it to explain everything. Akira Kazami was a newspaper reporter. Most of them were idle gossips. We were not stupid. We don't much like gathering together in groups, either."

[95] At the Liaison Conference, Army Minister Sugiyama and Vice-ACCcommander Tada concluded that such a Liaison Conference was harmful and it was better never to convene it again, and it never was (Boeicho, 1967a, p. 534). Sato (1976, pp. 144–5), who also demanded prompt termination of negotiations, recalled that it was Home Minister Suetsugu who met Tada in argument and recalled: "At that time there were signs that the Konoe Cabinet, at the Diet reopening soon, was going to take a very strong stand, and Home Minister Suetsugu was an extreme hard-liner."

[96] "The Basic Principle for Dealing with the China Incident," decided on 11 January at the Conference before the Emperor, stated: "Unless the present Chinese central government demands peace, *from this point the Empire will not expect to resolve the Incident with it.* Instead, supporting the establishment of the emerging provisional Chinese government, we would effect an arrangement of diplomatic relations and cooperate with it in rehabilitating new China" (my italics). Sato refuted popular criticism that he had written the proclamation (Sato, 1976, p. 145): "I took part in drafting the proclamation; however, it was not a proclamation as such. It gave a full account of our intention, and was more delicately written."

of the Republic of China, however, has not yet reached the stage of formal approval, and … we proceed to deny the National Chinese government and eliminate it."

As mentioned briefly in section 1–5–1, Boeicho (1967a, pp. 528–9) explained that "the Konoe Cabinet, ignoring the intentions of the ACCom, which was unsure about planning operations, abandoned the policy for a prompt resolution of the war." It referred to Strategy Section Chief Kawabe's commentary on the strategic judgment of the ACCom, ending with an impressive statement:[97] "In our judgment, Chiang Kai-shek will never give in to our force and surrender. Vice-ACCommander Tada and Strategy Division Chief Ishiwara firmly believed that Chiang would wage a long-drawn-out war of attrition. In contrast to this, most leaders, thinking little of China's power, expected to defeat China with one blow. They anticipated that China would surrender while Japan advanced from Shanghai to Nanjing…. The people were the most aggressive, the government was the next, and the ACCom, concerned about the country, was the least aggressive and most hesitant."[98]

---

[97] At this time, Strategy Division Chief Shimomura was ailing. For more details, see Miwa (2008, 3–6–1, pp. 185–7). In Sato (1976, pp. 146–7), I find an interesting note about the "private papers of Duke Konoe": "After Mr. Konoe committed suicide, *Staring at Dark Japan* was published, claiming to cite his private papers about an event that took place two years after the proclamation not to deal with Chiang's government. Explaining the drift of constructing '*shintaisei* (a new system)' and a 'new political party,' he wrote: 'In the summer of 1940, we established the Imperial Rule Assistance Association (*taisei yokusan-kai*). With the power of this national organization we intended to control the power of the military and resolve the China Incident.'

This might be relevant if the military in concert advocated terminating the negotiations and pressed this with the government. But the ACCom, the principal agency deciding military operations, advocated continuing negotiations, while the Army Minister advocated terminating them. Army opinion was split in two. If Konoe wanted fervently to end the war, he could have given a decision in favor of the ACCom. As Prime Minister, he could do it. Nevertheless, supporting Army Minister Sugiyama, he said, 'If the supreme command advocates continuation in any way, the Konoe Cabinet will resign.' In short, he had no need to control the power of the military. He needed only to make a decision in favor of the ACCom. There was no need even to create a national organization. Taking points like this into consideration, I suspect that someone else wrote these 'private papers.'" As mentioned in note 95, Sato demanded prompt termination of negotiations.

[98] In a preceding paragraph, Strategy Section Chief Kawabe reviewed the state of weapons preparation (Boeicho (1967a, p. 528): "Weapons preparation before the war was extremely deficient. Disastrously, the operation to capture Dachans (*daijo-chin*), a climax of the battle in Shanghai, took one more month [all-out attack began 15 October and ended 26 October]. Ratios of both light artillery to heavy artillery and shrapnel shell to high explosive were inappropriate. After the capture of Nanjing we planned to establish several divisions of troops, but to our surprise we could not obtain rifles and had to import them from abroad. War mobilization had not worked well, and we could not achieve the scheduled production goals because of worker shortage."

Around this time, according to the private papers of Military (*gunji*) Section Chief Shin'ichi Tanaka of the AM, there was little hope for prompt termination of the war:

The attitude that it would not deal with the National Chinese government reflects a determination to pursue a long, drawn-out war rather than hope for peace.... Were we to focus on the prompt termination of the war, we would deal with Chiang's government. When instead we pursue the route to a long war, we must support the emerging government to rehabilitate China, even if this takes 100 years. We have no other choice than to have as our basic goal the fundamental reconstruction of the Japan–China relationship. The question is, is such a great undertaking feasible, with Japan's present national capacity and in today's international conditions? In actual fact, we are steadily advancing toward a long war.

As we saw in section 2–2–3, after the Konoe Proclamation of 16 January, Strategy Section Chief Kawabe decided to wait until July to institute aggressive operations. He was able to secure consent for this delay from the ACCom, the AM, and also the Navy. The principal guideline of operations was approved on 16 February at the Conference in the Presence of the Emperor. But when Kawabe returned from his trip, he was met not with an order to implement the guideline, but a letter appointing him to Flight Training School at Hamamatsu. With the dismissal of the Strategy Section Chief, the nonescalation policy collapsed and Campaign Shandong and Campaign Xuzhou began, heading down the road to a long, drawn-out war of attrition or an impasse.[99]

2–4–3. War Leadership at Government Level

Conferences and Councils

Japan under the Meiji Constitution lacked a war leadership system. The Imperial Headquarters (IH) was established on 20 November 1937. Fukudome (1951, pp. 66–7) described it as "the IH of the armed forces for war leadership" and commented on its position and the division of roles among participants:[100] "The agenda of the IH Conference was limited

---

[99] Torashiro Kawabe was the War Leadership Section Chief when the War with China began. The War Leadership Section was abolished in the organizational change following the resignation of Strategy Division Chief Ishiwara, and Kawabe became the Strategy Section Chief on 26 October, succeeding Akira Mutoh.

[100] Fukudome was the Strategy Section Chief of the NCCom when the IH was established, and was the Strategy Division Chief when the Pacific War began. As shown in section 2–2–2, the only difference was that the ACCom was renamed the IH-AD and the NCCom became the IH-ND.

to operation plans issues, and it was nothing but a meeting between the NCCom and the ACCom. However, under the IH organization the Army Minister and the Navy Minister were members 'attending the IH'.... The essential role of the IH was leadership of operations decisions. The implementation of most operation plans was directly and indivisibly connected with military administration under the control of the military ministers. For this, the military ministers, as members of the IH, were to maintain close cooperation with the supreme command."

An arrangement made at the Cabinet meeting on 19 November 1937 established the IH-government Liaison Conference "as an organization for the sake of expedience." "Here the government and the IH agreed decisions on national policy, upon which on national affairs when necessary the Cabinet made decisions and asked for the Emperor's approval. Similarly, when necessary the ACCommander or the NCCommander asked the Emperor's approval for supreme command issues, and set them in motion" (Hara, 1987, p. 56).[101]

The details of the Cabinet meeting arrangement were as follows (Hara, 1987, p. 58)[102]:

(1) For liaison between the IH and the Cabinet, we create a consultative body for "conference as needed" between the IH and the government, and hold it when necessary. We neither attach any specific name to this conference, nor do we base it on the administration control rule. It is a de facto conference. (2) The conference consists of the ACCommander, NCCommander, Army Minister, Navy Minister, Prime Minister, and Ministers concerned. The Ministers to attend, together with the issues to be discussed, are selected by the Chief Cabinet Secretary and the Military Bureau Chiefs of both the AM and the NM. However, in actual implementation, neither the ACCommander nor the NCCommander attends the conference. Instead, in principle they are represented by the Vice-ACCommander and Vice-NCCommander. (3) For particularly important issues we ask to hold a Conference in the Presence of the Emperor, which is attended by the ACCommander and NCCommander, and, with royal permission, the Army Minister, Navy Minister, and Prime Minister (and

---

[101] Fukudome (1951, p. 67) called it "the government-supreme command liaison conference," and wrote that its first meeting was held on 27 July 1940. He argued that it was established at the suggestion of Prime Minister Konoe: "The Conference was not for decision making, but for liaison or discussion. When issues required decisions, the government made those concerning national affairs and the supreme command those concerning supreme command issues, both through their respective formal procedures.

Therefore, at the Liaison Conference the supreme command could not intervene in the authority of the government nor the government in the responsibility of the supreme command. The NCCom, at least, rigidly observed this limitation, and at the Conference never expressed views intervening with issues under the government's jurisdiction."

[102] It was based on the report of *Tokyo Asahi Shimbun* (Newspaper).

occasionally other Ministers). (4) The Chief Cabinet Secretary and the Military Bureau Chiefs both of the AM and the NM are to manage the conference.

Before the establishment of such "an organization for the sake of expedience" and the IH in November 1937, including the period following the Manchurian Incident, the Cabinet meeting discussed issues of war leadership as part of national affairs. In addition, it issued its decisions as Cabinet approvals. For example, the Outline of Guidelines for Handling Issues on Manchuria and Mongolia of 12 March 1932 was approved by the Cabinet.

In October 1933, on the initiative of Army Minister Araki, a Five Ministers Conference (Prime, Foreign, Finance, Army, and Navy) was held to discuss the Basic Outline of National Policy of the Empire. After that date, it became the convention to discuss and decide war leadership issues in Five or Four Ministers Conferences (the latter made up of the Prime, Foreign, Army, and Navy). They met in the spirit of a so-called small-and-strong, or war, cabinet. This convention persisted even after the establishment of the IH-government Liaison Conference, which the ACCom boycotted (Hara, 1987, p. 57).[103]

The Conference in the Presence of the Emperor during this period was essentially a kind of IH-government Liaison Conference. The conference proceeded ceremoniously in the presence of the Emperor on issues upon which the IH and the government had agreed. Its purpose was to convey the relevant information directly to the Emperor, which made it easy to obtain his approval later. The conference was held only for important issues of war leadership (Hara, 1987, p. 59).[104]

Conflict of opinions between the government and the IH-AD (ACCom) leading to the Konoe Proclamation of 16 January 1938 caused the ACCom's

---

[103] Hara continues: "The Army (Navy) Minister at Cabinet meetings or Five Ministers Conferences also spoke for the ACCom (NCCom), through which opinions of the supreme command were to be reflected indirectly." The participants of Five Ministers Conferences were all Cabinet members. The ACCom, part of the supreme command, boycotted the IH-government Liaison Conference, and the Five Ministers Conference is said to have played its part. However, the reality and actual performance of the Five Ministers Conference as a substitute for the IH-government Liaison Conference is not known at all. The issue that led the ACCom to boycott the conference was a clash with the Vice-ACCommander. It was not rare for opinions to differ between the ACCom (NCCom) and the AM (NM). If opinions of the ACCom (NCCom) were fully reflected through the Army (or Navy) Minister in decisions agreed at the Five Ministers Conference, it would not have been difficult to resume Liaison Conferences. In the first place, there was little need for establishing a mechanism such as the Liaison Conference.

[104] In addition, the Conference in the Presence of the Emperor differed from the Liaison Conference in that the Chairman of the Privy Council attended the former and joined the discussion. On this point, see Hara (1987, pp. 59–60) or Miwa (2008, p. 403, note 90).

boycott of the Liaison Conference, which now became a Liaison Conference in name only. Instead, war leadership was discussed at the Five Ministers Conference, and the Conference in the Presence of the Emperor was convened only once, on 30 November 1938, when it approved the Guideline for the Coordination of a New Japan–China Relationship (Hara, 1987, p. 60).

At the Four Ministers Conference of 26 November 1940, the IH-government Liaison Council was established on the suggestion of Army Minister Tojo. The council held regular meetings (every Thursday) at the Prime Minister's office. "It was a meeting to reach a decision on important national policies that needed to bring together the 'national defense' and 'operations' (supreme command) and the 'military administration,' not just a meeting for liaison and information exchange" (Hara, 1987, p. 62).[105]

Faced with a national state of emergency caused by the outbreak of the German–Soviet War on 22 June 1941, the term "Liaison Conference" was restored and the meeting was held at Court two or three times a week, including an IH-government information exchange meeting. With the start of the Koiso Cabinet in July 1944, to appeal for an improvement in war leadership, the title was changed to the Supreme War Leadership Conference. In effect, participants pretended they had improved and strengthened the mechanism for war leadership (Hara, 1987, p. 63).

IH-Government Liaison Conference Operations
It was the authorities concerned, such as ACCom, NCCom, the AM, the NM, and the Foreign Ministry, that actually drafted materials for national policies and held negotiations between the Army and the Navy and between the military and the government. Specifically, those at the core of this task were the following: for the Army, the Twentieth Subsection (the War Leadership Subsection under the direct control of the Vice-ACCommander) of the ACCom and the Military (*gunmu*) Section (Section Chief and Senior Officers) of the AM; for the Navy, a section under the Strategy Division of the NCCom and the Second Section (Section Chief and Senior Officers) of the Military Bureau of the NM; and for the Foreign Ministry, sections concerned (mainly Section Chiefs) and sometimes the General Affairs Section Chief of the Cabinet Secretary's office. The Strategy Section of the ACCom, the Military (*gunji*) Section of the AM, the Strategy Section of the NCCom, and the Military Bureau First Section of the NM (in

---

[105] This is from the memorandum of Arisue, who at that time was Twentieth Subsection Chief of the ACCom (Hara, 1987, p. 62). It wrote: "Obviously, it is not for the supreme command to attend the Four Ministers Conference."

each section, the Section Chief and Senior Officer) intervened strongly, too (Hara, 1987, p. 63).

Hara (1987, p. 63) describes the process for determining materials for national policies: "Above those authorities concerned were the Military Bureau Chiefs of the AM and the NM and the Strategy Division Chiefs of both the ACCom and the NCCom. The Army-Navy Bureau-Division Chiefs' Conference with those four military leaders (sometimes the relevant Bureau Chiefs of Foreign Ministry joined) virtually determined the destiny of the materials for national policies. Once approved by this conference, the materials almost automatically became the military (IH) draft. The military draft was usually to be regarded as the decision of the IH-government Liaison Conference."

The Army usually took the initiative in proposing national policy plans.[106] "Most national policy plans were proposed by the Army and put to the Navy. Through negotiation between the Army and the Navy, the participants started to determine the Army-Navy plan, that is, the IH-AD and IH-ND plan." This plan was propounded at the IH-government Liaison Conference. Once the IH-AD and IH-ND plan was decided, the government leaders seldom expressed opinions. On important national policies that determined the fate of the state, it was customary to adopt those policies with only one discussion meeting over several hours. The Outline of Imperial National Policy Implementation approved on 6 September 1941 was no exception (Hara, 1987, p. 64).[107]

2–5. Conclusion: No Way Out?

2–5–1. Impasse

The Vice-ACCommander's Evaluation of the Situation in October 1939
The War with China that began in July 1937 escalated further after the first Konoe Proclamation of 16 January 1938. After the capture of Hankou in

---

[106] Hara (1987, pp. 63–4) pointed out exceptions. For the Outline of Imperial National Policy Implementation approved at the Conference in the Presence of the Emperor on 6 September 1941 (which viewed war with the United States, the UK, and the Netherlands as inescapable), the Army waited for the Navy to take the initiative, because the Navy would play the principal role in the war. The Plan to Strengthen Alliance among Japan, Germany, and Italy (12 July 1940) was proposed by the First Section of the Foreign Ministry Europe-Asia Bureau, and the Policy Plan for the Military Alliance Negotiation (4 September 1940) was proposed by Foreign Minister Matsuoka.

[107] For more details, see Miwa (2008, 3–9, pp. 209–12).

October 1938, "without wiping out the main force of the Chinese military" (Boeicho, 1967a, p. 575), Japan reached the limits of its military strength and national capacity. With the second Konoe Proclamation on the "construction of a new order in East-Asia" on 22 December 1938, Japan followed a path toward a long, drawn-out war of attrition or impasse. Three years later, without any sign of improvement in the state of impasse, Japan began the Pacific War, that is, the war with the United States, the UK, and the Netherlands.

Lieutenant General Shigeru Sawada became the Vice-ACCommander on 2 October 1939, after the Nomonhan Incident. He had been a Division Commander in Manchuria. When he became the Vice-ACCommander, he investigated Japan's remaining capacity after the long war with China, asking for a rough estimate from all sides. He recalled the situation at the time (Boeicho, 1967a, p. 624)[108]:

Although behaving aggressively to the outside world, like a fruit rotten at the core, Japan's policy could not continue for long. Army Minister Hata shared the same view. We could not find a way to conclude the War with China through decisive engagement by force. A decisive war against China was impossible.... If Chiang Kai-shek gave up resistance against Japan, his government would collapse immediately. Therefore, even if he were driven into a corner, he would never surrender. On the other hand, we had withstood the enemy's winter offensive. It was unimaginable that we would be fought off by China even if we reduced our armed forces there to some degree. Unless Japan withdrew troops entirely from China, it was impossible to bring the war to a successful conclusion between the two countries. There was no other solution than to do it as part of global affairs (my italics).

At least after the second Konoe Proclamation on the "construction of a new order in East Asia" on 22 December 1938, most state leaders (and Army leaders in particular) concerned with decision making on national policies considered the position of the Vice-ACCommander and Army Minister obviously correct. Specifically, they believed the following: (1) Japan had already reached the limits of its military strength and national capacity. (2) Japan could not find a way to conclude the War with China through decisive engagement by force. A decisive war against the Chongqing government was impossible. (3) It was unimaginable that Japan would be fought

---

[108] As shown in section 1–5, the Head of Weapons Arsenals' summary at the end of June 1939 on the war mobilization in FY1938 stated that even though "we had not yet reached the stage of war that would exhaust the whole national power, we suffered from serious shortages of various materials," and could "not afford to obtain materials to fill the war demand from the military." Sawada was writing about the situation three months later than the time of this summary.

off by China. (4) It was at least politically infeasible for Japan to withdraw troops entirely from China. (5) Maintenance of the status quo over long periods was difficult for Japan.

Japan shifted its basic policy from traditional offensive action to a defensive strategy of waging a long, drawn-out war of attrition. With this shift, in 1939 the damage to the Japanese military increased, which at least some leaders must have anticipated.[109]

Leaders and Decision Making

In Japan, "nobody occupied the position of supreme national leader" (Tanemura, 1979, p. 22). As shown in the previous section, after the capture of Nanjing, Japan virtually rejected the achievement of the Trautmann peace overture, which started with an initiative from the Japanese side and was going to reach an agreement. The atmosphere in and around the government (the state) at that time symbolized the "tragedy."[110]

The next episode in Sato (1976, p. 138) showed another side of the tragedy. At the Cabinet meeting on 15 August 1937, after approving the dispatch of troops to Central China, including Shanghai, Army Minister Sugiyama cordially told Foreign Minister Hirota: "With this the time has come to begin an all-out war between Japan and China. As the Army Minister I am deeply troubled. *We are not allowed to complain before the enemies.* We sincerely hope to put diplomatic emphasis on the [China] Incident for peace" (my italics). This Army Minister's proposal, immediately after receiving approval to send troops to Central China, reflects the Army's hope for a prompt resolution of the China Incident. Hirota, firmly convinced that the Army had decided to wage war aggressively, was surprised to hear such words from the Army Minister.[111]

---

[109] In 1939, the damage to the Chinese military decreased considerably, whereas Japanese damage decreased hardly at all. On this observation, Boeicho (1967a, p. 622) commented: "In short, it demonstrated that in operations over a vast area of the Far East, the defensive operation entailed a larger force than the offensive one, although that had its own difficulties. It was a war lesson Japan learned from bitter experience in the Siberian Intervention and the Manchurian Incident."

[110] Shigeharu Matsumoto, then a news agency's reporter in Shanghai, recalled that General Iwane Matui, who led the Expeditionary Force to Shanghai, agreed with his opinion: "We must cease fire before arriving at Nanjing. Once we capture Nanjing, it will become an all-out war." Matsui responded: "I am devoting myself in secret to cease fire before Nanjing, but never mention this to anyone else." However, the retreat of the Chinese military was so fast that the Japanese had no other choice than to advance. See *ekonomisuto*, 14 May 1985 issue, p. 84. The serialization is published as Matsumoto (1986). Matsui's response was typical of the views regarding the tragedy.

[111] See also Boeicho (1975b, pp. 262–4) or Miwa (2008, p. 406, note 95).

With the escalation of the war, the gains and costs accumulated. As time went on, in each leader's mind the feasibility of peace, and the complete withdrawal of Japanese troops from China, must have decreased. As shown in the previous section, at the Liaison Conference on 14 December 1937, where Trautmann's peace overture was discussed, many participants revealed the same attitude as Sugiyama.[112]

State leaders, both in the government and in the military, must have recognized that Japan (the state) had fallen into a state of inertia. This situation worsened as the war escalated. They might have felt that they were forced to cover the losses due to failures of their predecessors.

In Ishii's recollection (Ishii, 1950, pp. 279–80), we find the following scene, which may have been universal. For leaders in the military and the government who had racked up victories in battles, this situation, the atmosphere and the individual leader's behavior, might represent the major cause of difficulty in peace overtures. On 30 July 1937, Prime Minister Konoe transmitted a message from the Emperor to Army Minister Sugiyama and Foreign Minister Hirota: "How about solving the problem around here through diplomatic negotiation?" Konoe and Sugiyama agreed to cease fire in North China and to open diplomatic negotiations. The Military (*gunmu*) Section Chief of the AM Shibayama, under Sugiyama's direction, met the Europe-Asia Bureau Chief of Foreign Ministry Ishii and declared: "We must obtain a cease–fire. However, it is not easy for the Japanese military to offer a cease-fire. We would be very pleased if we could receive a cease-fire proposal from the Chinese side. Will the Ministry of Foreign Affairs negotiate with the Chinese side to obtain such an offer from them?" Ishii began to make efforts, thinking: "The military were afraid of losing their prestige, and wanted to let China offer the cease-fire. How petty-minded they are. But there is no time to reproach them for it."

The Consequences of Inertia

As shown earlier in this chapter, immediately after his appointment in October 1939 Vice-ACCommander Sawada thought it would be impossible to achieve agreement on the end of the war between Japan and China; it would have to be done as part of global affair. There was no other way out. Key to this was a run of success by the German military. Japan was waiting for a German amphibious landing operation on the British mainland; however, this was never made. In the German–Soviet War, they waited in

[112] See also Miwa (2008, p. 406, note 96).

vain for a German victory. In the process, the Tripartite Pact was signed in September 1940.

The consequence of this lack of direction and search for an exit was the advance toward the south and finally the Pacific War – consequences that could be foreseen at least as early as the end of 1938.

On 22 July 1940, Hideki Tojo presented himself on an important political stage as the Army Minister of the second Konoe Cabinet. On 18 October 1941, fifteen months later, he became Prime Minister. Konoe's resignation, which resulted in Tojo becoming his successor, was triggered by Tojo's statement at the Cabinet meeting on 14 October, which summed up the situation of the Japanese state at the time:[113]

The Army is taking the issue of withdrawing troops seriously. If we take the claims of the U.S. at face value, our achievement in the War with China would be wiped out. Furthermore, it will endanger the existence of Manchukuo, and also destabilize the administration in Korea. Our Empire, with holy war objectives, has maintained the policy of nonannexation and nonreparation. Hundreds of thousands of soldiers were killed in the War with China. Those dead soldiers, together with the bereaved families, who number several times more, hundreds of thousands of wounded soldiers, millions of military, and a hundred millions of people, all suffered hardship both in the field and at home. We have already spent tens of billions yen of the nation's money. Japan, however, going against the convention of powerful countries and taking a permissive attitude, will have nothing to show for its efforts except its troops stationed in the country. We should not hesitate to express our demands to the world. We should not succumb to tricky oppression from the U.S.

If we don't stand firmly concerning North China, Mongolia, and Xinjiang, it will endanger the foundation of Manchukuo. Manifestly it will lead to serious problems in the future, and consequently the China Incident will arise again.

---

[113] For example, see Usui (1964, p. xxxvii). Not a few readers sympathize with Inada's (1969) recollection, "the third generation including the Emperor, every one ... contributed to the downfall of the nation," and following two comments: "Until the Russo–Japanese War of 1904–5 the first generation who had experienced hardships over the Meiji Restoration did good work.... Whether the military clique, the *Choshu*-clique, or the *Satsuma*-clique, any of them were all strong internally and well disciplined. But great men from then on were A-students. Under thoroughgoing care, they grew as Japan grew. In the Army, graduating from the Army War College with high marks, obtaining good positions in the AM or the ACCom, and studying abroad..., they were promoted steadily. Therefore, they were excellent clerks, ... peacetime clerks. But they were neither appropriate material for the supreme command nor for leaders. If all went well, they were good commanders and good staff officers. They could do nothing in unexpected situations, however, as they were not right people for turbulent times. So they did careless and disorganized work" (p. 97). "We should have solid and steady politicians. Not only the military but also politicians in the *Showa* era [the *Showa* era began in 1926] were A-students.... Many of them were indecisive. They were good men but shilly-shallied. Hajime Sugiyama headed the list" (p. 311).

Returning to the small-Japan before the Manchurian incident is no option.
Stationing troops is key. We must speak up about what we advocate. We have already
made concessions. If we make an additional one concerning troops stationed in
China, it is equivalent to surrender. It will embolden the U.S. further.[114]

2-5-2. War Leadership and Systematic War Preparations

"The supreme decision-making body was a motley collection of representatives from different parties." In Japan, "nobody occupied the position of
supreme national leader" (Tanemura, 1979, pp. 22–3). This basic structure
and mechanism of Japan's war leadership during this period decisively conditioned the effective and efficient implementation of systematic war preparations, war mobilization, and economic control.

Munitions were supplied in response to demand. Unless based on highly
reliable demand predictions, planned production would not proceed
smoothly, and confusion would result. Highly reliable munitions demand
predictions assumed highly reliable war and operation plans, based on precise forecasts from the field.

---

[114] Boeicho (1968, p. 520). Around the same time, ACCommander Sugiyama, at the meeting of IH Conference in Court, voiced his conviction (Fukudome, 1951, p. 54): "Since
the beginning of the China Incident, 100,000 have been killed and 200,000 wounded. It
is too late both for the maintenance of military discipline and for obtaining the public's
acceptance to withdraw troops now, leaving our reasons in the air." See Hiragushi (2006,
pp. 72–82) for how the evening editions of Tokyo newspapers reported the beginning of
the Pacific War at Pearl Harbor on the morning of 8 December 1941, which capture the
situation and atmosphere in Japan on that day. The announcement from the IH-AD was at
17:00, from the IH-ND at 21:00. In its editorial in the evening edition for that day, *Asahi
Simbun* wrote, in an article entitled "The Empire Declares War against the U.S. and the
UK": "Receiving the Imperial announcement of war, we are so deeply moved, and cannot
help but be highly stimulated and aroused with awe. One hundred millions of our fellow
citizens, in the line of battle or on the home front, will be putting our lives on the line. If we
die, we will die for a great cause of all our courage for the nation, with which, setting the
Emperor's mind at ease, we must be prepared not to be ashamed in front of our glorious
history.

Our enemies are rich in resources. The philosophy on which they depend is a recalci-
trant ambition of world domination. We must crush it, with which we establish the foundation of the Empire and construct a new order in East Asia. For however long the war
might continue, we, the citizens, must endure every hardship and overcome this 'ordeal
from heaven', and establish an everlasting basis for unshakable East Asia."

On the same evening, *Tokyo Nichinichi Shimbun* posted famous journalist-historian
Soho Tokutomi's "Righteous indignation of one hundred millions citizens" and *Yomiuri
Shimbun* famous poet Kotaro Takamura's "On a critical day."

The accuracy of prediction deteriorated with an interval between target time and prediction time. Likewise, the difficulty (and the cost) of making highly accurate predictions increased with the length of this time interval. The same held for plans and predictions of war and munitions demands. "Wars, when they come, are always different from the war that is expected" (Taylor, 1964, p. 116). Accordingly, with a war that was actually occurring and developing, the deterioration of predictive accuracy was tremendous.

The length of time that was necessary for formulating reliable war and operation plans based on accurate prediction on war development, and the value of those plans, depended on their purposes. Even highly standardized munitions, such as ammunition, took a long time to be manufactured in large quantities. The time required depended not only on the time directly necessary for production but also for procurement of materials and organization. If in addition it needed production capacity expansion, new product development, or product innovation, the time needed became longer. Munitions production in large quantities required production equipment and huge organizations.

Reliable plans and predictions were indispensable both for controlling activities in production organizations and for maintaining efficiency in coordinating the division of work. The unreliability and inaccuracy of the plans and predictions, together with the possibility of frequent changes, significantly damaged productive effectiveness and efficiency.[115]

Soon after the beginning of the War with China, Japan was to send troops outside the country in the greatest numbers in its history. Even if Japan could supply the munitions demanded from existing products (condition 1) and reliable plans and predictions about the war and its development were presented in advance to the supply side (condition 2), munitions supply must have suffered from serious disruption. In the War with China, neither condition was satisfied.

For Japan, the War with China began unexpectedly. No reliable war and operation plan had been prepared in advance for such a war. Moreover, when it abandoned the nonescalation policy it had adopted in the initial stages of the war, Japan escalated the war step by step to Shanghai, Nanjing, Xuzhou, Hankou, and Guangdong. A year into the conflict, even though the war had not reached the stage at which Japan was obliged to mobilize its entire national power, there were serious shortages of various materials and Japan could not afford to obtain materials to meet the demands of the

---

[115] For more details of this discussion, see Miwa (2008), particularly section 2–3, entitled "Peculiarities and Difficulties of 'War Mobilization' as a Policy Objective" (pp. 101–22).

military. Once it reached the limits of its military power and capacity to escalate the war further, with the second Konoe Proclamation in December 1938, Japan became resigned to a long, drawn-out war of attrition. After that, the no-way-out situation persisted, with no prospect of resolution or sign of improvement in war development. In the autumn of 1939, the Vice-ACCommander and the Army Minister agreed that Japan was "like a fruit rotten at the core," and predicted that the country's policy could not be maintained for much longer.

Chapter 1 detailed the reality of the second war mobilization over the course of the year ending in March 1939, three months after the second Konoe Proclamation. I find no sign in the following year of any improvement in the war situation. In the Army, the conflict of objectives intensified between rearmament for defense against the USSR and victory in the War with China. The constraints of the government budget had become much more binding. In addition, national exhaustion from the effect of long-term mobilization was beginning to take its toll on a wide variety of dimensions.

The conventional wisdom (or the dominant view) claims that Japan began and escalated the War with China on the basis of systematic war preparations. This view now seems not only false but also strange and bizarre.

The conventional wisdom also claims that Japan began the Pacific War in December 1941 on the same basis. However, Japan could already find no way out of a long, drawn-out war of attrition at least three years beforehand (December 1938). How could such Japan (or the Japanese military) have prepared systematically for the Pacific War? Some claim that Japan began systematic preparation for the Pacific War even before the beginning of the War with China or the Manchurian Incident in 1931. These claims are mere romance, and do not deserve careful review.

However, the task remains to specify when this drift toward no-way-out began.

2–6. Plans for Materials Mobilization, Production Capacity Expansion, and Manchuria

Many readers might still ask: "Everybody knows, at least in Japan, that there were many well-known plans, such as materials mobilization plans, production capacity expansion plans, and a five-year development plan in Manchuria. Why are you neglecting or denying even the existence of those plans?"

At the beginning of section 2–2, I called readers' attention to the meaning of expressions such as "plan," "forecast," and "vision," and the roles that those expressions have performed since the 1930s.[116] Independently of the pros and cons of my point, many readers are now more careful about the role that expressions such as "plan" could have played in the twentieth century, particularly in the 1930s. It is primarily because of the failure of the Soviet administrative-command economy, which "was the most important social and economic experiment of the twentieth century" (Gregory, 2004, p. 1).[117] Careful readers would be cautious about asking this question.

In the first two chapters of this book, I have shown that the existence and effectiveness of plans and visions are completely different things – as was the drawing up of plans and Japan's failure to respond promptly and appropriately to unexpected situations and events beyond the scope of the assumptions on which those plans were based. The key question is not whether such plans existed, but their effectiveness and the roles they performed.

A series of well-known plans (and related policies), such as materials mobilization plans and production capacity expansion plans, did not perform their roles effectively. This is the natural conclusion to the discussion in the last two chapters. In Part II, I take a case study approach to this conclusion, which constitutes an important part of this book and reinforces the discussion of the preceding chapters.

2–7. Appendix: Why Didn't Japan Stop the War on the Way?

Why didn't Japan stop the war on the way? Couldn't it simply stop? Suppose the peace negotiations had been successful. Could peace have been maintained? If so, for how long?[118]

At this stage, I hope that few readers still support the conventional wisdom about Japan's war plans and the development of the conflict with China. But many might be puzzled by these questions.

When the War with China began, Japan adopted a nonescalation policy based at least partly on a telling argument that the alternative was its commitment to a long, drawn-out conflict. The failure of the strategy to end the war

---

[116] For more details, see Miwa (2008), particularly sections 1–2 (pp. 43–56) and 2–2 (pp. 92–100) and subsection 2–3–4 (pp. 119–22).

[117] "The Nazi regime after 1936 was determined to transform the economy in ways which would serve the drive for empire and conquest." Preceding this, Overy (1994, pp. 16–17) wrote: "This process should not be seen in isolation. State intervention and 'planisme' was on the increase in all European economies. Arguments over the nationalization of industry emerged in Italy, France, and Britain in the 1930s.... Nor should this development be seen as a crude 'dualism', state on one side, industry on the other."

[118] This is the tenth puzzle in Miwa's (2008) Chapter 3, "10 Puzzles Associated with 'Wars', for Readers Supporting 'the Conventional Wisdom'" (pp. 213–18).

aggressively (the "one-blow theory") that had contained the nonescalation policy became apparent after the Battle of Shanghai. But the peace overtures following that battle did not end the war. During escalation of hostilities after the capture of Nanjing, the same pattern was observed repeatedly. At every stage, voices in Japan called for prompt resolution, which never manifested. Instead, the war ended in a complete defeat, after escalation into the Pacific War.[119]

In this appendix, I provide some background information that will answer readers' potential questions about processes and events that did not happen. These important issues have rarely been discussed, partly because of lack of clarity about past history and what actually occurred and the potent spell cast by the conventional, dominant view.

What would have been the consequence of stopping the war on the way? Could it have been done? Could the status quo[120] have been maintained, through a peace accord or voluntary withdrawal of troops? Suppose we look back from a vantage point a decade later; what would have been the feasible alternatives available to Japan?

For example, in December 1939 the ACCom proposed a radical change in its policy toward China to facilitate rearmament against the USSR, "[t]o withdraw military force step by step from Wuhan and Guangdong, and concentrate it both in the triangle zone of Shanghai, Nanjing, and Hangzhou and in the key areas of Mongolia and Xinjiang" (Boeicho, 1967a, p. 627).[121] Suppose this proposal had actually been executed? Or suppose the peace overture after the second Konoe Proclamation on a new order in East Asia had been successful, with China endorsing Japan's interest in some part of occupied areas?[122]

---

[119] Imoto (1978, pp. 185–6) wrote in the "afterword" to Chapter 1 on the situation in 1937: "On the whole, the Chinese military retreated without fighting, and abandoned the five vast provinces in North China. They put up long and stubborn resistance in Shanghai, largely because Japan countered with such small numbers of troops. When Japan increased the size of its force and made preparations for adequate operations, the Chinese began a full retreat, and abandoned fighting all the way to their capital Nanjing.

Yet China never surrendered, which was completely counter to the view dominant in Japan – and which had led Japan to escalate the war – that China would surrender at the first sign of force and that the war would continue for a further three months at most. What was needed at the time was a thorough reexamination of China's war plan. But this we could not do...."

[120] The same puzzles hold for scenarios such as "Japan could have stopped escalation of the war and maintained the occupied areas" and "the belligerent power could have surrendered."

[121] In December 1939, the ACCom reported to the Emperor the "Revised Armament Enhancement Plan." The change in policy toward China was proposed as its part. See Miwa (2008, 3-7-5, pp. 201–3).

[122] Around this time, there were many peace overtures through various routes. The most well known was the so-called *kiri-kosaku* (paulownia operation or overture) from the end of 1939 to mid-September 1940. See Miwa (2008, 3-7-5, pp. 201–3).

Few readers will propose optimistic answers to these puzzles. We tend to forget what a staff officer in charge of operations at the General Headquarters of the Japanese Expeditionary Force in China recalled (Imoto, 1978, pp. 400–1):

Japan had sent large armies of 700,000 to China, actually fighting at the front or getting ready to fight. Even inside our occupied areas, enemy forces put down roots and people were in spirit hostile to Japan, which made it hard even to maintain security. It was a false idea to promote policies inconsistent with the reality, neglecting the situation in China. It was based on a false illusion that the Chinese people in occupied areas were cooperative toward Japan, and shared Japan's attitude toward Chiang Kai-shek. In addition, the policy to instill in the Chinese the view that the Japan–China relationship was founded on cooperation and goodwill not only misled Japanese soldiers at the front but also attracted the scorn of the enemy.

Here more fundamental puzzles emerge: Was the temporary peace or cease-fire just a switch from an offensive to a defensive strategy, one moreover that was mediocre and undesirable? What feasible alternatives were available to Japan? And were they really feasible?

Suppose we could turn back the clock to the situation before the beginning of the War with China; and suppose Japan could withdraw troops to Manchuria and maintain this situation peacefully. Who could accomplish this, and how? Could the military, the Army in particular, that allegedly led Japan to war do it? Could the government do it? Was it a feasible option available to Japan at any point after the beginning of the War with China?

Again, there are few optimistic answers to these questions. Strategy Section Chief Kawabe's recollection of the situation from the capture of Nanjing to the first Konoe Proclamation "not to deal with the National Chinese government" (16 January 1938) summed up the situation (see section 2–4–2). The same holds for the situation just after the beginning of the War with China. At 8:00 P.M. on 11 July, the local cease-fire agreement for the Lukouch'iau Incident was established. Later that night, receiving a report that China accepted all the Japanese demands, the expectation of a nonescalation policy and local resolution became dominant among Army leaders. But the Kuanganment Incident of 25 July and the Langfang Incident of 27 July caused panic. On the morning of 28 July, "the Army began a battle to discipline the Chinese Twenty-Ninth Army. Journalists praised the government's resolution without reservation, and the general public with high excitement enjoyed the war without reflection. The situation changed radically, getting fired up beyond control" (Ishii, 1950, pp. 278–9).[123]

---

[123] Ishii was then the East Asia Bureau Chief of the Foreign Ministry. Boeicho (1967a, pp. 126–7) commented that similar phenomena were observed at the time of pacification

There was no possibility of reaching an agreement in the Japan–U.S. negotiation in 1941 "unless Japan had been prepared to return to the situation before the Manchurian Incident" (Hara, 1987, p. 156). Referring to the so-called Hull note[124] of 26 November 1941 that became the direct trigger of the Pacific War, Sejima (1995, p. 171) concluded that "in sum, it was a complete denial of Japan's policy toward the continent since the Meiji era": "There were two major points in our policy toward the continent. One was the interests that Japan acquired in the Treaty of Portsmouth following victory in the Russo–Japanese War: leasehold of South Manchurian Railways Company and Kwantung Leased Territory and the right to station troops there. It was U.S. President Theodore D. Roosevelt who mediated the treaty. It was an internationally approved definite interest. The other was the cultivation of Manchukuo, which was established as a consequence of the Manchurian Incident."[125]

The conventional view holds that the Manchurian Incident was to solve the so-called Mongolia-Xinjiang problem. Lieutenant Colonel Ishiwara, who played a key role in this Incident as a staff officer in the Kwantung Army, became convinced that (Boeicho, 1967a, p.310): "Japan had only

in both the Sino–Japanese War and the Russo–Japanese War. "In the Sino–Japanese War Japan won a victory not against the whole Shin Dynasty but against Li Hung Chang and his armies, including the Beiyang Fleet that he had established and controlled. In the Russo–Japanese War Japan did not fight against the whole country. Instead Japan defeated the Russian Imperial Army. Japan was assisted by the revolution movement in Russia." It also commented on the pacification of the Russo–Japanese War: "It was an extremely prudent choice for policy makers to obtain peace upon such unsatisfactory conditions. But not only during but also after the war they did not explain this truth to the public and the military. The general public, excitedly celebrating victory, did not understand the vulnerable reality of national defense, tending rather to disregard its importance." Chihaya (1982, pp. 123–4), a former Navy staff officer, also wrote: "In those wars the complexion of the war did not depend solely on the operations executed. I have a strong feeling that it was due rather to Providence or luck." Hara (1987, pp. 99–100) offered commentary in relation to the Tripartite Pact: "When Duke Konoe received an Imperial Order to form his second Cabinet in July 1940, public opinion, both all media organizations and political parties, spectacularly trumpeted and enjoyed the switch to pro-Axis diplomacy from pro–American-British diplomacy. It was the Tripartite Pact that the second Konoe Cabinet must tackle carefully as the top priority of tasks. But Duke Konoe, being pushed by overwhelmingly strong public opinion and instead going along with the wish of the public, at the time or prior to the Imperial Order decided to take the path to the Tripartite Pact." Hara's commentary continued: "also Navy Minister Oikawa attached his mind to public opinion" (pp. 101–3).

124 The Hull note (Outline of proposed basis for agreement between the United States and Japan) was the final proposal delivered to Japan by the US before the beginning of the Pacific War. It is named for Secretary of State Cordell Hull.

125 On the so-called "Mongolia-Xinjiang problem" and the Manchurian Incident, see also sections 6–3 and 6–4.

the alternative of full retreat or resolution by force. Now that China had acquired a greater sense of national independence and recovery of sovereign right, it was an infeasible dream to expect to secure the vested interest through Shidehara diplomacy." According to this view, the basic policy firmly maintained by succeeding Cabinets that "Japan must ensure the interests in Mongolia and Xinjiang that it acquired in the Sino-Japanese War and the Russo-Japanese War, at the cost of 100,000 war dead" would most probably result in a collision between Japan and China. This would have been the case even without the War with China and the Manchurian Incident.[126]

"What policy Japan should adopt toward China (the policy on the continent) after the RussoJapanese War was a really important issue for the course of Japan during the period that followed.... If Japan had established a policy consistent with the view of Hirobumi Ito, history would be different."[127] With this statement, Imoto (1978, pp. 25-7) introduced an episode at the *Genros* [founding fathers]-ministers Conference of 22 May 1906 on Manchurian problems. It was during the time of first Saionji Cabinet, and the conference was led by Ito, then Resident-General of Korea:

Emphasizing that "on this occasion, Japan should execute the foreign policy toward Manchuria and China it declared to major powers on the eve of the Russo–Japanese War," Ito presented a detailed execution plan. In relation to foreign policy he warned: "Without joining in the group of major powers grabbing overseas' interests, Japan must stand in its position as a leader to China and must prevent conflict

---

[126] "The Greater East Asian War began because the U.S. denied the Japanese policy on the continent. Even with Shidehara's diplomacy, or international collaboration, Japan would be forced to liquidate its continental policy." Hara drew this conclusion from the following view (Hara, 1987, p. 34). "Could Shidehara's diplomacy secure Japan's special position or vested interest in Mongolia and Xinjiang? The so-called special interest had not been approved in the Nine-Power Treaty of 1922. With the welling up nationalism in revolutionary China, Japan would ultimately be forced to abandon its vested interests as well. This would mean the complete liquidation of Japanese continental policy maintained since the Sino–Japanese War and the Russo–Japanese War. It might be the inescapable course of history; however the general public of the time could not endure it." Nishiura (1968, pp. 328–9) argued further that "without the Japan–U.S. negotiation there would have been no Hull note, and without the Hull note no war between Japan and the U.S.," and continued: "It was Japan's destiny finally to retreat completely from China or Manchuria, Korea, and Taiwan. What is not so clear is whether it was bad or not that the Japan–U.S. negotiation became a trigger to liquidate the Japan–U.S. disputes."

[127] There must be many different views about Imoto's conclusion: "If..., history would be different." Recall that the BNDP was for the first time formulated in 1907, and it originated from Marshal Duke Aritomo Yamagata's appeal to the Emperor in October 1906. He was the virtual Army leader during this period. See notes 42 and 43 earlier in this chapter. For the details of political situation of the time, see Oka (1958).

between the major powers and China. For this, Japan must take measures to create a Japan-friendly atmosphere in China and encourage the Shin Dynasty to trust Japan. However, Japan's policy after the achievement of peace has gone against this. Given this situation, Japan's attempts to overcome difficulties in Manchuria for the benefit of China will be disregarded, and our Empire will become a target of the hate and jealousy of the Shin Dynasty. It is really a false policy for the Empire." Having no other choice than to admit that Ito was right, the participants of the Conference superficially agreed. In fact, however, they hoped to secure and expand Japanese interests in Manchuria and to take a vantage point in mainland China. (Imoto, 1978, pp. 25–6).

At this time, too, neither policy makers nor the general public took sufficiently into consideration the truth that Japan's victories were largely due to the assistance of supporting countries, the UK and the United States in particular.

Hara (1987) wrote in the author's afterword (pp. 335–6)[128]:

Basically Japan lacked a body for war leadership, that is, to manage administration, war, and operations in an integrated fashion. Instead, Japan dealt with those issues through a council system with the ACCommander and the NCCommander as the heads of Army and Navy, and the Prime, Army, Navy, Foreign, and other Ministers as the heads of administration. It was usually called "the IH-government Liaison Conference." Of the Liaison Conferences, those held in the Presence of the Emperor were specifically called "*gozen-kaigi*".... Japan's war leadership was nothing more than the operation of this "Liaison Conference." With the tyranny of the military, particularly the Army, the self-righteousness of diplomacy, the conflict between the Army and the Navy, the fighting inside the supreme command, and so on, the Liaison Conference was preoccupied with controversy – like sheep without a shepherd. Establishing the war objectives, defining the advance limit of the military, understanding the measures for ending the war – those fundamental issues and basic principles of war leadership were never considered seriously.

Hara (1987, p. 71) concluded: "In this way, the independence of the supreme command ..., the posts of the military ministers on active service, together with the weak authority of the Prime Minister, the lethal conflict between the Army and the Navy, the infeasibility of legally establishing a

---

[128] Shiro Hara was a staff officer. When the Pacific War began, he was at the Twentieth Subsection (so-called the War Leadership Subsection) of the IH-AD, whose main task was to coordinate the administration of the government with the IH's war strategy. It was the administration authority of the IH-AD concerning war leadership. The author of Tanemura (1979) was in the same subsection. After the war, in the War History Chamber in National Institute for Defense Studies of Boeicho (Japan Defense Agency, now the Ministry of Defense [Japan]), he wrote *Details of the Beginning of the Greater East Asian War from the Side of the IH-AD* in 5 volumes, as part of Boeicho's *Library of War History* in 102 volumes. *The Beginning of a War Without a Grand Strategy* (Hara, 1987) was "a consideration to add his personal comments" on the content of *Details*.

permanent institution for war leadership, the military-first policy of the state, were all the outcome of the institutional framework under the Meiji Constitution. They were not the result of the tyranny of a high-handed military. Indeed, the structure of state power under the Meiji Constitution, although it appeared thoroughly concentrated and integrated, was in substance scattered."

It is my conjecture that, after absorbing these points, few readers will give optimistic answers to the questions posed presented at the start of this appendix.

PART II

MATERIALS MOBILIZATION PLANS, PRODUCTION CAPACITY EXPANSION PLANS, AND ECONOMIC CONTROL

Part II investigates government more than military competence by examining representative plans and policies for war mobilization and economic control in wartime Japan. This section focuses on the MMPlans and PCEPlans, particularly because they involved the supply and distribution of basic materials.

Introducing Part II, Chapter 3 discusses the historical context of the 1930s, when there was wide support for both planning and a planned economy, and for the idea of control and systems of control. Chapter 4 investigates in detail the practical effectiveness of the MMPlans. Chapter 5 investigates the details of the PCEPlans. Although the conventional wisdom emphasizes the PCEPlans as the backbone of systematic war preparations begun in the early 1930s, the Cabinet actually approved the outline for these plans in January 1939, a year and a half after the beginning of the War with China. This chapter also focuses on Japanese production capacity expansion policies not included in the PCEPlans. As Manchuria dominates both historical theories and the conventional wisdom about Japan, I devote Chapter 6 as a whole to the study of production capacity expansion policies in Manchukuo (Japanese-occupied Manchuria).

Part II concludes that Japan does not merit a high score for state competence, in a situation where its realization and manifestation were crucial. Japan's government is widely considered competent enough to have developed the nation into one of the world's most developed economies in over a century and a half. Nonetheless, I find the performance of this allegedly competent state, even when performance mattered most, desultory at best.

3

Economic Planning and Control in Wartime Japan: General Discussion

3-1. Overview

Starting in the autumn of 1937, Japan's economy rapidly shifted to a system under direct state control. "Plan" and "planning" were the key words that characterized this era. Admiration of socialist planned economies, due to the fact that the USSR had achieved its apparently rapid development through "the first Five-Year Plan" (Nakamura, 1989, p. 9) was an important historical precedent that prompted the radical adoption of state control just after the start of the War with China. The Russian model inspired Japanese plans and controls during this period and has until recently shaped historical and academic studies of wartime Japan.

Section 3-2, "Plans, Control and Planning: The Era, Situation, and Historical Background," begins by referring to a representative view of "the age of planning," and then discusses the planned economy under Stalin's dictatorship. Section 3-3 briefly reviews wartime control, critiquing the conventional wisdom about war preparations in Japan, and discussing the PCEPlans. Section 3-4 reviews major control laws, including the Temporary Import Export Grading (TIEG) Act of September 1937 and the National General Mobilization (NGM) Act of April 1938. Section 3-5 focuses on two other aspects of effective war mobilization: control associations and the Munitions Company Act of October 1943. Section 3-6 is a brief summary of this chapter and makes special reference to petroleum.

3-2. Plans, Control, and Planning: The Era, Situation, and Historical Background

3-2-1. Plans and Economic Control

After September–October 1937, Japan's economy rapidly shifted to a system under direct state control. "Plan" and "planning" were the key words that characterized this era. In 1989, leading economic historians in Japan published *The Japanese Economic History* (Umemura et al., pp. 1988–9) in eight volumes. The editor of volume 7, *Planning and Democratization*, which covers the period of 1937 to 1954, explains the historical background that prompted Japan's government to activate economic controls immediately after the start of the War with China, in July 1937.

Nakamura (1989, pp. 8–9) argues that the increase in public expenditure for the war caused a shortage of goods and inflation, increasing imports and tipping the international balance of payments toward catastrophe. The TIEG Act was enacted in September 1937. Under this act, the government designated items that it could restrict, prohibiting their import or export. The production, rationing, transfer, use, and consumption of products manufactured using designated items were also restricted.

According to Nakamura, in October 1937, the Planning Agency and Office of Resources were merged to form the Planning Council, which controlled planning and coordination for the expansion and use of total national power during both peacetime and war. Between October and December 1937, this new ministry took over the business of national general mobilization from the Office of Resources. It oversaw various plans, including the MMPlans, responsible for trade, finance, and labor mobilization, and the PCEPlans. The Planning Council assumed the role of the Central Command for Economic Control.[1]

Nakamura points out that widely accepted negative views of capitalism and laissez-faire economics played a critical role in decision making at this time.

Note that, as shown in Chapter 1, most important control laws were enacted after the beginning of the War with China. The TIEG Act was announced and came into force on 10 September 1937. The NGM Act was announced on 1 April 1938 and came into force on 5 May 1938.

---

[1] This is a translation of *sanbo honbu*, as I translate *rikugun sanbo honbu* into the Army Central Command. Chapter 4 of Johnson (1982) is entitled "Economic General Staff," which is a translation of *keizai sanbo honbu* (p. 117). Usually *keizai* is translated as "economic" or "economy."

In this historical context, various plans were formulated and economic controls implemented. However, the following six situations were anticipated to appear. Obviously, the existence of plans and visions does not guarantee their effectiveness; putting control laws and policies in place is not the same thing as enforcing them or to achieving policy goals. Verifying the effectiveness of such plans and controls requires careful examination.[2]

1. The state established a specialized institution (the Central Command of the Economy) that provided a framework for various plans, standardizing and coordinating them. This basic, overarching vision provided a foundation for various subsidiary plans.
2. It was assumed that every policy or action taken by a government office would conform closely to the basic vision. As this conformity was required when making a budgetary request, most policies proposed by government offices would naturally adopt formats that appeared to conform to the basic vision, while emphasizing their contribution toward achieving it.
3. As a consequence of these two points, institutions modeled on the Central Command of the Economy would be established throughout the government. Their primary task would be to formulate, oversee, and control plans formulated in the ministries to which they belonged. For this reason, the institutions exercising economic control would occupy a senior position relative to other units in the ministry. They would provide an environment conducive to plan formulation by other units, thus creating a flood of plans everywhere in the ministry.
4. The formulation and implementation of policies in conformity with the basic plan was consistent with the interest of all relevant parties. It became difficult to criticize such policies or to question their effectiveness, with the result that many ineffective plans were implemented and maintained. There was no feedback mechanism to bring these to the attention of the Central Command of the Economy or its equivalent

---

[2] The same applies to any policy that includes plans and controls. For example, it is generally argued that the Priority Production Scheme (*keisha seisan seido*, PPS) adopted in Japan just after the war to route crucial economic resources (such as coal) to critical sectors (such as steel) worked effectively and contributed greatly to the recovery of the Japanese economy after wartime destruction. But, as we saw elsewhere in Miwa and Ramseyer (2004a, 2005a, 2009a, 2009b), this view is based neither on clear logic nor persuasive evidence. Moreover, this view fundamentally contradicts empirical observations. In this sense, it is a false view, a misconception, or a myth that fatally deviates from the reality. The same holds true for the postwar Japanese industrial policy effectiveness theory. For this, see Miwa and Ramseyer (2002a, 2006).

institutions in the government offices responsible for formulating and implementing the basic vision and plans.

5. To call a set of related documents a plan tends to endorse and upgrade it. A discussion that is not a plan will not attract the attention or support of the general public, media, or politicians. For this reason, plans proliferate until they include even schedules for the quarterly purchase of materials, budgets, and theoretical concepts (paper or desk plans).
6. This proliferation causes interest in the effectiveness of plans and practical policy measures to decrease. With no accountability, ineffective plans and policies increase and flourish. Documents called plans quite often include budget requests and internal memos expressing general hopes and presenting wish lists.

These six situations can be seen as a natural consequence of the age of "planning and economic control," necessitating careful examination of the effectiveness of plans, policies, mobilization, and control. Readers should not accept without empirical evidence the conventional wisdom that Japan's plans, policies, mobilization, and control functioned effectively during this period.

Conditions Necessary for the Effective Functioning of Plans, Controls, and Mobilization

In confirming the effectiveness of mobilization and control policies and other plans, it is necessary to ask the following questions:

- What were the policy measures?
- Was government the central player implementing these policies?
- Did the right conditions exist for government to implement these policy measures effectively?
- Did existing conditions allow the policies to function effectively? For example, didn't the black market and similar factors invalidate controls?
- Could the government implement policy measures on a scale large enough to achieve its stated goals? For example, was it possible to fully fund its production capacity expansion plans?

Before examining the effectiveness of economic control, it is necessary to ask what the government actually controlled. Did it really control all goods? Were there no loopholes? What did the government hope to achieve through policies that restricted the use of some materials or foreign currencies? Careful examination of each target industry is necessary to confirm the effectiveness of individual controls. The existence of laws and government documents reporting on the effective implementation of controls does not provide sufficient evidence.

Control laws allowed the government, within specified limits, to impose restrictions on the freedom of choice of relevant decision-making bodies such as individuals and firms. It is extremely difficult to answer the following questions using either the laws themselves or the records of government bodies:

- Did the government actually impose restrictions?
- How strongly were the restrictions enforced?
- Were the restrictions binding and effective in controlling behavior?

Such well-known control laws as the TIEG Act and NGM Act are no exception.

Material Mobilization Plans (MMPlans)

Under the MMPlans, the control price of a targeted good was set below the market-clearing price, creating excess demand. The MMPlan was working effectively when the prioritized allocation of goods contributed to expanding the targeted industries. If targeted goods were resold at higher prices on the black market, then this plan was largely invalidated and ineffective.

MMPlans aimed to expand the production of targeted materials and products (for example, in the shipbuilding industry), but the most they could achieve was to increase the allocation of controlled materials, such as steel to shipbuilders. Many readers must wonder why the government did not simply raise the price of ships. To prove that the MMPlans worked effectively will require more evidence than this.

Restricting foreign currencies was an essential part of the MMPlans at the initial stage. By setting the price of foreign currency at a low level and creating excess demand, the government expected to achieve policy goals through prioritized allocation.

Production Capacity Expansion Plans (PCEPlans)

The PCEPlans also flourished during the period under study. To evaluate the effectiveness of the PCEPlans, it is indispensable to ask and examine the following questions:

- What policy measures were involved?
- Did the right conditions exist for the government to achieve its goals effectively?
- Did conditions allow the policies to function effectively?

The PCEPlans were designed not only to develop and improve products and to increase production in designated industries, but also to increase production capacity in related industries. Improvements to the machine tool industry, for example, would benefit all industries that manufactured machinery. To evaluate the effectiveness of the PCEPlans, it is therefore necessary to focus on five additional points:

1. Even in expanding production capacity for existing products, it is by no means easy to give private firms a sufficient incentive to realize investments. Capacity expansion and product development, however, have a long-term impact on a firm's profitability.
2. When creating a new industry or technical innovation, it is not enough for the government to appoint entrepreneurs and firms chosen from among motivated applicants; there is a risk of inefficiency. This was a weakness of the PCEPlans. For example, the aircraft manufacturing industry was required to produce five hundred heavy long-range bombers annually; this plan became all but meaningless and useless because it did not include specific information on who would implement it and how.
3. Even less innovative industries faced similar difficulties. A plan to manufacture more bearings with varied specifications raised the question of who would implement it and how. Only a limited number of firms could produce the required bearings.
4. Industries were mutually interdependent, and the performance of an individual industry's plan depended on the smooth functioning and efficiency of its suppliers, as they provided raw materials and equipment. When asked to cooperate with the automobile production capacity expansion plan in Manchuria, Yoshisuke Aikawa, the Chairman of Nissan Industries, immediately refused, citing underdevelopment in related industries.[3]
5. The Five-Year Development Plan in Manchuria set a precedent for other PCEPlans. As suggested by the Army in Tokyo, the ACCom in particular, representatives from the Kwantung Army, Manchukuo, and the South Manchuria Railways Company gathered together at a conference in Taggangzi (near Anshan), where, referencing a one-page memorandum from the ACCom, they compiled the basic plan in three days.[4] In Japan, creating a PCEPlan was difficult and took a long time. The military's total war regime idea, in vogue since the

---

[3] Hoshino (1963, p. 223). For the details, see section 4–6.
[4] Hoshino (1963, pp. 206–9). For the details, see section 4–6.

Manchurian Incident, was put into effect temporarily in Manchuria as the "Five-Year Development Plan in Manchuria," which was later evaluated quite favorably (Oishi, 1994, p. 14), thus implementing a plan described as "a test of the *living-body experiment* type for economic control" (Ando, 1972, p. 469; italicized text underlined in the original). Why was this plan put into effect first in Manchuria? Who implemented the plan, and did it work effectively? As I will show, no one has ever evaluated the Five-Year Development Plan's effectiveness or examined its policies in detail.

3-2-2. The Planned Economy Under Stalin's Dictatorship

Nakamura's (1989, p. 9) explanation of the historical background that prompted Japan's government to activate controls after the beginning of the War with China is still the dominant view, and became so just after the war. Today it is also believed that the postwar socialist government's plans were implemented effectively and efficiently, while its interventionist policies, represented by the so-called Priority Production Scheme (PPS), were remarkably successful.[5] Reflecting the perceived success of New Deal policies in the United States, highly interventionist government policies were introduced and accepted with wide support in Japan under the occupation.

What is remarkable and peculiar to Japan is the strength of this influence and the longevity of the conventional wisdom. Although support for this view peaked in the 1960s and began gradually to decline, it remains strong even in the twenty-first century. The following point illustrates the need for a full-scale review of the foundations of the conventional wisdom:

The Soviet administrative-command economy was the most important social and economic experiment of the twentieth century. Its failure continues to reverberate throughout those countries in Europe, Asia, and Latin America that adopted it, either forcibly or voluntarily.... The former administrative-command economies have had to confront their pasts as they make their transitions to market economies. Empirical studies show that the heavier the imprint of the administrative-command system, the more difficult has been the transition. (Gregory, 2004, p. 1)

What we witnessed during the confusion-to-collapse process of the former USSR demonstrates the failure of its administrative command economy

---

[5] On this view, recall note 2.

(ACE). The opening of formerly secret Soviet state and party archives in the early 1990s was an event of profound significance (Gregory, 2001, p. vii).

The remarkable onset and rapid development of the deregulation process in the majority of advanced market economies paralleled the confusion and collapse of the ACE in the socialist countries of the former USSR.

The USSR's much praised rapid development, the result of its "first Five-Year Plan" (Nakamura, 1989, p. 9), was an important part of the historical background that prompted Japan's radical adoption of economic control just after the beginning of the War with China. The Soviet model not only shaped plans and controls during this period, but it has influenced, at least until very recently, many studies of Japan. However, recent studies of the Soviet planned economy under Stalin's dictatorship demonstrate that it was not based on plans and systematically managed. Praise of the socialist planned economy was itself an important part of the historical background; thus, a key assumption was a misconception based on a misunderstanding about the Soviet planned economy.

As shown in Chapter 2, in Japan it was unclear who occupied the position of ultimate leadership in war; the country had neither dictators like Hitler and Stalin, nor strong leaders like Roosevelt, Chiang Kai-shek, and Churchill. Chapters 3 and 4 address the question: how would the socialist planned economy under Stalin's dictatorship have worked if there had been no Stalin?

A surprising archival discovery has been the near total absence of final approved plans from the USSR's ministries and enterprises of this socialist planned economy; the only plans found have been labeled "draft" or "preliminary." Gosplan was established in February 1921 to draft and implement a unified state plan for the whole economy, coordinating the plans of other economic departments (Gregory and Harrison, 2005, pp. 727, 729).

Stalin and his Politburo "guided the general direction of the economy by infrequent major decisions that set aggregate investment, which they poorly controlled, while reserving the right to make unlimited detailed interventions in current operations. Minor decisions were delegated from top to bottom through a hierarchy of 'nested' dictatorship. Formal rules were avoided in favor of ad hoc decision making. A compliant planning board was disengaged from responsibility for detailed allocation to guarantee its loyalty; the dictator was particularly loathe to delegate economic decisions to politically unreliable technocrats. As a result, delegation did not work well: subordinates funneled even trivial decisions upwards to limit their own exposure, placing a 'dictator's curse'[6] of excessive administrative burdens on their superiors at each level, most heavily on Stalin himself" (Gregory and Harrison, 2005, p. 753).

Faced with provisional plans and the prospect of endless interventions, enterprises and ministries sometimes refused to commit to plans; some enterprises operated without plans for years. Resource allocation by intervention rather than plan is consistent with the dictator's aversion to formal rules (Gregory and Harrison, 2005, p. 754).

The conventional wisdom that Gosplan exercised considerable executive power over allocation requires revision: Gosplan was important, but it was not powerful, and surprisingly sought to limit its own power (Gregory and Harrison, 2005, p. 727).

Symbolically, Stalin wrote in 1937: "Only bureaucrats can think that planning work ends with the creation of the plan. *The creation of the plan is only the beginning*" (Gregory and Harrison, 2005, p. 730; italics in the original text).

Calculation and incentive, the focus of the long-lasting socialist controversy, did not play an important role. The Soviet regime was indifferent to calculation, preoccupied by the need to punish and deter its enemies, and bent on implementing its decisions through a complex administrative hierarchy of agents motivated by threats and promises (Gregory and Harrison, 2005, p. 724).

Even today, in the twenty-first century, the conclusions of recent archival studies on Stalin's planned economy are not widely known in Japan. The same is true for studies reevaluating the U.S. New Deal and German economic policy and rearmament during the Third Reich.[7] Efforts have been made to introduce this research to Japan, but political scientists and historians who subscribe to the dominant view have discouraged them. Their opposition has made the introduction of such studies unprofitable and their acceptance difficult. It was in this environment that the eighth volume of *Japanese Economic History* was published, around 1989.

The same difficulties characterize the study of Japanese policies – including systematic war preparations, mobilization, and economic control – in the 1930s and 1940s. The conventional wisdom, epitomized by the key words "plan" and "planning" and a commitment to the remarkable performance of

---

[6] The result was a "dictator's curse": despite the intention to delegate, Stalin had to make many more decisions than he wished (Gregory and Harrison, 2005, p. 723).

[7] Similarly, in Japan there has been no reexamination of the dominant view of the UK during this period, or of the "declinist" view of twentieth-century Britain. See Taylor (1964), Overy (1994), Rockoff (1998), and Edgerton (2006), or briefly Miwa (2008, Introduction, pp. 5–8). Recall note 7 of the Introduction of this volume.

Stalin's socialist planned economy, has discouraged all efforts to reevaluate this period. As few Japanese academics or opinion leaders question the dominant view or call for the conventional wisdom to be reexamined, the dominant view has remained unchanged.

In Japan, planning and economic policy in prewar and wartime Japan are two sides of the same coin, reinforcing each other. Most commentators overvalue the competence of the state and assume outstanding performance in both areas.

The flaws in the Soviet planned economy became apparent to its leaders almost immediately (Gregory and Harrison, 2005, p. 724). It seems reasonable to assume that flaws in Japan's systematic war preparations, mobilization, and economic control must have been similarly apparent at least to its own leaders; this is consistent with the conclusions of this volume, particularly in Part II. The "outstanding performance" message was promoted among the public during wartime and became dominant after the war when the socialist government took power under the occupation; officials who had been on the spot kept almost entirely silent.

3–3. Wartime Control

3–3–1. An Overview: Oishi's Explanation

The view that I refer to in this volume as "the conventional wisdom" is taken from Kaichiro Oishi's introduction to *The History of Japanese Imperialism 3: The World War II* (1994), a collection of papers by Japanese economic historians, edited by Oishi. I refer to this introduction as a reference point for readers; although the views of economic historians have differed widely in their detail, they share the same basic framework. Oishi's explanation can be summarized in nine points[8]:

1. PCEPlans for a total war regime were established before the beginning of the War with China.
2. The idea of the military's total war regime, in vogue since the Manchurian Incident, was put into effect temporarily in Manchuria as the Five-Year Development Plan in Manchuria.

---

[8] On the view of Oishi (1994, pp. 14–15), summarized here and in detail, see Miwa (2008, pp. 93–9). Oishi's (1994) work includes many ill-defined and ambiguous key words. I choose his book because it is representative, encompassing most economic historians working on relevant issues. There seems to be neither a serious conflict of opinion among contributors nor any critical comments in the editor's *Introduction* by Oishi.

3. After the attempted coup of February 1936 (the so-called 2.26 Incident), the Japanese politico-economic system was reorganized along fascist lines.
4. The idea of a military total war regime was officially approved by the government and the business community early in 1937; with "the military-business embracing," it became the Three Principles of Public Finance and the Economy under the first Konoe Cabinet, formed in June.
5. Economic control began at the end of 1936 in response to an international payment crisis, focusing on import control.
6. Following the military total war regime, the Three Principles of Public Finance and the Economy first emphasized expanding production capacity, together with balancing international payments and coordinating the supply and demand of materials.
7. PCEPlans under state control were designed to develop military industries and other industries supplying basic materials, in order to create a production capacity system able to sustain a major war waged in both the homeland and the colonies. Effective policy enforcement assumed the effective implementation of economic controls (Oishi makes no distinction between policy and plan).
8. Immediately after the beginning of the War with China in July 1937 (before most leaders anticipated a long war), the government established the Applying the Munitions Industry Mobilization Act, the TIEG, and the Temporary Funds Coordination, and began economic controls.
9. The NGM Act was enacted in April 1938; as war escalated, controls expanded to include the whole economy.

Oishi's view, summarized in the preceding list, includes so many ill-defined key words and arguments that it is difficult to understand his intentions or meaning.[9] The following questions focus on the PCEPlans:

- What is the definition of the "military-business embracing"? Is its meaning clear? Was it a pact?
- Was the meaning of "officially approved by the government and the business community" clear?

[9] I thus present eight questions for readers to ask themselves in Miwa (2008, pp. 94–9). The first one begins: who were "the military" that led the process and executed "the military-business embracing"? Is there a common understanding and agreement among supporters of "the conventional wisdom" and "the dominant view"?

- What documents did they officially approve? (It cannot have been the PCEPlans, as these did not exist in 1937. The outline version was approved by the Cabinet for the first time in January 1939.)
- Did the Three Principles place the top priority on expanding production capacity? With increasing demand, particularly for goods containing imported materials and products, balancing international payments became an urgent policy priority. Next in order of importance was the coordination of the supply and demand of materials, enabling key resources to be allocated to specified areas at prices under inflation. Faced with difficulties in attaining those goals, the government chose to increase the supply of materials by expanding production capacity. Were they sure this could be effectively carried out and enforced? Might this have been a mere placebo or excuse?
- Was the expanding production capacity for key industries directly focused on the military industries?
- The conventional wisdom conflates two terms: the PCEPlans and the Production Capacity Expansion Policy. Oishi draws his conclusions from the PCEPlans,[10] even though they did not exist at the time. If the policy was being enforced before the Army presented its PCEPlans, who proposed, approved, and implemented it? Could this policy have been effective? Did it meet the Army's requirements, and if so, how? Why, in June 1937, did the Army present its Outline of a Five-Year Plan for Key Industries to the government?

3-3-2. The PCEPlans and the Production Capacity Expansion Policy

The PCEPlans are key to the conventional wisdom summarized by Oishi (1994), for the following reasons:

1. The PCEPlans were established before the beginning of the War with China.
2. They were designed to support total war.
3. They were put into effect temporarily in Manchuria as the Five-Year Development Plan in Manchuria.

---

[10] As I mentioned in section VI of the Introduction, Gregory (2004, p. 133) argues: "Early writers on the administrative-command economy ... paid little attention to the manner in which the dictatorship would organize its bureaucratic staff to manage producers.... Students of dictatorships also simplified it by assuming 'costless coercion'; namely, that the dictator could costlessly persuade subordinates to do his bidding." By assuming costless coercion, the distinction between a dictator's plan and its enforcement is unnecessary.

4. They aimed to create a new production capacity system for a major war.
5. Effective policy enforcement assumed the effective implementation of economic controls.

If the PCEPlans did not exist before the start of the War with China, Oishi's argument loses substance and proves nothing. However, only the Five-Year Plan for Key Industries formulated by the Army existed before the beginning of the war. On 17 June 1937, the Army presented an outline of its Five-Year Plan for Key Industries to the Planning Agency.[11] On 7 July 1937, when the War with China began, not even the deliberation framework had been established for the future PCEPlans. It was not until 17 January 1939, about a year and a half later, that the PCEPlans outline was adopted by the Cabinet. The outline included no specific policy measures, key individuals, or measures of feasibility and effectiveness.

Questions emerge also about the claim that the PCEPlans were put into effect temporarily in Manchuria as the "Five-Year Development Plan in Manchuria": Who put it into effect and how? How was it possible that this plan could have been used in Manchukuo while it had not yet been approved in Japan? Did it work effectively?

The Manchurian plan was designed to create a new production capacity system for major war. Was Japan expecting its war with China to become "major," or anticipating a Pacific War, or a war with the USSR that never occurred? Who was the imagined enemy? Was a major war really expected?

According to economic historian Yasuyuki Maeda (MITI, 1964, p. 125), expanding production capacity was seriously considered for the first time by the first Konoe Cabinet, formed on 4 June 1937. The Hayashi Cabinet, formed in February 1937, had laid the groundwork by discussing expansion of production capacity as a key policy. On 20 April, Finance Minister Yuuki described inflation as a social problem and spoke on the record about his view that the expansion of production capacity would naturally increase the supply of products. He called on individuals to contribute to national objectives through great creative activities. In line with the "enhancement of national defense" described in Finance Minister Baba's finance policy, Yuuki intended to hold down the inflation caused by a military budget increase by expanding production capacity. It is here that Yuuki's finance policy promoted the idea of a pact between the military aiming to enhance national

---

[11] For the original text of the plan and the outline, see MITI (1964, pp. 101–16).

defense dramatically and the business community fearing an escalation of inflation.

MITI (1964, p. 126) commented also on the joint statement and the Cabinet announcement of the Three Principles of Public Finance and the Economy by Finance Minister Kaya and Commerce Minister Yoshino of the first Konoe Cabinet. These Three Principles expand production capacity through balancing international payments and coordinating the supply of and demand for materials. Thus, they put the brakes on military demands while appealing to the business community to strengthen control over industry and trade.[12]

Although MITI did not describe specific policy details or evaluate effectiveness, it offered commentary, suggesting that some doubt about the Three Principles' feasibility remained (MITI, 1964, p. 127):

The government had serious reservations about whether, without friction with the business community, they could execute large-scale national defense enhancement or the five-year industry development plan that the military demanded.... However, with the beginning of the War with China in a month after the formation of the Konoe Cabinet, the conflict between the military and the business community temporarily calmed down, and the Japanese economy proceeded to the stage of wartime control.

3-3-3. Hara's Commentary on Fiscal Year Materials Mobilization Plans

Hara (1976a, p. 229) commented on a series of plans, including quarterly or fiscal-year materials mobilization plans. As we will see, his commentary is much more persuasive than the conventional wisdom represented by Oishi. Notice that even in July 1939, two years after the beginning of the War with China, Japan was increasing, rather than decreasing, its reliance upon the United States:

In 1939, together with the MMPlans, a general plan to mobilize the nation (trade, labor, the control of funds, transportation, and electricity) was tentatively prepared. There was little connection between the plans. The MMPlans, their backbone, were organized around the allocation of foreign currencies; this had to be revised in response to foreign trade forecasts. In July 1939, when Japan was negotiating with the UK about conflicts of interests in China, the United States warned Japan that it could abolish the Japan–U.S. Commerce and Navigation Treaty. It caused a major

---

[12] MITI (1964, p. 126) continued: reflecting the business community's fear of state control awakened since the Baba finance policy, control, or "planning of the national economy" took the form of voluntary control by business.

shock to Japan's controlled economy, increasing reliance upon the United States in munitions import.

July 1939 was nine months after the second Konoe Proclamation of "the creation of new order in East Asia," and three months before Vice-ACCommander Sawada and Army Minister Hata shared the view that, although its behavior toward the world was aggressive, "like a fruit rotten at the core," Japan's policy would not last long (Boeicho, 1967a, p. 624).

3-4. Major Control Laws

This book focuses primarily on systematic war preparations, war mobilization, and economic control during and prior to the first half of the War with China. The National General Mobilization (NGM) Act, the MMPlans and PCEPlans, and the Planning Council are the central topics of discussion. It is important to note that none of these existed before the beginning of the War with China.

During and prior to the first half of the War with China, none of these plans played a significant role in relation to PCEPlans or production capacity expansion policies for future rather than ongoing warfare.

In order to cope with developments, on 15 October 1937, the government appointed councilors to strengthen the Cabinet. These included veteran generals such as Kazushige Ugaki, Sadao Araki, Kiyokazu Abo, and Nobumasa Suetsugu, as well as Chuji Machida, Yonezo Maeda, Kiyoshi Akita, Seinosuke Go, Shigeaki Ikeda, and Yosuke Matsuoka. On 25 October, the Planning Agency merged with the Office of Resources to form the Planning Council, *kikaku-in*. On 20 November, the Imperial Headquarters (IH) was established, although this had almost no significance.

3-4-1. The National General Mobilization (NGM) Act

The NGM Act was announced on 1 April and came into effect on 5 May 1938. This huge act, consisting of fifty articles, was a powerful control law covering a wide range of areas that aimed to exploit every aspect of national power to attain the war objectives. It was all-inclusive legislation, in which most of the detail was passed over to Imperial Orders[13] (MITI, 1964, p. 135).

---

[13] There was a heated discussion in the Diet about the carte blanche character of this act. The NGM and Electricity Control acts became controversial for their national socialist thought. With these two acts, wartime control reached the stage of severely restricting the

It replaced the Munitions Industry Mobilization (MIM) and related acts. As it came into effect, the Army Factory Control Order, based on Article 13 of the NGM Act, and the NGM Council Order, based on Article 50, were enforced. At the end of 1938, three additional orders were enforced, with eight to follow by the end of March 1939. Most orders that came into effect in the year after the implementation of the NGM Act were related to wartime labor control and included the citizen registration system and the development of skilled workers. As before, industrial controls were based on existing temporary laws; the relevant stipulations of the NGM Act were pending (MITI, 1964, pp. 190–1).

After the capture of Hankou and Guangdong at the beginning of November 1938, Article 11 was invoked to control the distribution of funds and profits; the business world was shocked. These controls prevented companies that paid dividends of more than 10 percent of face value from further increasing their dividend payments. A discussion about new restrictions on the allocation of funds by financial institutions ended with the decision to continue studying adequate measures. Five more orders were enforced by the beginning of the Second World War in September 1939.[14]

On 3 March 1941, almost three years after becoming effective in May 1938, the Act to Revise the NGM Act was implemented. The revision expanded the coverage of controlled materials and activities, improved regulations to strengthen business and increase production, reinforced financial control regulations to release funds when needed, and strengthened the penalties for malicious crimes. Twenty-five of the act's fifty articles were revised or reinforced.

MITI (1964, pp. 453–4) offered commentary on this revision:

Penalties were strengthened for violations of the two major pillars of wartime control laws: the NGM Act and the Temporary Import-Export Grading Act. Together with the revision of the Criminal Law in the same session 76 of the Diet, this revealed a remarkable increase in control violations, indicating an escalation of problems in the controlled economy.

traditional working of a liberal economy (MITI, 1964, pp. 135, 182). Nakamura (1989, p. 10) presented another view, with which I agree: the former act was promoted by the military, and the latter by the Ministry of Transportation and Communication (*teishinsho*). Neither was implemented in response to an urgent need. Major Kikusaburo Okada, the War Mobilization Subsection Chief of the War Preparation Section (AM) after the war recalled concerns that without promptly resolving the War with China, it would be impossible to implement the PCEPlans. For this reason, the NGM Act was unnecessary at that time (Nakamura, 1989, pp. 65–6).

[14] For more details, see MITI (1964, pp. 189–92).

3-4-2. The Temporary Import Export Grading Act (TIEG Act) and Its Effectiveness as a Control Law

The seventy-second session of the Diet, during the period of 4–8 September 1937, enacted many important bills, including three acts (the Act for Applying MIM, the TIEG Act, and the Temporary Funds Coordination Act), which were important control laws (MITI, 1964, p. 134).

MITI (1964, pp. 134–5) evaluated the TIEG Act:

The TIEG Act was not a mere trade control law, but really a landmark law, representing industry control policies at the stage of emergency responses in Japan.... It aimed not only to restrict imports of unnecessary or non-urgent materials but also to control domestic products widely in cases where supply and demand coordination became necessary due to import restriction (Article 2). In addition, it was a so-called enabling legislation, delegating most of the enforcement to orders, whose characteristic as a delegated legislation fully manifested its power. Starting on 11 October 1937, when the announcement of a temporary regulation on import licenses became the first Commerce Ministry Order based on this act, myriad wartime control regulations (mostly Commerce Ministry Orders) dealing with production, rationing, consumption, use, and price were created; this went on until December 1941, when it was replaced by the Materials Control Order. In that sense, the TIEG Act was the basic law of materials control in Japan, not only during the stage of emergency responses but also during the War with China and the Second World War. The role it actually performed exceeded that of the NGM Act.

On 28 October 1937, the Commerce Minister ordered producers to supply a designated amount of nitric acid every month. It was an epoch-making order, the first production order in Japan, and was intended to increase dramatically the production of nitric acid, a critical raw material used in explosives.

The TIEG Act, together with related Commerce Ministry orders, might have enabled a temporary increase in the production of necessary materials. However, it could not have made a great contribution to systematic war preparations or the effective implementation of production capacity expansion policies. As it was not in place before the War with China began, it could not have been part of the preparations for this war.

Under the TIEG Act, numerous control orders, most from the Commerce Ministry, were enforced. It cannot be deduced from this that they were effective control laws or made an important and substantive contribution to the realization of control.[15]

---

[15] As Coase (1964, p. 194) rightly argued: What the regulatory commissions are trying to do is difficult to discover; what effect these commissions actually have is, to a large extent, unknown; when it can be discovered, it is often absurd.

A prosecutor's report (Kikuchi, 1947), entitled *A Study of the Causes of War Defeat from a Judicial Point of View*, written just after the end of the war[16] began the third part of the operation of a controlled economy, documented the failure in regulating violations, and the failure of the controlled economy and its causes. This documentation occupies the dominant part of the report. The failure of bureaucratic control has been discussed exhaustively from so many points of view that it has become a fashion. Kikuchi (1947, pp. 61–3) commented on prices and distribution, meeting the expectations of careful modern readers for a mid-twentieth-century wartime control success story:

Price control began with regulations on the sales price of goods, in accordance with the TIEG Act.... The Commerce Minister identified certain goods whose prices were rising rapidly, and controlled these prices. "However, such price controls were enforced without integration or coordination. There was no room to adopt measures focusing on basic causes of price increase.... As a result

  (a) Regulation was imposed on the greatly inflated prices of an extremely limited number of goods. Although those prices could be controlled, the prices of other goods increased in waves; no effective measures were in place to control the general inflation.
  (b) A big gap emerged between controlled and uncontrolled prices, creating a black market for controlled goods.
  (c) Control was enforced following a rapid price increase. It was therefore almost impossible to bring those prices back down to their original level.
  (d) Product specifications were not standardized in advance, so new controls resulted in the introduction of new products that could easily avoid regulation. There was no consistent regulation that included materials as well as final products. So, for example, a control imposed only on the materials needed to make an expensive, unrestricted final product encouraged black market trading in those materials.

For these and other reasons, the low price policy had a stormy passage.

Price control was a temporary expedient. The money supply continued to expand, causing inflation which further tightened supply and demand, resulting in a flourishing black market."[17] In fact, Japan's price control regime was doomed from the start. It was really a temporary expedient, launched with no preparation or organization.... Those defects were never corrected; in fact, they continued to escalate until the end of the war, leading to serious problems.

---

[16] This was the report of a study conducted from December 1945 to February 1946. The author, Ken'ichiro Kikuchi, was a prosecutor with several years' experience in the section in charge of economic affairs (Ogino, 2002, p. 73).

[17] Views shown in parentheses were quoted from prosecutor Teranishi's Report on Economic Control Violation Cases in the preceding issue of the same report series (pp. 188–).

3-4-3. The Temporary Funds Coordination (TFC) Act

The TFC Act was the first law designed to control funds directly; it aimed primarily to prevent industry equipment investment funds from flowing to unnecessary or non-urgent business. It was enforced through the self-regulation of financial institutions. Businesses were classified as A, B, or C so that the government could use funds to force industry to adapt to the wartime economy (MITI, 1964, p. 135). The TIEG Act controlled materials and the TFC Act funds (MITI, 1964, p. 161).

Little information is available about the effectiveness of the TFC Act in controlling funds, which were generally allocated in response to supply and demand. No one could be sure that this type of control law would effectively increase equipment investment in targeted industries; there is no evidence to prove that it did.[18] Particularly when war escalated and the proportion of military to nonmilitary goods rose dramatically, firms must have made it more of a priority to secure necessary materials than funds.[19]

3-5. Control Associations and the Munitions Company Act

3-5-1. Control Associations

The TIEG Act was the most important control law during the first half of the War with China.[20] The NGM Act announced in April 1938 established in 1941 control associations in key industries such as steel and coal

---

[18] It is not easy to control or manage the flow of funds. It is an extremely hard task to effectively influence resource allocation in an economy through the control of funds. Obviously, the enactment and enforcement of a law do not guarantee the effective enforcement of control. See Miwa and Ramseyer (2004b) for an examination of the effectiveness of credit controls in postwar Japan.

[19] The Budget Subsection Chief of the Military (*gunji*) Section of the AM recalled, in relation to securing materials (Nishiura, 1980, p. 114): "It was from the second year of the War with China that we began to emphasize materials securement in budget-making. Before then, the share of military goods in the economy was so small that there was no such a need.... Supply and demand coordination at the initial stage was by trial and error. Without reliable information, we could not grasp the reality of materials in the economy, although this later improved year by year. *Looking back later, however, I strongly feel that we just made up a cover story in desperation. At first, securing metals was at the core, and the Army Ministry as a whole became like a metal company*" (my italics).

[20] This subsection is based on Part I of Miwa (2004), where particular focus is placed on the machine tool industry.

mining. Then, in October 1943, the Munitions Company Act appointed a large number of munitions manufacturers as munitions companies. The government acted *only* at this stage, in response to urgent circumstances. The enactment of the Munitions Company Act in particular strongly suggests that control laws and related actions were not an essential part of Japan's systematic war preparations, contradicting the conventional wisdom. Many readers will be interested in their relation to war mobilization and economic control. As a precise understanding of economic control will be useful, I introduce briefly the control associations and the Munitions Company Act.

On 16 July 1940, three years after the beginning of the War with China, the Yonai Cabinet resigned en bloc. On 22 July, the second Konoe Cabinet was formed, giving a platform to the so-called New Order Movement.[21] On 26 July, the new Cabinet approved the Outline of Basic National Policy, demonstrating its intention to establish a national defense state system to underpin policies. In July and August, political parties dissolved in succession and joined the Imperial Rule Assistance Association (*taisei yokusankai*) established on 12 October. On 7 December, the Cabinet approved the Outline for Establishing the New Economic Order, a substantially revised version of the New Economic Order drafted by the Planning Council in September.[22]

On 3 March 1941, the Act to Revise the NGM Act was enacted for the purpose of strengthening penalties for malicious crimes.

The Imperial Order for Key Industry Associations (KIAss Order), establishing control associations, was made public on 30 August 1941. This was almost a year after the Konoe Cabinet's New Economic Order became a critical political issue in the autumn of 1940. The political debate centered on two issues. The first was economic. With a huge deficit in the international balance of payments, the economy had become extremely difficult to

---

[21] In June 1940, strongly advocating the New Order, Konoe resigned as Chairman of the Privy Council, a political-legal body separated from the parliamentary government. The Army responded to his resignation by withholding the Army Minister, and the Yonai Cabinet duly collapsed. See Nakamura and Hara (1972, p. 71) or Miwa (2004, pp. 30–1).

[22] The Planning Council almost determined the Outline of the New Basic Plan at the end of September 1940, when details of the plan were leaked to newspapers. Newspapers then reported that the plan would separate management from the business ownership. The business community reacted negatively, and the New Economic Order debate ensued, continuing until November. It was more serious than any other government–business debate that had occurred since the start of direct control. The so-called business offensive reached its peak in November, when even Cabinet members became involved (Nakamura and Hara, 1972, p. 96). For more details, see Miwa (2004, 1.2.5, pp. 30–4).

manage; this led to calls for the establishment of direct control over both materials and finance. The second was ideological, namely that both the political right and the Socialist Popular Party (both linked to the Army) argued strongly for reform of the capitalist system.[23]

The New Economic Order Plan declared its basic objectives in four points:

1. Establishing a national economic ideology that would support and contribute to the nation's security
2. Reforming the free enterprise system
3. Organizing the national economy into a totally planned production organ
4. Constructing a national security system to implement the nation's objectives

Readers will realize that what the Planning Council produced here was the conceptual foundation for wartime controls and therefore for the control associations.[24]

The private sector was, not surprisingly, fundamentally opposed to radical plans for reorganizing the economic system. Instead, firms in the private sector proposed that they themselves should reorganize the system of economic control because they best understood the real economy.

From the initial development of the plan to the establishment of the KIAss Order and the control associations, the private sector and bureaucracy struggled over interpretations of the plan and policies to implement it. Each worked to shift the policies to its private advantage (Nakamura and Hara, 1972, pp. 100, 102).

The publication of the KIAss Order was delayed until August 1941. The most serious cause of delay was a conflict of opinion among government institutions, particularly the Commerce Ministry and the Planning Council. The former was backed by the business community and the latter by reform bureaucrats. Furthermore, the Cabinet Order to designate key industries, expected to appear within two weeks of the Imperial Order, was also delayed (Nakamura and Hara, 1972, pp. 113–15).[25] Recall that the War with China began in July 1937, more than four years before this debate.

---

[23] See Nakamura and Hara (1972, p. 71) or Miwa (2004, p. 31).
[24] For more details, see Nakamura and Hara (1972). For the Outline of Basic National Policy, the Outline for Establishing the New Economic Order, the Act to Revise the NGMA Act, and the KIAssOrder, see MITI (1964, pp. 443–65).
[25] Also see Miwa (2004, pp. 33–4).

It was on 30 October that twelve industries, including steel and coal mining, were designated as key industries. Control associations were established in those two industries only before the beginning of the Pacific War, and in the remaining industries by the end of January 1942. The scheduled secondary designation of industries was delayed again because of a conflict of opinion among ministries. On 4 August, seven industries were newly designated, with control organizations established by the end of January 1943 (MITI, 1964, p. 507).

Besides control associations, in the shipping industry the Association for Shipping Operation was established on 1 April 1942, in accordance with the Wartime Ocean-Shipping Control Order of March 1942, through which the government controlled ships and sailors and enforced planned transportation. In the financial industries, the Finance Control Association was established on 23 May 1942, in accordance with the Finance Control Association Order of 18 April (MITI, 1964, p. 507).

In the controlled economy launched just after the beginning of the War with China, the government was directly responsible for control. It used existing self-control organizations such as cartels, industrial unions, and commercial unions to manage secondary rationing in individual industries. These organizations controlled various activities such as production, distribution, and consumption of key materials (Yamane, 1947, p. 79). The control associations were established five years after the beginning of the war, when Japan's war economy was in deep trouble. The justification for establishing a control association was both to ensure comprehensive control and to cooperate in formulating national policies for the industry (Article 4 of the KIAss Order).

3–5–2. An Illustrative Example: The Coal Control Association

After heated discussions and a complicated political process, control associations were established in key industries. Carefully conducted empirical studies are indispensable for identifying and evaluating the roles these well-known associations actually played and their importance. As we have shown elsewhere (Miwa and Ramseyer, 2004a), both in wartime and during the postwar period the effectiveness of the so-called control policies was extremely limited. The coal control association, which exemplifies the control association regime, was no exception.

The business of the control associations was twofold: to participate directly in formulating state policies and to implement national policy. In coal production, instead of direct state control, the government allowed the control association to operate at its own discretion. By respecting the ingenuity of the business community, it hoped to increase production. Commerce Minister Kishi gave these instructions at the inaugural meeting of the coal control association: "The control association is the culmination of years of trials and tribulations. Delegating implementation regarding production and distribution to the control association, the government will concentrate on determining the outline of national policy. We will maintain close coordination with the control association in governing the Japanese economy."[26]

The basic system and character of the coal control association remained unchanged throughout the period of wartime control. With the rapid deterioration of the war situation, the government adopted a wide variety of responses, including changes in system and organization. Within the coal control association, however, they remained unchanged. With the creation of the Ministry of Munitions (1 November 1943) and the enforcement of the Munitions Company Act (12 December 1943), major coal mining companies were designated as munitions companies. The Munitions Ministry could issue orders directly to those companies, bypassing the control association, without changing the association's role and activity. Despite radical changes in constraints and the environment, caused by the failure of the war, the control system at the starting point had been the optimal, robust choice for government.

3–5–3. Two Faces of the Control Associations

Before proceeding to the evaluation, note the two faces of the control associations.[27]

A control association, as finally established, had two faces: first, that of a trade association for private firms and, second, that of a government

---

[26] Hokkaido Coal-Mining and Steamship Co., ed. (1958, pp. 305–6).

[27] This part is from Miwa (2004, p. 34). For more details, see Miwa and Ramseyer (2004a, [1], pp. 36–9). The following episode from Atsushi Ohya (1964, p. 73) by the Chairman of the Light Metal Control Association is representative. Nippon Light Metal, for which the military had particularly large expectations, did not operate smoothly at the initial stage and could not supply products of satisfactory quality. Commerce Minister Kishi ordered Ohya and Suzuki, the Chairman and the President of Showa Denko, to conduct a site examination. Formally investigating the plant, they reported to Kishi that it would be best for the business to act independently, without third-party intervention. As before, Nippon Light Metal should be run by its management. Soon it began to supply the same quality products as others.

institution with influence over those private firms. Because of their character as private trade associations, there was no assurance that an association's control function would be used in the public interest, despite its transformation from a private cartel into a national control institution. Yet the new governmental aspect of these associations necessitated a tremendous administrative expansion – far beyond the administrative scale of the associations' former cartel headquarters.

An association also suffered from the need to coordinate jurisdiction with its supervising government agency, the bureaucratization of its own organization, and efficiency declines due to jurisdictional disputes with rival associations. The delegation of government authority to control associations was finally settled on 17 November 1942, an entire year after the control associations were established (Nakamura and Hara, 1972, p. 119).

3-5-4. The Evaluation of Control Associations

Control associations were established with ardent support from various sides. On 31 July 1942, the Chamber of Key Industries sent an enquiry to 142 members of five control associations asking for candid opinions about the latters' operation. The first declared improvement was this: that industry could rely on the control associations. In the past, industry requests, however fair, tended to be viewed skeptically, as partial and potentially self-serving. Now fair industry requests and opinions could be channeled through the control association directly to government. It played the role of a just notary. The defects included weaker leadership than expected. Lacking active and self-motivating leadership, the control associations were little more than government subcontractors. In addition, there was insufficient delegation by government authorities. The allocation of assignments between the government and the control associations required members to negotiate with both sides, resulting in "overlapping supervision," too many report requests, and the bureaucratization of association staff (Yamane, 1947, pp. 95–8).

Nakamura and Hara (1972, pp. 120–1) summarized the function of control associations through the following three points, with which I agree:

First, unable to operate effectively, the associations had no substantial impact on the behavior of individual firms or on aggregate industry supply. Most control associations were formed by restructuring established cartels. I do not claim that control associations did absolutely nothing. Rather, I would argue that the restructuring of the cartels into control associations had no substantial impact on the industry. Moreover, in the precision tool manufacturing sector, including the machine tool industry, the Precision Tool Section of the Commerce Ministry performed no substantial coordinating role.

Second, there was tremendous resistance to the establishment of control associations from the industry and within the government at every step of their establishment and operation. For instance, there was resistance to the enactment of the KIAss Order, under which the control associations were established; there was also resistance to the associations themselves and to their operating process, which involved the delegation of government control to strengthen and expand their roles. Because of this resistance, even stronger legal powers for the government would not have made it easy to operate the control associations effectively.

Third, widespread resistance to control associations declined when the expanding production in key industries, such as aircraft manufacturing, became a high priority. For once, the government displayed unity of purpose; direct state control of industry under the state-controlled enterprises designated under the Munitions Company Act became at least theoretically possible.

Under this system, the state appointed directors to private firms. Those directors then relayed government production instructions to the production managers at their companies and monitored their compliance. The state had the right both to discipline and to dismiss company directors and managers for noncompliance, and further had authority to order the alteration of corporate charters as necessary. This effectively put private enterprises under army-like organization, but whether it effectively expanded production is another question. Beyond the short-term impact, such a move seldom increases production and almost never improves efficiency.

I do not argue that the people directly in charge failed to understand the ramifications of this change. Army Lieutenant General Saburo Endo, the first Air Ordinance Bureau Chief of the Munitions Ministry, stated in an interview that, "I knew that public-owned enterprise was essentially inefficient ... If this system were to live long, managers and employees would grow listless, akin to public servants" (Ando, 1966, p. 307).

3–5–5. The Military and Control Associations

Another difficulty seriously impeded the activities of control associations. In the weapons manufacturing sector, absolutely independent of control associations, the Army Industry Association exercised stronger powers than control associations despite having no legal foundation. The difficulty began when the Army Weapons Manufacturing Association was established in May 1940 to provide better communication, friendly cooperation, and mutual technological assistance between the government and the private sector. In response, the Navy established twelve Navy Industry Associations and seven cooperative associations; in November 1942, the Army established the Army Aeronautical Industry Association. The Army Industry Association (joined initially only by large weapons manufacturing firms) expanded rapidly after the beginning of the Pacific War through the support and authority of the military. It grew into a huge organization, with twenty-one divisions and two subdivisions, covering the whole range of surface weapons (MITI, 1964, p. 517).

Every company controlled by the Army Industry Association was assigned a plant under the Army's control and supervision. Plants in the same industry were organized into a specialty division, which overlapped and was in conflict with the corresponding control association. The Weapons Administration Headquarters or Army arsenals that took over leadership of the association's operation conducted far more thorough and stringent production control and supervision than control associations did. For this reason, the status of the association surpassed that of the control associations (MITI, 1964, p. 517).

3–5–6. The Munitions Company Act and Munitions Companies

On 21 September 1943, the Cabinet approved the Outline of National Policy Operation Under the Current Situation. It adopted two goals, both emergency measures designed to increase munitions production, particularly for the Air Force. The first was to improve and strengthen the administrative system to produce munitions swiftly and simply under a unified framework. The second was to establish a system for responsible production, clarifying the public management of important munitions companies. The former was linked to the establishment of the Munitions Ministry and the latter to the enactment of the Munitions Company Act (MITI, 1964, p. 594).

The Munitions Ministry was established on 1 November 1943, amalgamating most divisions of the Commerce Ministry and the Planning Council with divisions of the Air Force Headquarters of the Army and the Navy responsible for supervising aircraft production in the private sector. The main goal was to increase production of munitions, particularly aircraft. To achieve this, the Ministry would consolidate the placement of orders, procurement, and aircraft production, which had previously been the responsibility of the

Air Force Headquarters of either the Army or Navy. The Planning Council's national mobilization activities were transferred to the Munitions Ministry. Thus, the Munitions Ministry took on overall responsibility for basic planning (formerly carried out by the Planning Council), exercising executive powers (formerly shared by the ministries) and distributing controlled goods (formerly done by control associations) (MITI, 1964, p. 593).

MITI (1964, p. 593) explained the background: Due to competition and resistance between the Army and the Navy, production planning and control in key industries, including aircraft manufacturing, fell into confusion. The inefficiency of the control associations inhibited the smooth operation of rationing and distribution, which also curtailed the function of control associations.

In November 1943, there were serious problems in even such core aspects of war mobilization and economic control as aircraft production. MITI (1964, p. 594) concluded: "Even with such major reforms in the system of administration … the conflicts between the Army and the Navy continued. They had practically no effect on improving the situation."

As shown in detail in Chapter 9, the defining moment of the Pacific War was the battle over Guadalcanal Island between August 1942 and January 1943. Almost a year after Japan's decisive defeat, reforms were proposed. By this time, Tojo had been Prime Minister for two years and Army Minister since July 1940. Nobusuke Kishi, a well-known reform bureaucrat, had been the Commerce Minister in the Tojo Cabinet. As a part of this reform, Tojo took on the additional role of Munitions Minister and Kishi became Munitions Vice-Minister. Etsusaburo Shiina, another well-known reform bureaucrat, was promoted from Vice-Commerce Minister to General Mobilization Bureau Chief. The Army Lieutenant General Endo became the Air Ordinance Bureau Chief of the Munitions Ministry, primarily responsible for strengthening aircraft production. In February 1944, Tojo also became the ACCommander. Despite such dramatic changes, the reforms had practically no impact on the situation.[28]

The essential points of the Munitions Company Act were:

1. It clearly articulated the state nature of company management.
2. It aimed to establish a system of responsible production.
3. It sought to improve the administration of munitions companies.

[28] Endo recalled that General Mobilization Bureau Chief Shiina allocated no materials to the Air Ordinance Bureau, forcing it to negotiate with the Army and the Navy for materials. As a result, the traditional separation of aircraft production within the Army and the Navy was preserved (Ando, ed., 1966, pp. 305–6).

MITI (1964, p. 598) explained the first point as follows: "the conflict of opinion between the military and the business community over the economic system was deep-rooted, and even after the beginning of the Pacific War the government's strong requests for dramatic production increases had been extremely hard to enforce because of the basic character of capitalist enterprises. So Article 3 of the act stipulated: A munitions company must respond with every effort to the state's request to strengthen military power and to responsibly implement munitions supply."

However, Shigeo Kitano, the Correspondence Section Chief of the Munitions Ministry, wrote in his book published in February 1944 (Kitano, 1944, p. 43): "Transforming the basic character of companies might disturb the foundation of the economic system, which would impede the very productivity improvement that is needed most urgently at the time of this decisive engagement. It was what we feared most."

To summarize, the government recognized serious defects in its industrial production and believed that a transformation in the basic character of companies was absolutely necessary. There were significant problems that had seriously disrupted attempts to strengthen military power. Transformation, however, involved great risks that worried many inside the government.

On 17 January 1944, a first round of 149 companies were designated "munitions companies," and on April 25 a second round of 424 companies were named, finally making a total of 688. The new munitions companies were automatically exempted from the Army Factory Control Order.

The Army Factory Control Order was based on Article 2 of the Munitions Industries Mobilization (MIM) Act. With the enactment of the NGM Act, the Order was reimplemented under its authority. Since the beginning of 1938, most munitions company plants had been under military control, via the Army Factory Control Order. In November 1943, even factories that had been under military control for a long time failed to accomplish the state's request to increase munitions production.

Serious defects in munitions production required a transformation in the basic character of companies, but overcoming their defects would not be easy. The reforms could not effectively achieve the goals.

Endo, when he was informally appointed to the Air Ordinance Bureau Chief, recognized that a dramatic increase in aircraft production would require the integration of directives from the Army and the Navy regarding not only production but also aeronautical technology. Accordingly, he proposed that the Army and Navy transfer their technology divisions to the Air Ordinance Bureau. Both refused, arguing that it would be impossible to separate their research, experimental, and trial production from military control. As a result, only production was transferred to the Munitions Ministry.[29]

Prosecutor Yamane's report (Yamane, 1947, p. 143)[30] concludes:

Except in aircraft production, the scheme to unify munitions production under the Munitions Ministry failed. As before, control associations had no opportunity to cooperate in munitions production. Orders from the military and the government remained divided and uncontrolled, while munitions manufacturing companies remained in disorder until the end of the war.

The Munitions Ministry was too weak politically to force through the integration of munitions production or the coordination of orders. After all, the Munitions Ministry was just the reorganized Commerce Ministry, traditionally powerless to resist the military. It must have been obvious that its reorganization into the Munitions Ministry would not increase its political power. The public considered it a crazy idea to remove munitions production from the military by creating the Munitions Ministry. It was seen as a life-extension program for Commerce Ministry bureaucrats who were going bankrupt.

3–6. Economic Control during the Period Prior to the War: Systematic War Preparations?

3–6–1. Industry Control and the Key Industries Control Act

The Key Industries Control (KIC) Act of 31 March 1931 was the first industry control law in Japan. This act grew out of the industry rationalization movement or industry rationalization policy. On 20 January 1930, the Office of Temporary Industry Rationalization was established as an agency affiliated with the Commerce Ministry. In order to rebuild the economy, the government asked it to recommend particular industries in which companies should be controlled and to suggest how this should be carried

---

[29] Boeicho (1975c, p. 404). Compare this with the policy reaction in the UK (Cairncross, p. 7): "Until May 1940 when Churchill took over the reins of the government there had been no Ministry of Aircraft Production; arrangements for the production of aircraft were the responsibility of the Air Ministry. The needs of the army, navy and air force were all catered for by that department. It is hardly surprising in these circumstances that the RAF enjoyed priority over the army and navy, or that the dive bomber and the seaplane were ranked well below the fighter and the heavy bomber. Churchill, who had been Minister of Munitions in the First World War, was a firm believer in taking away from Service departments responsibility for production of the weapons they used and took steps to put an end to the exercise of this responsibility by the Air Ministry. He set up a new department, hived off from the Air Ministry, to put fresh urgency into the production of aircraft." I don't argue that everything went fine in this new department, of course. On this point, see Edgerton (2006, pp. 73–4).

[30] See also Miwa (2008, 4–7–3, pp. 264–6).

out. In the same year, the Temporary Industry Rationalization Bureau was established as an agency affiliated with the Commerce Ministry. One of six permanent committees formed in the bureau was the Control Committee, where issues related to company control were discussed. The KIC Act was enacted in the Diet in accordance with the recommendations of this committee (MITI, 1964, pp. 47–52).

The industry control debate around 1930 focused on industry rationalization. The basic meaning of control (*tousei*) in this debate differed from the concept of wartime control (as reflected in the conventional wisdom dominant since the end of the war). In relation to industry rationalization, control was used in reference to empowering, promoting, or coercing cartels.[31]

MITI (1964, p. 47) declared: "The enactment of this act was the first step toward the full-scale development of industrial control in Japan." Arisawa (1937, p. 97) offered commentary on the significance of this act: "The enactment of this act was epoch-making. First, it cleared the path to form cartels in key industries, thereby taking control of large companies. Second, it established cartel-control as a control form."

Commerce Minister Sakurauchi explained its basic purpose as follows (MITI, 1964, p. 53): "This act imposes an adequate discipline and control on the current disarray in Japan's industries. By eliminating the source of instability, it intends to stabilize industries and make our whole economy prosper."

When asked whether the military applied pressure or lobbied for the act, Shinji Yoshino, the Industry Bureau Chief of the Commerce Ministry, said, "No. Nothing in particular. We did it by ourselves upon the opinion inside the Commerce Ministry.... In the Committee in the House of Representatives, we were criticized: 'Who would want to enact an Act to promote cartels and trusts?' Some also criticized the act for lacking any penalty for violations" (Yoshino, 1962, pp. 204–6).[32]

---

[31] A parallel example is the word "liberals," which has changed significantly since the nineteenth century. Manchester "liberals" of that era were the equivalent of today's Chicago free marketeers. "Most professional economists were hostile to planning, especially perhaps those who were directly involved in industrial planning and programming. Lionel Robbins was the head of the economic section of the Cabinet Office, a notable anti-planner. The successive directors general of planning in the MAP [Ministry of Aircraft Production] were Manchester liberals – John Jewkes and Ely Devons" (Edgerton, 2006, p. 72).

[32] This was the first occasion to use "control" in such acts. Yoshino explained that in the process of discussion, they found that it had been widely used in the Army. On this point, see Miwa (2007, [1], p. 21).

3-6-2. Stockpiling of Petroleum by the Petroleum Industry Act, and the Artificial Petroleum Manufacturing Industry

In Japan in the 1930s, most industry acts (or business acts) were introduced in connection with the Production Capacity Expansion Plans (PCE Plans) or PCE Policies. The Planning Council and its predecessor, the Planning Agency, were established in connection with MM Plans and PCE Plans.

For illustration, consider the effectiveness of the Petroleum Industry Act for the stockpiling of petroleum. This act, published in March and enforced on 1 July 1934, was the first industry act applied to a major private industry. It preceded the industry acts that appeared one after another in the heavy and chemical industries prior to and during the period of the War with China; these included the Automobile Manufacturing Industry Act enacted two years later and the Machine Tool Building Act of March 1938.[33] Those acts were designed to satisfy both the industry demand for anti-Depression measures and the national defense assistance required by the military.

The act placed petroleum refining and imports under a licensing system, which imposed the law by requiring relevant parties to stockpile petroleum. This ensured a supply of petroleum for urgent military use. The government requested importers and refining companies to hold back half (initially a third) of its total annual import for military use (Takahashi, 1985, p. 19).[34] The penalty for violating this act was no higher than 3,000 yen (Article 13).

Domestic companies completed their obligations by October 1935, and the government responded by offering a subsidy. However, two foreign companies (Standard and Rising Sun), which owned over 50 percent of the market, although holding the quantity equivalent to that of three months, failed to meet their target by the June 1936 deadline. Although Mitsui Bussan (Mitsui & Company) took over the stockpiling and temporarily resolved the conflict, no agreement was reached; the two companies never fulfilled their obligations. There was nothing the government could do. Beyond enacting the act, it had prepared little budgetary support for implementing its policy goal. With foreign companies refusing to meet

---

[33] Machine tools are the mother of the machinery industry, and the development of the machine tool industry was critical for systematic war preparation, rearmament, and mobilization. For another illustration of the effectiveness of an industry act, see Miwa (2004, pp. 86–102) on the Machine Tool Building Act enacted in 1938.

[34] It was stipulated in Article 6 of the implementation order and in Article 6 of the act.

their obligations, the government achieved less than half of its targeted stockpiling quantity (Takahashi, 1985, pp. 19–22).[35]

In June 1937, the Office of Fuel was established as an agency affiliated with the Commerce Ministry; seven militaries on active service joined. In 1936, the seven-year Plan for the Artificial Petroleum Industry was drawn up, with an initial target of 2 million tons per year, later revised to 4 million. On 10 August 1937, the Diet enacted the Artificial Petroleum Industry Act.[36] On 19 January 1938, the Imperial Fuel Industry Company was established as a national controlled corporation with 100 million yen in paid-in capital, half of which was invested by the government to promote the industry.

The act, with its target of controlling 50 percent of the petroleum market within seven years, aroused great hope within the industry. But by the time of the U.S. oil embargo on Japan in August 1941, the seven-year plan had become pie in the sky. The many artificial petroleum manufacturing plants constructed via the act all failed. The ratio of actual to planned production of more than 2 million kiloliters by FY1943 was only 11 percent (MITI, 1964, pp. 245–6; Takahashi, 1985, pp. 22–3). This ratio was even lower in gasoline production, just 3.7 percent in FY1940 and 4.7 percent in FY1941.[37]

Boeicho (1969a, pp. 710–11) summarized the plan and its actual achievements as follows[38]:

For its enforcement the related technologies and engineering capacity were too primitive. The artificial petroleum industry itself was too immature to standardize effectively. Moreover, because of the enforcement of the Army's and Navy's rearmament plan since FY1937 and because of the preparation for the War with China, materials allocation to this industry under the MMPlans was strictly regulated. In turn, this made the implementation of the plan extremely difficult.... The actual results were far different from those planned.

... The urgent necessity in the petroleum industry was emphasized. But, because materials needed were the same as those needed for rearmament, it became impossible to develop the industry satisfactorily.

---

[35] Takahashi, the author, was a bureaucrat with direct responsibility for enforcing the act.

[36] For example, Jilin Artificial Petroleum Co. expanded its production plan from 300,000 kiloliter per year to 1 million kiloliter per year. For more details, see Takahashi (1985, pp. 133–5). According to a summary table showing requisite funds for a key industry enhancement plan for Japan and Manchuria, the artificial petroleum manufacturing industry occupied a prominent place, second only to the electricity industry. See Horiba (1962, pp. 70–1).

[37] See Takahashi (1985, p. 9, Table 1) or Miwa (2007, [1], p. 22, Table 7–1).

[38] United States Strategic Bombing Survey (Report 51: Oil in Japan's War, p. 42) concluded: "Strategically, the contribution of Japan's synthetic oil industry to the war may be regarded as negative. The manpower and materials expended on it certainly impeded the national war effort more than the synthetic oil production aided it."

4

Materials Mobilization Plans (MMPlans)

Chapters 4 and 5 discuss the effectiveness of the MMPlans and PCEPlans (policies) that epitomized planning and control during this period. The Army's Five-Year Plan for Key Industries led to the PCEPlans, which in turn were superseded by the MMPlans. The Planning Council formulated and enforced both the MMPlans and PCEPlans. Section 4-1 includes a brief overview of those plans and the Planning Council. Section 4-2 examines individual MMPlans in more detail. If the goal of the MMPlans was to systematically prepare for and carry out a successful war, their effectiveness was minimal.

Sections 4-3 and 4-4 investigate the impact of MMPlans on economic control, with section 4-3 focusing on the plans themselves, and section 4-4 setting them in a wider context. These sections confirm that, although the MMPlans were considered central to Japan's wartime economic control, effective and efficient enforcement of economic control was extremely difficult to achieve.

Section 4-5 focuses both on the black market and on limitations to the effectiveness of the MMPlans. Section 4-6 investigates the military's role in economic control; although formally outside the MMPlans, the military was the key to war mobilization. Section 4-7 is a brief conclusion.

4-1. MMPlans, Production Capacity Expansion Plans (PCEPlans), and the Planning Council

4-1-1. The Planning Council and the PCEPlans

On 25 October 1937, the Planning Agency and the Office of Resources were reorganized into the Planning Council, which took over the business of planning and coordinating the growth and use of national power during peacetime and war. From the last quarter of 1937, this new ministry assumed responsibility for national general mobilization in place of the Office of Resources. The Planning Council oversaw various plans, including the MMPlans concerning trade, finance, and labor mobilization and the PCEPlans (Nakamura, 1989, pp. 8–9).

On 17 June 1937, the Army presented to the government its Five-Year Plan for Key Industries, together with an Outline of the Five-Year Plan for Key Industries to serve as a reference guide (Army plan) that its research institute formulated as a reference for its enforcement guide. The Army presented these to the Planning Agency, which had been established on 14 May 1937, through a reorganization of the Cabinet Research Office. The latter was itself a new institution established on 11 May 1935. For such new institutions, it was particularly hard to execute the huge, complicated task of finalizing the plan and making it enforceable.

Immediately thereafter, the War with China unexpectedly began, and the government adopted a nonescalation policy. Despite this, the war escalated rapidly for a year and a half, ending with the second Konoe Proclamation on a new order for East Asia. As a result, the finalization and implementation of the PCEPlans were postponed for a long time.

4-1-2. Difficulties in Systematic War Preparations, War Mobilization, and Economic Control

To achieve policy goals effectively, a plan must satisfy some critical conditions. First, policy goals must be presented clearly. Second, specific measures, including policy measures (such as incentives for manufacturers and other policy agents) must be clearly defined. And third, the technical feasibility and the availability of necessary resources, including materials and funds, must be effectively ensured. Formulating a specific plan with detailed enforcement measures and precise feasibility assessments is no easy task for a government or institution in any country at any time.

Stalin wrote in 1937: "Only bureaucrats can think that planning work ends with the creation of the plan. *The creation of the plan is only the beginning*" (Gregory and Harrison, 2005, p. 730; italics in the original text). Stalin's Soviet government primarily confronted peacetime conditions; in war mobilization, when faced with an explosive increase in munitions demand, a government encounters much more serious difficulties.

In theory, the Japanese government had a wide variety of ways to enforce its demands, including coercion, subsidies, persuasion, market trade, and even self-implementation. The gradual progress and quality of preparations for war decisively conditioned the effectiveness and efficiency of mobilization and the appropriateness, quality, and cost of munitions.[1] Japan's PCEPlans aimed to realize rapid expansion, new product development, and product improvements in many key industries over a long time. For the Japanese government, as for governments at any time, it was not easy to formulate a feasible plan with detailed policy measures to achieve its goals.

4-1-3. Example: Specificities of the Outline (Army Plan)

The Five-Year Plan that the Army presented to the government on 17 June 1937, with its accompanying outline, was not detailed enough to put the plan into action immediately.[2] To take one example, its recommendations for the coal industry (MITI, 1964, p. 107) were that the focus of coalfield development should be on the continent; the control of price and allocation should be unified throughout Japan and Manchuria, while importing coal from Manchuria to Japan should be promoted; and inferior firms should be integrated or closed in order to rationalize the industry.

---

[1] Although systematic war preparations, mobilization, and economic control are some of the most serious policy challenges for any government at any time, few Japanese studies are based on a clear recognition of this point. Miwa (2008, 2-3-2, pp. 107-12) listed seven entitling factors that make war mobilization a difficult policy agenda. Wars, when they come, are always different from the war that is expected. Victory goes to the side that has made fewest mistakes, not to the one that has guessed right (Taylor, 1964, p. 116). What makes these challenges most difficult is that a state mobilizes with a specific enemy in mind. On both sides, a country (or a group of countries) can choose from a wide variety of strategies, combining such components as the pros and cons of war, practical preparations, timing, battlefields, battle technique, and the basic war plan. The war and its consequences are the result of an intersection of choices made on both sides. Each country determines its own strategy, anticipating a particular consequence or payoff. Accordingly, the situation carefully prepared by one side tends never to materialize, because it cannot favor the other. Thus, war mobilization is decisively conditioned by the intersecting strategies of relevant parties. Progress in preparations on one side almost by necessity stimulates rearmament demand on the other side. Development and improvement in armaments or weapons on one side stimulate a countervailing movement on the other, as each demands better weapons than the other side. As precise information about the anticipated enemy is often quite poor, needs often emerge after war has begun (pp. 109-10).

[2] For the details of the outline, see MITI (1964, pp. 103-16).

In considering the machinery industry, which posed one of the most urgent challenges of the time, the Army simply wrote (MITI, 1964, pp. 108–9):

With the current production capacity of our country it is entirely impossible to provide for ourselves promptly all the machines necessary for enforcing this plan. We have no other choice than to import machines in areas of urgent need to fill the gap.

Although we expected to export domestic machines worth 1.7 billion yen over five years, the value of machinery imports will substantially exceed exports. Such a huge import surplus is unavoidable for a country still developing its heavy industries. Using imported equipment and technology, we must promptly achieve independence and self-sufficiency, and gain ground in the world market. To realize this goal swiftly we should adopt the following measures.

(1) We should establish a machine-producing company as a national policy concern. This firm would take charge of producing machines for which there is limited demand, including high-grade precision machine tools, machinery for coal liquefaction, and other equipment technologically or economically difficult for existing firms to produce.

(2) As a national policy, we should promptly import technology and equipment, and a national trading company should take charge of this task. The firm should control the orders abroad, study the capacity to increase imported goods, lower import prices, and provide import funds.

(3) We should promptly increase production capacity by standardizing products, rationalizing transactions in the home market, and controlling product items.

(4) We should control subcontractors, and thereby improve their capacity.

The Army's outline required 8.5 billion yen over five years to cover enforcement costs. Of this amount, the Japanese and Manchukuo governments would supply 1 and 0.5 billion yen respectively. The remaining 7 billion yen (82.6 percent of the total) would be provided by private investors. Allocating these funds to industries as requisite construction funds, the outline planned to enhance capacity.[3]

Nowhere have I found answers to such questions as: Who actually enhances those capacities? How would those capacity enhancements be realized? Are those enhancement plans feasible? Without clear affirmative answers that include specific details, one can only presume that the plan had poor feasibility at best.[4]

---

[3] See Horiba (1962, pp. 68–70) or MITI (1964, pp. 104–).

[4] The same applies to the Priority-Production Scheme (PPS) that the postwar Japanese government, particularly the Economic Stabilization Board, was alleged to have conducted effectively for Japan's economic recovery. We discussed this point in detail in Miwa and Ramseyer (2004a).

4–1–4. The Competence of the Planning Council

The conventional wisdom, as expressed by Oishi (1994) in section 3–3, takes it for granted that the PCEPlans were effectively enforced and that they contributed greatly to Japan's war preparations and mobilization. However, we must consider the competence of the institutions responsible for these activities, as well as the difficulty of their task. The Planning Council and the Munitions Ministry that succeeded it were seriously handicapped by a lack of human resources, accumulated experience, and relevant information; they lacked much ability to promote effective collaboration and cooperation.[5]

Unfortunately, there is little information available about the competence of the relevant institutions and their working mechanisms, both because little basic information remains and because scholars have not been encouraged to challenge the status quo.[6]

The recollections of the Budget Subsection Chief of the AM Military (*gunji*) Section are informative. He compared the Planning Council and the Munitions Ministry with the Military Budget Chief of the Finance Ministry (Nishiura, 1980, p. 113):

The Planning Council and the Munitions Ministry took charge of the MMPlans, but they could never seize the initiative. At one time, also in the Army, there was an argument in favor of transferring budget-making to the Planning Council, which I consistently opposed. In theory it might be correct; I opposed it because of the competence of the Planning Council, which was a motley collection of bureaucrats from different parties and unable to seize the initiative. It also had difficulty in maintaining confidentiality. If the Planning Council had seized the initiative as firmly as the Ministry of Finance did, the conflict between Army and Navy might have been much reduced.

4–1–5. From the Five-Year Plan for Key Industries to the PCEPlans: Commentary by Horiba (1962)

The Army anticipated difficulties in the enforcement of its Five-Year Plan for Key Industries. Colonel Kazuo Horiba, who had drafted the original version,

---

[5] The Planning Agency was established in May 1937 with great fanfare, and in less than half a year it was consolidated with the Office of Resources. One may question whether the conventional view (that the war was carefully planned, started, and developed on a foundation of systematic preparation) is consistent with such frequent reorganizations of the key institutions responsible for war preparations and mobilization. For the process of the establishment of the Planning Council, see Furukawa (1992, p. 52).

[6] Recall the commentary on the role of Gosplan presented in section 3–2–2. The conventional wisdom that Gosplan exercised considerable executive power over allocation "requires revision: Gosplan was important, but it was not powerful, and surprisingly sought to limit its own power" (Gregory and Harrison, 2005, p. 727).

joined the Planning Agency, the creation of which he had championed, to try to expedite the enforcement process.

Horiba joined the ACCom during the Manchurian Incident, having recently graduated from the Army War College. When the War with China began, he was the Head Staff Member in the War Leadership Section of the ACCom. He lived in the USSR and Poland as a resident officer for three years, enthusiastically studying Stalin's Five-Year Plan. Returning to Japan in February 1937, Horiba obtained a post in the newly established war leadership section of the ACCom. Strategy Division Chief Ishiwara ordered him to promote industry planning, including the Five-Year Industry Plan in Japan and Manchuria, and to formulate national defense policies.[7]

The war leadership authorities realized that after two successive Five-Year Plans and rearmament in the Far East, the USSR represented a serious threat to national defense and could threaten the defense of Manchukuo. The Japanese authorities reexamined Japan's national defense with a focus on Manchuria, and recognized that dependence on others in the defense industry (particularly heavy industry and the fragile national productive capacity) was a serious problem (Horiba, 1962, p. 61).

In explaining the Five-Year Plan for Key Industries and its Outline (enforcement guide), Horiba (1962, p. 62) wrote:

We had to formulate an unprecedented long-term integrated plan. Unfortunately, we lacked the comprehensive capacity even to formulate fiscal year plans, due partly to repeated organizational reforms. The government could not do it swiftly by itself. Hence, the war leadership authorities decided, in collaboration with their research institute, to formulate a plan by themselves and present it to the government. This was the Five-Year Plan for Key Industries. Originally, it was for the period FY1937–FY1941. It advised developing Japan and Manchuria comprehensively and importing materials in short supply from North China. The plan was transferred to the governments of Japan and Manchukuo. The Manchukuo government immediately adopted the plan and implemented it beginning in FY1937. In Japan, however, as usual, the government wasted time in discussions.

… In the newly established Planning Agency, 30 administrative officials discussed the plan. They had to take a broad spectrum of issues into consideration, and had limited capacity to cope with them. At that time, it was the Office of Resources that possessed basic statistics, … and the Planning Agency and the Office of Resources were consolidated into the Planning Council. The council restarted its study of

---

[7] I don't argue that Horiba's study of the Five-Year Plans was accurate and informative. His understanding was consistent with the conventional wisdom that had been dominant over several decades, at least until recently.

industry plans, but focused too much on the goals it intended to achieve in five years. Only in January 1939 did it finally reach the Outline of the PCEPlan.

It took almost two years to formulate the Outline, almost as long as to formulate the original plans. Horiba (1964, p. 63) commented:

For the promotion of the industry plan we spent half a year in persuading the AM and one and half years in persuading the government. This slow course was normal in administration at that time. Public events did not wait for the administration, however. Alas, the Outline we finally reached was almost the same as the original. What a pity for the country. After pushing the creation of the Planning Council, I obtained a seat there and took part in the process directly. I invited to the Planning Council as a prompter Major Kenkichi Shinjo, who had just returned from the USSR. Otherwise, the Outline would have been further delayed.

The Outline that the Army presented to the government advised the creation of "an administrative organ to conduct comprehensive guidance coercively and promote the plan as an unshakable national policy." However, neither the administrative organ nor the emergency measures was ever implemented. Horiba (1964, p. 73) offered the following commentary:

[The] immediate realization [of an administrative organ] being difficult, for the moment we must adopt the following emergency enforcement measures:

1. Establish the General Administration Agency as the central leadership control organ for enforcing the plan.
2. Create the Ministry of Trade to coordinate and control international trade.
3. Create the Air Ministry to develop civil aviation rapidly.
4. Create the Health Ministry to improve the health of citizens and cultivate a workforce.
5. Amend the job appointment rule for government clerks, so that talented men can be recruited from the private sector.
6. Prohibit the promotion of government clerks to the management of government-affiliated corporations.

In January 1939, the Cabinet approved the Outline of the PCEPlan of the Planning Council. Horiba suggests that it remained too abstract to work effectively. In order to make it workable as a plan, it needed further development[8]:

---

[8] Taking into consideration the difficulties inherent in the situation and the process by which Japan acquired the plan, readers might have doubts about the credibility of Horiba's comment that: "The Manchukuo government immediately adopted the plan and implemented it beginning in FY1937" (Horiba, 1962, p. 62). They might wonder whether the plan was

Using the basic idea proposed at the start, with strong determination and perfect cooperation, the government will devote every effort to enforcing this plan. To do this, the government aims to operate existing institutions and policies effectively to promote industrial development. As this plan aims for a rapid increase in production capacity, the government will adopt special measures to control and support business, supplying engineers, workers, funds, and requisite material.

As necessary, the government will also enact new laws and invoke the National General Mobilization Act.

4–2. The Effectiveness of the MMPlans as Measures for Systematic Preparation and the Enforcement of the War

4–2–1. 1938 MMPlans

The MMPlans, the core measure of wartime control and economic policy, were withdrawn before the plan for the second quarter of FY1945 had been formulated. The MMPlans, successively formulated since 1938, primarily concerned foreign exchange allocation and ocean transport capacity; they were defended and maintained by the continual efforts of many people (Tanaka, 1975, p. 651).

From October 1939 to the end of the war, from positions in the Planning Council and Munitions Ministry, Shin'ichi Tanaka participated in devising the MMPlans that defined the core of Japan's control economy.[9] Tanaka began his retrospective account as quoted here.

Few would deny that the MMPlans were at the center of Japan's wartime control economy. In the conventional wisdom, they and the PCEPlans occupied a key position and were considered effective. Therefore, examining the effectiveness of the MMPlans sheds light on the success of all systematic war preparations, as well as on mobilization and economic control in wartime Japan.

Most of the literature on the MMPlans is preoccupied with collecting, arranging, and interpreting facts, observations, or documents relating to what

---

actually enforced from FY1937 and whether it effectively achieved its policy goals. Nowhere in Horiba (1962) can I find any information about the effectiveness of the plan, either in Manchuria or Japan.

[9] Tanaka (1975, p. 1). Tanaka, from the South Manchuria Railways, became an employee of the Planning Council on a short-term contract (to work on the MMPlans). In May 1941, he became an investigating official of the Planning Council; following the November 1943 reorganization, he became an official in the General Mobilization Bureau of the Munitions Ministry.

aspects of the MMPlans were discussed, how the plans were documented, and what documents survive.

In the literature on the MMPlans, as with war mobilization, the PCEPlans, and various fiscal year plans, effectiveness is rarely questioned. In the preceding quote, Tanaka's emphasis on foreign exchange and ocean transport suggests that each MMPlan focused on the most precious materials at the time and aimed to realize the optimal allocation of resources for the most urgent policy target. The purpose and goal of the MMPlans also varied greatly over time. Evaluating the MMPlans' effectiveness depends on the standard of appraisal, which in turn depends on their purpose and goal.[10] That these were a moving target makes evaluation harder.

In this volume, I assume that the goal of the MMPlans was the systematic preparation for and execution of the war. Even if each MMPlan was effective in achieving a particular short-term goal, the MMPlans may have been ineffective overall. The goal of each MMPlan was not always clear; precise information about each plan's binding constraints is unavailable. However, together with the imposition of the economic embargo against Japan, I find evidence of actions that reduced the supply of materials. These included conflicts between the Army and the Navy, the military's suppression of private demand, the designation of munitions manufacturing plants, and the massive requisition of ships. The conclusion I must draw is that the MMPlans did not work effectively. This does not, however, imply that they had no impact on resource allocations.

4-2-2. The First MMPlan (1938)

The following passage describes the drafting of the first MMPlan (1938)[11] (MITI, 1964, p. 193)[12]:

The materials coordination after the beginning of the War with China depended both on import control through foreign exchange by the Foreign Exchange Control Act and on direct control of exports and imports, production, allocation, and consumption by the TIEG Act. For key materials such as steel, nonferrous metals, coal,

---

[10] According to Nakamura (1977, p. 111), an emergency measure adopted at the beginning of the War with China gradually expanded its coverage as war escalated. Around 1940, the government completed a network of control, covering materials, funds, prices, and wages. Although pulled together at the last minute, a system was somehow established.

[11] Obviously the MMPlans do not account for all activities that help to mobilize materials. Certainly, some materials were mobilized by the military or procured from the market outside the MMPlans.

[12] We find almost the same commentary in Shiina (1941, p. 307). Etsusaburo Shiina was the General Affairs Bureau Chief of the Commerce Ministry.

and machinery, the government formulated specific policies to increase production. Those policies were adopted in response to specific requests regarding individual materials, without any concern for interdependence. Accordingly, there was no macroeconomic, national perspective that could consider total supply, total demand and the requisite reduction in consumption.

As expectations grew for a long war, strong demand arose for the establishment of a comprehensive long-term materials supply and demand plan that focused on munitions supplies.... In October 1937, the Planning Council was established as an umbrella institution for the nation's general mobilization plans; the MMPlan was the first to be addressed.

Under the Planning Council, established on 25 October 1937, the First Committee was established and Planning Council Chairman Taki took the Chair. The committee was divided into eight sections, each of which focused on particular materials. Its task was to ensure the supply of munitions for the War with China while maintaining the balance of international payments. Based on plans drawn from sectional studies, ministries would take the measures necessary for industries in their jurisdiction.

The activity of the First Committee focused on the allocation of foreign exchange funds for materials purchased. On 9 November 1937 (two weeks after the Planning Council was established), Chairman Taki reported to Prime Minister Konoe that there had been an allocation of 470 million yen in import funds. This report showed that the MMPlans, in use continuously until the end of the war, maintained their original spirit. Due to wartime needs, military personnel from both Army and Navy took part in their formulation (Tanaka, 1975, pp. 20–1).

A series of puzzles emerges. What could actually be accomplished in such a short period of time? Could the committee collect information about supply and demand to underpin its plan? Was there any system for collecting information and did it work?

Tanaka (1975, p. 21) recalled, "the MMPlans continuously maintained the spirit of 1938 until the end of the War." Does this imply that the substance of the MMPlans did not change from beginning to end? Did the allocation of foreign exchange funds remain the foundation of successive MMPlans, even after the imposition of the economic embargo against Japan in the summer of 1941? How was the allocation of materials (including foreign exchange funds) decided? Was the allocation standard maintained, and who determined the allocation?

Following the work of the First Committee, the Planning Council established the Materials Mobilization Conference, which included representatives from the Planning Council, Army, Navy, Commerce, Agriculture, and other ministries. In late November, the committee began to draw up comprehensive guidelines for coordinating the supply and demand of materials. It took two months to create the first MMPlan, formally known as the Demand-Supply Comparison of Key Materials and Replenishment Measures. The Cabinet adopted it on 16 January 1938. The plan listed ninety-six items (including iron, steel ingot, pig iron, and scrap iron) and focused on basic materials and machinery. It formulated supply-and-demand plans for 1938 in eight sections: steel and iron, nonferrous metals, textiles, fuel, chemicals, machinery, food, and miscellaneous goods. During January and April, each section respectively discussed in detail an enforcement manual, "The Outline of Measures for the Situation Concerning 1938 Materials Mobilization" (Tanaka, 1975, p. 194).

The trade balance was the basis for the MMPlan. Restricting the mobilization of materials depended entirely on the purchase value of imports from outside Japan and its territories. Initially, the total annual value of imports was restricted to 3 billion yen. Under that assumption, the plan allocated import values of materials (expressed in terms of volume) among the military and the private sector. Adding domestic production, transfers from Manchuria and China, and recoveries from inventory, the plan then calculated the total supply available. Total demand was divided into two parts, to meet military and private sector demand. The priority was military demand; the assumption was that that would remain restricted. When there was lack of balance, supplementary plans were formulated, focusing on saving and substitution on the demand side and production increase and recovery from inventory on the supply side (MITI, 1964, p. 194; Tanaka, 1975, p. 23).

Initially, the plan allocated supply preferentially, first to the military and then to the private sector. It was then proposed to increase the military's allocation by suppressing the amounts allocated to the private sector. Finally, the total supply was increased by supplementing the funds available for import (Tanaka, 1975, p. 25). Note that "military demand" was for munitions production only, while industrial materials, such as steel, aluminum, and oil, were classified as private (Nakamura, 1977, p. 111).[13]

By forcing through those controls, the government hoped to ensure the supply of materials for urgent purposes. It aimed in practice to achieve its

---

[13] The Ministry of Finance was unable to curb military spending through the allocation of basic materials. Although allocation reduction occasionally occurred, in most cases the MMPlan accommodated the whole of the military demand (Tanaka, 1975, p. 25; Nakamura, 1977, p. 111). From the FY1939 MMPlan, private demand was classified into five groups: raw materials for munitions production; materials for production capacity expansion; government demand; materials for exports production; and private demand (Nakamura, 1977, p. 11; MITI, 1964, p. 208).

goals by inducing firms to accept these conditions voluntarily (Shiina, 1941, p. 309). Firms were expected to suppress demand to support the government's focus on the military (Tanaka, 1975, p. 25). The government proposed such measures as allocation controls, consumption suppression, and production expansion policies, hoping that private firms would agree to these voluntarily. To achieve that goal, it adopted the control association system (MITI, 1964, pp. 195, 507).

4–2–3. MMPlans Were Mobilization Plans for Inputs Rather than Outputs

As mentioned previously, the plan focused on basic materials, with the addition of machinery. It was a mobilization plan for inputs rather than outputs.[14] Tanaka (1975, p. 285) discusses the consequences of this approach[15]:

MMPlans of the time were generally input MMPlans. They estimated the expected supply of raw materials such as steel, cotton fiber, and electrolytic copper. They did not try to formulate plans about outputs. Because of this, *the planner's control ended with inputs allocation, and the recipients, particularly the military, were allowed to use the allocated materials as they wished* [my italics]. The Commerce Ministry tried various countermeasures, in particular to control the plants working with the materials. The result, however, was that it focused its attention on the small number of plants it could supervise, only to impose on them heavier constraints. By contrast, the military demand was almost entirely uncontrolled.

The allocation of inputs through the MMPlans was more than a system of distributing supplies among groups of recipients such as the Army, Navy, and private sector. The use of steel allocated to the Army was at the Army's disposal. Information about its actual use was not made available to government, even to the Planning Council.

Japan had no central planner to collect information and make comprehensive forecasts about the current situation and future trends. Hence, it was extremely difficult to predict future demand for basic materials. This made it more difficult to formulate and enforce the PCEPlans and prepare for the future.[16]

---

[14] In the United Kingdom, the key wartime controls did not relate to labor, important though this was. However, other inputs (raw materials, industrial plants) were controlled, as were outputs: *what* was produced (Edgerton, 1991, p. 68).

[15] This relates to the overall situation of production in the first half of FY1942, particularly production and allocation of machine tools in exceptional cases where actual production exceeded that which was planned. This point applies to the MMPlans as a whole.

[16] For more details, see Miwa (2008, 4–3, pp. 230–9).

In comparing aircraft production plans in Germany and the UK, Cairncross (1991, p. 148) pointed out, "The most striking difference is that whereas German planning seems to have revolved round the supply of materials, British planning – after 1941 at least – revolved round engine supply and development."

He continued (pp.148–9):

It was the allocation of materials that gave the German planners some purchase on the aircraft manufacturers; once the manufacturers had the necessary materials they were apparently able to look after all the other components .... It would be astonishing, however, if different manufacturers, using the same engine from the same suppliers, never found themselves in competition for an inadequate supply. When the big spurt in production occurred in 1943–4, there could hardly fail to be divergences between the rates of expansion in airframes and engines, not just in total but in each type of airframe compared with the engine fitted to it.

In British planning, these divergences were treated as inevitable, while raw material shortages were rarely the source of a hold-up in production.

Because of a shortage in aircraft engines and various components, the completion of many planes was seriously delayed in Japan. To search for and procure such components in times of shortage was the responsibility of the companies in charge of aircraft production.

4–2–4. Overview of the 1938 MMPlan Enforcement Concerning Common Steel

It was obviously easier to create an MMPlan than to enforce it. The case of common steel illustrates what could occur.

The focus of the first MMPlan was allocating common steel to the military and private sector, as the demand for steel was the key to national industrial capacity. This made the allocation of steel especially difficult. "No MMPlans without steel" was the unshakable belief of the Planning Council (Tanaka, 1975, p. 23).

The Overview of the 1938 MMPlan Enforcement (Planning Council document dated 16 May) summarized the steel situation on 1 May 1938 (Tanaka, 1975, pp. 23–4)[17]:

    1. [On allocation control] – Outline of the MMPlan: determine the ratio of steel by both item and use; control its production and allocation;

---

[17] See also MITI (1964, pp. 195–6). At the time, specific figures in the MMPlans were not made public.

carefully implement policies dealing with the price rise of steel due to saving and with unemployment.

2. State of enforcement: The Steel Control Conference was established within the Commerce Ministry to enforce the supply and demand plan determined by the Materials Mobilization Conference. Its role was to determine the volume of steel in production, sales, export and import, and consumption volumes by sector in a particular time frame. It would allocate steel to sectors such as the state, public organizations, and industries, including civil engineering, construction, railways, shipbuilding, machinery, gas, oil, and electricity, coordinating supply and demand in each sector. The allocation of volume in response to each sector's demand was finalized in April–June. Steel would soon be rationed through government certificates or coupons. The conference, chaired by the Mining Bureau Chief of the Commerce Ministry, was composed of representatives from relevant ministries, steel companies, sales organizations, and consumers.

3. To implement the rationing plan, the conference expanded traditional joint-selling cooperation programs to include tin plate and thin sheet manufacturers. It promoted joint-selling cooperation and put pressure on all steel producers to join.

4. In order to strengthen production controls, the conference aimed to organize a steel ingot association to increase the production of necessary steel and reduce the production of forms of steel not urgently needed.

5. To strengthen the control of steel rationing, the conference urged the organization of trade associations to help control intermediary rationing institutions as wholesalers do.

6. To rationalize demand, the conference decided to organize an institution for controlling purchase and rationing in each major steel consumption sector. Civil engineering and the construction industry would need a new conference, while the traditional shipbuilders' association would perform the role in the shipbuilding industry. In the machinery manufacturing industry, a conference would be established in each major sector; in addition, small firms would organize industrial unions to be integrated into the federation of industrial unions. This, like item 5, would need to be completed in a month.

7. [On consumption saving]: – Outline of MMPlan: enforcing 30 percent savings on 5 million tons in private demand, excluding the demand from the military, quasi-military, and government sectors. The saving ratio imposed on the private industries was: 55 percent for the civil

and construction industries, 18 percent for machinery, 50 percent for water and gas, 45 percent for private railways, 25 percent for rail vehicles, 15 percent for shipbuilding, 5 percent for mining, and 40 percent for others.

8. State of enforcement: The Steel Control Conference of the Commerce Ministry would enforce cuts in consumption, primarily through rationing control. Each sectional conference would conduct a survey to determine demand and rationing volumes by item and by use, tentatively for April–June. The conference aimed to ensure the consumption cuts by strengthening rationing control through certificates or ration coupons.

9. [On production]: – The MMPlan newly adopted for production increase, expansion, and transformation of equipment for steel making and rolling.

10. State of enforcement: In order to respond to national emergencies, the conference would issue guidance concerning the expansion of equipment for steelmaking and rolling at domestic steel companies. It would select the applicable items and their volumes. Regarding the transformation of steelmaking equipment under the MMPlan, the conference would ensure production by issuing orders to major domestic producers for April–June production. The conference, using these volume figures, would determine and implement the rationing volumes by use.

Note that this Overview (1 May 1938) referred to a plan for January–December 1938. In the initial stages, the state could not assume the existence of large-scale control. Without any preparation, it was forced to try to establish a system for control enforcement. The preceding summary gives a snapshot of what was thought to be necessary, particularly among the people in charge. The steel sector was known to have had a long history of cooperation and control, and most of the organizations mentioned in the summary were familiar with traditional joint-selling cooperatives. Even in this sector, most of the control organizations were to be in place by the end of May. No information about their effectiveness is available.

As a method for enforcing the MMPlans, the Planning Council adopted various measures, such as controlling rationing, consumption, and plans for increasing production. It delegated enforcement entirely to the Commerce Ministry's administration, which aimed to achieve the goal through voluntary agreements among industry members. The steel control system was designed to be adopted in other sectors. As a result of this scheme, innumerable control associations were later established in individual sectors (Tanaka, 1975, p. 23).

4-2-5. The Temporary Office for Materials Coordination (TOMC)

The Temporary Office for Materials Coordination (TOMC) was established by the Commerce Ministry on 7 May 1938 as an administrative organ exclusively responsible for supply-and-demand coordination by sectors. As an important organizational reform, it was set up in response to the establishment of the Planning Council as a comprehensive planning ministry (MITI, 1964, p. 143), but it survived for only one year.

The coordination of supply and demand for materials was enforced by the Commerce Ministry through temporary emergency measures that had been in place since the beginning of the War with China. The role of the Commerce Ministry was essentially negative. The National General Mobilization (NGM) Act was enacted in April and the revised MMPlan formulated in June 1938. To ensure the coordination of supply and demand for many key materials, the government decided to establish a new institution.

The TOMC, headed by the Commerce Minister, was a comprehensive institution for increasing the production of resources in short supply, coordinating import materials, and rationing resources (MITI, 1962, pp. 214–16).

At the time of the TOMC's establishment, the Commerce Ministry made it a planning institution. In combination with existing divisions in the Ministry and affiliated agencies, it aimed to enforce wartime commerce policies smoothly (MITI, 1962, p. 217). The system as a whole was established for the coordination of supply and demand. The Planning Council formulated the general outline, the TOMC formulated detailed enforcement plans, and the Commerce Ministry and its affiliated agencies (for example, the Offices of Fuel and International Trade) enforced them (MITI, 1964, pp. 143–4).

The operation of TOMC was not smooth. It soon became an integrated institution for planning and enforcing the coordination of key materials. With a few exceptions, most divisions of the Commerce Ministry became practically invisible. As the war developed, a more comprehensive enforcement of materials control and production capacity expansion became urgent. This was beyond the capacity of the traditional system. As part of a full-scale organizational reform, on 16 June 1939,[18] the Commerce Ministry (including TOMC) was reorganized into five new bureaus, which covered the industrial sectors of mining, steel, chemicals, textiles, and machinery. One year after it was established, the TOMC was abolished (MITI, 1964, pp. 146–7).

4-2-6. The Revised MMPlan (1938)

The first MMPlan failed to achieve its supply targets for many materials. MITI (1964, p. 196) attributed this to lack of experience and an undeveloped control system (launched prematurely when war began with China): "The biggest cause was the fact that import capacity (the foundation of the MMPlan) was derailed. That is, the volume of exports fell far below the target. In turn, this reduced import capacity."[19]

Imports decreased, and domestic production fell below the planned figures as well. At the same time, war escalated into the Xuzhou Campaign of May 1938. The demand for munitions increased rapidly. In response, the government revised the MMPlan to focus on imports (MITI, 1964, p. 197). On 23 June 1938, the Cabinet adopted the Revised MMPlan. Just when the Overview of 1938 MMPlan Enforcement concerning common steel was expected to complete its control system, the government had already begun to revise the MMPlan.

MITI explained that "the 1938 Revised MMPlan, based on actual patterns of international trade during the first half of the year, substantially reduced its estimate of import capacity for the second half. Correspondingly, it imposed a stricter restriction on materials allocated to private-sector demand. It placed its principal emphasis on the swift and sufficient allocation to the military and sacrificed all other demands. Thus, it revealed the extraordinary determination of the government to favor the military" (MITI, 1964, p. 197).

On the same day, the government proclaimed its determination to establish a wartime structure for a long, drawn-out war. It listed thirty-two items whose use would need to be restricted domestically. The Restriction on Manufacturing Cotton Products, enforced on 29 June through the TIEG Act, was the first manifestation of this (MITI, 1964, p. 137).

---

[18] Of all the organizational reforms from the establishment of the Commerce Ministry in 1925 to the reorganization into the Munitions Ministry in 1943, this was the most important (MITI, 1964, p. 147).

[19] See also Shiina (1941, p. 309).

In the case of common steel, where the Planning Council placed its principal emphasis, the plan began to derail. Steel was the basic material both for waging a war and for expanding production capacity. As supplies threatened to run short, the Planning Council focused more heavily on supplying the military and drastically reduced its allocation to other sectors. With this preferential allocation of common steel and reduction in the foreign exchange allocation, materials other than steel were the worst affected (Tanaka, 1975, pp. 24–5).

As MITI (1964, p. 204) summarized, "The 1938 Revised MMPlan was epoch-making. But still it could not eradicate its tentative and impromptu character, maintaining as its sole objective the fulfillment of the demand for combat weapons."

4-2-7. The FY1939 MMPlan

The MMPlan for January–March 1939, in transition from the 1938 MMPlan to the FY1939 MMPlan, was an extension of the 1938 Revised MMPlan. The government shifted to a fiscal-year term from FY1939, so that the term of MMPlan enforcement would conform to that of national budgets (MITI, 1964, p. 204).

Around September 1938, the Planning Council, in collaboration with other ministries, began to formulate the FY1939 MMPlan. Because of repeated delays due to various difficulties, it was not adopted by the Cabinet until 26 May 1939. This MMPlan was also based on the fiscal year's assumed import capacity; this capacity, conditioned by export trade and gold selling, was expected to decrease further, while the domestic inventory of materials was nearly exhausted. This made supply capacity much tighter than in the previous year. On the demand side, in addition to further increasing munitions demand, the government had to secure the preferential allocation of materials for production capacity expansion. This followed the PCEPlan launched in 1939, for which the Cabinet approved the Outline on 17 January 1939 (MITI, 1964, p. 204).

Tanaka (1975, p. 652), who was joining the MMPlan formulation working group in the Planning Council, recalled:

Unlike the previous year, the situation did not allow us to easily swallow the demands of the Army and the Navy. Ministries began to recognize the importance of the MMPlans ... both as a model of the so-called wartime economic control scheme and as a supreme national plan. This was the case even though it was not easy to understand. Gradually, negotiations among the relevant parties on the allocation of cuts in materials allocation intensified.

The *Shoko-gyosei-chosakai* (literally, Commerce Administration Research Team), in its report entitled *Information About Materials Control*, published in October 1939 soon after the Cabinet adopted the FY1939 MMPlan, declared (pp. 6–7): "At any rate, an almost perfect MMPlan has come along. Thus, our country has for the first time obtained a plan that we can call a 'real plan' with the FY1939 MMPlan." In a report entitled *A Long-Term Construction and the MMPlans*, it characterized the FY1939 MMPlan (pp. 6–7) as follows:

In FY1939 we proceeded to the first step of a war of long-term attrition.... In parallel with the battles in the War with China, we must achieve rearmament in both the Army and the Navy to secure the new order in the Far East and a production capacity expansion dramatic enough to establish Japan, Manchuria, and China as a coherent economic block. Toward that end, the plan must be more sophisticated, qualitatively and quantitatively, than the preceding three plans. Put more simply, we must establish a true MMPlan in response to the needs of the first year of this war of long-term attrition. Here we have obtained such a plan, the FY1939 MMPlan.

The plan listed 273 resources (the 1938 MMPlan had listed 96). Private-sector demand (including everything nonmilitary) was divided into five groups: production capacity expansion planning industries; authorities; Manchuria and China; exports to the third countries; and general private demand. In estimating the volumes of demand and production, the plan took into consideration consumption cuts and production increases. Thus, the demand figures in the plan represented allocation volumes by sector rather than mere demand estimates, and the production volumes were the planned volumes rather than mere production estimates.

In addition, the plan adopted varied enforcement measures, including a thorough reinforcement of consumption restrictions, cuts in national purchasing power, savings promotion, strengthening of fund control, the invocation of the NGM Act, improvements in the rationing system, production increases, and the promotion of substitute goods, as well as the further promotion of materials recycling. The plan made citizens aware of consumption cuts by strengthening the National General Mobilization Movement. When necessary, it would strengthen consumption control through the use of coupons (MITI, 1964, p. 208).

In January 1939, the Cabinet approved the Outline of the PCEPlan, in which production capacity expansion took shape as a policy objective in the four-year plan. It selected fifteen industries, including steel and coal. To promote enforcement, the PCEPlan adopted specific measures for business, labor, funds, and materials, while advocating stricter control enforcement through the invocation of the NGM Act when necessary. Most industry laws and materials control laws enacted during this period involved listed industries. Thus, the PCEPlans, together with the MMPlans for supply-and-demand coordination, constituted the basic economic plans that conditioned Japan for waging a long war (MITI, 1964, p. 139).

4-2-8. The Second World War Began in September 1939

In this volume, I divide the four years and five months, from the beginning of the War with China to the beginning of the Pacific War (in Japan traditionally called the period of the War with China), into two periods, separated by the start of the Second World War in September 1939. The primary focus of this book is on systematic war preparations, mobilization, and economic control during the two years and two months before September 1939 (the first half period of the War with China). This focus naturally spreads into both the second half of this period and the preceding period.

I therefore focus on the MMPlans for this period, from the first 1938 MMPlan to the first half of the FY1939 MMPlan, and examine their effectiveness.

It is hard not to draw the conclusion that MMPlans during the first half of the War with China bore little relation to planning, systematic preparations, or the war effort. They were entirely ineffective in achieving those objectives. This conclusion follows simply from three points.

1. The MMPlans integrated policies successively adopted in response to the rapidly increasing munitions demand and an escalating shortage of foreign exchange funds.
2. Their primary objective was to coordinate supply and demand in materials (rather than to allocate resources to designated sectors).
3. The conditions for their effective (and efficient) enforcement through an infrastructure capable of providing organization, information collection, and skill formation remained insufficient throughout the period.

4-2-9. The FY1939 MMPlan after Enforcement

Let's take a look at the effectiveness of the FY1939 MMPlan before evaluating the overall effectiveness of the MMPlans. The FY1939 MMPlan that the Cabinet approved on 26 May 1939 (celebrated as the nation's first real plan) immediately encountered obstacles. MITI (1964, p. 211) listed six:

1. Due to a drought in west, Japanese and Korean rice production decreased; as a result, Japan had to import 210 million yens' worth of rice and wheat.

2. Due to drought and then floods in North China and Manchuria, Japan could not import the planned amounts of rice.
3. Due to a coal shortage, overall domestic production decreased.
4. Due to an electricity shortage, overall domestic production decreased.
5. Japan faced economic pressure from the United States, the UK, and France, particularly in the form of a warning from the United States on 26 July that it might repeal the Japan–U.S. Commerce and Navigation Treaty.
6. Due to the beginning of the World War II, imports fell.

MITI concluded (pp. 211–12):

In particular, the outbreak of the World War II in September reduced imports from outside the Japanese territory, including European countries. This raised import prices, and caused grave obstacles to the implementation of the MMPlan.... Although the revision of the MMPlan was unavoidable, it was after the middle of the term and the government had no time to formulate a revised plan as it had in the previous year. Comparing the fiscal-year plan with its implementation plan, we find supply decreases in almost every sector. The actual performance of the FY1939 MMPlan revealed a 14 percent decrease in domestic production and a 20 percent decrease in total supply compared to the original MMPlan.

The situation became even worse. In his study of economic controls during the period of the War with China, *Beginning of the Wartime Control Economy*, Hara (1976a) pointed out that although a system of plans for national general mobilization (including the MMPlans and international trade plans) was established at least, there was little organic connection between those plans. Moreover, on every occasion when international trade forecasts were derailed, the government had to revise the foreign exchange funds allocation that was at the basis of the MMPlan formulation. The warning from the United States on 26 July that it might repeal the Japan–U.S. Commerce and Navigation Treaty (repealed six months later) caused a profound shock to Japan's control economy, which had been strengthening its munitions dependency on the United States (Hara, 1976a, p. 229).

He continued: "An electricity shortage intensified both due to a decrease in water-power generation because of exceptional drought and to a failure in securing coal by the Japan Electricity Generation and Transmission established in August 1938 through the state's electricity control mechanism. It resulted in supply cuts of both electricity and coal to manufacturing plants. As a result, from October 1939, the private-sector plants were forced to drastically curtail production, and several munitions plants were paralyzed as well. This became a serious obstacle to increasing munitions production" (Hara, 1976a, p. 230). In addition, "the 'interrelationship for materials-exchange inside the Japan-Manchuria-China Economic Block,' which was the central core of the 'Yen-block formation,' was in reality woefully fragile" (p. 232).

4-2-10. Efficiency Evaluation of the MMPlans
During the First Half of the War with China

September 1939, the midpoint of the term of the FY1939 MMPlan, was eleven months after the second Konoe Proclamation announcing a new order in East Asia. As shown in the previous chapter, it was also just before the time when the Vice-ACCommander and the Army Minister shared the view that Japan's policy would not last long.

Subsection 1–5–2 summarized the second Army war mobilization implementation plan (April 1938–March 1939) drafted on 30 June 1939 by the Head of Weapons Arsenals. This official took charge of procuring munitions, which he received, stored, and supplied. His opinion was: "Though we have not yet reached the stage of war that lays the whole national power on the line, we suffer from serious shortages of various materials" (Boeicho, 1970, p. 250).

However, the architects of the MMPlans could not obtain accurate information about the state of war mobilization.[20]

When the FY1939 MMPlan, considered "almost perfect," was put into effect, the War with China had unexpectedly escalated into a war that required the whole power of the nation. Japan was obliged to adopt a strategy for a long, drawn-out war aimed at building a new order in East Asia.

---

[20] Summarizing procurement performance (excluding ammunition) he reported (Boeicho, 1970, p. 243): "In spite of serious difficulties in distributing materials and machine tools to factories concerned and in recruiting engineers, we could improve the performance with developments of mobilization ... We could fill most of the demands from the military, and adjust ourselves to their operations." However, Nakahara (1981, p. 78), at the Military (*gunji*) Section of the AM in charge of procurement and supply of munitions, recalled: "Weapons production in the FY1937 comprised 42,600 rifles, 2,300 machine guns, 670 artillery, 330 tanks, and 879 airplanes, which was 10 times more than in FY1931. We had to urgently import from Italy 72 heavy bombers, 100,000 rifles and some observation airplanes for the artillery. As the shortage of ammunition was extremely serious, a big part of the budget was allocated to ammunition supply, occupying 56 percent of the weapons budget in FY1937 and 76 percent in FY1938, with which we could produce a small number of artillery and tanks."

4-2-11. Summary

The MMPlans were created in response to a war with China that began unexpectedly. When the war escalated, the plans also expanded and were forced to become more systematic.

- The MMPlans did not systematically prepare for coming wars. They constituted a short-term plan or agenda for coordinating supply and demand for a quarter-year, so that resources could be allocated to the production of munitions and related products.
- The MMPlans constituted an agenda for action with conditions. Important conditions remained ambiguous and uncertain, and often tended toward wishful thinking. A long-term reliable plan was hard to formulate, and in fact was not established. The plans were not precise or stable enough to serve as a reliable basis for the involved parties, particularly companies on the supply side, to make decisions and behave systematically.
- The MMPlans began full-scale operation on 26 July 1939, when the United States threatened to repeal the Japan–U.S. Commerce and Navigation Treaty. Upon repeal, in early 1940, importing important materials became extremely difficult. At that time, after a long war with China, Japan was at an impasse.
- Little preparation for effective control enforcement (including the collection of necessary information and coordination among relevant parties) preceded the MMPlans. The effectiveness of prepared and actual systems for control was, as shown in section 4–3, extremely limited.

4-3. Effectiveness of the MMPlans as Measures for Economic Policy

If we assume that the objective of the MMPlans was systematic preparation for and implementation of the war, their effectiveness was extremely limited.

In this and the following section, I investigate from a broader viewpoint the reality and impact of the MMPlans. Section 4–3 studies the effectiveness of economic control and section 4–4 considers the MMPlans from a wider perspective.

4-3-1. Steel at the Core of the MMPlans, and Coal at the Core of Energy

The FY1939 MMPlan, finally approved by the Cabinet three months after the beginning of its term, was described as "almost perfect." However,

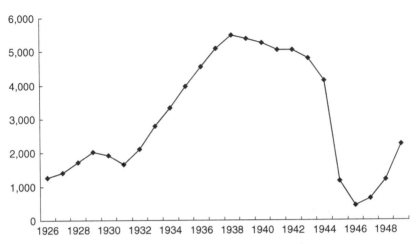

Figure 4–1. Steel Production: 1926–1949 (unit: 1,000 tons). Data from
Toyo keizai shimpo-sha (1950, p. 128).

it revealed an actual decrease of 14 percent in domestic production and
20 percent in total supply (MITI, 1964, p. 212). The munitions demand
increased, import capacity decreased, and imports from other countries,
in particular the United States, were disrupted. The MMPlans faced more
important objectives and more serious obstacles.[21]

As the ongoing long war with China was gradually undermining Japan's
national capacity, Tanaka (1975, p. 36) introduced the Outline Design
of MMPlan that the Planning Council drafted as a guide for the FY1940
MMPlan.

Although Tanaka (1975, p. 36) did not explain what he meant by the
"national capacity" of Japan, I see steel production as the core of the MMPlan
and coal as the key to energy. The Steel and Coal Control Associations were
the only two associations established before the beginning of the Pacific
War on 8 December 1941. They prove that steel and coal lay at the center of
wartime controls.

Figure 4–1 shows the annual production of steel for 1926 through 1949
in units of 1,000 tons (Toyo keizai shimpo-sha, 1950, p. 128). Production
peaked at 5,489,000 tons in 1938.

In January 1940, the Japan–U.S. Commerce and Navigation Treaty
expired. In June, the United States stopped exports of American machine

---

[21] Those export restriction measures caused the greatest difficulty in formulating the
MMPlans at the time (MITI, 1964, p. 361).

tools to Japan. In July, the U.S. government restricted aviation gasoline and scrap iron exports to Japan; the latter became an export prohibition in October 1941. Japan's average domestic supply ratio of scrap iron for 1935 through 1940 was 56 percent, and its scrap iron was imported mostly from the United States. The average blend ratio of pig iron to scrap iron during this period was 44:56.[22] The U.S. scrap iron embargo had a tremendously serious impact on steel production in Japan.[23]

After the Manchurian Incident, Japan adopted a rearmament policy. Together with the recovery of the world economy, this drastically increased the demand for coal from heavy industries and the chemical industry in particular. Production increased to 37,760,000 tons in 1935. After the beginning of the War with China, the demand for coal from the munitions industries (both as a source of power and for manufacturing) increased further. From 1939 to 1943, over 50 million tons of coal was produced annually. Production peaked in FY1940 at 57.3 million tons. Adding transfers and imports from Taiwan, Korea, Manchuria, and China, the total supply amounted to 67.4 million tons. Production decreased to 49.34 million tons in FY1944 and 22.34 million tons in FY1945 (Toyo keizai shimpo-sha, 1950, p. 5).

4–3–2. Subsequent MMPlans, Including the Emergency MMPlan

The Planning Council's outline design for the FY1940 MMPlan recommended allocating to each demand sector a percentage of the previous year's planned allocation: military was given 85 percent; materials for production capacity expansion planning industries was allocated 90 percent; authorities 80 percent; Manchuria and China 87 percent; raw materials for export production 105 percent; and general private-sector demand 80 percent. However, with a slump in imports from other countries, production fell below the planned level, making the supply-and-demand conditions much tighter. In March 1940, compressing allocations, the ratios were revised (Tanaka, 1975, p. 36). Although the military remained at 85 percent, materials for production capacity expansion planning industries and for Manchuria and China dropped to 75 percent. Authorities and the general private sector fell to 70 percent.

---

[22] See Toyo keizai shimpo-sha (1950, pp. 129–31). For the details of the export restriction measures taken against Japan, see Shiina (1941, pp. 271–3) or MITI (1964, pp. 361–2).

[23] For the details of steel production in Japan at the time, see Murakami (1994, p. 184) or Miwa (2007, [1], p. 54, note 53).

Many disasters befell Japan that year. The rice crop failed because of drought. In Taiwan and Manchuria, floods seriously impeded the production and transportation of materials. Due to the World War II, materials prices and the cost of ocean freight rose, and the yen/dollar exchange rate dropped. Consequently, Japan's import capacity decreased and it was obliged to reduce imports of materials.[24] Moreover, domestic production central to the supply capacity of the MMPlans was seriously impacted by the materials shortage and money-losing demand prices (through a shortage of skilled workers). As a result, the long-awaited PCEPlans made little progress (Tanaka, 1975, pp. 41–2). On 29 June 1940, the Cabinet approved the FY1940 MMPlan, based on poor national capacity and several overly optimistic assumptions (Tanaka, 1975, p. 61).

From about this time, there were strong indications that the international situation would deteriorate. Increasing the allocation to the military on the one hand, and anticipating the suspension of imports of important materials on the other, the government decided in June to accelerate the imports of scrap iron, special steel, and oil, until the end of August. It would rush to purchase special steel, nonferrous metals, and oil, taking the American attitude toward Japan into consideration (MITI, 1964, p. 360).

A record from the Imperial Headquarters' Outline of Policies for the Situation in summer 1940 reported: "Both in the Army and in the Navy there were few signs of a war with the U.S. and the UK.... Suddenly the Planning Council received a request from the Procurement Bureau of the AM to evaluate national capacity, from the following viewpoints." The result was the Tentative Draft for the Emergency MMPlan (Tanaka, 1975, p. 65).[25]

Work assumptions:

1. Imports from and exports to other countries are totally suspended.
2. Except for munitions, raw materials, and food, imports from the yen-block area has become difficult.
3. Materials transfer from outside Japan remains the same.

---

[24] The unit price of import materials rose 40 percent on average (MITI, 1964, p. 360).
[25] In mid-June, Lieutenant Colonel Tanemura of the ACCom's Twentieth Subsection proposed to Lieutenant Colonel Okada of the AM War Preparation Section: "Suppose, exercising the state's right to wage war, we make every effort to resolve the ongoing incident. This exercise might cause strong friction with the UK and the U.S., and we assume some armed conflict with them. Would you please clarify what then would occur on the MMPlans?" Okada treated this proposal as a clerical communication rather than an official request. With no more than a set of typed assumptions and the approval of War Preparation Section Chief Nakanishi, he made a request to the Chairman of the Planning Council (Nakamura and Hara, 1970, p. lxix).

Guidelines for formulating the MMPlans:

1. We formulate the MMPlan on major materials over three years, starting from FY1941.
2. In materials allocation, we emphasize the military demand sector and the production capacity expansion sector, suppressing the others as much as possible.
3. We study the influence of this suppression on private-sector demand.

The Tentative Draft drew several conclusions. The supply capacity of most basic materials would drop to less than half its current level. At this level, the supply of some materials would be insufficient to meet even the military demand. Many materials allocated for general private-sector demand would fall below 10 percent of the current level; at this point, the influence of allocation reduction would become too absurd to study seriously.

At the end of August, when the Planning Council presented the Tentative Draft, a heated debate arose between the council and representatives of the Army and Navy. The sober Tentative Draft was transformed by overexcited militants into emergency measures that stipulated first that the import of key materials would accelerate further; and second, that shipbuilding would accelerate to increase ocean transport capacity and the import of foreign ships and materials for shipbuilding (Tanaka, 1975, pp. 64–9).

Readers may be more surprised by the fact that the government, for the first time in the summer of 1940 (acting on an informal communication rather than a formal request), conducted this kind of national capacity evaluation than at the conclusions of the Tentative Draft or the reactions of the military. Already three years had passed since the beginning of the War with China, when Japan bombed Chongqing and Chengdu (Operation 101; see Chapter 8), and entered North Indochina, formalizing the Tripartite Pact.

With the announcement by the major powers that they would freeze the assets of Japan in July 1941, the Emergency MMPlan formulated on the assumption of import suspension became a true reality (Hara, 1994, p. 92).[26]

---

[26] For more details of the Tentative Draft, see Miwa (2008, p. 126, note 33; p. 144, note 56; pp. 168–9; and p. 246). See also the discussion in section 4–4 on juggling numbers.

4-3-3. An Effective and Efficient Use of Materials Allocated to the Military?

Here I review the effectiveness of the MMPlans from the viewpoint of specific sectors, rather than systematic war preparations and mobilization.[27] Before Japan's imports dried up, following the 1940 export embargo by major powers including the United States, the preferential allocation of key materials to the military was enforced effectively under the MMPlans.

Preferential allocation of key materials does not automatically result in their effective and efficient use. It is hard to believe that the military, responsible for all military production and the private production of munitions, really had the will, motivation, and capacity to achieve the most efficient use of key materials.

Even if the military leaders strongly wanted it, the realization of such efficiency would have been extremely difficult. To have managed production well, the Army would have needed to accomplish all the following:

- Recruit personnel with the skills to manage economic activities. It is a process of accumulating a wide variety of experiences, including many trials and errors over a long time, to be able to realize such efficiency.
- Train new staff, giving them the opportunity to gain competence, experience, and necessary skills.
- Organize staff into an efficient structure.
- Allow this management system to work effectively and efficiently.

This was an impossible challenge, even with the support of military leaders. When the war unexpectedly began, the Army faced an explosive demand for such capacity. As no systematic preparations preceded the war, the military had no choice but to rely on hastily built systems and coopted personnel.

Representing the Army, the War Preparation Section Chief of the Procurement Bureau (*seibi-kyoku*) of the AM participated in drawing up the MMPlans. The War Preparation Section, responsible for mobilization, was also in a position to speak for the Procurement Bureau as a whole.

---

[27] The MMPlans focused on the allocation of common steel. "According to its allocation to demand sectors, the military's share of demand came to more than 20 percent of the total in 1938 and 1939, and rose to over 30 percent in FY1940 and over 40 percent in FY1941. The share of demand for production capacity expansion industries remained consistently more than 30 percent, and the total share of other private demand sectors decreased gradually from more than 40 percent in FY1938 and FY1939 to just over 20 percent in FY1941.... Considering that 'private demand' incorporated indirect munitions demand, the degree both of increase in military demand and of decrease in pure private demand was amazing" (Hara, 1994, p. 89).

In collaboration with the Procurement Bureau (*heibi-kyoku*) of the NM, negotiating with the Planning Council and the Commerce Ministry, it formulated the MMPlans and secured materials for the Army. One official present at the Planning Council session (Tanaka, 1975, p. 61) recalled that the MMPlan was chiefly designed by Kikusaburo Okada, the War Preparation Section Chief of the AM.

Information about specific military demands was not available to the architects of the MMPlans. Did the War Preparation Section Chief who represented the Army fully understand the details of the military's demand? It is a decisively important question. Even a precise understanding of this demand would not have guaranteed that key materials allocated to the Army were used effectively and efficiently.

4-3-4. Demand Expansion Mechanism Under Rationing

The Resource Section in the Procurement Bureau took charge of the task of allocating the materials to relevant units. Takeo Takahashi (1985, p. 55) of the Resource Section offered the following important and persuasive commentary:

Switching onto a rationing system caused tremendous demand increases. Every material was insufficient. Everybody expected that he would receive much smaller allocations than his request. If he wanted to fulfill his responsibility, he would therefore make a request larger than his real demand. This amplification was repeated down the chain of command until the request grew into a huge volume; then, at the last stage, the materials were delivered from the munitions mobilization units to the Resource Section. Not having space for them, the Resource Section drastically curtailed the demands, beginning a process of restoration negotiation.

The trouble was that officials on the demand side did not understand the real demands accurately. It was a hastily formed system put in place out of necessity. The Resource Section making the allocation had no information about the history or past usage statistics of the individual units.

The official in charge at the end unit could not foresee exactly what his responsibilities would be in the coming term (whether a year, quarter, month, or week). In submitting a request larger than his real demand, he would take into consideration the need to respond flexibly to a wide variety of situations that might possibly occur. No penalty was imposed when his allocation resulted in a surplus; this rule applied to sections at every stage of the hierarchy. Munitions mobilization units that collected demands from the lower units and presented the aggregates had neither the capacity nor incentive to assess rigorously the appropriateness of individual demands.

End units had no incentive to report the surplus to any superior unit. Superior units had no incentive to uncover such surpluses. Moreover, surplus materials were sold on the black market to obtain useful provisions. Given these incentives, demand expanded under rationing, with no effective brake. No one had the time, capacity, or will to tackle the problem.[28]

Control associations, the Commerce Ministry, and other ministries received and summarized supply-and-demand information from private companies. Both types of organization helped to coordinate the distribution of materials to those companies. They had no more power or objectivity than the Resource Section or the War Preparation Section of the AM to take aggressive measures to contain demand expansion.

4-3-5. Illustration: The Case of Aviation Gasoline

The case of aviation gasoline epitomizes the difficulties in precisely understanding military demand. Even the Fuel Section of the AM Procurement Bureau could not precisely understand the Army's demand for aviation gasoline.

After threatening to repeal the Japan–U.S. Commerce and Navigation Treaty in July 1939 (it expired in January 1940), the U.S. government proposed a "moral embargo," prohibiting the sale and transfer of aviation gasoline manufacturing machines to designated countries.[29] In July 1940, it adopted a license system on exports to Japan, restricting scrap iron and oil products, including high-grade aviation gasoline.

The AM, acutely aware of the need for aviation gasoline, enforced the Army Fuel Arsenal Order on 1 August 1939. Before then, the Army had no body that managed the distribution of large quantities of oil (traditionally, the War Preparation Section was responsible for implementing the MMPlans). The Resource Section, renamed the Fuel Section in April 1941, became responsible for coal and oil issues, with other matters assigned to the War Preparation Section. For the first time, almost four years after the beginning of the War with China and eight months before the start of the Pacific War, the AM recognized the particular importance of fuel and established a Fuel Section to manage requests for coal and oil.

---

[28] Part of the military tended to disparage the MMPlans (Tanaka, 1975, p. 66), making the situation more difficult. However, this did not necessarily result in an abundant supply of materials to end units. See the recollection of Chihaya (1982, p. 104), a Staff Member at the Combined Fleets, quoted in section 9-6-2.

[29] See Boeicho (1975c, pp. 284–5).

How accurately did the Fuel Section understand oil demands? "The objective of its clerical work was not varied and complex products like machine tools. Our maximum effort for stockpiling was reaching a limit. In April–May 1941 there could be no hope of increasing oil imports from the U.S., even with our maximum effort" (Takahashi, 1985, p. 117).

The Fuel Section had no budget of its own. Instead, it oversaw many supply arsenals, called munitions mobilization units, which purchased, stored, and supplied the oil. The Fuel Section needed to collect from its supply arsenals information about the demand, supply, and storage of fuel in sectors. Relevant sections inside the AM took charge of those arsenals. Because the Army Fuel Arsenal was busy building oil refineries and had not been assigned the task of procuring and supplying fuel, the Fuel Section chose the Air Headquarters (nextdoor on the same site) to link with the supply arsenals responsible for aviation fuel (Takahashi, 1985, pp. 117–18).

As mentioned in section 3–6, the artificial petroleum project started with great fanfare. The Artificial Petroleum Industry Act was enacted in August 1937 and the Imperial Fuel Industry Company was established in January 1938. These measures already seemed unrealistic. For Takahashi, summarizing the supply and demand for aviation gasoline, the problem was on the demand side. Officials did not want to ask for necessary materials for demand estimation from the military administration side to the military command side. Supreme command, like a specter, got in the way (Takahashi, 1985, pp. 120–1).

Table 4–1, drawn up by Takahashi after the war, compares the forecast and result for Army aviation gasoline consumption. The prewar supply-and-demand forecast for consumption on the extreme right column shows that the Fuel Section cut the Air Headquarters' demand for 45,000 kiloliters per month for three months at the beginning of the war to 35,000 kiloliters per month. It was forecasted to decrease to 25,000 kiloliters per month starting in the fourth month. The result in the table shows that actual demand (probably the aggregate of demands for supply from end units, simply added together by the Head of Air Arsenals) did not increase after the War with China. The gap between demand and consumption gradually fell, until, in mid-1943, consumption caught up with demand. The Air Headquarters supply-and-demand forecast was far too high.

What shocked Takahashi more was the table showing consumption by octane number and item. The Air Headquarters required aviation gasoline to have an octane number higher than 92, suitable for aircraft with high-compression engines. The table showed that consumption for training

Table 4–1. *Comparison of forecast and result: army aviation gasoline consumption (unit: 1,000kl/Month)*

	Demand	Result			Consumption by Sector (%)				Prewar demand-supply Forecast for consumption Mostly octane number more than 92
		Consumption Octane number			Operation	Training	Transportation	Others	
		More than 91	Less than 87	Total					
									(45)
1941.2~42.3	15	3	6	9	30	30	30	10	35
1942.4~42.5	20	3	6	9	20	40	30	10	25
6~12	20	4	6	10	"	"	"	"	
1943. 1	30	7	8	15	25	35	30	10	
2	30	10	10	20	"	"	"	"	
3	30	12	13	25	"	"	"	"	
4	30	15	15	30	"	"	"	"	
5	30	16	16	32	"	"	"	"	
6~7	30	17	17	34	"	"	"	"	
8~11	30	17	18	35	"	"	"	"	
12	40	18	18	36	"	"	"	"	
1944. 1	40	19	19	38	"	"	"	"	
2	40	20	19	39	"	"	"	"	
3~6	40	20	20	40	30	30	30	10	
7	40	20	18	38	"	"	"	"	

8	40	20	16	36	"	"	"	"
9	40	20	14	34	"	"	"	"
10	40	20	12	32	"	"	"	"
11~12	40	20	10	30	"	"	"	"
1945. 1~4	40	20	10	30	40	20	30	10
5~8	40	20	5	25	30	30	30	10

Source: Takahashi (1985, p. 210, Table 10).

reached 30~40 percent, with two-thirds of the actual gasoline consumed having octane values below 87 (Takahashi (1985, p. 211).

Takahashi (1985, p. 213) recalled the "illusion of oil extinction": "After all, as the Section in the AM in charge of securing fuel for the Army, at least we could say that few operations had been obstructed because of a fuel shortage.... Due to a long-lasting fear of the 'illusion of oil extinction,' too much emphasis was placed on securing oil, from which we learned the lesson that we were too intuitive and illogical."

4-4. The Effectiveness of Economic Control as Measures for Economic Policy

4-4-1. Did the Rationing-Distribution System Function Effectively?

Economic control (the rationing system) took the planned aggregate supply volumes as given and cut or coordinated the aggregate demands to match those supply numbers. The government determined an allocation to each unit accordingly. The assumed control prices fell far below the market equilibrium prices. As a result, demand substantially exceeded supply, rationing became necessary, and the gap between the market equilibrating price and the control price created an opportunity for arbitrage. The size and attractiveness of the arbitrage opportunity depended on this price gap (or on the gap in volume between demand and supply). Black markets are always hard to eradicate, and they substantially inhibit the effectiveness of control.

At least three conditions had to be satisfied for the effective enforcement of economic controls such as the MMPlans:

1. The principal enforcing the control must have precisely forecast the supply of goods.
2. The principal must have precisely forecast the aggregate demand volume of the goods under control.
3. The principal must have taken appropriate action to block arbitrage.

Suppose, as with the MMPlans and economic controls closely connected with them, that the objective of the control was to enforce the preferential allocation of specified resources to predetermined sectors. If the supply volume fell below the planned volume, the preferential allocation might not be achieved. If the control principal did not estimate demand adequately, the preferential allocation would produce an inadequate result. Securing materials for preferential allocation might become impossible, causing uneven allocation among sectors. If the principal allowed the parties receiving preferential allocations to use the black market, then the objective of control would not be achieved.

Throughout the period of the War with China and the Pacific War, none of these three conditions was satisfied, as illustrated in the following subsections. Given the inadequate historical evidence, it is impossible to know the precise extent to which those conditions were not satisfied.

4-4-2. The Unredeemed Coupons Crisis

Few readers would believe that military officials were ever unable to exchange their rationing coupons. This is an episode described by Takahashi (1985, p. 57), then at the Fuel Section.

In the summer of 1940, when the United States introduced a license system governing scrap iron and oil, the supply of materials to every sector in Japan came apart at the seams. In 1941, the process of agreeing upon an MMPlan seemed endless. The primary cause of the delay was competition between the Army and Navy over materials in short supply, particularly major items of steel. As there was no change in the allocation-rationing system under the MMPlans, the connection between the supply plans with ration coupons and the actual flow of materials to be exchanged for coupons got out of control. This resulted in the unredeemed coupons crisis, first experienced by the general public. The government tried hard to contain the crisis by enacting laws, but parties routinely evaded them.

The coupons issued by the Army and the Navy were the strongest, and those issued by other ministries to meet private-sector demand were the weakest. Private-sector coupons were becoming mere scrap paper. Faced with mounting pressure from the Army and the Navy for production increases, managers in the munitions industries cried out for help – using private-sector coupons, they could barely obtain necessary materials. Quasimilitary coupons were issued, but these too became worthless. In addition to allocating materials to munitions mobilization units, the Fuel Section had to ask the Fuel Bureau of the Commerce Ministry for help in obtaining fuel and other materials for the munitions industries. Steel products for plant construction and repair were in such demand that officials themselves used quasimilitary coupons to try to obtain materials. Sometimes they were able to obtain military coupons from the AM's quota; as a last resort, they asked for help from the War Preparation Section.

Companies without access to these official and military countermeasures were in a far more serious situation.[30]

4-4-3. Number Juggling or Cosmetic Figures?

It is not hard to predict what will happen in a situation where the planned supply of key materials substantially falls below the aggregate demand. Japan's situation was exacerbated by the preferential treatment given to military and quasimilitary demand in the face of a limited import capacity, low stocks of important imports, and inadequate domestic production. Tanaka (1975) is full of descriptions that suggest how this prediction was realized.

At the outset, the parties involved urged the government to find a way and do something. The people in charge from the Army and Navy demanded a preferential allocation to the military demand. They realized that there had been a long-term conflict between the Army and the Navy, and that the interests within each organization were complex. They also realized that the military supply forecasts were related to national capacity and therefore represented national policy. Those situations and factors favored a resolution where numbers could be juggled, based on exaggerated supply forecasts.

The information used as a basis for the MMPlans was unreliable. Supply forecasts were conditional estimates that depended on various uncertain factors. There were varying opinions on the supply-estimating side. Factors such as wishful thinking were involved and necessarily influenced estimates of national capacity evaluation and a national policy.[31] It is no wonder that the plans were incompatible.

---

[30] Nakamura (1989, p. 16) offered commentary on the FY1940 MMPlan: control did not always work smoothly. Always and everywhere there were stories: ration coupons could not be exchanged for specified materials; on the one hand, there was too much stock; on the other hand, production was stopped due to a shortage of materials. Brokers intervened, and black market transactions prevailed. Also, during the postwar priority production scheme, the coupons for steel took two quarter years to be exchanged. For the details, see Miwa and Ramseyer (2004a, [1], 20–2).

[31] Summarizing several national capacity evaluations that preceded the beginning of the Pacific War, Nakamura and Hara (1970, p. xlii) concluded: "Obviously, there was the influence of the 'national capacity evaluation' on national policy and the distortion in evaluations caused by national policy. Setting aside 1938 and 1939, in 1940 and after it is beyond question that the 'evaluations' were overthrown by 'national policies.'" One of the evaluations included in their summary was introduced in Arisawa (1989, pp. 161–6). In February 1940, with the consent of Military (*gunji*) Section Chief Iwaguro and others in the AM, Lieutenant Colonel Jiro Akimaru (accounting officer) of the Military Bureau attracted economists, including Arisawa, to conduct research on countries such as Japan, the UK, the United States, Germany, and the USSR (the so-called Akimaru institution). Their conclusion from the summer and autumn of 1941 was that there is no possibility

One illustration is the reaction of the Army (as client) to the Tentative Draft for the Emergency MMPlan in the summer of 1940, described in section 4–3.[32] A similar case involved the allocation of steel by the FY1943 MMPlan. Having suppressed demand as much as possible, military officers still had to obtain essential materials. The Army and Navy Minister were unable to do so, even under tremendous pressure. The Navy Minister seemed poised to resign, and if he did, the Cabinet would collapse. The Planning Council was ordered to increase the supply capacity of steel (in other words, to pad the MMPlan) in order to avoid a crisis. After manipulating the figures, the council announced to the Army and Navy that it would be possible to increase steel production by 1 million tons. Army and Navy leaders understood that this assurance was unrealistic. The NM Military Bureau Chief Oka remarked (Tanaka, 1975, pp. 315–16): "We had negotiated an allocation for the Army and Navy of over 1.8 million tons of steel. One million tons of padding was unexpectedly large, and would destroy the MMPlans entirely."

A comparison of the initial plan, implementation plan, and actual achievement of the MMPlan shows that the supply capacity for steel was forced to decrease every year. Without exception, the initial plan was revised downward each year before implementation (Nakamura and Hara, 1970, p. xxix).

4-4-4. The Accuracy of Numbers as the Basis of the MMPlans

It is indispensable for the planner to grasp precise information about both the supply and the demand side. Otherwise, economic controls such as the MMPlans will not effectively achieve their desired goals. In addition, it is necessary to adopt an effective measure to eradicate opportunities for arbitrage (black market transactions) arising from gaps between the control

of increasing Japanese production capacity. German military capability was at its height, and the United States and UK could increase production. This conclusion was reported by Akimaru to the ACCom and the AM. ACCommander Sugiyama accepted that the research and method of evaluation were almost perfect, leaving no room for improvement. However, he also accepted that the conclusion was untenable, "against our national policy." He ordered all the copies of the report burned; the research institution was dissolved shortly thereafter.

[32] Another is turmoil in materials procurement between the Army and the Navy, in particular the well-known bloody battle between the Army and the Navy over munitions materials that occurred during the formulation of the FY1941 MMPlan. For the details of this turmoil, see Miwa (2008, pp. 133–44).

price and the market price. Moreover, the span of control must expand to all the relevant parties, including potential ones.

As described previously, even AM sections responsible for demand (the Fuel Section) and those involved in designing the MMPlan (the War Preparation Section) lacked precise information about actual Army demand. Accordingly, planners such as the Planning Council could not obtain it either.

Could planners have obtained precise information about the supply side? Suppliers had little incentive to present precise information to control associations or the Commerce Ministry. Those institutions had little incentive to report accurate information to umbrella organizations such as the Planning Council. The availability of arbitrage opportunities created an incentive to underreport production. The harsh reaction from umbrella organizations to any failure to attain the anticipated quantity of supplies must have made suppliers conservative with their numbers.

To quote Tadayoshi Obata (Ando, 1966, pp. 120–2) from Sumitomo corporate headquarters (later Vice-Chairman of the Planning Council in the second Konoe Cabinet):

I was in post for eight or ten months, and frankly had no idea what I was doing. Whether we could wage the war with the U.S. was the most basic question on which we formulated the MMPlans.... We spent time and energy just in feeling our way.... We could not draw any conclusion other than that Japan could not wage a long war. In addition, in Japan at that time, the numbers we had were unreliable. Many bureaucrats and military officials worked hard in the Planning Council. They drew conclusions with numbers, through accurate and complex calculations using detailed numbers .... Those numbers and statistics were reported by the private sector, however. Private sector numbers were wildly inaccurate from the start, since we ourselves had made them up. So long as they were based on those numbers, the MMPlans could not be reliable.[33]

At the end of October 1941, the IH-government Liaison Conference approved the following conclusion of the Planning Council as its National Capacity Evaluation before the beginning of the war:

We would be able to allocate on a steady basis marine vessels of 3 million tons (except at the initial stage it would be slightly less). In addition, as long as we maintain transportation with the South, it will be possible to maintain the national capacity (including common steel production) of 5 million tons per year while sustaining

---

[33] The same applies to those in charge of postwar economic control under the Priority Production Scheme (PPS), which Shiba, ed. (1948, p. 2) expressed as "a malady of desk-plan(ning)." For more details, see Miwa and Ramseyer (2004a, [1], p. 22) or Miwa (2008, p. 235, note 19).

people's minimum standard of living. Because Japan has a shortage of materials and is surrounded by the sea, the number of marine vessels and their allocation is the war leadership's major concern, both for waging war and for maintaining and cultivating the national capacity. (Tanemura, 1979, pp. 122–4)[34]

Recalling this National Capacity Evaluation, Tanemura concluded:

A comparison of actually observed numbers with the ones examined and adopted in late October vividly revealed how optimistic the judgment had been.[35] The forecast attrition rate of marine vessels, 800,000~1,000,000 tons per year, had not been based on careful investigation....The actual attrition rate stayed low in 1942, but after around August 1943 the volume of Japanese commercial ships sunk by U.S. submarines increased drastically. Between August and December 1943, 50,000, 100,000, 100,000, 100,000, and 130,000 tons were sunk. Between January and June, 1944, 150,000, 550,000 (the raid on Truk Islands), 300,000, 200,000, 250,000, and 350,000 (Saipan's fall) were sunk. Since then, the monthly average has been more than 250,000. These figures include only ships sunk; in addition there were nearly the same volume of fatally damaged ships. Moreover, these figures did not include naval vessels that were sunk or fatally damaged. (Tanemura, 1979, pp. 124–5)

4–4–5. Perspectives of the Relevant Industries and Companies on Economic Controls

As the MMPlans were part of economic controls, the accuracy of the numbers on which the MMPlans were based must be inextricably linked with the perspectives of the Japanese people, in particular, of those in the relevant industries and companies.

Responses to a questionnaire sent by the Japan Economic Federation to member companies on 17 January 1940 illustrate the industry view of economic controls. The questionnaire asked for feedback on flaws in the economic control system, industrial production and distribution, and specific countermeasures to correct those flaws.

---

[34] From his daybook on 29 October 1941, three days after the formation of the Tojo Cabinet, Tanaka (1975, p. 185) wrote: "Instead of foreign currency like the U.S. dollar and the sterling pound, ocean transportation became central to the wartime MMPlans. Before that date, there was almost no shipbuilding control" (Tanemura, 1979, p. 123).

[35] Concerning the National Capacity Evaluation, Imoto (1979, p. 50) recalled: "Upon examination, senior staff in charge of the AM concluded that due to the physical capacity of the nation it is impossible for Japan to wage a war against the U.S. Hearing this and its explanation, leaders in the ACCom and the AM experienced a major shock.... In the Planning Council the situation was almost the same.... After varied troublesome deliberations, however, they concluded that despite the difficulty in physical capacity, Japan would wage the war." See also the subsection "The Competence of the Planning Council" in section 4–1.

In this section, I summarize the opinions expressed through this questionnaire (MITI, 1964, pp. 431–4). The section on flawed economic controls is divided into three parts:

1. A general look at controls
2. A more detailed look at control laws and procedures
3. Other views of current economic controls[36]

In analyzing this sort of document, we should consider both the situation and historical background and ask relevant questions, such as, who expressed these opinions and with what intentions? Who produced the summary and why? Why did the Commerce Ministry need this summary? Was there an implicit understanding, not expressed in the document?

This summary reflects the perspectives of the Japanese people in relevant industries and companies.[37]

A General Look at Controls

- The national economy is an organic whole, and it is impossible to mechanically separate the war economy from the civilian one. It makes no sense to control industries, mechanically assigning them grades and establishing a hierarchy.

---

[36] The views summarized here are basically the same as the industry complaints and opinions raised at the roundtable conference on the current economy organized by the Japan Economic Federation in October 1938. The federation discussed this feedback with the Commerce Ministry. For more details, see MITI (1964, pp. 314–20).

[37] Yamane (1947, p. 133) argued: "The military neglected the very key to the nation's basic policy (a comprehensive planned economy established through government-private cooperation) and acted selfishly and self-righteously. This is a key to understanding the military's behavior during the Pacific War." Asking, "Why would the military adopt such autocratic (or ignorant and indiscreet) behavior?" Yamane next introduced business people who wanted to understand the military's behavior (pp. 134–5). His views are worth noting: "At the beginning, of course, the military made the effort to achieve cooperation with other ministries and industries to cultivate control associations. However, many military units in the field gave orders independently; the leaders could not fully control these. In addition, as war escalated, the military faced a huge demand for rearmament. It seemed more efficient, in dealing with emergency requests, for the military to negotiate directly with munitions plants rather than control associations. As the war intensified, this pattern increased, resulting in the enactment of the Munitions Company Act of October 1943. The conflict between business and the military over the MMPlans was not entirely the fault of the military, but also revealed the ignorance of businesspeople. The military refused to admit that the war situation was deteriorating. Businesspeople, ignorant of this reality, continued production in the same style as before, which irritated the military and made them distrustful, criticizing business as unpatriotic."

- In general, the controls are a mere desk-plan, deviating from the reality (in this case, metal refining, ammonium sulfate, and cement).
- Operations of national policy concerns overlap those of private companies, disturbing the priority system (mining).
- Communication and coordination are insufficient among controls (metal refining).
- Controls are entrusted to self-righteous bureaucrats, who are lax in their duties (metal refining).
- They enforce price control first before adopting allocation control, which inevitably promotes the use of the black market for procuring necessary materials (machine manufacturing).

A More Detailed Look at Control Laws and Procedures

- Various control procedures are extremely cumbersome (machine manufacturing, yarn-making, international trade, and fisheries).
- The letter of the law is flawed and difficult to apply (metal refining).
- Distribution channels are so complicated that the current control system just disrupts production (mining and yarn-making).
- There are too many control institutions; they dilute the control capacity (metal refining).
- Frequent improvement and elimination of control orders disturb business planning (textiles and others).

Other Views of Current Economic Controls

- Allocations and controls on particular items or materials are enforced arbitrarily, in an impromptu manner, without any unified comprehensive foundation (machine manufacturing, *tabi* or Japanese socks, shipbuilding, and fisheries).
- There is no consistency between production planning and materials allocation (cotton spinning).
- Lack of communication between ministries (machine manufacturing, shipbuilding, and silk fabric).
- It is unclear which ministry has authority, and so it is difficult to establish close communication with the industry (fisheries).
- Due to the increase in production costs, the current control price makes no business sense (mining, pharmaceuticals, cement, silk fabric, Japanese socks, and beer).

The following are responses from the private sector. The general view was that there is a strong feeling of opposition to bureaucratic control, and we should emphasize inventive ideas from the private side and their voluntary activities.

- There is no need to establish new control institutions. Instead, we should make use of existing institutions (metal refining).
- The government should restrict itself to supervising the basics of control; operations should be delegated to the private sector (shipbuilding).
- The government should hire experts who understand how industry works, and let them control the industry (cotton spinning).
- In enforcing controls, we should emphasize inventive ideas from the private sector. We should not create useless friction by establishing a national policy (mining in general).
- It is necessary to promote communication and cooperation between the government and the private sector (international trade).
- We should accept *zaibatsu* capitalists who respect tradition, capacity, and technology and prioritize production expansion. We should separate policies for rescuing inefficient industries from policies for expanding production (mining).

4–5. The Black Market and the MMPlans

4–5–1. Resisting the Black Market

Japan had a large black market, which had a significant impact on the management and working of the controlled economy. The term "black market" is difficult to define. Whatever definition we adopt leaves a gray zone. In the case of wartime Japan, there is neither detailed comprehensive information about its functioning nor accurate information about its size.

Nishida (1994) divided the period July 1938~August 1945 into quarters and discussed the gradual change in the character of economic crimes. He characterized each quarter as follows:

1. Supply shortage in important materials and increase in economic crimes – July 1938~December 1939
2. Pervasiveness of price control and explosion of price control violations – January 1940~December 1940
3. *kokumin-ka* (nationwide expansion) of economic crimes, becoming more serious in character – January 1941~March 1943
4. Collapse of the controlled economy and the breakdown of people's lives – April 1943~August 1945

About the third period, Nishida (1994, p. 386) explained: "According to the statistics, the number of economic crimes stabilized. In fact, the black market was taking over, and popular trust in the controlled economy substantially deteriorated."

On the fourth period, he offered this commentary: The Munitions Company Act enforced at the end of 1943 "effectively abolished the orders to control prices, wages, and accounting procedures that were, at that time, major bottlenecks of production. In the process, it provided a green light for the black market,"[38] in which the munitions companies and the military appeared as leading players.

Nishida studied the character of economic crimes committed by the military and munitions companies. These institutions were leading players and helped drive the controlled economy to collapse. Crimes of corruption dramatically increased after the first half of this period. Nishida (1994, p. 398) then concluded: "During the fourth period, economic crimes were so prevalent that people could not survive without the black market. The military and munitions companies themselves snatched up not only munitions materials but also private materials, including food. They neglected and paralyzed the controlled economy. This weakened the regulatory body policing economic crimes."

The Act to Revise National General Mobilization (the NGM Act) was enacted in March 1941, focusing on strengthening the penalties for malignant crimes. The maximum prison sentence allowed for violations of Article 8 (allocation control) and Article 19 (price control) changed from three to ten years, while the maximum fine rose from 5,000 to 10,000 yen. The TIEG Act was revised in the same manner, to strengthen penalties. Together with a revision of the criminal code in the same seventy-sixth Diet session, these acts exposed the escalation in control violations and deepening conflicts within the controlled economy (MITI, 1964, pp. 453-4).[39]

---

[38] Quoted from Kikuchi (1947, p. 27). Kikuchi continued: "Under the financial institution designation system for loans, munitions companies could obtain loans without restriction. Their profusion of funds went further, purchasing *machiai* [high-class traditional Japanese restaurants] as company dormitories and carrying on in luxurious clubs, which were subject to criticism recently and are still fresh in our memory. From this period, the divergence between finance and production plans expanded drastically, but the surplus did not return to the National Treasury. The military's high purchasing prices, supported by this huge temporary war expenditure, always attracted the attention of prosecutors. After the second half of 1943, aggressively distributed 'advance money' created a bigger money glut, from which the 'advance money broker' emerged."

[39] Furukawa (1992, p. 205), referring to shorthand minutes No. 12 of the House of Peers of the Imperial Diet, explained that those revisions were accounted for by the number of violations of the NGM and TIEG Acts, totaling more than nine hundred thousand. In

Nine months later, the Pacific War began. It lasted three years and eight months. Just after the end of the war, Prosecutor Kikuchi (1947) made three points:

- First, in the private sector, it was widely believed that bureaucrats and people with friends in politics could often obtain products at controlled prices. This was generally viewed as a crime and an abuse of power, lacking in common sense. Thus, in the public mind, controlled and black market prices were reversed; it was controlled prices that were associated with privilege and wrongdoing (Kikuchi, 1947, pp. 26–7).
- Second, from the beginning of economic control to the end of the war, many practitioners argued that the government should strengthen the penalties on brokers, but they argued in vain. The laws for materials and price control did not assume the existence of brokers. However, enormous numbers of brokers emerged during the war. Many had lost their jobs to the successive enterprise readjustments. From the first half of 1943, munitions companies aggressively used brokers for materials acquisition, further increasing their numbers. The activities of brokers fundamentally destroyed the controlled economy. Every law practitioners' meeting discussed the need to strengthen penalties, and local prosecuting offices tried to increase regulation, in part because of the weak penalties. However, brokers continued to proliferate (Kikuchi, 1947, p. 55).
- Third, the breakdown of Japan's controlled economy was caused by the following, rather than deterioration in moral principles among the public: (1) failures in control operations; (2) the corruption of leaders in the military, the government, and the bureaucracy; and (3) the black market, which was virtually endorsed by the military and government. Because rationing was not enough to live on, honesty did not pay. People could only obtain materials in the black market. Because the military and the government set an example, the black market was all pervasive, and black market entrepreneurs flourished. Because leaders became corrupt, production was inhibited and morale suffered (Kikuchi, 1947, p. 122).

In charting the failure of the controlled economy and its causes, Kikuchi, 1947, pp. 89–90) also noted:

his interpellation, Peer Akaike argued: "In a mere four years since the enactment of the NGM Act and the TIEG Act, the total number of persons under arrest exceeded 920,000, of whom more than 120,000 were punished. We had never seen laws creating such a huge number of criminals in a short time" (minutes, p. 95).

Violations by the military and munitions companies began with releasing war materials such as steel to the private sector through the black market. Those military-related sectors had an excess of materials and the private sector had only shortages. To meet military demand, materials were allocated to plants in volumes larger than their actual needs. This caused the military sectors to release surplus materials to the private sector. By 1941, major cases of this type had emerged.

As materials decreased, the black market for materials flourished. Without them, companies could not meet their deadlines for manufacturing munitions because of imbalances or the nondelivery of materials. Expecting future shortages, they stocked up on materials.... When finally the military authorities admitted and encouraged their use, some violators pretended to be patriots. Some recognized that violations would not be prosecuted if military demands were involved. Those tendencies created serious problems for prosecutors.[40]

Little information is available about the reality of the black market and its prices. The following episode, described by Yamaguchi (1946, p. 122), illustrates the situation:

The enterprise readjustment in the summer of 1943 involved the frequent transfer of machine tools, conspicuously raising their black market prices with no limit. With a roundup in November of machine tools on the black market, the authorities reclaimed more tools than expected, distributing these to sectors with shortages. They could also make a profit in metal and wool products. As the war situation deteriorated, the authorities urgently needed war materials and schemed to extract them. They established the public purchase corporation, which offered prices four times higher than the control prices. As a result, volumes were smaller than expected, showing the high profits brokers could make. In response to the high prices offered, some newly manufactured inferior products emerged.

4–5–2. The Basic Character and Coverage of the MMPlans

The MMPlans did not cover all resources and products. In the black market, supposedly controlled resources and products were traded. There were also markets where uncontrolled products were traded.

I focus here on markets that were not subject to the controlled economy. Unfortunately, investigating their influence on the MMPlans is beyond the scope of this book, primarily due to the lack of empirical information.

First, note that the MMPlans were designed for inputs rather than outputs. From beginning to end, the government calculated the supply capacity of materials such as common steel and allocated them to demand sectors

---

[40] See also Kikuchi (1947, p. 96) and Yamaguchi (1946, pp. 125–7, 133), as introduced in Miwa (2007, [1], p. 56, note 64).

such as the military and the private sector.[41] This impacted the MMPlans in two ways:

1. Whether it was military or private-sector demand, the planning authority did not supervise and control the entire process of distribution to the final demander. In the military demand sector in particular, almost the entire process was beyond the authority's control. From the end of 1941, control associations established in many key industries were expected to play an important role. As I showed in section 3–5, the Army (Navy) Industry Association was absolutely independent of and stronger than the control associations. Most major munitions companies were designated by the military and placed under their control and supervision, and joined this association. That is, most major munitions production related companies were virtually outside control associations.[42]

2. The planning authority did not involve itself with making, using, or distributing products, either to the military or to the private sector. Control associations in key industries were expected to become more involved, but intervention was partial and did not cover all sectors. The military-related companies were outside the control associations.[43]

Yamane (1947, pp. 123–4) reviewed the links between the government's production administration and the MMPlans. Control associations were established during the time of the Commerce Ministry. At that time, the

---

[41] Obviously, not all the materials were included in the MMPlans.

[42] People in other fields than the military were also not always cooperative with the planning authority. The following recollection on rail transport by Tanaka, the chief official in charge of transport in the General Coordination Section of the Planning Council, is indicative. "I firmly believed it necessary to introduce 'planning' in rail transport and make it compatible with the MMPlans and expand its capacity. With its long-cultivated professional awareness of the supremacy of railways, the Railways Ministry in charge of the National Railways was monomaniacal with a dogmatic pride, arguing that 'it was better to leave it to a specialist.' People in the Vehicle Assignment Section … simply preened themselves on their techniques, and behaved outrageously as if there were no MMPlans" (Tanaka, 1975, p. 269).

[43] Referring to the FY1942 MMPlan, Tanaka (1975, p. 243) commented: "The MMPlans had lost their independence. Materials ministries, first receiving allocations from the Planning Council, asked the Army and the Navy for additional materials when necessary. It was customary to receive materials from the military. The military obtained excess materials. It was a custom of the Railways Ministry and the Ministry of Home Affairs in particular to carry out construction work requested by the military and receive supplies. Public construction work appeared to be for the military. This was how the MMPlans lost their control power. With the help of the military, the government as a demand sector received an unexpectedly substantial allocation."

authority of the Commerce Ministry covered only 40 percent of important munitions production. The administration of war mobilization was disrupted by many ministries, including the AM and NM. Except for a few materials sectors such as steel and coal, control associations in most sectors were based on the private demand that occupied 20 or 30 percent of the market. At the start, the Cabinet agreed to cultivate and strengthen control associations, while ministries delegated some of their responsibility and authority to them. As the war developed, the quantity of war supplies in direct and indirect use increased tremendously, and the proportion of munitions industries (including military-controlled plants) in the economy rose. When the military placed those plants under its control and guidance, separating them from control associations, the comprehensively planned operation of munitions industries was headed for collapse.

4–5–3. Not All Listed Materials Were Covered by the MMPlans

Because the planning authority was not aware of all listed materials, the MMPlans did not necessarily cover them.

The following story from the oil sector may sound extreme, but other sectors also experienced a gap.

Engineer Lieutenant Takahashi, of the Fuel Section of the AM Procurement Bureau, was completely responsible for identifying the supply and demand of fuel in the AM. After the war, Takahashi, then an Army major, corresponded with the U.S. Strategic Bombing Survey's investigations into the oil industry. The gap between appearance and reality in Takahashi's analysis of fuel issues (1985, p. 232) is informative. According to the structural chart, first there were the MMPlans, under which the Planning Council controlled the whole supply of oil. The Army, Navy, and Munitions Ministry received their oil allocations based on the MMPlans. After the U.S. oil embargo in August 1941, the MMPlans collapsed. Once war began, the southern quarter became Japan's only major source of oil. Arguing that it was now part of the military operation under the supreme command, the Army and the Navy established the Oil Committee, leaving the Planning Council and the Munitions Ministry completely ignorant of the supply and demand of oil.

The correspondence between a Survey writer and Takahashi (1985, p. 233) is telling:

"So, you mean, for a long time you had been unable to formulate effective MMPlans. Almost all oil came from the southern quarter. The Army and Navy took most of this, and allocated a tiny remainder to the Planning Council and the Munitions Ministry."

"You are absolutely correct!"

Before the start of the Pacific War, ocean transportation was central to the MMPlans and war leadership. The most important issue for the Planning Council, evaluating national capacity in October 1941, was the supply of ships for ocean transportation. Assuming war with the United States and the UK, the council needed to take into consideration both the volume of ships requisitioned by the military and the volume sunk by enemy aircraft or submarines.

The Shipping Operation Committee was established on 1 April 1942, under the Wartime Ocean Shipping Control Order of March 1942. The committee took charge of controlling ships and crews and enforcing planned transport. However, many ships requisitioned by the Army and Navy were beyond the remit of the Operation Committee, and the increase in requisitioned ships decreased the number available for ocean transport.

The incident of 7 December 1942 involving the requisition of ships is well known. Strategy Division Chief Tanaka of the ACCom (the Army Division of the IH) shouted at Prime Minister Tojo in his office. For the battle over Guadalcanal Island, the ACCom asked the AM to increase ship requisitions by 370,000 tons for transporting new troops and for subsequent replenishments. The AM argued that its main responsibility was to improve the national capacity for waging the war, and that Japan should retreat from Guadalcanal and reorganize its war preparations. In addition, the Navy proposed to increase ship requisitions by 250,000 tons. The Planning Council, strongly criticizing the violation of the commitment to eliminate their ship requisitions of 2,600,000 tons, pressed the Army to resolve this unsettled issue before increasing its requisition (Tanaka, 1975, p. 280).

At the extraordinary Cabinet meeting of the night on 5 December, the government finalized its attitude toward the increase in ship requisitions. Recognizing that the ACCom had no choice but to halt the decisive battle over Guadalcanal, the Vice-ACCommander and the Strategy Division Chief urged Prime Minister Tojo to reconsider the issue, resulting in the previously described incident.[44] Ship allocation decisively affected not only the MMPlans but also the adoption of specific war operations.

In many sectors other than oil, materials were used and shipped outside the MMPlans. Unfortunately, no specific information is available.

---

[44] This is the well-known shouting incident. For more details, see Tanemura (1979, pp. 175–82) and Nishiura (1980, pp. 178–81), or Miwa (2008, pp. 244–5).

Most of the supplies included in the MMPlans were newly produced. Items that existed as working stock (for example, machine tools in operation) were not discussed. Beyond doubt, the immense amount of oil stockpiled by the Navy before the Pacific War remained outside the MMPlans.

On 13 May 1942, the Enterprise Readjustment Order was announced, legally enforcing enterprise reorganization for existing firms. On 1 June 1943, the Cabinet approved the Basic Outline of Enterprise Readjustment for Strengthening War Potential. This outline, which classified industrial sectors for readjustment into three categories, specifically indicated the industrial sectors that should make a significant contribution by delivering a workforce and scrapped metals and by diverting plants and equipment. In collaboration with enterprise readjustment, the government enforced policies for recovering material.[45]

4–6. Effectiveness and Efficiency in the Use of Materials for the Military Demand

4–6–1. The Consequence of an Administrative-Command (or Socialist Planned) Economy

In a report written just after the war, Prosecutor Yamaguchi (1946, pp. 123–4) explains the difficulties and questions involved in allocating materials for uncontrolled military demand. The military required materials that were well managed and allocated preferentially, and needed to use these effectively and efficiently. The report argued that the problems encountered were consistent with the predicted consequences of an administrative-command or socialist planned economy. These conditions were typical of systems and institutions that were hurriedly constructed and undeveloped:

Even if innumerable economic laws and orders stretched in a finely meshed pattern were effectively enforced, and even if required materials and the workforce were smoothly supplied to prescribed ends, we cannot directly conclude that the war economy was successful. Economic control was only a means to achieve a basic plan about the economy at a high level.... The more irrational factors the basic plan included, the less the war economy could have achieved its objectives. Did the basic plan respond effectively to the demands of the strategies of the Army or the Navy? Did it rationally exclude waste and bias? ... In response to the demands of the war, the military demanded strong control over the economy. At the same time, it must have enforced no less strong control inside the military.... I deeply fear that the military itself disturbed the smooth enforcement of the war economy.

---

[45] See MITI (1964, pp. 562–74). It judged the impact of the latter as fairly doubtful (p. 574).

It insisted on its demands as the number one priority, and ordered the government to provide what it required. "We need not explain, because our reasons are military secrets." Through the process, it obtained a larger workforce and more materials than necessary.

The military's approach to the economy was widely discussed for the first time after the war.

4-6-2. Example: The Construction of Large-Scale Battleships

It would not be true to say that materials allocated to the military were used systematically, effectively, or efficiently. Kenryo Sato, who, as the Military (*gunmu*) Section Chief and the Military Bureau Chief of the AM, spent most of the war trying to allocate materials between the Navy and Army, wrote as follows (Sato, 1976, pp. 283–4):

The Navy must have been restructured to be the Air Force–first principle, and Naval vessels became an assistant military power. In addition, during the Pacific War, convoy operations became extremely important, but the Navy did not reflect this in its basic policy. Convoy operations were the life force of the nation and the source of war capability. Without recognizing their importance, the Navy could not be well prepared. Preparations involving antisubmarine weapons and strategies were insufficient and crude. The Navy alone was not to blame. The Army should also have studied convoy operations and prepared more. However, when the Army began to prepare for escort transport and landing ships, it triggered condemnation from the Navy. Not only landing operations but also moves between islands and materials supply required self-defense to some extent. We could accomplish this by ourselves without help from the Navy when the task was small-scale. We understood this only after the Pacific War began – before that, it was beyond our ability to anticipate. In fact, the Army had not expected a war against the U.S. and UK over such a vast extent of sea.[46]

Sato continued, "Even after the start of the Pacific War, the Navy continued to devote huge amounts of steel and shipbuilding capacity to constructing large-scale battleships of seventy thousand DWT [deadweight tonnage]. These contributed nothing, and went to the bottom of sea. They had been inspired by the 'large-scale battleships with big cannons doctrine,' from which the Navy awoke too late. Indeed, the war ended without their

---

[46] A former Staff Member of the Combined Fleets recalled (Chihaya, 1982, p. 110): "After the war began, many emphasized the importance of ocean transport. What had the Navy been studying and doing for ocean transport before, I wonder? To my regret, I have never heard of specific studies undertaken by the Navy."

having ever awakened."[47] He concluded, "I bore a deep grudge against the large-scale battleships doctrine."

Such criticism was not rare among former Navy officers. A former Staff Member of the Combined Fleets recalled (Chihaya, 1982, p. 75): "Aircraft taking off from the task force's aircraft carriers achieved the great success of the surprise attack on Pearl Harbor. Land-based attack aircraft taking off from air stations in South French Indochina sank two UK battleships to the ocean floor off the Malay Peninsula. The subsequent unresisted advance in the southern quarter was primarily due to the good showing of the Navy Air Force. All that time, most of the battleship-centered fleets that the Japanese Navy had prepared as the backbone of its fleet of ships were unnecessarily anchored in Hiroshima Bay. Only four high-speed battleships took part in the attack, and none of them had an opportunity to fire a shot at their original target."

Japan's slow response after the hideously devastating defeat at the Battle of Midway in June 1942 is indicative. Chihaya wrote, "We painfully recognized that aircraft carrier–centered fleets were crucial, and that fleets without aircraft carriers, however overwhelming they might be, were a wheel without an axle."[48] He continued: "For the first time, the Navy hurried to build aircraft carriers and augment the air forces. *Shinano*, the third large-scale battleship of the *Yamato* type, was to be remodeled as an aircraft carrier. However, the Navy had not yet made the great transformation to the Air Force–first principle.... It was because Navy leaders firmly believed that the 46 centimeter naval guns of *Yamato* and *Musashi*, the centerpieces of the battleship gun first principle, would play a significant role. In fact, the purpose of the exercise of two battleships remained as before, a decisive battle between battleship fleets" (Chihaya, 1982, pp. 82–3). "It was in 1944 that the organization of the Combined Fleets was fundamentally restructured to become aircraft carrier–centered" (Chihaya, 1982, p. 252).

4–6–3. Two Additional Episodes for Illustration

The members of the War History Chamber of the Defense Agency that compiled the *Library of War History* in 102 volumes supplied valuable information and stories (Morimatsu, 1985) that have not attracted widespread

---

[47] The Navy devoted the First, Second, and Fifth Air Force fleets – that is, all the formal aircraft carriers that the Japanese Navy possessed at that time – to the Hawaiian Campaign. It was a subordinate action, however. Battleship fleets – including *Yamato*, the main force – were anchored in Hiroshima Bay (Chihaya, 1982, p. 252).

[48] Translation of *kanameno nai ougi*, literally a fan without a linchpin.

attention. The two episodes I recount in this section raise questions about the effective and efficient use of materials allocated to uncontrolled military demand.

The first episode is related to the so-called chairborne troops – ground support troops of the Army Air Force. The total size of the Army Air Force at the end of the war was approximately 690,000, of which 630,000 were ground support troops (if we include all members not in headquarters or the flying corps). These included a variety of troops responsible for area command, airfield construction, information and communication, weather observation, and measurement of air routes and speed, as well as supply and repair.

Some of these performed poorly, as a result of insufficient training. In many cases, the ground support troops were delayed when taking charge of battlefields. This resulted in inadequate research on the characteristics of these areas. Many ground support troops (including those responsible for airfield construction and air route measurement) were organized for war on an ad hoc basis. For troops of this type, there had been no peacetime research on their operations. Because of the short interval between their organization and operation, in many cases they could not achieve planned objectives. The Army Air Force was slow to organize its troops. One reason for this was a characteristically casual way of thinking about ground support: "When troops are organized with manpower and equipment, they will manage to achieve their ground support tasks somehow" (Nawata, 1985, pp. 178–80).[49]

The second episode is related to the curved runways that contributed to the elimination of the air forces on the ground. The Army Air Force broke

---

[49] The situation was almost the same in the Navy (Chihaya, 1982, pp. 220–8). Before beginning the Pacific War, the NCCom had paid no attention to airfield construction troops. In fact, there weren't any. When the Air Force became the leading player during the long, drawn-out war of attrition that developed between Japan's land-based attack aircraft and the United States, airfield construction troops became important, second only to fleets of airplanes. When the war ended, the Navy had more than two hundred airfield construction troops, with more than one hundred thousand personnel (not including troops destroyed by the Allied Powers, as in Guadalcanal). Troops were equipped with picks, shovels, and trams, with machines such as trucks and rollers at best. In 1944, even the most mechanized troops simply had many trucks. The Naval brigade, when they took over Wake Island, found bulldozers at a corner of an airfield. They marveled at the capacity of these machines, learning from a prisoner that they were used in constructing airfields, as each could do the work of more than one hundred people. NCCom leaders, without any experience or knowledge of civil engineering works, forced their troops to carry out extremely daring enterprises in civil engineering technology. In addition to the gap in technological capacity between airfield construction troops, such leadership greatly undermined the effective use of allocated materials. See also section 9–6.

into the southeast quarter. As there was mountainous jungle close to the beach, the Japanese military constructed airfields along the shore in a single line. Being narrow, the runways tended to be curved. It was not easy to improve on this, given the geographical features and lack of civil engineering machinery and materials. Nevertheless, the Army packed many fleets of airplanes into those defective airfields. When the airfields were filled with airplanes, the U.S. Air Force descended on them in large numbers. Japan's Air Force fought well, but performed poorly because of delayed information and poor airfield conditions.

Of the Army airplanes lost during August–December 1943, approximately 80 percent had accidents either during takeoff or landing or on the ground. Only 20 percent were lost in aerial combat. For this reason, people said that in the southeast, the Army Air Force was defeated during the airfield construction race. Ground forces in East New Guinea were unable even to withdraw. In order to maintain supplies for them, Japan needed to keep its advantage in the air. Although the ground forces cooperated with the airfield construction troops, elite units of the Army Air Force were swiftly depleted by defective airfields.

According to a senior official in charge of Air Force operations at the Army Headquarters, the Army did not want to send its Air Force to the southeast quarter, but was forced to do so by the situation. It was possible because of the relationship between the Army and the Navy and the status of the Army Air Force. Leaders at Headquarters caused the defeat by advancing troops without carefully investigating the characteristics of their battlefields or Air Force operations (Ikuta, 1985, pp. 182–4).

4-7. Summary

Economic control in wartime Japan, symbolized by the MMPlans, was ineffective in all stages of war preparation and mobilization, regardless of the criteria used to evaluate its functions and roles. It also failed to work effectively as a policy measure for planning and implementing systematic war preparations.

Resource allocation under the MMPlans (or economic control in general) was far from ideal. We must view with considerable skepticism the effective and efficient use of the uncontrolled military demand (Tanaka, 1975, p. 285).

Economic control began with little preparation for its effective implementation. There was no system for collecting the information needed for the effective and efficient enforcement of economic control. The War with China began unexpectedly, and economic control was introduced and extended in a hurry. It is noteworthy that this inadequate situation never improved before the end of the war. As the decision-making unit, the state (or the government, including the military) consistently demonstrated a poor understanding of the substance and limits of economic control and the conditions necessary for its effective enforcement. The state did not appreciate the damage created through poor preparations or the need to adopt effective countermeasures. This worsened the situation further. Thus, systematic war preparations, war mobilization, and economic control were all inadequate. Systematic preparations for identifying potential obstacles and implementing countermeasures were similarly inadequate.

The limits of economic control and the obstacles that blocked its effective enforcement could have been predicted by leaders familiar with business. However, from start to finish, economic control was managed by the military. These men were remote from the business world and ignorant of business activities. Popular criticism of capitalism and a laissez-faire economy (Nakamura, 1989, p. 9) also made the situation worse, even after the lessons of war might have provided a warning.

All of these points apply to the government's policies in general. Whether or not they were official plans, the government's market policies, including the production capacity expansion plans (policies) that I study in the next chapter, were ineffective.

4-7-1. "Bedtime Stories from the Business World"

How well did ordinary citizens understand the black market? Consider the following account from Taro Sagami (1940), entitled *Bedtime Stories from the Business World – the Armed Japanese Economy*, published in April 1940 by Banri-kaku. The book collects his recent articles written over one and half years for *Bungei Shunju*, a widely read monthly magazine. They reflect the state of society during the first half of the War with China. Sagami shows that most people did know about industry, economic controls, and the black market. It is interesting that the government never restricted the publication of these articles; clearly the existence of the black market was common knowledge at the time.

I sympathize with bureaucrats in the Commerce Ministry.... Whatever they might say out of politeness, most business people do not respect what the petty officials of the Commerce Ministry say.... When a bureaucrat receives an order to increase production, he willingly accepts it saying, "Sure," but postpones it – making excuses, and asserting that it makes no business sense.... Officers are chagrined, but those richly experienced in the business world are beyond their power. (p. 330)

The prevalence of the black market has recently intensified. The prosecutors' office, faced with a rapid increase in malicious offenders, has apparently decided to impose more severe punishments. Any company, whatever it may be, gets a lot of business.... Even a tiny munitions company can receive steel, coal, and other materials as allocations for the military demand. Quite often, it is said, the firms save some of those materials, or from the beginning demand more materials than they need. They then offer the materials to the private sector at higher prices, that is, on the black market.... You might say that the Commerce Ministry should send supervisors to regulate them, but bureaucrats in the Commerce Ministry are not economic police officers. They do not have the capacity to examine in detail how much steel and coal each company actually used for the military demand. They have many plants all over the place and managing them is beyond the capacity of amateurs. Even when black market dealers are arrested, it is a Sales Section Chief or Purchasing Section Chief who is punished. The President and Senior Managing Directors act all innocent. (Sagami, 1940, pp. 130–3)

Introducing these stories, the author quoted the Prime Minister of the time, Admiral Mitsumasa Yonai, speaking to the Diet while he was still the Navy Minister (from February 1937 to August 1939): "We must be careful not to enforce economic control excessively. We should not expand control over citizens' consumption" (Sagami, 1940, p. 99).

5

Production Capacity Expansion Plans and Policies

5-1. Overview

5-1-1. Toward the Production Capacity Expansion Plans (PCEPlans)

Chapter 5 focuses not only on the PCEPlans but also on production capacity expansion policies (PCEPolicies). Chapter 6 examines Japan's development plans and policies in occupied Manchuria (Manchukuo) and the relationship between "Team Manchuria" and the PCEPlans and PCEPolicies.

In Chapter 3, I introduced the conventional, dominant view promoted by Oishi (1994) that the PCEPlans were the foundation of Japan's economy in the 1930s and early 1940s. This conventional approach introduced but failed to clearly define a range of key concepts, involving a "total war regime," economic control, Manchurian development, the reorganization of Japan's politicoeconomic system along fascist lines, the "military business embracing," and the "Three Principles of Public Finance and the Economy."

On 17 June 1937, the Army presented the government's Planning Agency with a Five-Year Plan for Key Industries and an associated Outline (enforcement guide); this was the start of the PCEPlan development process.[1] As shown in subsection 1-4-3, the Army simultaneously began a fully fledged armament enhancement plan (during FY1937–FY1942), while the Navy began its landmark third replenishment plan (FY1937–FY1941). The Manchukuo Five-Year Industry Development Plan also began in 1937.[2]

---

[1] The historical importance of this Five-Year Plan for Key Industries was that it later became the prototype of the PCEPlans formulated as an axis of wartime control and planning. The Outline became the prototype for various pieces of legislation and policies for economic control, including the NGMAct of 1938 (Ando, 1976, p. 207).

[2] In accordance with the vision of Kanji Ishiwara, who became the Strategy Section Chief of the ACCom in August 1935, the Army formulated a large-scale expansion plan for munitions production. Ishiwara was firmly convinced that, while absolutely averting war for the next five years, Japan should dramatically expand its production capacity in heavy industries

It is not surprising that the PCEPlans have been at the core of the conventional wisdom and the dominant view of Japan's wartime economy. Most people believe that Japan's military leaders carefully and systematically prepared for war, adopting an effective and well-developed system of economic control. In reality, the Cabinet approved the Outline of the PCEPlans on 17 January 1939, a year and a half *after* the start of the War with China. Only the Outline was approved, while concrete plans for expanding and enforcing production capacity remained undecided.

In responding to the China Incident, the Five Ministers Conference of 24 June 1938 made clear that the Army and Navy both hoped to end the war that year. However, despite capturing Guangdong and Hankou in fall of 1938, Japan was unable to destroy the government of Chiang Kai-shek and end the war. After the capture of Hankou in October 1938, Japan's limited military strength and resources prevented it from completely defeating the Chinese military, creating an impasse. The second Konoe Proclamation of 22 December 1938 announced a new order in East Asia, setting Japan on the path toward a long, drawn-out war of attrition. It was not until 17 January 1939, nearly a month after the Konoe Proclamation, that the Cabinet approved the Outline of the PCEPlans.

5–1–2. Basic Observations on the PCEPlans and PCEPolicies

As described in Chapter 2, less than a year after the Outline was approved, the Vice-ACCommander and Army Minister agreed that the current policy could not last; even the maintenance of the status quo over a long period would be difficult for Japan. Following the second Konoe Proclamation, Japan's military position continued to deteriorate, although the Chinese position stabilized.

Two important observations can be made.

First, Japan had no PCEPlans and Policies before the second Konoe Proclamation.

to create a munitions industry both in Japan and Manchuria. He directed the Study Group on Finance and Economy in Japan and Manchuria to formulate a concrete plan (for more about this "Miyazaki Institute," see section 5–2–1). In August 1936, the study group presented the "Five-Year Revenue-Expenditure Plan for FY 1937, with an Outline of National Policy for Urgent Use." After repeated revisions, the Five-Year Industry Development Plan in Manchuria was enforced and the Japan-Manchuria Munitions Industry Expansion Plan finalized in 1937. The latter was presented to the Cabinet as the AM's Outline of a Five-Year Plan for Key Industries and Outline of a Five-Year Plan for the Munitions Manufacturing Industries (Hara, 1994, p. 78).

Second, by the time the Cabinet approved the Outline that laid the foundation for developing and enforcing PCEPlans, Japan's national power had been seriously exhausted by the War with China. The country needed immense resources to overcome damage and survive the long, drawn-out war of attrition. In addition, Japan's relationship with the United States was worsening, leading to new restrictions. It was becoming increasingly difficult to prioritize production capacity expansion for the future when allocating resources.

Expanding production requires both resources and time. To create a specific new capacity requires a plan. New production equipment must be designed, produced, and transported to factories where it can be installed and operated on a trial basis; also, management system must be established for its operation, including personnel training and skill-formation. Although the Cabinet approved the Outline of PCEPlans in January 1939, the time it took to implement the plans effectively was decisively important for the development of the war.[3] For example, the construction of two large-scale battleships, the *Yamato* and *Musashi*, started in the early summer of 1937. Although these ships were a centerpiece of Japan's military capacity, they were built on an existing production line and took four or five years to finish. In fact, they were completed *after* Pearl Harbor, on 16 December 1941 and 5 September 1942 respectively.

5-1-3. The PCEPlans and PCEPolicies

It is not unusual for a state or government to focus on expanding specific key industries; Japan's Commerce, Communication and Transportation, and Agriculture and Forestry ministries frequently targeted particular industries or firms.[4] The AM and NM likewise worked to build up munitions companies, while the Japanese and Manchukuo governments developed industries and companies in Manchuria. It could be argued that such aims and related state actions were, in effect, PCEPolicies, promoting systematic war preparations before the PCEPlans had been finalized.

Although the Army's presentation of its Five-Year Plan and related materials to the Planning Agency launched the formulation of the PCEPlans, the government would not have opted for plans that challenged preexisting

---

[3] A capacity expansion project that required radical innovation, the development of a new product, or the creation of a new industry might have been considered unfeasible.

[4] In legal terms, none of these ministries was subordinate to the military (Army, Navy, ACCom, NCCom, AM, NM, or IH) during the war period.

patterns, and could not have shaped or effectively enforced them without the support of most Cabinet members and government divisions.[5] As the War with China escalated, economic control began in earnest, and the MMPlans were drawn up and put into action. The moment had come when an individual policy was more likely to be adopted and enforced if it was consistent with the MMPlans and PCEPlans. The PCEPolicies clearly obtained broader support than the PCEPlans had done.

5–1–4. The Structure of Chapter 5

By the time the Cabinet finalized the implementation process for the PCEPlans, Japan had been at war with China for a year and a half. It is obvious, therefore, that the PCEPlans contributed little, if anything, to systematic preparations or to the development and enforcement of the war. Given the state of its economy in 1939, it is also clear that Japan could not afford the materials needed to expand production capacity in key industries. Thus, the PCEPlans neither contributed to systematic preparations or the development of war, nor offered any effective policies to achieve objectives.

In sections 5–3, 5–4, and 6–2, I examine the PCEPolicies in detail. Section 5–3 considers how they were used by individual ministries, including the Commerce Ministry, to manage industries under their supervision. Section 5–4 focuses on the Army and the Navy, applying PCEPolicies in the munitions industry. Proponents of the conventional wisdom admire the PCEPlans designed for occupied Manchuria and the central players who enforced them, often called "Team Manchuria." (Chapter 6 will focus on the Manchurian plans and policies, reinterpreting the myth of "Team Manchuria" and its key players, who included Tojo, Kishi, and Kanji Ishiwara.)

The MMPlans were formulated and enforced as a coordination measure, to deal with the shortage of foreign currency and key materials. Under the MMPlans, ministries needed authorization to achieve policy goals. For

---

[5] Both the Army and Navy took the PCEPlans seriously (Tanaka, 1975, p. 114); they obtained the support of key business personalities, including Nariaki Ikeda and Toyotaro Yuuki, for their Five-Year Plans (Hara, 1994, p. 78). According to Hara: "The Hayashi Cabinet formed at the beginning of 1937 appointed Ikeda Finance Minister and Yuuki Chairman of the Bank of Japan to strengthen 'the military-business embracing' and expand production capacity in accordance with the Army's vision of a Cabinet focused on Five-Year Plan enforcement" (p. 78). Although central players and decision makers cannot be clearly identified, many influential people outside the Army supported the expansion of production capacity. Readers should note that the Hayashi Cabinet collapsed in June 1937, only four months after its formation.

example, if the Commerce Ministry decided to expand a particular industry, it was confronted with the reality that key materials, funds, workforce, land, and foreign currency were difficult to secure. The MMPlans were, therefore, frustratingly difficult to enforce, a situation that also existed in Manchuria. The only exception was a policy implemented by the Army and Navy that privileged the munitions industry by allowing plants controlled by the military to obtain materials using a special military allocation. Given the lack of adequate preparations for war, this policy only made matters worse, as confirmed in section 5-4.

5-2. Production Capacity Expansion Plans (PCEPlans)

5-2-1. Formulation and Enforcement

An Outline of the PCEPlans at the Start

Although it took nearly two years to persuade both the AM and government to agree on revisions to the Outline, the final version was almost the same as the original[6] – still too abstract and general (Horiba, 1962, pp. 62–3). It could not be effective without substantial effort.[7] Although the plan was intended to be implemented in April 1938, the Cabinet did not approve the Outline until January 1939. At this point, the Cabinet set up the Production Capacity Expansion Committee (PCECmt) to implement the PCEPlans and coordinate the activities of relevant ministries (PCECmt Rule, Article 1).

The goal was to strengthen Japan's national defense by making it self-sufficient in the production of key materials. To achieve this, the plan targeted fifteen core industries[8]: steel, coal, light metals, nonferrous metal, oil

---

[6] It was in November 1938 that the Four-Year Plan for PCE was finalized, covering the period until 1941 (the so-called Revised Four-Year Plan); it was extensively cited in the Outline approved by the Cabinet on 17 January 1939. No detailed production schedule listing key materials was published at that time; at a Diet meeting on 8 March 1939, Aoki, the Chairman of the Planning Council, published only a comparison of production targets for individual materials in FY1941 and FY1938 (MITI, 1964, p. 213).

[7] As shown in section 4-1, the Outline presented by the Army as a policy guide advised creating an administrative organ that could compel adherence and promote the plan as an unshakable national policy. Acknowledging that this could not be immediately realized, it recommended adopting six enforcement measures (Horiba, 1962, p. 73). Almost none of these were put into practice.

[8] MITI (1964, p. 218) offered a commentary: "Ideally, we should formulate production increase plans through close cooperation with the industries involved. However, the broader the plan, the more unfocused it becomes. Given the intimidating situation, we had to adopt a priority system, selecting those industries most urgently in need of increased production … . We placed heavy industries like steel and mineral resources at the core, adding electricity as power resource and wool both as a consumption good and a key item

and its substitutes, soda and industrial salt, sulfate of ammonia, pulp, gold, machine tools, trains, shipping, automobiles, wool, and electricity.

Formulating and Enforcing the PCEPlans

Although the PCEPlans had a broad remit, covering fifteen industries and a geographical spread that included Manchuria and China, they were considered a single comprehensive initiative covering production, materials, financing, the workforce, and electricity. The body responsible for adapting these broad guidelines to meet the needs of individual plants, mines, and expanding industries had a particularly important role.

In March 1939, the PCECmt was formed, coopting the Chairman of the Planning Council and high officials from the Planning Council and other ministries. There were no members from the private sector. The PCECmt held eight session meetings, between 1 and 8 March; the first session meeting, for example, discussed the enforcement of PCEPlans for steel with the relevant ministries (MITI, 1964, pp. 220–1). Through these session meetings, the Planning Council coordinated plans submitted by the ministries. The Commerce Ministry was responsible for all but five planned industries. The Communication and Transportation Ministry was responsible for shipping and electricity, the Finance Ministry for industrial salt, and the Ministry of Agriculture for wool (MITI, 1964, pp. 221–2).

Every fiscal year, the Planning Council consulted with these ministries to set guidelines (involving both basic principles and structure) for individual plans. Using these guidelines, each ministry proposed long-term plans, detailing both goals and enforcement mechanisms, for the industries under its authority. Goals were further divided into production plans and lists of requisite materials. Enforcement measures were determined after deliberations at the General Coordination Session, at which all plans were summarized. Important conclusions were reported first to the PCECmt, and then by the Chairman of the PCECmt to the Cabinet (MITI, 1964, p. 222).

Although the scope and infrastructure of PCEPlans were large-scale and ambitious, a plan for enforcement was swiftly put in place. The PCECmt was formed in March 1939; on March 17, the committee drew up a set of Guidelines for Formulating FY1939 PCEPlans Enforcement, which were approved at the PCECmt's general meeting and published the same day. On 9 May 1939, in a spectacular and complex move, the committee published

for national defense.... Of the planned industries, the ones expected to stand on their own feet in Japan, Manchuria, and China by the end of FY1941 were steel, coal, light metals, zinc (nonferrous metal), soda, ammonium sulfate, pulp, trains, automobiles, and shipping."

enforcement plans governing the production and allocation of materials, funds, the workforce, and electricity.[9]

Both the PCEPlans and their enforcement plans were formulated by bureaucrats from the Planning Council and involved ministries. All the discussions were secret. Producers in planned industries were ordered by the relevant ministry to submit materials for drafting plans; after determination of PCEPlans, each producer received an allocation of materials needed for production. Given the PCEPlans, each ministry was responsible for enforcing the PCEPlans and putting them into action. Performance data were reported monthly to the Planning Council. In addition, each ministry was expected to investigate any discrepancy between its performance targets and actual performance, and to apply necessary measures (MITI, 1964, p. 222).[10]

Was the State Able to Ensure Cooperation Among the Private Sector Agents and to Use Their Ideas, Expertise, and Energy Effectively?

The PCEPlans and their enforcement guidelines were drawn up in secret by bureaucrats of the Planning Council and other ministries. No private-sector representatives were allowed to take part despite the "military-business embracing." Why did the government choose to exclude business from these deliberations? Could the PCEPlans have been managed effectively without private-sector participation? How did the state expect to ensure business cooperation in implementing and enforcing these plans? Was it really necessary for PCECmt discussions to be kept secret? Would it not have been useful to communicate with the private sector and encourage an exchange of information and opinions?

Some readers might wonder whether government leaders, including Cabinet members, unanimously supported the PCEPlans. Perhaps some decision makers considered them useless or unenforceable, a pretext to appease the military and its most aggressive supporters. However, it is important to recall two points: first, this took place in March 1939, more than eighteen months after the beginning of the War with China; second, it was the Army, not the government, that proposed these plans.

---

[9] For more details, see MITI (1964, pp. 223–35).

[10] The feasibility of plans was limited by the availability of imported materials, requiring macroeconomic coordination of the PCEPlans and MMPlans. "It was unclear how the government could ensure that companies implemented necessary business programs" (Yamazaki, 1996, pp. IV–V). Listing subsidy measures, such as tax exemptions over certain period, he concluded: "Those subsidy measures would not necessarily ensure the realization of the PCEPlans."

Was it possible for Japan, during this period of war preparations and mobilization, to ensure cooperation from the private sector, and to make use of its ideas, expertise, and energy?

As Cairncross (1991, p. 3) wrote:

War ... is a great centraliser. It is the government that conducts the war, decides what strategy to follow, and determines how the country's resources can best be used if the war is to be won.... Civilians are regarded as instruments for carrying on the war rather than as individual persons with separate and different objectives of their own.

Whether the state of Japan performed well in the role of the great centralizer is a central question in this book, which investigates the competence of the state, focusing on the performance of Japan's government during the war. As shown in Chapter 3, the military could not adequately fill this role. The government as a whole also fell short.[11]

One key task for a government performing the role of a great centralizer must be to recruit private-sector experts aggressively, ensuring cooperation among private agents and effectively making use of their ideas, expertise, and energy. One characteristic that Japan and Germany shared was a failure to encourage the active participation of private-sector experts, such as engineers and entrepreneurs, when formulating plans and enforcing war mobilization and economic control.

Overy (1980, p. 180) pointed out that, when it came to aircraft production[12]:

In all the Axis powers the common denominator was the exclusive role of the military in choosing designs and ordering modifications without sufficient attention to the economics of aircraft production. Without a coherent production plan, the firm responded by producing an unscheduled stream of designs. This satisfied the military demand for better and better weapons in theory only. In practice, the military failed to distinguish the best weapons, and found itself confused by promises

---

[11] Recall the discussions in subsection 1–4–4 on the surveys of munitions factories for Army control, those in section 4–1 on the competence of the Planning Council, and those in section 4–4 on numerical accuracy as the basis of the MMPlans.

[12] Comparing the aircraft production planning in Germany and the UK, Cairncross (1991, p. 148) concluded: "The most striking difference is that whereas German planning seems to have revolved round the supply of materials, British planning – after 1941 at least – revolved round engine supply and development." He explained (p. 115): "It is obviously much more important to establish whether the right decisions were made as to the scale of aircraft production, the type of aircraft to build, and the balance between different types than to pursue the question of how these decisions were translated into production programmes or how the activities of all the firms involved were coordinated." See also section 9–5.

from the firms which could not be fulfilled technically. Insistence on the pursuit of quality at all costs led to short production runs and constant interruptions to the flow of production which demoralized the producers and frustrated the soldiers.[13]

Government as a Great Centralizer in Aircraft Production

Winston Churchill, who had been Britain's Minister of Munitions during the First World War, firmly believed that service departments should not be responsible for producing their own weapons. He took steps to put an end to the exercise of this responsibility by the Air Ministry. When he took over the reins of government in May 1940, he set up a new department, the Ministry of Aircraft Production (MAP) (Cairncross, 1991, p. 7).

In Japan, the Army (AM) and the Navy (NM) chose to control their own aircraft production. Because the government and military rejected the participation of private-sector experts, Japan missed an opportunity to make the sort of bold decisions, described later in this section, that advanced military operations in the United Kingdom and United States.[14]

On the 15 May 1940, representatives of the British Ministry of Aircraft Production and Air Staff agreed to manufacture Wellingtons, Whitley Vs, Blenheims, Hurricanes, and Spitfires exclusively until the end of September. Monthly production of new fighters dramatically increased, from 256 in April to 467 in September. There were more than enough to cover previous losses, and Fighter Command emerged from the autumn "Battle of Britain" with more aircraft than it had possessed at the beginning. The most spectacular, as well as the most important, single incident in the history of war production was a great success (Postan, 1952, p. 116).

The German Blitz in the spring of 1940 brought about a complete reassessment of what was needed in American aircraft production. On 16 May

---

[13] In light of the importance of businessmen's participation in product selection, Overy (1983, p. 183) wrote: "The problem of product selection, like so many in the production of aircraft, was closely related to the extent to which industry was brought into the running of the war economy. That British and American businessmen were integrated into the organization and planning of aircraft production was not simply a reflection of a particular closeness between the government and commercial elites, but of an anxiety on the part of firms from the start in questions to do with contracts, production and particularly finance." Supporters of the conventional wisdom might argue that, by contrast, in Japan "reformist bureaucrats" (*kakushin kanryo*) such as Kishi, Hoshino, and Shiina played key roles. On this view, see Miwa (2008, pp. 252–3), where I discuss Puzzle 15–2. So, were "reformist bureaucrats" important? See also sections 6–4 and 9–6.

[14] Obviously the situation was far from the ideal also in these countries. See Overy (1980, pp. 181–2) and Rae (1968, pp. 121–2). Also recall the discussion in section 4–5's subsection "The Basic Character and Coverage of the MMPlans," particularly the basic character of the MMPlans as plans for inputs.

1940, President Roosevelt startled the nation, military, and aircraft industry by calling for the production of fifty thousand airplanes a year. The National Defense Advisory Commission was created at the end of May; one of its members, William S. Knudsen, left the presidency of General Motors to oversee production (Rae, 1968, pp. 113–14).[15]

Incentives for Private-Sector Cooperation?

Incentives play a crucial role in any attempt by government to obtain the participation and cooperation of private agents. Compared with the other major powers, Japan was surprisingly slow to use incentives to persuade the private sector to cooperate actively. For example, the Industrial Equipment Authority Act was enforced on 5 December 1941, almost five years after the beginning of the War with China. The Special Act for Promoting Weapons Manufacturing Industries was not implemented until 25 May 1942.[16]

On 17 November 1941, Commerce Minister Kishi explained to the Japanese Diet the need for an Industrial Equipment Authority Act[17]:

Growing tension in current affairs desperately demands a rapid and large-scale production increase in munitions, planned industries, and other key industries. Many private companies are struggling to maintain existing equipment or to acquire new machinery because their industries seem to have no future. It is therefore imperative that we, the state, create a new aggressive policy instrument to provide equipment.... To achieve this important objective, we will establish the Industrial Equipment Authority, which will invest in nationally important industries, and manufacture and lease equipment.

Government-owned, contractor-operated companies (known in the United States as GOCO) also began to appear in Japan (see section 5–3). In

[15] "Understandably, the most rapid progress in converting automotive facilities was in the manufacture of engines, which required a less drastic adaptation of concepts and techniques than did airframes. One difficulty that had to be surmounted was the desire of Secretary of the Treasury Henry Morgenthau to supervise the entire aircraft program.... However, when E. E. Wilson of Pratt and Whitney and Guy Vaughan of Curtiss-Wright pointed out the high degree of skill required to make aircraft engines and asked Morgenthau if he would be willing to accept the responsibility for casualties due to faulty production, Morgenthau abandoned the idea" (Rae, 1968, p. 130).

[16] As War Mobilization Subsection Chief Okada recalled after the war concerning the economy at the beginning of Army factory control in January 1938 (Boeicho, 1970, p. 109): "At that time there was a strong mood on the private business side not to welcome the military's factory control. In addition to a distaste for constraints on business freedom under a capitalist economic system, most worried about the expected loss that could occur through prompt resolution of the Incident."

[17] See Miwa (2008, pp. 76–7, note 31).

the UK, from 1936, the Air Ministry chose to pay private motor and other firms, to build and run "shadow" factories that remained state-owned. This structure, halfway between public and private, has remained important to the arms industry to this day (Edgerton, 1991, p. 75).

The Army's Miyazaki Institute Drafts the Outline

On 17 June 1937, the Army's Miyazaki Institute presented to the government its Five-Year Plan for Key Industries and an associated Outline. What was this research institute? When and why was it established? Who were its members, and what were their role and relationship to the Army? Was the institute established to systematize war preparations?

As mentioned in section 4-1, Horiba, the ACCom Staff Member who drafted the original Five-Year Plan, asked the Study Group on Finance and Economy in Japan and Manchuria to draft the Outline. The ACCom's Strategy Section Chief Ishiwara asked Masayoshi Miyazaki, Tokyo representative of the Economic Research Division of the South Manchuria Railway Company (SMR),[18] to form and lead an institute.

Masazumi Inada, ACCom Strategy Section Chief between March 1938 and October 1939, commented after the war on the Miyazaki Institute's plans (Inada, 1969, pp. 122-5):

A team appointed by Yosuke Matsuoka, the President of the SMR, began research with a budget of 50,000 yen. When Ishiwara became the ACCom Strategy Section Chief, he appointed Miyazaki a nonregular employee of the ACCom. When he was promoted to ACCom Strategy Division Chief in March 1937, the research shifted into high gear. Otherwise they could not obtain figures in military secrets. The Cabinet had neither reserve funds nor access to Army and Navy acquisitions and resources. As a result, the Cabinet could not make long-term plans for the economy or for war. The Army and the Navy formulated defense plans, rather than integrated war plans. Only the military could freely use military secrets, which the Miyazaki Institute could obtain. Their plans were logical.... *However, they were also sloppy, indeed ... in fact.*[19] (My italics)

---

[18] The so-called Miyazaki Institute, informally named after its chief, Masayoshi Miyazaki, was well known particularly among supporters of the conventional wisdom. For the dominant view of the Economic Research Division and Miyazaki, see Kobayashi (2005), particularly sections 2-2 and 2-3.

[19] In his statement that only the military could freely use military secrets, it is unclear whether Inada included the Army Minister and AM. As shown in subsection 4-2-1, the national defense operations that the ACCom controlled had a close connection with the AM-controlled military administration. In national defense and operations, the ACCom cooperated with the AM, and with government through the AM. However, the ACCom was an independent organization; the ACCommander and NCCommander were key figures in the Emperor's supreme command. The AM belonged to the Cabinet, and the Prime

When he became Chief of the new ACCom War Leadership Section in June 1936, Ishiwara tried unsuccessfully to persuade the AM to enforce a Five-Year Plan for industry. In March 1937, Ishiwara became the Strategy Division Chief and the AM adopted the ACCom plan. However, the Hayashi Cabinet favored by the Army collapsed. Its successor, the Konoe Cabinet, inherited an unrevised plan and then the War with China began.[20]

With the second Konoe Proclamation of 22 December 1938, the Japanese government prepared for a long, drawn-out war. In preparation, the ACCom and AM revised Japan's policy toward China, agreeing on 6 December 1938 to adopt a new policy toward China after the fall. This change was fundamental both for the role of the expeditionary force in China and for Japan's politics and war strategy (Boeicho, 1967a, pp. 573–5). When asked whether the "rearmament" planned by Ishiwara was mentioned in this policy, Inada (1969, pp. 125–6) said "You must be joking! Ishiwara's five-year 'Army Rearmament Plan' never made it to final draft stage.... Without an industry plan, we could not produce steel, making all rearmament plans useless. The five-year industry plan was a paper plan."

5-2-2. The Effectiveness of the PCEPlans

Three Points to Consider in Evaluating the Effectiveness of the PCEPlans
Both the formulation and the enforcement of the PCEPlans were kept secret; very little information has been archived or published. However, it is

Minister of the Cabinet was the Emperor's key political advisor. On matters of national defense and operations (including Inada's military secrets), the ACCom had no need to consult with either the AM or the Cabinet. To obtain information on munitions production or specific plans and budgets, the ACCom had to cooperate with the AM. In addition, as shown in section 1–4 (subsection 1–4–4 in particular), the AM and Commerce Ministry failed to conduct a careful survey of munitions plants coming under Army control. Involving the AM did not make the military's plans less "sloppy."

[20] With regard to the War Leadership Section, recall the comments of Inada and Nishiura in subsection 2–3–2, note 59. As a Staff Member in the Military (*gunji*) Section of the AM, Nishiura took charge of the Five-Year Plans for industry and for expanding production capacity. He commented about Masayoshi Miyazaki of the Miyazaki Institute (Nishiura, 1968, pp. 160–1): "As I was in the AM, I was not so friendly with him. In short, although an important person in the SMR's research division, he was a researcher type. He was a scholarly person, rather than a person of talent, and a political innocent. It was Horiba who, inheriting the Miyazaki Institute, provided money and human resources to support his research. Miyazaki lacked the initiative to do anything himself."

Inada (1969, p. 125) explained that Horiba worked for him and followed his instructions. He became a "great man" afterward by writing a book that has been widely read and cited. Horiba's book appealed to scholars who placed too much emphasis on "documents" and supported his views – for example, the authors of *The Road to the Pacific War* (Asahi-Shimbun-sha, 1962–3, in 8 volumes).

not difficult to deduce that the PCEPlans and PCEPolicies contributed little to systematic war preparations or policy objectives.

Consider three key points:

First, as time passed, the government's goals and policies changed radically – Tanaka (1975, p. 114) was frank on this point.[21] On 17 June 1937, the Army unveiled its Five-Year Plan for Key Industries and accompanying Outline. Both the Army and Navy were active in the PCEPlans. Originally, assuming that there would be no war, the policy was designed to enforce a rearmament plan under normal economic conditions. The actual expansion of production, carried out during the War with China at a time of military exhaustion, was completely different from the initial vision.

Second, from the start, the PCEPlans were stringently restricted. With the FY1939 enforcement plan formulated in May 1939, the PCEPlan after the first quarter of FY1939 began. Even between January and March 1939, the PCEPlans were derailed by a shortage of imports. Due to the lack of foreign currency, the number of imported machines allocated to the private demand fell to half of what had been purchased the previous year, making it almost impossible to maintain the status quo. Thus, even as they were being launched, the PCEPlans, designed to expand the production capacity of the basic industries, were already bankrupt and could not provide the machinery required to expand production (Hara, 1976a, p. 251).[22]

[21] Kanji Ishiwara, the Strategy Section Chief of the ACCom, represented a group that argued that building up armaments and expanding key industries was a necessary foundation. Assuming the establishment of the East Asia Federation thirty years later, as mentioned in subsection 2–3–2, he argued: "If a war breaks out tomorrow, we have no choice but to try for a short war. If we keep our war goals minimal, we can pursue a resolution of the war, leading to a surrender or cease-fire under extremely generous conditions" (Boeicho, 1967a, pp. 379, 393–4). Kenryo Sato recalled (1976, p. 124): "We intended to enforce the national defense policy, that is, rearmament and the Five-Year industry plans (it was the first trial in Japan. Even the USSR, a large country with rich resources, could not achieve its goals through its first Five-Year Plan, and had to develop second and third Five-Year Plans. Accordingly, in Japan, we were also prepared to try at least three times). This was in 1936; we resolved that for the next fifteen years (from 1937 until 1952) Japan would not become involved in border disputes between the USSR and Manchuria or China. We resolved never to begin a war. We never imagined that, when production capacity had expanded, we would begin a war with China."

[22] The Outline of January 1939 stated that, in order to enforce the PCEPlans in accordance with specific industry requirements, the government would enact a series of special measures to control and subsidize industry, ensuring a supply of engineers, workers, and funding. To achieve this, the government would enact new laws and orders when necessary, invoking the NGMAct (MITI, 1964, p. 219). Thus, no specific policy measures were specified.

Third, the timescale for implementing the PCE became a stringent constraint, as the following incident in the liquid fuel industry illustrates. The 1937 Outline included a table showing the funds needed to expand key industries in Japan and Manchuria. The liquid fuel industry's 1.325 billion yen was the second-largest, following 2.477 billion yen for the electricity industry and exceeding the 1.166 billion yen allocated to steel, pig iron, and iron-ore mining (Horiba, 1962, pp. 68–70).

The Tojo Cabinet, immediately after its formation on 18 November 1941, ordered the Planning Council to evaluate national capacity before the start of war with the United States and the UK. One key issue was whether the promotion of the liquid oil would be a measure for avoiding the war. Teiichi Suzuki, the Chairman of the Planning Council, told the IH-government Liaison Conference (Tanaka, 1975, pp. 179–80):

Suppose we decide to increase the production of liquid oil by 5.2 million tons per year:

1. To build equipment, we would need 2.25 million tons of steel, 1,000 tons of cobalt, 30 million tons of coal, 3.8 billion yen, and 380,000 workers.
2. Assuming that we obtain the requisite materials, we will need to construct factories. It will take six months to build low-temperature carbonization plants, two months to construct synthesizing plants, and approximately two years to create hydrogenation plants. Overall, it will take more than three years to complete all the necessary facilities.
3. We must also consider our limited engineering capacity, and particularly the difficulty we will have in manufacturing high-pressure reaction tubes and pipes. It will be almost impossible to establish self-sufficiency in liquid fuel or even oil in a short period of time. Even if we completely control implementation, we will need seven years at least.

For these reasons, a dependence on liquid oil will fatally compromise national defense for a significant period of time. It is particularly dangerous now, when we are at war with China.

Evaluation of the First PCEPlans

Judging by the ratio of goals achieved, the first PCEPlans (ending in FY1941) were miserably unsuccessful (Hara, 1976a, p. 251). Table 5–1 shows both targets and achieved goals.

Hara explained this failure as follows: "One problem was that the first PCEPlans ignored actual conditions on the ground in Japan, leading to

Table 5-1. *Achievements of the first PCEPlans*

		Four-year plan	Enforcement plan	Achievement
Common steel	1938	4,615	4,615	4,891
(1,000 ton)	1939	5,630	5,719	4,657
	1940	6,280	5,200	4,560
	1941	7,260	4,710	4,303
Artificial oil	1938	38	38	23
(or liquid fuel)	1939	74	68	29
(1,000 kl)	1940	159	89	40
	1941	536	73	58
Aluminium	1938	19	19	22
(1,000 ton)	1939	29	33	31
	1940	39	47	42
	1941	126	74	71
Shipping	1938	402	402	376
(1,000 ton)	1939	550	401	335
	1940	600	301	266
	1941	650	384	308

Note: Original source is the Industry Bureau of Economic Stabilization Board (*keizai antei honbu*), "The Summary Tables of MMPlans" (March 1951).
Source: Hara (1976a, p. 251, Table 16).

inflated expectations in the days before the war. As a result, the target values in each year's enforcement plan had to be set far below the Four-Year Plan targets, and even these revised targets were much higher than the amounts achieved. In some sectors, production fell below original levels. The primary cause of this low performance was a rapid increase in munitions demand, which year after year depleted the materials available for PCE planning. This situation was exacerbated by a trade crisis caused by the shortage of foreign currency" (Hara, 1976a, p. 251).

The production target for common steel was 5.72 million tons for FY1939, decreasing to 5.2 million tons for FY1940 and 4.71 million tons for FY1941. The achievement in each year fell far below the target: 4.66, 4.56, and 4.30 million tons respectively. During this period, the production of pig iron, iron-ore, and coal all increased, but the PCEPlans could not eliminate flaws in steel industry production technology. In FY1941, production remained at 60 percent of the target value of 7.26 million tons. In most other industries, production fell below the annual enforcement plan target; as a result, the production overall in FY1941 fell far below initial targets (MITI, 1964, p. 373).

Etsusaburo Shiina, the General Coordination Bureau[23] Chief of the Commerce Ministry, published a book in the fall of 1941, more than three years after the start of War with China but before Pearl Harbor. He described the PCEPlans as a policy for systematically developing Japan's economic capacity during the Showa era[24] (Shiina, 1941, pp. 177–9):

The international situations Japan has confronted since the Manchurian Incident have been complicated and full of difficulties. As a result, the formulation and implementation of the PCEPlans has become the most urgent and important political economic agenda item of the time. The government formulated the first PCEPlans, and asked the general public to cooperate in their enforcement. However, because it had not secured full political or economic support, the government was obliged to enforce the new policies using traditional measures. Essentially, they were pouring new wine into old skins. Now that the second Konoe Cabinet has adopted high national defense as national policy, ... *at last we can say that we are preparing to implement the PCEPlans in earnest.* (My italics)[25]

The Causes of Poor Performance

In launching the PCEPlans from the FY1939 MMPlans, the Cabinet reclassified private demand into five sections (Nakamura, 1977, p. 111).

In his chapter "The Process and Enforcement of the PCEPlans," Shiina (1941, p. 266) described various enforcement problems: "Only three years have passed since the first PCEPlans were put into effect in FY1938, but the situation both at home and abroad has changed frequently and drastically. To implement the plans, we had no choice but to tread a thorny path."

---

[23] The General Coordination Bureau (*soumu-kyoku*) was newly created during the Commerce Ministry's all-out organizational reform, enforced on 16 June 1939 in response to the situation. As the situation developed, a swift, smooth, and complete implementation of policies coordinating supply and demand became more urgent and also more difficult to achieve. The General Coordination Bureau was created to oversee the seven ministry bureaus, horizontally coordinating administrative affairs from an overall perspective (MITI, 1962, pp. 233–5). Shiina (1941) was published in the fall of 1941 under the name of General Coordination Bureau Chief Shiina. Due to the worsening situation, even if there was some dressing in his writing, there was little possibility of downward bias. In parallel with organizational reform, policies were also reviewed (Shiina, 1941, p. 253). The PCEPolicies were shaken to their foundations; a priority system and subsidy-incentive policies were enforced, increasing production of key materials such as steel, coal, electricity, and oil.

[24] The Showa era began in 1926.

[25] Shiina (1941, p. 179) continued: "We are now at a time of great historical transformation for the Japanese economy; the PCEPlans need to move us a large step closer to the planned economy of Showa Japan. We should not lament our slow progress. Instead, we should congratulate ourselves on the social, economic, and political reforms we have achieved in such a short period, despite the devastating Manchurian Incident, by building on the Imperial Rule Assistance Association Movement and Japan's historical strength."

This raises two questions. Were the PCEPlans physically, technically, and politically feasible? Was it true that the obstacles encountered could not have been predicted? After describing various obstacles, Shiina (1941, pp. 268–73) listed five factors that affected the implementation of the PCEPlans[26]:

1. We lacked a determined leadership capable of using political power to smoothly and adequately enforce the planned economy, obtaining the voluntary and active participation of all economic agents, including capitalists as business management agents, engineers, workers and merchants.[27]

2. The prolonged war with China seriously affected the PCEPlans in two ways: munitions manufacturers and the PCEPlans competed for materials while, at the same time, a large number of engineers and skilled workers were conscripted.

3. Preparations for state control of materials, funds and the workforce – the key to a controlled economy – were delayed or inadequate. Even at the beginning of the war, there were delays and difficulties in enforcing PCE policies. In FY1938, insufficient basic research had been done to enable materials to be allocated for expansion; there was no adequate system for controlling the allocation of materials. At first, funds and materials were not coordinated; in several cases, the government approved the production of new equipment without allocating the necessary materials.

4. We experienced problems due to the lack of comprehensive plans. In a controlled economy, there is no room for the equilibrating mechanism of the market. Instead, allocation totally depends on the content of the plans and the control techniques for their enforcement.... For various reasons, we had several bitter experiences, the most serious of which was the shortage and quality deterioration of coal in the fall of 1939.

5. The impact of the Second European War and the conclusion of the Tripartite Pact.

[26] For a table summarizing plans and achievements between FY1939 and FY1941, see MITI (1964, pp. 370–2).

[27] In the Outline, funds necessary for implementation over five years (from FY1937 to FY1941) totaled 8.5 billion yen, of which more than 7 billion yen (82.6 percent) was expected to come from the private sector, with 1 billion yen from the Japanese government and less than 0.5 billion yen from the Manchukuo government (Horiba, 1962, p. 68). There was no indication of how or from which private firms the government would raise these funds.

Subsequent PCEPlans or PCEPolicies

Following Yamazaki (1996, pp. X–XII), I conclude that no policy was effective in enforcing the PCEPlans or the PCEPolicies after FY1941.

After FY1941, the PCEPlans were transformed into production expansion plans, whose primary objective was not to expand production capacity overall, but to maintain the capacity utilization rate, particularly for quality equipment, in accordance with the human and physical resources available. The control associations established in 1941–2 were expected to have strong leadership, while industrial unions were responsible for enforcing the reduction and selection process among small private-sector businesses. However, the control associations failed to exert strong control, while there was little downsizing of small businesses.

At the beginning of FY1943, the final year of the plans, the primary objective of industry mobilization shifted from expansion to the buildup of production. Given a decrease in basic materials since the mid-FY1942, the government targeted production expansion by concentrating production resources in selected key industries, including aircraft, shipbuilding, steel, light metals, and coal. By the middle of FY1943, the government was concentrating resources on aircraft and aircraft-related industries, while controlling less important industries, including aluminum, steel and machine tools (in 1942), and magnesium (in 1943). The Munitions Companies Act was enforced in October 1943, and the Munitions Ministry established in November 1943.[28]

Even before FY1941, the situation was unfavorable (Yamazaki (1996, pp. VII–IX). The allocation of steel for the PCE sector in the FY1939 MMPlans was 2,008,000 tons in the initial annual plan, dropping to 1,675,000 tons in the quarterly enforcement plans. According to issued coupons, only 1,509,000 tons were produced. As a result, some capacity expansion projects were postponed for a second time. Materials allocated to the PCE sector in the FY1940 MMPlans remained at the level of the previous fiscal year. Steel allocation was 1,750,000 tons in the annual plan and 1,630,000 tons in the enforcement plan. This gap caused the FY1940 PCEPlans to adopt a preferential materials allocation policy, giving first priority to requests for repairs and equipment maintenance, and second priority to the immediate expansion of capacity in planned industries. Third priority requests involved materials needed for the production of machine tools, automobiles, and ships. Capacity expansions scheduled for the next fiscal year or beyond had to be carried out, if at all, using any remaining materials.

---

[28] For the impact of the general situation on the PCEPlans, see Tanabe (1943).

Enforcing the FY1941 PCEPlans presented a difficult challenge. The Guidance for formulating the plans required the following:

1. A special focus on the steel industry.
2. A strong preference for capacity expansion projects close to completion; longer-term projects could be considered only if urgent.
3. The exploitation of existing capacity.

Thus, the policy shifted its focus from increasing production capacity to maintaining the efficient use of existing capacity.

The first PCEPlans finished in FY1941; the second PCEPlans were designed to cover FY1942–FY1946 but could not be implemented as planned. The annual enforcement plans now focused on completing ongoing undertakings, authorizing the production of new equipment only in the most important cases.

5-3. Production Capacity Expansion Policies (PCEPolicies)

5-3-1. The Expansion of Production Capacity

On 17 January 1939, the Cabinet finally approved the Outline for the PCEPlans, which became Four-Year Plans, although the policies they promoted were already in place. "Since 1936, and particularly once the war began in 1937, we enforced aggressive policies from every side" (Shiina, 1941, p. 194).

As national defense expenditures increased, plans were formulated and policies adopted for the PCE. Given the international situation, all recognized the need for a rapid buildup of national defense. Expenditures sharply increased to cover the Manchurian Incident and emergency rearmament. It was clear that Japan needed an increased domestic supply of munitions to avoid shortages or a heavy reliance on imports. The PCE was designed to increase national defense expenditures; every Cabinet after the Hayashi Cabinet formally endorsed it as a key policy. Finance Minister Yuuki of the Hayashi Cabinet was the first to promote the PCE. The first Konoe Cabinet fully implemented its policies in the "Three Principles of Public Finance and the Economy of Finance Minister Kaya and Commerce Minister Yoshino" (Shiina, 1941, pp. 179–81).

In various sectors, industry laws were enacted and put into effect; most of these were triggered by the formulation and enforcement of the PCEPlans (Shiina, 1941, p. 226). Even before the beginning of the War with China, the Petroleum Industry Act and the Automobile Manufacturing Industry

Act were enacted and enforced. During the War with China, many industry laws were enacted in sequence, including the Artificial Petroleum Industry Act, the Steel Industry Act, the Machine Tool Building Act, the Aircraft Manufacturing Industry Act, the Shipbuilding Industry Act, and the Light Metals Manufacturing Industry Act.[29]

5–3–2. The Machine Tool Building Act and the Shipbuilding Industry Act

Here I examine the effectiveness of two industry laws, the Machine Tool Building Act and the Shipbuilding Industry Act, which symbolized the PCEPolicies but are not usually included in the PCEPlans.

Because of unanticipated events, neither the MMPlans nor the PCEPlans, although formulated and enforced as basic policies, achieved their initial goals. It is therefore not rational to expect that those industry laws would perform well after FY1939, when the government could not provide effective policy measures to support achievement. Accordingly, this book focuses on the period before FY1939.

It was obvious that machine tools and shipbuilding would decisively determine the conditions of war. Production expansion, PCE, and product improvements in these two industries and the capacity to manufacture high-precision machine tools were basic to military performance. They were an essential part of the government's systematic war preparations and a key to achieving its war objectives.

"The machine tool building industry is at the core of the PCEPlans and PCEPolicies.[30] As well as increasing the production of basic materials, we must expand production of machine tools. Without these, the Japanese economy will not achieve self-sustainability. The same applies also to rearmament and independence" (Shiina, 1941, p. 215).[31] Indeed, machine tools are the source of weapons and industry.

---

[29] For detailed information about industry laws, see MITI (1964, pp. 238–47), and for an overview, see Shiina (1941, p. 225).

[30] Concerning the Outline, Horiba (1962, p. 64) wrote: "We confronted many difficulties in enforcing industry expansion. Although policies to increase machine tool production and skilled workforce training were basic requirements, the tense international situation did not allow us to enforce such a two-stage approach. We relied on machine tool imports from the U.S., and our supply of skilled workers fell far below the planned level. We had to expand them, concurrently with other industries."

[31] This followed another statement (Shiina, 1941, pp. 214–15): "Modern civilization is the civilization of machinery. Machine tools, with which all machines are manufactured, are literally 'the mother of the machinery.' ... Every machine used in daily life and production

The first consequence of the termination of the Japan–U.S. Commerce and Navigation Treaty in 1940 was a prohibition on exporting machine tools to Japan. At the time, Japan imported most of its high-quality, high-precision machine tools; they were the Achilles' heel of its munitions industry. Japan produced very few machine tools usable in weapons production. At that time, the number of machine tools that Japan possessed for munitions production was one-eighth that of the United States. Although Japanese manufacturers of weapons, Naval vessels, and aircraft consistently suffered from a shortage of materials, the inferior quality of machine tools was an even more significant problem (Nakahara, 1981, pp. 87–8).

As mentioned in section 4-4, the MMPlans shifted focus from foreign currency to ocean transport once Japan's assets were frozen. At the end of October 1941, when the IH-government Liaison Conference approved the National Capacity Evaluation (Just Before the Beginning of War), the size, quantity, and allocation of marine vessels were the leadership's top concern, given geographical considerations and the shortage of materials. The problem affected both waging war and maintaining national capacity.[32] After 1943 in particular, the decline and collapse of the ocean transport capacity decisively conditioned the achievement of war objectives (Tanaka, 1975, pp. 185, 158–60, 653).

5-3-3. The Shipbuilding Industry Act and the Shipbuilding Control Association

The following is a brief summary of Miwa (2004, Part I).[33] Before the enactment and publication of the Shipbuilding Industry Act of April 1939, no noteworthy PCEPolicies had ever been enforced in this industry. Almost none were enforced after the act either.

The Shipbuilding Industry Act was published in April and implemented in December 1939. The government had taken a keen interest in the

is manufactured by machine tools. From naval vessels, aircraft, and tanks to rifles and bullets, all weapons are manufactured by machine tools.... It is true that supply capacity of key materials like steel, nonferrous metals, and light metals determines national capacity, but those materials are useless unless they are turned into machines and weapons."

[32] As Takushiro Hattori, the Strategy Section Chief of the IH-AD (at the outbreak of the Pacific War) later argued, the strength of the nation totally depended on the number of ships it possessed. The volume of ships was indeed of critical importance in the war effort (Hattori, 1965, p. 156).

[33] For more details, see Miwa (2004, ch. 1 ["The Machine Tool Industry Under Wartime Control"]). For the Shipbuilding Industry Act and the shipbuilding control association in particular, see Miwa (2004, pp. 38–48).

development of this industry for many years, preparing the legal foundation for active intervention in the sector by supervising shipping and providing subsidies to shipbuilders to ensure the smooth transportation of basic materials (Onozuka, 1962, p. 11).[34] The Five-Year Plan for Key Industries paid special attention to the shipbuilding industry and planned to expand Japan's production capacity from 500,000 tons to 860,000 tons in FY1941 (Nakamura, 1983, pp. 276–85). The NGMAct of April 1938 designated ships as mobilization materiel, and ship production and repair as a mobilization activity. In addition, the Factories and Workplaces Control Order, issued under the NGMAct in 1939, placed most major shipyards under government control. Furthermore, under the Shipbuilding Industry Act enacted in April 1939, the Shipbuilders Federation (established in 1937 by fourteen major shipbuilders) changed its name to the Shipbuilders Unions Federation and took responsibility for controlling the industry. Another organization, the Shipbuilding Control Association, was established on 28 January 1942 with fourteen members, mostly large shipbuilders; its membership eventually grew to include twenty-two domestic shipbuilders, three offshore shipbuilders, three shipbuilding machine manufacturers, and eight shipbuilders' control unions. A spinoff of the Shipbuilders Unions Federation, it restructured the then-voluntary association of large shipbuilders into a compulsory association. All large shipbuilders and related enterprises joined, with small shipbuilders and manufacturers of supplementary machinery forming associations in order to take part (Nakamura, 1983, p. 16).

Despite having legal authority, the government did not intervene or put its plans into action, presumably because the time was not ripe (Onozuka, 1962, p. 11). As Onozuka described it, the Shipbuilding Industry Act was better suited to peace than wartime. Its purpose was to provide a supply of good ships at lower prices and to promote management by the shipbuilders themselves, rather than preparing for industry control. As the wartime economy and international situation changed quickly, almost nothing could be achieved under this act.

---

[34] Seldom do we find either formal documents or descriptions of government policy or studies based on such materials. As the memoir of a member of the Naval Technical Department of the NM, with direct responsibility for shipbuilding control and planning, Onozuka's book (1962) is an exception. Ichiro Onozuka belonged to the Merchant Marine Subsection of the Fourth Section. Although published in 1962, his memoir was written between 1946 and 1951, shortly after the events it describes. According to historian Teratani (1993, p. 35), Onozuka's career is illuminating because he stayed at the center of the Planned Shipbuilding Section for the whole of this period. It is not too much to say that only through his record of experience can we reach a detailed understanding of planned shipbuilding.

Government took control of the shipbuilding industry in September 1939 through the newly approved Shipbuilding Approval System established by the Cabinet. Under this system, the Communications Ministry used industry standards to examine, and either approve or reject, plans for all ships more than 50 meters long. The new Shipbuilding Coordination Council, a branch of the Ship Management Committee, undertook these examinations. Chaired by the Chief of the Communications Ministry's Shipping Bureau, this body consisted of Department or Section Chiefs from the AM, NM, Planning Council, Finance Ministry, and Commerce Ministry, together with Section Chiefs of the Shipping Bureau, a representative from the Bank of Japan, and delegates from shipping and shipbuilders' associations. The standards adopted and applied were quite flexible (Onozuka, 1962, pp. 9–10).

Control shifted to a license system in February 1940, when the Shipping Control Order was established under the NGMAct. In practice, little changed.

Despite increased demand for more ships and faster production, the industry continuously missed deadlines, leading to a policy of planned shipbuilding between December 1942 and April 1944. This policy focused purely on volume-oriented production. Revising the Industrial Equipment Corporation Act, the government designated ships, aircraft, and liquid fuel as top-priority equipment. By inserting the phrase "building ships according to government standards and instructions" into the act, the government directed the corporation to order ships in bulk; it also arranged loans to enable ships to be ordered (Onozuka, 1962, pp. 36, 46, 24–6).

As 30 percent of private-sector shipbuilding capacity had been devoted to military vessels, it required smooth coordination to increase production of military ships without disrupting the scheduled production of commercial ships. Hoping that private shipbuilding would benefit from the military's immense power in the wartime economy, the government concentrated shipbuilding oversight and administration in large private plants managed by the Navy. Unfortunately, the Naval Technical Department was too busy building and repairing military vessels to focus on commercial shipbuilding. This department had no interest in controlling the shipbuilding industry or studying marine transport; it assumed it would be merely an executive body, overseeing shipbuilding using plans drawn up by the Communications Minister. However, there were no concrete policies, standardized designs, or production plans for individual shipyards, so the Naval Technical Department was forced to take responsibility for planning, eventually developing a real commitment to commercial shipbuilding (Onozuka,

1962, pp. 38–9). In short, the Navy was forced to accept responsibility for commercial shipbuilding, although it lacked the skills and time to implement effective industry control in the commercial shipbuilding industry.

In October–December, 1942, the Naval Technical Department sent a team headed by Technical Lieutenant General Niwata to carry out a nationwide investigation of all highly ranked shipyards, investigating the causes of bad performance and providing technical instructions on how to expand future production dramatically. This investigation enabled the Navy to evaluate precisely the technical competence of individual shipyards (Onozuka, 1962, pp. 49–50). Onozuka credited this tour with giving Japan's shipyards their first introduction to planned shipbuilding and mass production (p. 49). Note that this tour was conducted during October–December 1942.

Civilian and military ministries approached industry supervision and intervention in fundamentally different ways. For example, a Commerce Ministry civilian technical officer or administrator supervised only those industries that came within the jurisdiction of the Ministry. Communication with the Ministry was limited to defects and points to be improved. A military administrator, on the other hand, was responsible for demand; for example, he would supervise and coordinate the whole process of production and importation, advising on quantity, quality, and delivery times. He could work to eliminate obstacles to production by communicating with other ministries (Nakamura and Hara, 1972, p. 120). Even after the Navy had assumed responsibility for shipbuilding and its administration, the government struggled to assume effective control.

It seemed a perfect solution to centralize administration and shift responsibility for shipbuilding and the management of planned shipbuilding from the Communication Ministry to the NM. However, many legal constraints remained, complicating the management of industrial shipyards. The government attempted to sidestep these constraints by delegating all authority and responsibility for building high-quality ships to an official appointed by the Navy Minister rather than scattering responsibility across several ministries. In most cases, the Navy Minister appointed the chief Naval inspector of the Naval Technical Department; this structure was ratified in April–June 1943 as an extraordinary measure under the Act for Exceptional Wartime Administration Concerning Procedure and Jurisdiction (Onozuka, 1962, p. 30).[35]

Despite these efforts to sidestep direct legal constraints on the regulation of shipbuilding, shipbuilding under national control was regulated indirectly

---

[35] For this act, see Miwa (2004, section 1.2.4).

by many laws in addition to those directly concerned with shipbuilding and shipping. Among these indirect laws, the most important were the Order Regarding Ships for Air Defense, the Rule for Air Defense by Ships, the Act for Ship Protection, and the Implementation Rule for Ship Protection. The following regulations were also relevant: the Munitions Company Act (October 1943), the Order to Corporations for Sufficient Military Supply (January 1945), the Factories and Workforces Control Order (May 1938), the Order Regarding Facilities for National General Mobilization Tasks, the Special Subsidy Act for Arms Manufacturing Plants, the Temporary Funds Coordination Act, the Workforce Coordination Order, and the Materials Control Order (Onozuka, 1962, p. 32).

5-3-4. The Machine Tool Building Act and Precision Tool Control Association

The machine tool building industry was in much the same situation. Before the enactment of the Machine Tool Building Act in March 1938, no noteworthy PCEPolicies were in force in this industry; nor did this change after the act. Because the Precision Tool Section of the Commerce Ministry was in charge of the machine tool building industry, the control association to which machine tool builders belonged was the Precision Tool Control Association.[36] Most of its members were machine tool builders.

The Machine Tool Building Act was passed in March and enforced in July 1938. By introducing a licensing system for larger machine tool manufacturers, it aimed to rapidly expand their production capacity by providing various benefits to licensees. The act was revised in March 1941 (enforced in July). At the time of enforcement in July 1938, six firms were designated as licensees. Four more firms were added in October, one in December, and five in February 1939. Together with four firms licensed in November 1940, twenty-one firms (or twenty-four plants) were licensed before the revision.

Even before the 1938 act, the government and military were concerned about the machine tool industry. The Russo–Japanese War and World War I convinced at least part of the military of the importance of the machine tool industry. Before the Shanghai Incident in January 1932, the sector was in virtual hibernation; there were no active state policies to develop

---

[36] As political scientist Kyogoku (1983, p. 347) argued, in postwar Japan, "The basic unit of bureaucracy when the allocation of responsibility is concerned is the division in the main ministry that has jurisdiction over the industry ... within a given jurisdiction, each division of the ministry symbolizes the Japanese government." The same applied also to prewar and wartime Japan. For more details, see Miwa (2004, pp. 281–9).

the industry. In 1935, the Office of Resources developed policies for the machine tool industry.

The Resource Council also considered establishing policies to ensure a good supply of machine tool equipment for industry. Following intensive discussions, the Council, on 30 June 1937, submitted a report that acknowledged the need to train skilled engineers and workers, improve the quality of materials, and establish a coordinated system of materials rationing. The report proposed five courses of action, including a shift to domestic production of previously imported special machine tools, with temporary measures to allow imports if the domestic supply ran short (MITI, 1979, pp. 478–80).[37] The War with China began one week later.

The March 1941 revision of the act changed its character in two ways:

- The licensing threshold of two hundred machine tools was abolished; all machine tool manufacturers were made subject to the same licensing system.
- The act imposed mandatory rules concerning technical improvements.

The new rules enabled the government to issue orders regarding the following:

- Production, new equipment, and improvements
- Interfirm agreements
- Technical cooperation
- The use of sample machines and designs
- The transfer of business
- The use of designated designs, materials, and components
- Orders concerning the establishment of mandatory standards

One might ask why these measures came into effect only when the act was revised in 1941. Previously, Japan's basic policy had been to import most machine tools, particularly those that could not be produced domestically. This reliance on imports was designed to expand production capacity in key industries by supplementing local supplies and providing more technologically sophisticated machinery than could be produced domestically.

In June 1940, the United States prohibited the export of machine tools to Japan, and the Japanese government began active efforts to develop domestic

---

[37] For more details, see Miwa (2004, pp. 86–91). For the Office of Resources and the Resource Council, recall the discussion in subsection 1-4-2.

production. Although the General Mobilization Experiment and Research Order had been established in September 1939, under the NGMAct, it was put into operation on 23 January 1941.[38]

Three points are worth noting:

1. It took three years for the ineffective Machine Tool Building Act to be revised.
2. Even this revision failed to provide the government or the military with what it wanted.
3. Widespread dissatisfaction remained even after the revision, resulting in the establishment of the Precision Tool Control Association and the Munitions Ministry and Munitions Company Act. Despite these initiatives, wartime control had very limited success.

5-3-5. Evaluating the Machine Tool Building Act and the Precision Tool Control Association

The Machine Tool Building Act and its associated policies were modest, and had a limited impact for the following reasons.[39]

First, leading companies were not attracted by the new incentives and failed to expand production capacity. Many smaller companies (beyond the "Big Five," such as Ikegai Metalworks) received licenses. In total, twenty-one companies (twenty-four plants) were licensed under the act before its revision in 1941. In 1936, only six companies possessed more than one hundred machine tools. In addition to these six, licensed at the start in July 1938, four more producers were licensed in October, one in December, five in February 1939, and a further four in November 1940. Most of these firms possessed fewer than one hundred machine tools in 1936 but rapidly expanded their capacity. Many subsequently licensed companies were new entrants to the machine tool industry.

Second, by 1938, machine tool production had increased sharply. Comparing numbers of machines produced and the aggregate weight of machine tool production shows that output levels in 1938 were roughly thirty times higher than in 1932. As the act was established in March and implemented in July 1938, it could not have accounted for such a huge increase, for three reasons: (1) there were never more than twenty-one licensed producers and twenty-four factories, while the number of factories with more than one hundred workers had already reached ninety-three

---

[38] For additional details, see Miwa (2004, pp. 102–10).
[39] See Miwa (2004, pp. 94–102).

by 1938; (2) the average production share of licensed producers was low; and (3) incentives were effective only in increasing equipment acquisition beyond a threshold level.

Third, the government's policy focus was not merely to expand production capacity and volume, but to upgrade stock quality to include larger and more specialized machine tools. Many small producers made relatively useless low-quality tools, unsuitable for military production.[40] To counteract this situation, in September 1939, the government introduced its "Rules Concerning Machinery Equipment Control," which made the development and expansion of metal machine tool production and the allocation of equipment into machine tool production subject to government licensing.

Fourth, despite the preferential treatment of licensed producers under the act, a high proportion of machine tools were produced by unlicensed producers. In February 1938, the Steel Control Council was organized within the Commerce Ministry. Rules concerning steel rationing control were established in June, using a card system to control nationwide steel rationing. Hundreds of associations, including industrial unions, were designated control associations. One of these, organized by licensed producers, was the Japanese Machine Tool Builders Industrial Union. Small-scale manufacturers organized a branch of the First Machine Tool Builders Industrial Union in each major production prefecture. The National Federation of Machine Tool Builders Industrial Union incorporated these prefectural unions, boasting 403 members in August 1940. Excluded smaller producers set up the Second Machine Tool Builders Industrial Union; their members belonged to the Federation of Prefectural Local Industrial Unions.

The ratio of output from members of the Japan Machine Tool Builders Industrial Union, licensed producers, to those of the National Federation of Machine Tool Builders Industrial Unions in 1939 was 27:73 in terms of value and 14:86 in terms of the number of machines produced. In 1941, when the act was revised, these ratios had changed to 41:59 by value and 23:77 by number of machines produced (Sawai, 1984, p. 162, table 7). Clearly, licensed producers were in the minority.

Fifth, the act was based on the Office of Resources Report, which recommended the domestic production of special machine tools, with imports allowed under temporary measures when the domestic supply was not sufficient. Private companies and the military considered the second course of action a higher priority and regularly imported machine tools to supplement

---

[40] Japan Machine Tool Builders Association (1962, p. 117).

their stock.[41] Accordingly, machine tool imports showed increasingly rapid growth after the outbreak of the War with China. In 1939, they totaled 157.16 million yen, more than ten times the 1936 cost and 37.4 percent of domestic demand (10.6 percent in relation to the machines produced and 20.2 percent by aggregate weight).

The Precision Tool Control Association was established in January 1942 by the 1941 Imperial Order for Key Industries Association; the Commerce Minister designated firms as members. As of 1 December 1941, the membership included 318 manufacturers of machine tools, 40 of general tools, 19 of bearings, and 4 of precision tools. The President of the Osaka Kiko Company was appointed as the first Chairman. The association's main role was to provide additional administrative support to the Precision Tool Section of the Commerce Ministry's Machinery Bureau. As wartime control became stronger and more far-reaching in 1940–1, there were calls for a simpler, more efficient administration. The association, a powerful control organization managed by industry members, was designed to meet this need. It took charge of a wide variety of products categorized as precision tools, including machine and other tools, as well as bearings and measuring, optical, and experimental equipment.

The association, a private organization that relied fully on membership fees for its operation, made efforts to restructure the industry and coordinate the demand, supply, and price of products. It participated in the government's planned production and distribution of machine tools, as well as managing the supply and demand for production materials, equipment, finance, labor, and energy.

In contrast to the shipbuilding industry, the machine tools sector was characterized by a large number of firms offering a wide range of products. Legal regulations were similar to those governing shipbuilding, and in most cases weaker. While shipbuilding authority rested with the Navy, the Precision Tool Section of the Commerce Ministry was independent of the AM and NM and faced greater difficulties because of this decentralization. It was impossible for the Precision Control Association to play as important

---

[41] Overseas machine tool missions, conducted since 1937, resulted in the purchase of many tools. The Army's second purchasing mission to Europe and the United States, for instance, arranged to buy 985 machines in Europe and 848 in the United States (Japan's machine tool imports in 1938 and 1939 topped 7,000 in both years). However, war broke out in Europe before the machines had been shipped, interrupting the supply. In the autumn of 1939, the Army Air Service and Naval Aeronautics Departments sent a joint purchasing mission to the United States to acquire special machine tools, mainly for aircraft engine production. Most of these orders were canceled by the U.S. machine tool embargo of June 1940.

a role as the Shipbuilding Control Association or to contribute greatly to the PCEPolicies.

5–4. PCEPolicies Relating to the Army and the Navy

The Army and the Navy owned their own munitions manufacturing facilities. At the same time, they also purchased munitions from private companies and outsourced production to them. Munitions manufacturers were expected to manufacture equipment, increase production, and improve and develop products on demand. The Army and Navy had the budget and legal authorization to choose and promote their own policies; this control only increased once rearmament began in the mid-1930s. Even after the introduction of economic control, when the MMPlans were beginning to have an impact, the Army and Navy maintained their own policies.

Focusing on concrete examples, this section investigates the PCEPolicies enforced within this context. The following examples are drawn from industries and companies that produced munitions, rather than from industries supplying materials, which were prime targets of the PCEPlans. In relation to the former group, the military's policies were more direct and easily enforceable. Two additional points are important.

First, the AM and the NM took charge of military administration and their own budgets. Like other ministries, they had to submit a draft budget, negotiate with the Ministry of Finance, and obtain the approval of the Diet. They were expected to manage implementation and report results to the government and Diet. In the AM, the Military (*gunji*) Section of the Military Bureau played this role. War mobilization units were not allowed unlimited discretion.[42]

---

[42] Implementation of PCEPolicies could not have been easy for the Army and Navy, for three reasons: (1) Even during full war mobilization, early payment for munitions was considered a sufficiently effective enforcement measure. (2) As War Mobilization Subsection Chief Okada commented (subsection 1–3–2), "At the time, there was a strong instinct among private businesses not to welcome military control of factories. In addition to disliking constraints on business freedom under the capitalist economic system, businessmen worried about expected losses when the Incident was resolved." The black markets, exposed and described in "Bedtime Stories from the Business World" (in section 4–7) also had a strong impact on enforcement. (3) From the very beginning, prices were criticized for being too high, and the government had to deal with complaints of overpayment.

As mentioned both in subsections 1–3–3 and 5–4–2, the Japan Steel Works was a special Army and Navy munitions company. The company history contains this paragraph (Japan Steel Works, 1968, II, pp. 117, 120): "Items ordered from the Army and Navy, our dominant purchasers, were, except for some so-called educational- and trial-orders, priced using a rigid cost accounting principle. Particularly after the price stop order of

Second, precise enforcement of the large-scale PCEPolicies required a long-term plan (like the PCEPlans) based on reliable long-run demand forecasts. In reality, both before and after the start of the War with China and the Pacific War, long-term forecasts and plans were inaccurate and inadequate.[43]

For these reasons, I conclude that, despite having the freedom and authority to enforce them, the Army and Navy could not have implemented their PCEPolicies on a large enough scale to have been effective.

There is no way to confirm this conclusion directly, but the following episodes serve to support it.

5-4-1. Purchasing Machine Tools

As shown in subsection 1-4-2, on 26 June 1936 the Office of Resources finalized the second period general mobilization (GM) plan, a gigantic document in 104 volumes, including appendices and supporting materials. This plan declared that the supply capacity of machine tools, liquid fuel, and marine vessels was seriously insufficient and could lead to shortages. One target of the Army's 1937 Five-Year Plan for Key Industries was the PCE of machinery manufacturing (Boeicho, 1970, pp. 17, 79).

1939 and the subsequent series of low-price policies, regulations were extremely severe, and the company was strongly instructed to limit profits and dividend payments. With the Company Accounting Control Order of October 1940, this instruction became a legal regulation, prohibiting over 8 percent of dividend on equity capital.... The Army adopted a policy to set the purchasing price of munitions at 7 percent, below the '9.18 Stop Price,' and the Navy followed."

[43] This point is detailed in Chapter 2, in sections 2-5 and 2-6. Neither the Army nor the Navy was fully prepared for the start of the War with China, the long, drawn-out war of attrition that followed, or the Pacific War. As mentioned in section 4-6, Kenryo Sato, the Military (*gunmu*) Section Chief and the Military Bureau Chief of the AM, recalled, "The Army had not anticipated a war like the Pacific War against the U.S. and UK over such a vast extent of sea. Unsurprisingly, the Navy, the leading player on the sea, had never anticipated that securing such a long vein of transportation between the southern resource areas and Japan would become its major assignment" (Sato, 1976, p. 284). Nishiura of the Military (*gunji*) Section recalled: "From the beginning of 1941, we were beginning to prepare for the remote possibility that there would be an operation to the South" (Nishiura, 1980, p. 151). "The Army made a convulsive effort to reach an agreement in the Japan–U.S. negotiations that began in spring 1941.... It is true that the Army really wanted to reach an agreement, rather than [enter] the war. As it was their primary duty, they began to prepare for an operation to the South," he continued, "but this was before the decision to go to war. Although such was not the intention, it did fill gaps in the peacetime plans. We took it seriously, but didn't think it would be put into action soon" (Nishiura, 1980, p. 153).

The AM sent a purchasing mission to the United States to obtain high-quality, efficient machine tools. The mission set sail from Yokohama on 7 October and returned on 2 February 1938, having purchased machine tools on spot stock. The machines for artillery production were used as planned, but those for aircraft production were lent to private factories. It was the first occasion on which the Army lent equipment to private plants (Boeicho, 1970, pp. 80–1).[44]

The next case is important. In September 1939, the Army sent a purchasing mission to the United States headed by Colonel Saburo Atami of the Weapons Headquarters and including three employees from the Japan Steel Works; it was known as the Atami Purchasing Mission. Its assignment was to purchase urgently needed machine tools for artillery arsenals and factories. (Boeicho, 1970, p. 324, called it the Second Machine Tools Purchasing Mission, implying that there had been no mission sent to the United States during the previous two years. The Machine Tool Building Act was published on 30 March 1938.)

The Japan Steel Works was a special Army and Navy munitions company. The company history (Japan Steel Works, 1968, II, pp. 113–14) says: "Imports of materials became desperately scarce, while the control of domestic materials became more stringent. Even in top priority industries, it was becoming much harder to obtain materials for munitions production.... At first the only restriction (on machine tools) was the Exchange Control Act restriction on imports. Following the outbreak of World War II in September 1939, the U.S. prohibited machine tool exports to Japan; at that point it became impossible to import tools and our company was obliged to fundamentally reorganize its PCEPlans."

It was in this context that the company sent three employees on the purchasing mission, with high expectations. They set sail in September 1939 and negotiated hard in the United States, but were unable to achieve a notable result because of the international situation (Japan Steel Works, 1968, II, p. 114).[45]

---

[44] In Japan, most military aircraft were produced by private companies, 97 percent for the Army during 1937–45 and 95 percent for the Navy during 1941–5. For more details, see Miwa (2008, pp. 146–51). In some cases, it took a long time to receive machines purchased in the United States.

[45] The Mission had eight members, of whom four were from the private sector, three from the Japan Steel Works, and the remaining one from a trading company due to his business experience in the United States. They stayed in the United States until the end of March 1940. Boeicho (1970, p. 325) wrote: "The Mission succeeded in purchasing most items on the list. Most of the machines arrived in the spring or summer of 1940, fulfilling the contract. But special machines for gun manufacturing were canceled, and the equipment diverted to the U.S. Navy."

5-4-2. PCE in the Japan Steel Works

Soon after it was founded, the Japan Steel Works established an artillery production process that was unique among Japanese private companies and met the expectations of the Army and Navy in full. Together with Vickers-Armstrongs, Krupp, and Skoda (Japan Steel Works, 1968, II, pp. 172, 175), the Japan Steel Works was one of the four biggest weapons producers of the prewar period. As mentioned in subsection 1-3-3, both the Army and the Navy had a special interest in the use of a 10,000 ton press machine installed at its Muroran Factory. This was the only 10,000 ton press machine in Japan. Without it, the Army and Navy could not produce large-caliber guns, including anti-aircraft artillery.

The perspective of the Japan Steel Works (1968, II, p. 106) on the purchase and procurement of munitions was as follows: despite the severe financial crunch in mid-1937, an advance payment system for munitions allowed demand and purchasing power to increase, accelerating price increases for materials involved in munitions production. The government introduced profit regulation and then price control policies such as the Price Control Order of 20 October 1939 and the Rules Limiting the Production and Sales of Luxury Goods of 6 July 1940. These price control policies disrupted munitions production, forcing firms to adopt a uniform cost accounting system to achieve smooth and effective munitions procurement.

As the war escalated, Japan Steel Works supplied an increasing number of weapons to the Army and the Navy and PCE products to private companies. Demand increased drastically, particularly for new and upgraded products that required research, experimentation, and trial production. Some firms urgently needed funds and special-purpose equipment for weapons manufacturing. If products changed or an order was canceled, this equipment could not be used for other purposes. In July 1939, the government confronted this issue by publishing the Order on Business Equipment for GM Activities, which issued expansion orders and ensured future supplies. The order offered compensation for equipment losses. In 1942, it evolved into the government-owned, company-operated (GOCO) system based on the Act for Special Aid for the Weapons Manufacturing Business, or the Special Aid Act (Japan Steel Works (1968, II, p. 112).

In July 1939, the government promised to compensate the Japan Steel Works for equipment losses when necessary. It was not until 1942 that it adopted the GOCO system.[46]

---

[46] Under the Special Aid Act, published on 13 February 1942, weapons manufacturing companies were asked by the state to focus on producing munitions and improving productivity

In 1938, despite bad conditions, the Army instructed Japan Steel Works to build its Musashi factory as a special-purpose facility for tank production. The factory began operation on 1 May 1941. In August 1942, the Musashi factory was instructed to convert to artillery, in accordance with the priority production policies for aircraft. Even in this case, the Special Aid Act applied only to the conversion and did not cover tank production (Japan Steel Works (1968, II, pp. 166–7).

5-4-3. The Kobe Steel Works and Mitsui Shipbuilding

The Army designated the Kobe Steel Works a military control facility in January 1938. Following orders, the company formulated plans and applied for materials. The Kobe Steel Works passed on military requests to individual plants and coordinated their activities; it reported progress to the military. Army and Navy officers were sent to control and supervise the company. Additional full-time control and supervising officers were assigned to each plant. Production orders were issued by the Ministers and backed up with the allocation of necessary materials. It was assumed that factories encountered no difficulty in moving orders into production, but miscommunication among the Army, Navy, and Air Force ensured that companies encountered many problems (Kobe Steel Works, 1954, pp. 112–13).

According to Kobe Steel Works (1954, p. 118): "At that time, the Army operated an annual budget that did not clearly specify long-term production targets. As a result, private companies always felt uneasy when expanding production capacity. When orders decreased in 1939–1940, this problem attracted attention. Despite the 'Special Aid' Act of 1942, when the Army ordered a reduced quantity of bullets, it caused a serious problem for producers all over Japan, from large companies to small. Our company's order began to decrease in 1939 from one-half to one-third the previous amount.

as a primary business target; they maintained corporate responsibility by exercising creativity and making the best possible use of labor, materials, and funds. The government told the weapons manufacturing companies that it would adopt these policies: (1) lending production equipment without charge, while ordering companies to conduct business; (2) ordering companies to install at their own cost the equipment they borrowed; and (3) issuing construction orders on condition that companies regularly purchase products. These differed from simple subsidies or traditional incentives and were designed to compensate for deficiencies in the NGMAct, National Property Act, Loan Orders for Equipment Authority, and Wartime Loan Bank Act. By the end of the war, twenty-one private companies (twenty-six plants) expanded production capacity under this act. It applied to partial or complete pieces of equipment in four factories as well as the Yokohama factory of Japan Steel Works (Japan Steel Works (1968, II, p. 183).

By the beginning of 1940 we had scaled down capacity to one-third and converted it to specialty steel production...."

The account continued (Kobe Steel Works, 1954, p. 128): "At the request of the military, we built ten new factories, which required a huge investment. Regardless of whether or not we won the war, we could not finance this ourselves. Accordingly, apart from doubling our paid-in capital from 90 million yen to 180 million yen in March 1942, we adopted the GOCO system and used the Special Aid Act and Equipment Authority. For example, because they were special-purpose facilities for wartime use, we chose to build the bullet factory of Ohkubo and factories in Ohgaki and Kamii as Kobe Weapons Industries' GOCO factories under the Special Aid Act."

Before the Special Aid Act became available, neither the Army nor the Navy implemented any PCE policies at the Kobe Steel Works.

According to *35 Years of Mitsui Shipbuilding* (Mitsui Shipbuilding, 1953, pp. 109–10): "With the beginning of the Pacific War, we received orders from the Navy to invest heavily in capacity expansion. Toward that end, in March 1942 we established the Temporary Construction Headquarters to provide unified enforcement. Capacity expansions were planned and implemented entirely under the instruction of the Navy. We needed various approvals under the control laws, including the Temporary Funds Coordination Act and the Steel Industry Act. Since FY1942, the Industry Equipment Authority used government funds to expand shipbuilding capacity. In addition, the 'Temporary Treatment of New Factory Construction for Large Ships' was enforced in April 1943, allowing shipbuilders to receive preferential treatment."

Either way, the PCE policies began in FY1942 at the earliest, after the start of the Pacific War.

5-4-4. The Aircraft Manufacturing Factories of Mitsubishi Heavy Industries

Air power was essential to Japan's war effort after the mid-1930s, and it depended on tremendous improvements in aircraft and related instruments and weapons. If systematic war preparations had been planned and enforced during this period, it would have had an impact on product improvements and PCE for air armament.

I describe air armament (air power) in Chapter 7 (the Navy's PCE Policies toward Mitsubishi Heavy Industries for aircraft, in subsection 9-5-3). Here

Table 5–2. *Size of each aircraft body manufacturing plant of Mitsubishi Heavy Industries, at the end of each fiscal year*

Fiscal year	Nagoya	1st	3rd	11th	Mizushima	Kumamoto	Total
						Unit: 3.3 m^2	
1937	22,800						22,800
1938	66,000						66,000
1939	98,500						98,500
1940	117,012						117,012
1941	150,012						150,012
1942	189,074						189,074
1943	221,204						221,204
1944	200,900				65,025	66,218	332,143
1945	118,030	2,406	95,526	36,000	50,509	38,785	341,256

Source: Editorial Committee on the History of Air Industry, ed. (1948, p. 158).

I consider the effectiveness of the Army and Navy PCEPolicies, focusing on plans for aircraft engines and bodies.[47]

Together with the Nakajima Aircraft Company, Mitsubishi Heavy Industries was one of two major aircraft manufacturers. Table 5–2 shows the size of each Mitsubishi factory (where aircraft bodies were manufactured) at the end of each fiscal year (unit = 3.3 m^2). At the end of FY1941, the Nagoya factory was 6.5 times larger than in FY1937; it was 10 times larger in FY1943. In 1941, using GOCO, the Army and Navy established construction factories to manage the second PCE orders in Kumamoto and Mizushima. The Mizushima plant began operation at the beginning of 1944 and the Kumamoto plant in April 1944. With this increase in production, the Nagoya plant began to construct its fourth airport for experimental flights in Chita as a GOCO facility. It began operation in July 1945.

Construction of GOCO plants did not begin before 1941 at the earliest, and none were in operation before 1944. I find no information about

---

[47] Recall that, as mentioned in subsection 1–4–3, the Army started its fully fledged armament enhancement plan (the first Rearmament Plan) just before the War with China in July 1937. It aimed to build 41 divisions and 142 air squadrons by 1942. This plan, which focused on air armament, assumed that the Army's Five-Year Plan for Munitions Manufacturing Industries made capacity expansion in the aircraft manufacturing industry its top priority. In the same month, the Army asked the government to promote key industries necessary for the development of the munitions manufacturing industries (Boeicho, 1975c, pp. 117–18).

Table 5–3. *Size of each aircraft engine manufacturing plant of Mitsubishi Heavy Industries*

| | | | | | | Unit: m^2 | |
Year	Month	Nagoya	Shizuoka	Kyoto	16th (Ogaki)	Total	Index
1939	1–3	120,271				120,271	100
1940	1–3	211,437				211,437	176
1941	1–3	197,142				197,142	164
1942	1–3	207,091				207,091	172
1943	1–3	235,174				235,174	196
1944	1–3	274,939	73,113	1,368		349,420	291
1945	1–3	150,664	79,144	89,383	29,266	348,457	290
1945	4–6	12,038	16,603	58,033	66,602	153,276	127

Source: Editorial Committee on the History of Air Industry, ed. (1948, p. 236).

PCEPolicies governing aircraft body production at Mitsubishi Heavy Industries before FY1941.

Table 5–3 shows the size of each aircraft engine manufacturing factory owned by Mitsubishi Heavy Industries in January through March of each year (thus the figures for 1944 in Table 5–2 approximately correspond with those for FY1943 in Table 5–3, unit = m^2). Before 1938, the engines and bodies were made in the same factories, so separate figures were not available. In addition, Hiroshima's twentieth factory did not produce any engines.

New engine and body factories began operation in 1944 at the earliest. I find no information about the PCEPolicies governing aircraft engine production at Mitsubishi Heavy Industries before 1941.[48]

Although engine production increased year by year, the military increasingly placed orders without considering a company's production capacity. As shown in Table 5–4, backorders carried over to the next fiscal year built

---

[48] The Editorial Committee on the History of Air Industry, ed. (1948, p. 235) commented on the enforcement of the PCEPlans at Mitsubishi Heavy Industries: "We were well aware that, in our company, engine production, factory size, labor–management relations and machine tools were inseparably connected. Those three factors created the most serious bottlenecks when it came to increasing production. As the war changed, materials for plant construction also changed from reinforced concrete to wood and barracks; machine tools were remodeled into wartime versions, with low precision. To meet requirements, we enhanced recruitment, mobilized students, and increased the number of factory girls, thereby decreasing efficiency. Because of an imbalance in production materials and a failure to make use of every resource, it became harder to increase production. For aircraft engine production, the balanced increase in machine tools was critical. Imbalances resulted in the so-called 'headless' and 'flightless airplanes.'"

Table 5–4. *Number of orders received and production of aircraft engines by Mitsubishi Heavy Industries*

Fiscal year	Order received A	Production B	Carry-over A–B	Carry-over to the next fiscal year
1932	245	172	73	73
1933	274	206	68	141
1934	303	288	15	156
1935	239	145	94	250
1936	249	236	13	263
1937	520	530	−10	253
1938	1,306	1,312	−6	247
1939	2,525	2,254	271	518
1940	4,236	3,281	955	1,473
1941	5,790	4,594	1,196	2,669
1942	9,909	6,701	3,208	5,877
1943	16,176	9,710	6,466	12,343
1944	16,498	17,524	−1,026	11,317
1945	5,407	2,769	2,638	13,955
Total	63,677	49,722		13,955

Source: Editorial Committee on the History of Air Industry, ed. (1948, p. 237).

up rapidly, particularly after the beginning of the Pacific War. By FY1943, backorders exceeded production volume.

The military could not have carefully planned and effectively promoted PCEPolicies before the war, as it failed to ensure the necessary volume of munitions from companies.

6

PCEPolicies in Manchukuo (Occupied Manchuria)

6-1. Overview: Conventional Views of Manchuria and Japan

This chapter focuses on the nature and effectiveness of the PCEPlans and PCEPolicies in occupied Manchuria (Manchukuo), which has occupied a very special position in the dominant, conventional view of Japan.

Advocates of the conventional wisdom believe that during the century and a half since the Meiji Restoration, Japan has shown tremendous competence in economic planning and management. According to this view, Manchuria represents a model of economic development, from prewar development and wartime control through postwar economic growth.

Professor Kent Calder, Princeton political scientist, wrote (1993, p. 50)[1]:

[A]n influential vision of how industrial transformation should be pursued flowed from a central formative experience of many of postwar Japan's elite industrial bureaucrats: the forced creation of a formidable industrial base in Manchuria during the 1930s and early 1940s. .....[2]

---

[1] Calder (1993, p. 49) also wrote: "Chief among Japan's industrial strategists has long been the Ministry of International Trade and Industry and its predecessors ... As Chalmers Johnson points out, the emergence of self-conscious industrial strategy at MITI was an evolutionary process, with deep roots in the turbulent Depression and mobilization for World War II."

[2] Calder (1993, p. 50) continued, "This vision of a unitary, regimented industrial state, beyond politics, which could marshal resources flexibly to meet any threat to national goals, deeply inspired not only military leaders such as Ishiwara Kanji, operations officer to the Kwantung Army during the Manchurian invasion and a key Section Chief of the General Staff during the mid-1930s, but also many of the industrial bureaucrats who served there, such as Kishi Nobusuke (prime minister, 1957–1960), Shiina Etsusaburo (foreign minister, 1964–1966), and Sahashi Shigeru (Administrative Vice-Minister of MITI, 1964–1966). Many of them saw Manchuria, in Shiina's words, as 'the great proving ground for Japanese industry."

The underlying premise behind this model was common with that of Meiji Japan – that economic vitality and national security were inseparably linked. The model had three central tenets: (1) control over credit and nonfinancial resource allocation must be centralized in the hands of the industrial planner, thus cutting out the banker, (2) adequately directed growth could be achieved only through an alliance of the state with emerging, nonestablishment economic forces, and (3) coherent, planned economic growth could be brought about efficiently only in an environment devoid of pluralist politics.

Professor Calder's views echo most books on Japan's economic history written in English.[3]

The special position of Manchuria makes it the focus of conventional views of Japan's wartime planning and control, and general competence.

Section 6–2 focuses on the formation and outline of the Five-Year Industry Development Plan in Manchuria, a PCEPlan for Manchukuo. Section 6–3 reviews the historical background and investigates the effectiveness of the plan. Section 6–4 examines briefly the assumption that the "persons of influence in Manchuria" known as "Team Manchuria" and "2-ki-3-suke" were particularly influential in the systematic war preparations and "planned" enforcement' of the war.[4]

6–2. PCEPolicies and the Five-Year Industry Development Plan in Manchuria

6–2–1. Ando on Japan's Wartime Economy and the "New Bureaucrats"

According to Oishi (1994, pp. 14–15), the idea of a military total war regime, in vogue since the Manchurian Incident, was temporarily implemented in Manchuria as the Five-Year Development Plan in Manchuria: "After the 2.26 Incident, the Japanese politico-economic system was reorganized along fascist lines. The idea of a military total war regime was officially approved by the government and business community early in 1937 with 'the military-business embracing,' evolving into 'Three Principles of Public Finance and the Economy' under the first Konoe Cabinet.... Thus, the PCEPlans were

---

[3] The most famous of these include Johnson (1982), Lockwood (1955), Reischauer (1977), van Wolferen (1990), Pempel and Muramatsu (1995), Gao (1997), and Gordon (2003).

[4] Sahashi became the Vice-Minister of MITI in 1964 at the age of fifty-one. He joined the Commerce Ministry in July 1937 at the age of twenty-four, and got drafted and four months later was sent to China. He returned to the Commerce Ministry in October 1941 when Kishi became the Commerce Minister (Johnson, 1982, pp. 242–3). It would be interesting to know what Sahashi learned about Manchuria; there is no indication in Calder (1993).

formulated even before the start of war with China. Economic or import control began at the end of 1936 in response to the international payment crisis."

Ando (1972, pp. 469–70) commented more colorfully on Japan's wartime economy and "new bureaucrats":

"Team Manchuria" was a group of military officials that included the Kwantung Army Chief of Staff. The group was close to the Army's "control faction (*tosei-ha*)," which, inspired by the so-called Army pamphlet,[5] longed to enforce economic control policies in Japan. Under their leadership, bureaucrats linked to the Army's control faction and temporarily transferred to Manchukuo conducted *living-body-experiment*-type trials of economic control in Manchuria.

... Afterward, leaders of that time and staff of the Kwantung Army joined the military leadership at home, assuming important posts like Army Minister. Civilians in Team Manchuria also assumed important positions in the Finance and Commerce ministries. Thus, a coalition of control faction military officials and Manchurian new bureaucrats was re-created in Japan.... Some became Ministers and Vice-Ministers. It was just after the beginning of the War with China; and a system of wartime economic control was established and maturing. The coalition system epitomized by Team Manchuria reached its peak[6] during the Tojo Cabinet that began the Pacific War. At the same time, wartime economic control also peaked. Thus, the principles of the so-called Army pamphlet and the fruits of its Manchurian *living-body-experiments* in economic control were applied in this defining moment.

Many readers must feel dissatisfied with this view. The importance of Manchuria-related events and relevant observations must underpin the validity of the conventional wisdom. However, vague expressions and the absence of logical proof and empirical evidence must leave many readers dissatisfied.[7]

Sections 6–2 and 6–3 focus on the scale and effectiveness of the PCEPlans or PCEPolicies implemented by the Manchukuo or Japanese government, including the Kwantung Army and the South Manchurian Railway Company (the so-called Manchurian Railways, or *mantetsu*, hereafter SMR). Those sections illustrate that no such policies were implemented; if they had been, various factors, including their small scale, would have prevented them from achieving remarkable results. Oishi's statement that the idea of a military total war regime, in vogue since the Manchurian Incident,

---

[5] The so-called Army pamphlet is a pamphlet published on 10 October 1934 by the Newspaper Subsection of the AM, entitled "A Proposal for the Significance and Enhancement of the National Defense." It began, "War is father of creation, and mother of culture."

[6] He continued that the team included the Prime Minister and the Army Minister (later also the Munitions Minister) Hideki Tojo, the Commerce Minister (later the Vice-Minister of Munitions) Nobusuke Kishi, and the Chief Cabinet Secretary Naoki Hoshino.

[7] In Gordon (2003, p. 212), Kishi appears as one leading architect of the economic new order during this period in Japan.

was temporarily implemented in Manchuria as the Five-Year Development Plan in Manchuria is unsubstantiated. Ando's claim to have applied the fruits of its *living-body experiments* in Manchuria into economic control in Japan is simply untrue.[8]

6-2-2. The Timing of Implementation and the Historical Environment

With the PCE strongly endorsed both in Japan and in Manchuria and in response to the Army's request, the government began formulating the PCEPlans; just at that moment, the War with China began and escalated rapidly. As a result, the PCEPlans were postponed. Even after the Cabinet approved the Outline in January 1939, its implementation was impeded by the wartime situation and the scarcity of resources.

Both the PCEPlans and PCEPolicies were impacted by the war situation and faced severe constraints in securing budgets, foreign currencies, and relevant materials. As a consequence, the PCEPolicies in Japan had no real substance and were ineffective. How was the situation different in Manchuria? Was the Japanese government in Manchuria free from constraints and able to implement effective and functioning PCEPolicies? What arguments or evidence suggest that this was achieved?

The Cabinet approved the Outline of the PCEPlans in Japan on 17 January 1939. An MMPlans official, Tanaka (1975, p. 114), described the situation in Manchuria:

When the Cabinet approved the PCEPlans for Japan, those for Manchuria and North China were to be formulated. Industries targeted in the PCEPlans were selected to reinforce national defense by helping to establish self-sufficiency in important resources within Japan's sphere of influence. . . .

It was the Manchukuo government that was most interested in the PCEPlans across those areas. The Manchukuo government had already established both the Manchurian Heavy Industries Development Company [or *mangyo*; hereafter MHI] and the Five-Year Development Plan for Manchuria. It wanted build a steel company, larger than the Showa Steel Company controlled by SMR, in resource-rich southeastern Manchuria. Because officials in charge of the MMPlans strongly opposed this project, it never became a reality.

This example shows that if PCEPolicies were effectively enforced in Manchuria by the Manchukuo or Japanese governments, that enforcement must have happened before January 1939.

---

[8] Both Oishi and Ando were University of Tokyo professors of economic history.

6-2-3. The Five-Year Industry Development Plan in Manchuria

The Five-Year Industry Development Plan in Manchuria was formulated in October 1936.[9] Naoki Hoshino (1963, pp. 206–9), who was to become the Secretary General (*sohmu chokan*) of Manchukuo, recalled that in December 1936, the Kwantung Army, the Manchukuo government, and SMR attended a spring conference in Taggangzi (close to Anshan) and compiled the basic plan in three days.[10] Army leaders in Tokyo, particularly those with links to ACCom, suggested synthesizing existing plans to formulate a Five-Year Plan for industry development in Manchuria. They referred to a one-page ACCom memorandum concerning one- and five-year production capacity targets for twenty items, including heavy materials, industrial products, and important agricultural products.[11]

[9] There were serious clashes of opinion between the Finance Ministry and the AM, resulting in the dissolution of the Office Toward Manchuria (OM) (*taiman jimukyoku*) before details of the outline could be discussed. No compromise was reached until 14 April 1937, when an OM policy was formally decided. Postponing a discussion of the details and without obtaining the Cabinet approval, on April 26 the outline proposed by the Army was accepted, on condition that each item would go through the necessary formalities before being implemented (Suzuki, 1992, pp. 266–7). Accordingly, no plan could be put into action; the plan was a collection of items and called by various names, devised inserting the terms "industry development," "industry," "development," or "economy" between "Manchuria" and "Five-Year Plan." Takeo Iwaguro, a former Kwantung Army Staff Member and ACCom member/officer at the AM's Procurement Bureau of the AM worked from December 1934 to August 1936 at the OM. Iwaguro (1977, pp. 50–4, 76–7) recalled that there were serious problems rebuilding the Manchurian economy. These included SMR reorganization issues and the restructuring of institutions. During the first half of the 1930s, there were serious disagreements among the Kwantung Army, the Cabinet, and military leaders headed by Army Minister Araki. The OM was established in 1935 under the Cabinet Office, with the Army Minister as Head, reporting to the Prime Minister, and the ex–Bureau Chief of the Finance Ministry as Vice-Head. This was not the end of the conflict. The OM had three sections, with twenty-four or twenty-five members.

[10] There are differing versions of the conference dates, with Hoshino remembering December and Katakura October. Quoting the diary of a participant named Nango, Kobayashi (2005, pp. 102–3) locates it on 5–7 October, and estimates that discussions lasted for ten hours in total.

[11] Tadashi Katakura, Manchurian Subsection Chief of the AM, recalled the process of formulating the Five-Year Plan as follows (Katakura, 1978, pp. 221–3): In response to the ACCom Strategy Section Chief Ishiwara's request to the AM concerning armament enhancement in Manchuria, Katakura and other members consulted with the AM, ACCom, and Kwantung Army; on 3 August 1936, the Policy Outline Idea for Manchurian Development was finalized and issued to the Commander of the Kwantung Army. In the summer of 1936, the Miyazaki plan was completed in Japan. Ishiwara and Katakura agreed that, given Japan's situation, the plan could not be implemented immediately; it would be better to let the process start in Manchukuo. The Military and Procurement bureaus, collecting opinions from the Commerce and Agriculture ministries, presented ideas for

Hoshino (1963, pp. 209–10) argued that the conference was important because the Manchukuo government and SMR, having drawn up and enforced independent plans, discussed and implemented their plan together:

Before the formation of Manchukuo there were few modern heavy industries in the area, except for SMR and smaller Japanese businesses. Heavy industry production was concentrated in a narrow strip on the periphery. The SMR was a Japanese company, and Japanese administrators oversaw the foreign businesses in the peripheral industrial zones. This situation continued after the formation of Manchukuo. Manchukuo had no authority in those areas and did not intervene. However, the industrialized periphery lacked raw materials and needed space to expand production capacities. Factory sites in Manchuria were essential for the plans, and some of these were outside the industrial zone.

The following June, the Army presented its Five-Year Plan for Key Industries to the government Planning Agency. This directly triggered the development of the PCEPlans. In Japan, the government took more time to formulate plans. The military's "total war regime" was put into effect temporarily in Manchuria as the "Five-Year Development Plan in Manchuria" (Oishi, 1994, p. 14) in June 1937 at the earliest.

This book focuses on the substance and effectiveness of the PCEPlans and PCEPolicies in Manchuria between June 1937 and January 1939.

The Cabinet approved the PCEPlans Outline in January 1939. Despite the plans' temporary enforcement in Manchuria, basic questions remain unanswered. Who developed this idea? Was it feasible? If the original concept was intended for several regions, including Japan and Manchuria, how was it revised to suit Manchuria? If the 1937 War with China derailed implementation in Japan, weren't there also serious implications for Manchuria? How did the government overcome difficulties caused by changed conditions?

If the Five-Year Industry Development Plan had been enforced in Manchuria, one would expect the results of this successful, rapid (eighteen months) experiment in economic control to have been imitated later in Japan. I find no persuasive evidence or argument to suggest that this happened.

the five-year industry development plan in Manchuria. Once the plan was agreed to at the joint conference of the AM and ACCom and approved by superiors, Katakura went to the Headquarters of Kwantung Army at Changchun in September 1936 to explain the plan and obtain approval. The Kwantung Army revised the target ideas and organized an October conference at the Taggangzi spring. The Five-Year Plan for industry development in Manchuria was approved in October and the outline in November. Then, Katakura's target ideas were conveyed in a one-page memorandum in Hoshino.

6-2-4. The Five-Year Industry Development Plan in Manchuria and the MHI

The launch of the Five-Year Industry Development Plan in Manchuria coincided with the second term of an economy-building initiative. In its first term, the government had tried and failed to build the Manchurian economy by focusing on one company in one sector. Under the Five-Year Plan, Manchurian Heavy Industries (MHI) spearheaded and enforced economy building efforts. Instead of focusing on one company in one sector, the government adopted a development policy that resembled organically comprehensive management (Hara, 1976a, p. 228).

The Kwantung Army's control policy during the first economy-building period in Manchuria was influenced by the reformist military faction and heavily tinged with an anti-*zaibatsu* thought.[12] Although capital was needed, private investment in Manchuria was restricted; the contributions of private companies were therefore insignificant. The SMR became the primary channel for Japanese investment in Manchuria after the Manchurian Incident in 1931 (Suzuki, 1992, p. 268).

In June 1934, the Manchukuo government issued a statement to welcome private capital, encouraging firms to do business in Manchuria. As the Japanese economy was recovering from depression, investments did not increase. Between 1935 and 1936, the Kwantung Army began planning for a second-stage economy-building exercise in Manchuria, and published an Outline in which Army leaders explained their policy toward Manchurian investments. In accordance with the nature of each enterprise, the Japanese government would mobilize capital and encourage private companies to invest directly in Manchurian industries. The Kwantung Army collaborated with the Manchukuo government and SMR to quickly draft the outline of a Five-Year Plan. At the same time, Army leaders searched for industrial capitalists in Japan and invited them to visit Manchuria. Among the capitalists who accepted this request was Yoshisuke Aikawa, the Chairman of Nissan (Suzuki, 1992, pp. 268-9).

The Five-Year Industry Development Plan in Manchuria was enforced by MHI as the key to second-stage economy building. This chapter focuses on PCEPolicies enforced by the MHI in Manchuria before 1939.

On 22 October 1937, the Cabinet approved the Outline for Establishing the MHI; this was approved by the State Council of Manchukuo on 26 October. On 29 October, the governments of Japan and of Manchukuo announced

---

[12] For details, see Suzuki (1992, pp. 210-12).

the establishment of a Manchurian Development Company by relocating Nissan to Manchuria, a move endorsed by shareholders on 20 November. On 27 December, the MHI, with Aikawa as its President, was established as a Manchukuo government-affiliated corporation with 250 million yen in capital. In February 1938, the Manchukuo government accepted newly issued shares in exchange for 250 million yen, and in March transferred to the MHI the stocks it owned in private firms, including four purchased from the SMR: the Showa Steel Company, Manchurian Coal Mining, Manchurian Light Metals, and Dowa Motors. The MHI became a large national power and began operation, expecting to play a key role in Manchurian industrial development, in response to Japan's wartime demands (Suzuki, 1992, pp. 274–7).

6-2-5. The Manchurian Heavy Industries (MHI) Company

The Army expected Aikawa to develop the automobile and aircraft manufacturing industries in Manchuria to prepare for war against the USSR. Aikawa refused (Hoshino, 1963, p. 223) for the following reasons:

1. Even in Japan, the automobile industry has only just reached the scale needed to cover costs. It does not yet enjoy the scale economies of mass production. It will be impossible to develop this industry in the much smaller market in Manchuria.
2. The automobile industry needs many subcontractors, and there are none in Manchuria.
3. My capacity is that of all Nissan, not the one of Aikawa alone. Even if I send several people or go by myself, it won't be enough to develop the automobile industry in Manchuria.

Aikawa proposed his own vision for developing heavy industries in Manchuria. Its three features (Hoshino, 1963, p. 286) were the following:

1. We develop heavy industries comprehensively in Manchuria.
2. The MHI promotes this comprehensive development. The government will not give instructions directly to companies engaged in development. Instead, it will give them through the MHI.
3. For the development of Manchuria, we must import machines, technology, and capital at a large scale from foreign countries, the U.S. in particular.

The third feature was the most important. The War with China had begun, and the government was suffering from a shortage of foreign currency (import capacity). The Cabinet approved Aikawa's plan, and Finance Minister Kaya reaffirmed the emphasis on foreign capital, given the foreign currency shortage caused by the war (Suzuki, 1992, p. 274).

However, foreign capital was never imported and the machinery was never purchased. The development plan for resource-rich southeastern Manchuria collapsed. The SMR's economic research institute called this region the Saal of the East for its bountiful resources of iron-ore and coal. Aikawa conducted a resource survey and concluded that it would not be feasible to develop a steel industry using local iron-ore and coal. Developing this area influenced his decision to shift Nissan to Manchuria and to import foreign capital (Hara, 1976b, pp. 264–6).[13]

Twelve months was not enough time to develop heavy industries in Manchuria, and the War with China made it difficult to achieve this vision.

As shown in the next section, the Five-Year Plan ended in failure. "When the Greater East Asian War began, Japan could no longer afford to allocate capital, materials and personnel to develop Manchuria. We were left with a very basic doubt whether we should continue the development of Manchuria, for the next ten years as we had planned at the outset" (Hoshino, 1963, p. 302).

In July 1940, Naoki Hoshino, the Secretary of State of the Manchukuo State Council, returned to Japan and became the Chairman of the Planning Council. In 1942, concluding that his work in Manchuria had ended, Aikawa ceded the position of MHI President to Tatsunosuke Takasaki, the Vice-President of MHI; became an advisor; and returned to Japan (Hoshino, 1963, p. 302).

6-3. The Effectiveness of the PCEPolicies in Manchuria (Manchukuo)

6-3-1. The Location and Position of Manchuria

For advocates of the conventional wisdom that Japan began the war after careful, systematic preparations, Manchuria (or Manchukuo) has been a

---

[13] For more details, see Hara (1976b), pp. 248–74, in particular. Nissan's effort in large-scale machinery imports for Manchurian Motors, established in 1939, was also unsuccessful. Nissan succeeded in importing used equipment, which however arrived at Yokohama in 1940. Having given up constructing a new automobile production plant in Manchuria, and given the onset of war with the United States, Nissan used those machines for aircraft engine production in its Yoshiwara factory, which after the war contributed to automobile engine production for Nissan Motors (Hoshino, 1963, pp. 289–90). With the relocation of Nissan to the MHI, the registered head office was also transferred; this does not, however, mean that automobile production facilities were moved from Japan to Manchuria.

prime example. This was true of many Japanese politicians, bureaucrats, military officials, journalists, researchers, and ordinary citizens of the time, and it is also true today.

Before the Manchurian Incident in 1931, the so-called Manchurian problem had been one of the most basic issues for Japanese decision makers.[14] Succeeding Cabinets maintained as the basic policy that Japan must ensure the interests in Mongolia and Xinjiang that Japan acquired in the Sino–Japanese War and the Russo–Japanese War at the cost of the loss of one hundred thousand men (Boeicho, 1967a, p. 310). There were two major elements to Japan's policy toward the continent. One concerned the interests that Japan acquired in the Treaty of Portsmouth after victory in the Russo–Japanese War: the leasehold in the SMR, the Kwantung Leased Territory, and the right to station troops there. The other was the cultivation of Manchukuo, established as a consequence of the Manchurian Incident.[15]

In the mid-1930s' debates over national defense policy, observers often focused on plans and policies regarding rearmament and emphasized

---

[14] As mentioned in section 2–7, many people believe that the Manchurian Incident was to solve the so-called Mongolia-Xinjiang problem.

[15] Sejima (1995, p. 171). Another view of the Manchurian Incident is also telling (Taylor, 1964, pp. 62–4): "On 18 September [1931] Japanese forces occupied Manchuria, which was theoretically part of China. China appealed to the League [of Nations] for redress. It was not an easy problem. The Japanese had a good case. The authority of the Chinese central government – nowhere strong – did not run in Manchuria, which had been for years in a state of lawless confusion. Japanese trading interests had suffered greatly. There were many precedents in China for independent action – the last being the British landing at Shanghai in 1927.... The Washington naval treaty gave Japan a local supremacy in the Far East; and successive British governments confirmed this supremacy when they deliberately postponed the building up of their base in Singapore.... [T]he British government attached more importance to the restoration of peace than to a display of moral rectitude.... It was shared by the Labour party who at this time condemned not 'aggression' but 'war'.... The British had always regarded the League as an instrument of conciliation, not a machine of security.... The League set up the Lytton Commission, actually on a Japanese initiative, to discover the facts about Manchuria and to propound a solution. The Commission did not reach a simple verdict. It found that most of the Japanese grievances were justified. Japan was not condemned as an aggressor, though she was condemned for resorting to force before all peaceful means of redress were exhausted. The Japanese withdrew in protest from the League of Nations. But in fact, British policy succeeded. The Chinese reconciled themselves to the loss of a province which they had not controlled for some years; and in 1933 peace was restored between China and Japan. In later years, the Manchurian affair assumed a mythical importance. It was treated as a milestone on the road to war, the decisive 'betrayal' of the League, especially by the British government. In reality, the League, under British leadership, had done what the British thought it was designed to do: it had limited a conflict and brought it, however unsatisfactorily, to an end."

defense against the USSR.[16] Manchuria was located on the front line, and the Kwantung Army in Manchuria played a key role. The Army intended to systematically enhance and strengthen in the long run national defense against the USSR. The Army formulated the Outline of its Five-Year Plan for the Munitions Manufacturing Industries, and presented to the government the Outline of its Five-Year Plan for Key Industries. It then requested policies that would help it prepare the foundations. In response, the government began formulating the PCEPlans. Although, for various reasons, these were not effectively enforced in Japan, in Manchuria the plans were successfully implemented as the Five-Year Industry Development Plan in Manchuria. That is the conventional view.

The view that Japan systematically planned and executed its war with China and the Pacific War was widely accepted more than half a century ago, and has become the conventional wisdom and the dominant view, overwhelmingly popular and stable even today. As a consequence, most general readers accept without question the proposition that at least in Manchuria, Japan's PCEPolicies achieved a remarkable success. The understanding has not been questioned for a long time, and most people have lost interest.

By now, many readers may have changed their view. In the following subsection, I show that the PCEPlans had little substance, if any, and that the Five-Year Industry Development Plan in Manchuria was a failure.

6-3-2. The Five-Year Industry Development Plan in Manchuria

As shown in the preceding sections, the conventional wisdom has emphasized a series of observations concerning the PCEPlans (or PCEPolicies) suggesting that they were first implemented effectively in Manchuria, and then later in Japan. Key observations are as follows:

1. The Army emphasized national defense against the USSR.
2. Manchuria was the front line for that defense.
3. The government's PCEPlan deliberations were coordinated with the Army's plans and policies.
4. Although writing and enforcing the PCEPlans was a slow process in Japan, in Manchuria they were quickly converted into a five-year industry development plan.
5. The military, particularly the Army, spearheaded systematic war preparations.

---

[16] Recall the discussion in subsection 2-4-2.

Whether appropriate PCEPlans or PCEPolicies were formulated and effectively enforced in Manchuria is another issue. These observations alone do not prove the effectiveness of the PCEPlans.

Like every policy or choice, the Five-Year Industry Development Plan in Manchuria was chosen and implemented under constraints. The Japanese government could not choose from a rich set of effective plans and policies for the Five-Year Industry Development Plan in Manchuria, nor more generally for its PCEPlans and PCEPolicies.

Boeicho (1970, p. 21) wrote:

Both the Outline of Five-Year Plan for the Munitions Manufacturing Industries and the Army's Outline of the Five-Year Plan for Key Industries focused on munitions and other key industries on the continent, particularly in Manchuria. The Army served as a contact for leading Manchukuo, and upon the "Outline for Economic Controls in Japan and Manchuria," determined in March 1934, formulated the "Outline of Five-Year Industry Development Plan in Manchuria." In January 1937, the Kwantung Army Commander (concurrently serving as the Japanese ambassador to Manchukuo) asked the Manchukuo government to enforce it. The Manchukuo government developed the Five-Year Industry Development Plan from between FY1937 and FY1941, and enforced it from FY1937.

No information is available about the specific policies enforced from FY1937 or their impact. Boeicho (1970, p. 21) writes: "Just when the dramatic expansion of production capacity in the munitions industries and the expansion of key industries in Japan and Manchuria were about to begin, the North China Incident occurred. Accordingly, Japan was obliged to address the Incident, and subsequently the Greater East Asian War, before achieving any expansion in key industries or the PCE of the munitions industries." This statement suggests that the Five-Year Industry Development Plan in Manchuria lacked substance and that its enforcement had little effect. Given that the Japanese government was obliged to postpone its own PCEPlans because of the War with China, it seems unlikely it could have effectively implemented the PCEPlans or PCEPolicies through the Kwantung Army in Manchuria. There was much less preparation for the PCEPlans in Manchuria, and enforcement must have been difficult.

6–3–3. The Historical Background and Environmental Conditions

In 1938 and 1939, the Five-Year Industry Development Plan in Manchuria, PCEPolicies, and armament buildup were severely constrained.

In July 1937, the War with China began unexpectedly. The Japanese government was forced to address the drastically increased munitions demands, and rearmament against the USSR was postponed.

After the capture of Hankou and Guangdong on 22 December 1938, Prime Minister Konoe issued a proclamation on the new order in East Asia. Although previous aggressive operations had been successful, Japan could not eliminate the main force of the Chinese military; this led to an impasse. After the second Konoe Proclamation, it became a long, drawn-out war of attrition.

Japan conducted its second war mobilization until March 1939, three months after the second Konoe Proclamation. In June, the Head of Weapons Arsenals gave this summary: "Although we have not yet reached the stage of putting all our national power on the line, we suffer from serious shortages of various materials" (Boeicho, 1970, p. 250).

The new Vice-ACCommander, Sawada, evaluated this situation in October 1939: "Although behaving aggressively to the outside world, like a fruit rotten at the core, Japan's policy would not last long" (Boeicho, 1967a, p. 624). Army Minister Hata shared this view.

From the fall of 1938 to 1939, the ACCom studied two operation plans for FY1943 (the so-called Eighth Operation Plan) as a basis for a five-year rearmament effort against the USSR. Plan A (*koh-an*) focused on operations in the east and plan B (*otsu-an*) in the west. The Kwantung Army and the ACCom preferred the latter, but a joint-study meeting with the AM convinced the ACCom that there was little chance of adopting the latter. On 12 May 1939, Japan and the USSR clashed in the Nomonhan Incident (or Battle of Khalkhin Gol). Only a short time before, the ACCom had abandoned plan B, on the western front of Manchuria.[17]

---

[17] For the Eighth Operation Plan and the Nomonhan Incident, see pp. 584–7 and pp. 593–613 of Boeicho (1967a), respectively. See also Miwa (2008, pp. 196–7). Imoto participated in the investigation of the Eighth Operation Plan as a member of the Strategy Section of the ACCom, and reflected later, "there were other issues we should have investigated before this. I wonder if it was the most important" (Imoto, 1978, pp. 366–7). The first question was whether a decisive war at the national border was feasible or relevant. Troops would be transported from the homeland by ship and land, taking two months, then concentrated on the Soviet–Manchuria border to start the operation. The USSR, having assembled forces via the Trans-Siberian Railway, was expected to begin the war against the Japanese military. The Soviet military presence around Manchuria was four to five times that of the Japanese presence. If the Soviet military attacked soon, the Japanese forces in Manchuria would be defeated before troops could arrive from the homeland. The second point was that the Japanese Army was old-fashioned, dependent on transportation by horses. It was thought very hard to carry out operations in areas more than 250 kilometers away from the railroad; to fight in Transbaikal, it would be necessary to build a railway across the

In December 1939, the ACCom presented the Revised Rearmament Plan to the Emperor. Taking into consideration the escalation of the War with China and the lessons of the Nomonhan Incident, Army leaders revised the Rearmament Plan, hoping to enhance the quality and quantity of armaments. They decided to reduce the troops stationed in China and reallocate budgets and resources to the armaments against the USSR. As a matter of practice, however, it was infeasible to reduce the number of troops in China, and there was no other choice than to reduce the scope of plans on both sides. At that time, the national budget was in imminent danger, and it was impossible to enforce the Revised Rearmament Plan without reducing the troop levels in China. The Revised Rearmament Plan of December 1939 was enforced in July 1940 as the Renewed Rearmament Plan.

In this period, the MMPlans were central to plans and policies for materials allocation and production activities and formed their foundations. The MMPlans shifted into full swing in July 1939 when the United States threatened to abolish the Japan–U.S. Commerce and Navigation Treaty. The treaty was actually abolished in 1940, and it became extremely difficult to import important materials.

6-3-4. The Historical Background and Environment that Conditioned the Five-Year Industry Development Plan in Manchuria

The Japanese military and ACCom operated under constraints dictated by historical background and the environment. This situation in 1938 and 1939 conditioned the Five-Year Industry Development Plan in Manchuria and other policies. Even if the government hoped to build armaments and enforce PCEPolicies of substance, it was hard to do so effectively under such restrictive conditions. The Five-Year Industry Development Plan in Manchuria was subject to the following additional conditions.

The MHI was finally established by transferring Nissan to Manchuria, and Nissan's Chairman Aikawa assumed the presidency of the MHI.

Nobusuke Kishi was central to the conventional wisdom about the industry development "policies" in Manchuria of this time. Etsusaburo Shiina

---

Greater Khingan Range. Motor divisions and mechanized troops were proposed, but not considered feasible. At that time, in Japan, there were fewer than one hundred thousand motorized vehicles, including two-wheeled motor vehicles. Japan assumed that the USSR had similar limitations. If Japan, adopting plan B, moved forces to the west to fight with the Soviet military, the result would have been disastrous. The Nomonhan Incident, which occurred shortly after the investigation, vividly revealed the reality.

(then the chief official at the Industry Rationalization Bureau) arrived in Manchuria as the Planning Section Chief of the Business Division in October 1933, and other members of the Commerce Ministry followed. Nobusuke Kishi was the Correspondence Section Chief of the Commerce Ministry during this period, and Industry Bureau Chief at the time when the industry development plans were being decided.

Kishi left for Manchuria in 1936 as the Vice-Chief of the Industry Division, which he reorganized the following year into the Business Division. The Taggangzi spring conference was held in October 1936, and plans were being implemented when Kishi arrived. According to Kishi et al. (1981, p. 21), the Five-Year Plan was modeled on those of the USSR.[18]

As a member of the Office Toward Manchuria[19] since its establishment in 1934, Kishi had expressed his opinions on the plan and vision of industry development for Manchuria. He believed that the Fourth Section of the Kwantung Army was managing industrial policy in Manchuria badly. When the Kwantung Army exerted too much power, the business community in Japan backed off. The most talented officials in the Commerce Ministry should have gone to Manchuria to take industry policies away from the military.

Kishi argued that there were no managers capable of enforcing the Five-Year Plan in Manchuria. The existing managers were all old former bureaucrats or military leaders unqualified to manage businesses. They had enough money from the Japanese government, and had no need for Mitsui or Mitsubishi capital for the Five-Year Plan. Instead, they invited to Manchuria able managers from Japanese companies such as Mitsui and Mitsubishi. Aikawa and the Nissan managers transferred to Manchuria, were expected to contribute to developing Manchurian industry (Kishi et al., 1981, p. 23).

Apart from his optimism about developing Manchurian industry, Kishi's views were correct. Manchuria had not developed smoothly. One cause of

---

[18] Kishi et al. (1981, p. 17) recalled that the first Five-Year Plan of the USSR started in 1928: "I had strong doubts as to whether everything would proceed as planned. Vice-Minister Yoshino's view was much clearer, saying in disgust that there was no way it could." Kishi (1982, pp. 216–17) advised Park Chung-hee, two years before he became the President of South Korea: "I was the Chief Executive of Industry Development Policy in prewar Manchukuo. Developing countries want to realize industrialization by building large factories. From the experience then, however, large factories cannot flourish unless the undergrowth of small businesses and agricultural communities develops. Only through an increase in the purchasing power of the general public can large companies arise and develop. First you should focus on developing undergrowth, and raising the purchasing power of agricultural communities." Taking his advice, South Korea focused on the development of this undergrowth, which became the main engine of its economic growth.

[19] See note 9 of this chapter for the Office Toward Manchuria.

failure was the shortage of managers, and another was the Kwantung Army's intervention in industrial policy, which obstructed capital flow and business freedom. Commerce Ministry officials would be able to improve the situation. When the Kwantung Army was in charge of industrial policy, it actively solicited Japanese government money. New managers were needed to make this work, and to attract them, it was necessary to allow business freedom. The reputation of Manchuria's industrial policy was boosted by managers from successful companies, and particularly by Aikawa and Nissan.[20]

The transplanted managers should have achieved a remarkable success through MHI but the historical background and environment strictly conditioned their performance.

First, the Five-Year Industry Development Plan discussions at the Taggangzi spring conference raised two basic issues: how and where to increase production and how to obtain funds. Many feared that excessive production would weigh down domestic industry.[21] The Outline budgeted 8.5 billion yen to implement Five-Year Plans in both Japan and Manchuria. Of this amount, more than 7 billion yen (82.6 percent) was expected to come from the private sector, and the remaining 1 billion yen from the Japanese government. Less than 0.5 billion yen was expected to come from the Manchukuo government (Horiba, 1962, p. 68). At the start, the government counted on being able to acquire imported materials, machines, and foreign currencies.

Second, there was strong opposition to the plan from supporters of the existing policies, some of which straightforwardly reflected vested interests. In March 1937, Katakura, the Manchuria Subsection Chief of the AM, was transferred to the Kwantung Army. At that time, developing the automobile industry and aircraft manufacturing industries was a pressing issue. According to Katakura, the Military Bureau of the AM agreed to contribute to those industries in Manchuria by importing automobile technology and investment from the United States and aircraft technology from Germany. General Affairs Divisions Chief Suzuki and others in the Air Headquarters, from the standpoint of national defense against the USSR, opposed to the plan to build the aircraft manufacturing industry in Manchuria.

---

[20] In Manchuria, the military fastened a plaque reading "No Capitalists" to a gatepost, but Kishi persuaded the Kwantung Army to remove it. Otherwise, Mitsui and Mitsubishi would not come, he thought (Kishi et al., 1981, p. 25). According to Iwaguro (1977, p. 59), who as a member of the secret military division of the Kwantung Army took part in organizational reform issues in Manchuria, the sign meant "No Spoilers" rather than "No Capitalists." They thought it necessary to restrict access to Manchuria until tentative plans were formed; the restriction was lifted in 1933.

[21] See Hoshino (1963, pp. 210–12).

In June 1936, the Army Headquarters announced its plan to bring Nissan, with Aikawa, to Manchuria. Commander Ueda and Chief of Staff Tojo of the Kwangtung Army were reluctant to abandon the traditional method of economic control, which was to have one business in one sector. They worried that giving privileges to Aikawa would stir up trouble in the SMR. On the Manchukuo side, Secretary General Hoshino and Vice-Chief of the Industry Division Kishi agreed to the plan, but Planning Agency Chief Matsuda, Mining and Manufacturing Section Chief Shiina, and others argued that it would undermine the traditional method of economic control.[22]

At the Cabinet meeting on 7 July 1937, just after the beginning of the War with China, Interior Minister Baba told the Army Minister: "enforcing this plan will lead to the resignation of the president of the SMR, Matsuoka, and even the boycott by company members. However, I enthusiastically hope it will lead to the economic development of Manchuria, and enhance the national power of our country. Also, Finance Minister Kaya expects foreign capital imports to increase in earnest."[23]

Aikawa assumed that Nissan's transfer would be made possible by fresh supplies of capital and equipment from the United States. The Cabinet approved the Outline to establish the MHI on 12 October 1937, and on 12 December it was established and Aikawa became president.[24]

Kishi left Manchuria in October 1939 to become Vice-Minister of Commerce in the Abe Cabinet. In the two years since Aikawa had become president of the MHI, little had been achieved in either the automobile or aircraft manufacturing industries. As he left, Kishi announced: "We must now establish a rational priority system for all Japan and Manchuria, emphasizing the development in Manchuria of resources such as iron (pig iron and iron-ore), coal, and nonferrous metals." The same view was expressed by Planning Agency Chief Kanda: "Introducing a priority system to industry development in Manchuria changed the character of the Five-Year Plan drastically. At the start, it aimed to develop Manchurian industry to be self-sufficient and supply Japan with important materials. Those plans

---

[22] For details of the establishment process to the MHI, see Hara (1976b, pp. 228–48). As expected, in separating affiliated companies from the SMR and placing them under its control, the MHI had to realign the relationship between its head office and subsidiaries. Those subsidiaries, previously affiliates of the SMR, rejected their parent company (Hara, 1976b, p. 248). Also see Miwa (2007, [2], p. 55, note 121).

[23] For more details, see Katakura (1978, pp. 226–8).

[24] See Katakura (1978, p. 228). At that time in Japan, there was a strong opposition to importing, as it would risk a second Harriman Affair.

were abandoned completely, and the focus shifted to the development of a few sectors like steel and coal that had achieved significant results" (Suzuki, 1992, p. 369).[25]

As mentioned at the end of section 6-2, in July 1940 Hoshino returned to Japan and became the Chairman of the Planning Council. In 1942, Aikawa resigned from the presidency of the MHI and returned to Japan (Hoshino, 1963, p. 302).

6-3-5. The Failure of the Five-Year Plan

Suzuki (1992) began the first section, entitled "The Failure of the Five-Year Plan," of the last chapter, "The End of Manchukuo," of his bulky work *Japanese Imperialism and Manchuria, 1900~1945* with the following statement ([2], p. 367):

On 8 December 1941, the day Japan began the Pacific War, Emperor Puyi issued an Imperial Rescript, ... and appealed to the people "to support with all national capacity the war of an ally." On 22 December, the Manchukuo government, at the joint conference of the government and the private sector in Changchun, published its "Outline of Wartime Emergency Economic Policies," with nine emergency measures "to improve the wartime structure of industry and the economy ... and satisfy the urgent wartime demands from Japan." These included a measure to increase exports of steel, coal, liquid fuel, and agricultural and other products to Japan. However, the colonial economy of Manchuria was severely limited on every front. The Five-Year Plan at the last stage of FY1941 lacked funds, materials, and workforce; its goals were impossible to achieve.

The PCEPlans were first implemented as the Five-Year Industry Plan in Manchuria (1937~41).[26] When the War with China broke out, the government faced pressure to increase its scale, creating the Revised Five-Year Plan. As the Chinese war escalated and the second European and Pacific wars began, the role of Manchuria changed drastically.

It is difficult to evaluate plans or policies implemented under drastically changing environments. Merely comparing target with actual figures does not give a complete picture.[27] As policy measures were often ill defined, it is difficult to assess their impact.

---

[25] When he left Manchuria in 1939, Kishi rated his own performance during three years in Manchuria highly (Kishi et al., 1981, p. 34). "I was told on several occasions that I had achieved a considerable performance. At an interview in Dalian, on my way back to Japan, I explained that I had realized my vision for Manchuria; this has been frequently quoted. In any case, in a short period of three years, I created considerable results from the very beginning...."

[26] As mentioned in note 9, no such plan was approved by the government nor put into action.

[27] Suzuki (1992, p. 369), for example, wrote: "In the Revised Five-Year Plan's second year (FY1938) actual production of most items fell below the targets. Particularly in the mining

Nevertheless, it is possible to conclude that the plan to acquire substantial foreign funds and use them to import technology and machines from the United States and other countries was a failure. As this plan was central to the creation of the MHI, it underpinned the drive for heavy industries development in Manchuria, led by the MHI through the transfer of Nissan. The dominant view that the PCEPlans and PCEPolicies in Manchuria achieved a remarkable success must be based on appraisal standards very different from the ones adopted here.[28]

6-3-6. The PCEPlans in Manchukuo

Here I simply summarize Kaneko (1994, pp. 400–10) to review briefly the PCEPlans enforced in Manchuria.[29]

Economic development in Manchukuo had two objectives: self-suffi-ciency in munitions manufacturing, and the supply of resources to Japan; the first was the higher priority. When it came to financial planning, the focus was not on munitions but on industries providing energy and basic materials such as liquid fuel, steel, and electricity. Among the munitions industries, limited resources were allocated to weapons, aircraft, and auto-mobiles. These were primarily for the Manchukuo market, not for supply to Japan.

The expanded Revised Five-Year Plan changed the position and role of Manchuria radically, emphasizing the supply of resources to Japan. The plan listed the numerical targets for each item; 90 percent of the liquid fuel and 30~40 percent of the pig iron and aluminum produced in Manchuria was to be sent to Japan (munitions and steel were excluded).

The MMPlans were also applied to Japanese colonies and yen-bloc areas, including Manchuria. The MMPlans in Japan incorporated imports

and manufacturing sector where numerical targets were increased drastically in the revi-sion, actual production stayed at 857,000 tons (94 percent of the target) in pig iron, 585,000 tons (94 percent) in steel ingot, 349,000 tons (65 percent) in steel, 15.988 million tons (91 percent) in coal, 2,150 tons (83 percent) in zinc, 2,573 tons (85 percent) in lead, and 104 tons (27 percent) in copper. These ratios fell further in the third FY (FY1939) to 58 percent in pig iron, 80 percent in steel ingot, 89 percent in steel, and 94 percent in coal."

[28] Recall the symbolic statement of Ando (1972, p. 470) quoted in section 6-2: "Thus, the guiding principle of the so-called Army pamphlet and the fruits of its economic control experiment in Manchuria were applied in this defining moment."

[29] Clear answers to the following questions were unavailable: Were the plans enforced as planned? What were the primary policy measures? Were such measures appropriately implemented on a scale large enough to be effective? The plans were too poorly defined to investigate fully. The plans are not good enough to investigate fully.

from yen-bloc areas, such as Manchuria and North China, as part of the supply capacity, creating a yen-bloc areas category for materials allocation. Manchuria was expected to import many items from Japan, including common steel, specialty steel, nonferrous metals (zinc and lead), natural rubber, and machines. However, the foreign currency shortage, combined with priority allocations to the military, suppressed not only private demand but also PCE and the development of yen-bloc areas. The MMPlans for FY1939 cut 46 percent of materials for the PCEPlans and 53 percent of materials for yen-bloc areas.

The outbreak of the European war in September 1939 made the situation worse. In 1940 and 1941, the foreign currency shortage became more acute, and Japan instructed the yen-bloc areas to reduce their materials allocation and increase their supply of products to Japan. In Manchuria, the Five-Year Industry Development Plan underwent a fundamental transformation in 1940. Of its two original objectives, Manchuria's self-sufficiency in munitions had not been achieved. Although the imbalance between its two objectives was striking, the vision of comprehensive development was maintained until FY1939. The start of the European war exacerbated constraints, including the reduction in materials from Japan, the difficulty in importing equipment from Germany, and a shortage of funds and workers. In May 1940, the priority system was introduced. Designating steel, coal, electricity, and nonferrous metals as the priority sector, the new system aimed to increase production of materials for Japan.

In 1942, the PCEPlans and industry development plan in Manchuria moved to the second Five-Year Industry Development Plan in Manchuria (1942~6). It was no longer a comprehensive development plan; there was no choice but to expand production in response to Japanese instructions that reflected the change in the war situation (Kaneko, 1994, [2], pp. 400–10).

6-4. Roles of Prominent Individuals: Kanji Ishiwara, Hideki Tojo, Naoki Hoshino, Nobusuke Kishi, and Etsusaburo Shiina

6-4-1. Team Manchuria (Manchukuo) and *Living-Body-Experiments?*

Japan's supreme decision-making body was a motley collection of representatives from different parties; it was unclear who had ultimate leadership in war (Tanemura, 1979, pp. 21–2). Individual parties such as the ACCom and AM were neither completely independent nor isolated. There were few policy issues that a party could decide alone without obtaining agreement from other parties. Moreover, each party behaved as a unit, observing shared rules of organizational operation and restricted by its disciplines. Unit members shared responsibility for the work of the unit. A draft plan prepared by a unit underwent a predetermined process to be approved as an organizational decision. Even General Hideki Tojo, who concurrently served as Prime Minister, Army Minister, Interior Minister, and later Munitions Minister and ACCommander, was no exception.

The conventional wisdom argues that specific individuals or a handful of peopled planned and conducted systematic war preparations and led the mobilization and war: Kanji Ishiwara, Nobusuke Kishi, and Etsusaburo Shiina are mentioned in Calder (1993, p. 50), together with Hideki Tojo and Naoki Hoshino. They are often described as "Team Manchuria," the Army control faction or reformist bureaucrats.

The following quote from Ando (1972, p. 469) is representative:

Nobusuke Kishi, Naoki Hoshino, Etsusaburo Shiina, Chuichi Ohashi, Reisuke Matsuda, and others became important figures in the Secretary Agency, the Foreign Affairs Division, the Business Division, and the Industry Division of the Manchukuo government. Working closely with top officials of the Kwantung Army, including its successive Chiefs of Staff (Toranosuke Hashimoto, Kuniaki Koiso, Toshizo Nishio, Seishiro Itagaki, and Hideki Tojo), who virtually governed Manchukuo, those people controlled the government.... They were a unique group of "new bureaucrats," "Team Manchukuo" economic bureaucrats working together with the Army's "Team Manchuria." They became promoters of Japan's central economic policy and particularly wartime economic controls.

I encourage readers to ask themselves the following questions:

1. What would happen to the conventional wisdom if it could be proved that the Manchurian economic control experiments were ineffective?
2. What would happen if efforts to impose effective and efficient economic controls in Manchuria, creating a model for Japan, ended in complete failure?
3. Was it not, in fact, the case that the Team Manchukuo bureaucrats learned a painful lesson – that economic control was very difficult to enforce?
4. How persuasive is the argument presented in the preceding quote? Does it really prove anything?

The Five-Year Industry Development Plan in Manchuria neither mobilized powerful policy measures nor achieved remarkable results. Despite the transfer of Nissan and the plan of imports from the United States, heavy industries were not successfully developed in Manchuria. The "control faction" in the Army and "new bureaucrats" in Manchuria may have promoted Japan's economic policy and wartime economic controls, but did not find it easy to use Manchurian successes to prepare systematically and mobilize or to wage war. This is true of both the Team Manchukuo bureaucrats and the Army Team Manchuria, who virtually governed Manchukuo.

Readers must now have strong doubts about the dominant view that a few specific individuals in key roles planned and conducted systematic war preparations, leading the way for mobilization and war. This section focuses on the five members of Team Manchuria.[30]

6-4-2. Kanji Ishiwara and Hideki Tojo

In Calder (1993, p. 50) and other sources, Ishiwara typically takes center stage as a Kwantung Army strategic planner during the Manchurian Incident, and again on 1 August 1935 when he became the Strategy Section Chief of the ACCom.

Ishiwara was an impressive figure, well known even today for his global war vision (he attracted attention by arguing in favor of war against the United States). In June 1933, he submitted a paper to an Army enquiry, called "The Outline of Imperial Policies and Defense Plan from the Military Viewpoint." Boeicho (1967a, p. 379) summarized it as follows[31]:

In approximately thirty years, the East Asian Federation will be completed. If conflict breaks out before that, being unable to destroy the enemy, we will be forced to wage a long, drawn-out war. By the time of the establishment of Federation, Japan will have made remarkable progress in military affairs and have the capacity to wage a final war against the Anglo-Saxons, the last world war. To complete the federation, we must first cultivate and build up Manchuria and force the USSR to give up its eastward penetration. Once we have promoted friendship between Japan and China and established solidarity among Asian countries, the core part of the federation will be completed.... In the war against the U.S., we will have to hold a defensive position, however hard that might be. Without the East Asian Federation, we will be unable to carry out aggressive war operations.

Ishiwara, who became the Strategy Section Chief of the ACCom in 1935, argued that Japan could not conduct aggressive war operations without the East Asian Federation, which would take thirty years to implement.

---

[30] Recall the discussion in subsection 2–2–3, "Military Control of Japanese Politics," particularly "Personnel Changes in Top Military Posts," "Did 'the Military,' Particularly the Army, Control Politics?" and "Tojo: A Dictator?"

[31] For Ishiwara's outline, see Boeicho (1967a, pp. 378–9). Recall also the discussion in subsection 2–4–2.

In August, he spearheaded efforts to revise the Basic National Defense Policy (BNDP) and the Basic Outline of Operations. Little of this so-called Ishiwara Vision was reflected in the version approved in June, 1936. The view that the ACCom should focus on arming against the USSR lost support as the War with China developed. Even inside the ACCom, support gradually decreased, and on 23 September 1937 Ishiwara stepped down from the position of Strategy Division Chief. He had been at the ACCom for only two years, from August 1935 to September 1937.

Ishiwara's resignation came prior to the tempestuous period that included the capture of Shanghai and Nanjing, the outbreak of the German–Soviet war, the Soviet–Japanese neutrality pact, Japan's invasion of South Indochina, the formation of the Tojo Cabinet, and the outbreak of the Pacific War.[32] Ishiwara's time at the ACCom contributed little to the systematic preparations for the Pacific War or War with China.[33] There seems to be no relationship between Ishiwara's "argument for war against the U.S." and the Pacific War that actually occurred.

On 18 September 1931, when the Manchurian Incident occurred, Ishiwara was the Chief Strategy Staff Member of the Kwantung Army, together with senior Staff Member Seishiro Itagaki and two others. The Manchurian Incident was jointly planned by the AM and the ACCom, in particular its Information Division. In June 1931, the Kwantung Army officially proposed to the ACCom that the Manchurian issues be solved through military control. On 11 June, Army Minister Minami of the second Wakatsuki Cabinet secretly agreed to convene a national policy study meeting with leading Section Chiefs of the AM and ACCom, nominally to resolve the Manchurian and Inner Mongolian problems. The meeting was chaired by Major General Tatekawa, the Second Division Chief of the ACCom, and included two AM Section Chiefs, including Military (*gunji*) Section Chief Nagata and three Section Chiefs from the ACCom.[34] Nagata's idea of resolving the problems

---

[32] Sugita (1987, p. 52) commented on Ishiwara: "Judging from his 'outline of a national defense policy,' he knew virtually nothing about the U.S.... He deprived the Information Division of the ACCom of its role in assessing the situation; this suggests his poor understanding of value of information. I'm afraid he viewed the global situation only through his own strategic ideas."

[33] Bear in mind that he was a member of the ACCom, the Army, and Japan's bureaucracy, which oversaw both the Strategy Section and the Strategy Division.

[34] On 7 August 1931, Hideki Tojo, newly appointed Organization Section Chief of the ACCom, and Imamura, the new Strategy Section Chief, both joined. According to Hara (1987, p. 32), the Army's view since 1929 was that the problems of Manchuria and Inner Mongolia could be resolved only by ousting Zhang Xueliang and his troops. On 19 June 1931, an outline proposal to oust Zhang and establish a pro-Japan government was generally accepted by leaders in the AM. However, the resolution would be later than the next

by force was discussed.[35] On 19 June, the Policy Outline for Resolving the Manchurian Problems was issued (Boeicho, 1967a, p. 306). Military operations during the Manchurian Incident, conceived by Ishiwara and carried out by Itagaki, achieved remarkable results (Boeicho, 1967a, p. 310).

Hideki Tojo was the Chief of Staff of the Kwantung Army when the War with China began in July 1937. After leaving his position as Strategy Division Chief of the ACCom in September 1937, Ishiwara became the Vice-Chief of Staff of the Kwantung Army. When Itagaki became the Army Minister of the first Konoe Cabinet in June 1938, Tojo became the Army Vice-Minister. He and Ishiwara had a difficult relationship; the friction between them was noted by observers (Hoshino, 1963, p. 272; Ohtani, 1973, p. 122). In March 1941, Tojo had Ishiwara transferred to reserve duty.

Ishiwara was neither a "Team Manchukuo" bureaucrat nor a member of the Army's "Team Manchuria," which governed Manchukuo.

6–4–3. Hideki Tojo and Nobusuke Kishi

Hideki Tojo first came to Manchuria as Provost Marshal of the Kwantung Army in September 1935. Although he had lived in Korea when he was young, he had never worked in or studied Manchuria or China. He knew little about the economy, and almost nothing about the situation in North China (Hoshino, 1963, pp. 182–3).

In March 1937, Tojo succeeded Itagaki as Chief of Staff of the Kwantung Army. The Taggangzi spring conference was in October 1936, and it was in November 1936 that Kishi came to Manchuria as the Vice-Chief of the Manchukuo Business Division. Itagaki was the Chief of Staff of the Kwantung Army when Kishi arrived at Manchuria, and soon Tojo succeeded to the position. Upon arrival, Kishi proposed to Itagaki: "I will consult with you and ask your advice on the governance issues of Manchukuo and basic issues of politics, but give me a free hand over issues regarding the industry and the economy." To this, Itagaki responded: "I entrust them to you. That's my plan" (Kishi et al., 1981, p. 29).

Tojo trusted Kishi's advice on industry and the economy.[36] When he became the Vice–Army Minister in June 1938, he insisted on appointing

---

spring, and by that time they would make every effort both at home and abroad for its smooth implementation. See also Miwa (2007, [2], p. 56, note 131).

[35] As mentioned in subsection 2–3–3, Ishiwara's appointment as Strategy Section Chief in August 1935 was strongly supported by Military Bureau Chief Tetsuzan Nagata of the AM, who was killed in his office by Army Lieutenant Colonel Aizawa a day before Ishiwara's arrival.

[36] Kishi et al. (1981, p. 32) explained that this was because Tojo trusted Kishi. Tojo was a bureaucratic rationalist, not a politician (Kishi et al., 1981, p. 32). Kishi thought highly of

Kishi to the Vice–Commerce Minister post[37] (Kishi became Vice–Commerce Minister in October 1939 in the Abe Cabinet[38]). In July 1940, Tojo became the Army Minister in the second Konoe Cabinet.

In October 1941, Tojo became the Prime Minister. Kishi, after serving three successive Commerce Ministers – Godo, Fujiwara, and Kobayashi – as the Vice–Commerce Minister since October 1939, became the Commerce Minister in the Tojo Cabinet.[39]

We have already discussed Tojo during his Prime-Minister-cum-Army Minister period since October 1941, in subsection 2–3–3, in the section entitled "Tojo: A Dictator?"

On 18 July 1944, the day after Japan's defeat at Saipan, the Tojo Cabinet resigned en bloc. According to one version: "Tojo persuaded Ginjiro Fujiwara to become Munitions Minister on condition that Kishi, a state minister and the Vice-Minister of Munitions, would resign. Kishi refused.... The Cabinet had no way out, and decided to resign en bloc" (Tanemura, 1979, p. 225).[40]

According to Kishi, the final straw came when Tojo refused to consider his view that Japan could not continue the war after losing Saipan, by

---

Tojo, too. Takeo Iwaguro, as a staff under the Chief of Staff of the Kwantung Army, took charge of economic affairs in Manchuria. He remembered Tojo, Tanaka, and Kishi as follows (Iwaguro, 1977, pp. 116–17): "Tojo was probably a shallow-minded animal, learning by making mistakes. He was a man who moved instinctively and by impulse. Mr. Tanaka lacked intelligence.... He reasoned very subjectively and hated to lose. Tojo loved Tanaka." In response to the question of whether Kishi and other Japanese officials in Manchuria talked about the future politics of Japan, Iwaguro (1977, p. 74) answered, "I don't think so... Kishi liked politics from his early years. He was clever. When he became the Secretary General of the Japan Democratic Party and the Liberal Democratic Party, I predicted that he would make mistakes as Chairman or Prime Minister. But as a right-hand man or Secretary General, he was one of the best."

[37]   As Kishi et al. (1981, pp. 41–2) recall, for the second Konoe Cabinet, Kishi was asked to become the Chairman of the Planning Council and a state minister, but instead he recommended Noaki Hoshino. To the further request to become the Commerce Minister, he answered: "We are still in a semi-wartime structure, rather than a wartime one.... I would like to work as the Vice-Minister, and the Commerce Minister should be from the business community."

[38]   Hoshino (1963, p. 267) recalls, Commerce Minister Takuo Godo sought his appointment.

[39]   According to Sato (1976, pp. 366–7), the Military (*gunmu*) Section Chief, Kishi, preferred to become the Chief Cabinet Secretary rather than the Commerce Minister; the Army also was interested in having Kishi appointed Cabinet Minister. Military Bureau Chief Mutoh offered a strong opinion against the appointments of Hoshino to the Chief Cabinet Secretary and Suzuki to the Chairman of the Planning Council, but Tojo did not take his advice.

[40]   On the process, see Okada (2001, pp. 222–47) and Tanemura (1979, pp. 221–7). On Kishi's reaction, see Okada (2001, pp. 241–2) and Kishi et al. (1981, pp. 68–70).

saying: "It is the ACCom that should discuss such an issue" (Kishi et al., 1981, p. 68).[41]

6-4-4. Naoki Hoshino, Nobusuke Kishi, and Etsusaburo Shiina

Naoki Hoshino, Nobusuke Kishi, and Etsusaburo Shiina represented the Team Manchukuo economic bureaucrats who after working in Manchuria became important figures in the Japanese government.[42]

Manchukuo was established in March 1932, approximately half a year after the Manchurian Incident, where the Kwantung Army took indirect control. At first, the administrative machinery focused on bringing in more Japanese staff there. Although excited by the "state's founding ideal," they lacked administrative capacity. The Kwantung Army asked ministries to supply financial and economic specialists. In response, each ministry sent a few bureaucrats to Manchuria (Kishi et al., 1981, p. 19).

Naoki Hoshino (then the National Property Section Chief) led the first group of nine persons from the Finance Ministry in July, 1932. The Commerce Ministry sent former Chief Judge of the Patent Office, Kohjun Takahashi, to become Vice-Chief of the Manchukuo Business Division. In October 1933, Etsusaburo Shiina, then the Chief Administrative Official of the Industrial Rationalization Bureau, became the Manchukuo Planning Section Chief. As the Correspondence Section Chief of the

---

[41] At that time, Tojo was also the ACCommander. It was customary, if a Cabinet resigned, for distinguished members to be recommended for nomination by the Emperor to the House of Peers. General Tojo was so angry with Kishi that he did not recommend him (Tanemura, 1979, p. 228).

[42] Hoshino and Kishi were members of the well-known group, 2-ki-3-suke. This group, named for its two "ki" (Hideki Tojo and Naoki Hoshino) and three "suke" (Yosuke Matsuoka, Yoshisuke Aikawa, and Nobusuke Kishi), is generally considered responsible for systematic war preparations and enforcement. Here, Takashi Ito reflects the dominant view: "There was a plan, overwhelmingly backed by the Kwantung Army, to develop heavy industries in the agricultural state of Manchuria. It was challenging work for idealistic bureaucrats, as the intertwined issues included relationships with domestic capital, the Japanese government, and the SMR. Kishi was expected to deal with those issues well. ... It was symbolized in an expression, '2-ki-3-suke'" (Kishi et al., 1981, pp. 20-1). Kishi recalled being interrogated by an attorney at the International Military Tribunal for the Far East or the Tokyo War Crimes Tribunal (Kishi et al., 1981, p. 85): "It may sound funny, but the attorney asked me, 'Do you know 2-ki-3-suke?' (laugh). The attorney firmly believed that 2-ki-3-suke were the villains who invaded Manchuria." Nishiura (1980, p. 110) wrote as a scene at the Diet before the middle of the War with China: "Taneo Miyazawa at the Budget Committee mentioned the names of the Manchurian quintet, calling them '2-ki-3-suke.' This might be the origin of this popular expression."

Commerce Ministry, Kishi was involved in all these appointments (Kishi et al., 1981, p. 19).

Hoshino became first the Vice-Chief of the Manchukuo Finance Division and then, in 1936, Secretary General of the Manchukuo government.[43] The Secretary General was the Prime Minister's chief assistant, responsible for the Management and Coordination Agency (Hoshino, 1963, p. 191). Hoshino stayed in this position until July 1940, when he left Manchuria, becoming a state minister and Chairman of the Planning Council of the second Konoe Cabinet.

In November 1936, Kishi became the Vice-Chief of the Manchukuo Industry Division; he was soon promoted to Vice-Chief of the Management and Coordination Agency under Chief Hoshino. He left Manchuria in October 1939, becoming the Vice-Minister of Commerce under Commerce Minister Godo in the Abe Cabinet.

Shiina became the General Administration Section Chief of the Commerce Ministry in June 1939, and in December of the same year became the General Administration Bureau Chief. In the Tojo Cabinet, Kishi became the Commerce Minister and Shiina the Vice-Minister of Commerce. At the Munitions Ministry created in November 1943, under Tojo and Kishi, Vice-Minister Shiina became the General Mobilization Bureau Chief.

Hoshino, Kishi, and Shiina led industry and the controlled economy in Japan through the MMPlans and PCEPlans, from the second half of the War with China. The nature and poor performance of industry control and the controlled economy in Japan were consistent with the Manchurian experiments.

There is no real way of knowing their prior expectations about how effective the Manchurian *living-body-experiments* really were. Nevertheless, industry control and the controlled economy in Japan were modeled on the Manchurian experiments, the conventional view argues.[44]

---

[43] This was due to the resignation of his predecessor. "It was what I had expected least" (Hoshino, 1963, p. 18).

[44] In 1974, after the First Oil Shock, Japan suffered from a serious oil shortage. Being concerned with the shortage of materials and price increases, the Japanese government established the Act for Coordinating the Demand and Supply of Petroleum and the Act for Emergency Measures for Stabilizing People's Lives, the so-called Two Petroleum Acts. Mr. Shiina, the Vice-Chairman of the Liberal Democratic Party, then the ruling party, said at the debates: "Once we gain control, we will have to place even flowerpots under control." Nakamura (1974, p. 171) commented: "As a bureaucrat at the Commerce Ministry experienced in controlling activities in wartime Japan, Mr. Shiina warned against a self-expanding tendency of control."

6-5. Conclusion to Part II

For most Japanese leaders, the War with China began unexpectedly in July 1937. There were no effective plans or preparations; from beginning to end, war mobilization and economic control were in disarray. The Materials Mobilization Plans (MMPlans), created out of necessity after the outbreak of the war, consistently faced serious difficulties, including quantitative constraints on target materials, insufficient information about planned materials, chaotic environmental conditions, and incompetent preparation and planning. Before the War with China began, there were various discussions about plans and policies for expanding production capacity in key industries. None was put into action. The Japanese government and military found it very difficult to wage war against China. It was impossible to enforce effective policies for the future enhancement of production capacity.

In Part II, I have investigated the nature and effectiveness of the MMPlans, PCEPlans, and PCEPolicies in Japan and of the PCEPlans and PCEPolicies in Manchuria. Most of the existing literature supports the conventional wisdom, depending heavily on documents held in government ministries responsible for implementing those plans, policies, and relevant laws and orders. Most of this literature has assumed that the plans and policies worked effectively. I have examined the nature of those plans and policies and evaluated their real functions and roles.

Part II provides readers with the information necessary to address the question: How might the socialist planned economy under Stalin's dictatorship have worked if there had been no Stalin?

War is a great centralizer. The state, taking control over the entire economy and acting as "the sole consumer of the products of the economic system" (Cairncross, 1991, p. 3), must have determined how the country's resources could best be used if the war was to be won. In wartime Japan, the state of Japan was expected to achieve victory, despite impossible constraints. The conventional wisdom argues that Japan began and developed the war using carefully planned, systematic preparations; it carried out war mobilization and economic control. In Part II, I have shown that Japan was unsuccessful in enforcing war mobilization and economic control. In addition, Japan's competence in enforcing plans and policies, its overriding concern, was extremely poor.

The competence of the Japanese government has been questionable, raising strong doubts about the conventional wisdom that Japan's rapid economic development since the Meiji Restoration had been government-led.[45]

---

[45] See Gerschenkron (1962), Rosovsky (1961), Yamamura (1972), and Johnson (1982).

PART III

THE NAVY AIR FORCE: A STUDY OF A CENTRAL JAPANESE PLAYER

In Part III, I apply the analytic framework used previously to a study of the Navy Air Force, focusing on the air forces (and weaponry) such as carrier-based fighters and land-based attack aircraft (or bombers) that were developed, produced, and used by the Japanese Navy. The development and production of aircraft were under the direct control of the military and depended decisively on the supply of basic materials. It is therefore a representative case study, illustrating Japan's competence in wartime.

During the wars in China and the Pacific, Japan's Navy Air Force, rather than the Army Air Force, played a decisive role. It was a key player in the nation's systematic war preparations, mobilization, and economic control. Accordingly, Part III examines and evaluates the competence of the state in responding to unexpected situations, such as the battle of attrition over Guadalcanal Island in 1942 and 1943, discussed further in Chapter 9. I show that the Japanese state did not perform effectively, either in preparing for unexpected situations or in responding swiftly and adequately.

7

Preparations

7-1. Overview

7-1-1. Introduction to Part III

The conventional wisdom argues that Japan was a successful and competent state that prepared carefully for war, mobilizing and managing economic control effectively and efficiently. The case of the Navy Air Force confirms that this is a misconception, a myth that fatally deviates from the reality. It proves that conventional wisdom can be dangerous and harmful, impeding empirical inquiry.

The following is a summary of points made earlier:

1. Japan was ill prepared for its wars in China and the Pacific. After the outbreak of war, neither mobilization nor economic control was handled well.
2. Japan's competence, as reflected in its systematic war preparations, mobilization, and economic control, was extremely poor. There is no reason to believe that the Japanese state could have been competent but chose not to be.
3. The myth of Japan's competence was established and accepted immediately after the end of the Pacific War and continues to be believed today.

7-1-2. Three Reasons to Focus on the Navy Air Force

The Navy Air Force is an ideal candidate for an investigation of Japan's competence, for three reasons:

1. The Air Force was very important to the war effort.

2. Its case illustrates the incompetence of the state in making predictions and responding to unexpected situations.
3. The Navy Air Force faced unexpected events.

7-1-3. The Importance of the Air Force

Air weaponry decisively affected the development and outcome of the War with China and the Pacific War.[1] Both in the War with China and in the Pacific War, the Navy (not the Army) Air Force was the central player on the Japanese side and played the leading part.

Reflecting rapid developments in science and technology during the 1930s, the nature, function, and role of the Air Force changed remarkably. New weapons and new ways of using weapons promised to change the way war was waged in the future. Japan's government understood the need for competent predictions and responses to the new potential of air weapons.

As war developed, Japan consistently and significantly deviated from the basic policy outline and strategy of its Basic National Defense Policy. The functions and role of the Navy Air Force illustrate this deviation.

The following comment by Overy (1996, p. 322) highlights the importance of aerial weapons: "German ground forces were compelled to fight the last two years with limited or non-existent air support. When the last Luftwaffe chief-of-staff, General Karl Koller, sat down at the end of the conflict to address the question 'Why We Lost the War', he reduced it to a single formula: 'What was decisive in itself was the loss of air supremacy'. In Koller's view, partisan though it no doubt was, 'Everything depends on air supremacy, everything else must take second place.'"

7-1-4. The Competence of the State as Planner

This book focuses on the type of state competence needed to manage an economy; Japan's economy is thought to have been similar to the administrative-command economies of the USSR. "Wars, when they come, are always different from the war that is expected. Victory goes to the side that has made the fewest mistakes, not to the one that has guessed right" (Taylor, 1964, p. 116). What is necessary is that the state has the competence to respond to new situations in wartime as well as peacetime. It takes

---

[1] "Both the Japanese offensive and the Allied response were more dependent on the use of air power than was the case in Europe with its traditional and influential land armies" (Overy, 1980, p. 85).

competence for the state to anticipate carefully and prepare systematically for the situations that would occur with the beginning of "war" and to arrange human resources, systems, and organizational structures that allow it to make swift and adequate responses to unexpected situations and events.

Between the mid-1930s and the mid-1940s, the Japanese state played the role of planner in an administrative-command economy; competence was crucial. Understanding this, Japan must have tried to conduct its affairs as competently as possible. For the Japanese state more than any other at that time, the realization and manifestation of "the competence of the state" were crucial in playing the role as "the planner." I conclude that Japan's competence was not as high as the conventional wisdom has alleged, and was desultory at best.

7–1–5. Five Reasons Why the Issues Were Challenging

Japan found it difficult to play the role of planner in a planned economy for the following five key reasons. Reasons three and five are particularly important.

1. This was the largest mobilization Japan had ever attempted, in terms of its impact on the economy, its duration, and the quantity of resources involved.
2. The international situation and relationships in the mid-1930s were complicated and unclear, and the progress in weapons-related technology, particularly in the air forces, was remarkable. As a result, it was unusually hard for Japan to make predictions and to prepare for unexpected situations.
3. Air forces played a decisive role. Progress in the development of weapons-related technology was remarkable. At the same time, aircraft took a long time to design, develop, and produce. New aircraft had to satisfy ever more demanding requirements. In practice, the performance of an aircraft depended on the speed, power, and weaponry of the planes with which it was doing battle. In addition, the performance of air forces and the effectiveness of their uses heavily depended on aircraft models and their uses the belligerent power adopted. For this reason, Japan's ability to predict, prepare, and respond was crucial.[2]

---

[2] Readers will wish to have a rough idea of the extent of aircraft production during World War II. In 1940, the British MAP (Ministry of Aircraft Production) produced more than

4. Few Japanese officials anticipated that the war would escalate so dramatically or last so long. For this reason, the state was forced to respond to unexpected situations and events well beyond the scope of its assumptions.

5. Epoch-making new products (including electronic equipment) and improved model aircraft sprang up like mushrooms, while existing products realized new functions and remarkable improvements in efficiency. Moreover, each product or aircraft, even after the outbreak of war, created unexpected options for performance, function, and capacity. To respond swiftly and adequately, Japan needed great competence in making predictions and responding to unexpected situations.

7-1-6. Navy Air Weapons and Air Forces

"The competence of the state" can be observed more clearly in a situation in which the state needs swift and effective response to "unexpected situations"[3] During the Pacific War period, the Navy Air Force provided an ideal experimental laboratory for observing, identifying, and evaluating the competence of the state. Focusing on this laboratory most directly, the three sections from 9-3 to 9-5 are central to Part III. In these three sections, I focus on the "war of attrition" between land-based air forces over Guadalcanal Island from August 1942 to January 1943.

In particular, the war of attrition over Guadalcanal Island was a defining battle that decisively affected the outcome of the Pacific War and symbolized its basic character. The following three aspects of the Guadalcanal situation were completely unexpected, and it was unfortunate for Japan that the second and third occurred simultaneously:

1. Few Japanese leaders anticipated that the War with China would escalate into a Pacific War against Allied Powers including the United States and the UK. As a result, these leaders did not plan for such an engagement.

---

fifteen times the number of aircraft than it had in 1935, an economic expansion factor of thirty, and 50 percent more airframes and engines than Germany. Between 1940 and 1944, the economic weight of aircraft production trebled in Britain. In 1944, it was one hundred times greater than in 1935. MAP purchases reached nearly £900 million in 1943-4, with 1.5 million workers (8 percent of the mobilized or employed population) employed in aircraft production. This represented one-third of the labor force working in manufacturing (Edgerton, 1991, pp. 71-2).

[3] Here "unexpected situations" worked as "exogenous shocks." This is an attempt to identify "the competence of the state" through its responses to those exogenous shocks.

2. The Army, rather than the Navy, was expected to be the leading player in the "war" to come, and the War with China that actually occurred and escalated to the Pacific War. However, the leading player of this "war of attrition" was the Navy.
3. During the first half of the twentieth century, the Navy, under the Basic National Defense Policy, depended on a "large-scale battleships with big cannons" doctrine. Assuming that war in the western Pacific would be a one-game match between fleets of ships, the Navy treated the Air Force as a secondary concern. As the battle became a long-term war of attrition, land-based aircraft became Japan's most important resource, even more essential than carrier-based aircraft.[4]

The Japanese state did not expect the battle over Guadalcanal Island to happen at all, or to become part of a larger war of attrition between land-based air forces. Until the last minute, the government and Navy made little change in their plans and war preparations. Their response was so slow that the war ended without effective countermeasures. Both at the top of the state and in subordinate decision-making units, there was an absence of competence in responding swiftly or adequately to unexpected events.

7-1-7. The Structure of Chapter 7

Chapter 7 is preparation for Part III. As preparation for focusing on the Navy Air Force (NAF), sections 7–2 through 7–4 study the Army Air Force (AAF) to show why the NAF was more important than the AAF. Section 7–2 investigates the cooperative relationship between them. Section 7–3 discusses the preparations and role of the AAF. Section 7–4 examines the reality of cooperation between the NAF and the AAF. Section 7–5 provides an overview of the NAF, focusing on carrier-based fighter and land-based attack aircraft. Introducing alternative assessments of the NAF's active role during the War with China, section 7–6 evaluates the performance of the NAF. Similar to Chapter 6 in Part II, the last section of Chapter 9 concludes Part III.

7-2. The Army Air Force (AAF) and the Navy Air Force (NAF)

When the Navy split from the Army after the Russo–Japanese War of 1904–5, the two branches began to form competing concepts of national policy. On an equal footing, they competed against each other for enhanced armaments and national power. They formed distinct strategies and frequently

---

[4] Recall the discussion of the construction of large-scale battleships in section 4–6.

mistrusted each other. Side by side, they prepared, mobilized, and waged war in China and the Pacific. However, the conventional wisdom argues that the Army led systematic war preparations, beginning, and waging of the war.[5]

7-2-1. The AAF and the NAF at the Initial Stage of the War with China

The War with China began on 7 July 1937, the least convenient time possible for the AAF authorities, who were in the process of updating their aircraft and had no new models available. When the war began, Army leaders provided the North China Composite Air Corps with each two squadrons of reconnaissance aircraft, fighters (Kawasaki *ki*-10), and heavy bombers (Mitsubishi *ki*-1) assigned to the Kwantung Army. On 15 July, they organized for a temporary Air Corps to be sent from Japan to South Manchuria. The force included six squadrons of reconnaissance aircraft, five squadrons of fighters, four squadrons of light bombers, and three squadrons of heavy bombers – eighteen squadrons in total, including two hundred aircraft. Altogether, the AAF provided one-third of its fleet. The Army's new model aircraft began operations in March 1938, three months after the capture of Nanjing (Boeicho, 1975c, pp. 160–1).

Operations at the start of the war revealed inadequacies and defects in the flight performance and reliability of Army bombers, and this damaged the morale of the front-line Air Corps. The Army's Kawasaki *ki*-3, a type 93–1 single-engine light bomber, was old, with a short flight range; it was unable to conduct long-distance bombing. In contrast, when the war expanded to the Shanghai region in mid-August, the Navy conducted transoceanic bombing from Ohmura in Kyushu to the Shanghai region over a distance of 800 kilometers (for details, see section 7–4).[6]

As an emergency measure, the Army decided to import aircraft from abroad. At the end of August, it made a budget request for seventy-two heavy bombers (thirty-six initially, with thirty-six as backup). There was no hope of importing from Germany, so the Italian Fiat BR-20 was chosen. The BR-20s, produced since 1936, had proved effective in the Spanish Civil War. These planes were transported by sea and assembled in Manchuria; pilot

---

[5] Recall the discussion in section 2–3–3. See also of Miwa (2008, p. 422, note 6).

[6] Soon after the NAF's transoceanic bombing, Kanji Ishiwara, the Strategy Division Chief of the ACCom, inspected Yokosuka Naval Air Arsenal and made this comment: "we'd be better off giving all airplanes and relevant materials to the Navy" (NAFHistory, 1969, [1], p. 283).

training concluded on 11 March 1938. To put these dates in perspective, Nanjing was captured by Japan on 13 December 1937 and the first Konoe Proclamation was signed on 16 January 1938.

The BR-20 was highly ranked, with a structure that combined a welded steel tube with fabric covering the rear fuselage, powerful 1,000 horsepower engines, and a mounted 12.7 millimeter machine gun. The plane had a long flight range but carried so much fuel that it was too heavy to land on soft fields. In addition, its takeoff distance was too long for use on Japan's existing airfields (Boeicho, 1975c, pp. 161–4).

The primary targets of strategic air operations for the AAF and NAF were the Chiang government headquarters in Chongqing and the Chinese Air Force bases of Chengdu and Lanzhou. Japan could use only three airfields (Hankou, Yuncheng, and Baotou) to attack those inland regions. The distance between Hankou and Chongqing was nearly 800 kilometers, between Yuncheng and Chengdu 850 kilometers, and between Baotou and Lanzhou 800 kilometers. The Japanese air forces assumed a combat radius of 800 kilometers for the Army Type 97 Heavy Bomber model (Mitsubishi *ki*-21), 750 kilometers for the BR-20, and 900 kilometers for the Army Type 97 Command Reconnaissance Plane (Mitsubishi *ki*-15); all transporting 500 kilogram bombs.[7]

Japan hit Chongqing four times between 26 December 1938 and 15 January 1939 and aimed three times at Lanzhou in April 1939. These operations revealed that the BR-20 was neither bulletproof nor fireproof. As a result, the Army stopped using this aircraft (Boeicho, 1975c, p. 167).

After the battle over Shanghai in particular, the Air Force became important and central. In Japan, the role of NAF was far greater than that of the AAF.

7-2-2. The Army and Navy Air Forces in Offensive Inland Operations in China

For three years after 1939, Japanese bombers attacked inland Chinese targets, including Chongqing and Chengdu. Lieutenant General Eikichi Katagiri joined the joint Army-Navy operation in mid-January, 1941 as the

---

[7] Among fighters, the combat radius of the Army Type 97 fighter (Nakajima *ki*-27) was 450 kilometers – and 600 kilometers with additional fuel tanks providing an hour's allowance. Because of this short combat radius, fighters could not escort heavy bombers on long-range operations inland. In August 1940, three years after the outbreak of the War with China, the Navy's Type Zero Fighters began to provide an escort for long-range inland bombing (Boeicho, 1975c, p. 166).

General Officer commanding the Eleventh NAF at the Hankou base. The following comment by Katagiri suggests the overwhelming superiority of the NAF (NAFHistory, 1969, [1], pp. 283–4):

In 1941, when we were bombing Chongqing from the Hankou base, we shared the airfield with the AAF. I thought that the NAF had a far superior war capability than the Army's. The Army's bombers and fighters were clearly inferior to the Navy's "Zero" (Mitsubishi A6M Zero). Convinced that the Army's Air Force should be trained by the Navy, when I became Head of the Navy Air Headquarters, I proposed this directly to General Dohihara, Head of Army Air Headquarters, and General Tojo, the Army Minister. Although he blamed the Army's unsatisfactory fighters, Army Minister Tojo liked the idea.

A long time passed, and still we received no response from the Army to my proposal. At last, Major General Takijiro Onishi, the Chief of General Affairs at the Navy Air Headquarters, said that since there was no possibility of its realization, the Navy should not push the idea further. The idea was abandoned.

Operation 101 involved attacks on military facilities in and around the city of Chongqing; it was implemented over four months, beginning in May 1940. Roughly five to seven times as many Navy as Army aircraft participated, dropping ten times as many explosives.[8]

7–2–3. The AAF and NAF During the Pacific War

The Pacific War began on 8 December 1941. After the outbreak of war, the AAF played only a minor role.

On 7 August 1942, the U.S. Marine Corps attacked Guadalcanal Island in the South Pacific Ocean. Over that island, Japan and the United States waged fierce and continuous battles, during which the value of air supremacy became overwhelmingly important. The Army and Navy also held combined operations over the airfields (Boeicho, 1975c, p. 336). In late August, the IH-ND asked the IH-AD to send in the AAF. The IH-AD was unwilling, for the following intriguing reasons:

First, the AAF was already overstretched, trying to complete various important missions over a wide combat theater. These missions included controlling the enemy's air forces in the southern quarter, particularly on the Burmese front, air defense over the Palembang refinery, blocking air transportation from India to China, controlling Chinese air forces, defending Manchuria and Japan, and monitoring the northern Pacific Ocean. It had no capacity to devote to this operation. Second, the AAF had specialized in operations on the continent, and was not trained for

---

[8] From the Report of the Headquarters of the Combined Air Attack Troops, in Boeicho (1976, p. 120).

operations over the ocean. It had no land-based flight route to the South Pacific Ocean, air operation plans, or airfields; this situation made it inappropriate to send the AAF to this area (Boeicho, 1975c, p. 336).

After two months' heated debate, the Army agreed to send some forces for a limited period only.

On the role and contribution of the AAF during the Pacific War, and particularly over the Pacific Ocean, the following evaluation and comment on its causes are representative (NAFHistory, 1969, [1], p. 282):

The Greater East Asian War became far removed from the Basic National Defense Policy, which had assumed a war against one country. It became a war against several countries; on the continent the conflict spread from China to Burma. For this reason, the AAF was unable to devote appropriate resources to operations on the Pacific Ocean, and therefore could contribute little to the operation against the U.S. during the second stage of the war. When the situation in the southeast quarter grew tense after the fall of Guadalcanal Island at the beginning of 1943, in response to an eager request from the Navy, the AAF advanced into Rabaul, agreeing to share the tasks with the NAF. The New Guinea corner was assigned to the Army and the Solomon Islands to the Navy. In reality, however, Army aircraft were inept in operations over the ocean. Navy aircraft had to cover both New Guinea and the Solomon Islands, and they faced difficulties in their operations. The number of Army aircraft actually advanced to the area was small. The primary cause of their poor performance in the southeast corner was that their education and training during peacetime focused on cooperation with ground forces, and included little training in sea flights and attacks.

7–3. The Army Air Force (AAF): Preparations and Their Uses

Two points are important in understanding the position of the AAF mentioned in section 7–2. First, the War with China began just after the start of the full-fledged armament enhancement plan, which emphasized air forces. Second, the armament enhancement plan had assumed a war against the USSR.

7–3–1. Army War Preparations at the Start of the War with China

In Chapters 1 and 2, we examined the Army's preparations at the start of the War with China. Here, I briefly summarize the situation, focusing on the AAF. The following comment is from Imoto (1978, pp. 82–3).[9]

---

[9] Imoto was then on the staff of the ACCom Strategy Section.

Kanji Ishiwara, when he became the Strategy Section Chief of the ACCom in August 1935, recognized that operation plans full of dashing scenarios to overwhelm the Soviet military were empty statements; the strategy for defeating the USSR was bankrupt. The Army had a total force size of thirty ground divisions and forty-five air squadrons, far inferior in organization and equipment to the armies of powerful European countries, the U.S., or the USSR, Japan's anticipated enemy. At the Soviet–Manchurian border, the Soviet military completely dominated the Japanese. The Army needed an epoch-making armament enhancement, infeasible given national capacity of the time. Ishiwara thought that Japan should focus on improving and enhancing its national capacity and armaments. To achieve this, he thought, Japan must not enter into any war against a foreign country.

The armament enhancement plan emphasized air forces. Adapting the Basic National Defense Policy to a war drawn out over thirty years, the plan envisaged the development by 1941 of 41 ground forces divisions and 142 air squadrons, a military capable of waging full-scale war against both the USSR and China. The Ishiwara vision became the Army's formal armament enhancement plan, underpinning plans for each fiscal year. The implementation plan for FY1937 was established and enforced in June 1937, and one month later, the War with China began (Imoto, 1978, p. 353).

Nothing could be done to change the fact that the Japanese military was overpowered by the Soviet military, as well as in Manchuria and Korea. Japan's unsolved challenges were most serious and apparent in the area of Air Force enhancement. With basic industrial technology in poor shape, Air Force production could not be rapidly increased (Imoto, 1978, pp. 353–4).

At the end of 1938, Japan had thirty-three ground divisions, five mixed brigades, and seventy air squadrons in total (composed of ten reconnaissance planes, twenty-three fighters, twenty light bombers, and seventeen heavy bombers). Recognizing that Japan would be at war with China for a long time, the ACCom revised its rearmament plan. In the autumn of 1938, the policy subsection of the ACCom Strategy Section (previously the War Leadership Section) called, in its Five-Year Plan, for ninety ground divisions and three hundred air squadrons, impossible to acquire at the time. After a long-term investigation and negotiations between the AM and the ACCom from late 1938 to early 1939, the Revised Armament Enhancement Plan was formulated (Imoto, 1978, p. 354).

The AAF in South Manchuria was extremely weak when the war began, and the situation did not improve much, even in North China. Most members of the AAF believed their primary job was to fight an enemy's air forces, because air power would decide the tide of war. However, in the Army overall, most believed that ground battles were decisive. Imoto (1978, p. 356) wrote: "The foundation for increasing air forces was established. ...

this was not enough for its remarkable expansion, however. It was not easy to establish an actionable plan. In the end, the Army wrote a major plan demanding more than two hundred squadrons. We were worried and uneasy until the end of the war about such a vast increase in quantity without quality. Despite the enormous efforts of all parties concerned, during the wars with China and in the Pacific, the AAF remained inadequately prepared for excessive tasks."

After discussions with the Strategy Section, the ACCom agreed on a Five-Year Plan (1940–4) to increase ground forces by seventy-seven divisions and air forces by more than two hundred squadrons. It started negotiations with the Military (*gunji*) Section of the AM. The Military Section, however, preferred its own 1937 plan, very similar to the New Armament Enhancement Plan (the Second Rearmament Plan) presented, in outline form, to the Emperor on 20 December 1939. With slight modifications, this became the Renewed Armament Enhancement Plan (the Third Rearmament Plan) in July 1940. In the spring of 1942, after the outbreak of the Pacific War, it was again revised and became the Basic Armament Plan (the Fourth Rearmament Plan; Imoto, 1978, p. 360).

Thus, when the War with China began, the AAF had just started to expand its capacity. Its system for expansion was not well established or backed up. Budgetary constraints were severe, and basic conditions (for example, levels of industrial technology) were extremely limiting. Imoto was right: during both wars, the AAF remained unprepared for excessive tasks (Imoto, 1978, p. 356).

7–3–2. The AAF's Goals During the Late 1930s: Developing Bombers?

After 1935, the international situation was transformed by the rise of Nazi Germany and fascist Italy, the rapid development of the communist USSR, and the expansion of Japan's power from Manchuria to North China. The balance of power was radically changing. World War I and the dramatic development in air forces made most countries view national defense as a total war or establish a national-defense-first state.

What troubled the Army most was not Japan's international isolation after the Manchurian Incident but the rapid arms expansion of the USSR. After starting the discussion about full-scale rearmament in 1934,[10] the

---

[10] Kanji Ishiwara became the ACCom Strategy Section Chief in August 1935.

Army implemented its First Rearmament Plan in 1937, adding 41 ground divisions and 142 air squadrons.

The Soviet military force in the Far East had been reinforced since 1932. In mid-1934, five hundred aircraft, including three hundred strong, large planes, were deployed in Primorsky Krai Maritime Province. If Soviet long-range bombers attacked Japan, Korea, or Manchuria, not only Japan's people's lives would be threatened but their ability to mobilize, concentrate, and transport armed forces would be interrupted, bringing planned operations to a standstill.

During this time, the main role of the AAF changed from its traditional cooperation with ground forces to the destruction of enemy planes. A 1933 study on operations to destroy enemy air power convinced the Army to change focus in its FY1935 operational plan. As its opening gambit, the Army planned a raid to destroy enemy airfields and planes in South Primorsky Krai, while to the west and north, Japan's remaining force would engage in reconnaissance and cooperation with ground forces.

This change in AAF operation placed more emphasis on mobility and required many new aircraft models. Japan's research policy was revised twice, in 1935 and 1937, so that Army Type 97 aircraft could be developed as test models. The First Rearmament Plan was based on the premise that Japan's capacity to produce aircraft would be enhanced. In June 1937, the Army formulated its Five-Year Plan for Munitions Manufacturing Industries, giving top priority to aircraft industry development. The Army asked the government to promote those industries that supported munitions manufacturing.[11]

The First Rearmament Plan favored increasing the number of bombers and deploying most to Korea and Manchuria. From 53.3 squadrons in FY1937, Japan would increase its capacity to 142 in FY1942.[12]

New Type 93 and 95 aircraft were completed under the 1933 Equipment Research Policy, with which the Munitions Council was held on 29 October 1935 for revising the research policy.[13] The Aircraft Headquarters' proposal for revision thoroughly adopted the ACCom's request. When it was

---

[11] For more details, see Boeicho (1975c, pp. 117–18).

[12] Boeicho (1975c, p. 131).

[13] The Munitions Council was established on 16 May 1932, replacing the Army Technology Meeting. Chaired by the Army Vice-Minister, its remit was to discuss a research policy for Army munitions. On 7 February 1933, it had forty-five members, of whom four members were Air Headquarters Division Chiefs, and four organizers were also from the Air Headquarters (Boeicho, 1975c, p. 106).

revised, improvements included an increase in the speed of heavy bombers, the adoption of single-engine light bombers, an increase in reconnaissance aircraft models, and the redevelopment of super-heavy bombers. On 16 November, the result was reported to the Army Minister, and on 23 December the revision was transmitted to units concerned.[14]

The distance between Japanese airfields in Manchuria and Soviet frontline airfields required an offensive distance of approximately 300 kilometers. For this reason, it was more important for aircraft to be light than to have a long cruising distance. In order to move swiftly between air attacks in Primorsky Krai and the northern and western regions, both air bases and railway transportation needed to be improved. Japan needed some super-heavy bombers effective in long-distance bombing to destroy planes traveling between European Soviet areas and the Far East, attack enemies taking shelter, and interrupt the Trans-Siberian Railway. To intercept trains east of Lake Baikal, the radius of action must be over 1,500 kilometers.[15] Army aircraft would also need to be resistant to cold.[16]

The year 1936 was a transformational one for the AAF. When the AM underwent organizational reform in August, the AAF Order was revised, strengthening the authority of the Air Headquarters. Air Force administration beyond the basic level was transferred from the AM to Air Headquarters, enabling the Air Force budget to be managed in an integrated

---

[14] Boeicho (1975c, p. 135). In July 1935, the United States used a B-17 original model on a test flight, confirming that the Army Type 92 heavy bomber was technologically outdated. The U.S. Army planned to improve it in three years (Boeicho, 1975c, p. 136).

[15] In 1928, the Head of Air Headquarters proposed developing super-heavy bombers to attack Manila from Taiwan. With only a short cruising distance, existing Army aircraft could not get across the Bashi Channel, a total distance of approximately 400 kilometers. New bombers would need 1,000 kilometers as the radius of action, with more than 500 kilometers for action over the target and backup and 2,000 kilograms of bombs on board. A team was sent to Mitsubishi to supervise design and trial production. Obtaining a license from Junkers & Company of Germany, Mitsubishi decided to redesign the Junkers G38 and develop a bomber test model; in December 1929, it determined its basic specifications. Its test model production started in March 1930 and involved the whole engineering division of the Air Headquarters, together with Mitsubishi engineers. The first test model was completed in August 1931. After a review and practical trials, it was adopted on 2 August 1933 as a semiformal prototype of the Army Type 92 Heavy Bomber, the first and the last four-engine bomber of the AAF. Unfortunately, its performance at a horizontal velocity of 160 kilometers per hour was poor; by 1935, only six planes (including test models) had been produced. Ten years after the initial decision, research and training were stopped (Boeicho, 1975c, pp. 81–3). It was the Navy's Zero fighter planes that achieved air supremacy over the Philippines at the beginning of the Pacific War.

[16] Boeicho (1975c, p. 135).

fashion. Previously, administration had been inconsistent and inefficient, spread across several AM bureaus.[17]

On 29 July 1936, Army leaders released "On Aerial Weapons," transferring responsibility for aircraft machine-guns and their ammunition from the Army Weapons Arsenal to Air Headquarters. The authority to review armaments was transferred from the Army Technology Headquarters to the Air Technology Research Institute at Air Headquarters. Previously, aerial weapons had been reviewed by the Army Technology Headquarters and produced in munitions arsenals, leaving the Air Forces out of the loop.[18]

Once full authority for the development, production, and supply of air weapons was assumed by Air Headquarters, the Munitions Council convened its first meeting on 20 January 1937 and agreed to prioritize bombers. The Military (*gunji*) Section Chief argued that super-heavy bombers and transport aircraft should either be developed by the Navy or purchased from the private sector: "We should withdraw from research and model development and clearly define the focus of the AAF, as its technical capability is behind that of many countries and needs to improve." The ACCom responded: "We will need super-heavy bombers for operations by 1939 and hope they will be given the same research and development priority as heavy bombers and fighters." Air Headquarters backed the ACCom: "The Navy needs bombers with a longer flight range; it places less emphasis on flying speed than the Army. We need to develop aircraft for the Army." Research continued into the super-heavy bomber, but no test model was developed.[19]

The War with China began just after the Army had set up its full armament enhancement plan, emphasizing the Air Force. After Army Type 97 models were adopted in accordance with the existing research policy on 6 January 1938,[20] it became necessary to plan for the next period. The ACCommander submitted operational requests concerning aircraft performance to the Army Minister, emphasizing the need to increase flight ranges dramatically. Air Headquarters prepared a new research policy plan, taking the ACCom's requests and international trends into consideration, for the Munitions Council of 9 May. On 23 May, recommendations

---

[17] Boeicho (1975c, p. 126). In August 1936, less than a year before the start of the War with China, the Military (*gunji*) Section of the AM Military Bureau still was in charge of administration.

[18] Boeicho (1975c, pp. 126–8).

[19] Boeicho (1975c, pp. 139–41).

[20] Recall that Japan captured Nanjing on 13 December 1937 and the first Konoe Proclamation was issued on 16 January 1938.

were reported to the Army Minister, and a final decision was made on 1 July 1938.[21]

7-3-3. Army Aircraft Production

The Army's rate of production consistently fell below plan. Only 40 percent of planned airframes and 47 percent of aircraft engines were produced in FY1937, and 62 percent of airframes and 54 percent of engines in FY1938.[22]

The Outline for War Mobilization Plan for FY1941–FY1943 aimed to complete the Second Rearmament Plan. Majors Takasaki and Nakahara of the Materials Subsection in the AM Military (*gunji*) Section recalled (Boeicho, 1975c, p. 262): "Due to a lack of production capacity for the explosion in demand since the start of war with China, just over 70 percent of the munitions budget was used. This long-term plan promoted budget consumption, helping munitions companies expand production. As the situation grew more serious in February 1940, we shifted focus from supplying munitions for the war in China to preparing for new operations to the North and South."

Poor performance in aircraft production continued during the Pacific War. In May 1942, Army Minister Tojo announced a policy to prioritize aircraft production, but no remarkable improvement occurred.[23] As Prime Minister, Tojo believed that strong company managers could increase their firm's production by 20 to 30 percent. On 15 November 1942, he convened a roundtable conference of producers, circulating six requests from private companies (these were later given to supervising officers as guidelines). The requests, submitted five years after the beginning of the War with China, reveal the Army's management failures and the relationship between government and producers. Requests (1), (4), and (6) were as follows (Boeicho, 1975c, pp. 383–4):

(1) Even within the Army and Navy, orders to individual plants are uncoordinated, and it is difficult for producers to know which

---

[21] For the Weapons Research Policy of the Army Air Headquarters, see Boeicho (1975c, pp. 178–5). As shown in the policy, the primary objective of all bombers of the period – from light bombers with less than 300 kilograms of bombs on board to heavy bombers with up to 750 kilograms and long-range heavy bombers with up to 1,000 kilograms – was the destruction of aircraft and facilities, including airfields.

[22] For more details, see Miwa (2008, pp. 256–9).

[23] Boeicho (1975c, p. 380). This section is entitled "Production Crisis in the Second Half of FY1942."

ones come first. The government should manage the orders in an integrated fashion.

(4) To correct existing problems, the government should emphasize improving mass production technology.

(6) When it comes to technology research, the government should not dwell on past failures, discouraging new trials. Research should not be stopped before completion on grounds that "an egg is not a chicken."

7-3-4. Mass Production Technology

The request that demanded the most attention involved improving mass production technology. Describing the "lag in mass production technology," Boeicho (1975c, p. 384) explained: "Poor performance in aircraft production was attributed not only to a materials shortage but also to an outdated production system. It was a most urgent task to improve mass production technology. Until then, research on production technology and on mass production systems had been disparaged, and aircraft engineers tended to eschew it as frivolous research. The review attached too much importance to performance, downgrading durability, production, supply, and ease of repair and maintenance. In addition, the frequent need for revision and modification during production, caused by insufficient review and a plethora of production models, hampered aircraft production more seriously than was generally thought." (The same applies also to Navy aircraft production, as discussed in section 9-4.)

Boeicho continued, "We regulated materials' quality but not shape or dimension. The use of thin duralumin plate and an extrusion with a smaller cross-sectional area made production extremely difficult. No components other than nuts and bolts were standardized. No assembly components were standardized, either. Policies toward materials shortage lacked consistency; haphazard replacement and reducing standards disturbed the smooth flow of production."

Boeicho (1975c, pp. 384–5) argued that the worst bottleneck in aircraft production was the poor performance of machine tool industries. It listed its four causes:

(1) The shortage of machine tools, milling machines in particular. The conversion of factories making general machine tools to aircraft components did not alleviate this constraint.

(2) Most machine tools were of universal design. Production capacity was low, and they required a lot of skill to operate.

(3) Most manufacturers found it difficult to retain quality while shifting from handcrafting components to mass production.

(4) Design and casting equipment was inadequate. Poor design made it difficult to produce components, and inadequate casting equipment necessitated direct cutting using inefficient machines, as well as hand-forging.

7-4. Cooperation Between the Army and the Navy

7-4-1. Key Observations

With the split of the Navy from the Army after the Russo–Japanese War of 1904–5, the two branches formed distinct strategies, and frequently mistrusted each other. This conflict continued through the War with China on to the Pacific War, impacting the whole process from development, production, and supply to the use of air weapons by the Army and Navy.

In this section, I suggest that this conflict continued until the end of the Pacific War, impeding Japan's ability to produce and coordinate air weapons. In the next section, I focus on the NAF.

War is a great centralizer. To win, a government must perform the role of a strong central planner, choosing a combination of centralization and delegation and tackling the problem of coordination. In Japan, between the 1930s and mid-1940s, the Army and the Navy (or the military) strictly conditioned the decision making of the "government," and often decisively dominated it. The Army and Navy did not succeed in unifying for cooperation, despite their central role in planning systematic war preparations, mobilization, and economic control.

The following three observations strongly suggest a lack of cooperation between the Army and Navy throughout the wars over the whole process from the development to the use of air weapons. There had been consistently voices from various sides requesting cooperation, including actions for achieving it. However, even for air weapons, where its necessity was most earnestly emphasized, until the end of the Pacific War effective cooperation was never established.

First, because the Army and the Navy could not cooperate, the government was unable to perform its role as planner or to establish a system of control and implementation for tackling obvious problems. For example, although it was national policy to prioritize aircraft over other munitions, this policy could not be enforced.

Second, it constrained an effective utilization of scarce resources. The fierce competition between the Army and the Navy over foreign currency, basic materials, factories, engineers, and products such as steel, machine tools, and ships prevented the effective use of scarce resources. The enclosure of munitions factories and scarce engineers also had serious consequences.

Third, although the Navy surpassed the Army over the whole process from the development to the use of air weapons, the government failed to exploit its results, expertise, methods, or training procedures. There was no way for these resources to be fully exploited by the market without the intervention of a planner.

7-4-2. The Five-Year Plan for Munitions Manufacturing Industries and the Five-Year Plan for Key Industries

In June 1937, the Army launched its full-fledged armament enhancement plan (the so-called First Rearmament Plan) and the Navy began its landmark replenishment plan (the so-called Third Replenishment Plan). The complicated relationship between the Army, Navy, and government (with conflicting perspectives), together with conflicting perspectives inside the Army, caused the Army's liaison with munitions manufacturing industries and key industries to break down. The Army decided to deal with munitions industries on its own, and asked the government to cultivate and expand basic national capacity in key industries as a policy for national defense (Boeicho, 1975c, p. 153). On 17 June 1937, the Army Vice-Minister presented to the Vice-Director of the Planning Agency the Outline of the Five-year Plan for Key Industries.

Two points are important. First, this Outline was formulated without prior agreement from the Navy. Targeting operations against the USSR as a primary concern, it selected key industries to develop on the continent. The Outline also assumed the Army-master-and-Navy-subordinate principle.[24] For this reason, trying to reach an advance agreement with the Navy would just waste time and hold back the operation (Boeicho, 1975c, p. 155).

Second, the Outline aimed to build up key industries by 1941, so as to support Japan, Manchuria, and North China in any emergency. Its goal was to increase dramatically the national capacity in peacetime, thus establishing

---

[24] Recall the previous discussion in section 2-4-2.

the power to lead in East Asia. This goal was not agreed to with the Navy, but through a delicate relationship with the government (Boeicho, 1975c, pp. 153–7).

7-4-3. The Army-Navy Munitions Factory Mobilization Agreement on Aircraft Manufacturing Plants for FY1937

From the munitions procurement perspective, the Army and the Navy were independent and on an equal footing, causing a rivalry that made plans difficult to implement (Boeicho, 1970, p. 17). Both sides recognized the need for a reliable Army-Navy agreement on munitions procurement, and on 16 June 1937, the first step was accomplished: the Army-Navy Munitions Factory Mobilization Agreement on Aircraft Manufacturing Plants for FY1937.[25] Unfortunately, the start of the War with China interrupted this progress; no further steps were taken and Japan continued to suffer seriously from conflict and lack of communication between the Army and Navy. The scope and content, and therefore the effectiveness, of the agreement reached just before the outbreak of the war were woefully insufficient.

Once the War with China began, the Army's annual War Mobilization Plan became impractical. As both the Army and Navy needed to use factories to produce air weapons other than aircraft and engines, on 25 August, they signed the Air Weapons Acquisition Agreement for Dispatching Troops to Current Engagements. Needing a full-fledged agreement, on 18 November they signed the Army-Navy Munitions Industries Mobilization Agreement on Air Weapons in the China Incident (Boeicho, 1975c, pp. 195–6). The new agreement established boundaries and rules for discussion, requiring the two branches to communicate when necessary.[26]

---

[25] After the Manchurian Incident in 1931, many private companies aimed to grow by converting their business into munitions production. In response, the Army and Navy authorities competed fiercely for the leadership of those factories, bringing disputes to the surface. Each branch implemented its own armament improvements, so that the Army-Navy Aviation Agreement of December 1923 could no longer be enforced. On 29 August 1936, the Army-Navy Air Headquarters Consultative Committee was established to promote unification of standards and models in the Army and Navy Air Forces, to improve efficiency in aircraft production and the efficient use of materials. Its only accomplishment was this agreement. Previously, Army leaders had argued that it wasn't feasible to reach an agreement in peacetime. In wartime, it would become clear whether the Army-master-and-Navy-subordinate principle, or the opposite, would be adopted, making an agreement possible (Boeicho, 1975c, pp. 157–9).

[26] In various committees established before the Greater East Asian War, the Army and Navy attempted to coordinate technology and production. Given the independence of the two branches, and various territorial disputes, this attempt reaped few rewards. Japan lacked

7-4-4. The Musashi Factory of the Nakajima Aircraft Company and the Homare Engine

The Nakajima Aircraft Company built the Musashino Factory, a subsidiary of the Tokyo Factory, to specialize in engine production for the Army. Construction began in October 1937 and ended in April 1938. The Musashino Factory was the largest ever built in Japan, and it prompted the Navy to commission from Nakajima an equivalent factory for engine production at an adjacent site. Because the Navy did not like to share the name, the new factory, completed in 1941, was named the Tama Factory rather than Musashino Factory (Fuji Heavy Industries, 1984, pp. 31-2).

The Administration Inspector System was established in March 1943, and in October, Cabinet advisor Ginjiro Fujiwara was sent to Nakajima Aircraft as the first Administration Inspector. The Munitions Ministry ordered the Musashino and Tama factories to double their production, using existing facilities. Nakajima made a counterproposal to integrate the two factories with the same process separated by a wall and realize large-scale mass production by using assembly lines. Immediately adopting the proposal, the two factories were merged into a single Musashi Factory (Maekawa, 2000, pp. 114-15).

After with the Sakae, the Homare was Nakajima's best engine. Named by the Navy, the Homare began production in September 1942. As U.S. fighter planes rapidly improved their performance and fighting tactics, wreaking increasing levels of damage on Japan's Zero fighters, the military wanted more powerful engines, and the Homare satisfied this need (Maekawa, 2000, pp. 114-15).

Although the Homare engine was developed for the Navy, the Army quickly demanded the same, naming its own version the ha-45. Initially, the Homare and ha-45 were exactly the same, so that Tama and Musashino could exchange components with each other and improve productivity. However, as the Army and Navy demanded separate improvements, the engines evolved differently and lost interchangeability (Maekawa, 2000, p. 114).[27]

---

the competence to wage a sophisticated major war involving technology and supply with the Allied Powers (Boeicho, 1975c, p. 526).

[27] Maekawa, the author, was the person in charge of Homare's production (Maekawa, 2000, p. 122).

7–4–5. Interaction Between Two Air Forces, and the National Unification of Aircraft Technology

In May 1942, Army Minister Tojo introduced a policy giving priority to aircraft production over other munitions. No remarkable improvement in aircraft production occurred.

Since June and July, vigorous but ineffective efforts had been made to promote interaction between the two Air Forces. Some front managers hated unification and refused to compromise on even the specifications for a screw. When adopting the same fighter aircraft, both sides claimed that it was impossible to update factory production facilities. The standardizing of Army and Navy air weapons was an intractable problem. Aircraft manufacturing factories were not adapted for mass production and could not be rebuilt without a significant drop in productivity (Boeicho, 1975c, p. 380).

The Army and Navy needed to support each other in research and development because technology in Japan lagged significantly behind the United States. The Army-Navy Air Headquarters Consultative Committee established in 1936 was not sufficient, so on 9 August 1943, the Army-Navy Aircraft Technology Committee was established[28] to promote cooperative trial production, a topic outside the remit of the Consultative Committee (Boeicho, 1975c, p. 427).

As radiowave weapons became increasingly important, the Army-Navy Radiowave Technology Committee was established on 12 August 1943; it produced its Outline for Army-Navy Joint Research on Radiowave Weapons in September. On 29 December 1943, Japan established the Army-Navy Tube Production Committee to design new tubes for radiowave weapons; at the time, Japan's tube manufacturing industry merely copied imported tubes, leading to a lack of regulation and the overproduction of inferior products. As radiowave weapons depended on high-quality tubing, quality and quantity improvements were an urgent national requirement (Boeicho, 1975c, p. 428).

When a Comprehensive Policy for Science and Technology Mobilization was announced on 1 October 1943, the Research Mobilization Conference and the Wartime Researchers System was also established. This was the high command that would control and advance the unification of otherwise fragmented

---

[28] Because of the particular importance of the aircraft technology, this committee was newly established, a spin-off of the Army-Navy Technology Committee established on 13 June 1942 (NAFHistory, 1969, [3], p. 112).

research policies. After this, approximately 80 percent of research issues were cosponsored by the Army and Navy (Boeicho, 1975c, pp. 428–9).

None of these measures was realized before 1943 and disagreements on operations and aircraft performance persisted. "As the shortage of production materials and facilities became severe, the Army and the Navy competed over dwindling supplies. The scramble for materials, facilities, engines, and attachments intensified, and efforts to coordinate had little impact" (Horikoshi, 1950, pp. 604–5).

7–4–6. Cooperative Trial Production and the Unification of Standards

Cooperative Trial Production by the Army and Navy
After the May 1943 pronouncement on weapons research and trial production, the Army and Navy Air Forces embarked on the trial production of ki-87 models. Soon after establishing the Army-Navy Aircraft Technology Committee, eight additional models, including the ki-87 single-seat fighter (Nakajima), the ki-90 short-range bomber (Mitsubishi), and the ki-91 long-range bomber (Kawasaki), were added to the list.

Although this aircraft production was called a "trial," the models were not manufactured experimentally. If the Army or Navy proposed a higher-caliber trial test model, the other branch would adopt it as well. As communications remained difficult, each branch embarked on trial production independently, announcing its results only when the model was complete. As before, two sets of facilities were used for the same purpose (Boeicho, 1975c, pp. 429–30).

Separation of Development and Production
When the Munitions Ministry was established, Saburo Endo, the informal Head of the General Directorate Bureau for Air Weapons, pushed hard to include aircraft technology in its jurisdiction, arguing that unifying aircraft technology and production was essential. However, neither the Army nor the Navy was willing to give up control of research and trial production. Only final production was transferred to the Munitions Ministry (Boeicho, 1975c, p. 404).

The Need for Shared Standards
The unification of standards was a basic requirement for increasing production and improving efficiency in product use. Article 6 of the Aircraft Manufacturing Industry Act of 1938 legally constrained standards of aircraft

production.[29] It regulated the production of test models, but permitting the use of off-specification components and defining and in some cases waiving government, Army, Navy, and Commerce ministry clearances. Although aircraft standards were established and enforced by the state and all members of the Aircraft Industry Association were required to adopt them, in reality, it was impossible for factories to implement new standards immediately. As a result, military standards coexisted with the new aircraft standards, even after the Munitions Ministry's unification initiative (Boeicho, 1975c, p. 405).

7-5. The Navy Air Force (NAF): An Overview

7-5-1. Introduction

Why Focus on the NAF?
In both Japan's War with China and in the Pacific War, the Navy relied much more heavily on its Air Force than on battleships.

Aircraft carried out the attack on Pearl Harbor and dominated the naval battle off Malaysia at the start of the Pacific War. B-29 bomber staging air raids over Japan's mainland signaled the war's end. Describing key performances at the beginning of the Greater East Asian War, NAFHistory, 1969, ([1], pp. 14–15) wrote: "The great success of the operations at the beginning of the war to capture key areas in the southern quarter obviously was a result of attacks by an overwhelming power on weaker enemy forces, to which also the fine performances of the NAF contributed greatly. The surprise attack on Pearl Harbor, the naval battle off Malaysia, air warfare in the southern quarter including the Philippines, and operations on the Indian Ocean – in all of this the NAF carried all before it. It was not too much to say that its ability startled the world. Ahead of other countries, it proved that at the beginning of war, air forces were the backbone of sea forces."

In the Battle of Midway Island, many airplanes and aircraft carriers with skilled crew members were lost, dealing the Japanese Navy a heavy blow, and marking a watershed in the Pacific War. Similarly, land-based air forces took a leading role in the battle over Guadalcanal Island, a decisive conflict between Japan and the United States that determined the outcome of the war. Guadalcanal was a key encounter in the larger struggle over the Solomon Sea, a long war of attrition between land-based air forces.

---

[29] This was Japan's first case of industrial standards enforced by law (Boeicho, 1975c, p. 405).

Air Supremacy

As mentioned previously, Overy's comment on air supremacy reflects the important position and role of aircraft (Overy, 1996, p. 322).[30] In Koller's view, "Everything depends on air supremacy, everything else must take second place."

This was true for Japan. Shortly after the beginning of the War with China, on 11 July 1937, the Navy organized special air units, including the First Combined Air Corps (1st CAC) and the Second Combined Air Corps (2nd CAC).[31] "The 1st CAC was made up of land-based attack aircraft, and the 2nd CAC of planes based on ships. These two CACs, working with sea-based troops, were the first to attack Central China and secure air supremacy. Japan then added a 3rd CAC and developed air stations in Nanjing, Hankou, Hainan, and Hanoi. As the war expanded, the NAF carried out strategic bombing over the whole of China" (NAFHistory, 1969, [1], p. 13).

The NAFHistory (1969, [4], p. 440) concludes: "All in the military, without exception, became painfully aware of the decisive importance of air supremacy in land and sea operations when the situation deteriorated at the end of the Greater East Asian War." As the 2nd CAC confirmed, describing Army-Navy air cooperation in Shanghai and during the operation to capture Nanjing from Hangzhou Bay (1969, NAFHistory [4], p. 439): "The two armies were comparable when it came to military force, equipment, and deployment in those operations; Japan had no particular advantage. The biggest difference was that, while the enemy could not use air power

---

[30] For more details, see Miwa (2008, pp. 266–80).

[31] On 11 July, the Japanese government deferred a decision to dispatch troops to North China. Knowing that the two forces had reached an on-site agreement that night, Navy leaders judged it necessary to maintain the existing deployment and to observe subsequent developments carefully. On 12 July, they sent a secret telegram to Hasegawa, the Commander-in-Chief of the Third Fleet, asking him to continue the present policy and finalize preparations (Boeicho, 1974, p. 247). Recognizing that dispatching troops to North China was likely to cause war to spread across the whole country, the NM and the NCCom agreed to conduct rapid-response preparations and predetermined operation policies. Once war spread to the whole country, Japanese residents would need to withdraw from South and Central China. It would be necessary to ask the Army to send troops to protect residents in Shanghai and Tsingtao. The telegram was the final step (NAFHistory, 1969, [4], p. 144). On the morning of 22 July, Army leaders deferred the agreed-upon dispatch of troops from Japan to North China. Navy leaders, however, sent a secret telegram to Hasegawa on 23 July: "When the public learns of this agreement, anti-Japanese sentiment and the boycott of Japanese products will intensify; there will be trouble in Central and South China.... We are very concerned about the situation that will develop when the conflict reaches Central and South China" (Boeicho, 1974, p. 258).

against landing operations, we had complete air supremacy and used our Air Forces to full advantage."[32]

In air battles over the Philippines at the beginning of the Pacific War, it was the Navy Type Zero fighter planes that roared off from air stations in Taiwan, flew more than 500 miles, destroyed enemy planes in the air and on the ground, and achieved air supremacy. It was an absolute necessity to secure air supremacy over the Army's embarkation points, where transport convoys berthed. The U.S. Army had B-17 bombers deployed in the Philippines, powerful enough to deter an attack by the Japanese military (NAFHistory, 1969 [1], pp. 235–40).

The Supply of Air Weapons During the War with China

Reflecting on this period, the NAFHistory ([2], pp. 512–13) concluded that the supply of air weapons was managed smoothly during the War with China:

For the NAF, the four and half years from the start of war with China to the Pacific War were long and busy. The Fourth Rearmament Plan established and enforced during this period was designed "to prioritize the Air Forces ...," but in fact was implemented "placing a larger weight to Air Forces" at best. Although it is said that aircraft production increased unexpectedly with this plan, it only slightly improved the air armament situation at the start of the war. In these four and half years, however, most aircraft models, with the exception of training airplanes, were renovated and replaced by new models. As a result, Japan's NAF built up its arsenal of land- and carrier-based planes to a level equivalent to that of the Western countries. During the War with China, Japan produced a steady, smooth supply of air weapons; operations were never seriously disturbed.

Before the War with China, NAF had 800 aircraft, including training and reserve airplanes. By the start of the Pacific War, the total was approximately 4,500. By enforcing the first and second capacity expansion plans to increase production at government-owned-and-company-operated plants, Japan increased its supply capacity of air weapons.

The Supply Division was created in the Air Headquarters, and special air arsenals were established both in China and on the South Sea. In addition, the air arsenal in Japan was established to unify supply-repair institutions and strengthen their capacities.

---

[32] "If we were in the opposite situation, our Army would have faced serious difficulties. Without air supremacy, planes from both sides would have battled over the front. Then, not only would we have been overpowered at the front, but our rear troops, including artillery and logistics units, would have been too damaged to enforce the 'tete-de-pont' and other operations. Whenever our planes were in the air, the Chinese artillery fell silent and we were able to redeploy troops and supplies in the night. When bad weather forced the planes to land, enemy forces always increased" (NAFHistory, 1969, [4], p. 439).

7-5-2. Fighters and Bombers

From the beginning of the War with China until the first stage of the Pacific War, the air power of Japan, and particularly of its Navy, was first-class. The Navy Type 96 carrier-based fighter (the Mitsubishi A5M, code-named "Claude" by the Allies) and the Navy Type 96 land-based attack aircraft (the Mitsubishi G3M, code-named "Nell") were dominant at the start of the War with China. The Navy Type Zero carrier-based fighter (the Mitsubishi A6M) and the Navy Type 1 land-based attack aircraft (the Mitsubishi G4M, code-named "Betty") took the lead during the second half of the War with China. All of Japan's leading airplanes were designed by Mitsubishi for the Navy. Aircraft designers, pilots, and commanders felt confident that Japan's technology was world-class because of the excellent performance of the Type 96 carrier-based fighter and land-based attack aircraft, and its fourteen-cylinder, air-cooled, twin-row radial aircraft Kinsei or Venus engines made by Mitsubishi and Sakae engines made by Nakajima (Horikoshi, 1950, p. 595).

This section focuses on fighter and bomber fuselages. The NAFHistory (1969, [3], pp. 582–3) offers this overview: "Japan carried out a successful trial production of aircraft engines in 1930. Once it was possible to mass produce this key component, Japan became self-sufficient in engine production, allowing the Navy to enhance its Air Force dramatically. In 1932, the Navy established the Yokosuka Naval Air Technical Arsenal as a center for research and development, at the same time announcing its plan to develop a network of private companies to undertake trial production of new machines.... By 1940, Japan's domestically produced engines were comparable to those of Europe and the U.S. It is astounding that Japan was able to achieve such remarkable progress when industry development was generally so poor." The case of aircraft engines, which took longer to produce than fuselages (three to four years from trial production to practical use) was almost the same (NAFHistory, 1969, [3], p. 603).

The Type 96 and Type Zero Carrier-Based Fighters
On 19 November 1936, the Type 96 carrier-based fighter (the A5M1) was officially accepted by the Navy. In February 1934, the Navy ordered Mitsubishi and Nakajima to begin trial production of the 9-shi (literally "trial") single-seated fighter. At Mitsubishi, Jiro Horikoshi, the Chief Designer, focused on reducing air resistance and weight, problems he had encountered with the earlier 7-shi fighter.[33] On 1 October 1935, Mitsubishi

---

[33]In 1932, the Navy ordered Mitsubishi and Nakajima to begin trial production of the 7-shi carrier-based aircraft. In accordance with its original design (the Chief Designer was Horikoshi),

unveiled the first prototype, which had a bold design, speed, and climbing power – bypassing some requirements of carrier-based aircraft (NAFHistory, 1969, [3], pp. 412–14):

In the Navy, restrictions relating to speed, landing view, lift-size, and flight range often hindered the production of high-performance aircraft. During this period, aircraft were changing drastically through remarkable innovations, switching from biplane to monoplane, from wood and fabric to all-metal construction, and becoming larger, with far more powerful engines. Its out-of-date restrictions put the Navy at a serious disadvantage when designing airplanes.

The new plane demonstrated the impressive speed and climbing power of the world's most advanced aircraft.[34] Although some of the usual requirements were ignored, it was the first Japanese airplane to surpass world-class performance levels. After two years of modifications to adapt it for aircraft carriers, the Navy officially accepted the Type 96 carrier-based fighter (NAFHistory, 1969, [3], p. 416).[35]

Mitsubishi made the first low-wing monoplane prototype for the Navy. Nakajima remodeled the Nakajima Army Type 91 fighter to fit the Navy's requests. For a year (from June 1933), the Navy conducted performance tests on two machines, and concluded that neither met their requirements (NAFHistory, 1969, [3], p. 411). Once the Yokosuka Naval Air Technical Arsenal was announced in April 1932 and completed in 1936 (NAFHistory, 1969 [3], p. 133), the Navy focused on replacing imported aircraft bodies and engines with domestically designed and produced ones. As a first step, the Navy ordered private companies to compete in producing trial versions of the most important 7-shi models: carrier-based fighters, carrier-based attack aircraft, and reconnaissance seaplanes. Mitsubishi and Nakajima undertook the trial production of carrier-based aircraft while Nakajima, Aichi, and Kawanishi built reconnaissance seaplanes. Only the Kawanishi seaplane was officially accepted as the Navy Type 94 Reconnaissance Seaplane (Horikoshi, 1950, p. 601).

[34] After the 7-shi, the Navy ordered competitive trial production of several 8-shi and 9-shi models. Mitsubishi's prototype 9-shi single-seated fighter exceeded world-class performance levels and was officially accepted as the Navy Type 96 carrier-based fighter, enabling the Navy to cancel its foreign contracts. The 9-shi single-seated fighter performed better than the already completed and imported D510 Fighter made in France by Devoatin and the P35 Fighter made in the United States by Seversky (Horikoshi, 1950, pp. 601–2).

[35] After the producer had conducted basic test flights, new prototype planes were put through exacting flight tests by the Naval Air Technical Arsenal. The Yokosuka Navy Air Squadron tested the planes for operational suitability. Prototypes improved through testing were considered by the Navy before being officially accepted as weapons. The process took one or two years from prototype to official acceptance, even when the process proceeded smoothly.

Approved aircraft were sent to the front, so it was crucial that they should perform perfectly. However, front-line troops often faced maintenance and other problems (NAFHistory, 1969, [1], p. 915). The Navy Type 96 carrier-based fighter had engine troubles, both as a prototype and as an official weapon. The Navy was frequently obliged to replace its engines, reducing maximum speed and climbing power considerably (NAFHistory, 1969, [3], p. 416).

In October 1937, three months after the beginning of the War with China, the Navy delivered to Mitsubishi and Nakajima an order for a 12-shi carrier-based fighter so technically advanced that it was considered extremely difficult to achieve. At a joint meeting with business and the Navy Ministry, the government explained that from combat lessons of the War with China, it needed the best fighter in the world, able to outperform planes from other countries in speed, flight range, load, and maneuverability. Nakajima declined the challenge, but Mitsubishi accepted it (NAFHistory, 1969, [3], pp. 416–17).

The first prototype was designed by Jiro Horikoshi and completed in March 1939. On 13 September of the same year, two years after it was ordered, the company completed renovations and sent it to Yokosuka to be tested by the Flight Experiment Division. On 11 March 1940, the second prototype suffered an air breakup accident, and experiments were temporarily suspended. Because of the pressing demand for new weapons on the Chinese front, the Navy sent fifteen machines to Hankou in mid-July, before the Type Zero carrier-based fighter was officially accepted as a weapon on 24 July 1940. The Type Zero took two years and nine months from order to trial production, but its performance was marvelous. It was superior to all other contemporary fighters. Because Nakajima's Sakae engine passed a type test before the completion of the first prototype machine, Air Headquarters ruled that Zero fighters after the third series should have Sakae engines (NAFHistory, 1969, [3], pp. 417–21).

In November 1940, when Japan called off bombing by medium-sized attack aircraft, just twelve or thirteen Zero fighters effectively silenced the whole Chinese Air Force, destroying its planes and ending its air supremacy over the continent. After April 1941, Japan's Air Force focused on destroying enemy planes to prevent the sort of bomb damage experienced in Hankou in October 1939 and to stop China from rebuilding its Air Force. Japan combined bombing by attack aircraft with raids on Lanzhou and Chengdu, where Zero fighters trapped enemy aircraft hidden in shelters (NAFHistory, 1969, [4], p. 599).

In the attack on Pearl Harbor (known in Japan as the Hawaii Operation), the Air Force used the Type Zero carrier-based fighter model 21, the Type 99 carrier-based bomber model 11, and the Type 97 No. 3 carrier-based attack aircraft model 12.[36]

---

[36] For more details, see Boeicho (1967c, pp. 133–4).

The Type 96 Land-Based Attack Aircraft and the Type 1
Land-Based Attack Aircraft

In 1932, the Navy ordered the Hiro Naval Arsenal, which had most experience in developing large-scale, all-metal aircraft, to run a trial production of the 7-shi large-scale, long-range patrol-attack aircraft. Completed
in March 1933, the plane had a smoothly functioning engine and satisfied
all requirements. Although still classified as an experimental machine, in
June 1936 it was officially accepted as the Navy Type 95 land-based attack
aircraft (G2H1). This model needed significant reconstruction and was
already obsolete (replaced by the more advanced 8-shi medium-sized attack
aircraft) in 1935, when it finally passed all its tests. Four Type 95 land-based
attack aircraft were manufactured by Hiro Arsenal and two by Mitsubishi
(NAFHistory, 1969, [3], pp. 474–6).

In January 1933, the Navy ordered Mitsubishi to begin trial production
of a buoyant and higher-performance medium-sized land-based attack aircraft. Mitsubishi had developed significant expertise in large-scale all-metal
aircraft production. To make its technology more reliable, the Navy made
Mitsubishi build the 7-shi large-scale attack aircraft that the Hiro Arsenal
designed.

Mitsubishi's prototype (designed by Kiro Honjo) performed astonish-
ingly well. Its speed and maneuverability matched that of the world's best
fighters. It recorded a startling endurance capability of 24 hours and a flight
range of 2,500 nautical miles (1 nautical mile = 1,852 meters).[37] Although
only one experimental model was produced, its success convinced the Navy
that long-range, land-based attack aircraft were viable. The 8-shi special
or seacoast reconnaissance aircraft was renamed the 8-shi medium-sized
attack aircraft and became the prototype for all future medium-sized attack
aircraft (NAFHistory, 1969, [3], pp. 476–7).

When Mitsubishi began trial production of the 9-shi medium-sized
attack aircraft, its brief was to maintain the superb maneuverability of the
8-shi while fulfilling all necessary requirements of medium-sized attack

---

[37] It was the Navy's first all-metal monoplane with an undercarriage, considered the ultimate
fuselage structure. The Type 96 carrier-based fighter did not adopt the undercarriage. This
land-based reconnaissance aircraft featured not only the most advanced fuselage but the
best performance. With impressive acceleration capability, it could not be intercepted by
existing carrier-based fighters such as the Type 90 or the Type 95. Even the most advanced
Type 96 fighters could not overpower it in combat. Navy fighters were expected to demonstrate a 30 percent speed advantage over other planes. In 1934 and 1935, a claim that its
fighters were useless circulated within the NAF and stirred internal debate (NAFHistory,
1969, [4], pp. 262–3).

aircraft. The first prototype, designed by Kiro Honjo and completed in October 1935, performed better than any other aircraft in the world, with a maximum speed of 175 knots (1 knot = 1 nautical mile per hour) and a maximum flight range of 2,700 nautical miles. It was the Navy Type 96 land-based attack aircraft (G3M1).

In total, 1,040 planes were produced. They undertook some famous operations, including a transoceanic bombing on 14 August 1937 and a sea battle off Malaysia at the beginning of the Pacific War, when two British battleships were sunk simultaneously, resolving the question of whether battleships or aircraft were more powerful (NAFHistory, 1969, [3], p. 478).

In 1937, the Navy ordered a trial production of the 12-shi land-based attack aircraft. Based on lessons learned in the China war, the Navy demanded an increase in combat speed and an offensive flight range of more than 2,600 nautical miles. The first prototype, designed by Kiro Honjo, was officially accepted as the Type 1 land-based attack aircraft Model 11 (G4M1) in April 1941. It was introduced during the last days of the War with China, at the beginning of the Pacific War. Partnered with the Type 96 land-based attack aircraft, it was devastatingly effective in the sea battle off Malaysia and captured the world's attention. By the end of the war, 2,450 had been produced (NAFHistory, 1969, [3], pp. 479–80).

7–6. A First and Alternative Hypothesis

7–6–1. Did Everything Proceed as Smoothly as Planned Before the Pacific War?

Many readers might conclude that, at least until the initial stage of the Pacific War, the plans of the Japanese NAF proceeded smoothly. Let's call this the "first hypothesis":

First Hypothesis: After 1930, following careful preparations, the Japanese NAF resolved to end its dependence on imported air weapons. Once the Yokosuka Naval Air Technical Arsenal was established in 1932, the Navy worked with private contractors to carry out full-fledged aircraft production trials. Collaborating with the Army, the Navy achieved better-than-expected performance and expanded Japan's capacity to design, improve, and produce its own aircraft. The War with China revealed the strengths and weaknesses of Japan's airplanes, leading to design improvements and building the skill and experience of fighter pilots. As a result, the Japanese military began the Pacific War from a position of strength; in the early stages, everything proceeded smoothly.

After the Washington Naval Conference of 1921–2, the NAF established the foundations for future development (NAFHistory, 1969, [1], p. 15). Horikoshi (1950) divides the evolution of the NAF into three periods. The fifteen years spanning 1915 to 1930 was the second "imitative" period, following an initial "import" period. During the second phase, the Navy and its producers mastered engineering technology by purchasing from foreign producers the right to manufacture famous aircraft and engines and producing fuselages and engines under the direction of engineers invited from abroad. Foreign expertise gave Japanese producers the foundations of technological development. Although developments were protected by the military, private producers saw the potential in undertaking such work (Horikoshi, 1950, p. 595).

The third period of "independence" began in 1930. Horikoshi (1950, p. 595) wrote: "During this period, private companies began to develop the first fuselages and engines of Japanese design. The key driving force during this period was the Yokosuka Naval Air Technical Arsenal established in April 1932."

He also wrote, "In 1932, with the establishment of the Air Technical Arsenal, the Navy adopted an independent design policy, initially for fuselages and then for engines. The Army also adopted the same policy at the same time. This policy produced results earlier than expected" (Horikoshi, 1950, p. 603).[38]

The experience and performance of independence policy gave Japan a distinct advantage against China (NAFHistory, 1969, [4], p. 310): The Type 96 carrier-based fighter was used at the start of the War with China as if it were prepared for the war, and the Type Zero carrier-based fighter was developed during the war. Both models took advantage of the industry's rapid technological progress. On the contrary, the Chinese Air Force, which owned good-quality aircraft at the beginning of the war, soon found its weapons becoming obsolete as a consequence of its dependence on other countries.[39]

---

[38] Though the Army and Navy shared the same policy, the Army entrusted most research and design to private companies, concentrating on delivering orders and testing, critiquing, and repairing equipment. By contrast, the Navy established its own powerful research institution, not only providing materials but designing and manufacturing fuselages and engines. For this reason among others, the Navy's aircraft tended to be one step ahead of the Army's (Horikoshi, 1950, p. 604). On the Army's Air Technical Arsenal, see Horikoshi (1950, p. 599).

[39] NAFHistory (1969, [4], p. 598) also wrote (referring to the situation in 1941): "At the beginning of the War with China, the Type 96 fighter moved one step ahead of the

Lessons learned in China influenced air operations during the initial stage of the Pacific War. NAFHistory (1969, [4]. p. 750) wrote, "The air operations at the initial stage of the Greater East Asian War were battles between those with war experience and those without. With training it might not be impossible to raise the skill level to the coup de maître; however, it is another question whether existing skills could be fully exercised. The experience in actual fighting determined the performance in practice more decisively than any training operations. Although most air operations in the War with China were one-sided, the greatest contribution of the War with China was that it provided the Japanese Air Force with valuable opportunities for practice."[40]

7-6-2. Eleven Questions Concerning the First Hypothesis

In considering the hypothesis that, at least until the initial stage of the Pacific War, everything proceeded smoothly, the following questions arise[41]:

1. If the Navy was, as we have seen, the key player in air warfare, did it in fact lead the war? Alternatively, did the Army plan and direct the war, and the Navy take the lead in waging it?
2. The Army always assumed that the USSR would be its enemy; when war began with China, the Army was rearming against the USSR. The Navy, by contrast, expected a war with the United States (as mentioned in section 2-4-1, however, the Navy's policy against the United States was not so well established and robust as Army's policy

---

Chinese Air Force's aircraft, and the Type Zero one generation ahead of the Type 96. Relying on other countries for weapons, the Chinese Air Force was not able to make much progress in armament use. It was understandable that it avoided confronting the Type Zero."

[40] NAFHistory (1969, [4], p. 750) continued, "Air combat with multiple fighters, anti-aircraft explosions surrounding aircraft, and adverse circumstances where pilots were demoralized because of a deteriorating war situation with much damage – all these phenomena provided valuable experience. The air forces rapidly expanded just before the beginning of war with the U.S. and included many new conscripts. Seeing the perfect composure of experienced soldiers accustomed to the atmosphere of war, being led by experienced commanding officers enabled even those inexperienced men to control their emotions amid rising tension."

Obviously there were other factors. For instance, asking whether the engagement in operations on the continent lowered the skill level of airforces expected for offshore operations in the Pacific War, NAFHistory concludes: "in general, long-term engagement on the continent made the operations crude" (NAFHistory, 1969, [4], pp. 756–7). For more details, see note 38 of Chapter 8.

[41] Many other questions also arise in relation to the nineteen puzzles discussed in chapters 3 and 4 of Miwa (2008).

against the USSR); the air weapons designed for use against U.S. troops also worked well in China. The Army was the dominant player, with strongly held views. Assuming that the Army led (and the Navy accommodated) Japan's national defense policy (determining the enemy, priority, and timescale for armament enhancement), wouldn't one expect the NAF to have been poorly prepared for the beginning of the War with China?[42]

3. The Navy's basic policy was to focus on the large-scale battleships with big cannons, and to follow the "short-war-quick-outcomes, intercepting operation doctrine." Who would have expected Navy air weapons to play a major role in China and the Pacific? If this was planned, who planned it and how?

In "Reflections on the Operations and Preparations of the NAF," the author of NAFHistory (1969, [1], pp. 24–5) explains "the large-scale battleships with big cannon doctrine and the short-war-quick-outcome intercepting operation doctrine": "The Navy's operation and rearmament plans, based on the BNDP and Basic Outline of Operations, adopted the basic strategy of an intercepting operation against the U.S., which had been studied for a long time. Its fixation on large-scale battleships with big cannons prevented it from recognizing the changes in strategy and operations that were necessary because of the rapid development of air weapons. Moreover, understanding that it did not have the capacity to wage a long war, Japan favored the argument that war against the U.S. must be a short war with a quick outcome, in other words, a one-game match between fleets of ships."

The Third Navy Rearmament Plan was prepared as the London Naval Treaty was expiring, ushering in an era without naval disarmament; it was implemented just before the start of the War with China and centered around two large-scale battleships, the *Yamato* and *Musashi*, rather than aircraft or aircraft carriers.

Under these circumstances, how did the Navy come to build the air weapons that played such an important role in the wars after China? Why were air weapons prepared, assuming a short-war-quick-outcome operation, by a one-game match between fleets of ships, able to play such a role? Was it simply that, encountering unexpected

---

[42] In the so-called Ishiwara plan, war against the United States was a distant prospect, not expected for thirty years; for this reason, air preparations were not yet under way.

situations, the Japanese military tried to resolve them through a range of strategies and approaches?

4. Medium-sized land-based attack aircraft such as the Type 96 and the Type 1, together with the Type 96 and Type Zero fighters, played an enormous role in China and the initial stage of the Pacific War. How did the Navy come to develop medium-sized land-based attack aircraft that could not be loaded onto aircraft carriers? Who authorized these, in accordance with what plan?

5. Medium-sized land-based attack aircraft were particularly effective as part of long-range escort operations with fighters such as the 1940 Type Zero fighters. If the Navy (and the Army) understood this, why didn't the Navy build Type Zero fighters before the war?

6. The actual war against the United States was not a one-game match between fleets of ships but a long war of attrition using land-based air weapons over the Pacific Ocean. Had these air weapons been designed and produced at a time when Japan still expected a short sea war? Was it not, in fact, when Japan's plans failed that its war preparations finally got on track?

7. Was the war against the United States planned? The Strategy Division Chief of the NCCom recalled (Fukudome, 1951, p. 182): "There was no expectation of victory in the war with the U.S. unless the 'kamikaze (divine wind)' blew. There was no reason to expect anything except defeat." Had the Navy deliberately planned a war that, even if all went smoothly, was sure to end in Japan's defeat? Would such a plan deserve the name?

8. As shown earlier in this chapter, Mitsubishi's four Navy aircraft models, two carrier-based fighters and two land-based attack aircraft, were epoch-making successes. The outstanding performance of the 8-shi medium-sized attack aircraft encouraged the Navy to embark on a 9-shi trial production that led to the Type 96 land-based attack aircraft. The Type 96 carrier-based fighter was developed because the first Mitsubishi 9-shi single-seated fighter prototype delivered such a world-class performance. Success encouraged engineers to adopt a bold design, entirely emphasizing speed and climbing power, without worrying about the guidelines for carrier-based aircraft. As Nakajima declined, only Mitsubishi engaged in trial production of the Type Zero carrier-based fighter. What would have happened to Japan's military plans if Mitsubishi had delayed or failed to complete any of those trial productions, or if performance had faltered? Did those plans have any substance or detail? It was common knowledge in the mid-1930s that

Japan's technology lagged four years behind the United States in fuselages and six in engines.[43]

9. Had enemies and belligerents reacted as expected? Would Japan's plans have proceeded smoothly if the Chinese Air Force had been superior in strategy and fighting capability? Had Japan's plans assumed that bombers in low-altitude offensives would be shot down, that aircraft carriers could be bombed in the field, or that air stations could be easily attacked? For most in the Japanese government, the War with China began, developed, and expanded unexpectedly. The same applies to its subsequent rapid development and tremendous lengthening of the war. Were the NAF leaders really so accurate in predicting the war that they could make reliable plans? When the NAF leaders implemented their plans, did results match the expectations of government leaders?

10. The hypothesis that everything proceeded smoothly as "planned" was an interpretation of success stories, arrived at through hindsight. If cases of failure and missed success had also been considered, would analysts have recognized a lack of preparation? For example, the Japanese NAF lacked reconnaissance aircraft; this gap had a serious impact on strategy and operations. Similarly, Japan's bombs and bomb delivery technology worked well on warships, but not on onshore targets, such as air stations and related facilities.

11. War preparations, war mobilization, and economic control were implemented under various constraints, including government budget limitations, the state of the machine industry, the shortage of basic materials, the strength of the Japanese economy, and the political climate. Navy air weapons were restricted in every stage, from development and production to supply and usage. Technological expertise seriously conditioned industrial activities not only in

---

[43] In 1935, the office of Japan's Naval attaché in the United States obtained a U.S. Navy performance table that listed existing aircraft, those in trial production, and those planned for future trials. It was equivalent to the Japanese Navy's table of aircraft models and their performance standards, and of great value. It revealed the performance of U.S. Navy aircraft in trial production and the performance requirements for future trial production. This information was an extremely useful reference in establishing performance standards for aircraft in Japan. Lieutenant Colonel Takahashi of the Third Section (in charge of warships, aircraft, and mobilization) of the NCCom observed (NAFHistory, 1969, [1], pp. 407–8): "In the Japanese Navy, trial production took about four years for a fuselage and six years for an engine. The table revealed that the performance of existing U.S. aircraft was roughly equivalent to that of aircraft in trial production in Japan, implying that state-of-the-art in technology in Japan lagged four years behind the U.S. in fuselage design and six years in engine design." (This difference diminished, he believed.)

aircraft manufacturing, but also in industries and subcontractors manufacturing industrial materials, machine tools, electronics, and components. Japan had to work around the facts already on the ground: not only the weapons in use, but also bulldozers used to build airfields and transportation technology. The evaluation of plans and policies must take into consideration such constraints.

7-6-3. An Alternative Hypothesis

An entirely different view, or alternative hypothesis, can easily be reached by considering the preceding questions and the following factors:

1. How the Basic National Defense Policy and rearmament policies were actually developed, how Japan carried out operations and developed, produced and deployed weapons
2. Domestic conditions, including the political climate in Japan
3. Domestic conditions in countries assumed to be belligerent, and their impact on strategic choices
4. International events and the reactions of neighboring nations
5. Unplanned and unexpected developments, including rapid progress in weapons-related technology

A wide variety of conclusions, including the following alternative hypothesis, can be reached. There are no clear and adequate criteria for determining the most plausible view.

An Alternative Hypothesis: Japanese leaders did not expect the War with China and the Army and Navy did not welcome it. Similarly, no one in Japan's military or civilian leadership either expected or welcomed the war's rapid escalation and tremendous lengthening. The Air Forces, particularly the NAF, were most adaptable to unexpected developments in war. The Navy had built up a fleet of large-scale battleships with big cannons, on the assumption that there might be a short war against the United States, resolved in a one-game match by fleets of ships. In addition, some Navy leaders noticed the increasing importance and potential of air weapons; in 1930, the Navy began to manufacture its own aircraft. By chance, the War with China began just as this policy began to produce results. In October 1931, Air Headquarters appointed a new Head who favored developing flying-boat and large-scale land-based aircraft to support the Navy's ships and carrier-based aircraft. This led to the development of the Type 96 land-based attack aircraft.[44] Fortunately, the

---

[44] In October 1931, Shigeru Matsuyama became the Head of Air Headquarters, beginning the development of medium-sized land-based attack aircraft. He ordered Technical Division Chief Isoroku Yamamoto to start immediately the design and trial production

Navy also succeeded in developing a long-range escort fighter indispensable for its effective use.[45] Japan's greatest piece of good luck was that, with the escalation of tensions in Europe and the outbreak and escalation of World War II, the Chinese military failed to build international support, or to improve the quality and quantity of its forces.

The hypothesis that Japan's war proceeded smoothly as planned merely highlights a progression of accidental and lucky events. It is a *trompe l'oeil* constructed through hindsight. Already in the autumn of 1939, Vice-ACCommander Sawada and Army Minister Hata shared the view that Japan was like a rotten fruit at the core, with policies that would not last long. They thought that Japan had no idea how to end the War with China by force and believed that a decisive war against the Chongqing government was impossible, unless it became part of a larger global conflict (Boeicho, 1967a, p. 624). The war developed as they had expected and the Pacific War began in December 1941.

In the following chapters, I explain why the alternative hypothesis is more persuasive than the first hypothesis.

Tracing the progress of the war from its start through rapid escalation reveals deficiencies and problems with preparation, mobilization, and economic control. Problems became obvious and vigorous countermeasures were taken. The Pacific War was fought on a much larger scale than the War with China, and weapons were more advanced. However, by the time it began, Japan had had four years to recognize and take measures to correct deficiencies and problems due to insufficient preparation and unexpected events. In the sections that follow, I focus on the Pacific War, when many serious and intractable problems were carried over from the War with China.

The relative inadequacy of the Army's air weapons suggests that the alternative hypothesis applies more strongly to the Army than to the NAF.

---

of aircraft of this sort; Yamamoto ordered Misao Wada, Chief of Staff of the Technical Division, to begin research (NAFHistory, 1969, [1], p. 241).

[45] The ongoing debate about evaluations assumes that medium-sized land-based attack aircraft were successful in carrying out large-scale and continual long-range bombing on Chongqing and Chengdu. Important doubts exist about this assumption. NAFHistory (1969, [1], pp. 231–2) wrote: "The primary objective of land-based air forces was to ensure air supremacy by wiping out the enemy's air forces, and to block off supplies to the enemy and ruin its will to fight by bombing key areas and traffic routes. Although it achieved a great success in ensuring air supremacy by destroying the enemy's air forces, strategic bombing also increased hostility and the will to fight." As a member of the U.S. Strategic Bombing Survey commented: "The bombing conducted by the Japanese NAF during the War with China tactically achieved a tremendous outcome. Strategically, however, it was disastrous. There have been few operations so stupid in all of history."

The Navy Air Force during the War with China

8-1. Overview

In Chapters 8 and 9, I study the Navy Air Force (NAF), focusing on its preparations for – and performance in – the war. I divide the period of wartime into three phases and describe the activities of the NAF and its air weapons in detail. In Chapter 8, I focus on the first two phases of the War with China: the first extending from the first air attack to the capture of Nanjing (section 8-2) and the second covering the period after the capture of Nanjing (section 8-3). Chapter 9 focuses on the third phase, from the start of the Pacific War (section 9-3). Later sections discuss the performance of the NAF and the causes of its failure on various fronts, including aircraft development and production expansion.

Battlefield observers during the War with China generally evaluated Japan's competence highly. This view, that everything proceeded smoothly for Japan until the start of the Pacific War, underpins the conventional wisdom. Because Japan's superior fighters and attack aircraft were one step or one generation ahead of China's, the Japanese NAF maintained air supremacy over the continent. However, it is risky to conclude from such observations that the Japanese state was highly competent.

8-1-1. Two Additional Basic Facts

It is important to review two facts about the preparations and performance of the NAF, remembering (a) that Japanese leaders did not expect the War with China, (b) that the war began just after the Army and Navy had begun armament enhancement plans, and (c) that the NAF had just begun to deploy the epoch-making new aircraft models (such as the Type 96 carrier-based fighter and land-based attack aircraft) that were the fruits of its independence policy.

1. *The Navy Expected a One-Game Match Against the United States*

The Army and Navy prepared for future wars in accordance with basic government policies such as the BNDP and national defense plans. As previously discussed, the Navy expected to fight the United States in a one-game match between fleets of ships in the western Pacific, and prepared its air weapons accordingly. Needless to say, as the War with China was fought primarily on the continent, the Navy's weapons were inappropriate. There were also too few of them, due to a shortage of materials. This mismatch constrained operations and affected the morale of soldiers. The NAFHistory (1969, [4], pp. 750–1) explains[1]: "The Navy leaders were reluctant to lose in China air forces that had been prepared to fight a one-game match in the Pacific Ocean. Soldiers who had trained for the great sea battle did not want to lose their lives on the continent, and some became passively resistant."

---

[1] Throughout the War with China, the BNDP maintained its basic policy that the Navy's role was to prepare for a war against the United States that would be a one-game match between fleets of ships. In December 1937, after Japan abandoned its initial nonescalation policy, the war was developing around Nanjing in particular. It was extremely hard to judge the situation accurately, and the NCCom could not formulate an operation plan for FY1938, despite being under pressure to make preparations. At the beginning of December 1937, the NCCom was developing its FY1938 plan for operations (approved by the Emperor on 9 December), along the same lines as its FY1937 plan. Relations with the United States, the USSR, and the UK were expected to stay the same, while the operation in China would be modified when necessary and feasible. The ACCom obtained the approval of the Emperor for its operation in China and also for the FY1938 Imperial Army Operation Plan Outline, through which the ACCom and Kwantung, Korean, and Taiwanese armies started to prepare for the FY1938 operation plan.

When the spread of the war became apparent, negotiations began between the relevant administrative authorities from the ACCom (represented by Captain Kumao Imoto of the Strategy Division) and NCCom (represented by First Section Chief Lieutenant Colonel Chikao Yamamoto). (The latter is cited in this book as Yamamoto [1982], chief editor of the NAFHistory [1969, (1)~(40), and the former as Imoto [1978, 1979].) The FY1938 Imperial Navy Operation Plan was approved on 6 September 1937. "It initially defined the operational objective of the Imperial Navy as both conquering the Yangtze River and coastal area of China and commanding the sea surface in the East by destroying U.S. fleets and activity bases, and annihilating the main U.S. force in the East." The following understandings between administrative authorities from the ACCom and NCCom concern operations toward the United States: (1) The Army has primary responsibility for operations in China, basically along present guidelines. (2) The Navy devotes itself exclusively to U.S. operations but also blockades the Chinese coast and captures the Yangtze River area. (3) Naval marine landing forces retreat from Tsingtao, Shanghai, Amoi (Xiamen), and so on, and Army troops take over. (4) The Navy Air Force retreats from Central China and the Tsingtao area. "The role of the Imperial Japanese Navy's Third Fleet is to conquer the area downstream from Hankou on the Yangtze River and the coast, and collaborate with the Army to capture key areas in South China, including Fuzhou and Shantou. All other Navy troops are engaged in all-out operations against the United States" (Boeicho, 1975d, pp. 369–75). The Third Fleet was in charge of security in China.

In response to complaints that too few attacks were made by medium-sized attack aircraft early on in the War with China, Tomozo Kikuchi, Chief of Staff of the First Combined Air Corps, acknowledged: "We could not use too much force, because we had few soldiers, much attrition, and a poor supply capacity. We had to prioritize crew maintenance."[2]

2. Defects and Problems Are Conditioned by the War Situation

The extent of defects and problems (inadequate preparations, shortages, and mismatching) depends on the belligerent nations and the war situation. The NAFHistory (1969, [1], p. 235] comments: "The Chinese Navy was virtually nonexistent, and its Air Force was significantly inferior to ours, both in quality and quantity. Our forces had no strategic difficulty in any offensive operations on the coast, from North China to Central and South China. In transoceanic operations against the U.S. in the Philippines, the Japanese military understandably faced a powerful counteroffensive. For this reason, it was necessary from the start of the war to secure air supremacy over the Army embarkation point and transport convoy."

Depending on context, even an unexpected war situation can be resolved through flexible response and renovated equipment.

8-1-2. Before the Start of Battle

On 11 July 1937, the Japanese government deferred a decision to dispatch troops to North China, recognizing that such a move could escalate war to the whole country. Instead, Navy leaders decided to conduct rapid-response preparations and to decide operation policies. Their main objective was to protect the interests of Japan and its people. The Third Fleet was separately dispatched to guard key areas and the Naval ships in Magong and Ryojun; the Navy also prepared for future emergencies by organizing four special landing force units, as well as special air units; the latter included the First and Second Combined Air Corps (1st and 2nd CAC).

The 1st CAC was composed of the Kisarazu Air Squadron (two units of Type 96 land-based attack aircraft with twenty-four planes) and the Kanoya Air Squadron (1.5 units of Type 96 land-based attack aircraft with eighteen planes, and one unit of Type 95 carrier-based fighters with twelve planes).

---

[2] NAFHistory (1969, [4], p. 271). In later years, a medium-sized attack aircraft unit in operation consisted of twenty-seven to thirty-six airplanes and nine at night. During the War with China, however, air units were extremely small, usually three to six planes (NAFHistory, 1969, [4], p. 269).

The former advanced to Jeju, and the latter to Taipei. The 2nd CAC was reserved for the worsening situation in Tsingtao, and advanced on standby to Zhoushuizi in the Dalian suburb. It was composed of the Twelfth Air Squadron (six Type 95 carrier-based fighters, six Type 90 carrier-based fighters, twelve Type 94 carrier-based bombers, and twelve Type 92 carrier-based attack aircraft) and the Thirteenth Air Squadron (six Type 96 carrier-based fighters, six Type 90 carrier-based fighters, eighteen Type 96 carrier-based bombers, twelve Type 92 carrier-based attack aircraft, and one transport aircraft). Many aircraft were not advanced carrier-based fighters. Few of the most advanced carrier-based fighters and land-based attack aircraft were ready to deploy.[3]

The Navy also dispatched to Central and South China the First Carrier Division[4] (twenty-one carrier-based fighters, twelve carrier-based bombers, and nine carrier-based attack aircraft) and the Second Carrier Division (twelve carrier-based fighters, twelve carrier-based bombers, and eighteen carrier-based attack aircraft). Part of the 1st CAC in Jeju was sent to air stations in Shanghai, as were some of the air squadrons in the First and Second Carrier Divisions. The operation would begin with a collective surprise attack by air raiders, the First and Second Carrier Divisions on Hangzhou and the 1st CAC on Nanchang and Nanjing, with the 2nd CAC targeting North China. (NAFHistory, 1969, [4], pp. 148–51).

From mid-July, with hostility toward Japan intensifying in Shanghai, the risk of a collision between China and Japan increased rapidly. Violating the cease-fire agreement in place since the First Shanghai Incident in 1932, since the end of the previous year the Chinese military had begun fortifying the demilitarized zone and dispatching armed forces. After the start of the Incident, the concentration of military force in the area around Shanghai became more apparent; on 6 August, the Japanese Consul General in Shanghai ordered Japanese residents to find shelter in the concession. On the same day, learning that the Supreme War Council in Nanjing had declared an all-out war against Japan, upon the request of the Navy the Japanese government ordered Japanese residents in the Yangtze River area to withdraw to Shanghai. Japanese residents in South China began to withdraw on 12 August (NAFHistory, 1969, [4], p. 156).

---

[3] At the start of operations, Kisarazu Air Squadron possessed only twenty planes, fewer than the regulation twenty-four. The Kanoya Air Squadron had no machines for subsidiary use either. For more information, see NAFHistory (1969, [4], pp. 146–7) and Boeicho (1974, pp. 335–40).

[4] An air carrier unit of the Imperial Japanese Navy's First Air Fleet.

On 9 August, Lieutenant Ohyama was murdered; the next day, two units of the special landing forces waiting in Sasebo were ordered to advance. They arrived and landed at Shanghai on 11 August. On 12 August, the Commander-in-Chief of the Third Fleet reported a crisis situation around Shanghai and again offered to send Army troops. Meeting on 13 August, the Cabinet decided to send two divisions to Shanghai as planned. (NAFHistory, 1969, [4], pp. 156–7) At midnight on 12 August, the NCCom issued an order: the Commander-in-Chief of the Third Fleet, when attacked by the enemy, must protect Japanese residents in Shanghai and destroy the enemy's air forces. When the battle began, before 5 P.M. on 13 August, the Japanese had four thousand landing forces, including reinforcements, while the Chinese had about thirty thousand (NAFHistory, 1969, [4], p. 164).

Japan's first day of mobilization was 16 August. Some forces were scheduled to arrive at Shanghai on 21 or 22 August, but the main force would arrive between 28 August and 7 September.[5] In the meantime, a fierce battle began.

8-1-3. The Start of a Battle

At 11:30 P.M. on 13 August, in accordance with a plan to attack the enemy's air forces preemptively (Boeicho, 1974, p. 339), the Third Fleet ordered its air raiders to prepare for attack on the 14 August.

This preemptive air raid was suspended; instead, Chinese aircraft arrived. On the 14 August, the weather in Shanghai was bad. Clouds were hanging low in the sky, and the wind was blowing 20 meters per second and worsening. There was no chance of the first air raiders (the First Carrier Division) reaching their target. The second air raiders (the Second Carrier Division) could not take off or land. Transoceanic bombing by the third air raiders (the 1st CAC) waiting at Ohmura in Kyushu was considered impossible. At 5:30 A.M. on 14 August, despite the urgent situation, the Third Fleet Commander-in-Chief postponed the air attacks until the weather improved.[6]

---

5   Boeicho (1974, p. 317). In accordance with a previous agreement between the NCCom and ACCom, the Cabinet decided to send one division to Tsingtao (Boeicho, 1974, p. 317). On 23 August, the Army, Navy, and Foreign ministers reached an agreement: we have already sent troops to North China and Shanghai; it is not practical to send additional troops to Tsingtao. We should temporarily stop guarding residents on site in Tsingtao. On the following day, the Cabinet agreed not to guard residents in Tsingtao. The 2nd CAC was to be shifted, when the Shanghai air stations were ready, to the Third Fleet Commander-in-Chief's command (Boeicho, 1974, pp. 383–8). For details, see Imoto (1978. pp. 179–82).

6   See Boeicho (1974, p. 340); NAFHistory (1969, [4], p. 166).

At 12:15 A.M. on 13 August, a twin-engine monoplane bomber of the Chinese Air Force arrived over the concession and demonstrated for 30 minutes. On 14 August at 10:50 A.M., three Chinese fighters and a bomber launched an air attack on the Headquarters of the Japanese landing forces in Shanghai. At 10:55, five bombers struck the Eighth Squadron off Wusong, and at 11:22, three bombers struck Izumo, the flagship of the Third Fleet (with no dead shot).

Commander-in-Chief Hasegawa issued orders to completely destroy the enemy's air stations near Shanghai without waiting for the weather to improve. On 14 August, only carrier-based aircraft loaded on the Izumo, the Eighth Squadron, and the First Torpedo Squadron were available to carry out the attack. Carrier-based aircraft guarded warships, two aircraft each from the Izumo and Sendai (the flagship of the First Torpedo Squadron) struck Hongquiao Airport at 14:45, attacked the enemy's ground forces in the Zhabei District, and returned home (the Eighth Squadron could not use its aircraft because of high waves). Around 17:00, Japanese planes guarding Shanghai fought a battle with enemy aircraft and shot down two machines (Boeicho, 1974, p. 342).

The Kanoya Squadron of the third air raiders waiting at Taipei received the order to engage; at 14:50, eighteen aircraft left Taipei Airport, nine for Guangde and nine for Hangzhou. The weather was fine over the Taiwan Strait, but gradually worsened as they approached the continent, with cloud height at 500 meters. The planes were obliged to fly at low altitude in rain and clouds, and both units scattered into smaller units or a single plane. Two planes went missing before the attack and one, hit and with little fuel, fell into the Port of Keelung. Another was hit and had its wheels destroyed; it was very damaged on arrival. By 23:20, fifteen planes returned to Taipei Airport. The Second Carrier Division suspended attacks as high waves prevented takeoff, and the First Carrier Division was given no attack assignment (Boeicho, 1974, pp. 342–3).

The Third Fleet Commander-in-Chief decided to storm the enemy's airfields and completely destroy its air forces, in order to lead the ground troops in Shanghai to safety. At 19:00, he ordered an early dawn raid against the enemy's air forces, using all troops available. The main force would be medium-sized land-based attack aircraft units taking off from the Taipei and Kanoya Bases (Boeicho, 1974, p. 343).[7]

---

[7] On 15 August, from the second air raider (Second Carrier Division), sixteen Type 94 carrier-based bombers, thirteen Type 96 carrier-based attack aircraft, and sixteen Type 89 carrier-based attack aircraft took off at 5:30 A.M. from aircraft carrier Kaga in spite

On 15 August, due to fierce air defense gunfire from Nanjing and low-altitude bombing under bad weather, the Kisarazu Squadron was reduced by half: four planes were shot down by aircraft or ground fire, and six needed repairs. The epoch-making Type 96 land-based attack aircraft, which had generated controversy about the uselessness of fighters, were seriously damaged.[8]

8-1-4. Evaluation of the Three-Day Air Operations and Their Aftermath

Colonel Michitaro Totsuka, the 1st CAC Commander, confirmed that the offensive on 14–16 August inflicted heavy damage on the enemy, basically achieving the objective of completely destroying the enemy's air forces. In this offensive, the Kanoya Squadron lost five units of crew, including its Chief, and the Kisarazu four units. The number of aircraft still available for battle fell from eighteen to ten in the former and from twenty to eight in the latter (Boeicho, 1974, p. 347). The Navy had absolute confidence in its aircraft and crew. Understanding for the first time what air combat would really be like, it promoted the great value of fighters in particular (NAFHistory, 1969, [1], p. 232).[9]

---

of bad weather. In this attack, one bomber and two attack aircraft made a crash landing in Hangzhou Bay, and one bomber and six attack aircraft were lost. Thus the Second Carrier Division lost half of its force. At that time, Type 89 carrier-based attack aircraft were obsolete, and Type 96 carrier-based attack aircraft were being produced. Two factors contributed to the heavy damage: (1) the carrier-based attack aircraft on Kaga were not completely replaced by Type 96 attack aircraft; and (2) Japan lacked information to assess the true power of enemy aircraft and did not send fighters to escort its Type 89 attack aircraft (Boeicho, 1974, p. 345). The maximum speed of the Type 96 carrier-based attack aircraft was 150 knots, as compared with 123 knots for the Type 89. As for carrier-based fighters, the Type 96 Model 1 had a maximum speed of 219 knots, the Type 95 190 knots, and Type 90 158 knots (the Type 96 Model 4's speed was 235 knots). The Type 96 Model 11 medium-sized land-based attack aircraft had a maximum speed of 188 knots, and Model 21's speed was 201 knots (Boeicho, 1974, appendix table 2).

8   The speed of the Type 96 attack aircraft matched that of the Type 95 carrier-based fighter, a leading fighter at the start of the War with China. It was not easy for fighters with inadequate weapons to shoot down this attack aircraft. Japan overestimated its aircraft, although within the NAF many believed that the fighters were useless, a claim debated also in Europe and the United States. Fighters of the time were slow and had poor weapons. In addition, (1) they could not be used for escorting attack aircraft because of their short flight range, and (2) carrier-based attack aircraft were replacing fighters on board aircraft carriers. See NAFHistory (1969, [1], pp. 232, 287–93, and [4], pp. 262–5).

9   In concluding his detailed report about the day's combat, the 1st CAC Commander wrote: "The primary cause of the heavy damage in the offensive on 14–16 August was that we made an assault on military air bases under strict alert in bad weather. Judging it necessary

Boeicho (1974, p. 347) comments, "the damage was primarily because we pressed ahead with low-altitude daytime bombing in bad weather, and this caused the Navy to worry about the future of transoceanic bombing. The medium-sized attack aircraft squadron had been secretly prepared and trained as an offensive force for the interception operation against the U.S. A theory emerged among Navy leaders that Japan must be careful not to lose its 'nest eggs' in the operations against China.[10] ... After that, the Navy tried to minimize losses by prohibiting single operations, using defensive gunfire in formation, prohibiting ultra-low-altitude bombing, and avoiding enemy fighters through night bombing."

The landing forces in Shanghai faced a crisis. The size of the Chinese ground force was thirty thousand at the time of the first collision and seventy thousand by the 15 August. The size of the Japanese landing force was four thousand. Only the Navy air forces were available to help the landing forces and Japanese residents in Shanghai. For this reason, the air forces began to cooperate with ground operations. Some of the medium-sized attack aircraft continued the long-distance bombing that was possible only for them, and the carrier-based aircraft destroyed enemy air forces at the air stations around Shanghai. The rest of air forces cooperated with the ground forces (NAFHistory, 1969, [4], p. 206).[11]

After 23 August, the Army troops landed in Central China and the Navy air forces shifted the focus of their cooperation to the Army troops. With ground operations under way, carrier-based aircraft advanced to air stations around Shanghai, aiming once again to secure air supremacy over Shanghai and Nanjing. The cooperation with ground operations continued until 19 September, when the operation to capture Nanjing began (NAFHistory, 1969, [4], pp. 206, 210).

---

for the air raiders to attack, given the intimidating situation in Shanghai, we pressed ahead with this operation as if making an assault on the 203 Hill during the Russo–Japanese War" (NAFHistory, 1969, [4], p. 195). It was Navy policy to select the crew for a medium-sized attack aircraft from carrier-based fighter pilots with sufficient experience. For this reason, despite being new and rapidly expanding, the crew was a well-trained elite (NAFHistory, 1969, [4], p. 270).

[10] For more details, see NAFHistory (1969, [4], pp. 219–24).

[11] "The Chinese offensive on the morning of the 16 August was Japan's greatest crisis. On that day, the Chinese began an all-out assault at 1:00 A.M., and applied furious pressure to Japanese positions in the northern district. For a while, our lines seemed broken through, but the troops defended their positions at all cost. After a fierce battle spanning several hours, the Chinese military fell back at last, abandoning the aim of breaking through the Japanese positions" (NAFHistory, 1969, [4], p. 199).

8–1–5. Carrier-Based Aircraft Squadrons

After August, Japan's carrier-based aircraft squadrons engaged in operations to destroy enemy air forces. Carrier- and sea-based aircraft squadrons were struggling to assist the Navy and Army landing forces and ensuring air alertness over Shanghai; they were able to make only three attacks on air stations around Shanghai. Meanwhile, medium-sized land-based attack aircraft squadrons that had already been badly damaged engaged in the task of destroying the Chinese air forces. From 20 August, they flew to Hankou and Nanchang to destroy Chinese staging bases. When the first battles were over, more effective operations were established. At the beginning of September, the area of operations extended to South China (NAFHistory, 1969, [4], p. 216).

At 11:00 A.M. on 14 August, the Chinese air forces staged an attack using forty aircraft, while Japanese military had only five carrier-loaded sea-based aircraft in the Shanghai area – on the Izumo, the Eighth Squadron (Yura, Kinu, and Natori) and the Sendai. The Third Fleet deployed these five aircraft in both a ground attack and flying alert. Because of high waves, the aircraft on the Eighth Squadron off Wusong could not take off, and two aircraft on the Izumo and Sendai in Shanghai played a role (NAFHistory, 1969, [4], p. 208).[12]

The First and Second Carrier Divisions began cooperation with ground troops on 16 and 17 August. Together with all the sea-based aircraft on Shin'i, the Twenty-Second Air Squadron, Eighth Squadron, Izumo, and Sendai, they cooperated with the landing forces in Shanghai. Obtaining information that the Kuomintang (Chinese Nationalist Party) government was planning to destroy Japanese landing forces before Army troops arrived, Japan's planes attacked major railways and railroad bridges around Shanghai to block the enemy's reinforcements and supplies.

They also cooperated with the Army's advance team in a landing operation that began on 23 August. When the landing troops faced unexpected difficulties, the air forces fully supported them. With their support, the landing troops recovered from crisis, gradually advanced, and expanded the war fronts; at last, on 13 September, the Chinese military began to withdraw (NAFHistory, 1969, [4], pp. 209–10).[13]

[12] Only the Japanese Navy ever deployed sea-based scout aircraft in a flying alert. In this case, floatplanes with pontoons engaged in aerial combat with fighters and shot down two. This battle pioneered aerial combat against the Chinese military (NAFHistory, 1969, [4], p. 208).

[13] When the Cabinet on 13 August decided to send two Army divisions to Shanghai, the Army Minister accepted the decision with two reservations. First, the geography of the

From 15 August, the Chinese air forces attacked the Japanese warships, headquarters, landing forces, and concession every day, using more than ten fighters and bombers, but these caused little serious damage. From 20 August, Japan's air carrier battle groups began to patrol battlefields and to attack enemy airfields. Chinese Air Force reinforcements decreased radically after August. By the middle of September, the Japanese military had complete air supremacy over Shanghai (NAFHistory, 1969, [4], p. 221).

8-1-6. The Push for Air Superiority over Nanjing

The Chinese Air Force had countless airfields within easy reach of Shanghai that could be used for a wide variety of operations. Japanese air operations aimed to destroy the Chinese air forces based on airfields around Shanghai. The Japanese air forces had neither an onshore airfield for operations nor any available capacity to devote to it. Until late August, therefore, this operation was not implemented. In late August, most Chinese air forces, except for those remaining in Nanjing, retreated to inland China, and henceforth it was extremely rare to see Chinese aircraft on airfields around Shanghai (NAFHistory, 1969, [4], pp. 229–30).[14]

The 2nd CAC retreated from Zhoushuizi to Ohmura, and then received an order to advance to Shanghai by the end of August. The unit set off when Gongda Airport in Shanghai became usable and arrived on 10 September. At that time, Japan had air supremacy over Shanghai. The Japanese air forces had attacked a variety of Chinese airfields in the area. Nanjing, then the Chinese capital with several airfields and strong defensive positions, held approximately fifty fighters as well as powerful anti-aircraft guns, remaining a major base for the Chinese military. For this reason, Japan's assault by medium-sized attack aircraft without escort fighters suffered a heavy loss. It was urgent for the 2nd CAC to destroy the Chinese air forces in Nanjing and increase air supremacy, allowing it to extend its air attack to Nanjing (NAFHistory, 1969, [4], p. 233).

On 14 September, the Third Fleet Commander-in-Chief issued an order to attack Nanjing on 16 September, focusing on the enemy's air forces gathered there, military facilities, and major government buildings. Led by the

---

Shanghai area would make it difficult to implement operations as planned. Second, the Chinese military had improved more than expected; the odds were against the Japanese (NAFHistory, 1969, [4], p. 157).

[14] There were sporadic night attacks by Chinese aircraft in the Shanghai area (NAFHistory, 1969, [4], p. 230).

commander of the 2nd CAC, with sixteen Type 96 carrier-based fighters as its core force, the operation involved confronting the enemy's air forces and bombing various military, political, and economic institutions. There was no precedent for an offensive operation led by fighters with escorts from carrier-based aircraft and seaplanes. On 15 September, the Second Carrier Division air squadron also advanced to Gongda Airport in Shanghai (NAFHistory, 1969, [4], pp. 210, 233–5).

Forty Chinese fighters aggressively intercepted the first air attack on 19 September, and most were destroyed by the Type 96 carrier-based fighters and the Type 95 reconnaissance seaplanes. The second attack involved markedly fewer Chinese fighters, and from the seventh attack, on 22 September, no Chinese aircraft could be seen in the air over Nanjing. With air supremacy over the Shanghai-Nanjing area, the Japanese air forces could proceed with their next operations. They adopted a formation: within the area in which fighter squadrons could escort bombers (200 nautical miles from the fighters' or advance supply base), bombers acted under fighter escort, achieving an effective coalition. Beyond this escort area, bombers conducted nighttime attacks (NAFHistory, 1969, [4], p. 239).

Recognizing its political and strategic importance, the 1st CAC began attacks on Nanjing on 19 August. To prevent the loss of precious aircraft, it was obliged to bomb inaccurately from a very high altitude, escaping China's powerful anti-aircraft weapons at night or in the dim light of dawn. Japan set up widely scattered bombing-free zones for the many diplomatic missions of third countries. On 27 August, Japan ended the attacks on Nanjing by medium-sized attack aircraft and waited for the ground airfield to be finished and the carrier-based aircraft squadrons to arrive (NAFHistory, 1969, [4], pp. 241–2).

When the 2nd CAC arrived, attacks on military and political institutions in Nanjing restarted. The attacks were small-scale and at first there was little sign of the expected political response. Then on 20 November, as Japanese ground operations advanced, the Nanjing government announced that the capital was moving (NAFHistory, 1969, [4], p. 242).

8-1-7. The Type 96 Carrier-Based Fighter

Conditions were eventful for the Japanese military between the battle in Shanghai on 14 August and the issuance of air-raid orders in Nanjing on 14 September. Focusing on the Type 96 carrier-based fighters, it is clear that the realities of deployment and the use of Navy air weapons restricted the Japanese military's operations and battles during this period.

The Type 96 carrier-based fighter was designed to have the highest possible levels of performance, without needing the specific features of a carrier-based aircraft. At the start, it was thought to be unsuitable for aircraft carriers. With successive improvements, however, by the beginning of 1937 it was possible to load the Type 96 onto an aircraft carrier. Japan still did not have enough world-class aircraft. When the War with China began, there were six Type 96 fighters in the Thirteenth Air Squadron and several in the Ohmura Air Squadron. The Second Carrier Division had conducted landing training with Type 96 fighters in Ohmura and was satisfied with their performance. As the older Type 90 carrier-based fighters were inferior to Chinese fighters, the Navy demanded that they be replaced with Type 96 fighters.

As an emergency supply, aircraft with crew were transported by air from Ohmura Air Squadron directly to the mothership, Kaga. The Type 96 fighters participated in an actual fight for the first time on 22 August, escorting planes cooperatively with ground operations around Shanghai. Next, the inferior Type 89 planes were replaced with Type 96 carrier-based attack aircraft on Kaga. Of the Type 96 planes, there were five fighters and eighteen attack aircraft on 22 August, nine fighters and twenty attack aircraft on 25 August, eleven fighters and twenty attack aircraft on 5 September, and eleven fighters and twenty-three attack aircraft on 25 September.

The 2nd CAC also acquired Type 96 fighters before its redeployment to Shanghai. Overall, eighteen Type 96 fighters took part in the operation for air superiority over Nanjing, twelve from the Thirteenth Air Squadron and six from Kaga (NAFHistory, 1969, [4], p. 283).

On 15 August, the Second Carrier Division took off from Kaga for attacking Najing with thirteen Type 96 carrier-based attack aircraft, Suzhou with sixteen carrier-based bombers, and Guangde with sixteen Type 89 carrier-based attack aircraft. Unable to identify their first targets in the bad weather, the bombers attacked two other airfields and Type 89 attack aircraft on another airfield, where they fought many Chinese fighters. The Type 89 attack aircraft were already obsolete; although they shot down five enemy fighters, eight (half the force) were lost.

No escort fighters were provided, even to the vulnerable Type 89 attack aircraft, because of the bad weather. Fighter units would be scattered over enemy territory, and without navigation, the escorts would not make it home. In addition, the flight range of the Type 90 carrier-based fighters was too short even to reach Shanghai, so they could not escort attack aircraft to their first objective.

On Kaga, escorts were never discussed, mainly because fighter units on aircraft carriers still had as their primary role ensuring air supremacy over the sea surface, driving out enemy spotter planes, and escorting Japan's spotter planes. In 1937, when the War with China began, the aviation-related Research Meeting on the flagship Mutsu openly discussed reducing the number of fighters on aircraft carriers because they were "useless." The idea that fighters could escort attack aircraft was rarely raised (NAFHistory, 1969, [4], p. 266).

After this battle, fighters began to escort attack aircraft. The Second Carrier Division had only one aircraft carrier, Kaga, with only a few fighters to ensure air alertness. There weren't enough to escort every attack plane, so they focused on the vulnerable Type 89 aircraft. The Kaga fighters range of use was limited to cooperation with ground operations around Shanghai. After 22 August, the new Type 96 fighters provided air alertness over Shanghai, giving an indirect escort to the Type 89 attack aircraft.

On 10 September, the 2nd CAC arrived at Gongda Airport (hastily developed on the site of a golf course) in Shanghai. The runway was soft and unfinished, and it could barely be used for takeoff and landing. The runway became a muddy swamp either with shellfire from the unoccupied Pudong district (there was no direct damage to aircraft) or rain. In the first ten days, eleven precious Type 96 fighters either damaged their landing gear or were destroyed by rollover (NAFHistory, 1969, [4], p. 233).

The operation for air supremacy over Nanjing began on 19 September. The 2nd CAC's statement on Army-Navy cooperation in Shanghai and Nanjing explained (NAFHistory, 1969, [4], p. 439): "A month after the start of war with China, we transferred some aircraft units to an airport in Shanghai. We spent ten days improving the airport and ten days ensuring air supremacy over Nanjing. Fifty days after war began, we could finally cooperate fully with our ground operations. If we had been able to use onshore airfields much earlier, we could have circumvented to some extent the deadlocked operations in this area."

At the beginning of the War with China, within the NAF, fighters were not highly valued and their role was undefined. In total, there were not many Type 96 fighters and even fewer were deployed around Shanghai when the battle began. At first, having no onshore airfield near Shanghai, the Japanese military had no choice but to rely on planes loaded on aircraft carriers and seaplanes. The Third Fleet suspended its planned preemptive air attack on 14 August and was attacked by Chinese aircraft. Later, the operation to destroy enemy airfields around Shanghai was a limited success, achieved at great cost. To help residents and the landing forces in Shanghai, the priority of the moment, the air force began to cooperate with ground operations, while medium-sized attack aircraft units, at great cost to themselves, maintained long-range bombing. The Army landing operation also faced serious challenges on 19 September, when the operation for ensuring air supremacy over Nanjing started, after Type 96 fighters advanced to Gongda Airport at a heavy cost.

Only eighteen Type 96 carrier-based fighters were available when the operation for air superiority over Nanjing began; twelve of these belonged to the 2nd CAC at Tsingtao. During the first ten days at Gongda Airport, eleven Type 96 fighters were lost.

8-1-8. Cooperation with Landing Operations in Shanghai, Landing in Hangzhou Bay and Capturing Nanjing

After the operation for air superiority over Nanjing, military units returned to cooperate with ground operations in Shanghai. In early October, battle lines in the Shanghai area were unmoving, apart from troops who had landed on Chuansha making slight progress at the front. When Navy air forces launched an aerial bombardment on 4 October, the Army made significant progress. However, there was bad weather for the next few days, and the air force units could not operate. The Chinese military built up its antiaircraft defenses, greatly diminishing the impact of Japan's renewed bombing. Again the battle lines were fixed. In late October, the Chinese Army began to retreat. On 24 October, the Japanese military captured Dachans-town, reaching the Suzhou River on 27 October. Meanwhile, the 2nd CAC continued to cooperate with ground operations (NAFHistory, 1969, [4], p. 320).

In early November, before the Japanese Tenth Army landed in Hangzhou Bay, an agreement was reached between Army-Navy Headquarters and the Navy's 2nd CAC that the Navy would be primarily responsible for destroying enemy air forces in Central China, escorting the Army's transport convoy on the sea and supporting and cooperating with Army troops after landing. On 5 November, the Tenth Army landed on the north shore of Hangzhou Bay; by 9 November, the Chinese Army around Shanghai was in full retreat. In Hangzhou, the Chinese Army began its retreat on 11 November. On 13 December, the Japanese military captured Nanjing (NAFHistory, 1969, [4], pp. 321–5).

8–2. Review of Air Operations During the Initial Stage
of the War with China

8–2–1. Operations

The NAFHistory (1969, [4], pp. 258–87) reviewed air operations during the initial stage of the War with China, noting six points. First, on 12
August, the Third Fleet Commander-in-Chief received from the Imperial
Headquarters Navy Division (IH-ND) an order to destroy Chinese air forces;
on 14 August, the Chinese attacked the Third Fleet, which was not much
damaged by the preemptive attack (NAFHistory, 1969, [4], pp. 258–60).

Second, as in a gun battle between an onshore fortress and fleet of ships
in previous years, it was dangerous and an affront to common sense to
move aircraft carriers inside the attack zone of the Chinese air forces, even
to destroy enemy air forces and cooperate with ground operations. An aircraft carrier was at risk of sinking, and it was not the right sort of weapon to
counter an unsinkable onshore fortress. Given the assumption that aircraft
carriers would be needed for the one-game match against the United States,
it was not easy to send more than half the aircraft carriers available at the
time for operations on the continent.

Third, the perceived value of fighters was at its lowest point, and this had
a real impact, even within the NAF.

The fourth point concerns the use of medium-sized attack aircraft.
Their value was so high that, by comparison, it further diminished the
perceived value of fighters. The impact of a heavy shell on a warship was
different from an attack on an unsinkable onshore objective. On the sea,
pinpoint bombing by bombers in small units was more effective than those
in a big formation, for which the Navy crew had high skills. Airfields and
other onshore objectives had no fatal points and could not be completely
annihilated by the right shot. They typically presented a wide surface that
could be destroyed only by a collective attack. The review emphasized the
political and strategic importance of the attack on Nanjing, and argued
that it was time to absolutely prioritize destroying the enemy's air forces.

Fifth, it criticized the Navy for using sea-based scout aircraft to fly alerts
over Shanghai and to shoot down fighters and bombers. The Navy was also
criticized for using carrier-based aircraft units as escorts and for using seaplanes to assist ground battles in Shanghai.

The sixth point concerned six Type 95 land-based attack aircraft belonging to the Kisarazu Air Squadron. Judged unsuitable for warfare, they were
used as training aircraft and excluded from participating in the War with

China. In September, however, these planes were sent to Jeju and used in bombings. When the Shanghai and Nanjin ground operations were finished, it was thought wasteful to man these planes, and they disappeared from the battlefield, replaced by medium-sized attack aircraft. The shortage of medium-sized attack aircraft was so severe that training machines were mobilized. There was an equally severe shortage of crew members for medium-sized attack aircraft.

8-2-2. Armament and Weapons

The NAFHistory (1969, [4], p. 277) notes the lack of onshore reconnaissance aircraft: "The NAF lacked reconnaissance weapons, with which it could scout at high altitudes secretly, or force its way at high speed through the warning net of enemy fighters. There were successful examples of hit-and-run scouts who took an enemy by surprise, but they were exceptional and did not always succeed. The Navy had no direct way to study the condition of the enemy." It could not assess enemy strength when attacking, or cooperate with attack units by scouting out the enemy in advance.

The 8-shi land-based reconnaissance aircraft was converted into the Type 96 land-based attack aircraft. After conversion, no trial production for developing land-based reconnaissance aircraft was launched because the Navy recognized that the Type 96 attack aircraft was good enough to use as a reconnaissance aircraft. Three years later in the War with China, there was a lack of reconnaissance capacity. An emergency measure was adopted, but land-based reconnaissance aircraft could not be developed in time. During the Pacific War, when the combat between land-based aircraft became fierce around the Solomon Islands, the Type 2 land-based reconnaissance aircraft (JIN1-C) was produced but did not perform remarkably well. It was a blind spot of the Japanese NAF that it lacked interest in and understanding of reconnaissance.[15]

---

[15] The military use of aircraft began with search and reconnaissance. The Navy, when establishing its Air Force, primarily focused on the development of seaplanes. When it began to use land-based and carrier-based aircraft, initially it used seaplanes and flying-boats for reconnaissance. The Type 10 reconnaissance aircraft was completed in 1923, and the Type 97 was produced experimentally; neither were used on aircraft carriers. The Navy's policy was to use attack aircraft also for reconnaissance. It failed to recognize the need for land-based reconnaissance aircraft, which did not appear in an NCCom proposal until 1939, when lessons had been learned from the war. The Navy recognized this need during the War with China, but had no aircraft of this type; it therefore took over command center reconnaissance aircraft from the Army. No land-based reconnaissance aircraft

Another point concerned the preparation of bombs. Initially, medium-sized attack aircraft units had no onshore bomblets, and used 250 kilogram bombs even on airfields. However, in Nanjing on 24 August, they used 60 kilogram onshore bomblets. The war had begun unexpectedly, and some weapons and supplies were lacking.

8-2-3. Equipment

On the air raid of 14 August, the medium-sized attack aircraft's first fight in bad weather, the 1st CAC reported that the fighting capability of the aircraft was overwhelming. Each day's air raid could accomplish its mission, because of the reliability and scope of this aircraft and its superbly trained crew.

But the medium-sized attack aircraft had one egregious vulnerability: its fuel tank tended to catch fire. Navy leaders were aware of this problem and had conducted research into ways of addressing it. No solution had been proposed before the beginning of the War with China. As a result, the Type1 land-based attack aircraft was nicknamed "the One-Shot-Lighter" by the U.S. Air Force (NAFHistory, 1969, [4], pp. 280–1).[16]

were mentioned in the first proposed revision of 1940; they were reintroduced in 1943. Carrier-based reconnaissance aircraft appeared for the first time in 1943. Traditionally, the Navy had used carrier-based attack aircraft for reconnaissance, but war lessons learned in the Pacific War illustrated the need for land-based reconnaissance aircraft. The development of this reconnaissance aircraft, the Nakajima C6N Saiun (the name translates as "colored cloud") was delayed. A land-based reconnaissance aircraft, the Yokosuka R2Y Keiun ("beautiful cloud"), was not completed before the end of the war, largely because the Navy had traditionally emphasized spectacular offensives, such as aerial combat, aerial bombing, and torpedo bombing. During the war, the Japanese Navy suffered many losses because of its lack of special reconnaissance aircraft, both carrier- and land-based, (NAFHistory, 1969, [1], pp. 413–14).

[16] Kiro Honjo was Mitsubishi's Chief Designer of both the Type 96 and Type 1 land-based attack aircraft. Given the success of the Type 96 in the War with China, the Navy ordered the trial production of the Type 1 land-based attack aircraft exclusively instead of from Mitsubishi. Honjo (1982, pp. 55–8) recalled the first Navy–Mitsubishi preliminary meeting to discuss trial production. The success of the 8-shi and the Type 96 attack aircraft depended on the development and adoption of new technologies to improve performance, stability, and maneuverability. There had been no remarkable technological progress after the Type 96, so he had no choice but to soup up the engine, although little improvement was possible. The Navy's request was full of completely unreasonable demands, given the technological conditions of the time. Honjo thought there was an overemphasis on efficiency at the expense of strength and protection against enemy attacks; it needed to be more bulletproof, protected against fire and machine guns. It was possible to develop a fuselage that satisfied demands, but a small airframe with a long flight range called for fuel tanks everywhere on the body. The enemy would be sure to hit a fuel tank. A four-engine aircraft would require protection against bullets and fire, for both fuel tanks and crew. Following this explanation, he showed a four-engine aircraft plan he had prepared.

A second point concerned the Type 96 carrier-based fighter. In general, war capability equals the quantity of weapons multiplied by their quality, but a small difference in quality can make a very large difference in war capability. In the case of aircraft, this factor was particularly pronounced. In air combat between fighters (fighter versus fighter), the quality edge dominated. For this reason, great effort was put into quality improvement and advanced aircraft development (NAFHistory, 1969, [4], p. 281). The Type 96 carrier-based fighter, adopted as a weapon at the end of 1936, was of excellent quality and surpassed prior and existing fighters and the mainstay fighters of the Chinese Air Force. But the number of these aircraft manufactured and deployed was small. On 14 September, sixteen Type 96 fighters carried out the operation for air superiority over Nanjing. Despite that success, the situation did not improve.

The third issue concerned the lack of long-range fighters. When medium-sized attack aircraft units conducted ultra-low-altitude bombing in bad weather, they suffered heavy losses from anti-aircraft fire. By avoiding low-altitude bombing, these losses decreased, but many planes were still shot down by enemy fighters. Without an escort by fighter units, it was difficult to bomb an enemy's essential points; to destroy enemy air forces, it was necessary to destroy enemy fighters. The battle for air superiority over Nanjing demonstrated the essential role of fighters in destroying enemy air forces. Clearly perceiving the need for fighter-bomber combinations, the 2nd CAC argued that it was urgent to produce long-range fighters specialized in escorting air attack units (NIFHistory, 1969, [4], p. 284).

Learning its lesson, the Navy later built the Type Zero fighter out of a 12-shi carrier-based fighter already in development. It became available with the Zero fighter during the summer of 1940, three years after the beginning of the War with China.[17]

The fourth issue related to the large-caliber (heavy) machine gun. Traditionally, the Navy used 7.7 millimeter small-caliber machine guns

The Head of the Air Technical Arsenal, Misao Wada, was furious, declaring: "The military decides operational plans. Mitsubishi should just develop the twin engine attack aircraft it has been asked for. Forget this four-engine aircraft plan immediately." Honjo's most important proposal was rejected without deliberation; no one on the military side had the courage to defend it.

As the war situation deteriorated, Honjo's fears were realized. The military belatedly ordered Mitsubishi to make the plane more bulletproof, sacrificing fuel tank capacity; this had limited success. For more details, see Miwa (2008, 4–5–3, pp. 252–5).

[17] Taking these lessons on board, in 1938, the Navy began developing the 13-shi twin-engine fighter. It was not completed in time for operations on the continent, and had to be abandoned (NIFHistory, 1969, [4], pp. 284–5).

exclusively. Recognizing the power of medium-caliber machine guns in actual fighting, the Navy began to develop a 20 millimeter large-caliber machine gun, skipping the 13 millimeter medium-caliber machine gun. The 20 millimeter fixed machine gun was ready just in time to be used in the Type Zero fighter. Before the summer of 1940, there was no large-caliber machine gun in Japan.

8-3. Navy Air Forces and Air Weapons After Nanjing

Between the capture of Nanjing on 13 December 1937, the capture of Hankou on 26 October 1938, and the November operation to capture Guangdong and block enemy supply routes, the war expanded dramatically.[18] With the second Konoe Proclamation on 22 December 1938 opting to create a new order in East Asia, the Japanese government was committed to a long, drawn-out war. For three years after the fall of 1938, Japan conducted long-range mass bombing raids on inland China, focusing on Chongqing and Chengdu.

In this section on the second phase of the War with China, I focus on one uphill battle or difficulty in each phase of the air operations.

8-3-1. The Second Phase: Before the Capture of Hankou (October 1938)

Initially, the Navy was conservative and opposed sending troops from the homeland; once war had spread to Central China, the Navy did not hesitate to take draconian steps. Its role on the continent was limited to air, sea, and river operations. As the Army was conducting larger-scale operations during this period, the Navy tended to support Army requests (NAFHistory, 1969, [4], p. 298).

Japan's "operation to capture Wuhan" aimed to capture both Wuhan and Gangdong and to eliminate the Chiang government, ending the war in 1938. Around the time of the capture of Nanjing, Naval units on the river had built a water channel up to Wuhu. On 9 June, when the Chinese government ordered government institutions in Hankou to move inland (this move was suspended on 23 June), the Navy launched an up-the-river operation from Wuhu. On 11 June, the Japanese government notified third countries that it was beginning the operation to capture Hankou; it confronted

---

[18] For details of this process, see Miwa (2008, 3–6, pp. 185–92). For more on the operation to capture Guangdong, see Boeicho (1975a, pp. 54–65).

the enemy on Anqing on 12 June and captured Jiujiang on 26 July. On 27 October, it captured Hankou.[19]

After the operation to capture Anqing, Air Force units provided continuous support, scouting and helping to conquer enemy troops and positions, building a water channel, guarding Naval units on the river, and cooperating in ground operations. Sea-based aircraft units generally took charge of direct cooperation. While carrier-based aircraft bombed the enemy's positions on both sides of the river, land-based attack aircraft destroyed enemy air forces and bombed troop positions (NIFHistory, 1969, [4], p. 333).

The Uphill Battle of Fighter Units

Uphill battles of fighter units, particularly of a small number of the Type 96 carrier-based fighters, typified the air operations during the second stage. In collaboration with bombers, fighters struck Nanchang for the first time on 9 December 1937, using Guangde Airport as a staging base so that small fighter unit groups could conduct offensive operations within their flight-range limit. Indeed, the several months that followed were a period of hardship for the fighters (NIFHistory, 1969, [4], p. 434).

The majority Type 95 carrier-based fighters could not conduct offensive operations because of their quality and flight range; they were relegated to surveillance. Only the Type 96 fighters conducted offensive operations. When the War with China began, only a few Type 96 fighters were deployed to Air Force units in Yokosuka and Ohmura; there were none on aircraft carriers at the front. They were later allocated to the 2nd CAC. On 10 September, the 2nd CAC, including twelve Type 96 fighters, moved from Ohmura to Gongda Airport in Shanghai to carry out the operation for air superiority over Nanjing.

The Type 96 carrier-based fighters achieved remarkable results and were rarely lost in combat. However, losses due to muddy runways and a lack of airfield maintenance kept the 2nd CAC's fleet of Type 96 aircraft extremely small. There were never enough produced (NAFHistory, 1969, [4], p. 435).

The Fleet Headquarters in the Chinese quarter quickly destroyed the Chinese air forces in Nanchang-Hankou. Fighter units kept up an aggressive offensive, even with a small number of aircraft. In some cases, no enemy fighters were intercepted; when there was resistance, the number of enemy

---

[19] The operation was based on a guiding principle agreed to by the Five-Ministers Meetings (their final decision on was 8 July), following the Conference in the Presence of the Emperor on 15 June 1938. In accordance with the ancient tradition that "those who rule Wuhan rule China," the operation targeted the three boroughs of Wuhan, Hankou, and Hanyang as a strategic gateway to China and Guangdong (NIFHistory, 1969, [4], p. 299).

fighters was twice to four times that of the Japanese. Once the alarm was raised and transmitted to enemy bases, the Japanese air forces were intercepted by fighters flying at three levels: one group at 5,000 meters, another between 4,000 and 3,000 meters, and the third below 3,000 meters. Japan's forces were unable to escape (NIFHistory, 1969, [4], p. 436).

In this offensive operation, medium-sized attack aircraft led fighter units with no means of long-range navigation, and fighters escorted attack aircraft while also destroying enemy aircraft. A very small number of fighter units, fighting many more enemy fighters, shouldered the heavy burden of guarding attack aircraft. It was taboo for attack aircraft units to turn on a dime in enemy territory in order to maintain their air combat formation. Guarding these units was a heavy burden for fighter planes already fully engaged in air combat (NIFHistory, 1969, [4], pp. 436–7).

The fighter units were also assigned long-distance offensive operations, "caution in the air," and cooperation with ground operations. The airfields were poorly equipped, and many crew members suffered from heavy diarrhea. The fighter crews had a tired look; in offensive units, the commanding officers died one after another.

On 29 April 1938, thirty Type 96 carrier-based fighters bombed Hankou, at last improving the situation (NIFHistory, 1969, [4], p. 438).[20]

As the 2nd CAC report noted, the biggest difference was that, "ensuring perfect air supremacy, we took full advantage of our air forces. The same applied to the operations during this one year, in which the Type 96 fighters were central, although too few in number. Type 96 fighters shouldered too heavy a burden, and unexpected events such as delays in their deployment, must have caused confusion and necessitated serious changes to every operation."[21]

---

[20] The air combat in the sky over Hankou that day was fiercest of the war, and the greatest achievement of the Japanese Air Force. Learning that enemy aircraft were concentrated in Hankou, Japan sent eighteen medium-sized attack aircraft and twenty-seven carrier-based fighters to attack Hankou, destroying enemy air forces launching the reconstruction. With a dead shot, the Hanyang Military Arsenal was destroyed by fire. Japanese forces shot down fifty-one of seventy-eight intercepting fighters, losing only two attack aircraft and two fighters (Boeicho, 1975a, p. 68).

[21] According to the NAFHistory (1969, [1], p. 426), Japan's total achievement (destruction of enemy aircraft, including unconfirmed) and losses were as follows: until September 1937, the figures were 301 and 47, and from October 1937 to October 1938 1,112 and 64. After November 1937, the movement of Soviet aircraft became highly visible. In early 1938 (NIFHistory, 1969, [4], p. 375), there were three groups that formed the main force of the Chinese air forces; the most powerful had Soviet weapons and was directed by veterans of the Spanish Civil War. Chinese leaders confirmed that the Soviet aircraft and crew

8–3–2. The Third Stage: The Inland China Offensive and the Uphill Battle

The Uphill Battle of Medium-Sized Attack Aircraft Units

After the ground offensive was suspended in late 1938, there was no way to force the enemy into submission except by blocking transportation by land and sea and attacking the nation's capital, Chongqing. Having no alternative, the Navy carried out this operation as effectively as possible until just before the start of the Pacific War (NAFHistory, 1969, [4], p. 615).[22]

The attack on Chongqing demonstrated the uphill battle to medium-sized attack aircraft units: in FY1939, eighteen medium-sized attack aircraft were deployed to Central China and another eighteen to South China. This was hardly enough attack aircraft to force a country into submission. In the previous year, the 1st and the 2nd CACs had argued that a basic strategic unit needed twenty-seven to thirty-six machines,[23] but the deployment to Central China was reduced from thirty-six to eighteen. At that time, the Navy was rapidly expanding its attack aircraft units and needed space for crew training. In addition, it had to retain attack aircraft units for sea training (NIFHistory, 1969, [4], p. 616).[24]

---

were inferior to the Japanese; they were disappointed by the Soviet air forces in China. However, they had no alternative but to rely on the USSR to prepare and improve their aircraft and crew, and they planned to reconstruct the Chinese air forces through a mass import of Soviet aircraft. The Chinese had 350 to 450 aircraft and imported 70 to 80 aircraft per month. Imports from the USSR increased gradually until approximately half of China's aircraft were made in the USSR.

[22] In response to the question of whether it likely that bombing Chongqing would force the enemy into submission, and whether the Navy believed this, the NAFHistory (1969, [4], pp. 615–16) notes: "An official recollected that he had not been convinced that Japan could end the war by bombing Chongqing. In 1939, when the Japanese attacked Chongqing, no one had ever experienced a city bombing."

[23] See NAFHistory (1969, [4], pp. 427–8). This opinion was adopted by Navy Headquarters. On 26 June 1938, the Thirteenth Air Squadron and the Takao Air Squadron, full-time offensive units for the continental operation, decided to organize a unit with eighteen aircraft. Although the Takao Squadron remained a 0.5 unit with nine machines, the Thirteenth Squadron was reorganized into two units with thirty-six machines (NIFHistory, 1969, [4], p. 428).

[24] This was the third occasion since the beginning of the war that medium-sized attack aircraft had such a difficult battle. Before fighters advanced to the airport in Shanghai, medium-sized attack aircraft undertook search-and-destroy operations, while sea-based aircraft units intercepted enemy attacks. When the Chinese air forces withdrew beyond the range of Japanese fighters, only medium-sized attack aircraft could destroy them. After capturing airfields in Guangde, Wuhu, and Nanjing, Japanese fighters were able, through this system, to reach Nanchang and Hankou, where main Chinese Air Force bases were located (NIFHistory, 1969, [4], pp. 479–80).

The Situation

As shown in section 2-5-2, after the Shandong and Xuzhou campaigns, aiming to end the War with China within a year, Japan focused its whole national capability, Army forces in particular, on the capture of Wuhan and Guangdong. This was achieved in late October 1938.[25] Chinese resistance was strong, however, and there was no likelihood of a prompt resolution of the war. On 22 December, the Konoe Cabinet declared a new East Asian order. But, between China's statement: that "the real war is beginning now" and Japan's hopes for a peace overture and new order, there was a major disjunction (Boeicho, 1967a, pp. 570–1).

The Army had twenty-four divisions in China and nine divisions in Manchuria and Korea, leaving only the Imperial Guard (the Konoe Division) at home; it had lost the operational flexibility to continue the offensive. The Chinese operation had finished without destroying the enemy's main force. Japan was embarked on a long, drawn-out war of attrition with China, and was also beginning war preparations against the USSR. This combination was strategically extremely difficult (Boeicho, 1967a, p. 575).

After the capture of Wuhan and Guangdong, Japan restricted its ground operations. By maintaining security inside occupied areas, it hoped to establish long-lasting arrangements and institutions, and to support the development of the new government of Central-North China. The occupied areas were a collection of points and lines, too spreadout for the thinly deployed expeditionary forces to cover. Striking at weak points, the Chinese military employed gradual, hidden, and local resistance. The Japanese ground forces, forestalling plots and a hit-and-run strategy, warned against expanding the combat theater unless some extraordinary needs emerged.[26]

The Navy concentrated on enforcing air operations in inland China, while recognizing that devoting too much time and resources to this could impair combat capability on the sea, its key role. When the operation on the continent subsided, the air forces returned to the Combined Fleets and participated in sea training, switching roles (as policy required) with crew members deployed to the Combined Fleets. This policy was consistently maintained from spring 1938 to the end of the war. As part of the fiscal-year relocation of fleets and personnel, Air Force units in China were also reorganized (NIFHistory, 1969, [4], p. 465).

---

[25] For details of the process, see Miwa (2008, 3–6–2, pp. 187–9).
[26] See NAFHistory (1969, [4], pp. 475, 517). For details of the occupied areas and occupation policy, see Imoto (1978, pp. 399–410).

With changes to politics and strategy, greater emphasis was placed on inland air operations. The War with China became a long, drawn-out war of attrition, while Japan had to focus also on its own national defense. For this reason, after the attack on Hankou, Navy air forces in China were drastically reduced. The 1st CAC, the 1st Carrier Division on Kaga, the Second Carrier Division on Soryu, the Takao Air Squadron, and Chitose (mothership of seaplanes) were all sent home. At the beginning of 1939, Japan had 132 aircraft in China, a decrease of 40 percent from its peak. The Navy air forces in Central China totaled eighteen medium-sized attack aircraft of the Thirteenth Air Squadron, forty-four planes of the Twelfth Air Squadron, and eight planes in river units (Boeicho, 1975a, p. 106).[27]

The Inland Offensive in 1939

Beginning with the first attack on Chongqing on 3 May 1939, the Japanese military began an air offensive against Sichuan Province and Chongqing in particular.[28] The main Hankou airport was built on a racetrack and was vast enough to station two hundred aircraft.

The flight distance between Hankou and Chongqing was 420 nautical miles (780 kilometers), which took three hours each way for medium-sized attack aircraft. Given its cruising range, the Type 96 carrier-based fighters could make no inroads in this area. Attack aircraft units could only attack, eliminating for themselves the nuisance of enemy fighters.[29] At that

---

[27] The 1st CAC had already returned home in April 1938. Concentrating all the Type 96 attack aircraft, carefully reserved for a decisive war against the United States, the strategic bombing units had achieved excellent results. From the start until February 1938, thirty attack aircraft were lost. Recognizing that this would create a dangerous gap in defenses at the Pacific front, the Navy Central sent the 1st CAC home and retrained crew for the Type 96 Attack Aircraft. Thirty attack aircraft were deployed to the Thirteenth Air Squadron of the 2nd CAC, to take over the assignment of the 1st CAC (Boeicho, 1975a, p. 66).

[28] NAFHistory (1969, [4], p. 504). Actually, the first Japanese bombing of Chongqing was on 18 February 1938. Before the fall of Hankou, the Chinese government intended to continue the war against Japan, moving the capital to Chongqing. To demonstrate that wherever it moved to, the capital would not escape attack, Japan bombed Chongqing with three medium-sized attack aircraft (NIFHistory, 1969, [4], p. 380).

[29] Assuming fifteen minutes of air combat at its target destination, the cruising range of the Type 96 Fighter was 220 nautical miles when it traveled with the Type 97 carrier-based attack aircraft (with a maximum velocity of 200 knots, in contrast to the Type 96 Fighter's 219 knots). It managed less than 200 nautical miles when traveling with the Type 96 carrier-based attack aircraft, which had a maximum velocity of 150 knots. To leave more time for air combat, fighters were restricted to a range of less than 150 nautical miles. In attacking Nanchang (208 nautical miles) and Hankou (211 nautical miles), using Wuhu as a staging base and traveling with the Type 96 land-based attack aircraft, the Type 97 carrier-based attack aircraft could, with difficulty, achieve the standard cruising range (NIFHistory, 1969, [4], pp. 433–4). During the inland offensive of 1939, no reconnaissance

time, China had reconstructed its air forces, particularly its defense fighters (Iwaya, 2003, pp. 115–17).

On the afternoons of 3 and 14 October, Hankou airport was bombed by Tupolev SB-2 light bombers (made in the USSR). In the first bombing by eight SB aircraft, the first shot hit a place where top officials of the 1st CAC were gathered together, causing heavy human losses. In the second bombing, twenty SB aircraft attacked land-based attack aircraft of the Thirteenth Air Squadron and carrier-based aircraft of the Twelfth Air Squadron, causing the loss by fire of fifty to sixty aircraft.[30]

Three points are worth noting. First, Chinese SB bombers flew from various places, including Chengdu (950 kilometers from Hankou), keeping the Japanese forces at Hankou airport under constant threat of an air strike. Second, the forces in Hankou had no way to monitor surrounding areas. The Chinese could see Japanese attack planes take off from their base, and could make a successful surprise attack on Hankou at any time. Third, Chinese anti-aircraft guns were superior both in range and accuracy to those used by the Japanese. The Chinese also had more anti-aircraft guns. Important Japanese Navy air bases in China had small quantities, although they rarely hit their mark.[31]

The Thirteenth Air Squadron, in Hankou from late November 1939, recorded at the beginning of 1940 (NAFHistory, 1969, [4], pp. 619–20):

(1) A Japanese offensive was monitored immediately after it took off from the base. When we reached the attack destination, neither

---

aircraft could cooperate, and from beginning to end medium-sized attack aircraft units conducted the attack alone (NIFHistory, 1969, [4], p. 630).

[30] See Iwaya (2003, pp. 115–17) and NAFHistory (1969, [4], pp. 506–9).

[31] Basically, the Navy's anti-aircraft guns rarely hit their targets in low-altitude and low-velocity training (NAFHistory, 1969, [4], pp. 636–7). "Traditionally, the Chinese military rarely hit targets more than 3,000 meters high with anti-aircraft guns and more than 2,000 meters high with machine guns. However, the Chinese anti-aircraft guns gradually improved in power and accuracy even at ultra-high altitudes; during the offensive on Hankou and Hengyang, Japanese aircraft were generally hit even at 5,000 meters." On 25 June in Nanchang, evading clouds, aircraft flew up to 5,800 meters high, which was the upper limit for formation flying. Until higher-performance model aircraft became available, they had to attack at a height of between 4,500 to 5,000 meters (NAFHistory, 1969, [4], p. 431). This situation did not improve during the Pacific War. "The Chinese anti-aircraft guns were much better than the Japanese guns and inflicted heavy damage. Despite recognizing this situation, the Navy did not improve or increase its own air defense weapons. Although the importance of base defense was anticipated and emphasized in the second-stage operation, Japan's performance was as poor as before. The Navy and Japanese military in general had a fatally defective defense" (NAFHistory, 1969, [4], p. 768).

Chinese aircraft nor air weapons were left for bombing on the ground[32];

(2) The Chinese waited with the complete deployment of fighters and anti-aircraft guns for interception. We had no alternative but to fight with enemy fighters in the air;

(3) In consideration of third countries' interests, we could not bomb targets other than military facilities;

(4) Chinese aircraft were increasing, but the Japanese continued to have only eighteen.

In daytime attacks, the Japanese would suffer fairly heavy losses.

There was little chance of capturing enemy aircraft on the ground and destroying them. At least at night, although bombing accuracy somewhat decreased, there was the prospect of capturing and destroying enemy aircraft on the ground. For this reason, most inland offensives in 1939 were conducted as nighttime attacks.[33]

Inland Offensives in 1940 and 1941

In spring 1940, Type 96 medium-sized land-based attack aircraft in the Thirteenth and Fifteenth Air Squadrons were replaced by the renovated Model 23. The renovations improved its ultra-high-altitude performance so that the Model 23 could avoid the approach of Chinese fighters, supposedly eliminating the risk of attack. Operation 101, the concentrated attack of 1940, began on 18 May with twenty land-based attack aircraft in regular use. Following nighttime offensives over several days, the Japanese

---

[32] Labeling "the offensive as air attack almost useless," Iwaya (2003, pp. 159–60) explained as follows: "Since the offensive on Nanchang and Hankou in early 1938, the effectiveness of airfield attacks by land-based aircraft had significantly decreased from the initial stage of the war. By the time attack aircraft reached airfields, the large and transport aircraft had already gone, and fighters were waiting in the air. The few aircraft we captured on the ground were broken or in need of maintenance. Attack aircraft units were only able to destroy airbase facilities, hangars, and oil bankers and to make big holes in runways and airfields."

[33] Approximately two-thirds of inland offensives between January and October 1939 were undertaken at night, dawn, or twilight (NAFHistory, 1969, [4], pp. 620–2). During the day, medium-sized attack aircraft waited at Hankou airport and were vulnerable to attack from the air. Nor were nighttime offensives safe for aircraft. Although Chinese fighters were not good at night interception, Japan lost at least three medium-sized attack aircraft in nighttime offensives. If China had had special fighters for night interception, Japan's losses would have been far heavier. Japan was not prepared for night interceptions. Only in 1943 did the Japanese military begin to develop a nighttime fighter (NAFHistory, 1969, [4], p. 764).

forces switched to daytime attacks after 22 May, using the nights only for special purposes.

On 21 July, more than ten of the most advanced Type Zero carrier-based fighters were transported by air to Hankou; they attacked for the first time on 19 August.[34] On 6 and 10 September, respectively, the 1st CAC and expeditions of the 3rd CAC returned to their original units. The 2nd CAC, accompanying the excellent Zero fighters, continued an offensive on Sichuan Province. The Type Zero fighters needed to use Yichang as a staging base to Chengdu, but could reach Chongqing directly from Hankou (NAFHistory, 1969, (4), p. 570).

Operation 101 continued in 1941 as Operation 102. With the organizational reform of November 1940, the medium-sized attack aircraft units in China were dissolved, leaving only carrier-based aircraft and seaplanes on the continent (NAFHistory, 1969, [4], p. 593). After late July, the main forces of the Eleventh Air Fleet concentrated in Hankou and continuously attacked Chongqing with 135 medium-sized land-based attack aircraft. On 11 August, the Type 1 land-based attack aircraft of the Takao Air Squadron and Zero fighters in formation attacked Chengdu at dawn. With tension mounting between Japan and the United States, this massive short-term offensive was terminated at the end of August. In early September, medium-sized attack aircraft units retreated from the continent; on 15 September, carrier-based aircraft units returned home and were dissolved (NAFHistory, 1969, [4], pp. 599–606).

Particularly after the arrival of the Type Zero carrier-based fighters in summer 1940, medium-sized attack aircraft units achieved air supremacy in the inland offensive, in collaboration with powerful escort fighters.[35] However, they routinely suffered from difficulties arising from ambiguities in the strategic objective of the operation. The NAFHistory explained: "Until the capture of Hankou, we worked toward a common strategic objective in collaboration with all Army and Navy forces. After October 1938, however, further operations were suspended on all the war fronts, and medium-sized attack aircraft units had to continue the life-or-death battle

---

[34] On 24 August, it was formally adopted as a weapon. This machine still had problems that took some time to solve. Zero fighters achieved their first result on 13 September in the attack on Chongqing. While attack aircraft were bombing, thirteen Zero fighters captured thirty escaping enemy fighters, shooting down twenty-seven (Boeicho, 1975a, p. 157). Readers interested in Zero fighters should refer to Hakiri (2000).

[35] In Operation 101 in 1940, however, in all but 2 of 180 sorties, land-based attack aircraft attacked alone, without an escort of fighters (Iwaya, 2003, p. 147).

alone under difficult conditions, which had a negative psychological impact on crew members" (NAFHistory, 1969, [4], p. 620).

According to the NAFHistory, "We had a definite objective until the capture of Hankou and Guangdong. After that, the operational objective was abstract. In Sichuan Province, there were no big industries or decisively important strategic targets. The Chinese air forces retreated to the inland, and inland offensives were only for air combat with enemy fighters" (NAFHistory, 1969, [4], pp. 620–1).

In the NAF and Navy in general, most people believed it was a waste to lose medium-sized attack aircraft and crew in China; these had been developed and trained to wage war against the United States (NAFHistory, 1969, [4], p. 621). It was the primary role of the Navy to prepare for a one-game match between fleets of ships on the western Pacific against the anticipated enemy, the United States. This assumption was maintained consistently after the beginning of the War with China. The Navy had to divert aircraft and warships prepared for engagement against U.S. fleets into the War with China; it also developed new aircraft models, including new types of planes, such as the long-range escort fighter. But these were backward-looking responses; the focus was always on war with the United States. These views intensified as the War with China lengthened and tensions mounted between Japan and the United States.

8-3-3. Evaluation

Evaluation Depends on the Standard Used

An evaluation depends on the standard used. The activities of the Navy air forces do not receive high marks if the focus is their direct contribution to the victory against China and the surrender of Chiang's government. However, they receive an overwhelmingly high score when the focus is on the support and cooperation they offered to ground operations. If the Navy air forces had not ensured air superiority or cooperated successfully with ground operations in Shanghai and Nanjing, not only the inland offensive from Hankou but also the capture of Hankou and Guangdong would have been delayed substantially. The capture of Shanghai and Nanjing, as well as the Army landing operation, might have failed. Navy landing forces might have collapsed before the arrival of the Army troops.[36]

---

[36] It is difficult to give the Navy air forces a high score if one considers that Japan began the Pacific War against all odds and was crushingly defeated after a long war that inflicted

Here I emphasize two points essential for evaluating the Navy air forces in the War with China, keeping in mind the contrast with the "first hypothesis" mentioned in section 7–6 (that, at least until the initial stage of the Pacific War, everything proceeded smoothly as "planned").

Good Luck

Japan's situation would have been significantly different at various stages of the war if the Chinese air forces had been of higher quality. If the Zero-type carrier-based fighter had been delayed by one year, things might have been very different. Such factors could not have been accurately predicted before the war. The Japanese government had the good fortune to succeed with various risky projects.

The War with China began unexpectedly. If Japan had not managed to develop the Type 96 carrier-based fighter and the Type 96 land-based attack aircraft in time, the war would have developed differently. However, these advantages were fruits of the independence policy launched in the early 1930s in response to some Navy leaders who had noticed the importance and potential of air weapons. Medium-sized land-based attack aircraft, developed to cooperate with fleets of ships, ended up playing an important role in China. Nevertheless, the Navy continued to believe in the "large-scale battleships with big cannons" doctrine; moreover, it was the Army rather than the Navy that led the war. The Army had the good luck to be able to exploit the fruits of the Navy's independence policy.

The Unexpected War with China and the NAF

The War with China began unexpectedly, forcing the Army and Navy to react. As the war lengthened, the Army, unable to ignore the threat of the USSR, balanced its armaments and focus, restricting the impact of operations on the continent (NAFHistory, 1969, [4], p. 307).

---

terrible suffering on the people of many countries, including Japan. Even if Japan had conquered Chiang's government or realized peace after its initial victories, the Navy's activities would still seem unimpressive, arguing that, as the postwar history tells, it might only carry many reasons to fight for serious misfortunes. This evaluation would be reversed if it emphasizes the victory of the Chinese side represented by Chiang's government. Without the Type 96 carrier-based fighter and the Type 96 land-based attack aircraft, the War with China might have ended in the Battle of Shanghai, or earlier.

The Navy took both long-term measures to improve armaments and short-term flexible measures to respond to immediate issues.[37] When the abandonment of the nonescalation policy signaled a lengthening of the war, the Navy took measures to eliminate future intervention by third countries and to promote predetermined rearmament plans (NAFHistory, 1969, [4], p. 311).

The 1st CAC had the only medium-sized land-based attack aircraft units of the time, and had to develop and improve war skills in collaboration with fleets of ships. The Navy, however, had no choice but to send the 1st CAC into operations on the continent, despite the risk of exhausting its forces. The Navy also faced two more serious challenges:

1. Concentrating operations on the continent was degrading combat capability for the sea operations that were its primary duty.
2. The development of new sea weapons was stalled. For this reason, in March 1938, reorganizing the Thirteenth Air Squadron into medium-sized attack aircraft units, the Navy returned the 1st CAC to the Combined Fleets. However, the 1st CAC was sent to the front as a reinforcement unit at the peak of the Hankou Campaign. After 1939, it was repeatedly sent to reinforce operations on the continent (NAFHistory, 1969, [4], pp. 311–12).[38]

---

[37] As the Navy's rearmament could not be enforced quickly, it was hard to change direction in response to a temporary change in operations. The Navy could not control either operations in China to prepare for war against the United States or armament expansion to resolve the Incident (NAFHistory, 1969, [4], p. 307).

[38] As mentioned in section 8–3–2, the Navy concentrated its air forces efficiently to conduct operations in China. In order to save their strength for combat on the sea, the Navy returned its troops to the Combined Fleets for sea training when the operations subsided. It had a policy of returning units and crew members on the continent to the Combined Fleets for sea training. This policy was consistently maintained from the spring of 1938 until the end of the war (NAFHistory, 1969, [4], p. 465). See also note 27 earlier in this chapter. The NAFHistory (1969, [4], pp. 756–7) says: "the problem was most serious in those medium-sized attack aircraft units with the highest ratio of forces participating in operations." In response to the question of whether participation in operations on the continent degraded combat skill on the sea, the NAFHistory continued: "Overall long-term engagement on the continent led to careless maneuvers. As the war spread, losing sight of clear strategic goals, operations became infected with inertia, lacking responsiveness and flexibility. Enthusiasm and commitment decreased, leading to poor decisions, for example to jettison an attack too early because of poor weather conditions or to implement second-best alternatives too quickly. Nine aircraft in formation carpet-bombed ships blocked in Manila Bay just after the beginning of the war, shocking the Fleet Command Center. It was a dramatic contrast to the accurate bombing of airfields by three planes in formation at the beginning of the Incident."

The following opinions are those of a member of the NAF (NAFHistory, 1969, [4], pp. 288–9),[39] but they were widely shared outside the Navy.[40]

In this Incident, had Japan taken the political initiative in shaping its military action, gaining control of key points in North, Central, and South China at once, it could have dictated terms for peace. Under its nonescalation policy, Japan watched and reacted to movements on the Chinese side. Although Japan finally won control over key points on the continent, it spent more than a year on this effort. China did not surrender and Japan found it impossible to create the momentum for peace through military action. As a result, the war was prolonged.

Every year the NCCom and ACCom drew up detailed and well-considered plans relating to the UK, U.S., and USSR.... When it came to the Chinese operation, the plan was a simple few pages.... As a result, Japan was unprepared when the Incident occurred, and had no choice but to take temporary steps in response to the changing situation.

---

[39] See also Yamamoto (1982, pp. 264–7). Fukudome (1951, p. 223), the Strategy Section Chief of the NCCom at the beginning of the War with China (also the Strategy Division Chief of the NCCom at the beginning of the Pacific War), recalled: "In the War with China, the nonescalation policy politically adopted at the beginning was adhered to until the end. It seriously held back operations from beginning to end, making many decisions too late to win the game.... An operational objective was to destroy the enemy's will to fight.... It was of paramount importance, while aiming for victory, to capture and destroy the enemy's main force. In the War with China, although it was well within our capacity, we lost initiative, always conditioned by the enemy's political behavior."

[40] See, for instance, Imoto (1978, pp. 184–6). This ended reciprocal interference (between escalation and nonescalation, or expansion and nonexpansion) and inadequate war plans: "In total, two contradicting views of escalation and nonescalation conflicted; neither was adopted as the basic policy, so it was inevitable that the supreme command and war plans were ambiguous." Inada, who became the Strategy Section Chief of the ACCom in March 1938, described the War with China as a constrained dispatch of troops. He explained the operation plans of the Kwantung Army toward the USSR as follows (Inada, 1969, pp. 248–9): "The Kwantung Army's operation plans assumed that there would be no war with China. Although the war had been waged for a year, it still did not make sense to anybody; both its objective and end were unclear." As it was impossible to make plans, Japan had no choice but to maintain its previous one. Hilarious as it may seem, "mobilization plans for the divisions sent to China were formulated just as they would have been in Japan." At the end of each year, on-the-spot operation plans were drawn up. Agreements between the Navy and Army, ACCom, and the Army Ministry stipulated that mobilization plans (including munitions and supplies) be consistent with operation plans. As a result, Japan could not fight a war against the USSR. As it was a plan on the war unable to wage, no one cared of the composition from the Kwantung Army, just saying "uh-huh …, I see."

The Navy Air Force during the Pacific War

9-1. Overview

This chapter focuses on the 1942–3 war of attrition over Guadalcanal in the Solomon Islands, a defining battle involving air forces and land-based aircraft units, which changed the course of the Pacific War. I also discuss the Navy's air weapons and the third phase of the war, at the beginning of the Pacific War.

Guadalcanal was unexpected in three ways:

1. No government leader predicted that Japan's unplanned war with China would eventually develop into the Pacific War against the Allies.
2. The Navy, rather than the Army, was the central player.
3. Instead of the one-game match between fleets of ships predicted by the Navy, it was a war of attrition between land-based aircraft units.

Until the last minute, the Japanese state made little change in its war plans or preparations. In fact, its response to changed circumstances was so slow that the war ended without effective countermeasures. This incompetence and inability to respond promptly and adequately characterized every level of state decision making.

This chapter asks whether Japan's poor response to the unexpected battle over Guadalcanal was characteristic of its handling of the War with China. The War with China developed as a continual sequence of unexpected situations, each demanding a prompt and accurate response from the state. Given that Japan was still reacting incompetently to unexpected situations four years later, at the start of the Pacific War, it seems reasonable to infer that the War with China was similarly mishandled. As we have seen previously, the policies and responses of the Japanese government are consistent with this inference. It is therefore reasonable to assume that Japan was generally incompetent in responding to varied situations and policy issues. Guadalcanal provides an ideal experimental laboratory in which to observe, identify, and evaluate the function, performance, and competence of the state.

9–2. The Start and Initial Phase of the Pacific War

In this section, I focus on two types of aircraft that played a major role during the War with China: the Type 96 and Type Zero carrier-based fighters, and the Type 96 and Type 1 land-based attack aircraft. I also discuss how decision makers and their assumptions affected the Navy's armament enhancement plans before and at the start of the Pacific War.

The Pacific War began four and a half years after the start of the War with China. Of the leaders who directly or indirectly participated in Pacific War decision making, few, if any, predicted that the odds were in Japan's favor or that peace could be concluded on favorable terms.[1]

"In the NM and NCCom, neither leaders nor administrative authorities had any confidence in the war with the U.S. ... They felt confident about the initial stage, but not about long-term operations" (Hara, 1987, p. 93). General Sawamoto, the Vice-Navy Minister between 1941 and 1944, described the Navy conference of 6 October 1941 (Boeicho, 1968, p. 514): "On 6 October, Navy leaders put their heads together and reached this conclusion: 'it is incredibly foolish to fight with the U.S., given Japan's withdrawal from China. The situation must be solved through diplomatic measures.' The Navy Minister created great excitement by asking the NCCommander, in his professional capacity and as conference host: 'May I seriously disagree with the Army?' The NCCommander put out the flames, saying 'I'm not so sure about that.'"[2]

---

[1] For more details, see Miwa (2008, 3–2, pp. 162–70): "Puzzle 2: Was the Pacific War Part of the 'War' Referred to in Japan's 'Systematic War Preparations'?" In this connection, see also "Puzzle 1: 'The Cold Figures' Concerning Physical Productivity," in Miwa (2008, 3–1, pp. 100–2). It begins with the opening statement from "The Power of Victory: Munitions Output in World War II." by Raymond W. Goldsmith (1946, p. 69): "The cold figures of the output of airplanes, tanks, guns, naval ships, and ammunition, particularly when they are reduced to the still colder form of indices of aggregate munitions production of the major belligerents, probably tell the story of this war in its essentials as well as extended discussions or elaborate pictures."

[2] General Sawamoto continued: "If there had been no check by the NCCommander on this occasion, what would have been the consequence? Perhaps the resignation of the Navy Minister, the collapse of the Cabinet, intensified conflict between the Army and the Navy, and suspension of the progress toward war. However, the Vice-Minister, the Vice-

"On 20 October, two days after taking office, Navy Minister Shimada of the Tojo Cabinet asked a staff meeting with the NM and NCCom to reexamine the Outline for Implementing National Policy. Those present included the Minister, Vice-Minister, Military Bureau Chief, Vice-NCCommander, and Strategy Division Chief. Both the Minister and the Vice-Minister thought it was stupid to begin an unwinnable long war" (Sugita, 1987, pp. 210–11).[3]

The Army and Navy both considered the Navy the leading player in the war with the United States. Imoto (1978, p. 527) of the ACCom Strategy Section[4] recalled: "It was the Army that thoughtlessly advocated advancing southward. On this point, the Navy was cautious and hesitant. Both forces thought that the Army should aim to occupy resource-rich areas in the south, leaving the Navy to fight the U.S. Navy in the Pacific Ocean.[5] It was a shared view that underpinned operation plans. Without a detailed understanding of the situation, the Army believed in the strength of the Navy and was firmly convinced that Japan had a good chance of winning a war against the U.S."

Kenryo Sato, the Military (*gunmu*) Section Chief of the AM Military Bureau at the start of the war, and soon after the Military Bureau Chief, recalled (Sato, 1976, pp. 286–7): "How to end a war must be the main focus of leadership from the start. We had to think about it before beginning a

NCCommander, and the Military Bureau Chief said nothing, and after some silence, the conference adjourned" (Boeicho, 1968, p. 514).

[3] See also Yamamoto's booklet (1982, pp. 18–39), the section entitled "Everyone Opposed to Waging War Against the U.S. and the UK." General Osami Nagano, the NCCommander, did not clearly oppose the war at the IH-government liaison conference in November 1941 primarily because of the shortage of oil stocks. Yamamoto wrote that General Nagano considered Japan "a critically ill patient almost dying. There was no other remedy except to carry out drastic surgery. The country would die if left untouched; surgery gave it some chance of survival." They had confidence in the early battles, but not in a long war. Recall the Vice-ACCommander's evaluation of the situation in October 1939 discussed in subsection 2-6-1.

Readers may wonder what would have occurred if the NCCommander had strongly opposed the war, as discussed in the appendix to Chapter 2 (section 2-7). Why didn't Japan hold back? Could war have been averted, and peace maintained?

[4] Imoto, a Staff Member at the Strategy Section of the ACCom (IH-AD), told his boss, the Strategy Section Chief, that war with the United States and the UK was dangerous and should not be adopted as a national policy (Imoto, 1978, pp. 484, 516–17).

[5] "Based on the completely disrupted ideas of the national policy, the Army looked toward the continent (the USSR) and the Navy toward the sea (the U.S.). This led the Army and the Navy to think it a rule to fight strategically different wars. As a consequence, the Japanese military did not integrate its Army, Navy, and Air Force. That is, it lacked the integrated operation of three forces for a common objective under a common policy, which was strategically of absolute necessity in modern warfare" (Imoto, 1978, p. 37).

war. To my regret, in the recent war, we could establish neither our own plans nor a vision."[6]

According to NAFHistory (1969, [2], p. 998):

It was evident that Japan, with its national capability and armaments, was unable to bring simultaneous operations against more than two global powers to a successful conclusion. Therefore, the Basic National Defense Policy and Basic Outline of Operations stipulated that there would be no simultaneous operations against two countries.

It was a reckless action to begin a war against the U.S. and UK, after four and a half years of war with China, when Japan had exhausted a substantial portion of its national capability.

Japan made serious mistakes not only in starting and pursuing the War with China, but also in the Manchurian Incident, the Twenty-One Demands of 1915, and its continental policies since the Russo–Japanese War.

The BNDP, established soon after the Russo–Japanese War, was an early cause of the Pacific War.[7]

9-2-1. Navy Armament Enhancement Plans Prior to the Pacific War

The Navy did not manage operations in China in order to prepare for war against the United States, or enhance its armaments in order to resolve the Incident (NAFHistory, 1969, [4], p. 307):

---

[6] For his recollection on this point, see Miwa (2008, 3-2-4, pp. 169–70). Remember the recollection of the Strategy Division Chief of the NCCom (IH-ND) when the Pacific War began (Fukudome, 1951, pp. 182–3), quoted in section 2-2. He also introduced a view that Strategy Division Chief of the ACCom, Shin'ichi Tanaka, expressed at the meeting of the Imperial Headquarters before the beginning of the Pacific War (Fukudome, 1951, p. 239): "The German–Soviet War, now a half year since the beginning, is going into a stalemate, and as a whole the German momentum has passed a peak and is declining. It is dangerous for Japan to rely on help from Germany and Italy or to expect their victory. Once we begin to fight, we have to plan and determine to fight the war by ourselves to the end. Despite the opposition of Foreign Minister Matsuoka, Army Minister Tojo strongly supported continuing the U.S. negotiations that started in 1941." Akira Mutoh, the Military Bureau Chief, said: "We have been seriously troubled with the War with China. It is horrible in addition to begin a war against the U.S." (Fukudome, 1951, pp. 59–60). Already at Smolensk by July–August 1941, Barbarossa, which began on 22 June 1941, had run aground (Tooze, 2007, p. 668).

[7] Recall the discussion in section 2-7, the appendix to Chapter 2. Readers interested in whether the Japanese leaders planned to invade and/or conquer the United States should read section 3-2 of Miwa (2008, pp. 162–70). It discusses Puzzle 2, "Was the Pacific War systematically prepared for?" which includes Puzzle 2-1, "What were the primary ways and means the planners assumed for winning the war with the U.S.?" and Puzzle 2-2, "On what grounds did they judge the plan plausible and feasible?"

Without considering its own national capability, Japan foolishly embraced the no-arms-control-pact era, in which it entered into an unlimited arms race that followed the Third Rearmament Plan. It was indeed a foolish move. It was the objective of abolishing arms-control pacts, and to ensure its own national defense, Japan rejected fixed ratios between powers. Unfortunately, we could not do anything about the difference in national capability, and faced a horrible predicament.

At the start of war with the U.S., Japan had about 70 percent of America's fleets and related equipment. We could provide the same insufficient number of aircraft but our production capacity was extremely poor. We were far from having the capacity to sufficiently prepare, produce weapons, and train aircraft crew for a long war ... The rearmament plans were beyond the reach of our national capability. (NAFHistory, 1969, [2], pp. 1001–2)[8]

The drastic expansion of Navy armaments began in 1937. When the Washington Naval Treaty expired at the end of 1936, Japan abandoned arms-control pacts and began to build warships independently. The Third Rearmament Plan of 1936[9] called for the construction of seventy-one large and small vessels, including two battleships, the *Yamato* and *Musashi*, and two aircraft carriers, the *Zuikaku* and *Shokaku*. The Fourth Rearmament Plan of 1939 required the Navy to build ninety vessels, including two *Yamato*-class battleships and one *Taiho*-class aircraft carrier (Chihaya, 1982, p. 58). Under the First Plan (FY1931–6), the Navy built thirty-nine vessels (73,000 long tons in total) and sixteen air squadrons. Under the Second Plan (FY1934–7), it aimed to build forty-eight vessels (135,000 long tons in total) and eight air squadrons.

In parallel with (or in response to) Japan's armament expansion, the United States and UK expanded their Naval forces. Even after the completion of the Third Rearmament Plan in 1941, the Japanese Navy was under pressure to replace obsolete ships and cruisers. In response to the

---

[8] "Although they claimed to be self-sufficient in armaments production and emphasized the superior quality of individual vessels, they were content to build only super-battleships of the *Yamato* class.... To some extent, the focus was placed on the expansion of land-based air forces. As the conclusion of the Pacific War demonstrated, the *Yamato* and *Musashi* battleships that Navy leaders relied on were useless" (NAFHistory, 1969, [2], p. 1002).

[9] The Third Replenishment Plan, a so-called landmark replenishment plan, is mentioned in subsection 1–4–3. Almost at once, the Army began its full-fledged, six-year armament enhancement plan (from FY1937 to FY1942). In response, the AM drafted its five-year plan for Munitions Manufacturing Industries and Five-Year Plan for Key Industries Outline (Army Plan). On 17 June 1937, it forwarded requests regarding the Five-Year Plan for Key Industries to the Vice-Minister of the Planning Agency; this was just twenty days before the beginning of the War with China. For details of the Third Replenishment Plan, see Boeicho (1969b, pp. 475~).

development of new U.S. and UK armaments, the Navy created its six-year Fourth Plan, launched in 1939 (Boeicho, 1969b, p. 476).

In response to the U.S. Third Vinson Plan (effective until 1942) and the U.S. Two-Ocean Navy Act or "Stark's Plan" (effective until 1946), the Japanese Navy tentatively drafted the Fifth and Sixth Rearmament Plans. In September 1941, the NCCommander began negotiating the 1942 plan with the Navy Minister.[10] During the war, the Fifth Plan evolved into the Revised Fifth Plan, and the Sixth Plan disappeared (Boeicho, 1969b, p. 476).[11]

9-2-2. Air Weapons in the Third and Fourth Plans

The War with China began soon after the Third Plan was implemented. The rapid attrition of air weapons and equipment presented the Navy with a multitude of difficulties in implementing the Rearmament Plan and in organizing air forces. The escalation of war boosted the emergency budget for war expenditure and strengthened policies and motivations for production increase. As a consequence, emergency demand for various weapons

---

[10] After studying countermeasures to the Third Vinson Plan, the Navy recognized that Japan was already near the limit of its national power and industrial capability and predicted many difficulties in implementing further armament expansion. The Two-Ocean Navy Act enacted in July 1940 represented an astronomical increase. At the end of 1939, predicting that it would be impossible to maintain the traditional Japan–U.S. armaments ratio, the Navy refocused its policy of matching U.S. quality rather than quantity (Boeicho, 1976, pp. 86–7).

[11] It is not easy to answer the question of whether this series of large-scale rearmament plans constituted "systematic preparations" for an expected and imminent war with the United States. Readers interested in answering this question should consider the following four points: (1) In any country, the national defense authorities (in Japan, the ACCom and NCCom) simulate emergency situations and war operations in peacetime to train their armed forces (Sejima, 1995, p. 175). The Navy launched its Third Rearmament Plan in an atmosphere of heightened international tension, when the arms control pact had expired along with the Washington Naval Treaty. (2) The U.S. oil embargo and freezing of Japan's overseas assets caused relations between the two countries to deteriorate rapidly. Preparations for war began in the summer of 1940 (the war preparation itself formally started on 15 November). Before this, such a war seemed unlikely to occur. (3) After the rapid deterioration of relations, the Navy began to build armaments specifically to use against the United States. In August 1941, it was told to complete preparations for war by the end of September and to begin training. Immediately before the war, most Navy leaders, including the Vice-Minister, thought it was stupid to begin an unwinnable long war (Sugita, 1987, p. 210). (4) The two battleships, *Yamato* and *Musashi*, which symbolized the Navy's Third Rearmament Plan, were completed on 16 December 1941 and 5 September 1942, respectively, after the start of the Pacific War on 8 December 1941. Under the Fourth Plan, the *Shinano* battleship and aircraft carrier was completed on 19 November 1944, while another was suspended and finally canceled. Aircraft carrier *Taiho* was completed on 7 March 1944 (Boeicho, 1969b, pp. 506, 576–7).

and equipment was appended for the war, and the Navy succeeded in accelerating the implementation of the Third Plan:

1. Most land-based aircraft units (twelve squadrons, excluding medium-sized attack aircraft and flying boat units) were completed by the end of FY1938.
2. The attack aircraft unit was completed in FY1939, and the flying boat unit in FY1940.
3. Carrier-based aircraft units were completed between 1938 and 1941 to complement existing ships (with the exception of the *Musashi*, built in 1942).[12]

The Fourth Armament Enhancement Plan was implemented as soon as the Diet passed the FY1939 budget bill, which called for a rolling budget of 1.5 billion yen, providing seventy-five air squadrons in five years and eighty Navy vessels in six years. The Fourth Plan was huge in comparison with previous plans; the Navy hoped to double the size of its air forces in five years. Even while waging the War with China, Japan enforced the plan more quickly than scheduled. Planned growth was completed in 1941; that December, when Japan began the Pacific War, its Air Force met the targets set by the Fourth Plan. Thus the Fourth Rearmament Plan was extremely important for air armaments (NAFHistory 1969, [2], pp. 83–4).[13]

---

[12] See NAFHistory (1969, [2], pp. 57–8). The request from the NCCom of 22 August 1937, negotiated with the NM, included the unplanned procurement of seventy-five medium-sized attack aircraft. It doubled the existing number of such aircraft in half a year; those responsible for carrying this out faced serious difficulties. Despite difficulties and unsatisfactory outcomes, still they made progress. Even in peacetime, the attrition rate of air weapons was fairly high; it took a good deal of effort to maintain stocks through replenishment. It was difficult to maintain Japan's military strength while replacing forces lost in operations in China and also building new forces in accordance with the rearmament plans (NAFHistory, 1969, [2], pp. 67, 77). The Navy Armament Review Conference of 23 August 1937 announced the following strategy for promoting air armaments (NAFHistory, 1969, [4], pp. 305–6): (1) accelerate the scheduled completion time for twenty-five medium-sized attack aircraft units; (2) complete and deploy three medium-sized attack aircraft units to the Kanoya and Takao Air Squadrons in 1938; (3) complete the unplanned procurement of seventy-five medium-sized attack aircraft in FY1937; (4) combine armament enhancement with the replenishment of operating forces lost through attrition; (5) increase production capacity to 120 Navy aircraft per month; and (6) speed up the construction and redesign of aircraft carriers.

[13] Because the replenishment of armaments was restricted by arms-control pacts under the first three plans, these were referred to collectively as the ith Armament Replenishment Plan (i = 1, 2, 3). The Fourth Plan was called an Armament Enhancement Plan, reflecting Japan's determination to expand Navy forces aggressively, in response to America's Second Vinson Plan (NAFHistory, 1969, [2], p. 83).

However, as one author of the Fourth Plan (Chikao Yamamoto) remarked: "In the Navy, no proposal to build battleships could ever be turned down."[14] He explained (NAFHistory, 1969 [2], pp. 103–4): "The biggest issues in formulating the Third Plan were whether it was possible to produce enough aircraft and related equipment to dramatically increase air forces, and whether capacity expansion by the government and private sector would be achieved. At first most persons concerned were frightened by the enormity of the proposed Air Force expansion. Only Navy Minister Yonai thought that the 'Air Force expansion was still too slow.' The Fourth Plan appears to have adopted the theory of showing preference to air forces. From a broader perspective, however, at most it introduced a preference for air forces comparable to the traditional preference for Naval vessels."[15]

Observing that Navy air forces at the beginning of the Greater East Asian War fulfilled the goals of the Fourth Plan, NAFHistory (1969, [2], p. 105) pointed out[16] that its description of the Fourth Plan "is related to the procurement of aircraft. The production expansion in related weapons and the training of air crew did not keep pace. Both before and throughout the Pacific War, there was a bottleneck in air and general armaments affecting on-board weapons and aircraft crew."

9–2–3. The Situation Immediately Before the Pacific War

In the "Overview of the Position of the NAF at the Beginning of the War," Boeicho (1976, pp. 212–13) wrote: "At the beginning of the Pacific War, the Navy prepared air armaments to provide at least front-line units with excellent war capability.[17] However, the remarkable improvement in the war

---

[14] This applied not only to Japan but also to other major powers, including the United States. It was Major General Billy Mitchell of the U.S. Army, regarded as the father of the U.S. Air Force, who in the early 1920s first strongly advocated increasing investment in air power rather than battleships. Provoking the disapproval of military leaders, he resigned in 1926. See Yamamoto's section, entitled "Demonstration of the Useless Battleship Doctrine on a Big Stage" (1982, pp. 52–4).

[15] The ratio of expenditure on air forces versus ships increased in the Fourth Plan, from 1/5.49 in the First Plan to 1/7.2 and 1/10.73 in the Second and Third Plans to 1/2.82 in the Fourth (NAFHistory, 1969, [2], pp. 84– 5).

[16] To replace rather than enhance armaments, in 1940 and 1941 the Navy procured 75 carrier-based fighters, 37 carrier-based bombers, 36 carrier-based attack aircraft, 102 land-based attack aircraft, and 43 seaplanes – in total, 293 aircraft (NAFHistory, 1969, [2] p. 105).

[17] Chikao Yamamoto (1982, pp. 46–7), then Chief of the Aircraft Production Section of the Navy Air Headquarters, attended the last map exercise of the operation of the Combined Fleets of Ships against the United States and the UK in September 1941, conducted in the Naval War College in Tokyo. Among aircraft used to capture key areas in the south,

capability of the air forces created a demand for overly rapid expansion in air armaments. Given the national power and industrial capability of Japan, it was impossible to satisfy this demand. In addition, Navy leaders expected a one-game match between fleets of ships against the main U.S. force. Partly because they had not studied actual air combat sufficiently, they failed to realize that the attrition rate in air weapons would be extremely high and replenishment essential. At the beginning of the war, the Navy sent most of its air forces to the front lines, which created serious deficiencies in the supply and replenishment capacity indispensable for maintaining and growing air war potential." Boeicho concluded, "Thus, our NAF entered the war insufficiently prepared behind the lines."[18]

The doctrine of the one-game match between fleets of ships against the United States was still dominant in the Navy and NAF. The Navy's peacetime armaments also assumed that any conflict would be a one-game match. Due to inferior forces and insufficient national capability, the Navy could not afford to allocate sufficient resources to subsidiary forces and preparations behind the lines. In general, the Japanese military emphasized offensive strategies and downplayed the defenses necessary for maintaining the offensive (Boeicho, 1976, p. 466).[19]

[18] particularly fighters and medium-sized attack aircraft, the attrition rate was expected to be high. They would survive until Singapore was captured, but by February 1942, during the operation to capture Java and Sumatra, most fighters would be lost. For this reason, Combined Fleets strongly requested to obtain 150 more fighters than planned by January 1942. In November 1941, the monthly aircraft production capacity was just 180 for the Navy and 200 for the Army; this included the slightly larger training aircraft. Recognizing that 150 extra aircraft could not be produced by January 1942, Yamamoto responded that Air Headquarters would try but could not achieve such a huge production. General Isoroku Yamamoto, the Commander Admiral of the Combined Fleets, said indignantly: "For some time I have been asking the Navy Central to prepare one thousand medium-sized attack aircraft and one thousand fighters to wage the war with confidence. This is extremely frustrating." Lieutenant General Eikichi Katagiri, Head of the Air Headquarters, replied: "I know nothing about this request or a proposal. We cannot achieve such a production increase at this moment." At that time, the Fourth Rearmament Plan was being executed.

[18] Education, training, and the replacement of crew members were key factors for the air forces. As it took a long time to obtain high-level skills, training had to anticipate rearmament plans. On fatal defects in training, see Boeicho (1976, p. 467). "After the Battle of the Coral Sea (8 May 1942) and the Battle of Midway (5–7 June 1942), the Allied forces arrived in the southeast corner, where the Japanese military was involved in an air force war of attrition. At that point, supplies became difficult to maintain, too many crew members were young, and it was difficult to train in formation; as a consequence, the war capability of the air forces dropped rapidly" (Boeicho, 1976, p. 468).

[19] "On 6 November 1941, in the Presence of the Emperor, the NCCommander and Navy Minister held negotiations about vessel construction and air forces; the Basic Policy of the war was decided. The Basic Policy ranked forces in order of urgency and priority: (1)

The problem of ammunition that Chihaya (1982, p. 104), a Staff Member at the Combined Fleets, mentioned was typical: "Each fleet of ships that made a sortie from the harbor just before the beginning of the war in December 1941 was equipped with ammunition according to rule (although the volume was not large enough). The stock of ammunition for 25 millimeter machine guns that remained at the ammunition depots of Naval harbors such as Yokosuka, Kure, Sasebo, and Maizuru was next to zero. It was really a startling fact." He continued:

Throughout the war, this ammunition shortage was never overcome and only became more aggravated. Even after the middle of the war, surprisingly, the quota for anti-aircraft gunfire in the Japanese Navy was 200 for each anti-aircraft gun and 1,500 for each machine gun (enough to last for approximately 10 minutes). This was the total volume available. Whatever quantity of ammunition the forces might consume, they could not expect any replenishment. At the beginning of an air raid, the anti-aircraft guns might open fire, but they soon exhausted their ammunition. At most, they would only be allowed several dozen rounds of ammunition. In a Naval battle, it was possible to estimate the length of battle time. As the number of shells available to fire from a cannon was limited (120 shells for a large caliber cannon, for instance), it was possible to plan. They got into trouble, however, when they applied the same logic to anti-aircraft fire. It made no sense to apply the same logic to onshore batteries, always open to the threat of air attack. (Chihaya, 1982, p. 105)

9-3. Accuracy in Predicting the Future of the BNDP and Basic Policies: A War of Attrition Between Land-Based Aircraft Units

9-3-1. Overview

In the Army and Navy, war preparations, mobilization, and operations were implemented in accordance with the basic policies of government war plans and the BNDP; national defense policies were built around these plans as well. Because the Navy assumed that war would be a one-shot game against the United States, the NAF preparations were directed toward this goal.

However, the War with China, four and half years before the Pacific War, was not a one-shot game between fleets of ships but a series of ground battles on the continent. The Pacific War itself[20] was a war of attrition between aircraft taking off from aircraft carriers and onshore air stations.

---

aircraft, (2) submarines, (3) aircraft carriers, (4) defensive vessels, and so on to (6) cruisers, (7) battleships and large-scale cruisers, (8) other vessels" (Boeicho, 1969b, pp. 833–4).

[20] Recall the comment of a former Staff Member of the Combined Fleets (Chihaya, 1982, p. 75), quoted in section 4–6.

The government's basic and national defense policies and war plans, which shaped mobilization and war operations, were all irrelevant.

Assuming a one-game match, the Japanese Navy carefully prepared an interceptive operation.[21] Had the United States had actually challenged Japan in this arena, one might assume that it either had no information about Japan's plans or judged them ineffective. The former is unlikely and the latter improbable. Assuming rational decision making on both sides, it was natural for the United States to bypass a one-game match between fleets on the western Pacific and choose an alternative operation. That the Allied forces, primarily the U.S. military, began their counterattack in the southeast was not surprising. Due to its preparations and experience in China, Japan would have an advantage in a short war or during the initial stage of a long war. It was advantageous for the United States to emphasize its overwhelming superiority in industrial capability by planning for a long war. Given Japan's preparations and American superiority in industrial capability, a war of attrition between land-based aircraft, emphasizing strategic bombing by many long-range bombers, made sense.[22]

---

[21] This interceptive operation was modeled on Japan's victory in the Sea of Japan Naval Battle (the Battle of Tsushima) in the Russo–Japanese War. It aimed to intercept fleets of U.S. ships sent from the west coast to the Philippines in accordance with the 1933 War Plan Orange (Costello, 1981, p. 82). War Plan Orange was first formulated in 1904, however. See note 44 in subsection 2–3–1.

[22] It cannot be said that there was no Navy leader who thought beyond the one-game match. Isoroku Yamamoto, the Commander-in-Chief of the Combined Fleets, judged that, given well-developed air forces, there was little likelihood of a single sea battle. Even then, it would have been difficult for Japan to destroy the whole U.S. fleet of ships; a long war was therefore inevitable (Boeicho, 1976, p. 137; 1967c, p. 74). Shigeyoshi Inoue, the Head of the Air Force Headquarters, submitted to the Navy Minister a new rearmament theory, arguing that the NCCom's focus on a one-game match was obsolete given enhanced air forces. The Navy should focus on defending the western Pacific and the security of maritime traffic. However, this defensive stance, involving air forces widely scattered over key areas, raised questions of whether Japan had the capability to provide the required forces and whether key areas could be secured (Boeicho, 1976, p. 137). Given the supply of excellent, domestically produced aircraft since 1934–5 and the improvement in military skills and training, the air forces had become, since 1936, the Navy's strongest arm, leaving battleships relatively useless. In June 1937, the Navy's Conference on the Strength of Air Forces set out to collect materials and study plans for operations and armaments, to predict the key features of large aircraft that would be in common use in seven to ten years. Even at that time, both the NCCom and the Military Bureau of the NM maintained that it was speculative and premature to shift the focus of rearmament from battleships to air forces. The Air Force Headquarters, led by Takijiro Ohnishi, the Training Bureau Chief, made a strong case, and the Military Bureau was forced to agree. The conference report presented to the NCCommander and Navy Minister on 25 March 1938 (see NAFHistory, 1969, [1], pp. 153–92 and Chihaya, 1982, pp. 95–6) introduced a criticism of a student at an exercise class of the Naval War College on assuming a one-game match: "Would

9-3-2. The Need for Land-Based Aircraft Units to Confront Each Other

When carrier-based aircraft units fought, it was always a one-game match, with each side trying to destroy the other completely and ensure air supremacy. This was analogous to a one-game match in which fleets of ships fought and destroyed enemy naval forces. A decisive engagement between land-based aircraft units, however, was a long-term mission in which victory resulted from an accumulation of multiple successful operations. Destiny was not decided on the basis of a one-day battle (NAFHistory, 1969, [4], pp. 752-3).

The Japanese Navy had never trained for confrontations between land-based aircraft units; these were still being developed. There was little interest in the strategy of such battles. When it came to actual warfare, both in China and during the Greater East Asian War over the Pacific, land-based aircraft operations created an unbroken, uninterrupted, and long, drawn-out war (NAFHistory, 1969, [4], p. 753).

9-3-3. The Position of Land-Based, Medium-Sized Attack Aircraft (*Riku-Ko*, or *Chu-Ko*)

According to the BNDP, since the beginning of the twentieth century, Japan's Army had expected conflict with the USSR (Russia) while the Navy prepared to fight the United States. This focus was consistently maintained through the 1930s as the post–World War I arms control movement died down and the War with China began.

The Type 96 carrier-based fighter and the Type 96 land-based attack plane were Japan's main aircraft in the War with China. These models were developed under the independence policy of 1932, which continued to assume a one-game match between fleets. The attitude determined the use of land-based attack aircraft, as well as the organization and training of related troops.[23]

the U.S. Navy disadvantage itself by advancing to waters close to Japan to challenge the Japanese Navy to a one-game match?"

[23] Demand for aircraft models and performance changed with the evolution of operations and technology. As aircraft models and performance standards changed, Navy leaders understandably planned their battles using aircraft that satisfied various performance standards. For example, until 1936 there was only one type of fighter, the carrier-based fighter. In 1939 and 1940 plans, (land-based) local fighters and long-range fighters were added. Before the beginning of the War with China, the Navy assumed that carrier-based fighters would, be enough. With hindsight, the Navy acknowledged the need for two additional models. In the NCCom's first revision of the bill, the long-range fighter was

The Japanese Navy judged that a long war would be disadvantageous, given its inferior national capability. It aimed to fight a short war with an immediate resolution, hoping its ships could annihilate enemy fleets at an early stage. Japan favored the idea of a whittling operation that would gradually decrease the enemy's forces before the main engagement, allowing it to enter the one-game match with power at least equal to its enemy. Detailed scenarios were:

1. Before the enemy's main force arrived, the Japanese Navy would drive out its fleets in the East, ensuring Naval supremacy in the western Pacific. In collaboration with the Army, the Navy would completely destroy the enemy's base in the Far East and ensure trunk routes for commerce.
2. Submarines would monitor the enemy's main fleets. When enemy fleets made sorties, Japanese submarines would follow and pinpoint their location. With repetitive attacks, they would decrease the enemy's capability.[24]

renamed "fighter-cum-reconnaissance aircraft." There was little change in its performance standards; as before, its first task was to escort attack aircraft. A night fighter appeared on the list after February 1943. During the War with China, it was extremely rare for bases to be attacked by enemy aircraft. During the third stage of the Pacific War, however, Rabaul on the island of New Britain was often bombed at night by large aircraft, creating a great demand for night fighters; as a result, the *gekko* (moonlight) twin-engine night fighter was developed (NAFHistory, 1969, [1], pp. 408–10).

[24] The Strategy Division Chief of the NCCom (IH-ND) at the beginning of the Pacific War recalled their expectations about submarines (Fukudome, 1951, pp. 195–9). Since the Washington Naval Treaty, the Japanese Navy had expected much from submarine operations. Because of its lumbering performance under water, the primary objective of the submarine in most countries was to attack commercial ships, disturbing maritime transportation; warship attacks were secondary. The Japanese Navy, however, aimed to destroy the U.S. transoceanic fleets under the most heightened security. They expected much from their own submarine operations, while underestimating the performance of Allied submarines. In the Hawaii Operation (the attack on Pearl Harbor), together with air attacks on the U.S. fleets of ships, the Japanese Navy intended to use submarines to surround and blockade Oahu Island, not only to destroy any U.S. ships that survived the air attacks, but to complete the attack on Pearl Harbor by cutting off reinforcements and supplies from the mainland. Japan expected more from continuous submarine operations than from instantaneous air operations. But the achievement of submarine operations over more than a month defied their expectations completely. Only one of twenty-seven submarines was able to attack any U.S. vessel. The Navy admitted: "submarines can be useful in attacking commercial ships and should be used for this. The Imperial Headquarters and Combined Fleets, expecting too much from submarine operations, were extraordinarily shocked and deeply disappointed with the result. Japanese submarines could never achieve the expected results. By contrast, the Allied and particularly the American submarines played a remarkably active role, although we had written them off as nothing to be afraid of. Their attack was very damaging, not only to commercial ships, but also to warships under

3. Aircraft deployed over the South Pacific Islands would be used to locate the enemy. When enemy fleets advanced into the zone they controlled, Japanese land-based attack aircraft would attack.
4. High-speed battleships would decimate the enemy at night. At dawn, Japan's fleets would completely destroy the enemy's main fleets in a one-game match (NAFHistory, 1969, [1], pp. 256–7).

Land-based attack aircraft, such as the Type 96 and the Type 1, were developed and deployed in accordance with scenario 3.

The use of land-based aircraft units was peculiar to the Japanese Navy, and a major feature of operations. The mainstay of the land-based aircraft units was a twin-engine, medium-sized, land-based attack aircraft called the *chu-ko* (medium-sized attack aircraft) or *riku-ko* (land-based attack aircraft). The *chu-ko* distinguished itself in strategic bombing in various Chinese locations, and in both aerial warfare and attacks on enemy warships during the Pacific War. It had a major impact on Navy war planning (NAFHistory, 1969, [1], pp. 240–1).[25]

9–3–4. Causes of Failure in Land-Based Aircraft Unit Operations

Lieutenant General Tasuku Nakazawa[26] recalled (NAFHistory, 1969, [4], pp. 751–3): "When the Navy developed *chu-ko* for land-based aircraft units, it was planning to move and concentrate land-based aircraft units on the

heightened security. The damage to the latter in particular, even under heightened security, was considerable."

Yamamoto (1982, pp. 206–18) wrote as well: "The Japanese Navy intended to destroy U.S. transoceanic fleets under the most heightened security. For this, submarines needed to have both a long cruising distance and a high velocity. The Japanese Navy's weighed 2,500 tons, in comparison to German U-boats weighing 780 tons. Although Japanese shipbuilding was world-class when it came to marine vehicles, for submarines it was not. On average, one-third of all machines were broken down. The most perverse aspect of the last war was the poor performance of our submarines" (Yamamoto, 1982, p. 208). "Together with the poor performance of small vessels, including low-velocity antisubmarine vessels, the Navy's biggest miscalculation in the last war was in relation to escorting ships" (Yamamoto, 1982, p. 210).

[25] Land-based attack aircraft, peculiar to the Japanese Navy, were developed to compensate for the weakness created by the restrictions resulting from arms control treaties with Washington and London. From the War with China to the Pacific War, Types 96 and 1 medium-sized attack aircraft, *chu-ko*, were exclusively used in place of large-sized attack aircraft. During the Pacific War, the Navy produced two experimental models of large-sized attack aircraft, the Shinzan and Renzan, but both failed (NAFHistory, 1969, [1], pp. 412–13).

[26] He was Organization Section Chief and then Strategy Section Chief of the NCCom Strategy Division during the War with China, and became the Strategy Division Chief of the NCCom in June 1943, as Fukudome's successor.

sea. It would concentrate them in the North, in the Kuril Islands, and in the south, destroying enemy fleets on the Pacific. The Navy demanded a long flight range, but never expected the battles between land-based aircraft units that actually occurred. Pacific War operations formed an unbroken, uninterrupted, and long, drawn-out war. Warfare between land-based aircraft units was not a one-game match involving fleets of ships, but a long-term struggle to victory, through the accumulation of successful operations."

Land-based aircraft units played a spectacular role initially and during first-stage operations, enabling the Navy to capture key areas in the South. Later, the war situation deteriorated day by day. After the midpoint of the war, the Navy concentrated its efforts on improving and strengthening land-based aircraft units, but without success.

The NAFHistory (1969, [1], pp. 249–50) commented: "The Navy lacked data on and experience of land-based aircraft operations, and faced great difficulties on many fronts. As its problems stemmed from remote causes, no wartime emergency measure was effective. During the four and a half years of the War with China, Japan gained little experience of air warfare between land-based aircraft units. By focusing on major offensive operations, it failed to learn how to counter strong enemies. The Japanese Navy began the Greater East Asian War with insufficient research and training in both cooperative operations and retaliation against carrier-based aircraft units with excellent mobility."

The NAFHistory (1969, [1], p. 250) noted four lessons the Navy learned from the war[27]:

(1) In a long war, the Navy needed to launch a strong and enduring air war, not a one-game match operation between carrier-based units;
(2) The Navy could not continue to wage war without sufficient logistical support, including both personnel and equipment;
(3) Although Japan's aircraft were fast, they exercised full combat capability only when sufficient airfield preparations were in place. Their speed was therefore limited by their transport convoys;
(4) Air stations required in-depth preparations. The Navy could not continue to deploy all forces at the front. There had to be support troops at the back ready to engage in decisive operations.

---

[27] For details of the great difficulties they faced, see NAFHistory (1969, [1], pp. 250–4). They were (1) shortage in force size, (2) failure of cooperation between land-based aircraft units and carrier-based aircraft units, (3) defects in air stations, and (4) failures of the offensive by land-based aircraft units on enemy's task forces at a late stage of the war, particularly in the Aerial Battle of Taiwan-Okinawa, the Battle of the Philippine Sea, and the Battle of Okinawa.

9-3-5. The Battle over Guadalcanal Island

The battle over the air station on Guadalcanal Island was representative and instructive.[28] After the Battle of Midway,[29] the Allies directed their main force to the southeast. Recapturing Guadalcanal Island in August 1942, the Allies began a counterattack both in Solomon Islands and in East New Guinea. Lengthy, fierce battles developed in air, by sea, and on the ground. As air forces increased over Guadalcanal, the Allies secured air supremacy. Despite the six-month struggle between land-based air forces, reinforced by ground forces conducting repeated counterattacks, the Japanese military retreated from Guadalcanal in January 1943 (NAFHistory, 1969, [1], pp. 245–6).[30]

In the early morning of 7 August 1942, the Allied Powers came to Guadalcanal, two months after the Japanese defeat in the Battle of Midway. Judging this to be the enemy's main counterattack, Japan's Combined Fleets of Ships welcomed the move as a favorable opportunity to trap enemy aircraft carriers. The Navy ordered its Second and Third fleets to travel from Japan to the Truk Islands as quickly as possible. Fleets engaged in operations on the Indian Ocean were withdrawn to concentrate all forces in the southeast; the Navy Headquarters set up a base in Truk. The First Battle of the Solomon Sea (Savo Islands) was fought on 8 August. On

---

[28] See also Yamamoto (1982, pp. 95–116). The section is entitled "Guadalcanal, the Decisive Battle of the Pacific War."

[29] See Genda (1996, pp. 121–4) for the details of the Midway operation, the course of Battle of Midway, and causes of defeat. The author participated in the operation, on the First Fleet of Aircraft Carriers. As mentioned in subsection 8-2-2, concerning armament and weapons, one of the Japanese NAF's blind spots was a lack of interest in and understanding of reconnaissance (NAFHistory, 1969, [4], p. 279). This was illustrated by the choice of aircraft on carriers belonging to two forces that fought in the Battle of Midway, one cause of Japan's defeat. The *Yorktown* carrier had twenty-seven fighters, eighteen bombers, twelve torpedo bombers, and eighteen reconnaissance aircraft. *Shokaku*, Japan's newest aircraft carrier, had eighteen fighters, twenty-seven bombers, and twenty-seven attack aircraft. Japan used attack aircraft for reconnaissance (Genda, 1996, p. 220).

[30] According to the argument described in subsection 9-3-1, the Allied Powers made a rational choice in beginning the counterattack, avoiding a one-game match between fleets of ships and thus pulling the Japanese into a war of attrition between air forces, and land-based aircraft in particular. Even if Japan had won the Battle of Guadalcanal, it would have been pulled into a war of attrition over another air station, with similar consequences. After its defeat at Midway, Japan could not muster the well-equipped transport convoy or Air Force escort required by its huge landing force. Even if Japan had recaptured Guadalcanal, it would have been impossible to protect the air station from U.S. B-17 bombers. (As shown in note 35, even the 20 millimeter large-caliber fixed machine gun of the Type Zero fighter was not effective in shooting down B-17s.) The Japanese had no powerful, mechanized airfield construction troops to extend the airfield so that it could resist air attack or recover from destruction by bombing.

20 August, a patrol plane noticed an aircraft carrier to the southeast of Guadalcanal, and Japan received a report that carrier-based aircraft had moved to the Guadalcanal air station. In the Second Battle of the Solomon Sea on 24 August, the Allied Powers established a position of superiority over the Japanese military. The Japanese faced air combat when attacking the enemy's air forces on Guadalcanal, approximately 500 nautical miles from Rabaul. Without controlling the enemy at least temporarily, it was difficult to reinforce Army forces and capture the island (Boeicho, 1976, pp. 248–9).[31]

On 23 January 1942 the Japanese captured Rabaul; land-based air forces immediately moved in (Boeicho, 1976, p. 237).[32] In August, when the battle over Guadalcanal began, even Rabaul and Kavieng (on New Ireland Island, to the northwest of Rabaul) could not hold all the air reinforcements. In addition, Rabaul was 2,400 nautical miles from Japan, and the Japanese could not effectively replenish supplies. Given the shortage in aircraft production capacity and an inadequate replenishment system, distance seriously disturbed smooth operations (Boeicho, 1976, p. 266).

Air operations to destroy enemy air forces over a distance of more than 500 nautical miles (nearly 1,000 kilometers) were not easy to carry out. The dominant Type Zero fighters could spend only 15 minutes in air battle at their destination. Japan planned to construct additional airfields along the route, but had no forces or capacity to do it. Only in mid-October did the Buin air station, 300 nautical miles from Guadalcanal, become available (Boeicho, 1976, p. 221).[33]

The Allied Powers had an intelligence network over New Britain and the Solomon Islands.[34] Japan's offensive operation was reported in advance, and

---

[31] To attack Guadalcanal, the United States built an air station with a 1,800 meter runway for large-scale bombers on the Espiritu Santo Island in the Nouvelles-Hebrides. Two days after the completion of Japan's Guadalcanal air station (more than one and half months in construction), U.S. aircraft were taking off from the Espiritu Santo airfield, built in twenty days, and landing forces waiting on the Coral Sea began an amphibious operation. The Espiritu Santo was 150 kilometers closer to Guadalcanal than Rabaul. See Ishii (2006, pp. 41, 197–8).

[32] Rabaul was at the north end of New Britain Island, with a good port and airfields. Air warfare began immediately, with the enemy's air forces using Port Moresby as a forward base (Boeicho, 1976, p. 274).

[33] Buin was located at the southeast end of Bougainville Island. Using this air station, the Type Zero fighter could spend more than 30 minutes in battle. It was small, however, and could accommodate only smaller aircraft. There was great demand for an airfield that could accommodate medium-sized attack aircraft (Boeicho, 1976, p. 255).

[34] The major cause of failure in the June Midway operation, two months before the Battle of Guadalcanal, was that Japanese Naval codes were broken by the United States (Boeicho,

U.S. air forces on Guadalcanal were able to escape, taking shelter in the air (Boeicho, 1976, pp. 253, 266). By using aircraft such as the B-17, the so-called Flying Fortress, and the B-24, which were hard for the Japanese military to shoot down, the Allies freely inspected and attacked Japanese military bases. The Japanese could not conduct reconnaissance or carry out necessary surveillance or maritime patrol. It was difficult to defend Japanese bases such as Rabaul from attacks by large aircraft (Boeicho, 1976, pp. 263, 266-7).[35]

The Type 1 land-based attack aircraft was Japan's main medium-sized attack aircraft, but its defense capability was fatally flawed (Boeicho, 1976, p. 253). The Type Zero carrier-based fighter, used as an escort, could spend only 15 minutes in battle at its destination, which greatly restricted its

1976, p. 246). The same was true during the Battle of the Coral Sea in May (Boeicho, 1976, p. 243), when observers suspected that secrets had been leaked. However, the Japanese military, firmly convinced that their codes were rigorously protected, waged war to the end. It was hardly possible that Japan would win (Genda, 1996, p. 119). When the war was over, the Japanese military learned that Navy codes had been broken during the Battle of the Coral Sea (Imoto, 1979, p. 137). "Even at the Washington Naval Conference of 1921, the U.S. Army's most skilled code breakers were at work behind the scenes in a secret 'Black Chamber' in New York busily monitoring confidential cable exchanges with Tokyo. This gave Secretary Hughes an immense advantage" (Costello, 1981, p. 38). For details of how the Japanese Naval codes were broken, see section 9-6.

[35] In 1936, a B-17 made its successful first flight. When the Pacific War began, B-17 bombers were deployed in bases in the Philippines. The Japanese feared a preemptive attack on Taiwan by B-17s just after the beginning of the war (Boeicho, 1976, p. 225). As mentioned in note 44, subsection 2-4-1, in October 1941, General MacArthur received a message that, in response to a fatal defect of War Plan Orange, the U.S. military would consider it a primary option to deploy significant air forces, including B-17s, to the Philippines by May 1942. When war began, sixteen B-17 aircraft were deployed in the Philippines, although these were not used in a preemptive bombing of Taiwan (the proposal was rejected; see Costello, 1981, pp. 141-6). Following the Rainbow 5 War Plan, shown to MacArthur for the first time in September, they executed a well-rehearsed orange strategic retreat to hold the Bataan Peninsula (Costello, 1981, p. 104). The Type Zero fighter, with its 20 millimeter large-caliber machine gun, could easily shoot down any aircraft, fighter or bomber, except for the B-17. Even multiple dead shots could not bring down the B-17, make it catch fire, or cause a midair breakup (Genda, 1996, p. 238). Despite research on weapons and methods of attack, the Navy could find no effective countermeasure (Boeicho, 1976, p. 358). After November 1942, when the Army decided to send its air forces to the southeast corner, the Army struggled to find measures to deal with the B-17. Such a last-minute emergency effort could never achieve adequate results (Boeicho, 1975c, pp. 372-4). In the European theater, even in July and August 1940, eight out of twenty Fortresses had crashed or been shot down. Goebbels's propaganda was derisorily calling the wonder bombers "Flying Coffins," and the British condemned the B-17 for its trouble-plagued turbocharged engines, poor oxygen system, and tendency to ice up (Costello, 1981, p. 102).

activities.[36] During the war, the Japanese military made little progress in fire prevention measures.[37]

After its defeat at Midway, the Japanese military, and the Navy in particular, recognized the importance of air forces. With many aircraft carriers lost, however, it became difficult to formulate operation plans. Japan's Revised Fifth Rearmament Plan placed a higher priority on air forces (Boeicho, 1976, pp. 276–81). The annual attrition rate for aircraft fighting in the southeast reached 95 percent. Nor did production increase as planned. This aircraft shortage put the Navy at a tremendous disadvantage; the Revised Fifth Rearmament Plan began to collapse (Boeicho, 1976, p. 282).

Reflecting on this period, Boeicho (1976, p. 256) commented:

Because of insufficient forces and the condition of air stations, we could not destroy enemy air forces at the initial stage, before they increased their power. At that time, the war capability of our air forces far surpassed the enemy; one Type Zero fighter was said to be able to take on six enemy fighters. Because of insufficient personnel, crew members had to take on too many offensive operations and became very tired. In addition, the supply of equipment could not keep up with orders. As the enemy increased its air forces, our advantage disappeared. Consequently, our Navy concentrated most on its front-line forces and grew exhausted, while the war capability of the NAF deteriorated. By the end of 1942, the war capability of the Zero fighter units had fallen to a level equal to the enemy's.[38]

---

[36] In operations to capture key areas near the Java line, it was essential to ensure air supremacy. In air warfare between airbases, the Zero fighters had an outstanding record, accounting for more than 80 percent of successful missions. With the restructuring of wartime organization, the scale of land-based aircraft units gradually expanded. There were 288 medium-sized attack aircraft at the beginning of the war, increasing to 472 as a quorum on 1 April 1942. However, severe attrition meant that when the second stage began, there were no more aircraft than at the beginning (Boeicho, 1976, pp. 239–40, 273).

[37] During the War with China, it became apparent that Japanese large aircraft were built with little protective capacity, a problem that became more apparent after the start of war with the United States. This was impossible to correct, because of the flight range and volume of weapons on board. In France, bulletproof equipment was attached to airplane gas tanks. An aircraft suited to narrow battlefields in Europe was not right for air operations on the Pacific Ocean. Japan's technology was not well developed enough to satisfy all three requirements: offensive power, range, and protective capacity. The Japanese military placed too much emphasis on first offensives, range and weight saving, delaying research into bulletproof equipment (NAFHistory, 1969, [1], pp. 34–5). In addition, Japan could not produce enough artificial rubber to make bulletproof equipment (Boeicho, 1976, p. 358). Recall the comment of Kiro Honjo, the Chief Designer of the Types 96 and 1 attack aircraft, at the start of the Type 1 development, mentioned in subsection 8–2–3, note 16.

[38] Boeicho (1976, p. 267), declaring that the rate of attrition of Air Force units could not be precisely calculated, used materials as a reference: of the aircraft that did not return, 161 were medium-sized attack aircraft, 227 were Zero fighters, 39 were carrier-based bomber and attack aircraft, 32 were flying boats, 22 were seaplanes, and 19 were other models, in total 500; the onshore loss was 109. According to past statistics, the amount of equipment

Over time, U.S. forces grew more powerful, and it became hard to continue the operation to recapture Guadalcanal. The Allied Powers near New Guinea moved their air station to Buna (350 nautical miles from Rabaul; Boeicho, 1976, p. 221). Japan's prolonged operation gave crew members little time to rest, and many skilled workers were lost. Their replacements were young and unskilled. As insufficiently trained staff joined operations, war capability deteriorated. With the enemy forces strengthened, the attrition of the Japanese increased (Boeicho, 1976, p. 266). On 4 January 1943, the Japanese forces were ordered to retreat from Guadalcanal.[39]

9–3–6. Face-to-Face Air Warfare Between Land-Based Air Forces

Full-scale air warfare began in Guadalcanal Island and the Japanese military learned some valuable lessons about air power:

1. A battle becomes a war of attrition unless massive air power is immediately unleashed, securing air superiority.
2. Powerful airfield construction troops able to build well-equipped air stations quickly are essential.
3. Extra trained crew and planes are necessary to compensate for losses.
4. It is vital to provide investment and in-depth support for training, aircraft production, and a well-organized supply system.
5. The fact that Japan's medium-sized Navy attack aircraft were not bulletproof was a fatal flaw, made worse by the fact that the Navy could not shoot down U.S. B-17s.

The Navy had prepared armaments for the wrong sort of war; it was too late to take effective countermeasures, and the Japanese military finally reached breaking point (Boeicho, 1976, p. 274).

lost in combat nearly equaled that lost in non-combat. There is no doubt that the actual loss was far larger than calculated. Here we should also add the loss of carrier-based aircraft.

Replacing the F4F Wildcat (dominant at the beginning of the Pacific War) in February 1943, the F4U Corsair advanced to Guadalcanal as the U.S. Navy's main carrier-based fighter. Its advantage over the Zero in horizontal and descending speed gave the U.S. Navy a sense of confidence. On 1 September 1943, the first F6F Hellcat advanced to Marcus Island. With introduction of those two models, the tide began to turn against Japan. Until July 1943, Japanese and U.S. fighters remained on an equal footing, but the P-38J was easy to maneuver and excellent in both horizontal and descending speed (Boeicho, 1975c, pp. 376–7).

[39] For details of the retreat operation, see Boeicho (1976, pp. 260–3). For operations and battles over Guadalcanal Island, including the Japanese retreat operation, see Yamamoto (2001) and Imoto (1979, chs. 3, 4).

The Navy expected its air forces to engage in intercepting operations, taking off from existing front-line air stations. As a result, it neglected air base defense and the construction of air stations. Faced with fierce air warfare, Japan tried to react strategically, but could not build air stations in all the places where they were needed. The Navy had to select from a few feasible options, and construction took a long time. Existing air stations needed watch-houses, anti-aircraft guns, bulletproof facilities, and the organization and equipment to repair runways and damaged aircraft.[40] None of this was easy to accomplish. As Japan had never recognized the importance of reconnaissance, it had no high-powered reconnaissance aircraft (Boeicho, 1976, pp. 275–6).

Two Factors that Constrained Flexible Response

The NAF was part of a larger system, constrained by various factors that were out of its jurisdiction and control. Here I address two factors related to the training of crew members. As war intensified, the shortage of skilled personnel became as serious a cause of deteriorating war capability as the shortage of aircraft.

The first issue was raised by Colonel (later Major General) Yoshio Yamamoto, who claimed that the Finance Ministry's budgetary assessment of the Navy involved too little training. Yamamoto was the First Section Chief of the NM Military Bureau during the Pacific War (NAFHistory, 1969, [1], p. 29):

The trouble for air crew and sailors was that the Finance Ministry rigorously restricted and fixed the Navy's personnel expenditure budget. For instance, in the construction of a warship, it was customary to allocate a fixed number of sailors, without allowing for onshore activities. They thought that Naval battles would be of the Sea-of-Japan type; once a major sea battle occurred, it would be the end of the war. Either Japan would win or the warship would sink. It would take several years to rebuild the ship, and in this period the war would certainly be over. Therefore, additional personnel expenditures were unnecessary. As ridiculous as this might appear, it was a lesson learned from the Russo–Japanese War. Using this principle, the Finance Ministry tried hard not to increase the Navy budget or the personnel expenditure budget for Navy air crew. They never thought it necessary to allow a generous budget for reserve crew to replenish losses. (NAFHistory, 1969, [1], p. 30)

---

[40] Imoto (1979, pp. 49–50), then on the staff of the ACCom Strategy Section, recalled: "The Navy scarcely mentioned onshore armaments. It emphasized the importance of front-line air stations, but misidentified as impregnable the island stations on the Pacific that were almost as undefended as onshore bases. In addition, it constructed an undefended base on an isolated island that was too remote to be protected by land-based air forces. Moreover, more than was necessary, the Navy made unsupported sorties and collided with the enemy's integrated forces. As a result, the Navy wasted extremely little time in breaking its back, to which was attributed Japan's defeat in the Pacific War."

A related comment followed (NAFHistory, 1969, [1], p. 30): "To ensure many officers, it was necessary to increase the number of students accepted to the Imperial Naval Academy. The Bureau of Naval Personnel was reluctant to do this. Emphasizing that its personnel policy was trouble-free in peacetime, it firmly maintained a policy of promoting all Naval officers at least to the rank of Colonel. Increasing the number of students would make this difficult. However, military forces are designed for times of emergency, and training officers should be the highest priority. It was a big mistake to place the primary emphasis on personnel administration in peacetime, instead of on wartime preparations."

The second factor involved human resource mobilization. Until the end of the Greater East Asian War, air armaments, both materials and personnel, had been consistently and strikingly in short supply. The personnel shortage was particularly severe, a major flaw that impacted not only the air forces but the Navy in general. Why had such a situation occurred? One explanation is that Japan had such an over-optimistic view of the war that it did not thoroughly enforce mobilization, especially personnel mobilization. Another is that, because the Army enforced conscription, it was difficult for the Navy to achieve its personnel requirements. Moreover, until the war situation grew very strained, there was little agreement on personnel requirements even within the Navy (NAFHistory, 1969, [2], p. 1007).

A participant at the Third Section of the NM Bureau of Naval Personnel armament planning sessions recollected (NAFHistory, 1969, [1], pp. 1007–8):

In the middle of 1941, the basic framework of the Fifth Rearmament Plan was announced. It was an epoch-making major expansion of both air forces and vessels, for which a correspondingly large increase in personnel was required.... Claiming that in FY1942 the Navy should ensure personnel of at least 160,000, including 90,000 by conscription, the Bureau of Personnel began negotiations in June 1941 with the Personnel Armament Section of the AM Personnel Administration Bureau. Clashes of opinion prevented agreement, and the issue was taken up in negotiations between the Military Bureaus of the AM and the NM. Despite the NM Military Bureau's best efforts, on 4 January 1942, the Navy was forced to compromise on an increase of just 108,000. This caused a serious personnel shortage throughout the war.

9–4. Reaction Capabilities of the State at the Initial Stage of the Pacific War

9–4–1. Reaction Capabilities in Unexpected Situations

It is not plausible that the Japanese government would plan and carefully prepare for a war of attrition between land-based aircraft units, as happened during the Pacific War. It is therefore pointless to evaluate the accuracy of plans and the appropriateness of preparations, focusing on the discrepancy between unexpected situations and realized demands.

I therefore focus on the government or planners' ability to react to situations beyond the scope of their assumptions. If the government had made adequate preparations for the war that actually occurred, in the face of a complex international situation and rapidly changing technology, then it would have had the capacity to react with flexibility to unexpected challenges. If the government could react only poorly to such challenges as the beginning of the Pacific War and the development of a war of attrition between land-based air forces, it must have found it difficult to implement other appropriate policies before the War with China.

Systematic war preparations are difficult for any government at any time, and particularly when the international situation is unpredictable and technology is developing rapidly. A government unable to react quickly must recognize the recklessness of such a challenge. It is implausible that Japan did not even recognize the problem. Most governments with poor reaction capabilities would have postponed the challenge, modified it, or given it up.

The War with China rapidly expanded its battle lines and became protracted; both the war itself and each stage of battle line expansion was a situation beyond the scope of Japan's assumptions. Compared the Pacific War, however, the Chinese challenges must have been easier to handle. China's air forces were inferior and the Japanese military consistently maintained supremacy. It is therefore possible that its poor reaction capabilities went largely unrecognized. I therefore focus on the reaction capabilities of the Japanese government to unexpected situations, particularly to the development of a war of attrition between land-based air forces in the Pacific War. The conclusion that Japan's reaction capabilities were extremely poor is important to this book as a whole.

9-4-2. Reaction Capabilities, War Leadership and State Competence

I focus here on the competence of the state. The role and function of war leadership[41] can be investigated as an optimization problem under

---

[41] War leadership is a function of the supreme organ of the state in waging a war. Japan's government and military command organ (the ACCom and NCCom) jointly decided whether or not to begin a war (it was a cardinal rule to avoid war if at all possible). Once war became unavoidable, the state would lead politically and strategically, defining objectives

various constraints, including government choices and the reactions of other nations. One of the most important constraints was the competence of the state. Smooth enforcement of effective war leadership required a competent and strong government.

Leadership's ability to react to the unexpected situations determined the outcome of the Pacific War. For this reason, the war was an idea laboratory for testing the state's leadership capacity and competence. A state with poor leadership capacity in wartime must be poor in almost any situation.

From the mid-1930s to the mid-1940s, Japan had no supreme national leader who, facing a threat to national security, could devote his best efforts to determining strategies to follow in politics and war (Tanemura, 1979, p. 21). The government was neither competent nor powerful. The NAF leaders were an important but not dominant group. Because the NAF was recognized for its effectiveness and importance during the War with China, its leaders were respected within the government. As the Pacific War approached, the NAF leaders became more dominant.

I also focus on the NAF in studying the reaction capabilities of the state. For the state to respond well, three conditions were necessary:

1. The NAF leaders were capable of reacting.
2. The government accepted the reactions of the NAF.
3. There were sufficient technological, physical, and human resources to implement policies.

Neither the second nor third conditions were satisfied, as reflected in the Army–Navy scramble over materials that continued until the end of the war. The Navy's reliance on the "large-scale battleships with big cannons'" doctrine also interfered with government acceptance. The NAF cannot be evaluated highly with regard to the first condition, as discussed later in this section.

The Pacific War ended in total defeat for Japan; there were never enough good aircraft or front-line troops. We cannot directly conclude that:

1. The Japanese government had no capacity to react.
2. The government's reaction capabilities were not effectively exercised.

It is not possible to prove that NAF leaders lacked reaction capabilities, because this is not a black-or-white question, but a matter of degree.

In what follows, focusing on the development, production, and replacement of aircraft, I list ways to evaluate the reaction capabilities of the Japanese

and formulating plans, to achieve objectives, including victory, as soon as possible. At the last stage of war, the state aimed to end hostilities as soon as possible and achieve peace (Imoto, 1979, p. 32).

government and the NAF. Although I present my own critique, these details are primarily for readers to use in evaluating the government's response.

9-4-3. Prior Reactions: Airfield Construction Troops and Replenishment

Most government leaders in Japan hoped to avoid war with the United States. Since the beginning of the Chinese conflict, there had always been the threat of a broader Pacific conflict, particularly as the War with China dragged on and Japan launched its Southern Expansion Policy. Even those who hoped to avoid war had to prepare for it, formulating operation plans, developing national power and war capability, and establishing wartime organizations (Tanemura, 1979, p. 20).[42]

What war preparations had been made by the late 1930s? As discussed previously, the Navy prepared for the wrong sort of war, apparently not anticipating a war of attrition between land-based air forces.[43] As few effective countermeasures were adopted *ex-ante*, the NAF leaders did not react well to possible problems.[44]

---

[42] "At a conference in the Presence of the Emperor on 5 November 1941, the ACCommander explained the forecasted size of the enemy's front-line Air Force. Noting the combat capability of enemy's planes, including B-17 bombers, he expressed concern about the capability of the 562 aircraft scheduled for use in the southern theater. As the war would be long, Japan needed to anticipate future developments in technology on both sides, as they would determine the quality of weapons and production capacity. The development of enemy fighters was carefully discussed, particularly in sessions concerning air technologies. However, important national policies that would affect the fate of the nation were determined one after another, without emphasizing technological capability as a key factor in national power. It was only after suffering a serious counterattack from the enemy that the Army, in providing operational directions, really recognized the importance of technology" (Boeicho, 1975c, p. 293).

[43] Kazunari Miyo, who took charge of air operations and air armament planning for the NCCom Strategy Section after November 1939, was ordered to formulate the Fifth Air Armament Plan in response to the Third Vinson Plan for expanding Naval forces (1940-2) submitted to the U.S. Congress in November 1939. (Recall the discussion in section 9-2.) President Roosevelt, giving the Army Air Corps independence from the U.S. Army Chief of Staff in March 1939, ordered the production of many B-17s. Miyo realized that the United States would advance against Japan using large aircraft with long flight ranges to locate Japanese ships. Japanese fleets would have little room for undercover action, and less chance at a one-game match following whittling operations by submarines. The original draft of the Fifth Plan finalized at the end of January 1941 was based on this assumption. As mentioned later in this chapter, however, most officers in the NCCom had little knowledge of aircraft and revealed no reaction (Miyo, 1982, pp. 20-4). For the details of the U.S. operation plan against Japan, on which the Fifth Plan was based, see NAFHistory (1969, [2], pp. 137-40).

[44] Given rapid progress particularly since the mid-1930s in aircraft technology, and practical experience gained in the European and Chinese wars, aircraft were changing drastically. Regardless of basic policy, the Navy's plan needed flexibility.

The military operation to Rabaul in January 1942 was based on a 1940 Army-Navy agreement stating that, in an emergency, the Army would seize Rabaul (Sejima, 1995, p. 78).

The Navy's plan involved sending the main force of its Combined Fleets to Truk to engage the U.S. fleets, making use of the South Sea Islands (League of Nations) Mandate and the Marshall and Caroline Islands, the "unsinkable aircraft carriers." The Bismarck Islands (Rabaul) are only 1,200 kilometers to the south of Truk. Given rapid progress in aircraft technology, U.S. airfields in Rabaul would be well within range for an air attack, making it difficult for Japan to place its main force in Truk. If the main force stayed in the Palau Islands in a rearguard position, it might not reach the decisive engagement in time. Thus, the Army complied with the Navy's request, judging that, in operations over the Pacific Ocean, the Navy was the lead player and should have Army support.

An important point is that already, in early 1940, the Strategy Sections of the ACCom and the NCCom had agreed on ways to retaliate against attacks from Rabaul, 1,200 kilometers away from Truk.[45] This was two and half years before the Battle of Guadalcanal, 1,000 kilometers southeast of Rabaul. This was not just a discussion, but a formal agreement between Strategy Sections of the ACCom and NCCom.

Evaluation (1): Airfield Construction Troops and Their Capacity

As illustrated in the previous section on Guadalcanal, I found few notable reactions to situations beyond the scope of previous assumptions. Little was prepared. Few measures were taken to circumvent a war of attrition. I found no evidence of scenarios prepared after the beginning of a war of attrition.

Previously, I have considered airfield and aircraft defense, training, and the stockpiling of aircraft parts and ammunition.[46] Here I focus on airfield construction troops. If, in anticipation of U.S. airfields, Japan planned to occupy Rabaul, it must have considered how the island would be defended. To maintain occupied Rabaul, Japan needed a full-scale air station, for which it required competent airfield construction troops. When the battle

[45] Sejima was Army Chief in charge of this issue. Upon reporting the Navy's request to the Subsection and Section Chief, he included a sentence stating that in an emergency, the Army would seize Rabaul.

[46] In the postscript, Boeicho (1976, p. 466) noted as one of defects and weak points of the NAF: "The training and research focused on exerting offensive power through tactics, skills, and weapons, and the study of air warfare was neglected.... As a consequence, the leaders had little interest in such necessary factors as patrol, search, reconnaissance, contact, and training for those services, the protection of aircraft carriers and airfields, or the quick construction of air stations."

over Guadalcanal began, the air station in Rabaul was not large enough to hold all reinforcements.[47] The U.S. military was able to occupy Guadalcanal primarily because Japan spent too much time building its airfield. If Japan had had airfield construction troops capable of working more quickly, the Americans might not have taken Guadalcanal in August 1942. With more powerful air forces in Rabaul, Japan could have waged its war of attrition quite differently.[48]

On 23 December 1941, Navy landing forces occupied the Wake Island. A U.S. captive boasted that he could use one abandoned U.S. machine to do the work of three hundred men. Shocked at the high quality of U.S. machinery, the Navy Construction Headquarters planned to use U.S. machines and documents to produce bulldozers and other vehicles domestically. However, the Headquarters had little close relationship with private factories. Factories with a close connection to the Navy Technical Department and the Army were so busy producing weapons that they did not communicate with the Construction Headquarters. Nor did help come from Army factories with years of experience in manufacturing heavy vehicles such as tanks and tractors. A set of heavy construction vehicles manufactured in the mid-1943 performed poorly due to inferior production technology and defective materials, and frequently broke down (NAFHistory, 1969, [2], p. 358).[49]

Construction machines were not so special as to be used only for airfield construction. The research and development necessary to produce construction equipment were not very complicated.[50] It is clear that domestic

---

[47] The Navy Construction Troop that undertook construction and repair of air bases in occupied areas was the Special Construction Team organized just before the beginning of the Pacific War from civil construction officials and recruited workers. In February 1942, it was reorganized into the Special Construction Troop, under the command of a military officer. In May 1944, military construction troops were organized. In mid-June 1942, construction troops with two thousand members moved to Guadalcanal. The airfield was completed after one and half months' work. Just when Japanese aircraft were coming, the U.S. military captured and began to use it. The Japanese retreated in bitter disappointment (NAFHistory, 1969, [2], pp. 355–6).

[48] After Guadalcanal in August 1942, air base construction became so critical as to affect the outcome of air warfare decisively (NAFHistory, 1969, [2], p. 342).

[49] See also Yamamoto's (1982, pp. 97–100) "battle between bulldozer and man power." Asked for three hundred U.S. captives to repair bullet holes on runways, a U.S. officer answered that three would be enough. Japanese officers asked in surprise how many days it would take. "Less than a day," was the reply, and it actually took only a half day (Yamamoto, 1982, p. 97).

[50] Even before the Pacific War, many people in Japan had a basic knowledge of construction equipment from European and American magazines. Due both to unemployment relief work and the low-wage problem, interest and research were not sufficient. Japan did not

production of these machines was not an important government policy, even after the shock at Wake Island.

Until the end of the war, the Japanese government never prioritized airfield construction crews through policy. In the Navy, the rapid construction of airfields had fallen outside the focus of traditional operation plans. There was little understanding of airfield construction and few effective policies. The research for and development of construction equipment lagged far behind that of the U.S. military.[51]

Due to natural features, air bases constructed on the South Pacific islands were almost impossible to defend from air attacks. Due to weak reconnaissance capacity, air forces deployed there often suffered surprise attacks, and some of these were catastrophic. Colonel Chihaya Takahashi of the NCCom took charge of Air Force armament issues from 1935 to 1937. He refused a request from the NCCom Strategy Section to build onshore air stations in the Marshall Islands, reasoning that they would be hard to defend and might be captured and used by the enemy. He later commented (NAFHistory, 1969, [2], pp. 252-3):

At that time I firmly believed that we should have more than two runways in each airfield. Finding during the war that the enemy had more than three runways in Guadalcanal, and three in Port Moresby, ..., I realized that my plans had been inadequate.[52]

fully recognize the capacity of the U.S. military's construction equipment (NAFHistory, 1969, [2], p. 358).

[51] For more details, see NAFHistory, 1969, [2], pp. 359–60. The situation in the Army fell further behind. See Ishii (2006, pp. 174–206). Two episodes introduced in Fukudome (1951, pp. 204–5) were representative. After occupying Attu and Kiska in the Aleutian Islands, the Japanese military sent civil engineers to find the right spots for airfield construction. They concluded that there was no suitable place in occupied areas to complete an airfield in six months, with the exception of a small island close to Kiska where it would be possible in three or four months. When the Japanese began the construction on Attu, before counterattacking, the U.S. military occupied the small island Japan paid attention as an exception, and seventeen days later, small American aircraft were taking off from their airfield. In 1944, after experiments and training, the Navy moved its first mechanized construction troop to Guam. The equipment transported from Japan fell into disrepair in three months. By contrast, American machines captured at the time of occupation three years ago (two bulldozers, three transport lorries, and a dredger) continued to work effectively.

[52] Most airfields built before the war had two or three runways, but most built during the war had one runway along constant wind (NAFHistory, 1969, [2], p. 349). At that time, it was standard to land against the wind. For the details of Navy airfield construction in general, see NAFHistory (1969, [2], pp. 336–61). When U.S. runways were destroyed by gunfire or air attacks, construction troops with great mechanized capacity repaired the damage immediately, and no serious disturbance occurred in the function of airfields. The U.S. military included civil engineering machinery and construction materials whenever they sent reinforcements to Guadalcanal. In December 1942, when the Japanese decided to retreat

Evaluation (2): Replenishment

I can't help feeling that we were defeated because of replenishment problems. Neither the Air Force nor the Navy alone was to blame. Unlike the Sino–Japanese or Russo–Japanese wars, in the Pacific War, Japan fought alone without any partner. Therefore, it was a failure of the war leadership that it did not consider adequately the problem of replenishment capacity. The military as a whole must deeply regret that, expecting the U.S.–Japan War to be a total war, it failed to do careful research and preparation to ensure production and supply.

This quote is part of "Review of Air Weapons Replenishment" in NAFHistory (NAFHistory, 1969, [2], pp. 595–6). Confronting situations beyond the scope of the assumption, a war of attrition between land-based air forces instead of a one-game match between fleets of ships, replenishment became a major focus for a manifestation of the state's reaction capabilities. Yet the Japanese state performed poorly. The life of aircraft was short and its attrition rate was high.[53] Moreover, in the last war, production did not keep up with replenishment demand. As a result, the production capacity was equivalent to that of replenishment. The major cause of insufficient replenishment during the war was insufficient production (NAFHistory, 1969, [2], p. 568). In addition, both inadequate preparations for efficient replenishment and poor reaction capabilities to situations beyond the scope of the assumption in replenishments aggravated the problem.

Constantly communicating with fleets, the NCCom, the Military Bureau, and the Personnel Armament Bureau of the NM, as well with as replenishment staff offices in Naval and guard districts and Naval air arsenals, the Air Headquarters carefully surveyed production in government and private factories. The Air Headquarters drew up replenishment plans and implemented them. Replenishment was centralized in the Replenishment Division of the Air Headquarters, under which regional air arsenals cooperated (NAFHistory, 1969, [2], p. 514).

In the NAFHistory (1969, [2], p. 518) chapter titled "Types of Aircraft and Engines," one finds the following statement: "There were so many types of aircraft and engines; even under one name there were many models with different structure and features. This made replenishment complicated and

---

from Guadalcanal, there were (according to an Army aerial photo) four runways, including one for camouflage, and two more under construction. One was 1,800 meters long to accommodate large bombers (Ishii, 2006, pp. 41–2). For a U.S.–Japan comparison of airfield construction troops, see Ishii (2006, ch. 4). It was after the Japanese attack on Pearl Harbor that the U.S. Navy organized construction battalions, the so-called Seabees. More than half a year later, the Japanese organized airfield construction troops (Ishii, p. 192).

[53] The attrition rate of aircraft was so high that many said "aircraft are a commodity" (NAFHistory, 1969, [2], p. 476).

difficult to enforce. In addition, weapons and other equipment changed constantly, making replenishment even harder. Aircraft were redesigned and modified frequently during the three years and nine months of the Greater East Asian War. This seriously interfered with replenishment."

There were many types and models of aircraft and engines. For instance, in the Navy at the end of December 1942, there were forty-six types of air-cooled engines and six liquid-cooled, a total of fifty-two.[54]

Replacement air weapons had to be transported from Sumatra in the east and Andaman in the western Indian Ocean to the Aleutian Islands in the north, a distance greater than the entire western Pacific. It was a Herculean task to transport so many model-specific weapons quickly in the required quantities to troops scattered and moving across this vast territory (NAFHistory, 1969, [2], pp. 513–14).

As war spread across a wider geography, difficulties increased dramatically. Bombs and machine-gun bullets might be consumed rapidly during battle; actual consumption fluctuated drastically, according to the war situation. In addition to delivering stocks directly to fleets of vessels, it was necessary to prepare and store ammunition and other equipment in strategic key points. As of 1 September 1942, twelve types of weapon (or five times more, taking minor classifications and attachments into account) were stored in strategic key points.[55] The military had to transport, store, and

---

[54] "Well-organized product selection was vital in aircraft production. Too many aircraft in the programme diluted production effort, made standardization difficult, and reduced sharply the gains to be made from long production runs. Too many design changes to aircraft already in production, unless properly organized, could equally cost months of output because of the difficulty in changing tools, jigs, and installations to cope with the modifications, as well as producing constant interruptions to the flow of components and uncertainty in long-term production planning. The western Allies attempted to concentrate production. But more important than this, they concentrated considerable effort on the task of choosing aircraft types in such a way as to keep a balance between production and performance, between quantity and quality." In Italy and Japan, there existed simply too many types introduced at too fast a rate to guarantee sufficient output. In Japan, "during the war the navy produced 53 basic models with 112 variations, the army 37 basic models with 52 variations. America, by contrast, concentrated on the production of 18 models for the Army and the Navy together.... In addition modifications were forced upon industry in a bewildering stream, largely because of the influence of the front-line airmen whose views were regarded as the most important factor in considering changes to aircraft in production.... In Germany, the problem if less severe was still critical. It was the result of rather similar circumstances: poor technical and production appreciation, a high degree of interfirm design rivalry and a disproportionate influence of the air force itself on design changes.... In all the Axis powers the common denominator was the exclusive role of the military in choosing designs and ordering modifications without sufficient attention to the economics of aircraft production" (Overy, 1980, pp. 177–80). See also Postan (1952, pp. 166, 322, 326–7), Cairncross (1991, p. 115), and Miwa (2008, pp. 247–50).

[55] For details, see the table in NAFHistory (1969, [2], pp. 534–9).

supply in good time a wide variety of weapons to forces in the homeland and strategic key points over the Pacific Ocean,[56] from the Gilbert Islands in the east to Singapore in the west, from Kiska in the north to Rabaul south of the equator (NAFHistory, 1969, [2], pp. 533–9).

There is no replenishment without transportation. Production, transportation, and supply – these three provide an essential foundation for military force. During the Pacific War, Japan's lack of adequate transportation undermined replenishment. The Pacific War began before the leadership fully understood one lesson learned in China: the need to establish powerful air transportation units to supply air arsenals.[57] The Pacific War was a war of replenishment by long-distance air transportation over the Pacific Ocean. The Japanese military's failure to fully appreciate the importance of transportation diminished its performance (NAFHistory (1969, [2], p. 583).

The NAFHistory (1969, [2], p. 595) comments: "Replenishment territory expanded to a wide area over the western Pacific.... Due to increased transport restrictions and damage incurred in transit, together with the shortage of skilled personnel and production delays, on many occasions replenishment could not keep up with operational demands. With time it became increasingly difficult to prepare supplies in time, quantity, or quality, all essential in weapons replenishment, or to transport them efficiently to planned destinations. At the end of 1944, production material was running out and transport capacity had dropped. Shortages of air transportation crew and aviation fuel made replenishment more difficult."

9–5. Reaction Capabilities of the Government in Development and Trial Production, Production Capacity Expansion, and the Production of Aircraft

9–5–1. Aircraft Development

In section 9–5, focusing on development and trial production, production capacity expansion, and production of aircraft, I will investigate the government's reaction capabilities in air armaments, beginning with development and trial

---

[56] Eighty points in the table mentioned in note 55.

[57] On 18 February 1937, Navy transport aircraft appeared for the first time on the list of aircraft types. Most were experimental aircraft of foreign make or secondhand homemade trial production machines. The Fourth Rearmament Plan of 1939 listed thirty-five transport aircraft for the first time; the Fifth Plan of 1941 listed two units, forty-eight aircraft in total (NAFHistory (1969, [2], pp. 581–2). The Army also had a serious lack of air transportation capacity. Although a priority since the beginning of the Pacific War, the urgent need for front-line operation aircraft had left no room for developing it. In 1943, the Army finally shifted its attention also to transportation machines (Boeicho, 1975c, pp. 375–6).

production. Military operations always create a demand for higher-performance weapons, prompting technological progress. At the same time, advancing technology generates higher-performance weapons, enhancing military operations. Since the first airplane in 1903, aviation technology had made remarkable progress in a short time. Nevertheless, it was a hard task to harmonize technology and military operations (NAFHistory, 1969, [1], p. 400).

When the Navy was planning its one-game match against the United States, the Type 96 carrier-based fighter and Type 96 land-based attack aircraft were central players. As war progressed, fire prevention measures for fighters such as the Types Zero and land-based attack aircraft such as the Types 96 and 1 became more important. Yet there was still no development of high-speed reconnaissance or full-fledged transportation aircraft.

The Type Zero carrier-based fighter, first used in actual fighting in the summer of 1940, was the world's first long flight-range escort fighter. A successor capable of facing better-performing U.S. fighters was never developed.[58] The same was true in the case of a powerful large bomber.[59] No match was ever developed for America's B-17, the so-called Flying Fortress. In the final phase of the war, Japan faced much larger and more powerful B-29 bombers.[60]

---

[58] With lessons learned in China, the Navy developed Model 32, the so-called Zero-2 fighter, increasing air combat capability by giving it a 1 meter shorter wingspan, more horsepower, a better machine gun, and a slightly smaller fuel tank, although this reduced its flight range. The Zero-2 fighter was sent to Rabaul just before the U.S. military advanced to Guadalcanal. It could not be used in the battle over Guadalcanal because of its flight range, which became so serious a problem that the Head of Air Headquarters tendered his resignation. However, the plane could not have flown from Rabaul to Guadalcanal even with the original flight range (Boeicho, 1976, p. 287). Had it been used in a one-game match, sacrificing flight range for air combat capability would have been an advantage. Also recall the recollection of Kiro Honjo, the Chief Designer both of the Types 96 and 1 attack aircraft, at the start of the Type 1 development, mentioned in subsection 8–2–2. In 1940, the skeleton of a request for Reppu (storm wind), as a carrier-based fighter to succeed Zero, was presented to Mitsubishi. Its development started with Horikoshi as Chief Designer. However, Mitsubishi and the Air Technical Arsenal could not agree on its engine and wing loading, so the project did not achieve the expected result. The NAFHistory (1969, [3], p. 430) offers a harsh criticism: "the Air Headquarters, particularly the person in charge of engines, stuck with the Homare engine and ignored MK9A. He had unrealistic expectations that the exhaust gas turbine engine could be completed, grossly delaying the completion of Reppu and Shiden and also of Renzan and Saiun, then in trial production; this degraded the practical performance of those aircraft."

[59] Shinzan, Renzan, and Fugaku were never tried after the success of the Type 1 medium-sized attack aircraft. For details, see NAFHistory (1969, [3], pp. 481–4). The Army's large bombers, such as the Type 97 Heavy 2 Model, never worked at all (Boeicho, 1975c, pp. 374–5).

[60] It took at least three to five years for an airplane to be developed and used. Some experimental aircraft manufactured by 1942 could be used in actual battles. It is no wonder at

9-5-2. Performance Standards for Aircraft and Trial Production

On 6 December 1923, the NCCommander negotiated with the Navy Minister about aircraft types and performance standards for the first time. Subsequently, performance standards were revised roughly every three years, to take account of domestic and international technology levels.

Performance standards, determined through the following process, became the basis of the Air Headquarters' trial production plan for aircraft. Requests for aircraft were developed in the plan, and the companies and arsenals in charge were ordered to begin trial production (NAFHistory, 1969, [1], pp. 401-6): The NCCom drew up the original plan, which was revised through discussions with Air Headquarters, and then sent to the Yokosuka Naval District Staff Office, where the Air Technical Arsenal and Yokosuka Air Squadron reviewed it primarily from the viewpoint of production technology and practicality and submitted their own opinions. With this feedback, the Air Headquarters examined and revised the plan and reached a final decision at the Air Headquarters Technical Conference. The NCCom then formally presented it to the Navy Ministry. Before formally determining performance standards, the managers of relevant sections usually met for a careful discussion of operational and technological considerations. They sought

all, taking into consideration the time spent on fielding requests, designing, manufacturing, reviewing, and conducting practical trials, as well as mass producing the plane after the model was formally adopted as a weapon and training Air Force units. The Type Zero fighter, for example, experimentally manufactured under favorable conditions with extraordinary zeal, took more than three years to develop, from 19 May 1937 to its formal adoption at the end of July 1940 (NAFHistory, 1969, [3], p. 306). Particularly after the beginning of Pacific War, requests for new types of aircraft became more urgent and constraints, including shortages, more severe, leading to longer development times. The same applied to the Army. Boeicho (1975c, pp. 524-5) concluded that most aircraft active in the Greater East Asian War had been planned before it started; given Japan's development and production capability, it should have been possible to fast-track a few types and models of aircraft for trial production and actual use.

This problem was not specific to Japan. Almost every American airplane used in combat during the Second World War was at least on the drawing boards before the war began (Rae, 1968, p. 103). "In summer and autumn 1938, the new Hurricanes and Spitfires arrived in the squadrons. [B]y September 1939, Fighter Command, alone of the RAF's forces was ready for war" (Murray, 1999, p. 94). Me 109s and 110s, Dornier 17s, He 111s, Ju 87 Stukas, and Ju 88s were all on hand before the war began. With the sole exception of the FW 190, not a single new major aircraft type was added to the Luftwaffe until the last year of the war. The Luftwaffe reached its peak of effectiveness before the war had ever begun (Cairncross, 1991, p. 127). See also Miwa (2008, 4-8-2, pp. 271-4).

to identify achievable lines. This usually took more than six months, and sometimes more than a year.[61]

New and rebuilt aircraft models were generally developed by private companies; the government had the difficult job of controlling and supervising them through incentives and other basic policy measures. Both the quantity and quality of development work were uneven, making it hard to maintain and enhance capacities for trial production. In 1938, presenting standards for trial production capacity, the Navy asked manufacturing companies to expand trial production capacities (due to be completed in March 1941 for equipment and March 1943 for engineers). At the same time, the Navy ordered that production capacity expansion keep pace with the Fourth Rearmament Plan. Subsequently, it requested increases in production capacity for fuselage and then in the number of aircraft trial production; the standards were revised in 1942. To achieve such expansion, companies had to increase personnel and equipment for trial production by 2 to 2.5 times. They faced challenging problems and made fairly slow progress (NAFHistory, 1969, [3], pp. 282–5).

The NAFHistory (1969, [3], pp. 311–12) lists four key points:

(1) The aircraft manufacturing industry as a whole did not sufficiently prepare or develop trial production capabilities;

(2) The next trial production plan for aircraft, established in 1939 for FY1939–FY1942, at least considered trial production capabilities. In reality, however, the plan was not implemented systematically;

(3) Japan should have prioritized implementation and trial production;

(4) Concerning principal characteristics of individual models, in order not to become the best-laid plans, we should have guided trial productions from the beginning of discussion on requests for planning. We had not fully prepared for experimentally manufacturing high-performance aircraft incorporating new technology.[62]

Receiving various modification demands from the front, the Yokosuka Air Squadron and Yokosuka Air Technical Arsenal assessed their degree of urgency and made the changes. In fact, however, it was normal that they

---

[61] The Guidelines for Aircraft Model Renewal established in 1927 stated (1) that an old model aircraft would be replaced with a new one within the next fiscal year after its formal adoption as a weapon, and (2) that new aircraft models would not be renewed within four fiscal years of their introduction (NAFHistory, 1969, [4], p. 275).

[62] The government's role as a competent planner is to combine centralization, delegation, and coordination; Japan's leaders did not manage to provide this competence, although it was desperately needed and expected.

had to accept the demands from operating forces. Major General Toshitane Takada of the Combined Fleets, a former aircraft carrier Vice-Captain and Vice-Head of Yokosuka Air Squadron, recalled (NAFHistory, 1969, [3], p. 369): "It was characteristic of the NAF that there were many opinions on various issues. I sometimes felt overwhelmed by all these opinions. During the war, particularly when it came to modifications of aircraft models, it was so overwhelming that I struggled hard to make choices, as Vice-Head of Yokosuka Air Squadron. There were approximately three hundred modification demands for each model."

Performance standards were central to the Air Headquarters' trial production plan for aircraft; they determined how requests were formulated and projects delegated to companies and arsenals. It was unclear, however, who in this process would prepare for and take prompt and appropriate actions in response to the realization of situations beyond the scope of the assumption. Observations suggest that reactions were not solicited. The process of delegating trial productions to companies and arsenals was concluded inside the Navy, leaving managers and engineers in charge of the trials no opportunity participate or express their opinions.[63]

9-5-3. Production Capacity Expansion

Depending on the conditions of war, the demand for munitions can increase significantly. Moreover, it is almost impossible to predict precisely whether or when they will be needed. It is not easy for any government to obtain from private companies the precise munitions production capacity that it needs, as that capacity will necessarily change dramatically and unexpectedly.

---

[63] Recall the comment of Overy (1980, pp. 178–9) quoted previously: "in Japan modifications were forced upon industry in a bewildering stream, largely because of the influence of the front-line airmen whose views were regarded as the most important factor in considering changes to aircraft in production." He also commented (Overy, 1980, p. 180): "That British and American businessmen were integrated into the organization and planning of aircraft production was not simply a reflection of particular closeness between the governmental and commercial elites but of an anxiety on the part of firms to be involved from the start in questions to do with contracts, production and particularly finance." As mentioned previously, Churchill set up a new department, hived off from the Air Ministry, to put fresh urgency into the production of aircraft (Cairncross, 1991, p. 7). See also Edgerton (2006, pp. 73–4) and Miwa (2008, 4–5, pp. 247–54); As mentioned in note 35 of Chapter 7, aircraft were supplied to the front after exacting tests and should have been trouble-free. However, front-line troops generally experienced problems, particularly maintenance discrepancies (NAFHistory, 1969, [1], p. 915).

With use and technical progress, the value of aircraft increased rapidly after the mid-1930s. As production expanded, requests for increased and improved capacity also increased. Problems with munitions procurement were particularly pronounced in relation to aircraft. Incentives could have played a crucial role.

After the Third Rearmament Plan was put into effect in 1937, Japan's aircraft production increased strikingly. Before the plan, the Navy managed enforcement by informally notifying private firms of the next year's orders. This system no longer worked under the Fourth Plan; the Navy issued orders (*jitatsu*) to the private producers (NAFHistory, 1969, [3], p. 328).[64]

It was considered impossible to double production capacity from 1938 levels immediately. For this reason, the planned doubling took place in two phases. The first phase was ordered on 15 November 1938, with a March 1940 target of 3,024 fuselages and 5,700 engines (the date was later changed to March 1941). At the end of March 1941, there were still 2,600 unfilled orders for aircraft requested in 1939 and 1940. At the end of August 1941, this number had fallen to 300, delaying the completion of the first phase by about one year (NAFHistory, 1969, [3], pp. 328–33).

The first phase was implemented entirely through private means.[65] For the second phase, from April 1941 through March 1943, the government opted to use a government owned, contractor operated (GOCO) system to meet the requirements of the Fourth Rearmament Plan. Given the difference between wartime and peacetime funding, and between supplies and demand, the government recognized that private companies could not bear the whole cost of these plans. One hundred and fifty thousand workers had already been employed for the second phase; to complete in two years would not be easy.

Demand increased faster than capacity. The demand for fuselages in FY1942 (unofficially announced in summer 1941) was 3,757, while the actual FY1942 demand was 5,986 in June 1942. At the end of 1941, a first

---

[64] This *jitatsu* was considered equivalent to a production order based on the National General Mobilization Act. Although it had no legal foundation, it was a direct order from the Head of Air Headquarters, which was obliged to offer maximum assistance and cooperation to companies receiving orders. With the establishment of the Munitions Ministry in November 1943, the issue of legality was corrected (NAFHistory, 1969, [3], pp. 328–9).

[65] The target of 3,024 fuselages was more than three times the expected annual average. For this reason, even in the first phase, those involved argued heatedly about the procedure for issuing orders. Difficult questions included who would bear the cost of equipment, how to recruit workers, and what the state's warranty and indemnity should be. The Air Headquarters, obtaining the consent of all sections, began its enforcement (NAFHistory, 1969, [2], p. 572).

enforcement plan was implemented, to keep the Fourth Rearmament Plan on track for its March 1944 deadline. When the Revised Fifth Rearmament Plan was established, a third-phase capacity expansion plan was ordered (to meet increased demand by the end of March 1946), although the second phase was still in process (NAFHistory, 1969, [3], pp. 335–9).[66]

Two points are important.

1. Implementation of the plans to expand production capacity faced serious challenges, and actual aircraft production fell far short of rapidly increasing demand.
2. In the phase of expanding production capacity for the Fourth Rearmament Plan, ordered in April 1941, the government adopted GOCO in part to strengthen enforcement.

When, together with production capacity expansion of aircraft, the need to produce more airplanes became an urgent issue of the highest priority, the government adopted a GOCO system to make enforcement possible. At nearly the same time, the Tojo Cabinet enacted a series of laws, including the Industrial Equipment Authority Act, the Special Act for Promoting Weapons Manufacturing Industries, the Wartime Loan Bank Act, and the

---

[66] In the United Kingdom in July 1934, Neveille Chamberlain, then Chancellor of the Exchequer, overturned the recommendations of the government's Defense Requirements Committee by imposing drastic cuts on its proposals for Army and Navy rearmament. At the same time, Chamberlain directed that the strength of the Metropolitan Air Force be raised from the fifty-two squadrons proposed by the committee to eighty squadrons. This symbolic intervention established an order of priorities that was retained throughout the rearmament years. It was based on the belief that the next war would be an air war: a war that would be won or lost in the air. Through a process of consolidation, the key wartime contractors, Vickers, Hawker Siddeley, Bristol, De Havilland, and Rolls-Royce, were in place by 1935. These contractors were highly profitable and were able to gain considerable production experience before the commencement of rearmament. Nevertheless, consecutive Air Ministry studies demonstrated that the industry was not in itself capable of meeting the needs of war production, so plans were drawn up to augment the capacity of the professional airframe and aero-engine firms by employing automobile and other engineering companies as "shadows," to concentrate industrial resources into groups, and to create a state production organization to coordinate the output of the different sectors of the aircraft industry. It was expected that these plans might have to be implemented without notice to bridge the gap between Royal Airforce (RAF) requirements and industrial capacity in the first twelve months of a war, but in the event, Britain was granted a breathing space of some five years in which to rearm. A cohesive state production policy also developed in stages. In 1935, RAF specifications were relaxed, the Capital Clause was introduced to encourage investment, two-year contracts were allocated to certain firms, and the progress payment scheme was extended. In the following year, the government approved far more ambitious plans to re-equip the RAF with modern aircraft. Three-year contracts were placed, and further financial concessions were granted to the aircraft industry, with which the first shadow factories were set up (Ritchie, 1997, pp. 255–7).

Key Materials Control Authority Act, to provide incentives. None of those measures achieved anything significant by the end of the war.[67]

At the beginning of 1942, the government founded two arsenals: Kouza (in Kanagawa Prefecture) and Tsu (in Mie Prefecture). Whereas most Navy air arsenals specialized in repairs, these were designed for aircraft mass production. Although the Navy made construction a top priority, there was a delay in obtaining materials and machine tools, and the arsenals were opened unfinished in April 1944. Due to model changes and other obstacles, the Kouza arsenal produced only sixty Raiden fighters by the end of the war. The original annual production target of this arsenal was five thousand aircraft made by thirty-five thousand workers; it has been the largest fuselage manufacturing plant in the country. No engine was ever produced in the Tsu Arsenal (NAFHistory, 1969, [3], pp. 354–5).

9–5–4. The Causes of Failure in Aircraft Production Expansion

Aircraft production was strictly conditioned by the availability of resources. However, actual performance consistently fell far below the level that should have been attained given the resources available. The government was unable to coordinate the activities of producers, suggesting that its competence may have been low also in the areas of war planning, mobilization, and economic control. Here I focus on the weakness or insufficiency in production technology, particularly the one for mass production, and the absence or failure of policies to remedy and improve it.[68]

---

[67] For more details, see subsection 5–2–1. The establishment of the Munitions Ministry was 1 November 1943, and on 15 January 1944 the administration of aircraft production was transferred to the Munitions Ministry. It was in October 1944 when the leaders of the NM and the NCCom decided a significant diversion of equipment from the Navy Technical Department to enhancing air armaments, in order to shift the emphasis completely to the Air Force (NAFHistory, 1969, [3], p. 341).

[68] Obviously, improving mass-production technology was not the only problem that needed a solution. In "Deterioration in the Quality of Aircraft Produced," Boeicho (1975c, pp. 442–3) concluded that product quality was lost as technical skills evaporated and substitutes were used in place of scarce materials. In February 1944, two-thirds of manufactured aircraft were said to be unsuitable for front-line use. The Aircraft Review Division asked the Munitions Ministry to mass-produce precisely the prototype machine. The Munitions Ministry responded that most failures occurred after delivery, when planes were fully equipped by the military. Producers delivered aircraft to the military, after flight inspection, without any equipment except meters; the air arsenals fitted them out for the front line. See also Yamamoto (1982, pp. 199–200). He added: "During the War with China, we could use bomber engines continuously for 400 hours on an easy daily maintenance routine. At the end stage of the Pacific War, we had to overhaul engines entirely after 60 hours continuous

9-5-5. Controlling Aircraft Production

The systematic control of aircraft production was different from the production of other munitions:

1. Even in the same type of aircraft, frequent and radical modifications (model changes) were necessary.
2. Aircraft were constructed from a wide variety of components. As models were changed and new models introduced, modifications of many components became necessary.
3. The path from development to the mass production of a new type of aircraft was long. During the process, both underlying technological conditions and user demands changed radically.

I have already mentioned the third point on development and trial production. The development of new types and new models of aircraft was important, but frequent and radical modifications of established models were also significant.[69] As Postan (1952, p. 322) succinctly explained: "The quality of aircraft was subject to changes much more radical and more frequent than those of any other weapon, not excluding the tank. What ... is even more important is that, in their endeavours to maintain the quality of aircraft, the Air Minister and M.A.P. frequently had to sacrifice quantity. And here again, of no other weapon, not even the tank, can it be said that its output was equally subjected and sacrificed to considerations of quality. Had aircraft design and development been frozen or even retarded at the beginning of the expansion, or even at the beginning of the war, and no modifications or replacements been allowed to interfere with the flow of production, the output would have far outstripped the actual figures." He

---

use" (Yamamoto, 1982, p. 200).The number of aircraft accidents in FY1943 increased to 1.8 times that of the previous year. Although the faults were generally human, 12.9 percent were caused by equipment failure. The trend of increasing numbers of accidents did not stop in FY1944. (Boeicho, 1976, p. 210). Aircraft transportation also needed skilled crew members to reduce accidental losses, but the Navy could not provide them. The Navy judged the preparation of transport aircraft as secondary, and left them insufficiently prepared.

    Also recall the curved runway episode mentioned in section 4–6: of all the Army airplanes lost during August–December 1943, approximately 80 percent were due to accidents during takeoff or landing or to destruction on the ground.

[69] The Type 96 land-based attack aircraft was the most important land-based attack aircraft used in the War with China. As mentioned in section 8–3, for the concentrated attack, Operation 101, which began on 18 May 1940 the Type 96 Model 21 (G3M2) was replaced by its successor, Model 23 (G3M3). From an operational viewpoint, the greatest improvement was its ultra-high-altitude performance; it could avoid, and was said to have eliminated, attacks by Chinese fighters. That summer, the Type Zero carrier-based fighter was introduced. For more details, see Iwaya (2003, pp. 131–2) or Miwa (2008, p. 268, note 51).

noted as well: "The high average level of quality was a great achievement; but what from the point of view of production was more relevant was that the high quality was largely achieved not by frequent introduction of new designs, but by the constant modification and improvement of established types. Had the R.A.F. been entirely dependent for their technical progress on frequent replacement of old designs by new, an uninterrupted improvement in the quality of their aircraft would have been difficult to attain" (Postan, 1952, pp. 326–7).

Aircraft were constructed from a wide variety and huge number of components. According to the NAFHistory (1969, [2], p. 573): "The fuselage was composed of 10,000–20,000 different items, 100,000–150,000 in number. The engine was composed of 900 items, 8,500 in number. Most components were supplied by subcontractors, but when mass production began, those subcontractors and other companies were of little help."[70]

9–5–6. The Case of the Shiden and Shiden-Kai

Soon after the first test flight of the Kawanishi Aircraft Company's land-based fighter, Shiden (Violet Lightning, N1K-J), at the end of December 1942, the Navy ordered trial production of the Shiden-kai (N2K-J fighter, *kai* standing for "modified") in February 1943. A prototype flew on 1 January 1944, and the Navy judged it a fully satisfactory fighter. Mass production was scheduled for the start of 1944, involving not only Kawanishi but other producers and Navy arsenals.

In designing the Shiden-kai, as well as improving performance, the Navy set an additional target to make production easier. This involved reducing the number of components. Leaving aside the engine, propeller, bolts, nuts, and rivets, the Siden was composed of 66,000 components; this was reduced to 43,000 in the Shiden-kai. The number of components had a substantial impact on production, inspection, and management (Kikuhara, 1982, pp. 117–21).[71]

With the exception of the engine, undercarriage, and propeller, which were supplied by the government, the Shiden-kai's 43,000 components were

---

[70] "The automobile industry was similar in character to the aircraft industry. The U.S. automobile industry was a well-established mass-production assembly industry, relying on subcontractors that produced components and materials. Through a startling and beautiful concentration of production capacity, the U.S. converted its peacetime automobile industry into a wartime munitions industry, manufacturing a wide variety of air weapons" (NAFHistory, 1969, [2], p. 573). For details of aircraft production by the U.S. automobile industry, see Rae (1968, pp. 128–40).

[71] Yamamoto (1982, p. 199) recalled that in the final stage of the war, there were approximately one hundred Shiden-kai fighters at Ohmura under his command. "Due to overproduction

produced by many manufacturers of materials and functional components. When the Shiden-kai appeared, most private industries had already been forced to convert themselves into munitions production factories. Many became aircraft components factories; Kawanishi also directed production conversion and cooperated with 340 factories, not only in its own region of Hyogo but in Osaka, Kyoto, Tokushima, Fukui, and Ishikawa. Forty percent of the sheet metal processing parts and 50 percent of the machining process components in the Kawanishi fuselage were produced by those factories. As a result, Kawanishi could not produce the Shiden-kai unless those components were supplied by cooperative factories, regardless of its mass production equipment (Watanabe, 1995, p. 238).

As the government also failed to supply components on time, the Shiden-kai production did not proceed as planned. It was 1944 and everything was in short supply. Securing the rivets necessary for fuselage production was a particular challenge. The rivet-producing factory was located in Tsujido in Kanagawa. All factories producing aircraft were under enormous pressure, and there was severe competition (Watanabe, 1995, pp. 237, 239).[72]

As Cairncross (1991, p. 38) wrote: "Planning aircraft production … was quite unlike planning the production of ammunition where the same item was turned out month after month. It was necessary to decide months in advance which aircraft were to be produced and where, what modifications were necessary and when, what components of all kinds would have to be ready for use at each stage, and so on. The scale and pattern of output were always in flux and could only be reduced to order by comprehensive programmes that could not be suspended one day and reintroduced much later as if all the changes envisaged in the programmes were of no account."

9–5–7. Causes of Failure in Aircraft Production Expansion

To summarize these points, I will briefly introduce a well-written overall review from the NAFHistory ([3], pp. 367–70), which asks why aircraft

---

of inferior goods, only fifty could take off when needed. Moreover, when they landed after an air battle to refuel and take on bullets, only half could take off again. They could not respond to the secondary and tertiary attacks of U.S. aircraft."

[72] The Shiden-kai loaded the Homare engine Model 21, made by Nakajima Aircraft. Maekawa (2000, pp. 132–8), an engineer in charge of managing the production of Homare, recalled that serious confusion was caused not only by the technical difficulties specific to its production, but also by the smallest component, an oil filter, as the production of this auxiliary machinery fell behind.

production did not increase as expected. Six causes are listed. Here is the outline[73]:

1. The system of mass production was not well established. Many producers had the experience of asking many ministries for support without achieving their objectives.
2. Preparation for mass production was insufficient, as illustrated below:

    a. There was insufficient intelligent design to make mass production work efficiently. Aircraft were rushed from trial production to mass production. Designers knew nothing about engineering, and production engineers were inexperienced. It was necessary to review trial production drawings from a mass production viewpoint, as it was difficult to make big changes later.[74]

    b. Standardization remained poor. Without careful preparations, it was hard to accomplish it in a short time.

    c. The production of basic tools did not keep pace with aircraft production expansion. Basic tools were secondary in aircraft production policies. This caused serious troubles in starting and increasing production.

    d. The development of subcontracting factories was very poor. The Navy was too busy expanding the major parent companies that

---

[73] The NAFHistory (1969, [2], pp. 568–75) commented on productivity, as mentioned in the preceding discussion, listing sixteen causes of productivity failure, most of which are included in the six causes I introduce in the text. The last sentence read: "In design and trial production, aviation technology in our country had reached a world-class level. However, production and particularly mass production technology fell far short of the U.S. and European standard." The NAFHistory cited the startling and beautiful conversion of America's peacetime automobile industry into a munitions industry. Japan's automobile production at its prewar peak in 1941 was 46,498, (the U.S. figure was 4,840,000), equivalent to the U.S. output of 1907, which was 44,000). Japan's total production of 24,388 in 1938 corresponds to the U.S. output of 25,000 in 1905.

[74] Lieutenant General Ryutaro Shibuya, the last Head of the Navy Technical Department, early on became keenly aware of the need for the Navy Technical Department to support developing air technology. Recognizing that each aircraft producer had its own tradition and characteristics, he commented that Mitsubishi's aircraft construction was scientific and well organized. Fully understanding the design and production requirements of the Air Technical Arsenal, it made the prototype as much as possible through a gauge system that could produce one hundred to two hundred machines. Collaborating closely with engineers of the Air Technical Arsenal, Nakajima accepted difficult challenges, even if they seemed impossible to accomplish. As a consequence, some of their products were difficult to produce. Although its performance-first policy was intended to overcome production difficulties, Nakajima's yield rate was low (NAFHistory, 1969, [3], p. 353).

made fuselages and engines to develop subcontractors. Production capacity was quantitatively insufficient, but its qualitative improvement was further delayed. Nothing could be achieved without strengthening the foundation.

   e. Mass production requires full quality control that employs statistical methods; this was not carried out.

3. Demand for weapon renewal was overwhelming. The Navy began trial productions one right after another, and was soon exhausted.[75] It was natural to have rampant demand in wartime, but the lengthy development process meant that few new products launched after the war began were ever used in the battlefield.

4. Engineers were scarce; this affected production and repair in the Navy and its production companies because the priority of air armaments was low. Moreover, in principle, Navy arsenals were specialized in repair, rather than production. As a consequence, only a few specialized engineers took part in the production process. Capacity expansion and dispersion among production companies required expertise that was not available.[76]

5. The Navy was plagued by a flood of modification demands from operating forces. The Yokosuka Air Squadron and Yokosuka Air Technical Arsenal carefully assessed their urgency and implemented them. In fact, it was normal that they had to accept the demands from operating forces.

6. Even the points previously mentioned do not fully explain why Japan could not accomplish its production programs. Each production capacity expansion plan assumed many conditions that were not actually satisfied. In most cases, producers could do nothing to provide these conditions. Upon mutual agreement among persons concerned both in government and private, those plans were set

---

[75] By the end of 1941, Mitsubishi had produced approximately five hundred Zero fighters; after 1942, production was stalled and often disrupted. Naokazu Yui, the Mitsubishi manager, explained that the problems were caused by the startup of the 14-shi land-based fighter (Mitsubishi J2M, later called Raiden, which translates as "Thunderbolt") and by repeated changes in production program (Yui, 1982, p. 71).

[76] According to Lieutenant General Shibuya (mentioned in note 75 of this chapter), in the final stage of the war, many factories, including those producing components, had a yield of approximately 7 percent for products and components. Even among the best, more than 50 percent was rare. To produce the same aircraft, Japan was using much more aluminum than the United States or Germany: in fuselage production, 6–6.5 tons versus 5–5.5 tons per aircraft. This happened because Japanese producers were not careful with materials and did not prepare them well enough; many components had to be scrapped, resulting in a low yield rate (NAFHistory, 1969, [3], p. 352).

into action. The real consequences, however, were simply that they tried their best efforts. The assumed conditions were not satisfied, but targets were never modified. It was a natural consequence of the time that Japan strove to satisfy operational demands, while recognizing that this could not be done under the Material-Mobilization Plans.

The Causes of Failure

We must also consider the foundation and background underpinning these six causes of failure. Colonel Koi Kawamura, a Doctor of Engineering in the Navy Air Technical Arsenal, was consistently engaged in research on materials and production. His five requirements were (NAFHistory, 1969, [3], pp. 866–9):

(1) to establish basic industries;
(2) to strengthen research into industry technology;
(3) to have a supply of optimally sized materials;
(4) to cultivate among leaders a basic understanding of technology; and
(5) to recruit experienced experts from outside.

These lessons are summarized briefly. Readers should remember that the automobile and other mass production industries were at an early stage of development. Without waiting for active initiatives from private companies, the government enforced a government-led interventionist development policy.

1. It is extremely difficult, in creating a new industry, to be mindful of all the related basic industries. The government as planner should have taken care of both technological and political issues.
2. In prewar Japan, the development of production technology, particularly in forging and casting, was deficient. One cause of failure in the previous war was a low level of production technology in every industrial sector, generally requiring much time and money to improve.
3. The mass production of materials and components requires the mechanization or automation of machinery. The adoption of die-forging and casting and other machines required optimally sized, defect-free materials. Without carefully prepared materials, mechanization faced difficulties.

4. Most high-level policy makers had little understanding of technology. As a result, they often made mistakes or caused unnecessary confusion. This tendency became pronounced as productivity deteriorated after the beginning of the Pacific War.
5. Many sectors must cooperate to solve problems that arise in pursuing a common goal. I am deeply aware that Japanese people do not readily cooperate, and recommend that future cooperation be conducted smoothly and substantively in order to solve important national issues.

9–6. The Competence of Decision Makers and Managers in Allocating Human Resources

After the two preceding sections, many readers may ask the following:

- What were the causes of the deficiency, failure to improve, and poor policy measures?
- Why was the situation left unresolved?
- Why couldn't Japan bypass these problems? Hadn't the Japanese government anticipated them? Why did it not prepare adequate countermeasures?

Those questions lead us to the focus of this book: the competence of the state. Did the Japanese government take the country into war without anticipating the problems involved or preparing countermeasures? Did it lack the competence to anticipate such situations? Did it not realize how difficult these difficulties would be to resolve? Did Japan plan this war? Did it deliberately start, wage, and lead the war to crushing defeat? Was Japan competent to enforce systematic war preparations, mobilization, and economic control?

The Pacific War began four and a half years after the beginning of the War with China. Regardless of whether the War with China was unexpected, a competent state would not have left such a long list of urgent issues unresolved until the start of the Pacific War. In section 9–6, I focus on decision makers and managers, and investigate the placement and allocation of human resources.

Human-beings (or human resources) make up the government, make the rules that guide government, and thus condition and determine the competence and behavior of the state. Aircraft production during the Pacific War illustrates the peculiarity, insufficiency, and defects in the competence of the Japanese state.

9-6-1. Three Factors

Many related issues can be classified into three factors. All factors are mutually connected and interdependent.

1. The defective allocation of human resources, in particular specialists
2. The lack of decision makers and managers with necessary qualities, abilities, and knowledge
3. A weak or incompetent government

In the following subsections, I discuss the substance of factors 1 through 3 and their mutual interdependence.

9-6-2. Policy Measures Adopted for Production Expansion

The NAFHistory (1969, [3], pp. 353-60) listed ten measures adopted to boost aircraft production. It then discussed managerial theories as to why performance was lower than expected. The titles of ten measures were the following:

1. The issuing of orders on aircraft production capacity expansion to private producers
2. The integration of Army and Navy aircraft models and unifying aircraft production under the umbrella of the Munitions Ministry
3. The shortage of materials
4 The shortage of machine tools
5. The standardization of components
6. The investigation of designs for mass production
7. Improvement of efficiency
8. Implementation of modifications
9. Cooperation with the Navy Technical Department
10. Rationalization of military demands

None of the measures would prove very effective.

As the NAFHistory (1969, [3], p. 357) observes:

At that time, it was a rule to reexamine the structural design of any aircraft before making the transition from trial production to practical testing and mass production. However, the pressure to begin production was so intense that design modifications were adopted only when serious problems seemed likely. Even when there was enough time, it was not easy to implement design modifications. We must have examined the design on the drawing at the stage of trial production in order to make it suitable for mass production. Establishing a study group for production increase, we tried to examine the design of aircraft in production, like value analysis as we know it today, but we could achieve no remarkable result.

Why had the Japanese Navy or government not realized the importance of considering mass production when designing and trialing aircraft?

The next point concerning measure 7 is illustrative of the issue. In mid-1942, only one member of Air Headquarters was an expert in production technology and management. By applying the progress method that he used to manage components in air arsenals, he contributed to production increases in several companies. As the production volume of the Navy was small, however, fostering industrial engineers was not sufficient. It had few experts on production management in aircraft mass-production, and no organization working to resolve the problem (NAFHistory, 1969, [3], p. 359). Why weren't there more experts in charge of production technology and management in aircraft production?

Concerning measure 8, the NAFHistory commented: "It is natural that war lessons and operational needs led to modification demands. All demands were given equal weight, making the whole system uncoordinated. Despite emergency measures that (1) examined and evaluated individual demands, (2) reassigned tasks to air arsenals, and (3) urgently procured modification components, aircraft production was seriously affected. Why had the government failed to coordinate this process?" (NAFHistory, 1969, [3], pp. 359–60).

Concerning measure 9, the NAFHistory pointed out: "At the end of 1944, Navy leaders agreed to reorganize armament production and to prioritize the Air Force. The Navy Technical Department was to be substantially converted to air armaments. But preparations were insufficient and it was already too late" (NAFHistory, 1969, [3], p. 360). Why was this policy not adopted and enforced earlier and more effectively? Why was Air Headquarters unready to provide support?[77]

---

[77] Lieutenant General Shibuya, mentioned in previous notes, recognized the need to send Naval engineers, not only those in machinery- and shipbuilding but also trained to work with electricity, navigation, materials, machining, and fuel to the Air Force to develop aviation technology. He recalled that its realization had been extremely difficult, and explained (NAFHistory, 1969, [3], pp. 350–1): "Due to both the arrogance of young engineers in the Air Headquarters and the selfish attitude of engineers in the Navy Technical Department, we could not fully support Air Headquarters or boost cooperative production capacity.... It was not entirely due to the holding back of engineers by the Navy Technical Department, but also resistance with arrogant pride of engineers in the Air Headquarters played a part"; Some readers may wonder what would have happened had the Navy or Japanese government reorganized Navy armament production to focus on the Air Force before the beginning of the War with China. Those readers should refer to Miwa (2008, 4–9, pp. 280–5):

(1) The Human Resources Failure, and the Lack of Experts

Neither the Navy nor the government cultivated and recruited enough experts. Between the Battle of the Coral Sea in May and the Midway Operation in June 1942, Japanese Navy codes were broken by the United States. Fukudome (1951, pp. 219–20) described the malpractice committed by the Japanese Navy code-breaking section as wise after the event, and recollected: "Code-breaking was a reliable and fast way to understand the enemy's situation. The Japanese Navy made a great effort to break U.S. military codes but was not able to. Japanese Navy experts claimed that their own codes were the most advanced in Japan. Although there was a general lack of scientific knowledge throughout Japan, the Navy made things worse by insisting that its code-breakers must be Navy soldiers. With rare exceptions, soldiers under quick rotation were ill suited to this kind of task. Without experts, who had devoted their lives to specialized research, there could be no satisfactory progress."[78]

This point leads to the last lesson of Colonel Kawamura: the need to recruit outside experts: "It is most important for persons concerned in many sectors to cooperate in solving problems to achieve a common goal. The Japanese do not readily cooperate." As mentioned previously, performance standards became the foundation of the Air Headquarters' trial production plan for practical aircraft. Requests for trial production aircraft were formulated as part of the plan; production was delegated to companies and arsenals. This process took place within the Navy, giving engineers no opportunity to participate directly or indirectly by expressing their opinions and giving advice.[79]

Would the war have ended differently if Japan had converted to Air Force–centered rearmament at an early date? Would the outcome have been different if the Army and the Navy had cooperated smoothly?

[78] Genda (1996, p. 218) noted as the third cause of the Midway defeat: "There was a fundamental flaw in both counterespionage and code protection on our side and an advantage in espionage and code-breaking on the enemy's. For the Navy and government, it was a really serious problem."

[79] As shown in subsection 5-2-1, both the Production Capacity Expansion Plans (PCEPlans) and enforcement plans were formulated by bureaucrats of the Planning Council and other ministries. The discussions were secret; even representatives of the business community were not allowed to participate (MITI, 1964, p. 222). Many readers, particularly those familiar with the conventional view of wartime Japan, may recall the well-known term "reformist bureaucrats," or *kakushin kanryo*, mentioned in section 5-2, or "new bureaucrats" or "Team Manchuria" mentioned in Chapter 6. I encourage them to ask the following four questions: (1) Who were those reformist bureaucrats and how many were there? (2) Were they able to take an active role? Could they do more than formulate and enforce the PCEPlans for basic materials? Were they allowed to participate in producing aircraft, helping to decide the specifications of aircraft and their development and trial production? (3)

There were also serious problems in allocating scarce engineers and skilled workers. Maekawa (2000, p. 129), as an assistant to the chief promoter of Homare engine production, took charge of Homare production relationships for Nakajima Aircraft. In the section entitled "Losing a Partner," he criticized the disregard for technology that allowed his most important partner to receive a draft card just when production was on the right track. They never considered what an important military task this person was engaged in. In his place, they supplied technologically unskilled recruited workers and students, which caused great confusion in production.

Horikoshi (1950, p. 604) complained: "in 1940 and 1941, young engineering graduates were under mandatory military service. As a result, they were all recruited to the Army and the Navy. The supply of new engineers to the private sector almost ceased, reducing the number of engineers involved in the process of actual production. It was only in 1944 that some engineers were sent to private companies as engineering officers, instead of to military service."[80]

(2) The Deficiencies of Decision Makers and Managers

Particularly after the beginning of the war, the government could not expect the market alone to allocate adequate human resources to private companies responsible for munitions such as aircraft. For this reason, it was necessary for decision makers and managers at each stage of the government decision-making system to have the knowledge and capacity to recognize those human resources indispensable for key private companies. They must also recognize the grave consequences of misallocating of human resources.

The overwhelming scarcity of experts in charge of production technology and management illustrates the problem. Lieutenant General Shibuya, the last Head of the Navy Technical Department, pointed out (NAFHistory, 1969, [3], pp. 352–3): "Old leaders in the Air Headquarters had a poor understanding of production, leaving its management to their subordinates; high officers in charge of technological guidance did not understand technology; many young soldiers sent from Manchuria as supervisors for

Representative reform bureaucrats, such as Kishi and Shiina of the Commerce Ministry, were not engineers, but civil-service officials. Did they have adequate knowledge to play such a major role? (4) Like bureaucrats of the postwar Ministry of International Trade and Industry (MITI), could bureaucrats of the prewar Commerce Ministry intervene to shape the behavior of firms and industries? On question (4), see Miwa and Ramseyer (2002a), particularly chapters 7 through 9, or Miwa and Ramseyer (2006, ch. 6).

[80] Recall that Horikoshi was the Chief Designer of both Mitsubishi's Type 96 and Type Zero carrier-based fighters.

factory management had excessive self-confidence in moving others, and often disturbed operations that might have improved production."

Colonel Kawamura pointed out in his fourth lesson (cultivation among leaders of a basic knowledge of technology) that military leaders often made mistakes on technological issues and caused unnecessary confusion.

In the Navy, the NCCom requested trial productions of aircraft; the Air Headquarters, after discussions with the operational and technology sides, chose aircraft for trial production and delegated them to companies. Kazunari Miyo, in charge of air operations and air armament staff at the NCCom's Strategy Section, explained how the Fifth Rearmament Plan was presented in January 1940 to key NCCom personnel, including the NCCommander, the Chiefs of the Strategy Division, and the Third Division (Miyo, 1982, p. 24): "Only one participant from the Third Section of the First Division had any knowledge of aircraft, and he expressed no opinion. I insisted on expanding the air forces, particularly on increasing the number of large aircraft, by reducing warships like large battleships. I was prepared to make some degree of sacrifice."[81]

Chihaya (1982, p. 84), a former Staff Member in the Combined Fleets, pointed out that in the Navy, given the "large-scale battleships with big cannons" doctrine, many leaders were gunnery officers. Referring to the composition of operation leaders at the beginning of the Pacific War, he said:

the Navy could not completely dispel that traditional doctrine even after the failure of the Battle of Midway. Of the ten commander admirals including Yamamoto of the Combined Fleets, four were gunnery officers (Yamamoto, Takasu of the First Fleet, Kondo of the Second, and Takahashi of the Third), four were torpedo officers (Nagumo of the First Air Fleet, Hosogaya of the Fifth, Shimizu of the Sixth, and Ozawa of the Fleet-dispatched-to-the-south), while Inoue of the Fourth Fleet was a navigation officer. Tsukahara of the Eleventh Air Fleet was the only aviation officer. NCCommander Nagano and Chief of Staff of the Combined Fleets Ugaki were gunnery officers, Vice-NCCommander Itoh was a torpedo officer, and the NCCom Strategy Division Chief Fukudome was a navigation officer.[82]

---

[81]   The situation had been almost the same ten years before. As Lieutenant General (then Major) Kusaka of NCCom commented (NAFHistory, 1969, [1], p. 403): "It was the NCCom that received operational demands and relayed requests for aircraft models and improved performance to the Navy Ministry (NM). We were not allowed to demand impossible dreams, but there would be no progress if we simply accepted the budget, technology, and assumptions of the NM and the Air Headquarters. At that time, I was the only Air Staff Member in NCCom and had been only a few years in the aerial world. Having little knowledge or experience, I really suffered."

[82]   Referring to the new theory of armament planning that Inoue presented to the Navy Minister in January 1941, which was rediscovered in 1960s, Chihaya recognized his

(3) A Weak Government or an Incompetent Government?

The decision makers in government lacked the knowledge to understand what human resources were needed for the private companies under their management. Neither did they understand how important these human resources were. Unable to solve problems effectively, they were also reluctant to coordinate. As a result, the shortage in information and personnel was not resolved.

Neither the expansion of trial production and mass production capacity nor the concentration of trial production of new aircraft models proceeded smoothly. The Navy could not make the preparations necessary to manufacture prototypes or adopt new technologies in the face of rapidly advancing quality (NAFHistory, 1969, [3], p. 312). In response to floods of modification demands from operating forces, the Yokosuka Air Squadron and Air Technical Arsenal assessed urgency and executed orders; it was normal for them to accede to most demands (NAFHistory, 1969, [3], p. 369). Together with institutional incompetence, the lack of strong support and direction from higher-ranking decision makers must have been a major factor.

Within the Navy in the mid-1930s, although the Air Force was gaining ground, the mainstream "one-game match" view was still dominant. As Major General Isoroku Yamamoto, then Commander of the First Carrier Division, explained to young officers (Boeicho, 1976, p. 48): "It is so obvious. At the present moment it is too late to be concerned with it. We have no choice but to achieve remarkable results for transforming the obstinate opinions of gunnery officers. You must work hard at this."

The following two episodes raise two questions: (1) Were the policies of top leaders consistent and explicit? (2) Were those policies feasible and enforced during the war? Even if it could and did successfully recruit experts with adequate capacity and information, a government unable to reach an agreement on basic policies could not have achieved its goals effectively.

Competition in munitions production with the ground forces inside the Army was also a significant factor in the failure of aircraft production. The Weapons Administration Headquarters, established in October 1942 to consolidate the AM Weapons Bureau, the Weapons Arsenals, and the Army Technical Arsenal, disapproved of the emphasis placed on the Air Force as it downgraded ground forces, sowing the seeds of low morale. For this reason, the Army Minister directed the Air Headquarters to delegate nonemergency tasks to the ground forces, and to cooperate closely in

mistake in believing that Inoue favored the "battleships with big cannons" doctrine (Chihaya, 1982, p. 85).

technology development. Because of an increase in ocean vessel requisition after the beginning of the Pacific War, ships for the Materials Mobilization Plans (MMPlans) decreased, and the MMPlan for the second half of FY1942 was revised. Anticipating the revision, the AM section in charge unofficially announced a revision plan to reduce by 10 percent the steel meant for aircraft production, aiming to ensure the production of 6,400 aircraft planned for FY1942. It reduced with one blow the allocation of steel for aircraft production capacity expansion from 94,300 tons to 52,000 tons. This made an increase in aircraft production impossible and undermined the year's capacity expansion. This act was representative of the Army's instinct to diminish the Air Forces, even though Army Minister Tojo gave them preference. The FY1942 MMPlan appeared to reflect the aims of the Army Minister, who had won mental elbow-room through a victorious first battle and the acquisition of resources in the South corner. When the MMPlans were revised, preference seemed to revert to the ground forces (Boeicho, 1975c, p. 381).[83]

There was a fierce debate between the Army and Navy over the allocation of aircraft to be produced in FY1944. Army Minister Tojo signaled his intention to accept the Navy's proposal to allocate twenty-six thousand of forty-five thousand aircraft to the Navy; after a bitter dispute, the Army and Navy agreed to overstate the production to fifty thousand and split it in half. The allocation of aircraft was not only a competition over the number of planes but a choice of strategy and operations (Sato, 1976, pp. 328–37). Even at the end of FY1943, the Army and Navy could not agree on the best strategy operations.[84]

---

[83] The latent resources of American industry could in a measurable length of time have met any quantitative requirement within reason. Rae (1968, pp. 146–7) wrote: "in modern war, planning for production has to maintain a delicate balance between the need for immediate output and the need to keep one's own weapons at least equal in quality to the enemy's; there will seldom be agreement about the proper point of balance. All the belligerents of the Second World War had to wrestle with this problem, which was particularly acute in the field of aviation, where technical advance was rapid and unceasing." The people concerned with the air forces in Japan seemed unable to take the U.S. situation seriously.

[84] As mentioned previously, the original draft of the Navy's Fifth Rearmament Plan was explained to the NCCom at the end of January 1940. The final draft was explained to the NM at the end of February. After a year's careful investigation, it was approved in January 1941 and the outline plan determined in April–May. In June, the NCCom asked for a discussion with the ACCom to obtain its approval. The Army side agreed, but with so many conditions that it was practically a refusal: (1) the Navy plan would not restrict the Army's ability to recruit staff; (2) materials allocation would be separately agreed upon; and (3) the Navy's plan would have no impact on the Army's new armaments (NAFHistory, 1969, [2], pp. 131–3).

Arguing that that top leadership should achieve optimal performance in a comprehensive manner, Lieutenant General Shibuya wrote (NAFHistory, 1969, [3], p. 350): "As the supreme guiding principle of the nation, the Japanese military loudly proclaimed abstract slogans like 'faith for victory.' There was no concrete and comprehensive policy. Due both to inferiority in science and technology and to the materials shortage, policies addressing the situation by building up difficulties step by step followed a path to confusion. Instead of supreme leadership, immoderate exhibition of individual competence and sectionalism prevailed; the harmful effects of these accelerated the defeat."

9–7. Concluding Remarks on Part III

Part III is a study of the Navy Air Force (NAF), in which I have applied the analytic framework and previous discussion to a specific side of the war, and confirmed their validity. During the War with China and the Pacific War, the NAF (and its weaponry) was the central player in the Japanese military. Part III systematically studies war preparations, mobilization, and economic control in relation to the NAF. It investigates and evaluates the function, role, competence, and performance of the Japanese state, focusing on moments when competence was desperately needed and expected. "Wars, when they come, are always different from the war that is expected. Victory goes to the side that has made fewest mistakes, not to the one that has guessed right" (Taylor, 1964, p. 116). Such was the War with China and the Pacific War for Japan. Part III focuses on the importance of the air forces, as demonstrated in the battle of attrition over Guadalcanal Island in 1942–3, and highlights the competence of the state in predicting and responding to unexpected situations and events.

As stated at the opening of Part III, the NAF is, for three reasons, the best candidate for a study of the competence of the Japanese state:

1. Air forces (or air weapons) decisively affected the outcome of World War II; they also played a decisive role in the Pacific War. Also in the War with China that preceded the Pacific War, consistently the air forces decisively affected its development and consequences. During the War with China and Pacific War, the Navy (not the Army) Air Force was the central player on the Japanese side.
2. Reflecting rapid progress in science and technology, the substance, function, and role of air forces changed dramatically. The changes in weapons and the ways in which they were used had the possibility

of dramatically changing the wars that would come. The government recognized the need for competence in making predictions and responding to unexpected situations.

3. The development of the War with China and of the Pacific War consistently and heavily deviated from the basic policy outline and strategy assumed in Japan's Basic National Defense Policy. The gap between the planned and actual role of the NAF is representative.

The focus of this volume can be summarized in three points:

1. The War with China began and developed when Japan was desperately ill-prepared for war. War mobilization and economic control after the outbreak of the war remained unsatisfactory. This applies also to the Pacific War.

2. Japan's competence of the state, as reflected in its systematic war preparations, mobilization, and economic control, was extremely poor. There is no reason to think that the Japanese state had competence but chose not to exercise it.

3. The conventional wisdom that Japan prepared for war and waged wartime economy with outstanding competence is a misconception, a myth that fatally deviates from the reality. This view was established and accepted immediately after the end of the Pacific War on the misguided assumption that the state of Japan had an outstanding competence in policy planning and its enforcement.

Conclusion

This book examines the competence and performance of the state through a study of Japan's war policies (including plans, preparations, mobilization, and control) between the 1930s and mid-1940s. Although there continues to be overwhelming public support for the conventional view of Japan's wartime competence, it is a myth that fatally deviates from reality.

Summary of Study Results

War is a great centralizer, and government is the central planner that conducts the war, deciding what strategy to follow and how to use national resources to achieve victory. Government assumes all necessary powers, taking control of the entire economy and acting as "the sole consumer of the products of the economic system" (Cairncross, 1991, p. 3). The Japanese government, which supposedly began and waged war following careful planning and systematic preparations, gave a woefully ineffective and incompetent performance.

This book reaches three main conclusions:

1. Japan was desperately ill-prepared to begin and wage war with China. War mobilization and economic control were unsatisfactory throughout the War with China, and also during the Pacific War, which started four and half years later.
2. Japan's systematic war preparations, war mobilization, and economic control were extremely poor. There is no reason to think that Japan had competence in these areas and chose not to exercise it.
3. The myth of Japan's wartime competence was accepted immediately after the end of the Pacific War and continues to be believed.

Those results raise fundamental doubts about the Japanese government's performance in other areas. One must question the assumption that the country's spectacular post-Meiji economic development was government-led.

Misunderstanding and Myth

In Japan, even today, there is wide support for the idealized picture of a socialist planned economy effectively enforced by the competent state. By discouraging the discussion of real problems, Japanese opinion leaders have misrepresented the state of the economy and the role and function of government in Japan. This has resulted in seven critical misunderstandings, which I list in this section. The first three in particular suggest that the myth has distorted thinking about all aspects of Japan, from the economy to politics, society, history, and life in general.

1. The conventional wisdom, established and widely accepted immediately after the war, has never been seriously questioned and is strongly supported today.
2. The conventional view that the mid-1930s to mid-1940s was the era of planning has convinced many people that Japan's postwar plans, such as the Priority Production Scheme (PPS) policies, contributed significantly to Japan's economic recovery. Similarly, many argue that succeeding plans and interventionist policies (generally called "industrial policy") led to high economic growth.
3. Japan's national plans, developed between the 1930s and the end of the war, are believed to have functioned well. Most Japanese people believe that the government effectively managed the development and growth of the economy, and that Japan's post-Meiji economic development was government-led.
4. The Japanese intelligentsia, including economists, political scientists, and historians, joined with the media in promoting the idea that the socialist planned economy, characterized by planning, was a highly effective model.
5. Popular opinion both reflects and reinforces this academic bias, leading to a public bias in favor of socialist planned economies. The conventional wisdom is accepted because it is consistent with the dominant thought of the time and at once contributes to the reinforcement of the status of the dominant thought.
6. In the second half of the 1930s, long-term plans and economic controls were put into effect. Capitalism and the laissez-faire economy

were heavily criticized (Nakamura, 1989, p. 9), leading to public distrust of market mechanisms in favor of interventionist policies. More than half a century later, this conventional view still influences the government's actual policy making and implementation.

7. The myth of Japan's successful wartime planning has influenced every field in social science. Although the dissolution of the former USSR and the collapse of the administrative-command economy (ACE) under Stalin's dictatorship had an immediate impact on economics and economic history, they were much slower to impact the scholarly research agenda. Perhaps the more entrenched the conventional wisdom becomes, the more difficult it is to make a transition.

Japanese public opinion is shaped by strong expectations of government and frustrations with it, reflecting an overvaluation of the competence of the state. Thus, the original myth continues to cause serious damage to public opinion and policy making in Japan.

The worldwide appeal of Marxism, communism, and the radical left remains remarkably unaffected by the collapse of communism (Gregory, 2004, p. 3). Particularly since the collapse of the former Soviet Union, Japan has become a poster child for the planned economy under strong government control. The myth of Japan's competence has therefore had an impact on international issues.

This book raises fundamental doubts about the competence of Japanese state and calls for a reevaluation of Japan's performance since the Meiji Restoration, not only with regard to economic policy, but spanning history, society, culture, and life.[1]

Beyond Japanese Competence

For this study of government competence (rather than its motives), I chose World War II Japan as a laboratory, demonstrating that its systematic war preparations, mobilization, and economic control were extremely poor.

[1] In collaboration with Professor J. Mark Ramseyer, I have written many articles and books both in English and Japanese challenging and criticizing dominant views and the conventional wisdom about the Japanese economy since the Meiji Restoration (Miwa and Ramseyer, 2000a, 2000b, 2002b, 2002d, 2003a, 2005b). Their most basic and important common foundation is the myth of Japanese competence described in this volume. Eight points for illustration are listed in Miwa (2008, pp. 47–8). The first point, for instance, is: "We have serious reservations about the conventional wisdom that the state led the impressive economic development in Japan since the Meiji Restoration." Also see Miwa and Ramseyer (2006).

Nowhere in this book have I argued that Japan is unique or different from other countries. Japan may not have been more incompetent in waging war than the UK, the United States, the USSR, China, Germany, France, or Italy. Although I have included a few suggestive comparisons with the UK, I have never argued that the Japanese fell behind other countries in any particular time period or policy. The conclusions of this book may fit other countries as well.

The modern economy entails government intervention at many levels. To choose the appropriate foci for government policy, one must understand accurately what government can and cannot do. Such understanding requires an empirical basis, facts developed through a careful study of when, how, and to what effect governments have intervened in the past. As one contribution to the broader empirical project of understanding government competence, this book supplies a case study. It is my hope that other studies, focusing on government competence in different countries, eras, and situations, will follow.

References

Ando, Yoshio [1972] "Nihon senji keizai to 'shin-kanryo" (Japan's Wartime Economy and "New Bureaucrats") in Kohachiro Takahashi, Yoshio Ando, and Akira Kondo, eds. *Shimin shakai no keizai kozo* (Economic Structure of Civil Society), Tokyo: Yuhikaku.

[1976] "History of Wartime Economic Control," in Ando, ed. [1976].

Ando, Yoshio, ed. [1966] *Showa keizai-shi heno shogen* (Testament to the Economic History of Showa), 2, Tokyo: Maincihi shimbun-sha.

[1976] *Nihon keizai seisaku-shi ron* (Studies on the History of Economic Policies in Japan), 2, Tokyo: University of Tokyo Press.

Arisawa, Hiromi [1937] *Nihon kogyo tosei-ron* (Theory of Industry Control in Japan), Tokyo: Yuhikaku.

[1989] *Gakumon to shisou to ningen to* (Academics, Thought, and Man), Tokyo: University of Tokyo Press (originally published in 1957 from Mainichi shimbun-sha).

Berliner, Joseph S. [2001] "The Contribution of the Soviet Archives," in Gregory, ed. [2001].

Boeicho (Japanese Defense Agency), [*Boei kenshujo* (National Institute for Defense Studies), *Senshi shitsu* (War History Chamber)] [1967a] *Daihon'ei Rikugun-bu* (Imperial Headquarters Army Division) *(1): showa 15nen 5gatsu made* (Until May 1940), *Senshi-sousho* (War History Library) 8, Tokyo: Asagumo shimbun-sha.

[1967b] *Rikugun gunju doin* (Army War Mobilization) *(1): keikaku-hen* (Planning), War History Library 9, Tokyo: Asagumo shimbun-sha.

[1967c] *Hawai sakusen* (Hawaii Operation), War History Library 10, Tokyo: Asagumo shimbun-sha.

[1968] *Daihon'ei Rikugun-bu* (Imperial Headquarters Army Division) *(2): showa 16nen 11gatsu made* (Until November 1941), War History Library 20, Tokyo: Asagumo shimbun-sha.

[1969a] *Kanto-gun* (Kwantung Army) *(1): taiso senbi, nomonhan jiken* (Armament Toward the USSR and the Nomonhan Incident), War History Library 27, Tokyo: Asagumo shimbun-sha.

[1969b] *Kaigun gunsenbi* (Navy Armament), (1): *Showa 16nen 11gatsu made* (Until November 1941), War History Library 31, Tokyo: Asagumo shimbun-sha.

[1970] *Rikugun gunju doin* (Army War Mobilization) *(2): jisshi-hen* (Implementation), War History Library 33, Tokyo: Asagumo shimbun-sha.

[1974] *Chugoku-homen kaigun sakusen* (Navy Operations in China) *(1): showa 13nen 3gatsu made* (Until March 1938), War History Library 72, Tokyo: Asagumo shimbun-sha.

[1975a] *Chugoku-homen kaigun sakusen* (Navy Operations in China) *(2): showa 13nen 3gatsu ikou* (Since March 1938), War History Library 79, Tokyo: Asagumo shimbun-sha

[1975b] *Shina jihen rikugun sakusen* (Army Operations in the China Incident) *(1):* Until January 1938, War History Library 86, Tokyo: Asagumo shimbun-sha.

[1975c] *Rikugun kouku heiki no kaihatsu, seisan, hokyu* (Development, Production, and Supply of Army Air Weapons), War History Library 87, Tokyo: Asagumo shimbun-sha.

[1975d] *Daihon'ei kaigunbu, rengo-kantai* (Imperial Headquarters Navy Division, Combined Fleets) *(1): kaisen made* (Until the Outbreak of the Pacific War), War History Library 91, Tokyo: Asagumo shimbun-sha.

[1976] *Kaigun kouku gaishi* (Summary History of the Navy Air Force), War History Library 95, Tokyo: Asagumo shimbun-sha.

Cairncross, Alec [1991] *Planning in Wartime: Aircraft Production in Britain, Germany and the USA*, Basingstoke: Macmillan.

Calder, Kent E. [1993] *Strategic Capitalism: Private Business and Public Purpose in Japanese Industrial Finance*, Princeton: Princeton University Press.

Chihaya, Masataka [1982] *Nihon kaigun no senryaku hassou: haisen chogugono tsuukon no hansei* (Strategic Ideas of the Japanese Navy: Painful Reviews Immediately After the War Defeat), Tokyo: Prejidento-sha (mostly written in 1946).

Coase, Ronald H. [1964] "Comment," *American Economic Review*, May.

Costello, John [1981] *The Pacific War*, London: Collins.

Davies, R. W. [2001] "Making Economic Policy," in Gregory, ed. [2001].

Dower, John W. [1999] *Embracing Defeat: Japan in the Wake of World War II*, New York: W. W. Norton.

Edgerton, David [1991] *England and the Aeroplane: An Essay on a Militant and Technological Nation*, Basingstoke: Macmillan.

[2006] *Warfare State: Britain, 1920–1970*, Cambridge: Cambridge University Press.

Editorial Committee on the History of Air Industry (*Kouku kogyo-shi hensan iinkai*), ed. [1948] "*Minkan koukuki kogyo-shi*" (Commercial Aircraft Manufacturing Industry), mimeographed.

Fuji Heavy Industries [1984] *Fuji juko 30-nenshi* (30 Years of the Fuji Heavy industries), Tokyo: Fuji Heavy Industries.

Fukudome, Shigeru [1951] *Kaigun no hansei* (Remorse of the Navy), Tokyo: Nihon shuppan kyodo kabushikikaisha.

Furukawa, Takahisa [1992] *Showa senchu-ki no sougou kokusaku kikan* (Institutions for Comprehensive National Policy During the Showa Wartime Era), Tokyo: Yoshikawa kobun-kan.

Gao, Bai [1997] *Economic Ideology and Japanese Industrial Policy: Developmentalism from 1931 to 1965*, New York: Cambridge University Press.

Genda, Minoru [1996] *Kaigun kouku-tai shimatsuki* (Memories of the Navy Air Force), Tokyo: Bunshun-bunko (originally published in 1962 from Bungei-shunju-sha).

Gerschenkron, Alexander [1962] *Economic Backwardness in Historical Perspective: A Book of Essays*, Cambridge, MA: Harvard University Press.

Goldsmith, Raymond W. [1946] "The Power of Victory: Munitions Output in World War II," *Military Affairs*, Vol. 10, No. 1.

Gordon, Andrew [2003] *A Modern History of Japan: From Tokugawa Times to the Present*, New York: Oxford University Press.

Gregory, Paul R. [2001] "Preface," in Gregory, ed. [2001].

Gregory, Paul R., ed. [2001] *Behind the Façade of Stalin's Command Economy: Evidence from the Soviet State and Party Archives*, Stanford, CA: Hoover Institution Press.

Gregory, Paul R. [2004] *The Political Economy of Stalinism: Evidence from the Soviet Secret Archives*, Cambridge: Cambridge University Press.

Gregory, Paul and Mark Harrison [2005] "Allocation Under Dictatorship: Research in Stalin's Archives," *Journal of Economic Literature*, VLIII, September.

Hakiri, Matsuo [2000] *Ozora no kessen: zero-sen toujo-in kuusen-roku* (Battles in the Sky: Air Battle Records of a Zero Fighter Pilot), Tokyo: Bunshun bunko.

Hannah, Leslie [1995] "Afterthoughts," *Business and Economic History*, 24–2, Winter.

Hara, Akira [1976a] "Senji tosei-keiseki no kaishi" (Beginning of Wartime Control Economy), in *Iwanami-koza* (Iwanami Course) *Nihon-rekishi* (The Japanese History) *20, kindai* (Modern Era) *7*, Tokyo: Iwanami-shoten.

[1976b] "'Manshu' niokeru keizai tosei seisaku no tenkai: mantetsu kaiso to mangyo setsuritsu wo megutte" (Development of Economic Control Policy in "Manchuria": Reorganization of the South Manchurian Railways and Establishment of the Manchurian Heavy Industries) in Ando, ed. [1976].

[1994] "*Keizai so-doin*" (Economic General Mobilization) in Oishi, ed. [1994].

Hara, Shiro [1987] *Daisenryaku naki kaisen: kyu-daihon'ei ichi-bakuryou no kaisou* (The Beginning of a War Without Grand Strategy: Memoires of a Staff of Imperial Headquarters Army Division), Tokyo: Hara-shobo.

Hattori, Takushiro [1965] *Daitoa senso zenshi* (The Whole History of the Greater East Asian War), Tokyo: Hara-shobo.

Hayase, Toshiyuki [2007] *Nankin-sen no shinjitsu: Matsui Iwane shogun no munen* (The Truth of the Battle over Nanjing: Chagrins of General Iwane Matsui), Tokyo: Kojin-sha (originally published in 1999 from Kojin-sha, as *Shogun no shinjitsu* (The Truth of the General)).

Hayek, Friedrich, A. [1945] "The Use of Knowledge in Society," *American Economic Review*, September.

Hiragushi, Takashi [2006] *Daihon'ei houdo-bu: genron tosei to sen'i kouyou no jissai* (Imperial Headquarters News Service: The Truth of Gag and Will-to-Fight-Raising), Tokyo: Kojin-sha (originally published in 1980 by Tosho shuppan-sha).

Hokkaido tanko kisen kabushiki kaisha (Hokkaido Coal-Mining and Steamship Company), ed. [1958] *Sekitan kokka tousei-shi* (History of Coal Control by the State), Tokyo: Nihon keizai kenkyujo.

Honjo, Kiro [1982] "Chuko, zerosen, zerokan no sekkei" (Designing Medium-Sized Attack Aircraft, Zero Fighter, and Zero Reconnaissance Aircraft) in NAF Private History [1982].

Horiba, Kazuo [1962] *Shina jihen senso shidou-shi* (War Leadership History During the China Incident), Tokyo: Jiji-tsushin-sha.

Horikoshi, Jiro [1950] *Koukuki kogyo* (The Aircraft Manufacturing Industry), in Toyo keisai shimpo-sha [1950].

Hoshi, Takeo and Anil Kashyap [2001] *Corporate Financing and Governance in Japan: The Road to the Future*, Cambridge, MA: MIT Press.

Hoshino, Naoki [1963] *Mihatenu yume: Manshukoku gaishi* (Unfulfilled Dream: A Private History of Manchukuo), Tokyo: Diyamondo-sha.

Ikuta, Atsushi [1985] "Magatta kassouro: chijo de kaimetsushita kouku senryoku" (Curved Runways: Air Forces Destroyed on Ground) in Morimatsu, ed. [1985].

Imoto, Kumao [1978] *Sakusen nisshi de tsuzuru shinajihen* (The China Incident in Strategy Diary), Tokyo: Fuyo shobo.

[1979] *Sakusen nisshi de tsuzuru daitoa senso* (The Greater East Asian War in Strategy Diary), Tokyo: Fuyo shobo.

Inada, Masazumi [1969] *Inada Masazumi shi danwa sokkiroku* (Shorthand Record of Discourse by Mr. Masazumi Inada), Tokyo: Kido nikki kenkyu-kai & Nihon kindaishi kenkyu-kai.

Inomata, Keitaro [1959] "Nakano Seigo no higeki" (The Tragedy of Seigo Nakano), Tokyo: Kon'nichino mondai-sha.

Ishii, Itaro [1950] *Gaiko-kan no isshou* (Life of a Diplomat), Tokyo: Yomiuri shimbun-sha.

Ishii, Masanori [2006] *Gijutsu chujo no nichibei senso* (The Japan–U.S. War for an Engineering Lieutenant General), Tokyo: Kojinsha NF bunko.

Iwaguro, Takeo [1977] *Iwaguro Takeo shi danwa sokkiroku* (Shorthand Record of Discourse by Mr. Takeo Iwaguro), Tokyo: Kido nikki kenkyu-kai & Nihon kindaishi kenkyu-kai.

Iwaya, Fumio [2003] *Raigekitai, shutsugeki seyo: kaigun chuko-tai no eikou to higeki* (Sortie, the Torpedo Bombers Squadron: The Glory and Tragedy of the Navy Medium-Sized Attack Aircraft Squadron), Tokyo: Bunshun-bunko (originally published in 1956 by Shuppan kyodo-sha).

Japan Machine Tool Builders Association (*Nihon kosakukikai kogyo-kai*) [1962] *Nihon no kosakukikai kogyo hattatsu no katei* (Development Process of the Machine Tool Industry in Japan), Tokyo: Kikai kogyo shinko kyokai.

Japan Steel Works [1968] *Nihon seiko-jo shashi shiryo II* (Materials for the Company History of Japan Steel Works II). Tokyo: Japan Steel Works.

Johnson, Chalmers [1982] *MITI and the Japanese Miracle: The Growth of Industrial Policy, 1952–1975*, Stanford: Stanford University Press

Joho, Yoshio [1979] *Rikugun-sho gummu-kyoku* (Military Bureau of the Army Ministry), Tokyo: Fuyo-shobo.

Kaneko, Fumio [1994] "Shokuminchi, senryochi shihai" (Governance in Colonies and Occupied Areas) in Oishi, ed. [1994].

Katakura, Tadashi [1978] *Kaisou no manshu-koku* (Manchukuo in Retrospect), Tokyo: Keizai ourai-sha.

Kershaw, Ian [2000] *The Nazi Dictatorship: Problems & Perspectives of Interpretation*, fourth edition, London: Edward Arnold.

Kikuchi, Ken'ichiro [1947] "Siho no menyori mitaru haisen gen'in no kenkyu" (A Study on the Causes of the Defeat from the Judiciary Point of View), *Shiho kenkyu*, Report 34–5, September.

Kikuhara, Shizuo [1982] "Shiden-kai monogatari" (A Tale of *Shiden-kai*), in NAF Private History [1982].

Kishi, Nobusuke [1982] *Nijuseiki no riidaa-tachi* (Leaders in the 20th Century), Tokyo: Sankei shuppan.

Kishi, Nobusuke, Kazuo Yatsugi, and Takashi Ito [1981] *Kishi Nobusuke no kaiso* (Memoires of Nobusuke Kishi), Tokyo: Bungei-shunju-sha.

Kitano, Shigeo [1944] *Gunju-sho oyobi gunju-kaisha-ho* (Munitions Ministry and Munitions Company Act), revised edition, Tokyo. Shoko-gyosei-sha.

Klein, Burton H. [1948] "Germany's Preparations for War: A Reexamination," *American Economic Review*, 38.

[1959] *Germany's Economic Preparations for War*, Cambridge, MA: Harvard University Press.

Kobayashi. Hideo [2005] *Mantetsu chosa-bu: "ganso shinkutanku" no tanjo to hokai* (Research Division of the South Manchurian Railway Company: The Birth and Collapse of "the First Think-Tank,") Heibonsha-shinsho 209, Tokyo: Heibonsha.

Kobe Steel Works [1954] *Kobe seiko-jo 50 nenshi* (Fifty Years of Kobe Steel Works), Kobe: Kobe Steel Works.

Kyogoku, Jun'ichi [1983] *Nihon no seiji* (Politics in Japan), Tokyo: University of Tokyo Press.

Lea, Homer [1909] *The Valor of Ignorance*, New York: Harper.

Lockwood, William W. [1955] *The Economic Development of Japan: Growth and Structural Change 1868–1938*, London: Oxford University Press.

Maekawa, Masao [2000] *Nakajima hikouki monogatari* (A Tale of the Nakajima Aircraft Company), Tokyo: Kojin-sha NF bunko (originally published in 1996).

Matsumoto, Shigeharu [1986] *Showa-shi heno ichi shogen* (A Testament to the Showa History), Tokyo: Mainichi shimbun-sha.

McCloskey, Donald N. [1990] *If You're So Smart: The Narrative of Economic Expertise*, Chicago: University of Chicago Press.

Meulen, Jacob Vander [1995] *Building the B-29*, Washington: Smithonian Institution Press.

Minobe, Tatsukichi [1927] *Kenpo satsuyou* (Essentials of the Constitution), revised fourth edition, Tokyo: Yuhikaku.

MITI (Ministry of International Trade and Industry, *Tsusho sangyo sho*) [1962] *Gyosei kiko* (Organization for Administration), Vol. 3 of *The History of Commerce Policies*, Tokyo: Shoko seisakushi kanko-kai.

MITI [1964] *Sangyo tosei* (Industry Control), Vol. 11 of *The History of Commerce Policies*, Tokyo: Shoko seisakushi kanko-kai.

[1979] *Kogyo gijutsu* (Industrial Technology), Vol. 13 of *The History of Commerce Policies*, Tokyo: Shoko seisakushi kanko-kai.

Mitsui Shipbuilding [1953] *Mitsui zosen 35 nen-shi* (35 Years of Mitsui Shipbuilding), Tokyo: Mitsui Shipbuilding.

Miwa, Yoshiro [1996] *Firms and Industrial Organization in Japan*, Basingstoke: Macmillan (originally published in Japanese in 1990 by the University of Tokyo Press).

[2004] *State Competence and Economic Growth in Japan*, London: RoutledgeCurzon (originally published in Japanese in 1998 by Yuhikaku as *Seifu no noryoku* (The Competence of the State).

[2007] "Busshi doin keikaku, seisanryoku kakuju keikaku (seisaku), keizai tosei" (Materials-Mobilization Plans, Production-Capacity-Expansion Plans [Policies], and Economic Controls in Wartime Japan), *Keizaigaku ronshu* (*Journal of Economics of the University of Tokyo*), 73–3, 73–4.

[2008] *Keikakuteki senso junbi, gunju doin, keizai tosei: zoku seifu no noryoku* (Wartime Planning, Mobilization, and Economic Control in Japan: Further Studies in "the Competence of the State"), Tokyo: Yuhikaku.

Miwa, Yoshiro and J. Mark Ramseyer [2000a] *Seisaku kin'yu to keizai hatten: senzen-ki nihon kogyo ginko no ke-su* (Policy Finance and Economic Growth: The Case of the Prewar Industrial Bank of Japan), *Keizaigaku ronshu*, 66–3.

[2000b] "Corporate Governance in Transitional Economies: Lessons from the Prewar Japanese Cotton Textile Industry," *Journal of Legal Studies*, 29, January.

[2001] *Nihon-keizai-ron no gokai: "keiretsu" no jubaku kara no kaiho* (Misunderstandings in the Theory of the Japanese Economy: Liberation from the Spell of the "Keiretsu"), Tokyo: Toyo keizai shimpo-sha.

[2002a] *Sangyo seisaku-ron no gokai: koudo seicho no shinjitsu* (Misunderstandings About Industrial Policy: Truth About Japan's High Growth), Tokyo: Toyo keizai shimpo-sha.

[2002b] "Banks and Economic Growth: Implications from Japanese History," *Journal of Law & Economics*, 45–1, April.

[2002c] "The Fable of the Keiretsu," *Journal of Economics & Management Strategy*, Vol. 11, No. 2.

[2002d] "The Value of Prominent Directors: Corporate Governance and Bank Access in Transitional Japan," *Journal of Legal Studies*, 31, June.

[2002e] "The Myth of the Main Bank: Japan and Competitive Corporate Governance," *Law & Social Inquiry*, 27–2.

[2003a] "Capitalist Politicians, Socialist Bureaucrats? Legends of Government Planning from Japan," *Antitrust Bulletin*, Fall.

[2004a] "Keizai kisei no yukousei: "keisha seisan" seisaku no shinwa" (The Effectiveness of Economic Controls: The Myth of the Priority-Production-Scheme [PPS]) (1)(2), *Keizaigaku ronshu*, 70–2, 70–3.

[2004b] "Directed Credit? The Loan Market in High-Growth Japan," *Journal of Economics & Management Strategy*, 12–1, Spring.

[2005a] "The Good Occupation," Harvard Law and Economics Discussion Paper No. 514, available at http://papers.ssrn.com/abstract=729463

[2005b] "Japanese Industrial Finance at the Close of the 19th Century: Trade Credit and Financial Intermediation," *Explorations in Economic History*, 43.

[2006] *Fable of the Keiretsu: Urban Legends of the Japanese Economy*, Chicago: University of Chicago Press.

[2009a] "The Good Occupation? Law in the Allied Occupation of Japan," *Washington University Global Studies Law Review*, 8–2.

[2009b] "Good Occupation – or Vindicative?" in *Law and Practice in Postwar Japan: The Postwar Legal Reforms and Their Influence*, Tokyo: Blakemore Foundation and International House of Japan.

Miyo, Kazunari [1982] "Kaigun no kouku gunbi keikaku" (Air Armament Plans of the Navy), in NAF Private History [1982].

Morimatsu, Toshio, ed. [1985] *Haisha no senkun* (Losers' War Lessons), Tokyo: Toshoshuppan-sha.

Murakami, Katsuhiko [1994] "Gunju sangyo" (Munitions Industries) in Oishi, ed. [1994].

Murray, Williamson [1999] *War in the Air 1914–45*, Washington: Smithonian Books.

NAFHistory [1969] See Nihon kaigun kouku-shi hensan iinkai [1969].

NAF Private History [1982] See Nihon kaigun kouku gaishi kankoukai [1982]

Nakagane, Katsuji [2007] "Ikou-keizai-ron: shakaishugi taisei ikou no rekishiteki hai-kei to rironteki konkyo" (Theory of Economic Transition: Historical Background and Theoretical Foundation of Regime Shift from Socialism), (1), *Aoyama kokusai seikei ronshu*, No. 72, May.

[2010] *Tasiei-ikou no seiji-keizaigaku: naze shakaishugikoku ha shihonshugi ni mukatte dassou sunonoka* (The Political Economy of Transition: Farewell to Socialism), Nagoya: University of Nagoya Press.

Nakahara, Shigetoshi [1981] *Daitoa-hokyusen: waga senryoku to kokuryoku no jittai* (The Greater East Asian Supply War: The Reality of Our War Capacity and National Power), Tokyo: Hara shobo.

Nakamura, Takafusa [1974] *Nihon no keizai tosei: senji, sengo no keiken to kyokun* (Economic Control in Japan: Wartime and Postwar Experiences and their Lessons), Tokyo: Nikkei shinsho.

[1977] "Senji keizai to sono hokai" (Wartime Economy and Its Collapse) in *Iwanami-koza* (Iwanami Course) *Nihon-rekishi* (The Japanese History) *21, kindai* (Modern Era) *8*, Tokyo: Iwanami-shoten.

[1983] *Economic Growth in Prewar Japan*. New Haven, CT: Yale University Press.

[1989] "Gaisetsu: 1937–54" (Overview: 1937–54) in Nakamura, ed. [1989].

Nakamura, Takafusa, ed. [1989] *"Keikakuka" to "minshuka"* ("Planning" and "Democratization"), Vol. 7 of *The Japanese Economic History*, Tokyo: Iwanami shoten.

Nakamura, Takafusa and Akira Hara [1970] "Shiryo kaisetsu" (Commentary of the Materials) in Nakamura and Hara, eds. [1970].

Nakamura, Takafusa and Akira Hara, eds. [1970] *Gendaishi shiryo* (Materials in Contemporary History) *(43): kokka sodouin* (The National General Mobilization) *(1)*, Tokyo, Misuzu shobo.

Nakamura, Takafusa and Akira Hara [1972] "'Keizai shin-taisei'" (New Economic Regime), in Nihon seiji-gakkai, ed. *"Konoe shin-taisei" no kenkyu* (Studies on the Konoe New Regime), FY1972 Annual Report, Tokyo: Iwanami shoten.

Nawata, Takeshi [1985c] "Chijo kinmu-in: rikugun kouku no kiban butai" (Groundwork Troops: Support Troops of the Army Air Force), in Morimatsu, ed. [1985].

Nihon kaigun kouku gaishi kankoukai (Society for Private History of the Japanese Navy Air Force) [1982] *Umiwashi no kiseki: Nihon kaigun koukuu gaishi* (History of Sea Eagles: Private History of the Japanese Navy Air Force), Tokyo: Hara shobo.

Nihon kaigun kouku-shi hensan iinkai (Editorial Committee on the History of Japanese Navy Air Force) [1969] *Nihon kaigun kouku-shi* (The History of Japanese Navy Air Force) *(1)~(4)*, Tokyo: Jiji Tsushin-sha ([1]: Book on Operations, [2]: Book on Armament, [3]: Book on Institutions and Technology, and [4]: Book on War History).

Nihon kindaishi kenkyu-kai, ed. [1971] *Nihon riku-kaigun no seido, soshiki, jinji* (Institution, Organization, and Personnel in the Japanese Army and the Navy), Tokyo: University of Tokyo Press.

Nishida, Yoshiaki [1994] "Senjika no kokumin seikatsu jouken: senji yami-keizai no seikaku wo megutte" (People's Life Conditions in Time of War: Attributes of Wartime Black Markets) in Oishi, ed. [1994].

Nishiura, Susumu [1968] *Nishiura Susumu shi danwa sokkiroku* (Shorthand Record of Discourse by Mr. Susumu Nishiura), Tokyo: Kido nikki kenkyu-kai & Nihon kindaishi kenkyu-kai.

[1980] *Showa senso-shi no shogen* (Testament to Showa War History), Tokyo: Hara shobo (originally published in July 1947 for private circulation).

Ogino, Fujio [2002] "'Keizai shiho' no senzen to sengo" (Prewar and Postwar of "Economic Judiciary") in *Keizai geppo, kaidai, soumokuji* (Monthly Economic Reports, Annotated Bibliography, and Integrated Table of Contents) Tokyo: Fuji shuppan.

Ohtani, Keijiro [1973] *Kenpei: jiden-teki kaiso* (The Military Police: Autobiographical Recollection), Tokyo: Jinbutsu orai-sha.

Ohya, Atsushi [1964] *Sangyo ichiro* (Dedication to Industry), Tokyo: Kagaku keizai kenkyujo.

Oishi, Kaichiro [1994] "Dainiji sekaitaisen to nihon shihonshugi: mondai no shozai" (World War II and the Japanese Capitalism: Basic Issues) in Oishi, ed. [1994].

Oishi, Kaichiro, ed. [1994] *Nihon teikoku shugi-shi* (History of the Japanese Imperialism), *3, dainiji taisenki* (The World War II Period), Tokyo: University of Tokyo Press.

Oka, Yoshitake [1958] *Yamagata Aritomo*, Tokyo: Iwanami shinsho (in Japanese).

Okada, Keisuke [2001] *Okada Keisuke kaikoroku* (Memoires of Keisuke Okada), Tokyo: Chuko-bunko (originally published in 1977 from Mainichi shimbun-sha).

Okazaki, Tetsuji and Masahiro Okuno-Fujiwara, eds. [1999] *The Japanese Economic System and Its Historical Origins*. Oxford: Oxford University Press.

Onozuka, Ichiro [1962] *Senji zosen-shi: Taiheiyo senso to keikaku zosen* (History of Wartime Shipbuilding: The Pacific War and Planned Shipbuilding), Tokyo: Nihon kaiji shinko-kai.

Overy, Richard J. [1980] *The Air War 1939–1945*, London: Europa.

[1994] *War and Economy in the Third Reich*, Oxford: Clarendon Press.

[1996] *Why the Allies Won*, New York: W. W. Norton.

Pempel, T. J. and Michio Muramatsu [1995] "The Japanese Bureaucracy and Economic Development: Structuring a Proactive Civil Service," in Hyung-Ki Kim, Michio Muramatsu, T. J. Pempel, and Kozo Yamamura, eds. *The Japanese Civil Service and Economic Development*, Oxford: Clarendon Press.

Postan, M.M. [1952] *British War Production*, London: H.M.S.O.

Rae, John B. [1968] *Climb to Greatness: The American Aircraft Industry, 1920–1960*, Cambridge, MA: MIT Press.

Rees, E. A. [2001] "Leaders and Their Institutions," in Gregory, ed. [2001].

Reischauer, Edwin O. [1977] *The Japanese*, Cambridge, MA: Harvard University Press.

Ritchie, Sebastian [1997] *Industry and Air Power: The Expansion of British Aircraft Production, 1935–1941*, London: Franck Cass.

Rockoff, Hugh [1998] "By Way of Analogy: The Expansion of the Federal Government in the 1930s," Michael D. Bordo, Claudia Goldin, and Eugene N. White, eds. *The Defining Moment: The Great Depression and the American Economy in the Twentieth Century*, Chicago: University of Chicago Press.

Rosovsky, Henry [1961] *Capital Formation in Japan, 1868–1940*, New York: Free Press of Glencoe.

Sagami, Taro [1940] *Zaikai yawa: Buso seru nihon keizai* (Bedside Stories from the Business World: The Armed Japanese Economy), Tokyo: Banri-kaku.

Sato, Kenryo [1976] *Sato Kenryo no shogen* (Testament of Kenryo Sato), Tokyo: Fuyo shobo.

Sawai, Minoru [1984] "Senji keizai tosei no tenkai to nihon kosakukikai kogyo: Nicchu senso-ki wo chushin to shite" (Development of Wartime Control and the Machine Tool Industry: Focusing upon the War with China Period), *Shakai kagaku kenkyu* (Social Science Studies), 36(1).

Schumpeter, Joseph A. [1947] *Capitalism, Socialism, and Democracy*, second edition, New York: Harper & Brothers.

Sejima, Ryuzo [1995] *Ikuyamakawa: memoires of Sejima Ryuzo* (in Japanese), Tokyo: Sankei shimbun-sha.

Shiba, Minoru, ed. [1948] *Keizai tosei no jittai karamita keizai-hanzai sousa no youtei* (Essence of Economic Crime Investigation in View of the Reality of Economic Control), Tokyo: Keisatsu jiho-sha.

Shidehara, Kijuro [1951] *Gaikou 50-nen* (Fifty Years in Diplomacy), Tokyo: Yomiuri shimbun-sha.

Shiina, Etsusaburo [1941] *Senji keizai to busshi chosei* (Wartime Economy and Materials Coordination), Tokyo: Sangyo keizai gakkai.

Shoko-gyosei-chosa kai (Commerce Administration Research Team) [1939] *Busshi tosei no chishiki* (Information About Materials Control), Tokyo: Shoko gyoisei-sha.

Shoko gyosei-shi kanko-kai (Society for History of Commerce Administration) [1955] *Shoko gyosei-shi* (History of Commerce Administration), *(3)*, Tokyo: Shoko gyosei-shi kanko-kai.

Smith, Adam [1776] *An Inquiry into the Nature and Causes of the Wealth of Nations* (London). Modern Library edition, 1937, New York: Random House.

Spulber, Nicholas [2003] *Russia's Economic Transitions: From Late Tsarism to the New Millennium*, Cambridge: Cambridge University Press.

Stigler, George J. [1965] "The Economist and the State," *American Economic Review*, March.

[1988] *Memories of an Unregulated Economist*. New York: Basic Books.

Sugita, Ichiji [1987] *Joho naki senso shidou: daihon'ei joho-sanbo no kaisou* (War Leadership Without Information: Memories of an Information Staff of the Imperial Headquarters), Tokyo: Hara shobo.

Suzuki, Takashi [1992] *Nihon teikokushugi to manshu* (The Japanese Imperialism and Manchuria): *1900–1945, (2)*, Tokyo: Hanawa shobo.

Takahashi, Takeo [1985] *Yudan no gen'ei: ichi gijutsu shouko no mita nichibei kaisen no uchimaku* (Illusion of Oil Extinction: An Engineer Officer's Inside View of the Outbreak of the Japan–U.S. War), Tokyo: Jiji Tsushin-sha.

Takeyama, Morio [1971] "Riku-kaigun chuo-kikan no seido hensen" (Institutional Change in the Army- and the Navy Central Agencies) in Nihon kindaishi kenkyu-kai, ed. [1971].

Tanabe, Tadao [1943] "Seisan-ryoku zoukyono zentei" (Prerequisite for Production Capacity Expansion), *Chuo-khoron* (monthly), January.

Tanaka, Shin'ichi [1975] *Nihon senso keizai hishi* (Secret History of Japan's Wartime Economy), Tokyo: Konpyuta eiji-sha.

Tanemura, Suketaka [1979] *Daihon'ei kimitsu nisshi* (Confidential Diary of the Imperial Headquarters), Tokyo: Fuyo-shobo (originally published in March 1952 by Daiyamondo-sha).

Taylor, A. J. P. [1964] *The Origins of the Second World War*, second edition, London: Penguin.

Teratani, Takeaki [1993] *Zosengyo no fukko to hatten* (Recovery and Development of the Shipbuilding Industry), Tokyo: Nihon keizai hyoron-sha.

Tooze, Adam [2007] *The Wages of Destruction: The Making and Breaking the Nazi Economy*, London: Penguin.

Toye, Richard [2003] *The Labour Party and the Planned Economy, 1931–1951*. London: Royal Historical Society/ Boydell Press.

Toyo keizai shimpo-sha [1950] *Showa sangyo-shi* (Showa History of Industry), Vol. 1, Tokyo: Toyo keizai shimpo-sha.

Umemura, Mataji et al., eds. [1989] *The Japanese Economic History*, in 8 volumes, Tokyo: Iwanami-shoten.

Usui, Katsumi [1964] "Shiryo kaisetsu" (Commentary of the Materials) in *Gendaishi shiryo* (Materials in Contemporary History) *(9): Nicchu senso* (The War with China) *(2)*, Tokyo, Misuzu shobo.

Watanabe, Shin'ichi [1995] *Shiden-kai bikkuri deeta 99 no nazo* (The Mystery of Ninety-Nine Surprising Data on Shiden-kai Aircraft), Tokyo: Futami shobo.

Watt, Donald C. [1965] "Appeasement: The Rise of a Revisionist School?" *Political Quarterly*, Vol. 36, No. 2.

Wolferen, Karel van [1990] *The Enigma of Japanese Power: People and Politics in a Stateless Nation*, London: Papermac.

Yamaguchi, Tetsushiro [1946] "Keizai jihan bouatsu no kantenyori mitaru keizai kensatsu no jitujo ni tsuite" (The Reality of Economic Prosecution for Preventing Economic Crimes), *Shiho kenkyu*, Report 34–2, October.

Yamamoto, Chikao [1982] *Daihon'ei kaigunbu* (Imperial Headquarters Navy Division), Tokyo: Asahi-sonorama.

Yamamoto, Chikuro [2001] "Gadarukanaru tettai" (Retreat from Guadalcanal) in Arichika Rokuji et al., *Tettai* (Retreat), Tokyo: Kojin-sha (originally published in *Maru*, separate volume No. 5, March 1987).

Yamamura, Kozo [1972] "Japan 1868–1930: A Revised View," in Rondo E. Cameron, ed. *Banking and Economic Development: Some Lessons of History*, New York: Oxford University Press.

Yamane, Tadashi [1947] "Eidan tousei-kai sonohoka touseidantai no kouzai" (Merits and Demerits of Control Organizations Like Authorities, Control Associations, Etc.), *Shiho kenkyu*, Report 34–7, December.

Yamazaki, Shiro [1996] "Kaisetsu: seisanryoku kakuju keiaku shiryo" (Commentary on Materials for Production Capacity Expansion Plans), in Akira Hara and Shiro Yamazaki, eds., *Seisanryoku kakuju keikaku shiryo* (Materials for Production-Capacity-Expansion Plans), Vol. 1, Materials for Planning *(1)*, Tokyo: Gendai shiryo shuppan.

Yoshino, Shinji [1962] *Omokaji torikaji* (Right and Left), Tokyo: Tsusho sangyo kenkyu-sha.

Yui, Naokazu [1982] "Mitsubishi ni okeru kaigun-ki no seisan" (Navy Aircraft Production in Mitsubishi), in NAF Private History [1982].

Index